ANNOTATED CHECKLIST

OF THE BIRDS OF KENTUCKY

Third Edition

By

Brainard Palmer-Ball, Jr.

This book is dedicated to the memory
of my parents, Brainard, Sr., and Ida Thames,
who never discouraged me from spending way too much time birding

ACKNOWLEDGMENTS

The records contained in this work represent countless hours of field effort by hundreds of observers. The second edition contained an Appendix listing many of the individuals who had contributed reports, but some fifteen years later this is no longer possible without including the hundreds of additional contributors to the eBird database maintained by the Cornell Lab of Ornithology. Suffice it to say that such a summary could not be produced without the contributions from many, many individuals.

I am indebted to Carol Besse, Ronan O'Carra, Chris Sloan, and Mike Stinson, all of whom reviewed drafts of the manuscript and contributed many helpful suggestions that improved its content. Greg Abernathy (Ky. Natural Lands Trust), Amy Covert (Ky. Energy and Environment Cabinet), and James Wheat provided invaluable assistance in producing the maps that accompany the text, and Mary Yandell converted files into various formats required for printing. Gratitude is also extended to Pam Spaulding for designing the front and back covers. Again, many thanks to all.

Finally, as I did in the Acknowledgements section of the second edition of the *Checklist*, I remain compelled to call attention to the dedicated efforts of Anne L. Stamm, who served as unofficial record keeper of Kentucky bird sightings for nearly three decades (roughly from 1970 through the late 1990s). Subsequent to the publication of Robert Mengel's *Birds of Kentucky* (1965), there was a need for someone to step in and continue to compile and maintain Kentucky's ornithological records. During an era of typewriters and white-out—and certainly long before the arrival of the internet, home computers, word processing, and database software—Anne kept track of notable observations in a set of meticulously coddeled notebooks, reviews of which remained invaluable in preparing this expanded update.

Photo credits:

Front cover: Kentucky Warbler by Pam Spaulding. **Back cover**: Baird's Sandpiper by Jamie Baker, Osprey by Jim Johnson, Palm Warbler by Jackie Elmore, and Yellow-crowned Night-Heron by Pam Spaulding. **Page vi**: Red-bellied Woodpecker by Jackie Elmore. **Page 2**: Bonaparte's Gull by Jamie Baker. **Page 4**: Buff-breasted Sandpiper by the author. **Pages 9 and 10**: Eastern Kingbird and Rose-breasted Grosbeak by Jackie Elmore.

INTRODUCTION

For more than fifty years, the benchmark for ornithological study in Kentucky has been (and remains) Robert Mengel's comprehensive work, *The Birds of Kentucky*. In 1988, the Kentucky Ornithological Society published the first edition of an *Annotated Checklist of the Birds of Kentucky*, which served to summarize (in an abbreviated fashion) the occurrence of the state's birdlife. This work, the *Checklist's* third edition, serves to update and expand slightly on the second edition, published in 2003.

The *Annotated Checklist* summarizes the status of 390 species of birds in Kentucky, including 384 species documented by specimen or photograph; six others (Greater Prairie-Chicken, Passenger Pigeon, Whooping Crane, Black Skimmer, Ivory-billed Woodpecker, and Carolina Parakeet) have been substantiated on the basis of at least one multiple-observer sight record or accounts in the historical literature. Eight of the 390 species are regarded as extinct or extirpated, and seven are introduced species. An additional eight species are regarded as having occurred hypothetically based on either single-observer sight records or details that are vague enough to raise some doubt as to their validity. Exotic species presumed to be escaped or of unnatural origin and not established are omitted; in this category are several species of waterfowl, gallinaceous birds, parakeets, and finches.

Subsequent to the publication of the first edition of the *Annotated Checklist*, the Kentucky Ornithological Society established the Kentucky Bird Records Committee (KBRC). During the fall of 2001, the KBRC reviewed those species that had been reported in Kentucky but for which photographic or specimen documentation was lacking. As a result of that review, several species that were included as accepted members of the state's avifauna in the first edition were omitted in the second edition (Purple Sandpiper, Fork-tailed Flycatcher, Kirtland's Warbler and Pine Grosbeak). These species had been reported either by single observers or on the basis of vague details. All are now excluded from the Official List (see pp. 259-260). Recent reassessment of the single report of another species, Masked Duck, has resulted in the omission of that species from the state's official list (see p. 260). Finally, taxonomic changes as published by the American Ornithologists' Society resulted in the lumping of Iceland Gull and Thayer's Gull into one species since publication of the second edition.

Any contemporary resource on the avifauna of a geographical or political area would not be complete without reference to the impact that the Cornell Lab of Ornithology's "eBird" database has had on collection and summarizing of ornithological data. For decades the published record remained the single source for the vast majority of ornithological occurrence information. At the time of the publication of the second edition of this work, the internet and personal database programs had only begun to impact the landscape of ornithological record-keeping.

In the early 2000s, contemplating how to tap into the vast supply of useful bird data being gathered by the ever increasing masses of birders, staff at the Cornell Lab created a powerful online geographic information and database system they named "eBird." They hoped eBird would be embraced by the birding community, and that the acceptance of the system would allow the Cornell Lab to gather an enormous amount of information and feed it into a management system to utilize for conservation purposes. The Cornell Lab's vision has now blossomed into probably the single most significant advance in tracking bird occurrence in history. Along with the popularity of eBird has come the expected subset of unreliable data. As with any data source there are an unknown number of questionable or erroneous records, but with the help of a network of regional "reviewers" much of the flawed information is being sorted out. It is my belief that eBird has become as reliable a data set as any published or unpublished resource based primarily on sight and photo-documented data. This level of reliability in our state would not have been possible without the efforts of Kentucky's primary eBird reviewer, Roseanna Denton, who is to be commended for her diligence at setting useful regional "filters" that flag unusual data and for reviewing the entire state's data set for more than 10 years.

As a result of the evolution of eBird into such a significant data source, I found it impossible to reliably update the status of Kentucky's birdlife without undertaking a systematic search of the information now contained in the eBird database. With the help of Cornell Lab staff and Kentucky's regional reviewers (most particularly Roseanna Denton), I was able to complete a review of eBird records in a reasonably efficient manner. Review of this new resource, however, involved an immense amount of time. I began the process of searching eBird data early during 2018 but was not able to complete the work until March 2019. Because observers are constantly entering current and historic data, it is certain that searches I completed during 2018 likely missed an unknown number of records that have been subsequently entered. This is always a problem when creating a cut-off for data collection for such a summary, but readers should be aware of the potential for missing data, particularly from eBird. I have made an attempt to include all of the more recent data of significance, but some records certainly will not appear herein.

In *The Birds of Kentucky*, Robert Mengel included a variety of well-founded cautionary notes concerning the validity of records that were not based on verification with specimens. Since that time, birding has increased in popularity to a level likely never envisioned by early ornithologists, while the collection of specimens has become quite rare. With the meteoric evolution of photographic technology, especially the recent advances in digital capability, photographic documentation has become more frequent and is highly desirable in substantiating unusual observations. I cannot overemphasize the value of photo-documenting observations.

As with all other data sources, I had to make a call on certain records for which supporting details were lacking or incomplete. In reviewing Kentucky's ornithological literature in preparation of this edition, I continued to be conservative in the acceptance of unusual records, especially if they were based solely on sight reports and lacked any obtainable details. For this reason, I have continued to step back from some of the extreme dates of observation listed in previously published summaries including some published in the first and second editions of this work. By applying a more conservative standard for inclusion of these records, I intend only to elevate the credibility of this resource and the birders who have contributed to it. In a few cases, my assessment of reliability of reports differed from those of eBird reviewers and/or previous authors and editors of published information. Those differences are typically noted in the text.

This checklist reflects the cooperative effort of many members of the Kentucky Ornithological Society and the birding community at large. It draws upon the notes and reports of a variety of past and present birders, and includes published records through 28 February 2019 (*The Kentucky Warbler*, Vol. 95, No. 2). A few significant observations made subsequent to that date (during spring and early summer 2019) are also included. Nomenclature and the order in which the species are presented follow the *American Ornithologists' Society Check-List of North American Birds* (Chesser et al. 2019a) and the 60th Supplement (Chesser et al. 2019b).

Previous editions of the *Checklist* have included a table of bar graphs summarizing the occurrence of each officially accepted species in the state. The utility of this resource has been diminished somewhat since the appearance of the Cornell Lab of Ornithology's eBird database. A component of that resource is customizable bar graphs that can summarize information for the state, as well as individual counties or "hotspots."

SPECIES ACCOUNTS

The species accounts are arranged in phylogenetic order following the AOS (Chesser et al. 2019a; Chesser et al. 2019b) and typically contain two sections. The first section includes the following information: (1) a brief statement of status in the state; (2) a breakdown (if one occurs) in regional occurrence of the species within the state; (3) a brief statement regarding habitats in which the species can be expected to be found; (4) if appropriate, a brief account of breeding occurrence in the state; (5) if pertinent, miscellaneous notes on habitats, numbers of the species to be expected, and behavior; and (6) for those species being monitored by state and federal wildlife agencies, a special notation concerning the state and/or federal conservation status of that species as designated by the Office of Kentucky Nature Preserves (state) or the United States Fish and Wildlife Service (federal). For most species with fewer than a few dozen records, each record is listed below the brief status summary.

A second section cites specific information on maximum counts and extreme seasonal dates of arrival and departure, as well as individual dates for out-of-season records. Most of this information is self-explanatory. Maximum counts are not included for all species. For a few species where maximum numbers may vary seasonally, more than one season is covered (e.g., maximum counts for both spring and fall). Also, for some species for which maximum counts vary regionally within the state, high numbers have been listed for more than one region (e.g., maximum counts are included for far western as well as central and/or eastern Kentucky). For extreme dates of occurrence, those that lie beyond what might be considered "normal" are included; in some cases when no abnormally early or late records are known, only the single or few earliest or latest date(s) is(are) given. When many early or late dates have been established in recent years, more dates may be listed simply for the recognition of the amount of new information. In some cases, the year of an observation included in this summary was not given in an original source; those dates for which the actual year of observation is not known are given as "18—" or "19—."

A few abbreviations are utilized in the lists of records in the second section as follows: (ba.) means a bird was banded; (*ba.) means a previously banded bird was recaptured; (ph.) or (vt.) means the report is substantiated by photograph or video evidence; (vo.) means the report is substantiated by voice recording evidence; and (sp.) [when in parentheses as shown "(sp.)"] means that a specimen was collected or obtained. Ages of birds are abbreviated as follows: adult (ad.); immature (imm.); juvenile (juv.); young (yg.). The reader should be aware that the terms "nesting" and "breeding" are used interchangeably. Additional standard abbreviations used in the second section include ones for directions (n., s., e., w., ne., etc.) and public land units (NP = Nature Preserve; SP = State Park; SNP = State Nature Preserve; SRP = State Resort Park).

Also included in the second section are **unaccepted records**. These records, which typically represent observations that either fall outside of an established pattern of seasonal occurrence and/ or represent numbers that are not typically observed during the season reported, lack some level of accompanying documentary information that I regard as necessary to conclusively consider them part of the accepted data set. The subset of observations treated in this summary as unaccepted certainly contain some valid records; however, in my opinion unequivocal documentary information for them is lacking. Reports considered to be hypothetical by other authors typically are included under the unaccepted category; exceptions are so noted. A few reports are noted as being accepted herein "provisionally;" these are reports for which documentary evidence appears to be conclusive but are qualified for the reason(s) explained in the text.

Finally, in assembling information for the various editions of the *Checklist*, I have run across a number of obvious or probable errors in previous publications, including the *Checklist's* first two editions. Thus, **published errors** represent definite or apparent errors that have been published in one source or another. Some of these errors were corrected by original observers, but others became apparent upon review of original reports or summaries. The source for such mistakes typically appeared to be simple typographical errors. In addition to the list of published errors, the reader will occasionally find an erratum statement, [usually enclosed in square brackets], embedded within the text of this section. Such notations typically call attention to errors in published dates or locations of otherwise valid records.

In this third edition of the Checklist, I also have attempted to tease out, typically at county level, individual reports of rarer species, both as breeding birds and non-breeding birds. This attempt has resulted in some additional lists or summaries of bird occurrence by county. It is hoped that this presentation will allow for additional data to come to light as the information presented is reviewed by readers. Readers are referred to the final paragraph of this introductory section for contact information regarding corrections or submission of new data.

SYMBOLS AND NOTATIONS

Symbols used in the species accounts are as follows:

[s] when placed before the common name of a species, denotes that it has not been documented in the state on the basis of specimen or photograph evidence, but simply on the basis of multiple observer sight record(s) or historical account(s).

[e] when placed before the common name of a species, denotes that it has become extinct or extirpated from Kentucky. Two species, Trumpeter Swan and Whooping Crane, are technically still within this category, even though members of introduced populations are being regularly seen again.

[*] when placed before the common name of a species, denotes that it has been verified by specimen, photographic, or written documentation to have bred on at least one occasion in Kentucky.

A few of dozen localities cited in the text are familiar enough to most readers as to be included with an abbreviated name and without reference to the county in which they are situated. These localities are listed with full name and county(ies) of occurrence in Figure 1 (pp. 6-7).

In many species accounts, references to specific regions of the state are made. These regions are shown on Figure 2 (p. 8). The physiographic boundaries shown on Figure 2 are adapted from a variety of sources.

STATUS DESCRIPTIONS

The following definitions apply to the descriptive occurrence terms used in the species accounts:

Resident: a species that is present throughout the year, although numbers and local abundances may vary widely from season to season as a result of influxes of transients or seasonal residents.

Summer resident: a non-resident species that is known to breed in the state.

Winter resident: a non-resident species that is known to winter in the state.

Transient: a non-resident species that regularly passes through the state during migration.

Visitant: a species that has been recorded at a given season, but for which breeding (summer), wintering (winter), or regular occurrence as a transient (spring or fall) has not been documented.

Vagrant: a species for which reoccurrences generally are not to be expected.

Extirpated: a species formerly present in Kentucky that has disappeared from the state, although still present elsewhere in North America.

Extinct: a species formerly present in Kentucky that is no longer in existence.

Definitions of the various levels of abundance used in the species accounts are defined as follows:

Common: Numerous and widespread, and should always be found in appropriate habitat.

Fairly common: Observed most of the time when searched for in appropriate habitat.

Uncommon: Often observed, but may require a diligent effort to locate, even in preferred habitat.

Rare: Observed infrequently and difficult to find, but usually seen every year.

Extremely rare: Observed very infrequently and not seen every year, but an apparent pattern of occurrence is established.

Accidental: Species with single or only a few scattered records, and without an apparent pattern of occurrence.

SOURCES

Periodical journals and several additional sources that are cited frequently in the Species Accounts appear there in abbreviated fashion. Citations for several other less frequently cited publications, web sites, and reports are found at the end of the Species Accounts section in a more traditional format.

AB	–	*American Birds*, National Audubon Society
AFN	–	*Audubon Field Notes*, National Audubon Society
AOU Checklist	–	*The A.O.U. Check-list of North American Birds*. 7th ed. 1998. American Ornithologists' Union. Allen Press, Lawrence, KS
Auk	–	*The Auk*, American Ornithologists' Union
BBS data	–	Breeding Bird Survey data, United States Department of the Interior, 1966-2019
Birding	–	*Birding*, American Birding Association
BNA	–	*The Birds of North America*, The Academy of Natural Sciences and the American Ornithologists' Union
BO	–	*The Beckham Observer*, Beckham Bird Club, Louisville
FN	–	*Field Notes*, American Birding Association and National Audubon Society.
IAQ	–	*The Indiana Audubon Quarterly*, Indiana Audubon Society
KBBA	–	Palmer-Ball, Brainard L., Jr. 1996. *The Kentucky Breeding Bird Atlas*. University Press of Kentucky Lexington, KY. 372 pp.
KW	–	*The Kentucky Warbler*, Kentucky Ornithological Society
Mengel	–	Mengel, Robert M. 1965. *The Birds of Kentucky*. American Ornithologists' Union Monograph No. 3
Migrant	–	*The Migrant*, Tennessee Ornithological Society
NAB	–	*North American Birds*, American Birding Association and National Audubon Society
WB	–	*The Wilson Bulletin*, Wilson Ornithological Society

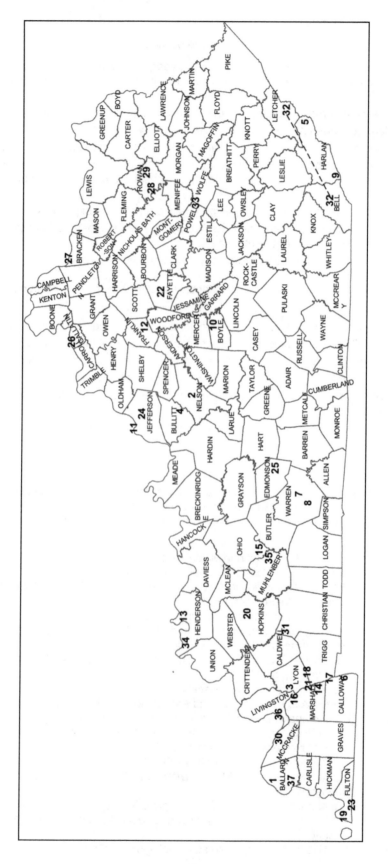

Key to Figure 1 locations.

(1) Ballard Wildlife Management Area, Ballard Co.
(2) Bardstown, Nelson Co.
(3) Barkley Dam, Livingston/Lyon Cos.
(4) Bernheim Forest, Bullitt/Nelson Cos.
(5) Black Mountain, Harlan/Letcher Cos.
(6) Blood River Embayment, Kentucky Lake, Calloway Co.
(7) Bowling Green, Warren Co.
(8) Chaney Lake/McElroy Lake (the "transient lakes" or "karst lakes," Warren Co.
(9) Cumberland Gap National Historical Park/Cumberland Mountain, Bell/Harlan Cos.
(10) Danville, Boyle Co.
(11) Falls of the Ohio, Jefferson Co.
(12) Frankfort, Franklin Co.
(13) Henderson, Henderson Co.
(14) Jonathan Creek Embayment, Kentucky Lake, Marshall Co.
(15) Ken Unit, Peabody Wildlife Management Area, Ohio Co.
(16) Kentucky Dam (Ky Dam), Marshall/Livingston Cos.
(17) Kentucky Lake (Ky Lake), Calloway/Lyon/Marshall/Trigg Cos.
(18) Lake Barkley, Lyon/Livingston/Trigg Cos.

(19) Lake No. 9, Fulton Co.
(20) Lake Peewee/Madisonville, Hopkins Co.
(21) Land Between the Lakes, Lyon/Trigg Cos.
(22) Lexington, Fayette Co.
(23) Long Point Unit, Reelfoot National Wildlife Refuge, Fulton Co.
(24) Louisville, Jefferson Co.
(25) Mammoth Cave National Park, Edmonson/Hart Cos.
(26) Markland Dam, Ohio River, Gallatin Co.
(27) Meldahl Dam, Ohio River, Bracken Co.
(28) Minor Clark Hatchery, Rowan Co.
(29) Morehead, Rowan Co.
(30) Paducah, McCracken Co.
(31) Pennyrile State Forest, Christian Co.
(32) Pine Mountain, Bell/Harlan/Letcher Cos.
(33) Red River Gorge Geological Area, Powell/Wolfe Cos.
(34) Sauerheber Unit, Sloughs Wildlife Management Area, Henderson Co.
(35) Sinclair Unit, Peabody Wildlife Management Area, Muhlenberg Co.
(36) Smithland Dam, Ohio River, Livingston Co.
(37) Swan Lake/Barlow Bottoms Wildlife Management Area, Ballard Co

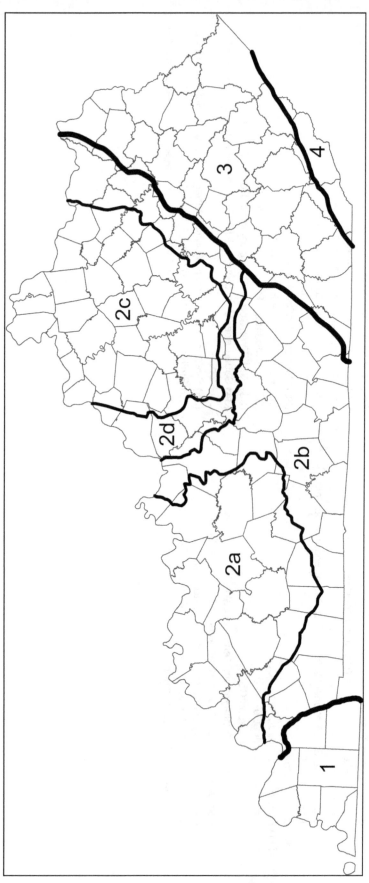

Figure 2. Map of Kentucky showing regions referred to in the text. 1) that part of the state west of the Land Between the Lakes (the Jackson Purchase); 2) central Kentucky from Land Between the Lakes east to the Cumberland Plateau; 2a) Shawnee Hills (Western Coalfield), 2b) Highland Rim (Pennyrile or Pennyroyal), 2c) Blue Grass, 2d) Knobs subsection of the Blue Grass; 3) Cumberland Plateau; 4) Cumberland Mountains. System of naming and boundaries are adapted from a variety of sources.

CONSERVATION STATUS DESIGNATIONS

Those species for which **State Breeding Status** designations are given are included on the Office of Kentucky Nature Preserves (OKNP) list of *Endangered, Threatened, Special Concern, and Historic Biota of Kentucky* (latest publicly available version on OKNP's web site is from 2012, although there have been a few subsequent additions and status changes [*fide* S. Fulton, pers. comm.] that have been incorporated herein). These species are tracked by OKNP through the recording and monitoring of specific breeding sites. The special designations pertain only to the breeding status of these species in Kentucky and do not necessarily imply rarity or a need for conservation at other seasons. A few species also are federally listed by the United States Fish and Wildlife Service, and a **Federal Status** designation is included for them. These species also are monitored by OKNP. The following definitions, adapted from KSNPC (2000), apply to the conservation status designations:

State Status Categories

Endangered: A species that is in danger of extirpation and/or extinction throughout all or a significant part of its nesting range in Kentucky.

Threatened: A species that is likely to become endangered within the foreseeable future throughout all or a significant part of its nesting range in Kentucky.

Special Concern: A species that should be monitored because: a) it exists in a limited geographical area, b) it may become threatened or endangered due to modification or destruction of habitat, c) certain characteristics or requirements make it especially vulnerable to specific pressures, d) experienced researchers have identified other factors that may jeopardize it, or e) it is thought to be rare or declining but insufficient information exists for assignment to the threatened or endangered status categories.

Historical: A species that has not been reliably reported breeding in recent (past 20-40) years.

Federal Status Categories

Endangered: ". . . any species which is in danger of extinction throughout all or a significant portion of its range . . ."

Threatened: ". . . any species which is likely to become an endangered species within the foreseeable future throughout all or a significant portion of its range."

SUMMARY

Readers should recognize that in order to summarize occurrence and abundance information so that it represents the status of a species over the entire state, generalizations must be made. The local status of a species may differ from the generalized statewide status indicated in this summary. Although Kentucky does not have the extreme size or latitudinal range of some adjacent states, there is still some regional variation in the occurrence and abundance of its birds. Much of this variation can be explained by habitat differences, such as the predominance of forested areas and the lack of waterbird habitat in the mountainous regions of eastern Kentucky as compared to the greater amount of open land and waterbird habitat in the central and western portions of the state. However, patterns of bird migration also play a role; for example, the proximity of western Kentucky to the Mississippi Flyway accounts for the greater number of some species of waterbirds observed in that region. In contrast, some passerine migrants such as the Cape May Warbler and Black-throated Blue Warbler can be unusually scarce in the western portion of the state although they are more numerous in the east because of their migration patterns.

For further information readers are referred to the very complete work by Robert M. Mengel (*The Birds of Kentucky*) from which much of the information assembled in this summary is taken. While now dated by more than fifty years, much of the information contained in Mengel's work cannot be found elsewhere, and it remains the major reference to Kentucky's avifauna.

It is doubtless that some errors have been made or records omitted. It seemed that every time I delved into the ornithological literature, I could find additional records of significance that had eluded me during previous forays. In order to ensure that occurrence information may be kept up to date for future revision, it is requested that all changes in abundance, errors, or extensions of extreme dates, as well as any records of extremely rare or accidental species, be sent to either the author or the Secretary of the KBRC (see inside of front cover for contact information).

SPECIES ACCOUNTS

OFFICIAL LIST

*BLACK-BELLIED WHISTLING-DUCK *Dendrocygna autumnalis*

Status: Extremely rare spring and summer visitant (but increasing in occurrence); one recent breeding record. This species has been expanding remarkably during the past couple of decades. There are now 22 records.

Early spring dates: 18 Apr 2015, Madison Co. (*KW* 91:64, 2015); 4 May 2019, Lexington (R. O'Carra, eBird data); 11 May 2018, Larue Co. (*KW* 94:68, 2018).

Late fall dates: 1 Dec 2018, Calloway Co. (J. Lowery, pers. comm); 16 Sep 2016, McCracken Co. (*KW* 93:4, 2017); mid-Sep 2013, McCracken Co. (*KW* 90:4, 2014).

Chronological list of records

1) 19 Aug 2000, 2 at Mitchell Lake, Ballard WMA (*KW* 77:4/35, 2001)
2) 20 May 2010, 5 (ph.) sw. Rumsey, McLean Co. (*KW* 86:53/63, 2010)
3) 13-19 Jun 2010, 1 (ph.) at McElroy Lake (*KW* 86:77/90, 2010)
4) 14-16 May 2011, 10 (ph.) sw. of Rumsey, McLean Co. (*KW* 87:82/100, 2011)
5) 23 Jun–20 Jul 2012, 2 (ph.) outside Elizabethtown, Hardin Co. (*KW* 88:92/104, 2012)
6) mid-Jul–7 Aug 2013, 4 (ph.) in sw. Logan Co. (*KW* 90:4/20, 2014)
7) 21-25 May & mid-Sep 2013, 2 in s. Todd Co. (*KW* 90:4, 2014)
8) 18 Apr–19 May 2015, 1 (ph.) at Lake Reba, Madison Co. (*KW* 91:64/80, 2015)
9) 22 May 2016, 4 (ph.) at Iuka, Livingston Co. (*KW* 92:56, 2016)
10) 31 May–16 Sep 2016, up to 9 (ph.) at West Paducah, McCracken Co. (*KW* 92:77, 2016; *KW* 93:4, 2017) with up to 16 (ph.) returning to the same location late Apr–17 May 2017 (*KW* 93:70, 2017)
11) 16 May 2017, 1 (ph.) at Ledbetter, Livingston Co. (*KW* 93:70/105, 2017)
12) 11-13 May 2018, 2 (ph.) at Hodgenville, Larue Co. (*KW* 94:68, 2018)
13) 14-16 May 2018, at Pembroke, Christian Co. (K. Greenfield/C. Bliznick, eBird data)
14) 19-31 May 2018, up to 6 (ph.) nr. and at Morgan Pond (*KW* 94:68, 2018)
15) 30 Jun 2018, n. of Glasgow, Barren Co. (*KW* 94:103, 2018)
16) 30 Jun–18 Aug 2018, 4 (ph.) n. of Simpsonville, Shelby Co. (*KW* 94:103/124, 2018; *KW* 95:4, 2019)
17) 1 Aug 2018, 2 (ph.) n. of Wickliffe, Ballard Co. (*KW* 95:4/5, 2019)
18) summer/fall 2018, 1-2 nr. New Concord, Calloway Co. (*KW* 94:103, 2018; *KW* 95:4, 2019) with a family group of an ad. and 13 yg. present during Oct 2018 representing a first confirmed breeding record for the state (J. Lowery/P. Hahs, pers. comm.); ad. and five yg. were last seen ca. 1 Dec 2018 (J. Lowery, pers. comm.) and the pair returned spring 2019 (J. Lowery, pers. comm.)
19) 4-12 May 2019, 5 (ph.) at Lexington (R. O'Carra et al., eBird data)
20) 10 May 2019, 7 (ph.) at Hawesville, Hancock Co. (T. Lucas, photos/pers. comm.)
21) late May 2019, a pair (ph.) using a Wood Duck box for nesting at Kevil, Ballard Co. (B. Jerrell, photos/pers. comm.)
22) 11 Jun 2019, 4 (ph.) along Bayou de Chien, Hickman Co. (C. Bliznick, eBird data)

FULVOUS WHISTLING-DUCK *Dendrocygna bicolor*

Status: Accidental vagrant. This duck shows up occasionally well north of its normal range. It has been documented in Kentucky twice.

Chronological list of records

1) 8 May 2008, 5 (ph.) at and nr. Open Pond, Fulton Co. (Yandell and Yandell, *KW* 84:93/100, 2008; *KW* 84:53, 2008)
2) 28 Jul 2008, (9) at Blood River (*KW* 84:83, 2008)

SNOW GOOSE *Anser caerulescens*

Status: Rare to locally fairly common transient and winter resident; extremely rare during summer. This species is numerous along the Mississippi and lower Ohio rivers and regular throughout the remainder of central and western portions of Kentucky, but relatively infrequent across the eastern portion of the state. A recent increase in the North American nesting population has resulted in a dramatic increase in numbers in Kentucky, especially in the western portion of the state. Peak of abundance occurs from late Nov to early Mar. There was a nesting attempt of presumed wild birds near Goshen, Oldham Co. in 1973 (*KW* 52:43, 1976); injured birds undoubtedly now account for an increasing number of summer observations. In Kentucky, both the blue morph (Blue Goose) and white morph (Snow Goose) are well-represented.

Maximum counts: more than **200,000** total from Ballard to Fulton cos., 15 Feb 2007 (*KW* 83:44, 2007); ca. **150,000** at Ballard WMA, 6 Feb 2006 (*KW* 82:44, 2006); ca. **150,000** at Doug Travis WMA, Carlisle Co., 31 Jan–3 Feb 2017 (*KW* 93:44, 2017); **137,870** at Ballard WMA, 20 Jan 2008 (*KW* 84:41, 2008); ca. **130,000** in Ballard Co., 6 Feb 2007 (*KW* 83:44, 2007); ca. **125,000** in the vicinity of the Long Point Unit, 8 Jan 2004 (*KW* 80:40, 2004); ca. **100,000** at Ballard WMA, first week of Mar 2002 (eBird data; C. Wilkins, pers. comm.); **90,000** at the Long Point Unit, 11 Jan 2008 (*KW* 84:41, 2008); **76,000** in Ballard Co., 3 Feb 2004 (*KW* 80:40, 2004); **40,000-50,000** at Ballard WMA, 26 Dec 2004 (*KW* 81:56, 2005); **30,000-60,000** at Ballard WMA, winter 1997-1998 (C. Wilkins, pers. comm.); **35,000** at the Long Point Unit, 27 Dec 2010 (S. Rogers/M. Riggs, eBird data); **27,000** at the Long Point Unit, 23 Jan 2018 (*KW* 94:53, 2018); **22,500** at the Long Point Unit, 14 Dec 2007 (eBird data); **15,000-20,000** at Ballard WMA, 19 Dec 1989 (*KW* 66:36, 1990); **15,000-18,000** at Ballard WMA, winter 1990-1991 (*KW* 67:28, 1991); **15,000** at the Sauerheber Unit, first week of Feb 2007 (KW 83:44, 2007); **15,000** at the Sauerheber Unit, 13 Jan 2016 (*KW* 92:40, 2016); **15,000** in w. Henderson Co., 5 Jan 2017 (*KW* 93:44, 2017); **12,000** at the Sauerheber Unit, late Feb 2006 (*KW* 82:44, 2006); **10,000** at the Long Point Unit, 24 Jan 2002 (C. Dirks, pers. comm.); **10,000** at the Sauerheber Unit, 25 Jan 2008 (*KW* 84:41, 2008); **8000** s. of Rumsey, McLean Co., 23 Jan 2017 (*KW* 93:45, 2017).

Late spring dates (apparently uninjured birds): 16 Jun 1973, Oldham Co. (*AB* 27:875, 1973); 3 Jun 1999, Warren Co. (*KW* 76:9, 2000); 2 Jun 2018, Franklin Co. (*KW* 94:103, 2018).

Early fall dates (other than presumed injured birds): 17 Aug 2002, Ky Lake, Calloway Co. (*KW* 79:5, 2003); 17 Aug 2003, Minor Clark Hatchery (*KW* 80:4, 2004; also, see *KW* 80:64, 2004 & *KW* 82:4, 2006); 29 Aug 1983, Ballard Co. (*KW* 60:15, 1984); 10 Sep 1983, Lexington (*KW* 60:15, 1984).

Out-of-season records (summer): in recent years there has been an increase in the number of summer reports, in large part due to the presence of injured birds.

Hybrid records: See Greater White-fronted Goose and Ross's Goose.

ROSS'S GOOSE *Anser rossii*

Status: Rare to locally uncommon transient and winter visitant/resident. Unrecorded prior to the 1980s, perhaps to some degree by being overlooked; however, a dramatic increase in the North American breeding population has resulted in an increased occurrence in the United States during the non-breeding season. First recorded in Kentucky 30 Nov–7 Dec 1986 at Ballard WMA, where at least four were found in the company of a flock of several thousand Snow Geese (Palmer-Ball and Robinson, *KW* 63:66-67, 1987). Since the early 1990s, the species has become annual in Kentucky, especially at the state's three largest wintering areas for Snow Geese at Ballard WMA, Ballard Co., Reelfoot NWR, Fulton Co., and Sloughs WMA, Henderson Co. Small numbers also have become annual in the company of flocks of waterfowl (usually geese) at other locales including the transient lakes near Woodburn, Warren Co. Individuals or small flocks also are occasionally found with feral waterfowl. In recent years, the species has become annual in other parts of Kentucky, currently as far east as Cave Run Lake. Peak of abundance occurs from late Nov to early Mar. With the increase in populations of Ross's Geese and Snow Geese, hybridization between the two species has become more apparent, resulting in a number of reports across the range. Some of these individuals, particularly backcrosses, are quite difficult to detect. Subsequent to initial reports in the region, I have tended to monitor the occurrence of these hybrids less critically.

Maximum counts: **109** total (tallies of 82 and 45 in two different flocks) in the Lower Hickman Bottoms, 2 Feb 2018 (*KW* 94:53, 2018); **95** in the Lower Hickman Bottoms, 22 Feb 2007 (*KW* 83:44, 2007); up to **80** at the Long Point Unit, 10 Feb 2002 (B. Palmer-Ball, eBird data); at least **79** (ph.) along Horseshoe Road, w. Henderson Co., 22 Feb 2016 (*KW* 92:40, 2016); at least **65** in the Lower Hickman Bottoms, 13 Feb 2017 (*KW* 93:45, 2017); **54** at the Long Point Unit, 18 Dec 2004 (*KW* 81:55-56, 2005); at least **40** at the Sauerheber Unit, 1 Dec 2010 (*KW* 87:57, 2011); **37** at Open Pond, Fulton Co., 6 Feb 2005 (*KW* 81:56, 2005); at least **30** at the Long Point Unit, 21 Dec 2008 (*KW* 85:44, 2009); **26** at the Sauerheber Unit, 28 Jan 2006 (*KW* 82:44, 2006); **26** at the Sauerheber Unit, 21 Nov 2007 (*KW* 84:4, 2008); **23** (ph.) in Todd Co., 16-18 Feb 2018 (S. Arnold, eBird data); **22** (ph.) in w. Hardin Co., 20-21 Nov 2017 (*KW* 94:4, 2018); ca. **20** at the Long Point Unit, 11 Dec 2009 (*KW* 86:40, 2010); **20** at the Long Point Unit, 29 Jan 2018 (M. Todd, eBird data); **19** nr. Woodburn, Warren Co., 23 Dec 2017 (A. Hulsey, eBird data); **18** at McElroy Lake, 18 Jan 2017 (*KW* 93:45, 2017); at least **16** at the Long Point Unit, 17 Feb 2013 (*KW* 89:44, 2013); **16** in the Lower Hickman Bottoms, 5 Jan 2016 (*KW* 92:40, 2016); **15** at McElroy Lake,, 24 Feb 2008 (*KW* 84:41, 2008); **15** in Shelby Co., 2 Jan 2016 (*KW* 92:25, 2016); **15** nr. Needmore, Ballard Co., 18 Dec 2017 (C. Bliznick/B. Palmer-Ball, eBird data); at least **14** at Ballard WMA, 19 Dec 2016 (*KW* 93:45, 2017); **13** at McElroy Lake, 21 Feb 2014 (*KW* 90:44, 2014); **13** (ph.) at Wooton Pond, Pulaski Co., 4-7 Jan 2018 (R. Denton, eBird data); **12+** at the Sauerheber Unit, 13 Jan 2001 (*NAB* 55:176, 2001); **12+** at the Sauerheber Unit, 11 Jan 2007 (*KW* 83:44, 2007); **9** in e. Allen Co., 24 Dec 2016 (*KW* 93:18-19, 2017); **9** at Lake Reba, Madison Co., 8-9 Jan 2018 (C. Titus, eBird data); **9** (ph.) at Frogue Pond, Todd Co., 23 Dec 2016 (S. Arnold, eBird data).

Late spring dates: 28 May 1999 (*KW* 75:4/24 1999; L. Doyle, notes); 28 May 2017, Hardin Co. (*KW* 93:70, 2017); 25 May 2012, (ph.) Franklin Co. (*KW* 88:71, 2012); 19 May 2009, Warren Co. (*KW* 85:64, 2009); 12 May 2018, Bowling Green (*KW* 94:68, 2018); 25 May 2019, Bowling Green (m. ob., eBird data); 4 May 2011, Hardin Co. (*KW* 87:82, 2011); 12 Apr 1996, McElroy Lake (eBird data).

Early fall dates: 11 Aug 2010, Falls of the Ohio (*KW* 87:11, 2011); 20 Aug 2018, (ph.) Bowling Green [possibly summered] (*KW* 95:4, 2019); 26 Aug 2009, (ph.) Falls of the Ohio (*KW* 86:4, 2010); 4 Nov 2017, (ph.) Lake Linville, Rockcastle Co. (*KW* 94:4, 2018); 5 Nov 2004, Ohio Co. (*KW* 81:4, 2005); 10 Nov 2017, (ph.) Frogue Pond, Todd Co. (A. Troyer, eBird data); 11 Nov 2015, (ph.) Sinclair Unit (*KW* 92:4, 2016); 13 Nov 2010, Sinclair Unit (*KW* 87:11-12, 2011); 15 Nov 2010, Calloway Co. (*KW* 87:12, 2011); 15 Nov 2017, (ph.) two locations in Wayne Co. (R. Denton, eBird data); 17 Nov 2012, Boone Co. (*KW* 89:4, 2013); 17 Nov 2014, Pulaski Co. (*KW* 91:4, 2015); 17 Nov 2017, (ph.) Pulaski Co. (R. Denton, eBird data); 18 Nov 2017, Calloway Co. (H. Chambers, eBird data); 19 Nov 2003, Warren Co. (*KW* 80:4, 2004); 19 Nov 2017, (ph.) Fayette Co. (L. Combs, eBird data); 20 Nov 2010, (ph.) Russell Co. (*KW* 87:12, 2011); 20 Nov 2013, Trigg Co. (*KW* 90:4, 2014); 20 Nov 2012, Sauerheber Unit (*KW* 89:4, 2013); 20 Nov 2013, Trigg Co. (*KW* 90:4, 2014); 20 Nov 2017, (ph.) Hardin Co. (C. Bliznick/P. Spaulding, eBird data).

Hybrid records (Ross's Goose x Snow Goose): 21 Mar-20 Apr 2006, imm. (ph.) in Warren Co. (*KW* 82:65, 2006); 22 Feb 2007, Lower Hickman Bottoms (*KW* 83:44, 2007); 17 Feb 2008, Todd Co. (*KW* 84:41, 2008); 21 Mar 2008, McElroy Lake (*KW* 84:56, 2008); 15-20 May 2018, (ph.) Calvert City, Marshall Co. (*KW* 94:68, 2018; T. Smith, eBird data).

Summary of records by county

Allen (*KW* 84:41, 2008; *KW* 89:23, 2013; *KW* 90:24, 2014; *KW* 91:64, 2015; *KW* 92:40, 2016; *KW* 93:18-19/22, 2017)

Ballard (annual since 1986)

Barren (*KW* 80:40, 2004; *KW* 85:44, 2009; *KW* 89:24, 2013)

Boone (*KW* 80:4, 2004; *KW* 81:56, 2005; *KW* 85:36/44, 2009; *KW* 85:44, 2009; *KW* 88:36/44, 2012; *KW* 89:4, 2013; *KW* 93:45/70, 2017)

Boyle (*KW* 64:27, 1988; [*KW* 73:28, 1997; M. Flynn, et al., 1996 pers. comm.]; *KW* 85:44, 2009)

Bracken (*KW* 87:57, 2011; *KW* 90:44, 2014)

Bullitt (L. McMahon et al., 2018 eBird data)

Calloway (*KW* 82:65, 2006; *KW* 87:12, 2011; *KW* 91:64, 2015; *KW* 92:56, 2016; H. Chambers, 2017 eBird data)

Campbell (*KW* 82:44, 2006; *KW* 93:45, 2017)

Carroll (*KW* 84:32/41, 2008; *KW* 85:35/44, 2009)

Fayette (*KW* 85:10/44, 2009; *KW* 87:12, 2011; *KW* 88:71, 2012; *KW* 89:25/44, 2013; *KW* 90:44, 2014; *KW* 91:48, 2015; *KW* 92:40, 2016; *KW* 93:45/70, 2017; m. ob., 2017 eBird data; *KW* 94:68, 2018; m. ob., 2018 eBird data)

Franklin (*KW* 85:44, 2009; *KW* 88:71, 2012; *KW* 90:44, 2014; *KW* 93:45, 2017; R. Chadwick et al., 2017 eBird data; *KW* 94:68, 2018)

Fulton (annual since the late 1990s)

Graves (H. Chambers, 2018 eBird data)

Hardin (*KW* 85:44, 2009; *KW* 87:57/82, 2011; *KW* 89:44, 2013; *KW* 90:44/64, 2014; *KW* 91:48/64, 2015; *KW* 93:70, 2017; *KW* 94:4, 2018; J. Snyder et al., 2018 eBird data)

Hart (*KW* 89:32/44, 2013; *KW* 90:44, 2014; *KW* 91:48, 2015; J. Sole, 2017 eBird data; *KW* 94:68, 2018)

Henderson (annual since the early 2000s)

Henry (*KW* 88:44, 2012)

Hopkins (A. Morgan, 2002 notes; *KW* 86:40, 2010; *KW* 91:64, 2015; *KW* 94:68, 2018; T. Graham, 2018 eBird data)

Jefferson (*KW* 85:64, 2009; *KW* 86:4, 2010; *KW* 87:11, 2011; *KW* 90:64, 2014; R. Falls, et al., 2015 eBird data; *KW* 93:70, 2017; *KW* 94:68, 2018)

Kenton (*KW* 89:44, 2013; *KW* 93:45, 2017)

Larue (*KW* 87:31, 2011; *KW* 88:44, 2012; *KW* 94:27, 2018; J. Snyder et al., 2017 eBird data)

Laurel (*KW* 92:40, 2016)

Logan (*KW* 82:65, 2006; *KW* 85:44, 2009; *KW* 87:57/82, 2011; F. Lyne, 2017 eBird data)

Lyon (*KW* 80:64, 2004; J. Sole, 2013 eBird data; J. Hall/S. Arnold, 2017 eBird data)

Madison (*KW* 85:64, 2009; *KW* 88:71, 2012; *KW* 89:44, 2013; *KW* 90:44, 2014; *KW* 93:45, 2017; *KW* 94:32, 2018; D. Lang et al., 2018 eBird data)

Marshall (*KW* 78:32, 2002; *KW* 88:44, 2012; *KW* 90:44, 2014; *KW* 91:48/64, 2015; D. Simbeck, 2017 eBird data; A. Lydeard, 2019 eBird data)

McCracken (*KW* 88:44, 2012; T. Wolff, eBird data)

McLean (*KW* 93:45, 2017)

Meade (*KW* 79:27/44, 2003)

Mercer ([W. Kemper, 2000 pers. comm.; B. Palmer-Ball, 2000 eBird data]; *KW* 79:44, 2003; *KW* 93:45, 2017)

Monroe (*KW* 90:44, 2014)

Muhlenberg ([*KW* 77:18, 2001; *KW* 78:21/32, 2002]; *KW* 78:21, 2002; *KW* 87:11, 2011; *KW* 89: 44/64, 2013; *KW* 90:23/44, 2014; *KW* 92:4/40, 2016; B. Yandell, 2018 eBird data)

Nelson (*KW* 78:22, 2002; *KW* 82:20/44, 2006; *KW* 87:29/57, 2011; *KW* 92:40, 2016)

Ohio (*KW* 79:20/44/66, 2003; *KW* 80:19/40, 2004; *KW* 81:4/55, 2005; *KW* 82:19/44, 2006; *KW* 83: 8/23/44, 2007; *KW* 84:41, 2008; *KW* 89:44, 2013; C. Bliznick, 2017 eBird data; *KW* 94:68, 2018)

Oldham (B. Palmer-Ball/L. McNeely, 2002 eBird data; *KW* 79:44-45, 2003; *KW* 84:41, 2008; *KW* 85:44, 2009; *KW* 86:40, 2010; *KW* 87:57, 2011; *KW* 89:44, 2013; *KW* 90:44, 2014; B. Woerner, 2015 eBird data; C. Bliznick, eBird data)

Pulaski (*KW* 82:44, 2006; *KW* 84:56, 2008; *KW* 89:44, 2013; *KW* 91:4, 2015; *KW* 93:45, 2017; R. Denton, 2017 eBird data; *KW* 94:68, 2018)

Rockcastle (R. Denton, 2017 eBird data)

Rowan (easternmost record) (*KW* 73:52, 1997; G. Robe, 2002 notes; *KW* 80:40, 2004; *KW* 83:44, 2007)

Russell (*KW* 87:12, 2011)

Shelby (*KW* 92:25, 2016)

Taylor (*KW* 85:44, 2009)

Todd (*KW* 84:41, 2008; *KW* 91:20/48, 2015; *KW* 93:22/45/70, 2017; A. Troyer/S. Arnold, et al., 2017-2018 eBird data)

Trigg (*KW* 84:41, 2008; *KW* 85:44, 2009; *KW* 90:4/64, 2014; *KW* 91:48, 2015)

Union (*KW* 89:64, 2013)

Warren (*KW* 66:54, 1990; essentially annual since the mid-1990s)

Wayne (*KW* 83:25/44, 2007; *KW* 84:56, 2008; *KW* 93:45/70, 2017; R. Denton/R. Bontrager, 2017 eBird data; *KW* 95:29, 2019)

GREATER WHITE-FRONTED GOOSE *Anser albifrons*

Status: Locally rare to fairly common transient and winter resident; extremely rare during summer. This goose was seen regularly by Audubon during the early 1800s, at least in western Kentucky (Mengel:175). After many decades of absence, the species reappeared during the early 1970s, initially as an extremely rare visitant. During the 1990s it became remarkably more widespread (especially across the western third of the state), but in recent years the species has become annual in central and western Kentucky and not unexpected anywhere in the state. As a result of the overall increase in presence, the number of known or likely injured birds that have lingered into or through summer also has increased. The maximum counts given below include several from earlier years and from central Kentucky to demonstrate the increase in numbers and distribution over the past 20 years.

Maximum counts: **35,498** in the vicinity of the Long Point Unit,11 Jan 2008 (*KW* 84:40, 2008); **21,650** in the vicinity of the Long Point Unit, 8 Jan 2004 (*KW* 80:39, 2004); **17,750** at the Sauerheber Unit, 10 Dec 2015 (*KW* 92:40, 2016); **16,000** at the Sauerheber Unit, 31 Dec 2014 (*KW* 91:47, 2015); **13,250** in the vicinity of the Long Point Unit, 2 Jan 2007 (*KW* 83:44, 2007); **10,050** at the Sauerheber Unit, 21 Nov 2018 (*KW* 95:4, 2019); ca. **10,000** at Doug Travis WMA, Carlisle Co., 3 Feb 2017 (*KW* 93:44, 2017); **8750** at the Sauerheber Unit, 14 Dec 2016 (*KW* 93:44, 2017); **8700** at Ballard WMA, 3 Jan 2013 (*KW* 89:44, 2013); **8530** at Ballard WMA during the last week of Dec 2016 (*KW* 93:44, 2017); **7300** at Ballard WMA during the second week of Dec 2014 (*KW* 91:47, 2015); **7000** at the Sauerheber Unit, 29 Jan 2007 (*KW* 83:44, 2007); **5800** at the Sauerheber Unit, 9 Jan 2008 (*KW* 84:40, 2008); **5580** at Ballard WMA, 20 Jan 2008 (*KW* 84:40, 2008); **5390** at Ballard WMA, 11 Feb 2004 (*KW* 80:39, 2004); **5000** at the Long Point Unit, 31 Dec 2002 (*KW* 79:44, 2003); **4500** at the Long Point Unit, 24 Jan 2002 (C. Dirks, pers. comm.); **3500** at the Sauerheber Unit, early Jan 2003 (*KW* 79:44, 2003); **3000-4000** at Ballard WMA, first week of Feb 2007 (*KW* 83:44, 2007); **3210** at the Sauerheber Unit, 18 Jan 2012 (*KW* 88:43, 2012); **2300** at the Sauerheber Unit, 4 Jan 2006 (*KW* 82:44, 2006); **1500** at the Sauerheber Unit, 24 Jan 2002 (M. Morton, pers. comm.); up to **1500** at the Long Point Unit, winter 2000–2001 (*NAB* 55:176, 2001); more than **1000** at the Long Point Unit, 19 Feb 1998 (B. Palmer-Ball, eBird data); **800+** at the Long Point Unit, 29 Dec 1999 (*KW* 76:28, 2000); ca. **350** at Ballard WMA, 31 Dec 2001 (B. Palmer-Ball, eBird data); **150** at Hodgenville, Larue Co., 31 Dec 2017 (J. Snyder, eBird data); **58** at A.J. Jolly Park, Campbell Co., 3 Nov 2005 (*KW* 82:4, 2006); **51** at the Reformatory Lake, Oldham Co., 10 Jan 2014 (*KW* 90:44, 2014); **40** at Lake Linville, Rockcastle Co., 23 Dec 2016 (*KW* 93:44, 2017); **30** at Cave Run Lake 20-21 Feb 2014 (*KW* 90:44, 2014).

Late spring dates (reports after late Mar/early Apr may be mostly or all injured birds): 19 May 2018, (ph.) Henderson (*KW* 94:68, 2018); 17 May 1970, Louisville (Robertson, *KW* 46:56, 1970); 13 May 2017, Hardin Co. (K. Thomas, eBird data); 3 May 2013, Sauerheber Unit (*KW* 89:64, 2013); 3 May 2014, w. Henderson Co. (*KW* 90:64, 2014); 21 Apr 2007, Sauerheber Unit (*KW* 83:72, 2007); 12 Apr 2004, Ballard WMA (*KW* 80:64, 2004); 19 Apr 2015, Minor Clark Hatchery (*KW* 91:64, 2015); 6 Apr 2012, Ballard WMA (*KW* 88:71, 2012); 5 Apr 2015, Pulaski Co (*KW* 91:64, 2015); 1 Apr 1989, McElroy Lake (Palmer-Ball and Boggs, *KW* 67:39, 1991); 29 Mar 2016, Fulton Co. (*KW* 92:56, 2016); 27 Mar 2009, Ballard WMA (*KW* 85:64, 2009); 21 Mar 2003, Ballard WMA (*KW* 79:65, 2003); 21 Mar 2007, Ballard WMA (*KW* 83:72, 2007); 15 Mar 1998, Fulton Co. (B. Palmer-Ball, eBird data).

Early fall dates: 18 Sep 1982, Ballard Co. (*KW* 59:14, 1983); 1 Oct 2009, Jefferson Co. (*KW* 86:4, 2010); 4 Oct 2018, Union Co. (*KW* 95:4, 2019); 7 Oct 1991, Ballard Co. (B. Palmer-Ball, eBird data); 9 Oct 2013, Sauerheber Unit (*KW* 90:4, 2014); 10 Oct 2012, Marshall Co. (*KW* 89:4, 2013); 10 Oct 2017, (ph.) Union Co. (*KW* 94:4, 2018); 12 Oct 2015, Calloway Co. (*KW* 92:4, 2016); 13 Oct 1990, Henderson Co. (*KW* 67:4, 1991); 14 Oct 2011, Calloway Co. (*KW* 88:4, 2012); 15 Oct 1989, Ohio Co. (*KW* 66:5-6, 1990).

Out-of-season records (late-spring/summer and likely or confirmed injured): through the summer of 2005 at Ballard WMA (*KW* 81:82/104, 2005; *KW* 82:4, 2006); through the summer of 2012 at the Sauerheber Unit (*KW* 88:71, 2012); summer 2013, (2) at Ballard WMA (*KW* 89:92/100, 2013; *KW* 90:4, 2014); 1 May 2016, (3) at Ballard WMA (*KW* 92:56, 2016); 30 May 2017, (ph.) in w. Fulton Co. (*KW* 93:70, 2017).

Hybrid records: Presumed Greater White-fronted Goose x Snow Goose at the Long Point Unit, (ph.) 17 Dec 2004 (M. Todd, eBird data) and 2 Dec 2005 (*KW* 82:44, 2006).

Published error: 4 Oct 2000, Henderson Co. (*KW* 77:4, 2001); date should have read 21 Oct (*fide* B. Palmer-Ball, notes).

County records east of Bowling Green

Allen (2008 eBird data; *KW* 90:24/44, 2014; *KW* 91:4, 2015)

Allen/Barren (Barren River Lake [S. Stedman, 2004 eBird data; *KW* 86:40, 2010; *KW* 87:57, 2011; *KW* 90:44, 2014; T. Durbin, 2017 eBird data])

Barren (*KW* 80:40, 2004)

Bath/Rowan (Cave Run Lake [*KW* 67:28, 1991; A. Newman, 2011 eBird data; *KW* 89:44, 2013; *KW* 90:4/44/64, 2014])

Bell (*KW* 80:4, 2004; D. Ledford, 2017 eBird data)

Boone (28 Nov 1976, 2 collected [K. Maslowski, pers. comm.]; *KW* 74:32, 1998; B. Palmer-Ball, 2000 eBird data; *KW* 80:31/40, 2004; *KW* 81:23, 2005; *KW* 82:44, 2006; *KW* 85:36/44, 2009; m. ob., 2018 eBird data)

Boyle (*KW* 85:27, 2009)

Bracken (W. Hull, 2016 eBird data)

Bullitt (J. Sole, 2018 eBird data; J. Sole, 2018 eBird data)

Campbell (*KW* 75:4, 1999; *KW* 82:4, 2006; *KW* 90:44, 2014)

Carroll (*KW* 87:39, 2011)

Carter (*KW* 81:82, 2005)

Clark (*KW* 91:47, 2015)

Fayette (*KW* 85:44, 2009; *KW* 89:44, 2013; *KW* 90:44/64, 2014; *KW* 91:47, 2015; m. ob., 2016 eBird data; *KW* 93:44, 2017; R. O'Carra et al., 2017 eBird data; m. ob., 2018 eBird data)

Fleming (*KW* 88:44, 2012; *KW* 90:64, 2014)

Franklin (*KW* 87:57, 2011; *KW* 89:44, 2013; *KW* 90:27, 2014; *KW* 91:47, 2015; *KW* 93:4, 2017; R. Chadwick et al., 2018 eBird data)

Gallatin (*KW* 83:44, 2007; B. Palmer-Ball/L. McMahon, 2018 eBird data)

Hardin (late Dec 2000–mid-Jan 2001, at least 2 off and on at Freeman Lake [R. Healy, pers. comm.]; *KW* 79:44, 2003; *KW* 83:44, 2007; *KW* 85:44, 2009; *KW* 85:44, 2009; *KW* 87:57, 2011; *KW* 91:47, 2015; J. Snyder/J. Sole, 2016 eBird data; *KW* 93:44, 2017; K. Thomas, 2017 eBird data; J. Sole et al., 2017 eBird data; J. Snyder et al., 2018 eBird data)

Hart (*KW* 91:47, 2015; J. Sole et al., 2017 eBird data; J. Sole/J. Rose, 2018 eBird data)

Henry (*KW* 94:30, 2018)

Jefferson (14 Mar 1970, 1 on the Ohio River at Louisville [Holding, *KW* 46:55, 1970]; 20 Apr–17 May 1970, probably the same bird (ph.) at Cave Hill Cemetery, Louisville [Robertson, *KW* 46:56, 1970]; *KW* 86:4/40, 2010; M. Callan, 2011 eBird data; *KW* 91:47, 2015; *KW* 92:4, 2016; *KW* 93:4, 2017; P. Bell et al., 2018 eBird data)

Kenton (*KW* 90:44, 2014)

Larue (*KW* 91:47, 2015; *KW* 94:27, 2018; B. Woerner et al., 2017 eBird data; J. Sole, 2018 eBird data)

Laurel (*KW* 93:44, 2017)

Lincoln (*KW* 90:64, 2014; *KW* 91:64, 2015)

Madison (C. Elliott, 1992/1996/1997 notes & pers. comm./eBird data; *KW* 86:40, 2010; *KW* 90:27, 2014; D. Lang et al., 2018 eBird data)

Meade (*KW* 92:4, 2015)

Mercer (*KW* 61:43, 1985); *KW* 90:44, 2014; *KW* 93:44, 2017; F. Mitchell, 2017 eBird data; R. Denton, 2018 eBird data)

Nelson (*KW* 77:19, 2001); *KW* 90:44, 2014)

Oldham (*KW* 80:40, 2004); *KW* 83:44, 2007; *KW* 85:44, 2009; *KW* 86:40, 2010; *KW* 90:44, 2014; *KW* 91:47/64, 2015; *KW* 93:44, 2017; B. Wulker, 2017 eBird data; m. ob., 2018 eBird data)

Pendleton (*KW* 90:44, 2014)

Pulaski (*KW* 76:28, 2000; *KW* 84:41, 2008; R. Denton, 2010 eBird data; *KW* 91:47/64, 2015; *KW* 93:44, 2017; *KW* 94:28, 2018; R. Denton et al., 2018 eBird data)

Rockcastle (*KW* 83:44, 2007; *KW* 85:44, 2009; *KW* 90:44, 2014; *KW* 93:4/44, 2017; J. Abrams, 2017 eBird data)

Rowan (*KW* 72:40/52, 1996; *KW* 80:4, 2004; *KW* 89:44, 2013; *KW* 90:4, 2014; G. Robe, 2014 eBird data; *KW* 91:64, 2015)

Russell (R. Bontrager, 2018 eBird data; R. Denton, 2019 eBird data)
Shelby (*KW* 90:44, 2014; B. Palmer-Ball/A. Henze, 2017 eBird data)
Taylor (Kessler and Dale, *KW* 72:34, 1996; R. Denton, 2000 eBird data; *KW* 85:44, 2009)
Wayne (*KW* 66:36, 1990; R. Denton, 2000 eBird data; *KW* 81:4/55/62, 2005; R. Denton, 2011 eBird data; *KW* 90:27/37/44, 2014; R. Bontrager, 2017 eBird data; R. Denton, 2018 eBird data)

BRANT *Branta bernicla*

Status: Extremely rare visitant. Based on occurrence of this species in nearby states, it should be expected to occur occasionally during migration and winter, but so far it has only been reported in Kentucky three times (single individuals once each during fall, winter, and spring)

Unaccepted record: 3 Jan 2012, Long Point Unit (*KW* 88:44, 2012; see *KW* 92:89, 2016).

Chronological list of records

1) Dec 1991, (sp.) adjacent to Ballard WMA that is currently housed as a mounted specimen at Doug Travis WMA headquarters (Walter Maples/Jack Sloan, pers. comm)
2) 7 Nov 1993, (ph.) with a mixed flock of waterfowl at the Falls of the Ohio (Palmer-Ball and Ebel, *KW* 70:26-27, 1994)
3) 14-28 May 2005, (ph.) nr. Somerset, Pulaski Co. (*KW* 81:82, 2005)

CACKLING GOOSE *Branta hutchinsii*

Status: Rare to locally uncommon transient and winter visitant/resident. This species was formerly considered a race of the Canada Goose, but it was elevated to full-species status in 2004. The first photo-documented record for the state occurred 5 Mar 1978 at Louisville and at least one extant specimen exists; that individual was collected in Ballard Co. in 1989 or 1990 (Palmer-Ball, KW 83:57-59, 2007). Records accumulated primarily since 2004 indicate the species occurs annually in small numbers with all but one record to date originating from west of the Cumberland Plateau. Peak of abundance occurs from late Nov to early Mar.

Maximum counts: at least **46** at the Reformatory Lake, Oldham Co., 19 Feb 2006 (*KW* 82:44, 2006); **43** (ph.) at the Reformatory Lake, Oldham Co., 9 Dec 2018 (C. Bliznick, eBird data); **40-50** at the Reformatory Lake, Oldham Co., 15 Jan 2009 (*KW* 85:44, 2009); at least **35** at the Reformatory Lake, Oldham Co., 16 Dec 2004 (*KW* 81:56, 2005); **35** at the Reformatory Lake, Oldham Co., 25 Feb 2015 (B. Woerner, eBird data); **35** at the Reformatory Lake, Oldham Co., 5 Jan 2018 (*KW* 94:54, 2018); **30** at the Reformatory Lake, Oldham Co., 5 Dec 2010 (*KW* 87:57, 2011); **28** at Ballard WMA, 17 Dec 2007 (*KW* 84:18/41, 2008); **28** at the Reformatory Lake, Oldham Co., 9 Feb 2014 (*KW* 90:44, 2014); **23** at the Long Point Unit, 10 Dec 2009 (*KW* 86:40, 2010); **21** in Allen Co., 30 Dec 2017 (*KW* 94:24, 2018); ca. **20** at the Reformatory Lake, Oldham Co., 1-26 Jan 2008 (*KW* 84:41, 2008); up to **20** nr. Woodburn, Warren Co., 11-20 Feb 2009 (*KW* 85:44, 2009); ca. **20** at the Reformatory Lake, Oldham Co., 26 Nov 2011 (*KW* 88:4, 2012); up to **20** at the Reformatory Lake, Oldham Co., mid-Feb 2016 (*KW* 92:40, 2016); **15-20** at the Reformatory Lake, Oldham Co., 29 Jan 2007 (*KW* 83:44, 2007); **17** at Griffin Park, Warren Co., 5-6 Feb 2009 (*KW* 85:44, 2009; D. Brown, eBird data); at least **15** at the Sauerheber Unit, 15 Dec 2005 (*KW* 82:44, 2006); **15** at Spindletop Farm, Fayette Co., 26 Jan 2014 (*KW* 90:44, 2014).
Early fall dates: 20 Oct 2016, (ph.) Jefferson Co. (*KW* 93:4, 2017); 26 Oct 2007, Marshall Co. (*KW* 84:4, 2008); 27 Oct 2007, Sauerheber Unit (*KW* 84:4, 2008); 4 Nov 2016, Reformatory Lake, Oldham Co. (*KW* 93:4, 2017); 10 Nov 2017, Todd Co. (*KW* 94:4, 2018); 12 Nov 2017, ne. Jefferson Co. (*KW* 94:4, 2018); 14 Nov 2004, Muhlenberg Co. (*KW* 81:4, 2005).
Late spring dates: 6 Apr 2009, Trigg Co. (*KW* 85:64, 2009); 6 Apr 2019, (ph.) Wayne Co. (R. Bontrager, eBird data); 23 Mar 2013, Trigg Co. (*KW* 89:64, 2013); 23 Mar 2019, Wayne Co. (R. Bontrager, eBird data); 9 Mar 2015, Jefferson Co. (*KW* 91:64, 2015); 6 Mar 2008, Oldham Co. (*KW* 84:56, 2008); 6 Mar 2014, Shelby Co. (*KW* 90:64, 2014); 5 Mar 1978, Louisville (*KW* 54:43, 1978); 5 Mar 2013, Fayette Co. (*KW* 89:64, 2013).

Summary of records by county

Allen (*KW* 84:41, 2008; *KW* 86:40, 2010; *KW* 87:57, 2011; *KW* 89:44, 2013; J. Beachy, 2018 pers. comm.)

Ballard (Palmer-Ball, *KW* 83:58, 2007; *KW* 81:56, 2005; *KW* 82:44, 2006; *KW* 84:41, 2008; *KW* 85:22/44, 2009)

Barren (*KW* 86:40, 2010; *KW* 87:57, 2011)

Boone (*KW* 84:31/41, 2008; *KW* 85:36/44, 2009; *KW* 86:23, 2010; *KW* 89:25/44, 2013; *KW* 90:44, 2014)

Bullitt (*KW* 81:56, 2005; *KW* 85:44, 2009; *KW* 92:40, 2016; J. Sole, 2018 eBird data)

Calloway (*KW* 82:44, 2006; *KW* 84:41, 2008; H. Chambers, 2011 eBird data)

Campbell (B. Wulker, 2011 eBird data)

Daviess (*KW* 81:56, 2005)

Fayette (*KW* 85:44, 2009; *KW* 86:40, 2010; *KW* 89:44/64, 2013; *KW* 90:44, 2014; *KW* 91:48/64, 2015; *KW* 92:40, 2016; *KW* 93:45, 2017; *KW* 94:54, 2018; m. ob., 2017/2018 eBird data)

Fleming (*KW* 88:44, 2012; *KW* 89:44, 2013)

Franklin (*KW* 86:40, 2010; *KW* 92:40/52, 2016; A. Melnykovych, 2018 eBird data)

Fulton (Mengel:175; R. Denton/B. Palmer-Ball, 2002 eBird data; *KW* 82:44, 2006; *KW* 83:44, 2007; M. Todd, 2007 eBird data; 2009 eBird data; J. Hall, 2016 eBird data)

Greenup (*KW* 85:44, 2009)

Hardin (*KW* 83:44, 2007; *KW* 84:41, 2008; *KW* 85:44, 2009; *KW* 87:57, 2011; *KW* 92:40, 2016; *KW* 93:45, 2017; J. Snyder, 2018 eBird data)

Henderson (*KW* 82:44, 2006; *KW* 84:4/41, 2008; *KW* 87:57, 2011; *KW* 89:4, 2013; C. Crawford, 2013 eBird data; *KW* 92:40, 2016)

Henry (*KW* 95:31, 2019)

Hopkins (B. Palmer-Ball, 2000 eBird data; T. Graham, 2018 eBird data)

Jefferson (Palmer-Ball, *KW* 83:58-59, 2007; *KW* 54:43, 1978; *KW* 58:28, 1982; *KW* 81:56, 2005; K. Lee, 2013 eBird data; *KW* 91:48/64, 2015; *KW* 92:22/24/40, 2016; *KW* 93:4/45, 2017; *KW* 94:4/54, 2018/m. ob., 2017/2018 eBird data)

Larue (*KW* 86:24/40, 2010; *KW* 87:31, 2011)

Livingston (*KW* 78:32, 2002)

Logan (*KW* 85:44, 2009)

Madison (*KW* 86:40, 2010; D. Lang, 2018 eBird data)

Marshall (*KW* 84:4, 2008; *KW* 85:44, 2009; *KW* 90:26/44, 2014; H. Chambers, 2015/2018 eBird data)

Mercer (*KW* 57:36, 1981)

Muhlenberg (*KW* 81:4, 2005; *KW* 84:41, 2008; D. Lang, 2009 eBird data)

Oldham (*KW* 81:56, 2005; *KW* 82:44, 2006; *KW* 83:44, 2007; *KW* 84:41, 2008; *KW* 85:44, 2009; *KW* 86:40, 2010; *KW* 87:57, 2011; *KW* 88:4/44, 2012; *KW* 89:44, 2013; *KW* 90:44, 2014; *KW* 91:48, 2015; *KW* 92:40, 2016; *KW* 93:45, 2017; *KW* 94:54, 2018; m. ob., 2017/2018 eBird data)

Ohio (2003 eBird data; *KW* 81:4, 2005)

Pulaski (*KW* 85:44, 2009; *KW* 91:48, 2015; *KW* 93:45, 2017; R. Denton, 2018 eBird data)

Rockcastle (*KW* 83:44, 2007; *KW* 90:44, 2014; *KW* 91:48, 2015; *KW* 93:45, 2017)

Russell (*KW* 89:44, 2013)

Shelby (*KW* 87:57, 2011; *KW* 90:64, 2014; *KW* 93:45, 2017)

Taylor (*KW* 82:44, 2006)

Todd (*KW* 91:20/48, 2015; *KW* 94:4/54, 2018/S. Arnold/J. Hall/A. Troyer, et al., 2017/2018 eBird data)

Trigg (*KW* 81:56, 2005; *KW* 84:41, 2008; *KW* 85:44/64, 2009; *KW* 88:44, 2012; *KW* 89:64, 2013)

Warren (Mengel:175 [probable]; *KW* 78:32, 2002; *KW* 81:22/56, 2005; *KW* 82:44, 2006; *KW* 84:41, 2008; *KW* 85:44, 2009; *KW* 86:40, 2010; *KW* 94:54, 2018)

Wayne (R. Denton, 2004 eBird data; *KW* 89:25/44, 2013; *KW* 95:29, 2019)

*CANADA GOOSE *Branta canadensis*

Status: Uncommon to fairly common transient, uncommon to locally common winter resident, locally rare to fairly common summer resident. Recorded statewide, but generally much more numerous west of the Cumberland Plateau. Flocks are sometimes seen flying over during spring and fall migratory periods, but they are also seen resting on open water or feeding in open fields. The status of this species has changed dramatically over the past several decades; the presence of migrant birds from farther north (*B. c. candensis*) has declined remarkably, while numbers of the population of reintroduced, formerly rare but resident, subspecies (*B. c. maxima*) has soared. Huge wintering numbers are seldom seen in far western Kentucky any longer, but overall the population of resident birds has spread statewide. Nesting of resident birds is now occurring locally throughout much of the state, chiefly west of the Cumberland Plateau (*KBBA*:36-37). Generally encountered in flocks of up to a few hundred birds, but tens of thousands formerly wintered on public lands in Ballard, Fulton, and Henderson cos.

Maximum counts: **170,000** at Ballard WMA, 19 Dec 1989 (*KW* 66:6/36, 1990); **135,000** at Ballard WMA, 8 Feb 1979 (*KW* 55:29, 1979); **130,000** at Ballard WMA, winter 1976-77 (J. Moynahan, notes); **130,000** at Ballard WMA, Feb 1978 (*KW* 54:27, 1978); **130,000** at Ballard WMA, 11 Feb 1985 (*KW* 61:28, 1985); **49,500** at the Sauerheber Unit, 15 Feb 1986 (M. Morton, notes).

SWANS *Cygnus* spp.

Status: During most of the 20th century, the Tundra Swan was the only species of swan occurring in the wild in Kentucky. However, during the past several decades, the increase in the feral Mute Swan population in the northeastern United States as well as the success of Trumpeter Swan restoration programs in the Great Lakes region have resulted in the appearance of both of those species in Kentucky on a somewhat regular basis. The result is that all three swan species are now almost equal in probability of occurrence. The subtleties in differentiating the three species is a very underappreciated issue for birders, especially for individuals in immature plumage. Great care should be exercised when identifying swans in the field.

*MUTE SWAN *Cygnus olor*

Status: Introduced. Rare to (occasionally) uncommon transient and winter resident (formerly absent, then extremely rare, but has become more regular in recent years), extremely rare summer resident. Recorded at scattered localities across the state, but chiefly west of the Cumberland Plateau. A few individuals and pairs of this Old World native have always been present as members of private waterfowl collections. Some of these individuals are free-flying and may have even successfully raised young. As a resident population has become established on the Great Lakes, the number of birds retreating south from this region, particularly during especially cold winter weather, has increased. This has resulted in an increase in the number of Mute Swans seen in Kentucky, especially during winter. Interestingly, winter site fidelity of such birds apparently has been occasionally exhibited (e.g. a flock at Bernheim Forest, in multiple years during the 2000s [*KW* 80:40, 2004; *KW* 81:55, 2005; *KW* 82:44-45, 20; *KW* 85:45, 2009; *KW* 86:41, 2010]). The appearance of birds from established populations on the Great Lakes has blurred the status of Mute Swans observed in Kentucky; some continue to originate from private collections, especially individuals that are present for long periods (particularly outside of winter). It is likely that some Mute Swans traditionally seen in Fayette, Oldham, and Shelby cos. are such feral birds of local origin (see *KW* 93:45, 2017). In 2001, a pair of unknown origin raised a cygnet on a swamp along Cypress Creek, Muhlenberg Co., where they were observed into early Jul (Palmer-Ball and Moosman, *KW* 78:40-42, 2002); likely this same pair was observed at the same location 15 Jul & mid-Sep+ 2002 (B. Palmer-Ball, eBird data & *KW* 79:5, 2003) and 8 Aug 2004 (*KW* 81:4, 2005). In more recent years, probably this same pair has taken up residence at Adkins Swamp, Sinclair Unit, where they have successfully raised young most years (e.g. *KW* 90:64/87/112, 2014; *KW* 91:64, 2015. T. Graham, et al., 2017/2019 eBird data). Most records are for single birds or pairs, but more recently the species has been reported in flocks of up to a dozen or more individuals. Peak of abundance occurs from late Nov to mid-Mar.

Maximum counts: **25-30** at Bernheim Forest, mid-Dec 2005–Feb 2006 (*KW* 82:44-45, 2006); **21** at Cooley's Pond, Wayne Co., 27-28 Dec 2004 (*KW* 81:55, 2005); most of **22** along the Ohio River, Gallatin Co., 10 Feb 2014 (*KW* 90:44, 2014); **17** on Lake Barkley, 26 Dec 1989–3 Jan 1990 (*KW* 66:36, 1990); **14** in Warren Co., Dec 1985 (*KW* 62:26, 1986); up to **14** in Boyle Co., in late Feb

2005 (*KW* 81:55, 2005); up to **14** at Bernheim Forest, Dec 2008 (*KW* 85:45, 2009); **13** on the Ohio River, Bracken Co., 12 Feb 2014 (*KW* 90:44, 2014).

Late spring dates (other than breeding records): 20 Apr 2014, Franklin Co. (L. Flowers, eBird data); 13 Apr 1986, Henderson Co. (*KW* 62:42, 1986); 6 Apr 1986, Madison Co. (*KW* 62:42, 1986).

Early fall dates (presumed free-flying, non-resident): 1 Aug 2010, Minor Clark Hatchery (*KW* 87:12, 2011); 17 Aug 2006, Falls of the Ohio (J. Galitzine/C. Farmer, eBird data); 19 Aug 2006, (ph.) Wayne Co. (*KW* 83:8, 2007); 13 Sep 1975, Falls of the Ohio (*KW* 52:42, 1976); 27-28 Sep 1999, Smithland Dam (*KW* 76:4, 2000).

Out-of-season records (summer away from single known nesting location): 10 Jun/22 Jul 2008, at two different locations in Pulaski Co. (*KW* 84:83, 2008); 22 Jul 2008, Ohio River, Bracken Co. (*KW* 84:83, 2008).

Hybrid record? (possible Mute Swan x Trumpeter Swan): (2) in Pulaski and Laurel cos., winter 2007-2008 (*KW* 84:41, 2008).

[e]TRUMPETER SWAN *Cygnus buccinator*

Status: Extirpated. Formerly (into the early 19th century) distributed locally across much of North America but nearly extirpated by over-harvesting. At the time of settlement this swan was apparently a common transient and winter resident in Kentucky, especially in the western part of the state, occurring as late as the mid-1800s (Mengel:172-173). A single specimen exists from the Ohio River, Boone Co., collected in Dec 1876 (Mengel:173). A variety of conservation measures initiated during the mid-1980s, mostly in a few Great Lakes states, has resulted in a significant increase in numbers. The species is now considered reestablished in the western Great Lakes, an area from which occasional individuals, pairs, and flocks now seen in Kentucky apparently originate. Such reports (most documented with photographs) have now been documented from at least 18 counties across the western two-thirds of the state.

Hybrid record?: See Mute Swan.

Unaccepted record: 5 at Swan Lake, Ballard Co., 11 Feb 1986 (Logsdon, *KW* 62:30-31, 1986).

Summary of recent reports (post 1989) by county

Boone (17 Feb 2018, 2 (ph.) in w. Boone Co. (*KW* 94:54, 2018)

Bracken (23 Jan 2014, 3 above Meldahl Dam [B. Wulker, notes] this record has not been validated in eBird)

Caldwell (29 Dec 2009, 3 (ph.) at Otter Pond [J. Rice, photos/eBird data; *KW* 93:105, 2017]; 29 Jan 2011, 14 at Otter Pond [eBird data])

Campbell (19 Dec 2005, 3 (ph.?) at A.J. Jolly Park [F. Renfrow, eBird data])

Fulton (14 Mar 2009, 3 (ph.) in w. Fulton Co. [B. Yandell et al., photos/eBird data; *KW* 93:105, 2017]; 5 Mar 2010, 3 (ph.) at Lake No. 9 [R. Griffin photos/eBird data; *KW* 93:105, 2017]; winter 2018-2019, 3 (ph.) in the Lower Hickman Bottoms (*KW* 95:46/47/59, 2019)

Hardin (28-31 Dec 2013, 4 (ph.) at and n. of Stephensburg, Hardin Co. [C. Logsdon, pers. comm.; B. Palmer-Ball, eBird data; *KW* 93:105, 2017]; 1-17 Feb 2018, 2 sw. of Elizabethtown, [*KW* 94:54, 2018)

Hart (20 Jan–late Feb 1996, a banded ad. at a farm pond nr. Munfordville, Hart Co. [*KW* 72:40, 1996])

Henderson (17 Dec 2002, 3 at the Sauerheber Unit [*KW* 79:45, 2003]; 7 Mar 2009, 2 (ph.) at unspecified location in Henderson Co. [D. Brown photos/eBird data; *KW* 93:105, 2017])

Larue (late Dec 1989–Feb 1990, (2) at the Larue Co. Sportsman's Lake and McDougal Lake, Larue Co. [J. Elmore, notes/B. Palmer-Ball eBird data])

Lyon (22-24 Jan 2011, 14 at Honker Bay, LBL [C. Szwed et al., eBird data])

Madison (12 Nov 2014, Wilgreen Lake, Madison Co. [R. Crinean, eBird data])

Marshall (18 Dec 2010, 1 on Ky Lake [H. Chambers, eBird data])

McCracken (20 Jan–early Feb 2001, 2 at West Paducah [*KW* 77:27, 2001; R. Denton, eBird data])

Metcalfe (15 Jan 2015, 2 (ph.) at Dunham Lake, Metcalfe Co. [R. Denton, photos/eBird data; *KW* 93:105, 2017])

Muhlenberg (29 Dec 2013, 1 (ph.) Sinclair Unit [B. Palmer-Ball, eBird data; *KW* 93:105, 2017])

Ohio (16 Jan 2010, 7 (ph.) in Ohio Co. (A. Hulsey, eBird data)

<u>Warren</u> (13-18 Mar 1996, 1 (ph.) in the company of an ad. Tundra Swan at McElroy Lake (B. Palmer-Ball, eBird data)

<u>Wayne</u> (18 Dec 2008–7 Jan 2009, 1 (ph.) at Cave Lake, Wayne Co. [R. Denton, photos/eBird data; *KW* 93:105, 2017])

TUNDRA SWAN *Cygnus columbianus*

Status: Extremely rare to rare transient and winter visitant; very locally uncommon winter resident. Recorded chiefly west of the Cumberland Plateau. Generally encountered on the larger lakes and rivers, but occasionally seen on smaller bodies of water. An individual seen on a small lake near Chenoa, Bell Co., 8 Mar 1971 (Harm, *KW* 49:16-17, 1973) represents the only report from the Cumberland Plateau. Over the past 20 years, the Sauerheber Unit of Sloughs WMA, Henderson Co., has become the state's only regular wintering site, with a flock of up to 100-200 birds present every year. Generally seen singly or in small flocks of up to a half-dozen individuals. Peak of abundance occurs from late Nov to mid-Mar.

Maximum counts: **216** at the Sauerheber Unit, 31 Dec 2014 (*KW* 91:48, 2015); **197** at the Sauerheber Unit, 3 Feb 2016 (*KW* 92:40, 2016); **174** at the Sauerheber Unit, 21 Nov 2018 (*KW* 95:4, 2019); **152** at the Sauerheber Unit, 30 Jan 2012 (*KW* 88:44, 2012); **150** at the Sauerheber Unit, 28 Nov 2014 (*KW* 91:4, 2015); **140** at the Sauerheber Unit, early Feb 2010 (*KW* 87:57-58, 2011); **118** along Horseshoe Rd., w. Henderson Co., 24 Feb 2013 (*KW* 89:44, 2013); **117** at the Sauerheber Unit, early Feb 2011 (*KW* 87:57, 2011); **115** at the Sauerheber Unit, early Jan 2014 (*KW* 90:45, 2014); **94** along Horseshoe Road, w. Henderson Co., 22 Feb 2016 (*KW* 92:40, 2016); **93** at the Sauerheber Unit, 25 Jan 2008 (*KW* 84:41, 2008); **70** at the Sauerheber Unit, 7 Jan 2009 (*KW* 85:45, 2009); **62** at the Sauerheber Unit, 2 Jan 2010 (*KW* 86:41, 2010); **57** at the Sauerheber Unit, 17 Dec 2007 (eBird data; M. Morton, pers. comm..); **56** at the Sauerheber Unit, 1 Feb 2006 (*KW* 82:45, 2006); **40+** on Cave Run Lake, 13 Nov 2014 (*KW* 91:4, 2015); **29** at the Sauerheber Unit, 1 Mar 2004 (*KW* 80:64, 2004); **24** on Dewey Lake, Floyd Co., 3-5 Jan 2012 (*KW* 88:44, 2012); up to **24** at the Sauerheber Unit, mid-Jan–mid-Feb 2002 (M. Morton, pers. comm.; B. Palmer-Ball, eBird data); **19** in flight along the Ohio River nr. Petersburg, Boone Co., 23 Nov 1985 (*KW* 62:4, 1986).

Late spring dates: 16 Apr 2018, Ohio Co. (*KW* 94:68, 2018); 13 Apr 1991 (*KW* 67:76, 1991); 10 Apr 2011, w. Henderson Co. (J. Meredig, eBird data).

Early fall dates: 13 Oct 1937, Louisville (Mengel:172); 29 Oct 2012, Sauerheber Unit (*KW* 89:4, 2013); 30 Oct 1993, Boone Co. (*KW* 70:6, 1994).

Unaccepted records: 27 Sep 1933, Hopkins Co. (Bacon, *KW* 9:[14-16], 1933; Mengel:172); 29 Sep 19— [year published as 1929, but may have been 1955 – see ref.], (6) at Dale Hollow Lake (*KW* 31:71, 1955); 12 Mar 1966, 42 nr. Bernheim Forest (Weller, *KW* 42:31, 1966 [description contained therein does not rule out – and somewhat suggests – Sandhill Cranes]); 29 Aug 1982, Barren Co. (*KW* 59:14, 1983); 17 Dec 1983, 25 birds on the Lexington CBC (*KW* 60:12, 1984 [description contained therein again suggests a migrant flock of Sandhill Cranes]); 19 Jan 1985 (*KW* 61:1-2, 1985 [photograph is inconclusive]).

*WOOD DUCK *Aix sponsa*

Status: Fairly common to common transient and summer resident, rare winter resident. Recorded statewide, but less numerous (although perhaps increasing) on the Cumberland Plateau and Mountains. Generally encountered on streams, ponds, sloughs, and flooded backwater areas, especially if wooded, but sometimes seen resting with other waterfowl on open water of the larger lakes and rivers during migration. Peak of abundance occurs from mid-Mar to late Sep. Breeding is widespread in the western portion of the state and along the Ohio River upstream to Cincinnati, somewhat more localized and less numerous in the rest of the central and eastern parts of the state (*KBBA*:38-39). Usually seen singly, in pairs, or small groups of up to a dozen birds, but hundreds occasionally gather in favored feeding areas, especially during fall. A few birds seem to linger throughout the winter, especially during milder years, but the species is scarce or absent in most areas.

Maximum counts: **500** on a pond in Jefferson Co., 20 Oct 1978 (*KW* 55:14, 1979); **350** on Lake No. 9, 26 Jul 2006 (*KW* 82:79, 2006); **300** at Dade Park Slough, Henderson Co., 6 Oct 1976 (*AB* 31: 183, 1977); **300-400** at Lake No. 9, late Jul 2007 (*KW* 83:103, 2007); **250** on Honker Bay, LBL, 30 Sep 2008 (*KW* 85:10, 2009); **250** at the Sauerheber Unit 15 Aug 2010 (*KW* 87:12, 2011); **250** at the Sauerheber Unit, 25 Jul 2011 (C. Crawford, eBird data); **250** at the Sauerheber Unit, 22 Aug 2013 (C. Crawford, eBird data); **225** on Honker Lake, LBL, 1 Sep 1985 (*KW* 62:4, 1986); **237** on the Louisville CBC, 15 Dec 1991 (*KW* 68:32, 1992).

Hybrid record: male Wood Duck x Mallard at the Reformatory Lake, Oldham Co., 1 Jan 2002 (B. Palmer-Ball, eBird data)

*BLUE-WINGED TEAL *Spatula discors*

Status: Fairly common to common transient, extremely rare to rare summer resident, extremely rare during winter. Recorded chiefly west of the Cumberland Plateau but likely regular on water bodies in eastern Kentucky during migration. Encountered in a great variety of shallow aquatic habitats from small ponds to flooded fields, but also seen resting with other waterfowl on open water of the larger lakes and rivers during migration. Peaks of abundance occur from mid-Mar to early May and from late Aug to late Sep. The species is occasionally found in central and western Kentucky during summer, but breeding rarely occurs (currently documented from only ten counties). There are a few well-documented winter records, but generally the species is absent from late Nov to mid-Feb. Generally seen in small to medium-sized flocks of up to 50 birds, occasionally in larger groups of up to a hundred or more. **State Breeding Status**: Threatened.

Maximum spring counts: **1500** at Morgan Pond, 3 Apr 2018 (*KW* 94:68, 2018); **825** e. of Hickman, Fulton Co., 17 Apr 2015 (*KW* 91:65, 2015); **800+** in the Upper Hickman Bottoms, 20 Apr 2014 (*KW* 90:65, 2014); at least **750** nw. of the Sauerheber Unit, 7 Apr 2016 (*KW* 92:56, 2016); ca. **600** at the Sauerheber Unit, 2 Apr 2013 (*KW* 89:64, 2013); **550+** in w. Henderson Co., 5 Apr 2014 (*KW* 90:65, 2014); **400** at McElroy Lake, 10 Apr 1997 (Roemer, et al., *KW* 73:79-83, 1997); **320** adjacent to Obion WMA, Fulton Co., 30 Mar 2013 (*KW* 89:64, 2013).

Maximum fall counts: **665** and **275** at two sites in e. Union Co., 7 Sep 2012 (*KW* 89:4, 2013); **620** e. of Morganfield, Union Co., 2 Oct 2013 (*KW* 90:4, 2014); **550** at McElroy Lake, 4 Sep 2016 (*KW* 93:4, 2017); **500+** at Lake No. 9, 2 Sep 2001 (B. Palmer-Ball, eBird data); **500** at Morgan Pond, 28 Sep 2016 (*KW* 93:4, 2017); ca. **500** e. of Morganfield, Union Co., 10 Oct 2017 (*KW* 94:4, 2018); **400-500** at McElroy Lake, early Sep 1989 (Palmer-Ball and Boggs, *KW* 67:40, 1991); **400** at the Sauerheber Unit, 7 Sep 1986 (*KW* 63:7, 1987); **440** total between two sites in Union Co., 10 Sep 2015 (*KW* 92:4, 2016); **350+** at Ballard WMA, 9 Sep 2000 (*KW* 77:5, 2001); **350** at Morgan Pond, 11 Jul 2008 (eBird data).

Early spring dates: 3 Feb 1999, Warren Co. (*KW* 75:24, 1999); 4 Feb 1999, Pulaski Co. (R. Denton, eBird data); 6 Feb 1966, Calloway Co. (E. Larson, eBird data); 13 Feb 2016, Ky Lake, Marshall Co. (*KW* 92:40, 2016 [date erroneously published as 18 Feb therein]); 14 Feb 1997, Warren Co. (Roemer, et al., *KW* 73:79-83, 1997); 15 Feb 2017, Wayne Co. (R. Bontrager, eBird data); 18 Feb 1999, McElroy Lake (R. Denton, eBird data); 18 Feb 2017, Marshall Co. (*KW* 93:46, 2017).

Late fall dates (occasionally lingers into early winter): 19 Dec 2015, Frankfort (*KW* 92:23/40, 2016); 19 Dec 2017, Fayette Co. (L. Combs et al., eBird data); 18 Dec 2001, a pair at Camp #11 Mine, Union Co. (B. Palmer-Ball, eBird data); 18 Dec 2004, a pair at the Long Point Unit (*KW* 81:56, 2005); 17 Dec 2005, a male in Fayette Co. (*KW* 82:45, 2006); 24 Nov/15 Dec 2000, an injured bird on Ky Lake above the dam (B. Palmer-Ball, eBird data); 14 Dec 2008, (2) Lake Barkley, Lyon Co. (*KW* 85:45, 2009); 11 Dec 2007, (2) Barren River Lake (*KW* 84:42, 2008); 1 Dec 2014, Hart Co. (*KW* 91:48, 2015); 27 Nov 2015, Green River Lake, Taylor Co. (*KW* 92:4, 2016); 19 Nov 2016, Lexington (R. Chadwick, eBird data); 18 Nov 19—, Louisville area (*KW* 52:44, 1976).

Out-of-season records (winter): 24 Dec 1957, at Danville noted as incapable of flight (*AB* 12:160, 1958; *KW* 34:14, 1958); 15 Jan 1976, Lake Peewee (J. Hancock, notes; *fide* A. Stamm, historical archive files); 25 Dec 1999, Ky Lake above Ky Dam (*KW* 76:28, 2000; D. Roemer, notes); 4 Jan 2002, a female at Freeman Lake (B. Palmer-Ball, eBird data); 19 Dec 2004–28 Jan 2005, a female in Warren Co. (*KW* 81:20/56, 2005); 7 Jan 2006, a male (ph.) in Wayne Co. (*KW* 82:45, 2006); 23/27 Dec 2007 & 17 Jan 2008, Falls of the Ohio (*KW* 84:42, 2008); 3 Jan 2010, Glasgow CBC (*KW* 86:16/41, 2010, [erroneously reported as 4 Jan 2010 at *KW* 86:41, 2010]); 9 Jan 2017, Barren River Lake (*KW* 93:46, 2017).

Unaccepted records: this species probably has been reported falsely numerous times during Dec and Jan in Kentucky; it typically winters along the Gulf Coast and south into Middle America. While occasional birds (perhaps sometimes injured) remain into the winter, this duck does not occur regularly and numerous winter reports (perhaps including some that have been included above) are likely not valid. Numerous others that have been published, as well as some that have been entered into eBird, are not included herein (e.g. *KW* 78:14, 2002; *KW* 79:18, 2003; *KW* 80:23, 2004; *KW* 88:25/44, 2012; *KW* 89:19/44, 2013; *KW* 92:4, 2016; *KW* 94:54, 2018; eBird data for 16 Dec 2012 [2]; 21 Nov 2013 [2]). Observers are encouraged to make every effort to photo-document mid-Nov through mid-Feb sightings of the species.

Hybrid records (Blue-winged Teal x Cinnamon Teal): 6-8 Apr 1987, a male in ne. Jefferson Co., (*KW* 63:48, 1987); 4 May 1996, a male at Island No. 8 Slough, Fulton Co., (B. Palmer-Ball, eBird data; erroneously published in the 2nd ed. of this work as 10 Apr 1996 [*fide* B. Palmer-Ball, notes]); 9 Apr 2000, a male at the Sauerheber Unit (*NAB* 54:288, 2000; B. Palmer-Ball, eBird data); 17 Apr 2002, a male (vt.) at Morgan Pond, Christian Co. (*KW* 78:48, 2002); 9-27 Apr 2005, a male at Chaney Lake (*KW* 81:82, 2005); 5 Apr 2008, a male (ph.) in the Lower Hickman Bottoms (*KW* 84:56, 2008); 5 Apr 2014, a male (ph.) in Henderson Co. (*KW* 90:65, 2014); 21 Apr 2014, a male (ph.) in Hart Co. (*KW* 90:65, 2014).

Hybrid records (Blue-winged Teal x Northern Shoveler): 10 Apr 1996, a male at McElroy Lake (B. Palmer-Ball, eBird data); 5 Apr 2011, a male at Chaney Lake (*KW* 87:82, 2011); 27 Mar 2015, a male (ph.) in Jefferson Co. (*KW* 91:65/80, 2015).

Hybrid record (Blue-winged Teal x Green-winged Teal): 18 May 2006, a male at the Sauerheber Unit (*KW* 82:65, 2006; B. Palmer-Ball, eBird data).

Summary of confirmed breeding records by county

Caldwell (B. Palmer-Ball, 1997 eBird data)
Christian (*KBBA*:42; *KW* 73:72, 1997; D. Roemer, 2002 notes; *KW* 84:56/83, 2008; *KW* 87:111, 2011; *KW* 89:92, 2013; J. Hall, 2015 eBird data; *KW* 94:104, 2018; J. Hall et al, 2019 eBird data)
Fulton (*KW* 69:55, 1993; B. Palmer-Ball, 1993 eBird data; *KW* 84:84, 2008)
Hardin (*KW* 84:83-84, 2008)
Jefferson ("near Louisville") (Mengel:183; Stamm and Jones, *KW* 42:39, 1966; *KW* 52:43-44, 1976)
Jessamine (*KW* 79:80, 2003)
Logan (*KW* 89:92, 2013)
Trigg (*KW* 65:85, 1989; *KBBA*:42; B. Palmer-Ball, 1997 eBird data; *KW* 84:83, 2008)
Union (*KW* 79:80, 2003; *KW* 82:79, 2006)
Warren (primarily on the karst lakes south of Bowling Green) (Wilson, *KW* 16:13-21, 1940; Wilson, *KW* 24:54-55, 1948; *KW* 65:84-85, 1989; Palmer-Ball and Boggs, *KW* 67:40, 1991; *KBBA*:42 [including Simpson Co.]; Roemer, et al., *KW* 73:79-83, 1997; Roemer, *KW* 74:93/94, 1998; D. Roemer, 2002 notes; *KW* 80:80, 2008; *KW* 84:56/83, 2008; *KW* 86:90, 2010; *KW* 87:111, 2011)

CINNAMON TEAL *Spatula cyanoptera*

Status: Extremely rare spring and fall transient/visitant. There are at least 13 records (11 during spring, two during fall).

Hybrid records: see Blue-winged Teal.

Unaccepted records: fall of 1952, a Cinnamon Teal was reportedly killed by hunters on the Ohio River, but no specimen was ever examined (Mengel:184); 30 Aug 2003, a bird retaining some rufous feathers in the body at Lake No. 9 [but hybrid could not be eliminated] (*KW* 80:5, 2004); 15 Apr 2008, a possible female at McElroy Lake (*KW* 84:57, 2008).

Chronological list of records

1) 20 Mar 1951, a male on a backwater pond just east of Cincinnati, Ohio; this bird was seen on several occasions flying out over the Ohio River, thus into Campbell Co. (Mengel:184)
2) 30 Apr 1985, a male (ph.) at the Long Point Unit (*KW* 61:43, 1985)
3) 23-24 Apr 1989, a male (ph.) on a pond just outside of Bowling Green (Palmer-Ball, *KW* 66:47, 1990)
4) 6 Apr 1991, a pair nr. Maceo, Daviess Co. (Stinson, *KW* 67:66-67, 1991; *KW* 68:12, 1992)

5) 4 Apr 1994, a male at Kentucky Bend, Fulton Co. (T. Heatley, pers. comm.)

6) 30-31 Mar 1995, a male (ph.) on the Westvaco WMA, Carlisle Co. (*KW* 73:28, 1997; M. Toon, pers. comm.)

7) 19-22 Apr 1997, a male (ph.) at McElroy Lake (Roemer, et al., *KW* 73:79-83, 1997)

8) 8-19 Apr 2000, a male (vt.) at the Sauerheber Unit (*KW* 76:44, 2000; B. Palmer-Ball, eBird data)

9) 8-10 Apr 2006, a pair (ph.) at the Sauerheber Unit (*KW* 82:65/76, 2006)

10) 28 Mar–7 Apr 2013, a male (ph.) at Lexington (KW 89:65/74, 2013)

11) 12-15 Feb 2014, a male (ph.) at McElroy Lake (*KW* 90:45/60, 2014)

12) 10 Sep 2016, a male with orange irides (ph.) at Jacobson Park, Lexington (*KW* 93:4/36/105, 2017)

13) 6 Sep 2018, a male with orange irides (ph.) e. of Morganfield, Union Co. (*KW* 95:5, 2019)

*NORTHERN SHOVELER *Spatula clypeata*

Status: Uncommon to fairly common transient, rare to locally uncommon winter resident, extremely rare summer resident. Recorded chiefly west of the Cumberland Plateau but likely regular on water bodies in eastern Kentucky during migration. Encountered in a variety of shallow aquatic habitats from small ponds to flooded fields, but also seen resting with other waterfowl on open water of the larger lakes and rivers during migration. As of the mid-1960s, the species was not considered to winter in the state (Mengel:186), but in recent years this dabbler has become more regular during the winter months and it now appears to regularly winter. Peaks of abundance occur from mid-Mar to mid-Apr and from early Sep to mid-Oct. The species occasionally lingers into early summer and may have bred in the vicinity of McElroy Lake in 1989 (Palmer-Ball and Boggs, *KW* 67:41, 1991; Palmer-Ball, *KW* 74:61, 1998). Breeding was confirmed near Morgan Pond, Christian Co., in 1997 and again in 2008 (see below). Generally seen in small flocks of fewer than 20 birds, especially during fall when the species is much less numerous; up to a hundred or more birds are sometimes reported during spring. **State Breeding Status**: Endangered.

Maximum spring counts: at least **1000** in the Upper Hickman Bottoms, 18 Mar 2016 (*KW* 92:56, 2016); up to **1000** at the karst lakes in Warren Co. in the spring of 1952 (Wilson, *KW* 28:46, 1952); **780** on Ky Lake above the dam, 27 Mar 2000 (*KW* 76:44, 2000); **750** at Morgan Pond 3 Apr 2018 (*KW* 94:68, 2018); **700** at the Sauerheber Unit, 26 Mar 2018 (*KW* 94:68, 2018); **650** in the Lower Hickman Bottoms, 30 Mar 2018 (C. Bliznick/J. Wheat, eBird data); **550** in the Lower Hickman Bottoms, 18 Mar 2016 (*KW* 92:56, 2016); ca. **500** in w. Fulton Co., 20 Mar 2009 (*KW* 85:64, 2009); **500** at the Sauerheber Unit, 27 Mar 2015 (*KW* 91:65, 2015); **500** at the Sauerheber Unit 15 Mar 2016 (*KW* 92:56, 2016); **458** at the Sauerheber Unit, 13 Apr 2013 (M. Autin, eBird data); **400** at the Sauerheber Unit, 5 Apr 2014 (*KW* 90:65, 2014); **400** in s. Warren Co. (with 350+ at McElroy Lake), 16 Apr 1994 (R. Denton/B. Palmer-Ball, eBird data); **360** at the Sauerheber Unit, 8 Mar 2017 (*KW* 93:70, 2017); **335** in w. Henderson Co., 10 Apr 2007 (*KW* 83:72, 2007); **320** at McElroy Lake, 6 Apr 2011 (eBird data); a few hundred at Ky Dam, 28 Mar 2007 (*KW* 83:72, 2007); **250+** at Ballard WMA, 21 Mar 2007 (*KW* 83:72, 2007); **250** at the Long Point Unit, 8 Apr 1989 (*KW* 65:64, 1989); ca. **250** at the Long Point Unit, 16 Mar 2005 (*KW* 81:82, 2005); ca. **250** at and nr. the Long Point Unit, 7 Mar 2009 (*KW* 85:64, 2009); **250** at the Sauerheber Unit, 11 Mar 2006 (*KW* 82:65, 2006); **200+** at McElroy Lake, 31 Mar 1991 (B. Palmer-Ball, eBird data); **200** in Warren Co, 22 Apr 1939 (Wilson, *KW* 15:31-32, 1939); ca. **200** at McElroy Lake, 28 Feb–8 Mar 1989 (Palmer-Ball and Boggs, *KW* 67:40, 1991).

Maximum winter counts: **775** counted on an aerial survey in the vicinity of the Long Point Unit, 8 Jan 2004 (*KW* 80:40, 2004); ca. **500** at the Sauerheber Unit, 13 Feb 2012 (*KW* 88:44, 2012); **495** at the Long Point Unit, 14 Dec 2007 (eBird data); **441** at the Long Point Unit, 2 Jan 2007 (*KW* 83:44, 2007); **400** at the Sauerheber Unit, 6 Dec 2014 (*KW* 91:48, 2015); **400** at the Sauerheber Unit, 5 Jan 2016 (*KW* 92:40, 2016); **350-400** at the Long Point Unit, 15 Dec 2007 (*KW* 84:42, 2008); **350** at the Long Point Unit, 16 Jan 2016 (*KW* 92:40, 2016); **350** at the Long Point Unit, 27 Feb 2017 (*KW* 93:46, 2017); **300** in the Lower Hickman Bottoms, 23 Feb 2005 (eBird data); **300** at the Sauerheber Unit, 13 Feb 2013 (*KW* 89:45, 2013); **300** at Ballard WMA, 17 Feb 2017 (*KW* 93:46, 2017); **250** at the Long Point Unit, 28 Feb 2009 (M. Autin, eBird data); **220** at the Long Point Unit, 10 Feb 2002 (B. Palmer-Ball, eBird data); **179** at Honker Lake/Honker Bay, LBL, Lyon/Trigg cos., 23 Dec 2006 (*KW* 83:44, 2007); **130** at Lake No. 9, 1 Feb 2004 (*KW* 80:40, 2004); **106** at the

Long Point Unit, 2 Feb 2002 (B. Palmer-Ball, 2002 eBird data); **99** on Ky Lake, Marshall Co., 28 Jan 2000 (*KW* 76:28, 2000); **93** on the Reformatory Lake, Oldham Co., 6 Jan 2013 (*KW* 89:44, 2013); at least **90** on the Ballard WMA, 31 Dec 2001 (B. Palmer-Ball, eBird data).

Maximum fall counts: **110** at the Sauerheber Unit, 20 Nov 2016 (*KW* 93:4, 2017); **100** at the Sauerheber Unit, 1 Nov 2012 (K. Michalski, eBird data); **100** at the Sauerheber Unit, 23 Oct 2013 (A. Gatham, eBird data); **73** at Murl Pond, Wayne Co., 20 Nov 2017 (R. Denton, eBird data); **58** over e. Jefferson Co., 23 Oct 2013 (*KW* 90:4, 2014); **50** at Jacobson Park, Lexington, 6 Nov 2014 (*KW* 91:4, 2015).

Late spring dates (has lingered into early summer on a few occasions): 26 Jun 2011, (4) at McElroy Lake (*KW* 87:111, 2011); 24 Jun 2014, Jefferson Co. (*KW* 90:65/87, 2014); 23 Jun 2018, McElroy Lake (*KW* 94:104, 2018); 13-22 Jun 2008, Henderson/Union Co. line (*KW* 84:84, 2008); 19 Jun 1935, Warren Co. (Mengel:186); 14 Jun 1998, McElroy Lake (Roemer, *KW* 74:94, 1998); 13 Jun 1989, (pair) at McElroy Lake (Palmer-Ball and Boggs, *KW* 67:40-41, 1991); 12 Jun 2015, Morgan Pond (*KW* 91:83, 2015); 10 Jun 2008, Chaney Lake (*KW* 84:84, 2008); 4 Jun 2014, Henderson Co. (*KW* 90:87, 2014); 27 May 2012, Sauerheber Unit (*KW* 88:71, 2012); 26 May 2017, (ph.) Jefferson Co. (*KW* 93:70, 2017).

Early fall dates: 17 Jul–Aug 1989, possible breeding birds, Warren Co. (Palmer-Ball and Boggs, *KW* 67:40-41, 1991); 20 Jul 1998, possible summering bird, McElroy Lake (Roemer, *KW* 74:94, 1998); 20 Jul 2007, Lake No. 9 (*KW* 83:103, 2007); 20 Jul 2015, ne. Jefferson Co. (*KW* 91:83, 2015); 22 Jul 2000, Muhlenberg Co. (*KW* 76:55, 2000; M. Bennett, notes); 22 Jul 2006, Ballard WMA (*KW* 82:79, 2006); 6 Aug 2017, (ph.) Lexington (M. Oliver, eBird data); 11 Aug 1999, possible summering bird, Warren Co. (*KW* 76:4, 2000); 11 Aug 2001, (2) in Union Co. (B. Palmer-Ball, eBird data); 12 Aug 2013, (2) in Union Co. (*KW* 90:4, 2014); 15 Aug 1999, Fulton Co. (*KW* 76:4, 2000.

Unaccepted record (hybrid): 21 Dec 2010, a bird thought to be a Mallard x Northern Shoveler at First Creek Lake, Mammoth Cave NP, Edmonson Co. (*KW* 87:28, 2011).

Hybrid records: see Blue-winged Teal.

Summary of confirmed breeding records by county

Christian (nw. of Oak Grove, Jun 1997 [Palmer-Ball, *KW* 74:60-62, 1998] and Jun 2008 [*KW* 84:84, 2008])

*GADWALL *Mareca strepera*

Status: Fairly common transient and winter resident, extremely rare during summer (one record of nesting). Recorded chiefly west of the Cumberland Plateau but likely regular on water bodies in eastern Kentucky during migration. Encountered in a variety of shallow aquatic habitats from small ponds to flooded fields, but also found resting with other waterfowl on open water of the larger lakes and rivers during migration. Peak of abundance occurs from mid-Nov to late Mar. Generally seen in small to medium-sized flocks of up to 50 birds, but larger groups of several hundred or more have been reported. This species has definitely increased in occurrence over the past couple of decades.

Maximum counts: **11,927** at the Long Point Unit, 14 Dec 2007 (eBird data; possibly included some birds in Tennessee); **7822** at the Long Point Unit, 2 Jan 2007 (*KW* 83:44, 2007; possibly included some birds in Tennessee); **4000** at Honker Bay, LBL, Lyon/Trigg cos., 25 Dec 2017 (*KW* 94:54, 2018); **3180** estimated in the upper Hickman Bottoms, 5 Feb 2002 (P. Hahs, notes); **3000+** along the Mississippi River, Carlisle, Fulton, and Hickman cos., 13 Feb 2012 (*KW* 88:44, 2012); **2500** on Honker Lake, LBL, Lyon Co., with at least 500 more on each of Energy Lake and Hematite Lake, LBL, Trigg Co., 23 Nov 2008 (*KW* 85:10, 2009); **2250** at Sloughs WMA, Henderson Co., 28 Nov 2006 (*KW* 83:8, 2007); **11,927** at the Long Point Unit, 14 Dec 2007 (eBird data); **920** on Lake Barkley, Lyon Co., 7 Jan 2013 (*KW* 89:44, 2013); ca. **2000** at Bailey's Hollow embayment of Ky Lake, Calloway Co, 7 Jan 1993 (*KW* 69:33, 1993); ca. **1100** at Boatwright WMA, Ballard Co., and **1600** at Duck Island, Lake Barkley, Trigg, Co., both 23 Nov 2011 (*KW* 88:4, 2012); **1200-1300** at Jonathan Creek, 13 Nov 2012 (*KW* 89:4, 2013); ca. **1200** at Sloughs WMA, Henderson/Union Co., 22 Nov 2011 (*KW* 88:4, 2012); ca. **1000** on the Bailey's Hollow embayment of Ky Lake, Calloway Co., 16 Oct 1993 (*KW* 70:7, 1994); at least **1000** at Jonathan Creek, 17-27 Nov 2010 (*KW* 87:12, 2011); **1000** in the Upper Hickman Bottoms 1 Feb 2017 (*KW* 93:46, 2017); **975** at Ballard WMA, 13

Feb 2012 (*KW* 88:44, 2012); **800+** at Jonathan Creek, 7 Nov 2000 (*KW* 77:4, 2001; B. Palmer-Ball, eBird data); ca. **700** in the Lower Hickman Bottoms (with ca. 500 at Open Pond), Fulton Co., 24 Mar 2010 (*KW* 86:63, 2010); **530** on Cave Run Lake, 6 Nov 2014 (*KW* 91:4, 2015); **500** at the Long Point Unit, 4 Jan 2004 (R. Denton, eBird data); **500+** at the Long Point Unit, 15 Dec 2007 (*KW* 84:41, 2008); **500** on Hematite Lake, LBL, Trigg Co., 30 Nov 2009 (*KW* 86:4, 2010); ca. **500** at the Sauerheber Unit, 23 Feb 2010 (*KW* 86:41, 2010); **500** at the Sauerheber Unit, 6 Dec 2017 (A. Hulsey, eBird data); at least **500** at Ballard WMA, 18 Dec 2017 (C. Bliznick, eBird data); **500** along the Ohio River at Wabash Island, Union Co., 30 Dec 2017 (K. Michalski, eBird data); **500** at McElroy Lake, 8 Mar 2018 (*KW* 94:68, 2018); **462** on Cave Run Lake, Rowan Co., 23 Jan 2008 (*KW* 84:41, 2008); **450** at Island No. 8 Slough, Fulton Co., 8 Feb 2016 (*KW* 92:40, 2016); at least **400** at Jonathan Creek, 13 Nov 2008 (*KW* 85:10, 2009); **400** on Cave Run Lake, 1 Dec 2009 (*KW* 86:41, 2010); ca. **400** at Sloughs WMA, Henderson Co., 8 Mar 2013 (*KW* 89:64, 2013); **400+** at the Long Point Unit, 17 Apr 2013 (*KW* 89:64, 2013); **400** at Jonathan Creek, 5 Nov 2013 (H. Chambers, eBird data); **400** at the Sauerheber Unit, 17 Mar 2017 (*KW* 93:70, 2017); **400** at the Sauerheber Unit, 22 Mar 2018 (J. Meredig, eBird data); at least **350** in Union Co., 3 Nov 2010 (*KW* 87:12, 2011); ca. **300** at Morgan Pond, Christian Co., 23 Mar 2008 (*KW* 84:56, 2008); **300** at McElroy Lake, 11 Mar 2015 (*KW* 91:64, 2015); at least **160** at the Falls of the Ohio, 22 Nov 2008 (*KW* 85:10, 2009).

Late spring dates: lingering male to 12 Aug 2016 at Morgan Pond (*KW* 92:77, 2016; *KW* 93:4, 2017); lingering birds to 20 Jul 1989, McElroy Lake (Palmer-Ball and Boggs, *KW* 67:41, 1991); a pair lingered in Fayette Co. to 27 Jun 2017 (*KW* 93:98, 2017) with perhaps the same pair lingering in Fayette Co. to 23 Jun 2018 (*KW* 94:104, 2018); 23 Jun 2018, (3) at Chaney Lake (*KW* 94:104, 2018); 18 Jun 2014, Cumberland Co. (*KW* 90:87, 2014); 15 Jun 2011, Christian Co. (*KW* 87:111, 2011); 14 Jun 2010, s. Jefferson Co. (*KW* 86:90, 2010); 12 Jun 1994, McElroy Lake (M. Bierly, notes); 11 Jun 2019, (ph.) Fayette Co. (D. Lang, eBird data); 10 Jun 2015, Fayette Co. (*KW* 91:83, 2015); 3 Jun 1953, Warren Co. (*KW* 38:7, 1962); 3 Jun 2004, Lake Barkley, Lyon Co. (*KW* 80:80, 2004); 30 May 2008, Chaney Lake (*KW* 84:56, 2008); 28 May 2019, Christian & Warren cos. (J. Hall & T. Durbin, 2019 eBird data); 28 May 1975, Louisville area (*KW* 52:43, 1976).

Early fall dates (birds prior to mid-Aug could be summering?): 25 Jul 2018, (ph.) Morgan Pond (*KW* 94:104, 2018); 3 Aug 1997, Morgan Pond, Christian Co. (D. Roemer, notes); 14 Aug 2006, Lake No. 9 (*KW* 83:8, 2007); 18 Aug 1950, Warren Co. (Wilson, *KW* 27:4, 1951); 23 Aug 2006, Union Co. (*KW* 83:8, 2007); 27 Aug 2002, Ky Lake, Calloway Co. (*KW* 79:5, 2003); 30 Aug 1985, Falls of the Ohio (*KW* 62:4, 1986).

Hybrid records (Gadwall x Mallard): 15 Dec 2005, a male at the Sauerheber Unit (*KW* 82:45, 2006); 10 Dec 2010, a male (ph.) in Pulaski Co. (*KW* 87:58/72, 2011) with possibly the same individual at a nearby location in Pulaski Co., 17 Nov/29 Dec 2015 (*KW* 92:4/40, 2016), 11/15 Nov 2016 & 17 Feb 2017 (R. Denton, photos/eBird data; *KW* 93:46, 2017), and 13 Nov/25 Dec 2017 & 30 Mar 2018 (*KW* 94:4/54/68, 2018); and 23 Dec 2017, a male in Wayne Co. (*KW* 94:54, 2018). Also see Northern Pintail.

Summary of breeding records by county:

Union (2003, former Camp #11 Mine (Palmer-Ball, *KW* 80:32-35, 2004; *KW* 79:80, 2003; *KW* 80:5, 2004)

EURASIAN WIGEON *Mareca penelope*

Status: Extremely rare late winter and spring visitant. This species has been documented in Kentucky on only seven occasions (and not in more than 30 years). Based on its occurrence in nearby states, it also could occur during fall.

Hybrid records (Eurasian Wigeon x American Wigeon): 7 Apr 1992, a male (ph.) on the Ken Unit Peabody WMA, Ohio Co. (B. Palmer-Ball, eBird data); 10 Feb 2002, a male (vt.) in w. Fulton Co. (B. Palmer-Ball, eBird data).

Unaccepted records: 10 Dec 2007, a male at the Sauerheber Unit [hybrid with American Wigeon could not be eliminated] (M. Morton, pers. comm.; *KW* 84:42, 2008); 17 Dec 2007, Ohio River floodplain nr. South Shore, Greenup Co. [hybrid with American Wigeon could not be eliminated] (J. Brunjes, pers. comm.; *KW* 84:42, 2008).

Chronological list of records

1) 22-28 Feb 1939, two males and a female (male specimen collected 28 Feb) at Lentz's Pond nr. Louisville (Monroe and Mengel, *KW* 15:40, 1939)
2) 25-26 Mar 1950, a male on a backwater pond just east of Cincinnati, Ohio, that flew out over the Ohio River and into Campbell Co. (Mengel:184-185)
3) 19 Apr 1957, a male nr. Louisville (Mengel:184; *KW* 52:44, 1976 [date published incorrectly as "late Feb and 18 Apr 1957" in *AFN* 11:349, 1957; *fide* A. Stamm, historical archive files]);
4) 12 Apr 1958, a male at Chaney Lake (Wilson, *KW* 34:43-44, 1958)
5) 8 Apr 1961, a male at Chaney Lake (*KW* 37:43, 1961; *KW* 38:7, 1962)
6) 20 Mar 1967, three males nr. Louisville (*KW* 52:44, 1976)
7) 17 Mar 1988, a male on the Ohio River above Meldahl Dam, Bracken Co. (J. Stenger, notes; *KW* 88:99, 2012)

*AMERICAN WIGEON *Mareca americana*

Status: Fairly common transient, uncommon winter resident, extremely rare during summer (one breeding record). Recorded chiefly west of the Cumberland Plateau but likely regular on water bodies in eastern Kentucky during migration. Encountered in a variety of shallow aquatic habitats from small ponds to flooded fields, but also seen resting with other waterfowl on open water of the larger lakes and rivers during migration. Peaks of abundance occur from mid-Mar to early Apr and from late Oct to mid-Nov. The species has occasionally lingered into summer at the transient lakes in Warren Co., and a breeding record was documented in Ballard Co. in 2007 (see below). Generally reported in small to medium-sized flocks of fewer than 50 birds.

Maximum counts: **2256** counted on aerial survey in the vicinity of the Long Point Unit, 8 Jan 2004 (*KW* 80:40, 2004; possibly included some birds in Tennessee); **1300** in the Upper Hickman Bottoms, 5 Feb 2002 (P. Hahs, notes); **1807** at the Long Point Unit, 2 Jan 2007 (*KW* 83:44, 2007); **989** on the Long Point Unit, 14 Dec 2007 (eBird data; possibly included some birds in Tennessee); ca. **825** at Duck Island, Lake Barkley, Trigg Co., 23 Nov 2011 (*KW* 88:4, 2012); **590** at the Sauerheber Unit, 18 Jan 2010 (*KW* 86:41, 2010); **520** at and immediately adjacent to the Long Point Unit, 17 Feb 2017 (*KW* 93:46, 2017); **479** at Ballard WMA, 20 Dec 2010 (*KW* 87:25, 2011); **430** at Lake Peewee, 25 Nov 1978 (J. Hancock, notes); **400** at the Long Point Unit, 15 Dec 2001 (C. Sloan, eBird data); **400** at Honker Lake, LBL, 31 Oct 1991 (*KW* 67:4, 1991); ca. **400** at Island No. 8 Slough, Fulton Co., 8 Feb 2016 (*KW* 92:40, 2016); "aggregations of **200-400** being not unusual in mid-Mar, especially on backwaters nr. rivers and larger lakes" (Mengel: 185); ca. **350** at Sloughs WMA, Henderson/Union cos., 23 Nov 2011 (*KW* 88:4, 2012); **310** at the Sauerheber Unit, 5 Jan 2016 (*KW* 92:40, 2016); **300+** at Lake No. 9, 16 Mar 2005 (*KW* 81:82, 2005); **300** at McElroy Lake, 25 Mar 1989 (Palmer-Ball and Boggs, *KW* 67:41, 1991); ca. **300** at Lake No. 9, 25 Feb 2010 (*KW* 86:41, 2010); **300** at Ballard WMA, 13 Feb 2012 (*KW* 88:44, 2012); **300** in the Upper Hickman Bottoms, 1 Feb 2017 (*KW* 93:46, 2017); **300** at Open Pond, Fulton Co., 22 Mar 2018 (*KW* 94:68, 2018); **200-300** at the Sauerheber Unit, 19 Nov 2004 (*KW* 81:4, 2005); **265+** at the Sauerheber Unit, 15 Dec 2005 (*KW* 82:45, 2006); ca. **250** at the Long Point Unit, 15 Dec 2007 (*KW* 84:42, 2008); **250** at the Long Point Unit, 8 Feb 2016 (*KW* 92:40, 2016); **210+** at the Sauerheber Unit, 21 Nov 2007 (*KW* 84:4, 2008); ca. **200** at McElroy Lake, 22 Mar 1991 (B. Palmer-Ball, eBird data); **200** at the Long Point Unit, 16 Dec 2005 (*KW* 82:45, 2006); **200** at the Sauerheber Unit, 1 Dec 2015 (C. Crawford, eBird data); **200** at the Sauerheber Unit, 6 Dec 2017 (A. Hulsey, eBird data); **200** at McElroy Lake, 2 Mar 2018 (S./J. Kistler, eBird data); **175** on Honker Lake, LBL, 13 Nov 1988 (*KW* 65:5, 1989).

Late spring dates (has occasionally lingered into summer with the following records): 10 Jul 1949, Warren Co. (*KW* 38:8, 1962); 19 Jun 1949, a few at Chaney Lake (Mengel:185); 15 Jun 1965, Louisville area (*KW* 52:44, 1976); through early Jul 1989 at McElroy Lake (Palmer-Ball and Boggs, *KW* 67:41, 1991); 6 Jun 2013, Parsons Pond, Logan Co. (*KW* 89:93, 2013); summer 2013, an injured bird summered e. of Morganfield, Union Co. (*KW* 89:93, 2013; *KW* 90:4, 2014).

Early fall dates: 25 Aug 1950, 10 [possibly summered – see Mengel:185] at Chaney Lake (Wilson, *KW* 27:4, 1951); 25 Aug 2015, Blood River (H. Chambers, eBird data); 27 Aug 2002, Ky Lake, Calloway Co. (*KW* 79:6, 2003); 28 Aug 1988, (3) in Fulton Co. (*KW* 65:5, 1989); 29 Aug 1976, Falls of the Ohio (J. Elmore, notes); 29 Aug 1988, McCracken Co. (*KW* 65:5, 1989).

Hybrid records: see Eurasian Wigeon.

Summary of breeding records by county

Ballard (summer 2007, an injured female (present with a male earlier in the season) was accompanied by yg. at the Ballard WMA [*KW* 83:103, 2007]).

*MALLARD *Anas platyrhynchos*

Status: Resident; common during migration and winter, uncommon during summer. Recorded statewide but generally less numerous on the Cumberland Plateau and Mountains. Encountered in a great variety of aquatic habitats from small ponds and flooded fields to the larger lakes and rivers. Peak of abundance occurs from mid-Nov to early Mar. Breeding regularly at scattered localities throughout central and western Kentucky (*KBBA*:40-41). Feral forms of this species and hybrids between it and some exotic waterfowl account for many reports of the species in settled areas. Often seen in flocks of up to a hundred or more birds, but larger concentrations of thousands of individuals are regularly reported during winter in western Kentucky.

Maximum counts: **430,000** in the Ohio River bottoms of Henderson/Union cos., Feb 1958 (*AB* 12: 282, 1958; Soaper, *KW* 34:19-22, 1958); nearly **90,000** at the Long Point Unit, 14 Dec 2007 (eBird data); **tens of thousands** along the Ohio River, Henderson/Union cos., 22 Feb 1953 (Rhoads, *KW* 29:34, 1953); ca. **60,000** in Ballard Co., 23 Nov 2011 (*KW* 88:4, 2012); **31,590** in the Upper Hickman Bottoms, 5 Feb 2002 (P. Hahs, notes); **25,000** at the Long Point Unit, 16 Dec 1995 (B. Foehring, eBird data); the majority of **19,000-20,000** in Ballard Co., 19 Dec 1989 (*KW* 66:6, 1990).

Hybrid records: see Wood Duck, Gadwall, American Black Duck, and Northern Pintail.

AMERICAN BLACK DUCK *Anas rubripes*

Status: Uncommon to fairly common transient and winter resident (but far less numerous in recent years), extremely rare during summer. Recorded chiefly west of the Cumberland Plateau, although the species is generally more numerous in central and northeast Kentucky than in the far west. Encountered in a great variety of shallow aquatic habitats from small ponds to flooded fields, but also seen resting with other waterfowl on open water of the larger lakes and rivers during migration. Peak of abundance occurs from early Nov to early Mar. Individuals occasionally linger into or throughout the summer, but the potential for confusion with vagrant Mottled Ducks may cloud the validity of some reports, especially in the past. However, with this species formerly being much more numerous, it is likely that most summer reports during the 20th century were valid. Generally seen in small flocks of up to a dozen or so birds, but larger groups of up to several dozen or more are regularly observed during winter.

Maximum counts (western Kentucky): **31,000** in the Ohio River bottoms of Henderson/Union cos., Feb 1958 (*AB* 12:282, 1958; Soaper, *KW* 34:19-22, 1958); perhaps **tens of thousands** along the Ohio River, Henderson/Union cos., 22 Feb 1953 (Rhoads, *KW* 29:34, 1953); **500** at the Sauerheber Unit, 19 Feb 2015 (*KW* 91:48, 2015).

Maximum counts (eastern & central Kentucky): aerial survey total of **1480** in ne. Kentucky [primarily Cave Run Lake and upper Ohio River], 7 Jan 2014 (*KW* 90:45, 2014); aerial survey total of at least **1200** in the same area, 21 Jan 2009 (*KW* 85:45, 2009); aerial survey total of **804** in the same area, 23 Jan 2008 (*KW* 84:42, 2008); **423** on Cave Run Lake, 22 Jan 2009 (A. Newman, eBird data); **250-300** at Louisville, 16 Feb 1985 (*KW* 61:28, 1985); **250** on Green River Lake, Taylor Co., 8 Jan 1984 (eBird data); **250+** in Pulaski Co., 18 Jan 1992 (*KW* 68:32, 1992).

Hybrid records (American Black Duck x Mallard): individuals are regularly observed in small numbers annually.

MOTTLED DUCK *Anas fulvigula*

Status: Extremely rare visitant. The origin of extralimital Mottled Ducks is not clear; introduction efforts have been undertaken in a few areas in past decades. The relatively recent appearance of the species in midwestern states seems unlikely to be wholly the result of greater awareness on the part of birders. An expansion of birds from introduced populations, or a change in status of the species due to climate change or introgression from feral Mallard populations could also be involved. There are seven records (three during spring, three during summer, and one during fall).

Unaccepted records: early 1800s, species reported as breeding up the Mississippi River to the mouth of the Ohio (see Mengel, p. 520); 14 Aug 1941, Marshall Co. (see Mengel, p. 520).

Chronological list of records

1) 22 Mar 2000, (2) at Lake No. 9 (*KW* 84:74, 2008)
2) 20 May 2005, (ph.) in w. Henderson Co. (*KW* 81:82, 2005)
3) 4-5 Sep 2008, (ph.) at Lake No. 9 (*KW* 85:10/40, 2009)
4) 31 Jul 2009, (ph.) at Lake No. 9 (*KW* 85:90, 2009)
5) 3-7 Jul 2010, (vt.) at McElroy Lake (*KW* 86:90, 2010)
6) 10-16 Jul 2010, (ph.) in w. Fulton Co. (*KW* 86:90/104, 2010
7) 30 Mar–7 Apr 2018, (ph.) in w. Fulton Co. (*KW* 94:68-69, 2018)

NORTHERN PINTAIL Anas acuta

Status: Transient (uncommon to fairly common during spring, uncommon during fall); rare to uncommon winter resident; accidental during summer (one breeding record). Recorded chiefly west of the Cumberland Plateau; occurrence generally increasing from east to west with greatest numbers present from Henderson Co. to the west along the floodplains of the larger rivers. The species is a very early spring migrant, often peaking in numbers during Feb. Peaks of abundance occur from late Jan to early Mar and from late Aug to late Sep. Encountered in a variety of shallow aquatic habitats from small ponds to flooded backwater areas, but also seen resting with other waterfowl on open water of the larger lakes and rivers during migration. This species is not numerous during fall, when it is generally seen in small flocks of fewer than a dozen birds; in contrast, larger groups of up to several dozen are regularly reported during late winter and spring, and extraordinary concentrations of thousands have been reported occasionally during the peak of northward migration. A single breeding record was documented in Shelby Co. in 1973 (see below).

Maximum late winter/spring counts: extraordinary concentrations of **53,200** estimated in Fulton Co., 17,550 estimated in Ballard Co., and 16,720 estimated in Hickman Co., all on 5 Feb 2002 (P. Hahs, notes); **20,000-30,000** collectively in Ohio River bottoms of Henderson/Union cos., Feb 1958 (Soaper, *KW* 34:19-22, 1958); ca. **15,000** along the Mississippi River, Carlisle, Fulton, and Hickman cos., 13 Feb 2012 (*KW* 88:44, 2012); ca. **13,000** at Lake No. 9, 25 Feb 2010 (*KW* 86:41, 2010); **4948** at the Long Point Unit, 14 Dec 2007 (eBird data; possibly included some birds in Tennessee); **2395** counted on aerial survey in the vicinity of the Long Point Unit, 8 Jan 2004 (*KW* 80:40, 2004); **2000** in Walnut Bottoms of Ohio River in western Henderson Co., Feb 1958 (Soaper, *KW* 34:19-22, 1958); ca. **2000** in Warren Co., 22 Mar 1960 (Wilson, *KW* 36:59, 1960); **1000** at the transient lakes, Warren Co., 15 Apr 1952 (Wilson, *KW* 28:45, 1952); **1000** in w. Henderson Co., 1 Mar 2006 (*KW* 82:65, 2006); ca. **900** at Boatwright WMA, Ballard Co., 13 Feb 2012 (*KW* 88:44, 2012); **600** along the Mississippi River, Hickman Co., 3 Feb 2007 (M. Riggs, eBird data); **600** in the vicinity of Lake No. 9/Open Pond, 6 Mar 2018 (*KW* 94:68, 2018; M. Greene, eBird data); **500** in w. Fulton Co., 20 Feb 1999 (*KW* 75:24, 1999); possibly **500** along Horseshoe Road, w. Henderson Co., 16 Feb 2012 (*KW* 88:44, 2012); **400** in ne. Hopkins Co., 15 Mar 2015 (*KW* 91:65, 2015); **350** at Cedar Creek Lake, Lincoln Co., 7 Mar 2015 (*KW* 91:65, 2015); **350** at McElroy Lake 11 Mar 2015 (*KW* 91:65, 2015); **350** in ne. Hopkins Co., 14 Feb 2018 (*KW* 94:54, 2018); **335** along the Ohio River at Louisville, 7 Mar 2015 (*KW* 91:65, 2015); **300** in the Lower Hickman Bottoms, 23 Feb 2005 (*KW* 81:56, 2005); **300** in the Lower Hickman Bottoms, 13 Feb 2017 (*KW* 93:46, 2017); **250** in ne. Hopkins Co., 13 Feb 2019 (B. Carrico, eBird data); ca. **200** at McElroy Lake, 8 Feb 2009 (*KW* 85:45, 2009); **200** at Barren River Lake, 2 Mar 2015 (*KW* 91:65, 2015).

Maximum fall counts: ca. **600** in Ballard Co., 23 Nov 2011 (*KW* 88:4, 2012); ca. **100** at Sloughs WMA, Henderson/Union cos., 23 Nov 2011 (*KW* 88:4, 2012); **60** over Ky Lake, Marshall Co., 21 Oct 2008 (*KW* 85:10, 2009); **53** e. of Morganfield, Union Co., 3 Nov 2010 (*KW* 87:12, 2011); **50** on Ky Lake, Calloway Co., 10 Oct 1992 (*KW* 69:5, 1993); **45** total along the Mississippi River, Carlisle Co., 14 Sep 2008 (*KW* 85:10, 2009); **40** at Barren River Lake, 20 Nov 2018 (R. Bontrager, eBird data); **35-40+** in e. Union Co., 22 Oct 2011 (*KW* 88:4, 2012); ca. **30** e. of Morganfield, Union Co., 1

Oct 2003 (*KW* 80:5, 2004); **25** at Jonathan Creek, 29 Aug 1998 (*KW* 75:4, 1999); ca. **25** at the Sauerheber Unit, 27 Oct 2007 (R. Denton/B. Palmer-Ball, eBird data): **23** along the Ohio River, Gallatin Co., 25 Oct 2007 (*KW* 84:5, 2008).

Late spring dates: family group from above-noted Shelby Co. nesting record was observed to 8 Aug 1973 (Robinson, *KW* 50:18, 1974); injured female that lingered to 22 Jun 1937 at McElroy Lake (*KW* 38:7, 1962); 9 Jun 1997, injured female at Lake No. 9 (B. Palmer-Ball, eBird data); 26 May 2018, McElroy Lake (*KW* 94:68, 2018); 23 May 1993, Oldham Co. (*KW* 69:44, 1993).

Early fall dates: 25 Jul 2014, Union Co. (*KW* 90:87, 2014); 5 Aug 2002, Livingston Co. (*KW* 79:6, 2003); 8 Aug 1989, McElroy Lake (Palmer-Ball and Boggs, *KW* 67:40, 1991); 16 Aug 2016, Mitchell Lake, Ballard WMA (R. Denton, eBird data).

Hybrid record (Northern Pintail x Gadwall): 16 Nov 1948, Ohio River nr. Henderson, Henderson Co. (Mengel:182).

Hybrid records (Northern Pintail x Mallard): 6 Mar 1996, Ballard Co. (B. Palmer-Ball, eBird data); 21 Feb 2003, (ph.) Sauerheber Unit (*KW* 79:66, 2003); 25-26 Dec 2007, Petros Pond, Warren Co. (*KW* 84:42, 2008); 25-26 Feb 2009, Freeman Lake (*KW* 85:45, 2009); 18 Jan 2010, Sauerheber Unit (*KW* 86:41, 2010); 8 Feb 2014, w. Fulton Co. (*KW* 90:45, 2014); 16 Jan 2017, (ph.) Freeman Lake (*KW* 93:46/56, 2017).

Summary of breeding records by county

Shelby (summer 1973, on a large farm pond south of Eminence (Robinson, *KW* 50:18, 1974)

GREEN-WINGED TEAL *Anas crecca*

Status: Uncommon to fairly common transient, rare to locally uncommon (formerly less numerous) winter resident, extremely rare during summer. Recorded chiefly west of the Cumberland Plateau but likely regular on water bodies in eastern Kentucky during migration. Encountered in a variety of shallow aquatic habitats from small ponds to flooded fields, but also seen resting with other waterfowl on open water of larger lakes and rivers during migration. Peaks of abundance occur from mid-Mar to early Apr and from late Aug to mid-Oct. This small duck has increased remarkably in abundance as a winter resident during the past few decades. Generally seen in small flocks of up to several dozen birds, but larger groups of up to 50 or more birds are regularly reported during winter and spring. The Eurasian subspecies (*A. c. crecca*) has not been documented in Kentucky.

Maximum spring counts: **10,850** total (including 8700 in the Upper Hickman Bottoms) along the Mississippi River, Carlisle, Fulton, and Hickman cos., 13 Feb 2012 (*KW* 88:44, 2012); at least **3100** in the Lower Hickman Bottoms (including 2100 at and e. of Open Pond and 1000 at Lake No. 9), 31 Mar 2018 (*KW* 94:69, 2018; C. Bliznick/J. Wheat, eBird data); at least **1230** in the Lower Hickman Bottoms, 1 Apr 2016 (*KW* 92:56, 2016); at least **1050** in the Lower Hickman Bottoms and ca. **1000** in the Upper Hickman Bottoms, both 18 Mar 2016 (*KW* 92:56, 2016); **900+** at the Long Point Unit and **300-500** at Obion WMA, Fulton Co., both 16 Mar 2005 (*KW* 81:82, 2005); **750-1000+** adjacent to Obion WMA, Fulton Co., 28 Mar 2013 (*KW* 89:65, 2013); ca. **600** in the Lower Hickman Bottoms, 24 Mar 2010 (*KW* 86:63, 2010); ca. **600** in the Upper Hickman Bottoms, 17 Mar 2012 (*KW* 88:71, 2012); **600** at the Sauerheber Unit, 3 Mar 2017 (*KW* 93:71, 2017); **600** at the Sauerheber Unit, 18 Mar 2018 (J. Meredig, eBird data); at least **550** at the Sauerheber Unit, 28 Mar 2016 (*KW* 92:56, 2016); ca. **500** at the Long Point Unit, 23 Mar 2013 (*KW* 89:65, 2013); ca. **500** at the Sauerheber Unit, 15 Apr 2018 (C. Bliznick et al., eBird data); ca. **450** in w. Henderson Co., 10 Apr 2007 (*KW* 83:72, 2007); ca. **450** at the Sauerheber Unit, 23 Mar 2014 (*KW* 90:65, 2014); ca. **400** in the Lower Hickman Bottoms, 7 Apr 1996 (B. Palmer-Ball, eBird data); ca. **400** at the Long Point Unit, 24 Mar 2002 (D. O'Brien, eBird data); ca. **375** at the Long Point Unit, 21 Mar 2014 (*KW* 90:65, 2014); **375** at Blood River, 23 Mar 2017 (H. Chambers, eBird data); at least **300** at the Long Point Unit and at least **250-300** at and adjacent to Obion WMA, Fulton Co., all 20 Mar 2009 (*KW* 85:64, 2009); **325+** in the Upper Hickman Bottoms, 20 Apr 2014 (*KW* 90:65, 2014); **320+** nr. the Long Point Unit, 21 Feb 2001 (*NAB* 55:176, 2001); **300+** at Ballard WMA, 27 Mar 2009 (*KW* 85:64, 2009); **260** at the Long Point Unit, 17 Feb 2000 (B. Palmer-Ball, eBird data); **250** at the Sauerheber Unit, 3 Mar 1996 (B. Palmer-Ball, eBird data); **245** at Morgan Pond, 8 Mar 2018 (J. Hall, eBird data); **225** at the Sauerheber Unit, 27 Mar 1992 (*KW* 69:44, 1993).

Maximum fall counts: ca. **1050** at Ballard WMA, 23 Nov 2011 (*KW* 88:4, 2012); at least **500** e. of Morganfield, Union Co. 31 Oct 2010 (*KW* 87:12, 2011); ca. **350** e. of Morganfield, Union Co., 10 Oct 2017 (*KW* 94:5, 2018); **330** at Sloughs WMA, Henderson Co., 28 Nov 2006 (*KW* 83:8, 2007); **315** e. of Morganfield, Union Co., 20 Nov 2012 (*KW* 89:4, 2013); **250-300+** at Mitchell Lake, Ballard WMA, 20 Oct 2008 (*KW* 85:10, 2009); **250** in Union Co., 14 Nov 2000 (*KW* 77:5, 2001); **200+** e. of Morganfield, Union Co., 9 Nov 2006 (*KW* 83:8, 2007); at least **200** at the Sauerheber Unit, 29 Oct 2011 (*KW* 88:4, 2012).

Maximum winter counts: **1300** at Ballard WMA, 19 Dec 2016 (*KW* 93:46, 2017); up to **1000** along the Tennessee River s. of Ledbetter, Livingston Co., late Jan 2015 (*KW* 91:48, 2015); ca. **600** at the Sauerheber Unit, 22 Feb 2016 (*KW* 92:41, 2016); **525** in the Lower Hickman Bottoms, 17 Feb 2017 (*KW* 93:46, 2017); **506** at Mitchell Lake, Ballard WMA, 31 Dec 2001 (*KW* 78:15, 2002); **500** in the Lower Hickman Bottoms, 23 Feb 2005 (*KW* 81:56, 2005); **450** at the Long Point Unit, 8 Feb 2016 (*KW* 92:41, 2016); **400** on Lake Barkley, Lyon Co., 7 Jan 2013 (*KW* 89:45, 2013); **293** at Mitchell Lake, Ballard WMA, 21 Dec 1999 (*KW* 76:14, 2000; B. Palmer-Ball, eBird data); **270** in s. Todd Co., 14 Dec 2016 (*KW* 93:46, 2017); **238** in s. Todd Co., 3 Dec 2017 (J. Hall/S. Arnold, eBird data); **200** on Hematite Lake, Trigg Co., mid-Dec 1966 (Able, *KW* 43:32, 1967).

Late spring dates: 8 Jun 1989, Mercer Co. (*KW* 65:84, 1989); 1 Jun 1989, McElroy Lake (Palmer-Ball and Boggs, *KW* 67:40, 1991); 1 Jun 2018, Lexington (*KW* 94:104, 2018); 28 May 2008, Lower Hickman Bottoms (*KW* 84:57, 2008); 22 May 1982, Fulton Co. (*KW* 58:49, 1982).

Early fall dates: 1 Aug 1964, Falls of the Ohio (Stamm, et al., *KW* 43:7, 1967); 1 Aug 2003, e. of Morganfield, Union Co. (*KW* 80:5, 2004); 13 Aug 1978, ne. Jefferson Co. (B. Palmer-Ball, eBird data).

Out-of-season records (summer): a male, possibly or likely injured, on Lake Barkley, Lyon Co., 13 Jul 2005 (*KW* 81:104, 2005); 11/17 Jul 2011, McElroy Lake/Chaney Lake (*KW* 87:111, 2011/B. Palmer-Ball, eBird data).

Hybrid record: see Blue-winged Teal.

CANVASBACK *Aythya valisineria*

Status: Uncommon to fairly common transient, rare to uncommon winter resident (formerly more numerous), extremely rare during summer. Recorded chiefly west of the Cumberland Plateau but likely regular on water bodies in eastern Kentucky during migration. Generally encountered on the larger lakes and rivers, but also occurs on smaller bodies of water and flooded backwater areas, especially during migration. Peaks of abundance occur from mid-Feb to mid-Mar and from mid-Nov to early Dec. Individuals have lingered into early summer on a few occasions, with one record of apparent summering (perhaps an injured bird). Most often observed in small flocks of fewer than 25 birds, but occasionally larger flocks of a hundred or more birds are seen.

Maximum counts: survey total of **2738** in ne. Kentucky [mostly Cave Run Lake and upper Ohio River], 5 Feb 2009 (*KW* 85:46, 2009); **1150** on Lake Barkley above Barkley Dam, 14 Feb 1988 (*KW* 64:28, 1988); over **1000** in flooded bottomland nr. Swan Lake, Feb 1986 (C. Logsdon, notes); ca. **1000** on Lake Barkley above Barkley Dam, 10 Feb 1996 (B. Palmer-Ball, eBird data); at least **1000** on Lake Barkley, Lyon Co., 23 Jan 2010 (*KW* 86:41, 2010); **600** in ne. Hopkins Co., 5 Mar 2018 (*KW* 94:69, 2018); ca. **550** above Smithland Dam, 5 Jan 2010 (*KW* 86:41, 2010); ca. **500** above Meldahl Dam, Bracken Co., 13 Feb 2011 (*KW* 87:58, 2011); at least **500** above Smithland Dam, 19 Jan 2018 (*KW* 94:54, 2018); at least **400** on the Ohio River, Gallatin Co., 10 Feb 2014 (*KW* 90:45, 2014); **350-400** on the Ohio River, Bracken Co., 12 Feb 2014 (*KW* 90:45, 2014); **350** above Barkley Dam, 21 Feb 2007 (*KW* 83:45, 2007); "**several hundred**" on Lake Barkley, Lyon Co., 16 Jan 2004 (*KW* 80:40-41, 2004); **300** above Uniontown Dam, Union Co., 10 Feb 2007 (*KW* 83:45, 2007); **270** on Lake Barkley, Trigg Co., 11 Mar 2015 (*KW* 91:65, 2015); **240+** on the Ohio River at Louisville, 17-19 Feb 2007 (*KW* 83:45, 2007); ca. **240** above Smithland Dam, 1 Jan 2009 (*KW* 85:45-46, 2009).

Late spring dates: a female lingered at Morgan Pond to 5 Jun 1997 (B. Palmer-Ball, eBird data); a female lingered at Morgan Pond to 1 Jun 2018 (*KW* 94:104, 2018); 24 May 1952 (Wilson, *KW* 28:46, 1952).

Early fall dates: 3 Sep–21 Oct 1984, possible summering bird at Falls of the Ohio (*KW* 61:14, 1985); 3 Sep/5 Oct 2008, likely summering bird on Lake Barkley above the dam (*KW* 85:10, 2009);12 Oct

1974, Louisville area (*KW* 52:44, 1976); 19 Oct 1992, Jonathan Creek (*KW* 69:5, 1993); 21 Oct 2017, Lexington (*KW* 94:5, 2018).

Out-of-season records (summer): Jun-Jul 1997, a male was present at the Minor Clark Hatchery (*KW* 73:72, 1997); 27 Jun-15 Jul 2002, a female capable of flight was present at Morgan Pond, Christian Co. (*KW* 78:61, 2002); summer 2009, likely injured bird on Lake Barkley above the dam (*KW* 85:90, 2009); 12-26 Jul 2014, Little Sandy River, Greenup Co. (*KW* 90:87, 2014).

REDHEAD *Aythya americana*

Status: Uncommon to fairly common transient, rare to uncommon winter resident, extremely rare during summer. Recorded chiefly west of the Cumberland Plateau but likely regular on water bodies in eastern Kentucky during migration. Generally encountered on the larger lakes and rivers, but also found on smaller bodies of water and flooded backwater areas, especially during migration. Peaks of abundance occur from mid-Feb to mid-Mar and from early Nov to early Dec. Individuals have lingered into early summer on a few occasions, and summering has been documented on at least one occasion. Generally seen in small numbers with other diving ducks, but large flocks of hundreds of birds are occasionally reported during migration.

Maximum late winter/spring counts: a survey total of **2147** at LBL, 18 Mar 1975 (*AB* 29:697, 1975); **1600** in ne. Hopkins Co., 5 Mar 2018 (*KW* 94:69, 2018); over **1000** in flooded bottomland nr. Swan Lake, Feb 1986 (C. Logsdon, notes); ca. **1000** along the Ohio River at Louisville, 11 Mar 2015 (*KW* 91:65, 2015); **1000** on Lake Barkley, Trigg Co., 27 Feb 1985 (*KW* 61:28, 1985); **800** at McElroy Lake, 9 Mar 2018 (B. Wulker et al., eBird data); **600** on the Ohio River at Louisville, 10 Mar 1978 (B. Palmer-Ball, eBird data); **500** at Barren River Lake, 22 Feb 2018 (C. Besse et al., eBird data); **350** on Barren River Lake 28 Feb 2014 (*KW* 90:45, 2014); ca. **300** on McElroy Lake, 12 Mar 2011 (*KW* 87:82, 2011); **300** on the Ohio River, Campbell Co., 15 Mar 2015 (*KW* 91:65, 2015); **165** on McElroy Lake and **185** on Walton Pond, Warren Co., both 23 Feb 2014 (*KW* 90:45, 2014); **281** at Minor Clark Hatchery 24 Feb 2013 (*KW* 89:45, 2013); **250-300** on the Ohio River at Louisville, 5 Mar 2014 (*KW* 90:65, 2014); **251** Owsley Fork Lake, Madison Co., 6 Mar 2014 (*KW* 90:65, 2014); **200** on Owsley Fork Lake, Madison Co., 28 Feb 2010 (R. Foster/R. Bates, eBird data); **200** on Lake Linville, Rockcastle Co., 13 Feb 2014 (*KW* 90:45, 2014); **200** on Green River Lake, Taylor Co., 18 Feb 2014 (*KW* 90:45, 2014); **200** at Sloughs WMA, Henderson Co., 14 Mar 2014 (*KW* 90:65, 2014); **200** in Jessamine Co., 8 Mar 2015 (S. Penner, eBird data); **200** at McElroy Lake, 11 Mar 2015 (J. Sole, eBird data); **200** at Walton Pond, Warren Co., 28 Feb 2016 (*KW* 92:41, 2016); **110** above Meldahl Dam, Bracken Co., 19 Feb 2007 (*KW* 83:45, 2007);.

Maximum fall/early winter counts: ca. **8100** [60% of 13,400 diving ducks] on Barren River Lake, 3 Dec 2014 (*KW* 91:48, 2015); at least **2500** on Lake Cumberland, Pulaski Co., 30 Nov 2015 (*KW* 92:4, 2016); **1430** total on Lake Cumberland, Russell Co., 3 Dec 2014 (*KW* 91:49, 2015); **925** on lakes at the Bluegrass Army Depot, Madison Co., 2 Dec 2015 (*KW* 92:41, 2016); at least **900** on Lake Cumberland, Russell Co., 9 Dec 2013 (*KW* 90:45, 2014); **800** on Lake Vega, Bluegrass Army Depot, Madison Co., 3 Dec 2014 (*KW* 91:49, 2015); **700** at Lexington and **700** on Lake Cumberland, Russell Co., both 1 Dec 2016 (*KW* 92:41, 2016); **350+** on Lake Cumberland, Pulaski Co., 5 Dec 2005 (*KW* 82:45, 2006); **315** on Lake Cumberland, Pulaski Co., 2 Dec 2014 (*KW* 91:48, 2015); **300** on Lake Peewee, 1 Dec 2015 (*KW* 92:41, 2016); **300** at Lake Cumberland, Wayne Co., 15 Nov 2018 (R. Denton, eBird data); **280** on the Ohio River at Louisville, 8 Dec 2003 (D. O'Brien, eBird data); **275** at Lake Cumberland, Pulaski Co., 16 Nov 2018 (R. Bontrager, eBird data); **250** at Fagan Branch Lake, Marion Co., 17 Feb 2018 (J. Sole, eBird data); **205** at Lake Peewee, 3 Dec 2014 (*KW* 91:48, 2015); **200** on the Ohio River at Louisville, 29 Nov 2015 (*KW* 92:4, 2016); at least **100** on the Ohio River at Louisville, 19 Nov 2010 (*KW* 87:12, 2011).

Late spring dates: a male lingered to 15 Jul 1991 at Morgan Pond, Christian Co. (B. Palmer-Ball, eBird data); a male on the Ohio River, Campbell Co., 21-25 Jun 2009 (*KW* 85:90, 2009); a male in n. Pulaski Co. to 22 Jun 2007 (*KW* 83:103, 2007); (2) lingered to 19 Jun 1949 at Chaney Lake (Mengel:189; *KW* 38:8, 1962); 17 Jun 2018, Ohio River, Campbell Co. (*KW* 94;104, 2018); 8 Jun 2013, McElroy Lake (*KW* 89:93, 2013); 25 May 2013, Morgan Pond (*KW* 89:65, 2013); 23 May 2018, Morgan Pond (*KW* 94:69, 2018); 22 May 2015, (pair) on Cedar Creek Lake (*KW* 91:65, 2015); 20 May 2002, Sinclair Unit (eBird data); 20 May 2002, Morgan Pond, Christian Co. (B. Palmer-Ball, eBird data); 19 May 2010, s. Warren Co. (*KW* 86:63, 2010); 18 May 2004, Union Co.

(*KW* 80:64, 2004); 14 May 1989, Warren Co. (Palmer-Ball and Boggs, *KW* 67:41, 1991); 14 May 2009, ne. Jefferson Co. (*KW* 85:64, 2009).

Early fall dates: 18-19 Sep 2017, (possibly a summering bird?) (ph.) above Ky Dam (*KW* 94:5, 2018); 5 Oct 19—, Hopkins Co. (Mengel: 189); 12 Oct 1988, Ballard WMA (*KW* 65:5, 1989); 13 Oct 2012, Minor Clark Hatchery (*KW* 89:4, 2013).

Out-of-season record (summer): a male (ph.) summered at Freeman Lake, during 2016; it was observed 19 Jun–8 Jul, 11 Sep, and 22 Oct (*KW* 92:77, 2016; *KW* 93:5, 2017).

Published error: based on a review of a number of sources, I believe that the late spring date of 24 Jun [1974] published by Monroe, et al. (1988) is erroneous, the result of a transcription error (*fide* A. Stamm, historical archive files /J. Hancock, pers. comm.).

RING-NECKED DUCK *Aythya collaris*

Status: Fairly common to common transient, uncommon to fairly common winter resident, extremely rare during summer. Generally widespread and numerous west of the Cumberland Plateau, uncommon during migration on the reservoirs of eastern Kentucky. Encountered in a variety of aquatic habitats; most often observed on protected, shallower portions of the larger lakes and rivers and on flooded backwater areas, but also occurs on open water with other waterfowl and not infrequently on smaller lakes and ponds, especially during migration. Peaks of abundance occur during Mar and Nov. The species occasionally lingers into or throughout the summer without evidence of breeding. Most often seen in small to medium-sized flocks of up to a hundred birds, but flocks of several hundred or more are regularly observed, especially during migration.

Maximum counts: **4500** estimated on and adjacent to Ballard WMA and **1760** estimated on and adjacent to Swan Lake, both on 5 Feb 2002 (P. Hahs, notes); **4435** at Ballard WMA and **3200** at Swan Lake WMA, 22 Dec 2009 (*KW* 86:41, 2010; P. Hahs, notes); **3600** at Boatwright WMA, Ballard Co., 13 Feb 2012 (*KW* 88:45, 2012); **3390** at Ballard WMA, 18 Jan 2012 (*KW* 88:45, 2012); **1500-2000** on the Ohio River at Louisville, 21-28 Mar 1939 (Monroe and Mengel, *KW* 15:38-44, 1939); **1500** on Lake Peewee, 29 Dec 1974 (J. Hancock, notes); **1400** in ne. Hopkins Co., 9 Mar 2018 (*KW* 94:69, 2018); up to **1150** at Lake Peewee, winter 1978-79 (*KW* 55:29, 1979); **1100** on Lake Barkley, Lyon Co., 9 Nov 2000 (*KW* 77:5, 2001); at least **1000** on McElroy Lake, 11 Mar 2015 (*KW* 91:65, 2015); **1000** at Lake Peewee, 6 Nov 1989 (*KW* 66:6, 1990); **750-1500** at Lake Peewee, 26 Dec 1987 (*KW* 64:28, 1988; B. Palmer-Ball, eBird data); **800** at McElroy Lake, 4 Mar 1979 (*KW* 55:47, 1979); **800** e. of Central City, Muhlenberg Co., 2 Jan 2010 (*KW* 86:41, 2010); **600** at McElroy Lake, 27 Feb 2018 (*KW* 94:54, 2018); **500** at Fagan Branch Lake, Marion Co., 6/26 Dec 2017 and 5 Dec 2018 (J. Sole, eBird data).

Unaccepted record: tally of 693 at the Long Point Unit, 14 Dec 2007 (eBird data) possibly or probably pertains to the Tennessee portion of the Long Point Unit.

TUFTED DUCK *Aythya fuligula*

Status: Accidental vagrant. Although the possibility of an escaped bird is always a concern with this Eurasian species, it is a regular visitant to the Atlantic coast and occasional across the inland United States. Details of the single report indicated that there was no reason to suspect that it did not occur naturally.

1) 5-15 Apr 1997, a male (ph.) at the transient lakes nr. Woodburn, Warren Co. (Autin, et al., *KW* 74:86-87, 1998)

GREATER SCAUP *Aythya marila*

Status: Rare to uncommon transient and winter resident, extremely rare during summer. All records currently from west of the Cumberland Plateau; generally encountered on the larger lakes and rivers, but also occurs on flooded backwater areas and smaller bodies of water, especially during migration. Peak of abundance occurs from mid-Dec to late Feb. Known primarily as a winter species, occurring only in small numbers during the peaks of migration of other species during Nov and Mar. There are now a couple of summer records, likely of injured birds. Most often seen in small numbers with other waterfowl (especially Lesser Scaup), but also occurs in flocks distinct from other species, occasionally in groups of several dozen or more birds.

Maximum counts: ca. **2850** on Ky Lake, Marshall Co., 21 Feb 2007 (*KW* 83:45, 2007); **most of 2000** diving ducks on Lake Barkley above the dam, 6 Feb 1994 (B. Palmer-Ball, eBird data); **at least half, maybe most, of 1000** scaup sp. on Lake Barkley above the dam, 21 Feb 1993 (B. Palmer-Ball, eBird data); **450** on Lake Barkley above the dam, 23 Feb 2001 (*KW* 77:28, 2001); **403** on Ky Lake, Marshall Co., 22 Feb 2006 (*KW* 82:45, 2006); **360** on Lake Barkley above the dam, 8 Feb 1992 (*KW* 68:33, 1992); up to **270** on the Ohio River at Louisville, mid-Feb 2014 (*KW* 90:45-46, 2014); **250-300** on the Ohio River, Bracken Co., 12 Feb 2014 (*KW* 90:46, 2014); **150** on the Ohio River at Louisville, 26 Feb 2015 (*KW* 91:49, 2015); **125** on the Ohio River, Gallatin Co., 10 Feb 2014 (*KW* 90:46, 2014); **110** on the Ohio River, Campbell Co., 15 Mar 2015 (*KW* 91:65, 2015); **80** on the Ohio River at Meldahl Dam, Bracken Co., 3 Mar 2003 (*KW* 79:66, 2003); **70** on the Ohio River at Louisville, 30 Dec 1962 (*KW* 39:8/10, 1963).

Early fall dates: 22 Oct 1985, Lexington (*KW* 62:4, 1986); 25 Oct 1988, Ohio River at Louisville (*KW* 65:5, 1989); 26 Oct 2008, Lake Barkley, Lyon Co. (eBird data).

Late spring dates: 19 Jun 1949, Chaney Lake (Mengel:192); injured male [likely Greater] lingered in Muhlenberg to 13 Jun 2003 (*KW* 79:80, 2003); 8 Jun 2013, McElroy Lake (*KW* 89:93, 2013); 29 May 2015, Ohio River at Louisville (*KW* 91:65, 2015); 24 May 2008, McElroy Lake (*KW* 84:57, 2008); 18 May 2008, Union Co. (*KW* 84:57, 2008); 14 May 2014, Jefferson Co. (*KW* 90:65, 2014); 14 May 2017, Ohio River, Campbell Co. (L. Walters, eBird data); 14 May 2019, McElroy Lake (m. ob., eBird data); 12 May 1945, Chaney Lake (Wilson, *KW* 22:10, 1946).

Out-of-season records (summer): two females and a male (probably injured) remained on the north end of Lake Barkley, Lyon Co. throughout the summer of 2000 (B. Palmer-Ball, eBird data; R. Denton, eBird data; D. Roemer, notes); at least one and perhaps a few birds likely summered again in 2001 (B. Palmer-Ball, eBird data); at least a couple of injured birds remained into summer 2004 on Lake Barkley, Lyon Co. (*KW* 80:80, 2004).

*LESSER SCAUP *Aythya affinis*

Status: Fairly common to common transient, uncommon to fairly common winter resident, extremely rare during summer. Generally widespread and numerous west of the Cumberland Plateau, uncommon during migration on the reservoirs of eastern Kentucky. Typically encountered on the larger lakes and rivers, but also occurs on flooded backwater areas and smaller lakes and ponds, especially during migration. Peaks of abundance occur from mid-Mar to early Apr and from mid-Nov to early Dec. A nesting record (listed under "*Aythya* spp. scaup" by Mengel: 191) originated from a small marsh along the Ohio River near Carrollton, Carroll Co., 3 Jun 1950 (Webster, *KW* 27:21-22, 1951). The species occasionally lingered into or through summer historically; in recent years, small numbers of possibly or likely injured birds have summered in the LBL vicinity every year, particularly on Lake Barkley, Lyon Co. Most often seen in small to medium-sized flocks of up to a hundred birds, but migratory and wintering concentrations of more than a thousand birds have been reported.

Maximum counts: **30,000** on Ky Lake, Marshall Co., 17 Feb 2018 (*KW* 94:55, 2018); ca. **11,400** on Lake Barkley above the dam and **5000** on Ky Lake, Marshall Co., both 21 Feb 2007 (*KW* 83:45, 2007); several flocks of **5000-10,000** observed on the Ohio River, Campbell Co., during the period 2-10 Nov 1945 (Mengel:192; under scaup sp.); ca. **10,000** on Lake Barkley, Lyon Co., 10 Mar 2001 (*KW* 77:49, 2001); ca. **9500** on Lake Barkley, Lyon Co., 27 Dec 2000 (*KW* 77:28, 2001); ca. **5400** on Lake Barkley above the dam and **2200** on Ky Lake above the dam, 21 Mar 2000 (*KW* 76:44, 2000; D. Roemer, notes); **5000+** on Lake Barkley, Lyon Co., and **2000** on Ky Lake, both 10 Jan 2005 (*KW* 81:57, 2005); **3500+** on Lake Barkley above Barkley Dam, 17 Nov 2004 (*KW* 81:5, 2005); a **majority of 6000** ducks on Ky Lake, Marshall Co., 26 Feb 2011 (*KW* 87:58, 2011); ca. **3000** on Lake Barkley above the dam 24 Feb 1998, 12-15 Dec 1998, and 2 Apr 1999 (D. Roemer, notes); "**thousands**" on Lake Barkley above the dam, 9 Nov 2009 (*KW* 86:4, 2010); ca. **2700** [20% of 13,500 diving ducks] on Barren River Lake, 3 Dec 2014 (*KW* 91:49, 2015); ca. **2000** on Ky Lake above the dam, 4 Apr 1989 (*KW* 65:64, 1989); **2000** on Lake Barkley, Lyon Co., 22 Feb 2006 (*KW* 82:45, 2006; erroneously published as 21 Feb therein [*fide* D. Roemer, notes]); **1700** on Lake

Barkley above the dam, 3 Mar 2018 (*KW* 94:69, 2018); **1215** on Lake Cumberland, Pulaski Co., 9 Dec 2018 (R. Bontrager, eBird data); **1200** on Lake Barkley, Lyon Co., 11 Mar 2015 (*KW* 91:65, 2015); more than **1000** nr. Swan Lake, late Feb 1986 (Logsdon, *KW* 62:30-31, 1986; C. Logsdon, pers. comm.); up to **1000** at the transient lakes and on the Ohio River at Louisville in various years (Mengel:191; under scaup sp.); ca. **1000** in ne. Hopkins Co., 24 Mar 2015 (*KW* 91:66, 2015); ca. **1000** in ne. Hopkins Co., 7 Mar 2018 (J. Sole/D. Lang, eBird data).

Out-of-season records away from Ky Lake/Lake Barkley & Christian/Warren Co. transient lakes (summer/early fall): 11 Jul 2008, Fish Pond, Fulton Co., (*KW* 84:84, 2008); 1 Aug 2014, Lake Linville, Rockcastle Co. (*KW* 91;5, 2015); 16 Sep 2016, Mercer Co. (*KW* 93:5, 2017); 10-13 Jun 2017, w. Henderson Co. (*KW* 93:98, 2017); early Jun–4 Jul 2018, Ohio River at Louisville (*KW* 94:104, 2018); 22 Jun 2018, sw. of Hopkinsville, Christian Co. (*KW* 94:104, 2018).

KING EIDER *Somateria spectabilis*

Status: Extremely rare late fall and winter visitant. This primarily coastal species occurs infrequently in the inland eastern United States. It has been documented in Kentucky three times.

Chronological list of records

1) 26 Dec 1959, an imm. female was shot by a hunter on the Ohio River, Boone Co., across the river from Rising Sun, Indiana (Mengel:195)
2) 2 Jan 1971, a female was shot by a hunter on the Ohio River nr. Cincinnati (*AB* 25:585, 1971; OSUMZ 15821 [*fide* B. Whan. pers. comm.]; B. Peterjohn, pers. comm.)
3) 25 Nov–10 Dec 2017, a female (ph.) on the Ohio River upstream from Chilo, Clermont Co., OH, that roosted out in the main channel, thus in Bracken Co. (*KW* 94:55/64, 2018).

HARLEQUIN DUCK *Histrionicus histrionicus*

Status: Extremely rare winter and spring visitant. This duck winters primarily in coastal areas and is infrequently reported inland. It has been documented in Kentucky on two occasions.

Chronological list of records

1) 8 Mar 1967, a male was seen by many observers on a small pond adjacent to the Ohio River nr. Louisville (Gresham and Moore, *KW* 43:65, 1967)
2) 26 Feb 2008, a female (ph.) on the Ohio River at New Richmond, Ohio, that a few times swam and flew out into Campbell Co. (D. Morse, 2008 notes; B. Palmer-Ball, eBird data; *KW* 84:37/42, 2008)

SURF SCOTER *Melanitta perspicillata*

Status: Rare fall transient, extremely rare winter resident and spring transient. Recorded chiefly west of the Cumberland Plateau. This scoter has increased noticeably during the past four decades, and it now occurs regularly in small numbers, especially during the peak of fall migration from late Oct to early Dec. Typically absent as a wintering bird, but as numbers have increased, an occasional bird has wintered and a perceptible peak in spring migration has been noted during Apr. Generally to be expected to occur regularly only on the larger lakes and rivers, but the species can turn up on smaller bodies of water, especially during migration. Most records are of single birds or small flocks of up to a half-dozen birds. Birds in female/imm. plumage far outnumber adult males.

Maximum fall counts: **34** (including 10 ad. males) on the Ohio River at Louisville, 3 Dec 2000 (*NAB* 55:176, 2001); **27** on the Ohio River at Louisville, 8 Dec 2001 (*KW* 78:32, 2002); **22** on the Ohio River at Louisville, 27 Oct 1988 (*KW* 65:5, 1989); two flocks of **13** and **9** on Lake Cumberland, Pulaski Co., 5 Dec 2005 (*KW* 82:45-46, 2006; **15** on the Ohio River at Louisville, 21 Oct 2003 (*KW* 80:5, 2004); **13** at Jonathan Creek, 26 Oct 2007 (*KW* 84:5, 2008); **13** on the Ohio River at Louisville, 19 Nov 2010 (*KW* 87:13, 2011); **10** on the Ohio River at Louisville, 31 Oct 2002 (B. Palmer-Ball, eBird data); **9** on the Ohio River at Louisville, 24 Oct 1984 (*KW* 61:15, 1985); **9** on Barren River Lake, 7 Nov 2003 (*KW* 80:5, 2004).

Maximum spring counts: **13** on the Ohio River at Louisville, 29 Apr–1 May 2005 (*KW* 81;83, 2005); **10+** above Ky Dam, 30 Mar 2007 (*KW* 83:73, 2007).

Late spring dates: 23-28 May 2005, (ph.) w. Henderson Co. (*KW* 81:83, 2005); 23 May 2008, (ph.) McElroy Lake (*KW* 84:57, 2008); 20-22 May 2012, Marion Co. (*KW* 88:71, 2012); 14 May 2008, (ph.) Lake Cumberland, Pulaski Co. (*KW* 84:57, 2008); 5-9 May 2008, above Ky Dam (*KW* 84:57, 2008); 25 Apr–7 May 2000, Barren River Lake (*KW* 76:44, 2000); 5-6 May 1989, Minor Clark Hatchery (*KW* 65:64, 1989); 6 May 2000, Big South Fork, McCreary Co. (Stedman 2019); 4 May 1988, above Ky Dam (*KW* 64:45, 1988); 4 May 1998, Lake Barkley above the dam (B. Palmer-Ball, eBird data); 2 May 2010, (ph.) Lake Linville, Rockcastle Co. (*KW* 86:63, 2010); 1 May 2005, Ky Lake and Louisville (*KW* 81:83, 2005); 1 May 2009, above Ky Dam (*KW* 85:65, 2009); 30 Apr 1991, w. Hardin Co. (*KW* 67:53, 1991); 28 Apr 2003, above Ky Dam (*KW* 79:66, 2003); 25 Apr 2014, Ohio River at Louisville (*KW* 90:66, 2014); 21 Apr 1991, Lexington (*KW* 67:53, 1991); 21 Apr 2007, Greenup Co. (*KW* 83:73, 2007); 21 Apr 2014, above Ky Dam (*KW* 90:66, 2014); 19 Apr 2013, Freeman Lake (*KW* 89:65, 2013); 19 Apr 2016, (ph.) Ohio River at Louisville (*KW* 92:57, 2016); 18 Apr 2003, Boone Co. (*KW* 79:66, 2003); 17 Apr 2004, Fulton Co. (*KW* 80:64, 2004); 17 Apr 2008, Campbell Co. (*KW* 84:57, 2008); 14 Apr 2012, Adair Co. (*KW* 88:71, 2012); 13 Apr 2012, Campbell/Kenton cos. (*KW* 88:71, 2012); a wintering bird lingered on the Ohio River at Louisville to 9 Apr 1995 (B. Palmer-Ball, eBird data); another lingered on Lake Barkley above the dam to 29 Mar 1998 (*KW* 74:52, 1998).

Early fall dates: 16 Oct 1940, Ohio River, Meade Co. (Mengel: 195); 17 Oct 2009, (ph.) Russell Co. (*KW* 86:4, 2010).

Unaccepted record: 28 Mar 1934, 4 with a flock of White-wingeds at McElroy Lake (Wilson, *KW* 16:18, 1940 [see Mengel:196]).

WHITE-WINGED SCOTER *Melanitta deglandi*

Status: Rare transient and winter resident. Most records from west of the Cumberland Plateau but the species has occurred statewide. Historically reported chiefly from the Ohio River, but can be expected to occur on any of the state's larger lakes and rivers, and occasionally on smaller bodies of water. During the 20th century, this species of scoter was the most likely to occur, particularly during mid-winter. It is now typically outnumbered by other scoters during migratory periods, but remains more likely during mid-winter. Peak of abundance occurs from early Nov to mid-Mar. Unprecedented numbers appeared on the Ohio River during the late winters of 2014 and 2015, accounting for the largest numbers ever reported in the state (see below). Typically observed singly, in pairs, or in small flocks of only a few birds. Females and imms. have far outnumbered adult males except during the remarkable events noted above.

Maximum counts: **187** on the Ohio River, Lewis/Mason cos., 6 Mar 2014 (*KW* 90:66, 2014); **158** on the Ohio River at Louisville, 14 Feb 2014 (*KW* 90:46, 2014); **61** on the Ohio River, Bracken Co., 6 Mar 2014 (*KW* 90:66, 2014); **71** on the Ohio River, Oldham Co., 21 Mar 2014 (*KW* 90:66, 2014); **61** on the Ohio River, Jefferson Co., 8-9 Mar 2015 (*KW* 91:66, 2015); **56** on the Ohio River, Gallatin Co., 10 Feb 2014 (*KW* 90:46, 2014); **56** on the Ohio River, Bracken/Mason Cos., 21 Mar 2015 (*KW* 91:66, 2015); **52** total on the Ohio River Boone/Gallatin cos., 16 Feb 2014 (*KW* 90:46, 2014); **40** on the Ohio River at Meldahl Dam, Bracken Co., 10 Jan 1971 (*AB* 25:585, 1971); **39** on the Ohio River at Dayton, Campbell Co., 15 Feb 2014 (*KW* 90:46, 2014); **18** on the Ohio River, Oldham Co., 2 Mar 2008 (*KW* 84:57, 2008); **13** on the Ohio River at Louisville, 3 Mar 2008 (*KW* 84:57, 2008); **8** on Ky Lake, Lyon Co., 29 Mar 2011 (*KW* 87:83, 2011); up to **7** on the Ohio River at Louisville, mid-Feb 1974 (*AB* 28:647, 1974).

Early fall dates: 24 Oct 1984, Ohio River at Louisville (*KW* 61:14-15, 1985); 24 Oct 2007, Barren River Lake (*KW* 84:5, 2008); 29 Oct 2002, Ohio River at Louisville (*KW* 79:6, 2003).

Late spring dates: 18 May 2019, (possibly injured) Lower Douglas Lake, Hardin Co. (M. Lehman, eBird data); 1 May 2011 McElroy Lake (*KW* 87:83, 2011); 24 Apr 2014, Lake Peewee (*KW* 90:66, 2014); 22 Apr 2014, Ky Lake, Marshall Co. (*KW* 90:66, 2014); 21 Apr 2018, (ph.) above Ky Dam (*KW* 94:69, 2018); 15 Apr 2018, (ph.) Oldham Co. (*KW* 94:69, 2018); 12 Apr 2008, Ky Lake, Trigg Co. (*KW* 84:57, 2008); 10 Apr 1999, Ohio River at Meldahl Dam, Bracken Co. (*KW* 75:42, 1999); 9 Apr 1995, Ohio River at Louisville (B. Palmer-Ball, eBird data); 7 Apr 1964, Louisville area (*KW* 52:45, 1976); 6 Apr 2014, Ohio River at Louisville (*KW* 90:66, 2014); 4 Apr 2013, Ohio River

Bracken Co. (*KW* 89:65, 2013); 4 Apr 2014, Cave Run Lake (*KW* 90:66, 2014); 29 Mar 2011, Ky Lake, Lyon Co. (*KW* 87:83, 2011); 24 Mar 2013, Ohio River at Louisville (*KW* 89:65, 2013); 26 Mar 2015, Lake Cumberland, Pulaski Co. (*KW* 91:66, 2015); 23 Mar 2019, Ky Dam & Lower Douglas Lake, Hardin Co. (J. Hall/S. Arnold, eBird data & M. Lehman, eBird data); 22 Mar 1981, Louisville (*KW* 57:55, 1981).

BLACK SCOTER *Melanitta americana*

Status: Transient (extremely rare during spring, rare during fall); extremely rare winter visitant/resident. Generally to be expected regularly only on the larger lakes and rivers, but occurs occasionally on smaller bodies of water. Peak of abundance occurs from late Oct to early Dec. This species is seldom found during mid-winter, but a few individuals have been documented to remain through the winter in recent years. Likewise, only a few spring records have been documented, most relatively recently. Females and imms. far outnumber adult males. Usually encountered singly or in small flocks of up to a half-dozen birds.

Maximum counts: **18** on the Ohio River at Louisville, 3 Nov 2010 (*KW* 87:13, 2011); **13** on the Ohio River at Louisville, 2 Dec 2014 (*KW* 91:49, 2015); **11** on the Ohio River at Louisville, 28 Oct 1985 (*KW* 62:4, 1986); **7** on Green River Lake, Taylor/Adair Cos., 31 Oct 1993 (*KW* 70:7, 1994); **7** on the Ohio River at Louisville, 12-13 Nov 2016 (*KW* 93:5, 2017).

Late spring dates: 6 May 2004, Herrington Lake, Boyle/Garrard cos. (*KW* 80:64, 2004); 4 May 1992, Ky Lake, Marshall Co. (B. Palmer-Ball, eBird data); 24 Apr 2013, an ad. male above Ky Dam (*KW* 89:65, 2013); 13-17 Apr 2008, Campbell Co. (*KW* 84:58, 2008); 14 Apr 2012 (ph.), Green River Lake, Adair Co. (*KW* 88:71, 2012); 23 Mar 2002, Ohio River at Louisville (a bird that wintered) (*KW* 78:49, 2002); 23 Mar 2015, Ohio River at Louisville (*KW* 91:66, 2015); 2-23 Mar 2017, (ph.) Lexington (*KW* 93:71, 2017); 20 Mar 2009, Ballard WMA (*KW* 85:65, 2009); 18 Mar 2008, Ohio River at Louisville (*KW* 84:58, 2008); 6 Mar 2006, Ohio River, Hancock Co. (*KW* 82:65, 2006); 5 Mar 2006, Ohio River at Louisville (*KW* 82:65, 2006); 18 Mar 2004, Ohio River, Campbell/Kenton cos. (eBird data); 17 Feb 1957, Ohio River at Louisville (Sommers, *KW* 33:56-57, 1957).

Early fall dates: 20 Oct 1978, Ohio River at Louisville (*KW* 55:15, 1979) 25 Oct 2007, Ohio River at Louisville and Ohio River, Gallatin Co. (*KW* 84:5, 2008).

Unaccepted record: 3 Dec 2014, (24) Ohio River, Boyd Co. (eBird data).

Note: On two occasions, all three species of scoters have been reported in a single flock: 24 Oct 1984, on the Ohio River at Louisville – nine Surf, one White-winged, and four Black (*KW* 61:14-15, 1985); and 11 Nov 1997, on Freeman Lake – two Surf, one White-winged, and three Black (R. Healy, pers. comm.).

LONG-TAILED DUCK *Clangula hyemalis*

Status: Extremely rare to rare (formerly uncommon) transient and winter visitant. Recorded chiefly west of the Cumberland Plateau, but there are a few reports from reservoirs in eastern Kentucky. Typically encountered on the larger lakes and rivers, but occasionally seen on smaller bodies of water. Peak of abundance occurs from mid-Nov to early Mar, although bouts of extremely cold weather can result in the appearance of small numbers from farther north at any time during the winter. Usually observed singly or in small flocks of fewer than a half-dozen birds.

Maximum counts: flocks of **30** and **55** were reported on the Ohio River nr. Louisville on 9 Jan 1947 and 10 Jan 1948, respectively (Mengel:195); flocks of **17** on Lake Barkley above Barkley Dam and **25** on Ky Lake above Ky Dam, both on 31 Mar 1984 (*KW* 60:41, 1984); **32** on the Ohio River at Louisville, 19 Mar 2014 (*KW* 90:66, 2014); **20** on Lake Barkley, 16 Feb 1975 (J. Pasikowski/L. Smith, notes); **18** (ph.) on Lake Cumberland, Pulaski Co., 10 Jan 2004 (*KW* 80:41, 2004); **17** on the Ohio River at Louisville, 5 Nov 1967 (L. Brecher, notes); **16** on the Ohio River, Bracken Co., 6 Mar 2014 (*KW* 90:66, 2014); **15** on the Ohio River at Louisville, 19/21 Nov 1969 (*AFN* 24:54, 1970); **14** on Ky Lake above the dam, 21 Mar 1987 (*KW* 63:48, 1987).

Early fall dates: 26 Oct 2016, (ph.) Lexington Reservoirs #2/#3 (*KW* 93:5, 2017); 1 Nov 2014, Ohio River at Louisville (*KW* 91:5, 2015); 3 Nov 1995, Ohio River at Louisville (B. Palmer-Ball, eBird data); 4 Nov 19—, Ohio River (Mengel:194).

Late spring dates: 4 May 1965, Ohio River at Louisville (*KW* 41:43, 1965; *KW* 52:44, 1976; A. Stamm, notes); 2 May 2015, Lake Barkley, Lyon Co. (*KW* 91:66, 2015); 16 Apr 1947, Ohio River at Louisville (Mengel:194); 16 Apr 2015, (ph.) Lake Liberty, Casey Co. (*KW* 91:66, 2015); 11 Apr 2015, (ph.) w. Henderson Co. (*KW* 91:66, 2015).

BUFFLEHEAD *Bucephala albeola*

Status: Fairly common transient, uncommon winter resident, extremely rare during summer. Recorded chiefly west of the Cumberland Plateau, but probably uncommon during migration on the reservoirs of eastern Kentucky. Generally encountered on the larger lakes and rivers, but occasionally reported on smaller bodies of water, especially during migration. Peaks of abundance occur from early Mar to early Apr and from early Nov to early Dec. On a few occasions, individuals (some possibly or likely injured) have lingered into or through summer. Generally seen in small to medium-sized flocks of up to a few dozen birds, larger groups being only rarely reported.

Maximum counts: **380** (including a single flock of 250) on Ky Lake above the dam, 18 Dec 2015 (*KW* 92:41, 2016); **375** on Lake Barkley, Lyon Co., 8 Apr 2014 (*KW* 90:67, 2014); "at least **a few hundred**" on Ky Lake, Marshall Co., 13 Dec 2009 (*KW* 86:41, 2010); **300** on Lake Barkley, Lyon Co., 16 Jan 2004 (eBird data); **300** on Lake Peewee, 1 Dec 2015 (*KW* 92:41, 2016); more than **250** on the Ohio River, Lewis Co., 27 Jan 2010 (*KW* 86:41, 2010); **250** at Minor Clark Hatchery, 31 Mar 1989 (*KW* 65:64, 1989); **245** total (including flocks of 100 and 98) at several sites on Lake Cumberland, 30 Nov 2011 (*KW* 88:5, 2012); **200+** in several flocks on the Ohio River at Louisville, 17 Dec 1999 (R. Dever, notes); **180** on Lake Cumberland, Russell Co., 3 Dec 2014 (*KW* 91:50, 2015; number erroneously published as 190 therein [*fide* R. Denton, eBird data]); **160** on Lake Cumberland, Pulaski Co., 9 Dec 2018 (R. Bontrager, eBird data); **163** total in several flocks on the Ohio River at Louisville, 27 Nov 2009 (*KW* 86:5, 2010); **150** at Cave Run Lake, 19 Mar 1989 (*KW* 65:64, 1989); ca. **150** on the Ohio River at Louisville, 18 Mar 2008 (*KW* 84:58, 2008); **144** on Barren River Lake, 2 Dec 2014 (*KW* 91:50, 2015); **143** on Lake Cumberland, Pulaski Co., 8 Dec 2013 (*KW* 90:47, 2014); **142** on Ky Lake, Calloway Co., 27 Dec 2013 (*KW* 90:47, 2014); **137** on Lake Cumberland, Pulaski Co., 2 Dec 2014 (*KW* 91:50, 2015); **126** on Cave Run Lake, 23 Jan 2008 (*KW* 84:43, 2008).

Late spring dates: 3 Jun 2004, Lake Barkley, Lyon Co. (*KW* 80:80, 2004); 1 Jun 1999, Ky Lake above the dam (*KW* 75:60, 1999); 27 May 1999, Lake Barkley above the dam (B. Palmer-Ball, eBird data; date erroneously published as 29 May in 2nd edition of this work [*fide* author's notes]); last week of May 2007, Ky Lake above the dam (*KW* 83:73, 2007); 19 May 2013, Morgan Pond (*KW* 89:66, 2013); 16 May 2012, Lake Barkley, Lyon Co. (*KW* 88:71, 2012); 15 May 1991, Ky Lake (*KW* 67:53, 1991); mid-May 2008, Ky Lake above the dam (*KW* 84:58, 2008); 23 May 2019, McElroy Lake (m. ob., eBird data); 9 May 1984, Pulaski Co. (*KW* 60:41-42, 1984).

Early fall dates: 18 Oct 1988, Ky Lake (B. Palmer-Ball, eBird data); 24 Oct 1990, LBL vicinity (*KW* 67:5, 1991; C. Peterson, notes.); 24 Oct 2014, e. of Morganfield, Union Co. (*KW* 91:5, 2015); 25 Oct 2007, Lake Cumberland, Pulaski Co. (R. Denton, eBird data); 27 Oct 2011, Sauerheber Unit (*KW* 78:6, 2002; location published erroneously therein as Falls of the Ohio [*fide* D. O'Brien, eBird data]).

Out-of-season records (summer): a presumably injured female or immature male summered at McElroy Lake, mid-Apr–2 Sep 1989, when remains of its body were found (Palmer-Ball and Boggs, *KW* 67:42, 1991); 12 Jul 2005, male Ky Dam Village (*KW* 81:104, 2005); 13 Jun 2015, Ky Dam Village (*KW* 91:83, 2015).

COMMON GOLDENEYE *Bucephala clangula*

Status: Uncommon transient, uncommon to locally common winter resident. Recorded chiefly west of the Cumberland Plateau; known primarily as a winter species, typically occurring in small numbers during the peaks of migration for most other diving ducks during Nov and Mar. Generally encountered on the larger lakes and rivers, but a few are regularly seen on smaller bodies of water, especially during migration. Most frequently observed in small flocks of up to about 15-20 birds, but regularly reported in flocks of several dozen or more on Ky Lake and Lake Barkley.

Maximum counts: **20,000** on Ky Lake, Marshall Co., 17 Feb 2018 (*KW* 94:55, 2018); ca. **9235** on Ky Lake, Marshall Co., 21 Feb 2007 (*KW* 83:45, 2007); perhaps **most of several thousand** diving ducks on Ky Lake at Birmingham Point, Marshall/Lyon cos., 15 Feb 1997 (B. Palmer-Ball, eBird data); **2000-3000** on Ky Lake above the dam, Livingston/Marshall cos., 16 Jan 1998 (D. Roemer, notes); **2350** on Ky Lake, Marshall Co., 22 Feb 2006 (*KW* 82:46, 2006); "**thousands**" on Ky Lake, Marshall Co., 15 Jan 2010 (*KW* 86:41, 2010); **1000+** on Ky Lake, Marshall/Lyon cos., 6 Feb 2000 (B. Palmer-Ball, eBird data); **750-1000** on Ky Lake, Marshall Co., 18 Feb 2012 (*KW* 88:45, 2012); **720** on Ky Lake, Marshall Co., 18 Dec 2010 (*KW* 87:58, 2011); **600** on Lake Barkley above the dam, 19 Jan 2018 (*KW* 94:55, 2018); ca. **550** on the west side of Ky Lake, mid-Feb 1985 (*KW* 61:28-29, 1985); ca. **500** on upper Lake Barkley, 23 Jan 1981 (*KW* 57:36, 1981); ca. **500** on Kentucky Lake/Lake Barkley, Jan–early Feb 1983 (*KW* 60:24, 1984); **500** on Lake Barkley above the dam, 16 Jan 2015 (*KW* 91:50, 2015); **450** on Lake Barkley above the dam, 2 Feb 2019 (R. Bontrager, eBird data); **210+** on the Ohio River, Lewis/Mason cos., 6 Mar 2014 (*KW* 90:67, 2014); **150-200** on the Ohio River, Bracken Co., 12 Feb 2014 (*KW* 90:47, 2014).

Late spring dates: 30 May 2018, (ph.) above Ky Dam (*KW* 94:69, 2018); 29 May 1999, Lake Barkley above the dam (B. Palmer-Ball, eBird data); 29 May 2005, Lake Barkley above the dam (*KW* 81:83, 2005); 29 May 2013, Ballard WMA (*KW* 89:66, 2013); 26 May 1988, Ky Lake above the dam (*KW* 64:45, 1988); 24 May 2007, (likely injured) Lake No. 9 (*KW* 83:73, 2007); 19 May 2013, Union Co. (*KW* 89:66, 2013); 18 May 2013, above Ky Dam (*KW* 89:66, 2013); 16 May 2011, above Ky Dam (*KW* 87:83, 2011).

Early fall dates: 27 Oct 1992, Jonathan Creek (*KW* 69:6, 1993); 2 Nov 1984, Ohio River at Louisville (*KW* 61:15, 1985).

Out-of-season records (summer): a presumably injured female apparently summered on Ky Lake above the dam during 2008 (*KW* 84:58/84, 2008; *KW* 85:11, 2009); 6-16 Jul 2015, three different birds on Lake Barkley/Ky Lake (*KW* 91:83, 2015).

Hybrid record: Common Goleneye x Hooded Merganser, (ph.) 10-11 Feb 2011 on Barren River Lake (*KW* 87:58, 2011).

HOODED MERGANSER *Lophodytes cucullatus*

Status: Fairly common transient, uncommon to fairly common winter resident, rare summer resident. Recorded chiefly west of the Cumberland Plateau. Most often encountered on larger lakes, rivers, and flooded backwater areas during migration, more often on smaller bodies of water including slow moving streams at other times. Peaks of abundance occur from mid-Mar to early Apr and from mid-Nov to early Dec. The species has been reported during summer (and likely breeds) at scattered localities on backwater sloughs and ponds along the Ohio and Mississippi rivers, occasionally elsewhere. It has increased in distribution as a breeder over the past few decades with confirmed breeding records from 19 counties (see limited distribution documented by Mengel:197, KBBA:44-45, and summary below). Usually seen in small flocks of fewer than 25 birds, but groups of more than a hundred are occasionally reported. **State Breeding Status**: Threatened.

Maximum counts: **890** in a single flock on Honker Bay, Lake Barkley, Lyon Co., 29 Nov 1987 (*KW* 64:16, 1988); at least **750** on Honker Lake, LBL, Lyon Co., 4 Dec 2008 (*KW* 85:46, 2009); **623** on the LBL CBC, 18 Dec 1987 (*KW* 64:28, 1988); **576** on the LBL CBC, 23 Dec 1968 (*KW* 45:12, 1969); **551** at Lexington, 1 Jan 2015 (*KW* 91:50, 2015); **500** on Energy Lake, Trigg Co., early Dec 1989 (*KW* 66:37, 1990); **500** at Lexington, 14 Jan 2016 (*KW* 92:41, 2016); **500** at Lexington, 15 Dec 2016 (*KW* 93:47, 2017); ca. **500** on Honker Bay of Lake Barkley, Lyon Co., 26 Nov 1988 (*KW* 65:5, 1989); **500** at Lexington, 1-3 Jan 2018 (*KW* 94:55, 2018); ca. **400** on Barren River Lake, 11 Jan 2010 (*KW* 86:42, 2010; date erroneously published as 8 Jan therein [*fide* D. Roemer, notes]); **400** on Barren River Lake, 8 Mar 2013 (*KW* 89:66, 2013); **350** on Honker Bay, LBL, Lyon Co., 30 Nov 2009 (*KW* 86:5, 2010); **265** on Lake Peewee 7 Feb 2014 (*KW* 90:47, 2014).

Hybrid record: see Common Goldeneye.

Summary of confirmed breeding records by county:

Ballard (*KW* 80:64, 2004; *KW* 81:83, 2005; *KW* 84:58, 2008)
Boone (*KW* 82:66, 2006; *KW* 83:73, 2007; *KW* 84:58, 2008)
Crittenden (*KW* 91:84, 2015)

Fulton (Able, *KW* 43:27, 1967; B. Palmer-Ball, 1995/1996 eBird data; *KW* 78:61, 2002; *KW* 84:84, 2008; *KW* 85:65, 2009; *KW* 86:64, 2010; *KW* 88:72, 2012; *KW* 91:67, 2015; C. Bliznick, 2018 eBird data)

Hardin (*KW* 85:65, 2009; *KW* 86:64, 2010)

Henderson (*KW* 62:66, 1986; *KW* 68:56, 1992; *KW* 79:67, 2003; *KW* 81:83, 2005; *KW* 82:66, 2006; *KW* 83:73, 2007; *KW* 84:84, 2008; *KW* 85:91, 2009; *KW* 86:90, 2010; *KW* 88:72, 2012; *KW* 91:84, 2015; *KW* 92:57/72/78, 2016; C. Crawford, 2017 eBird data; *KW* 94:104, 2018; C. Crawford, 2018 eBird data)

Jefferson (Monroe, *KW* 23:57-60, 1947; Lovell, *KW* 27:59, 1951; Hays, *KW* 33:3, 1957; Mengel:197; *KW* 79:67/80, 2003; *KW* 81:83/104, 2005; *KW* 83:73, 2007; *KW* 84:58, 2008; *KW* 86:64, 2010; *KW* 89:66, 2013; *KW* 90:67, 2014; *KW* 91:67, 2015; *KW* 92:57, 2016; *KW* 94:104, 2018; B. Yandell, 2019 eBird data)

Laurel (A. Kayser, 2018 eBird data)

Livingston (B. Palmer-Ball, 1996/1997 eBird data; *KW* 86:90, 2010)

McCracken (C. Nicholson, 2000 notes/eBird data)

Menifee (Haight and Reeder, *KW* 73:26, 1997; *NAB* 55:305, 2001)

Muhlenberg (*KW* 88:72, 2012)

Ohio (*KW* 82:66, 2006; *KW* 83:73, 2007)

Owen (*KW* 85:91, 2009)

Pulaski (*KW* 69:56, 1993)

Rowan (*KW* 82:66, 2006; *KW* 84:58, 2008; *KW* 85:65, 2009)

Trigg (*KW* 87:83, 2011; *KW* 88:72, 2012; *KW* 91:67, 2015; *KW* 92:57, 2016; R. Denton et al., 2017 eBird data; P. Theobald, 2018 eBird data)

Union (*KW* 81:83, 2005; *KW* 89:66, 2013)

Warren (Palmer-Ball and Boggs, *KW* 67:42, 1991; Roemer, *KW* 74:93-94, 1998; *KW* 86:90, 2010)

*COMMON MERGANSER *Mergus merganser*

Status: Rare to locally uncommon transient and winter resident, extremely rare summer resident. Recorded chiefly west of the Cumberland Plateau during the non-breeding season; formerly known primarily as a winter species, being most numerous during mid-winter spells of extremely cold weather when birds from farther north arrive. In contrast, only a few birds are typically observed during the peaks of migration of most other diving ducks during Nov and Mar. Generally encountered on larger lakes and rivers, but a few can be found on smaller bodies of water. Abundance varies greatly from year to year depending on severity of the weather. During the past few years, a pronounced expansion of breeding range has been documented in the southern Appalachian Mountains including a few locations in eastern Kentucky (see below). Most often seen in small groups of up to a dozen birds, but sometimes reported in larger flocks during mid-winter, especially on Lake Barkley and Ky Lake.

Maximum counts: **1500** on Lake Barkley at the Silo Overlook, Lyon/Trigg cos., 28 Jan 1984 (*KW* 60:24, 1984; *AB* 38:322, 1984); **800** on Ky Lake, 19 Mar 1979 (*KW* 55:47, 1979); **600** on Lake Barkley at Silo Overlook, Lyon/Trigg cos., 10 Feb 1985 (*KW* 61:29, 1985); **600** on the Kentucky Woodlands CBC, 29 Dec 1964 (*KW* 41:10, 1965); **450-500** on the Ohio River, Bracken Co., 12 Feb 2014 (*KW* 90:47, 2014); more than **400** on Honker Bay, Lake Barkley, Lyon Co., 5 Jan 1990 (*KW* 66:37, 1990).

Late spring dates (other than recent breeding birds) 10 Jun 1939, injured bird in Warren Co. (Wilson, *KW* 16:18, 1940); 6 Jun 1997, Lake Barkley, Lyon Co. (*KW* 73:72, 1997; M. Bennett, notes); 16 May 2009, Minor Clark Hatchery (*KW* 85:65, 2009); 10 May 2003, Boone Co. (*KW* 79:67, 2003); 5 May 1982, Lake Barkley (*KW* 58:49, 1982); 5 May 2013, Minor Clark Hatchery (*KW* 89:66, 2013); 4 May 1996, Fulton Co. (*KW* 72:53, 1996).

Early fall dates: 14 Oct 1972, Lake Cumberland (*KW* 48:68, 1972); 16 Oct 1976, Louisville (*AB* 31:183, 1977); 1 Nov 2006, Ohio River at Louisville (*KW* 83:9, 2007); 4 Nov 2012, Ohio River at Louisville (*KW* 89:4, 2013).

Out-of-season records (probable summering birds): 1 Sep 1986, (4) in heavy molt on Lake Barkley, nr. Kuttawa, Lyon Co. (*KW* 63:7, 1987); at least 18 Jul–25 Nov 1999, a female below Smithland Dam (*KW* 76:5/9, 2000); 14 Sep 2002+, a female above Ky Dam (*KW* 79:6, 2003).

Unaccepted record: 2000 on Lake Barkley, Lyon Co., 14 Feb 1965 (E. Larson, eBird data); this record may well be correct, similar to the Jan 1984 concentration, but lacks any details.

Recent records of confirmed breeding by county

Jackson (28 Apr 2017 & 20 Apr–25 Jun 2018, Middle Fork Rockcastle River [Palmer-Ball, *KW* 94:118-121])
Menifee (25 May 2018, East Branch Indian Creek [Palmer-Ball, *KW* 94:118-121])
Rockcastle (30 May/25 Jul 2017 & 18 Jun 2018, Skegg Creek [Palmer-Ball, *KW* 94:118-121])

Recent records of probable breeding by county

Pike (31 Oct 2016, 8 on the Levisa Fork [*KW* 93:5, 2017])
Pike (27 May/6 Jun 2017, 8 & 2 on the Russell Fork, Big Sandy River at Breaks Interstate Park [*KW* 93:71 & 98, 2017])

RED-BREASTED MERGANSER *Mergus serrator*

Status: Fairly common transient, rare to uncommon winter resident, extremely rare during summer. Recorded chiefly west of the Cumberland Plateau, but probably uncommon on the reservoirs of eastern Kentucky during migration. Peaks of abundance occur from mid-Mar to mid-Apr and from mid-Nov to early Dec. Typically encountered on the larger lakes and rivers, but also occurs on smaller bodies of water, especially during migration. An occasional bird (perhaps injured) turns up during summer. Generally observed in small groups of up to 25 birds, but larger flocks of up to a hundred or more are occasionally reported during migration.

Maximum fall counts: **1500** on the Ohio River at Louisville, 18 Nov 1972 (*KW* 52:45, 1976); **1042** on Barren River Lake, 2 Dec 2014 (*KW* 91:50, 2015); **810** on Lake Cumberland, Russell Co. and **301** on Lake Cumberland, Wayne Co., both 3 Dec 2014 (*KW* 91:50, 2015); more than **800** on Lake Cumberland, Russell Co., 9 Dec 2013 (*KW* 90:48, 2014); ca. **500** on Cave Run Lake, 29 Nov 1986 (*KW* 63:7, 1987); at least **450-500** in scattered flocks on the Ohio River at Louisville, 17 Nov 1991 (B. Palmer-Ball, eBird data); **475** in three flocks on Lake Cumberland, Russell Co., 30 Nov 2008 (*KW* 85:11, 2009); **463** on Lake Cumberland above Wolf Creek Dam, 24 Nov 2009 (*KW* 86:5, 2010); **350** on Lake Peewee, 3 Dec 2014 (*KW* 91:50, 2015).

Maximum spring counts: **700+** on Lake Barkley, 21 Mar 1987 (*KW* 63:48, 1987); **several hundred** on Lake Barkley above the dam, 1 Apr 1990 (*KW* 66:55, 1990); **327** on Lake Barkley, Lyon Co., 22 Feb 2006 (*KW* 82:46, 2006).

Late spring dates: occasionally lingering into Jun, latest being 22 Jun 1958, Woodburn lakes (*KW* 38:9, 1962); 12 Jun 2012, Ky Dam Village (*KW* 88:92, 2012); 9 Jun 2018, (ph.) Ky Dam (*KW* 94: 104, 2018).

Early fall dates: 28 Oct 2012, Blood River (H. Chambers, eBird data); 30 Oct 2006, Lake Cumberland, Wayne Co. (R. Denton, eBird data).

Out-of-season records (mid-summer/early fall): 12 Sep 1959, Jefferson Co. (Stamm, et al., *KW* 36:5, 1960; *KW* 37:27, 1961; Mengel:199); 20 Jul [probably 1967 or 1968], Falls of the Ohio (A. Stamm, notes); 4 Aug 1962, Ohio River at Louisville (Stamm, et al., *KW* 43:7, 1967); 13-14 Jul 2005, Falls of the Ohio (*KW* 81:104, 2005); 10-16 Jul 2016, (ph.) Falls of the Ohio (*KW* 92:78, 2016).

Unaccepted records: 13 Oct 2011, Grayson Lake, Carter Co. [more likely Common?] (eBird data).

Published error: 18 Jul 1999, Smithland Dam (*KW* 75:60, 1999; this bird was a Common Merganser [*fide KW* 76:9, 2000; D. O'Brien, notes]).

*RUDDY DUCK *Oxyura jamaicensis*

Status: Fairly common transient, rare to uncommon winter resident, extremely rare during summer (one breeding record). Recorded chiefly west of the Cumberland Plateau, but probably uncommon during migration on water bodies in eastern Kentucky. Generally encountered on the larger lakes and rivers, but also occurs on smaller bodies of water, especially during migration. Peaks of abundance occur from early Nov to early Dec and from mid-Mar to early Apr. Occasionally lingers into or through summer with one documented breeding record (see below). Most often seen in small flocks of up to a couple of dozen birds, but larger groups of more than a hundred are occasionally observed, especially at favored wintering sites.

Maximum counts: **700+** on Lake Barkley above the dam, 29 Oct 2013 with possibly **up to 1000** there 15 Nov 2013 (*KW* 90:5-6, 2014); **650** on Lake Barkley above the dam, 4 Jan 2013 (*KW* 89:46, 2013); **546** on Lake Peewee, 26 Mar 2006 (*KW* 82:66, 2006); **400** on Lake Peewee, 1 Dec 2015 (*KW* 92:41, 2016); ca. **350** on Lake Barkley, Lyon/Trigg cos., 30 Mar 2007 (*KW* 83:73, 2007); **339** on Lake Peewee, 21 Jan 2004 (*KW* 80:41, 2004); at least **325** on Lake Barkley above the dam, 18 Feb 2012 (*KW* 88:45, 2012); **306** at Jonathan Creek, 21 Feb 2016 (*KW* 92:41, 2016); ca. **300** on Lake Barkley above the dam, 15 Feb 2005 (*KW* 81:57, 2005); **300** on Molloy Bay, Lake Barkley, Lyon Co., 14 Dec 2008 (*KW* 85:46, 2009); **300+** on Cedar Creek Lake, Lincoln Co., 1 Dec 2015 (*KW* 92:41, 2016); **250-300** on Lake Barkley above the dam, 28 Mar 2007 (*KW* 83:73, 2007); ca. **250** on Lake Barkley at the Lyon/Trigg co. line, 27 Jan 2010 (*KW* 86:42, 2010); **237** on Lake Peewee, 2 Nov 1989 (*KW* 66:7, 1990); **225** on Lake Peewee, 28 Nov 1987 (*KW* 64:16, 1988); **208** on Ky Lake, Calloway Co., 4 Jan 2013 (*KW* 89:46, 2013); **200** at Jonathan Creek, 11 Mar 2002 (*KW* 78:49, 2002); ca. **200** on Barren River Lake, 16 Nov 2010 (*KW* 87:13, 2011); **200+** on Lake Barkley above the dam, 30 Nov 2005 (*KW* 82:5, 2006).

Late spring dates: birds occasionally linger well into early summer, the latest being 22 Jul 2002 nr. Morganfield, Union Co. (*KW* 78:61, 2002); 6 Jul 2005, Union Co. (*KW* 81:104, 2005); 5 Jul 2008, Morgan Pond (*KW* 84:84, 2008); 28 Jun 2002, Morgan Pond, Christian Co. (*KW* 78:61, 2002); 20 Jun 1998, McElroy Lake (*KW* 74:72, 1998); 15-18 Jun 2013, Parsons Pond, Logan Co. (*KW* 89:93, 2013); 17 Jun 1997, s. Logan Co. (B. Palmer-Ball, eBird data); 12 Jun 1962, Warren Co. (*KW* 45:33, 1969); 9 Jun 1989, McElroy Lake (Palmer-Ball and Boggs, *KW* 67:42, 1991); 9 Jun 2010, McElroy Lake (*KW* 86:90, 2010); 5 Jun 1997, Morgan Pond (B. Palmer-Ball, eBird data).

Early fall dates: 29 Aug 1950, Warren Co. (Wilson, *KW* 27:4, 1951); 4 Sep 1987, [location unspecific] (*KW* 64:16, 1988); 7 Sep 2002, Union Co. (*KW* 79:7, 2003); 17 Sep 2006, Lake Barkley above the dam (*KW* 83:9, 2007); 29 Sep 2016, Morgan Pond (*KW* 93:5, 2017); 4 Oct 1975, LBL (*KW* 51:79, 1975; A. Stamm, notes); 4 Oct 2012, Pendleton Co. (C. Cone, eBird data); 10 Oct 2009, Boone Co. (*KW* 86:5, 2010); 10 Oct 2017, Union Co. (*KW* 94:5, 2018); 11 Oct 1989, Lake Peewee (*KW* 66:7, 1990).

Out-of-season records (summer): a bird remained on a small pond nr. Louisville throughout the summer of 1952 (Mengel:196); Jun–Jul 1964, a bird at Lake Peewee (Hancock, *KW* 41:17, 1965); Jul 1963, a bird at Louisville (*KW* 52:45, 1976); 17-20 Jul 1989, (1-2) at McElroy Lake (Palmer-Ball and Boggs, *KW* 67:42, 1991); 2-6 Aug 1999, a female in Warren Co. (*KW* 76:5, 2000); a male remained at the Brown Power Plant, Mercer Co. throughout the summer of 2000 (*KW* 76:44/55 2000; *KW* 77:5, 2001; R. Denton, notes) with another present there 3-18 Aug 2001 (R. Denton, eBird data); 29 Jul 2006, Ballard WMA (*KW* 82:79, 2006); mid-Jul–late Oct 2006, Lexington (*KW* 82:79, 2006; *KW* 83:9, 2007); 30 Jun 2008, w. Henderson Co. (*KW* 84:84, 2008); summer 2011, a male summered on Lake Reba, Madison Co. (*KW* 87:83/111, 2011; *KW* 88:5, 2012); 17 Aug 2016, Morgan Pond (*KW* 93:5, 2017); 2 Jul 2018, Morgan Pond (*KW* 94:105, 2018).

Published error: 13 in LBL area, 17 Jul 1999 (*KW* 75:60, 1999) (correction *fide KW* 76:9, 2000).

Confirmed record of nesting

Union (Jun 2003, female with a brood of small young [*KW* 79:80, 2003; Palmer-Ball, *KW* 80:32-35, 2004]

*NORTHERN BOBWHITE *Colinus virginianus*

Status: Locally rare to uncommon resident (formerly much more widespread and numerous). Recorded statewide except in heavily forested portions of eastern Kentucky; most numerous in semi--open farmland with brushy cover. Breeding throughout the state in suitable habitat, but quite local in heavily forested areas. The wild population has been supplemented with game stock in some areas; however, the species has declined substantially during the past four decades and is no longer common anywhere across the state. Typically heard calling and sometimes seen in coveys of up to a dozen or more birds.

Maximum count: **45** at Davis Bend NP, Hart Co., 27 Jan 2013 (J. Sole, eBird data).

*RUFFED GROUSE *Bonasa umbellus*

Status: Locally rare to fairly common resident. Formerly occurred throughout the state (Mengel: 223-224); currently restricted primarily to more rugged, wooded areas of the Cumberland Plateau and Mountains. Largely unsuccessful attempts to reintroduce the species have occurred at scattered locations in central and western Kentucky as far west as Pennyrile State Forest and LBL (*KBBA*: 70). Occurs most frequently in wooded areas with a well-developed shrub layer and/or abundance of openings and edge. Most often the unique "drumming" of males is heard, especially during early spring, but single birds or family groups can be flushed from woodlands and woodland edge, and are sometimes seen foraging along or crossing rural roadsides. This species has two color morphs, red and gray, but only the red morph is encountered in Kentucky (J. Sole, pers. comm.).

e/sGREATER PRAIRIE-CHICKEN *Tympanuchus cupido*

Status: Extirpated. Formerly resident on the "barrens" (prairies) of central and western Kentucky, with breeding reported north and east as far as Bardstown, Nelson Co. However, the species essentially disappeared from the state by the mid-1800s (Mengel:225). A modern sighting (1940) from near Madisonville, if correct, probably represented a wanderer from the then extant southern Illinois population fewer than 50 miles to the west (Mengel:225). Although many were likely eaten by early settlers, no specimen appears to have ever been preserved!

*WILD TURKEY *Meleagris gallopavo*

Status: Uncommon to fairly common resident (somewhat locally distributed but increasing). Once considered common in woodlands throughout the state, Wild Turkeys virtually disappeared from Kentucky during the first part of the 20th century. Birds of wild stock are probably restricted to the LBL area and perhaps portions of the Cumberland Mountains. After a prolonged period of scarcity during much of the 20th century, the species has increased dramatically during the past few decades, in large part due to a very successful reintroduction program (*KBBA*:72). Occurs in wooded and semi-open habitats; most numerous in rural farmland with scattered patches of woodland. Generally seen singly or in flocks of up to a couple of dozen birds, but larger flocks of 50 or more are sometimes seen, especially during winter.

Maximum counts: **326** in a single flock in se. Muhlenberg Co., 3 Jan 2009 (*KW* 85:24/47, 2009); **296** in sw. Todd Co., 22 Dec 2017 (A. Troyer, eBird data); at least **239** in a flock in se. Muhlenberg Co., 3 Jan 2004 (*KW* 80:19/41, 2004); **215+** in a single flock in se. Muhlenberg Co., 30 Dec 1996 (B. Palmer-Ball, eBird data); **200** at Big Bone Lick SP, Boone Co., 10 Apr 2014 (I. Horn, eBird data).

*PIED-BILLED GREBE *Podilymbus podiceps*

Status: Fairly common transient, uncommon to (locally) fairly common winter resident, extremely rare (formerly uncommon) summer resident. Recorded statewide in a variety of aquatic habitats from small ponds and marshes to the largest lakes and rivers. Peaks of abundance occur from mid-Mar to early Apr and from mid-Oct to late Nov. Summering has been documented from scattered localities in central and western Kentucky, but confirmed breeding records have come from only ten counties (see below). Most often seen singly or in small flocks of up to a dozen birds, but larger groups of several dozen are occasionally seen, particularly during migration. **State Breeding Status**: Endangered.

Maximum counts: **223** on Green River Lake, Adair/Taylor cos., 31 Dec 2013 (*KW* 90:48, 2014); **175** above Ky Dam, 24 Jan 2012 (H. Chambers, eBird data); at least **165** on Lake Peewee, 1 Mar 2008 (*KW* 84:58, 2008); **165** (including family groups) on Morgan Pond, 8 Oct 2016 (*KW* 93:5, 2017); up to **164** on Lake Peewee, 26 Oct 1972 (*AB* 27:67, 1973); **150-200** on Lake Barkley above the dam, 27 Mar 2013 (*KW* 89:66, 2013); **162** on Ky Lake, Calloway Co., 3 Jan 2012 (E. Huber, eBird data); **146** on Lake Peewee, 15 Nov 1975 (*AB* 30:78, 1976); **140** on Lake Peewee, 11 Dec 2008 (*KW* 85:47, 2009); **125** on Barren River Lake, 8 Nov 2013 (*KW* 90:6, 2014); **113** on Lake Nevin, Bernheim Forest, 27 Oct 2012 (*KW* 89:5, 2013); **110** on Barren River Lake, 9 Mar 2013 (*KW* 89:66, 2013); **125** on Green River Lake, Taylor Co., 15 Feb 2014 (*KW* 90:48, 2014); **109** on Lake Peewee, 15 Nov 1983 (*KW* 60:14, 1984) and 15 Oct 1987 (*KW* 64:15, 1988); **103** on Lake Peewee, 20 Oct 1986 (*KW* 63:6, 1987); ca. **150** in scattered flocks on the Ohio River at Louisville, 4 Nov 2000 (*KW* 77:4, 2001); **112** total on Ky Lake, Marshall Co., 17 Dec 2011 (H. Chambers, eBird data); **112** on Lake Peewee, 30 Dec 2013 (*KW* 90:48, 2014).

Summary of confirmed breeding records by county

<u>Christian</u> (*KW* 73:71, 1997; *KW* 84:84, 2008; *KW* 86:90, 2010; *KW* 87:111/124, 2011; *KW* 88:5, 2012; *KW* 89:66/93, 2013; *KW* 92:57/78, 2016; *KW* 93:5, 2017)
<u>Fulton</u> (Mengel:155; *KW* 74:71, 1998; *KW* 79:79, 2003; *KW* 85:91, 2009; Palmer-Ball, *KW* 74:85-86, 1998; *KW* 93:98, 2017)
<u>Henderson</u> (*KW* 78:60, 2002)
<u>Hopkins</u> (Mengel:155)
<u>Jefferson</u> (Mengel:155)
<u>Logan</u> (*KW* 86:90, 2010; *KW* 89:66/93, 2013)
<u>Menifee</u> (Kenawell and Reeder, *KW* 78:39-40, 2002)
<u>Trigg</u> (Mengel:155)
<u>Union</u> (*KW* 79:79, 2003; *KW* 81:104, 2005; *KW* 82:80, 2006)
<u>Warren</u> (Mengel:155; Palmer-Ball, *KW* 67:86-87, 1991; Roemer, et al., *KW* 73:79-83, 1997; Roemer, *KW* 74:93, 1998/*KW* 75:3, 1999; *KW* 79:79, 2003; *KW* 87:111, 2011; *KW* 86:64, 2010; *KW* 94:105, 2018)

HORNED GREBE *Podiceps auritus*

Status: Fairly common transient, rare to locally uncommon winter resident, extremely rare during summer. Recorded chiefly west of the Cumberland Plateau, but probably uncommon during migration on the reservoirs of eastern Kentucky. Generally encountered on the larger lakes and rivers, but sometimes found on smaller bodies of water, especially during migration. Peaks of abundance occur from mid-Mar to early Apr and from late Oct to early Dec. Historically quite rare during mid-winter, but in recent years at least a few birds have wintered on some of the larger reservoirs of southern and western parts of the state (e.g., Dale Hollow Lake, Barren River Lake, Green River Lake, Ky Lake, Lake Cumberland). Lingering spring migrants are usually seen in their distinctive breeding plumage and occasionally remain into early summer. Generally seen in small to medium--sized flocks of a few to a couple of dozen birds.

Maximum fall/winter counts: **2161** on Ky Lake, Marshall Co., 28 Nov 2008 (*KW* 85:11, 2009); at least **980** on Ky Lake, Marshall Co., 27 Nov 2007 (*KW* 84:5, 2008); at least **750** on Ky Lake, Marshall Co., 13 Dec 2009 (*KW* 86:42, 2010); **500** at Lexington, 1 Dec 2015 (*KW* 92:42, 2016); **455** in scattered flocks on the Ohio River at Louisville, 3 Dec 2000 (*NAB* 55:176, 2001); **450** on Dale Hollow Lake, Clinton Co., 2 Dec 2017 (*KW* 94:55, 2018); ca. **400** on the Ohio River at Louisville, 18 Nov 1972 (*AB* 27:67, 1973); **380** on Lake Cumberland, Wayne Co., 17 Nov 2018 (R. Bontrager, eBird data); at least **375** on Lake Barkley, Lyon Co., 18 Feb 2012 (*KW* 88:45, 2012); **308** on Lake Cumberland, Russell Co., 13 Feb 2012 (*KW* 88:45, 2012); **305** on Lake Peewee, 3 Dec 2014 (*KW* 91:51, 2015); **300** total on the Ohio River at Louisville, 30 Nov 2015 (*KW* 92:5, 2016); nearly **300** on Lake Cumberland, Russell/Wayne cos., 5 Dec 2014 (*KW* 91:51, 2015); **200-300** above Ky Dam and **100** on Lake Barkley above the dam, both 26 Nov 2003 (*KW* 80:5, 2004); at least **280** on the Ohio River at Louisville, 1 Dec 2008 (*KW* 85:47, 2009); **280** on Barren River Lake, 2 Dec 2014 (*KW* 91:51, 2015); **276** on Lake Cumberland, Russell Co., 24 Nov 2009 (*KW* 86:5, 2010); **254** on Ky Lake, Marshall Co., 14 Dec 2013 (*KW* 90:48, 2014); ca. **250** on the Ohio River at Louisville, 23 Nov 2009 (*KW* 86:5, 2010); at least **250** on the Ohio River at Louisville, 9 Jan 2014 (*KW* 90:48, 2014); **250** on Lake Peewee, 1 Dec 2015 (*KW* 92:42, 2016); at least **230** on the Ohio River at Louisville, 19 Nov 2010 (*KW* 87:13, 2011); **215** above Ky Dam, 15 Dec 2006 (*KW* 83:46, 2007); at least **215** on the Ohio River at Louisville, 4 Nov 2011 (*KW* 88:5, 2012); **210+** on Barren River Lake, 16 Nov 2002 (*KW* 79:4, 2003); **202** on Barren River Lake, 19 Nov 2007 (*KW* 84:5, 2008); **200** on the Ohio River at Louisville, 1 Dec 2015 (*KW* 92:41-42, 2016); ca. **200** in scattered groups on the Ohio River at Louisville, 3 Nov 1986 (*KW* 63:6, 1987); **four flocks of 50 or more** on the Ohio River at Louisville, 29 Nov 1953 (Stamm, *KW* 30:13, 1954); **200+** on Ky Lake, Marshall Co., 10 Jan 2005 (*KW* 81:57, 2005); **189** on Green River Lake, Adair/Taylor cos., 31 Dec 2013 (*KW* 90:48, 2014); **189** on Green River Lake, Adair Co., 5 Dec 2014 (*KW* 91:51, 2015); **175** on Lake Cumberland, Russell Co., 2 Dec 2017 (R. Bontrager, eBird data); **170** on Barren River Lake, 16 Nov 2002 & 7 Nov 2003 (eBird data & *KW* 80:5, 2004); **162** on Lake Linville, Rockcastle Co., 16 Nov 2018 (R. Denton, eBird data); **156** on Freeman Lake, 3 Dec 2014 (*KW* 91:51, 2015); **150** on Cave Run Lake, 2 Dec 2015 (*KW* 92:42, 2016); **146** on Lake Cumberland, Pulaski Co., 2 Dec 2014 (*KW* 91:51, 2015); **145** on Lake Cumberland, Russell/Wayne cos., 9 Dec 2013 (*KW* 90: 48, 2014).

Maximum late winter/spring counts: **450** on Ky Lake, Marshall Co., 22 Feb 2006 (*KW* 82:46, 2006); **231** on Lake Cumberland, Russell Co., 23 Feb 2008 (*KW* 84:43, 2008; R. Denton, eBird data); **204** on Green River Lake, Taylor Co., 9 Mar 2013 (*KW* 89:66, 2013); **200+** on Lake Barkley and Ky Lake, 10 Mar 2001 (*KW* 77:48, 2001); **165** at Meldahl Dam, 5 Mar 2005 (*KW* 81:84, 2005); **149** on Green River Lake, Taylor Co., 13 Mar 2014 (*KW* 90:68, 2014).

Early fall dates: 1 Oct 2006, Cedar Creek Lake (*KW* 83:9, 2007); 6 Oct 1978, Jefferson Co. (*KW* 55:14, 1979); 12 Oct 1974, Louisville (*AB* 29:64, 1975); 13 Oct 2002, Blood River (*KW* 79:4, 2003); 13 Oct 2015, Adair Co. (*KW* 92:5, 2016); 14 Oct 1820, Boone Co. (Mengel:154).

Late spring/summer dates: has lingered to 17 Jun 1934, Louisville (Mengel:154); 25 May–4 Jun 1947, Louisville (*KW* 52:41, 1976); an injured bird lingered at McElroy Lake from spring to 12 Sep 1989, when it was captured and released elsewhere (Palmer-Ball and Boggs, *KW* 67:38,91, 1991); one was observed into May 1999, and then 26-29 Jun 1999 on Ky Lake above the dam, Marshall Co. (*KW* 75:59, 1999; H. Chambers, notes); 17-18 & 22 Jun 2018, (ph.) KenLake SRP, Marshall Co. & just s. on Ky Lake, Calloway Co. (*KW* 94:105/124, 2018).

Unaccepted records: those during fall earlier than the early fall date of 1 Oct given above and including 10 Sep 1994, Rowan Co. (*KW* 71:3, 1995); 24 Sep 1980, Ky Lake (*KW* 57:19, 1981) [descriptions do not rule out Eared Grebes, which are more likely in Sep]; also 3 Oct 1980, LBL vicinity (eBird data).

Published error: 2 in Hart Co., 10 Sep 1997 (*KW* 74:4, 1998) (*fide* M. Sturgeon, pers. comm.).

RED-NECKED GREBE *Podiceps grisegena*

Status: Extremely rare transient and winter visitant, accidental during summer. Most historical records originated from the Ohio River and the transient lakes in Warren Co., but the species has now been reported in more than 50 counties across the state. During Feb 1994 and Mar 2014, unprecedented fallouts of this species occurred on inland lakes in the southeastern United States. These birds apparently originated from the eastern Great Lakes, which had mostly frozen over immediately prior to the grebes' appearance. During 1994, one to five were observed at seven locations in the state (*KW* 70:31/49, 1994; *KW* 72:32, 1996; C. Elliott, 1994 notes). An even more remarkable fallout occurred during Mar 2014, when no fewer than 260 individuals were documented with one to 27 reported on nearly 60 bodies of water in Kentucky (Palmer-Ball, *KW* 90:78-81). Most records are of single birds.

Maximum counts: **10-27** on ten different bodies of water during Mar 2014 (Palmer-Ball, *KW* 90:78-81, 2014); **5** on Owsley Fork Lake, Madison Co., 6 Mar 1994 (*KW* 70:49, 1994).

Late spring dates: 27 May 1939, Warren Co. (*KW* 38:5, 1962); 7 May 2006, Ky Lake above the dam (*KW* 82:66, 2006); 25 Apr 2014, e. Jefferson Co. (*KW* 90:79/80, 2014).

Early fall dates: early Sep 18—, by Audubon (Mengel:153); 16 Oct 1986, Jackson/Madison cos. (*KW* 63:6, 1987); 23 Oct 1938, Jefferson Co. (Monroe and Mengel, *KW* 15:38, 1939); 3 Nov 2002, Brown Power Plant, Mercer Co. (*KW* 79:4, 2003).

Out-of-season record (summer): 1-2 on McElroy Lake, 1-4 Jul 1950 (Wilson, *KW* 27:4, 1951; Mengel:153).

Unaccepted records: 16 Dec 1995, Danville CBC [no details] (*KW* 72:18, 1995); 13 Nov 2002, Ky Lake, Marshall Co. (*KW* 79:4, 2003; see *KW* 92:89, 2016).

Summary of records by county

Adair (*KW* 90:79, 2014)
Allen (*KW* 87:59, 2011; *KW* 90:79, 2014)
Anderson (*KW* 90:79, 2014)

Barren (*KW* 78:31, 2002/D. Roemer, 2002 videotape; *KW* 87:59, 2011; *KW* 90:79, 2014)

Bath (*KW* 90:6/48/79, 2014)

Bell (*KW* 90:79, 2014)

Boone (*KW* 70:49, 1994; *KW* 90:79, 2014)

Boyle (*KW* 54:42, 1978)

Bracken (*KW* 74:4, 1998; *KW* 83:46, 2007; *KW* 84:43, 2008; *KW* 87:59, 2011; *KW* 89:5, 2013; *KW* 90:79, 2014)

Bullitt (*KW* 90:79, 2014)

Calloway (*KW* 90:79, 2014)

Campbell (Mengel:153; *KW* 90:79, 2014)

Casey (*KW* 95:5, 2019)

Daviess (*KW* 82:66, 2006)

Fayette (*KW* 72:32, 1996; *KW* 82:46, 2006; *KW* 87:13/44/59, 2011; *KW* 89:5, 2013; *KW* 90:79, 2014; R. Graham, 2019 eBird data/photo)

Fleming (*KW* 90:79, 2014)

Franklin (*KW* 90:79, 2014)

Gallatin (*KW* 72:19/44, 1996/*KW* 73:28, 1997; *KW* 90:79, 2014)

Hardin (*KW* 70:31, 1994; *KW* 90:79, 2014)

Harlan (*KW* 90:79, 2014)

Henderson (Mengel:153; *KW* 64:44, 1988)

Hopkins (*KW* 91:51, 2015; *KW* 94:5/56, 2018)

Jackson (*KW* 63:6, 1987; *KW* 70:31, 1994; *KW* 90:79, 2014)

Jefferson (Mengel:153; *KW* 52:40-41, 1976; *KW* 55:29, 1979; *KW* 57:35, 1981; *KW* 83:9, 2007; *KW* 90:6/80, 2014; *KW* 91:51, 2015; *KW* 95:5, 2019)

Kenton (*KW* 90:80, 2014)

Knott (*KW* 90:80, 2014)

Knox (*KW* 90:80, 2014)

Larue (*KW* 90:80, 2014)

Laurel (*KW* 60:41, 1984; *KW* 90:80, 2014)

Letcher (*KW* 90:80, 2014)

Lewis (*KW* 90:80, 2014)

Lincoln (*KW* 90:80, 2014)

Lyon (*KW* 63:6, 1987; *KW* 79:18/44, 2003; *KW* 84:58, 2008; *KW* 91:18/51, 2015)

Madison (*KW* 63:6, 1987; *KW* 70:31, 1994; C. Elliott, 1994 eBird data; *KW* 87:59/84, 2011; *KW* 90:80, 2014; *KW* 91:5, 2015)

Marshall (*KW* 74:4, 1998; *KW* 78:48, 2002; *KW* 79:4, 2003; *KW* 80:65, 2004; *KW* 82:66, 2006; *KW* 95:48, 2019/m. ob. 2019 eBird data)

Mason (*KW* 90:80, 2014)

Meade (*KW* 90:80, 2014)

Mercer (*KW* 68:3, 1992; *KW* 79:4, 2003)

Nicholas (*KW* 90:80, 2014)

Oldham (Mengel:153)

Pike (*KW* 79:44, 2003)

Pulaski (*KW* 83:9, 2007; *KW* 95:5, 2019)

Rockcastle (*KW* 90:80, 2014)

Rowan (*KW* 70:31, 1994; *KW* 90:6/48/80, 2014)

Russell (*KW* 87:84, 2011; *KW* 90:80, 2014; *KW* 91:51, 2015)

Scott (*KW* 90:80, 2014)

Spencer (*KW* 90:80, 2014)

Taylor (*KW* 70:31, 1994; *KW* 83:25/46, 2007; *KW* 85:27/47, 2009; *KW* 88:25/45, 2012; *KW* 89:46, 2013; *KW* 90:48/80, 2014; *KW* 94:56, 2018)

Trigg ([*AB* 32:210, 1978; C. Peterson, notes]; *KW* 90:80, 2014)

Union (*KW* 90:80, 2014)

Warren (Mengel:153; *KW* 38:5-6, 1962; *KW* 90:80, 2014)

EARED GREBE *Podiceps nigricollis*

Status: Extremely rare transient and winter visitant, accidental during summer. Over the past few decades this species has been found annually, but it is unknown if this is due to a real increase in the number of birds or better birding coverage. It occurs on a variety of water bodies from small lakes to the largest rivers and reservoirs. Typically encountered singly, but more than one have been seen on a few occasions. Most reports have involved the observation of birds for short periods of time, but an individual wintered on Freeman Lake 1992-93 (*KW* 69:32, 1993; R. Healy, pers. comm.) and 1-2 have wintered on Lake Cumberland 2017-2018 and 2018-2019. The few early fall reports are apparently indicative of a limited movement of birds prior to the peak migration period during late fall.

Maximum count: 5 at McElroy Lake, 8 Apr 1997 (Roemer, et al. *KW* 73:79-83, 1997).

Early fall dates: 27 Aug 1989, (2) at McElroy Lake (Palmer-Ball and Boggs, *KW* 67:38, 1991); 28 Aug 1992, Lexington (R. Reid, notes) [this record was not accepted by the KBRC (*KW* 70:13, 1994) but details appear to be complete and it is accepted herein]; 1 Sep 2001, Union Co. (B. Palmer-Ball, eBird data); 4 Sep 2001, (ph.) Barren River Lake, Barren Co. (*KW* 78:4, 2002); 6 Sep 2008, Barren River Lake (*KW* 85:11, 2008); 20 Sep 1996, Mercer Co. (B. Palmer-Ball, eBird data); 20 Sep 2003, Ohio River at Louisville (*KW* 80:5-6, 2004); 1 Oct 2012, (ph.) Ohio River at Louisville (*KW* 89:5, 2013); 9 Oct 2013, (ph.) e. of Morganfield, Union Co. (*KW* 90:6, 2014); 10 Oct 2009, s. Jefferson Co. (*KW* 86:5, 2010); 3 Nov 2010, Ohio River at Louisville (*KW* 87:13, 2011); 5 Nov 2004, Lake Cumberland, Pulaski Co. (*KW* 81:5, 2005).

Late spring dates: 3-4 Jun 1980, Lake Cumberland, Wayne Co. (Hines and Watson, *KW* 56:88, 1980); 24 May 1988, Louisville (*KW* 64:44, 1988).

Out-of-season record (summer): 25 Jun 1999, (vt.) Warren Co. (*KW* 75:60, 1999; L. Doyle, notes).

Unaccepted record: 25 Oct 2018, Hardin Co. [details not complete] (*KW* 95:5, 2019).

Summary of records by county

Allen/Barren (*KW* 75:3/24, 1999; *KW* 77:27, 2001; *KW* 78:4, 2002; *KW* 85:11, 2008)
Bracken (*KW* 73:52, 1997)
Bullitt (*KW* 52:41, 1976)
Calloway (*KW* 54:42, 1978/J.T. Erwin, notes; *KW* 83:24/46, 2007)
Christian (*KW* 78:48, 2002)
Fayette (R. Reid, 1992 notes)
Hardin (*KW* 69:32, 1993/R. Healy, pers. comm.)
Hopkins (*KW* 66:4, 1990; B. Palmer-Ball, 1998 eBird data; *KW* 80:42, 2004)
Jefferson (*KW* 29:12, 1953; Wiley, *KW* 32:18-19, 1956; *KW* 37:24, 1961; Wiley, *KW* 38:52-53, 1962; *AB* 22:532, 1968; *KW* 52:41, 1976; *AB* 27:67, 1973; *AB* 28:645, 1974; *AB* 30:724, 1976; *KW* 64: 44, 1988; *KW* 65:62, 1989; J. Withgott, 1995 pers. comm.; B. Palmer-Ball, 1997 eBird data; *KW* 80:5-6, 2004; *KW* 86:5, 2010; *KW* 87:13, 2011; *KW* 89:5, 2013; *KW* 91:51, 2015)
Livingston (*KW* 74:31, 1998; *KW* 75:3, 1999)
Lyon (*KW* 75:24, 1999; *KW* 84:5, 2008; *KW* 84:58, 2008; *KW* 85:11, 2008)
Marshall (*KW* 76:4, 2000/D. Roemer, videotape; *KW* 77:48, 2001; *KW* 78:48, 2002; *KW* 83:46/73, 2007; *KW* 85:47, 2009; *KW* 86:5, 2010; *KW* 86:64, 2010; *KW* 87:59, 2011; *KW* 90:6, 2014; *KW* 95:27/48, 2019)
Meade (R. Healy, 1997 pers. comm.)
Mercer (W. Kemper, 1993 pers. comm.; *KW* 70:49, 1994; B. Palmer-Ball, 1996 eBird data)
Muhlenberg (*KW* 83:46/73, 2007)
Oldham (B. Palmer-Ball, 2000 eBird data)
Pulaski (*KW* 81:5, 2005)
Russell (*KW* 94:5/56/70/96, 2018; *KW* 95:5/28/48/60, 2019)
Taylor (*KW* 69:12, 1993; B. Palmer-Ball, 2001 eBird data; *KW* 91:51, 2015)
Trigg (*KW* 83:76, 2007)
Union (B. Palmer-Ball, 2001 eBird data; *KW* 90:6/40, 2014)
Warren Co. (Mason, *KW* 61:19-20, 1985; Palmer-Ball and Boggs, *KW* 67:38, 1991; *KW* 66:35, 1990; *KW* 70:49, 1994; B. Palmer-Ball, 1994 eBird data; Roemer, et al., *KW* 73:79-83, 1997; Roemer, *KW* 74:92-93, 1998; *KW* 75:60, 1999; *KW* 89:66, 2013)
Wayne (Hines and Watson, *KW* 56:88, 1980)

WESTERN GREBE *Aechmophorus occidentalis*

Status: Extremely rare spring, fall, and winter visitant. There are at least 22 records (8 during fall, two during mid-winter, 12 during spring), all but one of single birds. Generally to be expected only on the larger lakes and rivers. All records included below are considered to pertain to the more widespread species of *Aechmophorus* grebe (formerly known as the "dark morph"), rather than the more localized, less migratory, and southern species, CLARK'S GREBE (*A. clarkii*; formerly known as the "light morph"). Most all vagrants occurring east of the Mississippi River should be the former (and hybrids occur regularly in the west), but a few well-documented records of *A. clarkii* apparently exist for the eastern United States. Most photographs and/or descriptions accompanying older records are not definitive; however, photographs and written descriptions of birds observed more recently have typically substantiated them as *A. occidentalis*.

Late spring dates: 25 May 1949, Ky Lake, Marshall Co. (Morse, *KW* 25:74-75, 1949); 18-21 May 1977, Pfeiffer Fish Hatchery, Franklin Co. (D. Coskren, pers. comm.); 1-8 May 2005, (ph.) on Lake Barkley above the dam (*KW* 81:84, 2005).

Early fall dates: 1 Nov 1972, Ohio River at Louisville (Robertson, *KW* 49:19, 1973); 6 Nov 2002, (ph.) Lake Cumberland, Pulaski Co. (*KW* 79:4, 2003).

Unaccepted records: 18 Dec 1981, Ohio River at Louisville (*KW* 58:10, 1982; B. Palmer-Ball, notes) [no details available]; 27 Mar–2 Apr 1994, (at least 4) at McElroy Lake (*KW* 70:49, 1994).

Chronological list of records

1) 25 May 1949, Ky Lake, Marshall Co. (Morse, *KW* 25:74-75, 1949)
2) 6-21 Dec 1958, Ohio River at Louisville (*KW* 35:6, 1959; *KW* 37:24, 1961)
3) 1-2 Nov 1972, Ohio River at Louisville (Robertson, *KW* 49:19, 1973)
4) 16 Dec 1972+, Grider's quarry lake, Bowling Green (*KW* 49:12, 1973)
5) 17 Dec 1975–21 Jan 1976, Ohio River at Louisville (*KW* 52:41, 1976)
6) 18-21 May 1977, Pfeiffer Fish Hatchery, Franklin Co. (D. Coskren, pers. comm.)
7) 8 Nov 1977, Ohio River at Louisville (Parker, *KW* 54:15, 1978)
8) Jan 1981 (for three weeks), Barren River Lake, Allen/Barren cos. (*KW* 57:35, 1981)
9) 29 Feb–8 Mar 1992, (ph.) Green River Lake, Taylor Co. (*KW* 68:43, 1992; *KW* 69:23, 1993; B. Palmer-Ball, eBird data)
10) 27 Nov 1993, Ohio River above Markland Dam, Gallatin Co. (ph.) (*KW* 70:6, 1994; *KW* 72:33, 1996)
11) 2-4 Dec 1995, Green River Lake, Taylor Co. (B. Palmer-Ball, eBird data)
12) 2-6 Feb and 21 Mar–21 Apr 2000, (vt.) Ky Lake above the dam, Livingston/Marshall cos. (*KW* 76:28/43, 2000; D. Roemer, notes [date published incorrectly as 21 Feb in *NAB* 54:183, 2000]; the early Feb observations reported as *Aechmophorus* sp. but included as this species herein)
13) 10 Apr 2002, (vt.) Ky Lake above the dam, Livingston/Marshall cos. (*KW* 78:48, 2002)
14) 6-30 Nov 2002, (ph.) Lake Cumberland, Pulaski Co. (*KW* 79:4, 2003)
15) 1-8 May 2005, (ph.) on Lake Barkley above the dam (*KW* 81:84, 2005)
16) 6 May 2006, above Ky Dam (*KW* 82:66, 2006)
17) 28 Mar–18 Apr 2007, 2 (vt.) above Ky Dam (*KW* 83:76, 2007)
18) 26-27 Apr 2008, (vt.) on Lake Barkley above the dam (*KW* 84:58, 2008)
19) 4 May 2010, Ky Lake, Marshall Co. (*KW* 86:64, 2010)
20) 15 Mar–12 Apr 2013, (ph.) Ohio River at Louisville (*KW* 89:66-67/74, 2013)
21) 18 Apr 2013, above Ky Dam (*KW* 89:67, 2013)
22) 27 Mar 2015, Morgan Pond (*KW* 91:67, 2015)

*ROCK PIGEON *Columba livia*

Status: Introduced. Locally rare to common resident. Recorded statewide but quite scarce in heavily forested areas. Breeding statewide, but generally restricted to cities and towns, as well as open agricultural areas; also occasional on cliffs in natural situations.

BAND-TAILED PIGEON *Patagionenas fasciata*

Status: Accidental vagrant. This resident of the western United States is very infrequently reported in the east, and it has been reported in Kentucky only once.

1) ~20 Nov–1 Dec 1973, a presumed wild bird (ph.) that frequented a yard at Eddyville, Lyon Co. (Peterson, *KW* 50:18-19, 1974; *AC*, 2nd ed., p. PHOTOS - 9).

*EURASIAN COLLARED-DOVE *Streptopelia decaocto*

Status: Introduced. Locally rare to fairly common resident. Increasing but still quite locally distributed; perhaps somewhat less numerous (or at least harder to find) during winter. First recorded at La Center, Ballard Co., about 1997 (H. Chambers/E. Webb, pers. comm) with confirmed nesting by local residents by 1998 (E. Webb, pers. comm.). During late spring/early summer 1999 the species also was reported from Owensboro, Daviess Co. (*KW* 75:44, 1999; D. Dugas, notes); Hickman, Fulton Co. (*KW* 75:44, 1999), and Bowling Green (J. Elmore, pers. comm.; D. Roemer, notes) with nesting first confirmed in the state at Hickman that year. By the end of summer 2002, the species had been reported from more than a dozen localities from Bowling Green and Owensboro west- ward, as well as a few sites in central Kentucky as far east as Harrison Co. (*KW* 78:64, 2002), Knox Co. (D. Roemer, 2001 notes), and Shelby Co. (*KW* 78:64, 2002). Most frequently encoun- tered in cities and towns, but also locally distributed in rural farmland and settlement. Apparently largely avoids urban areas dominated by Rock Pigeons, preferring residential areas; also generally absent in heavily forested areas. The spread of this species seems to have slowed in recent years, and how much more widespread and common it may become is uncertain. Generally seen singly in pairs, or small groups of up to a half-dozen birds.

Maximum counts: **90** in w. Daviess Co., 12 Nov 2005 (*KW* 82:48, 2006); **25** in Meade Co., 20 Dec 2005 (*KW* 82:48, 2006).

e/sPASSENGER PIGEON *Ectopistes migratorius*

Status: Extinct. Formerly a fairly common to locally common transient and uncommon to locally com- mon resident, disappearing by the beginning of the 19th century. Apparently nested at least occa- sionally in large numbers in the state during the 1800s (Mengel:267-269). Unfortunately, it appears that no specimen from Kentucky remains extant.

INCA DOVE *Columbina inca*

Status: Accidental vagrant. This dove has been reported with increasing regularity north of its normal range, and it may become regular in occurrence in the future. The species has now been docu- mented in Kentucky four times.

Chronological list of records

1) 1 Oct 2000, an individual was shot during a dove hunt in ne. Carlisle Co., and the specimen was preserved (*KW* 77:7, 2001; S. White, pers. comm.; G. Burnett, pers. comm.)
2) 9-11 Feb 2002, (ph.) at Hickman, Fulton Co. (Yandell, *KW* 79:32-33, 2003)
3) 19 Aug 2010, in the Lower Hickman Bottoms, w. Fulton Co. (Monroe et al., *KW* 86:100, 2010)
4) 7-9 Aug 2016, (ph.) at Schochoh, Logan Co. (*KW* 93:1/10/36, 2017)

COMMON GROUND DOVE *Columbina passerina*

Status: Accidental vagrant. This dove is a resident of the southern United States and Middle Amer- ica, but it has been in decline over the last several decades. The species has been suitably docu- mented in Kentucky on two occasions.

Unaccepted record (a previously reported, single-observer sight record has not been reviewed by the KBRC): 25 Jul 1999, Westvaco WMA, Carlisle Co. (J. Quinn, notes).

Chronological list of records

1) 23-30 Nov 2002, (ph.) nr. Lake No. 9 (Chambers and Denton, *KW* 81:66-67/68, 2005)
2) late Dec 2004–11 Apr 2005, (ph.) ne. of Union Mills, Jessamine Co. (*KW* 81:59/88, 2005)

WHITE-WINGED DOVE *Zenaida asiatica*

Status: Extremely rare visitant. This dove of the southwestern United States has been occurring with greater regularity in the eastern United States, and it has become an annual visitant in Kentucky during recent years. All reports have been of single birds. The vast majority of individuals in the east are considered to be of natural origin. There are 24 records (17 during spring, three during summer, and four during fall). A noticeable peak in occurrence occurs from mid-Apr to late May (16 of 24 records).

Chronological list of records

1) 14-22 Apr 2002, (ph.) at Murray, Calloway Co. (Mowery, *KW* 78:39, 2002; C. Peterson, notes)
2) 17-21 Apr 2002, (ph.) at Aurora, Marshall Co. (Mowery, *KW* 78:39, 2002; S.L. White, pers. comm.)
3) 6-7 May 2003, (ph.) at Hickman, Fulton Co. (*KW* 79:70, 2003)
4) 1-2 Jun 2003, (ph.) at Berea, Madison Co. (*KW* 79:83, 2003)
5) 23 Aug 2009, at Independence, Kenton Co. (*KW* 86:11, 2010)
6) 22 May 2011, at Panorama Shores, Calloway Co. (*KW* 87:91, 2011)
7) 2-6 Apr 2012, (ph.) nr. Sharkey, Rowan Co. (*KW* 88:61/77, 2012)
8) 6 May 2012, (ph.) at Lexington (*KW* 88:77/84, 2012)
9) 9 May 2013, nr. Scottsville, Allen Co. (*KW* 90:55, 2014)
10) 12 May 2013, (ph.) at Henderson (*KW* 89:73/75, 2014)
11) 11-12 Jun 2014, (ph.) at Murray, Calloway Co. (*KW* 90:89, 2014)
12) "summer" to 18 Sep 2015, (ph.) at Bowling Green (*KW* 92:10, 2016)
13) 15-16 Apr 2016, (ph.) at Erlanger, Kenton Co. (*KW* 92:64, 2016)
14) 29 Apr 2016, (ph.) at Benton, Marshall Co. (*KW* 92:62/64, 2016)
15) 24-26 Nov 2016, (ph.) at Lexington (*KW* 93:10/36, 2017)
16) 30 May 2017, (ph.) in nw. Scott Co. (*KW* 93:71, 2017)
17) 2-3 Jun 2017, (ph.) at Midway, Woodford Co. (*KW* 93:105, 2017)
18) 21 May 2018, (ph.) ne. Hopkins Co. (*KW* 94:70/96, 2018)
19) 24-25 May 2018, Cadiz, Trigg Co. (*KW* 94:70, 2018)
20) 2-3 Jun 2018, (ph.) Midway, Woodford Co. (*KW* 94:105, 2018)
21) 8-9 Apr 2019, Murray, Calloway Co. (M. Easley, eBird data)
22) early Apr–5 June 2019, (ph.) at Lexington (E. Molle et al., eBird data)
23) 2-3 May 2019, (ph.) nr. Briensburg, Marshall Co. (T. Rice, pers. comm)
24) 12 May 2019, (ph.) ne. Hopkins Co. (B. Carrico, eBird data)

*MOURNING DOVE *Zenaida macroura*

Status: Common resident. Numerous in settled areas throughout the state, but much less wide-spread in heavily forested habitats, especially in eastern Kentucky. Breeding statewide in a great variety of habitats from open farmland to suburban parks and yards. Aggregations of this species in open farmland may number a hundred or more birds, especially during late summer and fall.

Maximum count: **1200-1500** in ne. Shelby Co., 12 Jan 2010 (B. Palmer-Ball, eBird data).

GROOVE-BILLED ANI *Crotophaga sulcirostris*

Status: Accidental vagrant. This species formerly exhibited a regular pattern of vagrancy into the eastern United States, with a clear peak during the latter half of Oct; however, the U.S. population has declined significantly since the early 1990s, and few are now reported extralimitally. It has been reported in Kentucky twice.

Chronological list of records

1) 30 Oct 1979, (ph.) e. Calloway Co. (Brines, *KW* 56:65-66, 1980)
2) 22-23 Oct 1981, Lexington (Hobbs, *KW* 58:19-20, 1982)

*YELLOW-BILLED CUCKOO *Coccyzus americanus*

Status: Uncommon to fairly common transient and summer resident. Recorded statewide during migration in a variety of forested and semi-open habitats from mature woodlands and woodland borders to suburban parks and yards. Breeding statewide; generally more widely distributed across central and western portions of the state (*KBBA*:94-95). Most numerous in open woodlands and along woodland borders. Peak of abundance occurs from early May to mid-Sep. Generally far out-numbers the following species at all seasons.

Maximum count: **32** at Mammoth Cave, 31 May 2007 (S./J. Kistler, eBird data).
Early spring dates: 10 Apr 1968, south-central Kentucky (*KW* 45:35, 1969); 18 Apr 1982, Boyd Co. (C. Thompson, eBird data); 20 Apr 2006, Jefferson Co. (*KW* 82:71, 2006).
Late fall dates: 18 Nov 1975, Jefferson Co. (*AB* 30:80, 1976; J. Elmore, notes [date published incorrectly as 27 Nov in *KW* 52:52, 1976]); 9 Nov 2002, Pulaski Co. (*KW* 79:12, 2003); 2 Nov 1989, Hart Co. (*KW* 66:12, 1990).
Published error: 1 Apr 1995, Madison Co. (*KW* 71:42, 1995) should have read 1 May (*fide* A. Ricketts, pers .comm.).

*BLACK-BILLED CUCKOO *Coccyzus erythropthalmus*

Status: Rare to uncommon transient (seems to be decreasing), extremely rare summer resident. Recorded statewide during migration in a variety of semi-open habitats; most often encountered along woodland borders and in successional thickets. Modest peaks of abundance occur from late Apr to mid-May and from mid-Sep to early Oct. Breeding not well documented, but probably occurs locally throughout the Cumberland Plateau and Mountains and at least occasionally at scattered localities across central and western Kentucky.

Maximum count: **4** along Elkhorn Creek, Franklin Co., 19 May 2012 (J. Sole, eBird data).
Early spring dates: 16 Apr 1967, Warren Co. (*KW* 43:69, 1967); 20 Apr 2017, Pennyrile State Forest, Christian Co. (*KW* 93:71, 2017).
Late fall dates: 22 Oct 1982, Rowan Co. (*KW* 59:17, 1983); 21 Oct 1979, Louisville (*KW* 56:16, 1980); 19 Oct 1935, south-central Kentucky (*KW* 38:14, 1962); 19 Oct 1981, Calloway Co. (*KW* 58:16, 1982); 19 Oct 2016, Louisville (*KW* 93:10, 2017).

Summary of confirmed breeding records by county

Crittenden (*KW* 30:14, 1954)
Fayette (D. Svetich, 1996 pers. comm.)
Franklin (*KW* 44:25, 1968)
Jefferson (*KW* 65:69, 1989; *KBBA*: 92)
Lyon (W.H. Brown, 1976 notes)
Madison (*KW* 66:87, 1990; *KBBA*:92)
Martin (*KW* 67:77, 1991; *KBBA*:92)
Mercer (*KW* 86:94-95, 2010; *KW* 87:19, 2011)

*COMMON NIGHTHAWK *Chordeiles minor*

Status: Fairly common transient, uncommon but locally distributed summer resident. Recorded statewide but absent from heavily forested portions of eastern Kentucky. The species has been reported to be declining in some parts of its range, but the status of population trend in Kentucky is unclear. During the breeding season nighthawks are most numerous about cities and towns where they typically nest on gravel rooftops; however, the species is occasionally encountered nesting in other open, gravelly areas including abandoned roads and railroad rights-of-way, parking lots, and reclaimed surface mines. More widespread and numerous during migration, occurring in a variety of semi-open and open habitats; especially numerous during the peak of its fall movement from late Aug to mid-Sep when the species is most conspicuous and can be encountered in loose flocks of several dozen or more birds. Most often observed flying overhead at dusk or around outdoor lights at night, but sometimes seen roosting on tree limbs and utility wires during the day.

Maximum counts: **1300** at Lexington, 31 Aug 1974 (D. McWhirter, eBird data); **1000** in Jefferson Co., 26 Aug 1979 (*KW* 56:15, 1980); ca. **1000** in a single flock over n. Pulaski Co., 31 Aug 2005 (*KW* 82:11, 2006); **800-1000** over Rineyville, Hardin Co., 29 Aug 2006 (*KW* 83:15, 2007); **780** and **705** s. of Mt. Zion, Allen Co., 10 & 11 Sep 2011, respectively (*KW* 88:12, 2012); **550** ne. of Red Hill, Allen Co., 8 Sep 2011 (*KW* 88:12, 2012); **500** in Jefferson Co., 30 Aug 1987 (*KW* 64:18, 1988); **500** in Jefferson Co., late Aug or early Sep 1986 (*KW* 63:10, 1987); ca. **500** over Nolin Lake, Grayson Co., 9 Sep 2011 (*KW* 88:12, 2012); **497** counted in Louisville, 2 Sep 1978 (*KW* 55:16, 1979); **350+** in Calloway Co., 10 Sep 1978 (*KW* 55:16, 1979); **336** in Jefferson Co., 2 Sep 1992 (*KW* 69:9, 1993).

Early spring dates: 26 Feb 2009, Mt. Sterling, Montgomery Co. (*KW* 85:51, 2009); 16 Mar 2003, Lexington (*KW* 79:70, 2003; date erroneously published as 18 Mar therein [*fide* S. Marsh, pers. comm.]); 2 Apr 1980, Louisville (*KW* 56:61-62, 1980); 11 Apr 1965, south-central Kentucky (*KW* 45:35, 1969); 14 Apr 1991, Jefferson Co. (*KW* 67:56, 1991); 16 Apr 1952, south-central Kentucky (*KW* 38:15, 1962); 16 Apr 2019, Lexington (D. Svetich, eBird data); 17 Apr 1967, Murray, Calloway Co. (E. Larson, eBird data); 19 Apr 1964, Murray, Calloway Co. (E. Larson, eBird data); 20 Apr 2012, Murray, Calloway Co. (*KW* 88:78, 2012); 22 Apr 1952, Louisville area (*KW* 52:53, 1976); 23 Apr 1893, Pulaski Co. (Mengel:285).

Late fall dates: 1 Dec 2009, (ph.) s. Jefferson Co. (*KW* 86:45, 2010); late Nov 1995, an injured bird at Louisville (T. Love, pers. comm.); 19 Nov 1997, Warren Co. (T. Durbin, pers. comm.); 17 Nov 2006, Pulaski Co. (*KW* 83:15, 2007); 16 Nov 1998, Louisville (P. Bell, pers. comm.); 13 Nov 2007, Louisville (*KW* 84:12, 2008); 11 Nov 1982, Louisville (*KW* 59:17, 1983); 9 Nov 2002, Louisville (*KW* 79:12, 2003); 7 Nov 1986, Bowling Green (*KW* 63:10, 1987).

Unaccepted records: 13 Mar 19— (see Mengel:285); 21 Mar 1992 (3) in Grayson Co. (*KW* 68:46, 1992).

Published error: the early spring date of 28 Mar [1978] published by Monroe, et al. (1988) is erroneous, the result of a transcription error (*fide* A. Stamm, historical archive files).

*CHUCK-WILL'S-WIDOW *Antrostomus carolinensis*

Status: Uncommon to fairly common but locally distributed summer resident. Recorded chiefly west of the Cumberland Plateau, although there are several records from eastern Kentucky (see below). Extremely scarce as a transient, occurring occasionally in forested and semi-open habitats during spring, but essentially unknown away from breeding areas during fall. Breeding is fairly widespread but has been documented only west of the Cumberland Plateau, and very locally across much of central Kentucky; most numerous in the Highland Rim and Jackson Purchase (*KBBA*:108-109). Peak of abundance occurs from late Apr to mid-Jul. Usually found in less extensively forested areas than the Whip-poor-will. Mostly heard, but individuals can be seen on rural roads at night or occasionally flushed from wooded areas during the day when they are roosting on or near the ground on fallen logs or tree limbs.

Maximum counts: **24** in n. Pulaski Co., 9 May 2015 (R. Denton, eBird data); **18** in n. Pulaski Co., 10 May 2014 (R. Denton, eBird data).

Early spring dates: "mid-Mar" 1950 in Daviess Co. (Powell, *KW* 27:9, 1951); 2 Apr 2017, Calloway Co. (*KW* 93:72, 2017); 4 Apr 1988, Grayson Co. (*KW* 64:48, 1988); 6 Apr 1973, Grayson Co. (C. Noland, pers. comm.); 6 Apr 1991, Grayson Co. (*KW* 67:56, 1991); 6 Apr 1993, Grayson Co. (*KW* 69:46, 1993).

Late fall dates: 13 Sep 1987, Hopkins Co. (*KW* 64:18, 1988); 9 Sep 1986, Calloway Co. (*KW* 63:10, 1987).

List of records from Cumberland Plateau by county

Breathitt (C. Young/S. White, 2014 eBird data)
Elliott (*NAB* 54:390, 2000; *KW* 83:106, 2007; *KW* 84:68 2008)

Laurel (Mengel:283)
Menifee (J. Wheat, 2019 eBird data)
Morgan (*KW* 80:84, 2004)
Whitley (Mengel:283; *KW* 94:105, 2018)

*EASTERN WHIP-POOR-WILL *Antrostomus vociferus*

Status: Uncommon to fairly common summer resident. Recorded statewide during migration in a variety of forested and semi-open habitats, but generally scarce as a transient away from nesting areas; especially rare during fall when very few reports of birds presumed not to be lingering breeders have occurred. Peak of abundance occurs from late Apr to mid-Jul. Breeding statewide but quite local in some regions as follows: most numerous in predominantly forested areas with an abundance of openings and edge; least numerous in open farmland of the Inner Blue Grass, Highland Rim and Jackson Purchase. Mostly heard, but not infrequently seen on rural roads at night, and can be flushed from wooded areas during the day when they are roosting on the ground or fallen logs.

Maximum count: **30** in LBL, Lyon Co., 8 May 2018 (*KW* 94:70, 2018).
Early spring dates: 17 Mar 1992, Grayson Co. (*KW* 68:46, 1992); mid-Mar 1950, Daviess Co. (Powell, *KW* 27:9, 1951); 20 Mar 1948, Louisville (Young, *KW* 24:42, 1948); 21 Mar 1991, Hopkins Co. (*KW* 67:56, 1991); 23 Mar 1945, Bowling Green (Young, *KW* 24:42, 1948); 24 Mar 2003, Hart Co. (*KW* 79:70, 2003).
Late fall dates: 14 Nov 1978, Louisville (*KW* 55:16, 1979); 15 Oct 2003, Grayson Co. (*KW* 80:11, 2004); 13 Oct 2011, Trigg Co. (*KW* 88:12, 2012); 9 Oct 1965, Louisville area (*KW* 52:53, 1976).
Published errors: the late fall date of 26 Oct [1975] published by Monroe, et al. (1988) is erroneous, the result of a transcription error (*fide* A. Stamm, historical archive files); 18 Oct 1998, Louisville (*KW* 75:6, 1999) (correction *fide KW* 75:61, 1999).

*CHIMNEY SWIFT *Chaetura pelagica*

Status: Fairly common transient and summer resident. Widespread and recorded statewide during migration when swifts can be encountered foraging over virtually any habitat type. Peak of abundance occurs from mid-Apr to mid-Oct. Breeding locally statewide; most nests are now placed in human structures acounting for the species' relative abundance in settled areas. Also occurs in forested areas where hollow trees are likely utilized for nesting. Occasionally encountered in flocks of a hundred or more birds during fall prior to the major movement south.

Maximum counts: **2000** at the Falls of the Ohio, 7 Aug 1979 (*KW* 56:15, 1980); ca. **2000** in Martin Co., Aug 1960 (Reed, *KW* 36:67, 1960); **1750** going to roost at Lexington, 8 Sep 2018 (*KW* 95:5, 2019); **1500** going to roost at Somerset, Pulaski Co., 9 Oct 1991 (eBird data); **1300** going to roost at Lexington, 13 Sep 2014 (*KW* 91:11, 2015); ca. **1200** at the Falls of the Ohio, 30 Sep 2010 (*KW* 87:19, 2011); ca. **1100** going to roost at Somerset, Pulaski Co., 13 Sep 2008 (*KW* 85:17, 2009); ca. **1000** at Louisville, 7 Oct 1978 (*KW* 55:16, 1979); ca. **1000** at the Falls of the Ohio, early Oct 1985 (*KW* 62:9, 1986); **1000** going to roost at Paducah, 5 Oct 2018 (*KW* 95:5, 2019).
Early spring dates: 17 Mar 1981, Murray, Calloway Co. (*KW* 57:57, 1981); 21 Mar 1966, Murray, Calloway Co. (E. Larson, eBird data); 25 Mar 1945, south-central Kentucky (*KW* 38:15, 1962).
Late fall dates: 29 Nov 1975, Louisville (*KW* 52:53, 1976); 4 Nov 1925, south-central Kentucky (*KW* 38:15, 1962); 30 Oct 2018, Lexington (*KW* 95:6, 2019); 29 Oct 2018, e. Louisville (*KW* 95:6, 2019).

MEXICAN VIOLETEAR *Colibri thalassinus*

Status: Accidental vagrant. This resident of Mexico and Central America wanders widely, accounting for several dozen records in the eastern United States and Canada, mostly during summer. It has been documented in Kentucky once.

1) 25-27 Aug 1999, an ad. male (ph.) at Taylor Mill, Kenton Co. (McNeely, *KW* 76:22-23, 2000)

*RUBY-THROATED HUMMINGBIRD *Archilochus colubris*

Status: Fairly common to common transient and summer resident. Widespread and recorded state-wide in a variety of forested and semi-open habitats from mature woodlands and woodland borders to suburban parks and yards. Peak of abundance occurs from late Apr to late Sep. Breeding state-wide; most commonly in fairly mature woodlands but sometimes in rural and suburban yards. Individuals sometimes linger into mid-Oct and occasionally into Nov, but banding efforts have shown that most late fall hummingbirds in the eastern United States are other species, especially Rufous Hummingbirds. For this reason, all hummingbirds observed after the middle of Oct should be studied very carefully. Generally encountered singly, but loose groups of up to a dozen or more birds can be observed in late summer frequenting favored feeding areas.

Maximum counts: **174** were banded in a two-day period, 1-2 Aug 1997, at the LBL Nature Station, Trigg Co. (R. Sargent, pers. comm.); estimates of **150** at the LBL Nature Station, mid- to late Aug in various years (J. Pollpeter, eBird data); **65** (ba.) at Middletown, Jefferson Co., 3 Sep 2007 (*KW* 84:12, 2008).

Early spring dates: 24 Mach 2010, Louisville (*KW* 86:70, 2010); 25 Mar 2009, at Paducah and in Calloway Co. (*KW* 85:73, 2009); 25 Mar 2010, Rockcastle Co. (*KW* 86:70, 2010); 25 Mar 2011, Marshall Co. (*KW* 87:91, 2011); 29 Mar 1945, south-central Kentucky (*KW* 38:15, 1962).

Late fall dates (only a few of the following records have been confirmed by in-hand examination or definitive plumage; the remainder are accepted provisionally based on written descriptions and/or photographs): 2 Jan 2008 (ba.), Oldham Co. (*KW* 84:45/52, 2008); 2 Jan 2008 (ph.), Warren Co. (*KW* 84:45, 2008); 28 Nov 2008, Jefferson Co. (*KW* 85:17, 2009); 25 Nov 2009 (ph.), Lincoln Co. (*KW* 86:12, 2010); 22 Nov 2018, Lyon Co. (*KW* 95:8, 2019); 19 Nov 1995, Bourbon Co. (E. and J. Perry, pers. comm.; eBird data); 19 Nov 2007, an ad. male in Jefferson Co. (*KW* 84:12 2008); 18 Nov 1983, an adult male at Leitchfield, Grayson Co. (*KW* 60:18, 1984); 15 Nov 2002, (ph.) in Morgan Co. (*KW* 79:12, 2003); 14 Nov 2015, Kenton Co. (*KW* 92:11, 2016); mid-Nov 1986, a bird at Bowling Green that was reported without details as a Ruby-throated (*KW* 63:10, 1987); mid-Nov 2002, Woodford Co. (*KW* 79:47, 2003); 11 Nov 2005, Warren Co. (*KW* 82:11, 2006); 9 Nov 2004, Lexington (*KW* 81:11, 2005); 9 Nov 2009, Campbell and Jefferson cos. (*KW* 86:12, 2010).

BLACK-CHINNED HUMMINGBIRD *Archilochus alexandri*

Status: Extremely rare fall/winter visitant. This summer resident of the southwestern United States and Mexico is found regularly in the eastern United States. It has been recorded twice in Kentucky.

Chronological list of records

1) early Nov–16 Dec 1998, an imm. male (ph./ba.) at Reidland, McCracken Co. (Sloan, *KW* 75:32-34, 1999)
2) 28 Oct 2015–14 Jan 2016, an imm. male (ph./ba.) in ne. Calloway Co. (T. Gemeinhardt, photos; *KW* 92:11/37/44, 2016)

RUFOUS HUMMINGBIRD *Selasphorus rufus*

Status: Extremely rare visitant and winter resident. The increase in this hummingbird represents one of the more remarkable changes in status of a Kentucky bird species during the past few decades. It was first confirmed during the late 1980s and has become annual in occurrence since the late 1990s with several reports of wintering now documented during milder years. Although an ex-tremely cold spell of weather during January 2014 has resulted in a decrease in the number of re-ports in recent years, there are now almost 80 confirmed records scattered across nearly the entire state. Most reports are of immature and adult females, but some immature males and about 20 adult males have now been documented. Because an effort to carefully document the species has been ongoing for nearly 30 years, all reports are listed below.

Early fall dates: 28 Jul 2006, Corbin, Knox Co. (*KW* 82:82, 2006); 29-31 Jul 2013, (ph.) Owensboro, Daviess Co. (*KW* 89:97/104, 2013); 1 Aug 1997, LBL Nature Station, Lyon/Trigg cos. (R. Sargent, pers. comm.); 7 Aug 2013, (ba.) s. of Haywood, Barren Co. (*KW* 90:13, 2014).

Late spring dates: 19 Apr 2013, (ba.) Pike Co. (*KW* 89:49/76, 2013); 13 Apr 2016, (ba.) Murray, Calloway Co. (*KW* 92:65, 2016); 11 Apr 2017, (ba.) Salt Lick Bend, Cumberland Co. (*KW* 93:72, 2017); 9 Apr 2013, (ba.) Campbell Co. (*KW* 89:49/76, 2013); 7 Apr 2004, (ba.) n. of Rich Pond, Warren Co. (*KW* 80:46/69, 2004).

Unaccepted records: 28 Aug 2002, Warren Co. (see *KW* 79;12, 2003); early Oct 2006, ad. male in Calloway Co. (see *KW* 83:16, 2007)

Tally of records by county

Barren (4); Boone; Bourbon (2); Boyd; Boyle; Bullitt; Calloway; Campbell; Carlisle; Clark; Crittenden; Cumberland (2); Daviess (2); Fayette (3); Franklin (2); Garrard; Grayson (2); Hardin (2); Harrison; Hart (3); Henderson; Jefferson (7); Jessamine; Kenton; Knox (2); Lincoln; Logan (2); Lyon; Madison; Marshall; Meade (2); Menifee; Muhlenberg; Nelson; Oldham (2); Pike; Pulaski (2); Scott (2); Shelby (4); Simpson; Taylor; Trigg (2); Warren (5); Wayne; Whitley; Woodford

Chronological list of records

1) 25 Sep–16 Dec 1989, ad. male (ph.) in Grayson Co. (Clay, *KW* 66:44-46, 1990)
2) 11 Nov 1996–2 Jan 1997, female (ba.) nr. Canton, Trigg Co. (*KW* 73:8, 1997; R. Sargent and B. Hainey, pers. comm.)
3) 1 Aug 1997, ad. male at LBL Nature Station, Lyon/Trigg cos. (R. Sargent, pers. comm.)
4) mid-Nov–30 Dec 1998, imm. male (ba.) nr. Bardwell, Carlisle Co. (Sloan, *KW* 75:32-34, 1999)
5) mid Nov 1998–4 Jan 1999, ad. female (ba.) at Lexington (Sloan, *KW* 75:32-34, 1999)
6) early Nov–16 Dec 2000, ad. female (ba.) nr. Brandenburg, Meade Co. (*KW* 77:8, 2001)
7) 15 Nov–30 Dec 2000, ad. female (ba.) in e. Jefferson Co. (*KW* 77:8, 2001; B. Regan, pers. comm.)
8) 31 Oct–18 Dec 2000, ad. female (ba.) at Louisville (*KW* 77:8, 2001; B. Ashley, pers. comm.)
9) early Nov–26 Dec 2000, (2) ad females (ba.) at Briensburg, Marshall Co. (*KW* 77:8, 2001 [location erroneously published as Meade Co. therein]; B. Kane, pers. comm.)
10) 23 Sep–17 Dec 2000, ad. female (ba.), at Rockholds, Whitley Co. (*KW* 77:8, 2001; F. Moore, notes; S. Helton, pers. comm.)
11) early Nov 2001–1 Jan 2002, ad. male (ph.) at Paris, Bourbon Co. (B. Palmer-Ball, eBird data; V. Sanders, pers. comm.)
12) 22 Oct 2002–24 Jan 2003, ad. female (ba.) at Danville (*KW* 79:12/48, 2003)
13) 15-30 Nov 2002, ad, female (ph./*ba.) at Bowling Green (*KW* 79:12/48, 2003)
14) late Oct 2002–22 Jan 2003, imm. male (ba.) at Louisville (*KW* 79:12/48, 2003)
15) mid-Aug–mid-Nov 2003, ad. male (ph.) at Bowling Green (*KW* 80:11, 2004; J. Elmore, pers. comm.)
16) 12 Oct 2003–6 Jan 2004, ad. female (ba.) at Rich Pond, Warren Co. (*KW* 80:11/46, 2004)
17) 8 Nov 2003–7 Apr 2004, ad. female (ba.) n. of Rich Pond, Warren Co. (*KW* 80:11/46/69, 2004)
18) late Oct–12 Dec 2003, imm. female (ba.) in Logan Co. (*KW* 80:11/46, 2004)
19) fall 2003–14 Dec 2003, imm. female (sp.) in Boone Co. (*KW* 80:46, 2004)
20) fall 2003–26 Jan 2004, ad. male (ph.) at Mt. Washington, Bullitt Co. (*KW* 80:46, 2004)
21) 29 Sep–17 Dec 2004, ad. female (ba.) at Lexington (*KW* 81:11/59, 2005)
22) 11 Oct–2 Dec 2004, imm. male (ph.) in Warren Co. (*KW* 81:11/59, 2005)
23) late Oct 2004–31 Jan 2005, ad. female (ba.) in Harrison Co. (*KW* 81:11/59, 2005)
24) 25 Nov 2004–15 Feb 2005, ad. male (ba.) at Louisville (*KW* 81:11/59, 2005)
25) ca. 25 Sep–2 Oct 2005, imm. male (ba.) in Oldham Co. (*KW* 82:11/49, 2006)
26) 20 Oct 2005–29 Mar 2006, ad. male (ba.) in Knox Co. (*KW* 82:11/49/71, 2006)
27) 7 Oct–mid-Dec 2005, imm. male (ba.) in Scott Co. (*KW* 82:12/49, 2006)
28) mid-Nov–27 Dec 2005, imm. female (ba.) in Jessamine Co. (*KW* 82:12/49, 2006)
29) ca. 17-27 Nov 2005, imm. male (ba.) in Shelby Co. (*KW* 82:12/49, 2006)
30) 23-25 Nov 2005, ad. male (*ba.) in Daviess Co. (*KW* 82:12/49, 2006)
31) mid-Oct 2005–26 Jan 2006, imm. male (ba.) in Jefferson Co. (*KW* 82:49, 2006)
32) 28 Jul 2006, ad. male at Corbin, Knox Co. (*KW* 82:82, 2006)
33) 26 Oct–5 Nov 2006, imm. female (ba.) in Shelby Co. (*KW* 83:16, 2007)
34) 28 Oct–mid-Nov 2006, ad. female (ba.) in Shelby Co. (*KW* 83:16, 2007)
35) late Nov 2006–18 Mar 2007, ad. female (ba.) at Louisville (*KW* 83:50/82, 2007)
36) early Nov 2006–15 Feb 2007, imm. female (ba.) at Frankfort (*KW* 83:50, 2007)

37) 3-6 Oct 2007, ad. male (ph.) in Grayson Co. (*KW* 84:12, 2008)

38) early Nov 2007–9 Feb 2008, imm. male (ba.) in Oldham Co. (*KW* 84:12/45, 2008)

39) 6-10 Nov 2007, imm. female (ba.) in Shelby Co. (*KW* 84:12, 2008)

40) late Oct–29 Dec 2007, imm. female (ba.) in Garrard Co. (*KW* 84:45, 2008; early date *fide* V. Roark, pers. comm.)

41) 12 Dec 2007–3 Jan 2008, ad. female (ba.) in Bourbon Co. *KW* 84:45, 2008)

42) early Nov 2007–ca. 1 Feb 2008, imm. female (ba.) in Hardin Co. (*KW* 84:45, 2008; early date *fide* M. & G. Whelan)

43) early Dec 2009–4 Jan 2010, ad. male (*ba.) in Hardin Co. (*KW* 86:37/45, 2010)

44) late Oct 2009–5 Jan 2010, imm. female (ba.) in Crittenden Co. (*KW* 86:45, 2010)

45) 14 Nov–12 Dec 2010, ad. female (ba.) at Bardstown, Nelson Co. (*KW* 87:19/63, 2011)

46) 18 Oct–31 Dec 2011, imm. female (ba.) nr. Dot, Logan Co. (*KW* 88:13/49, 2012)

47) late Oct 2011–14 Jan 2012, imm. female (ba.) in Pulaski Co. (*KW* 88:13/49, 2012)

48) 3 Nov 2011–26 Mar 2012, imm. female (ba.) in Barren Co. (*KW* 88:13/49/60/77, 2012)

49) 12 Nov–26 Mar 2012, ad. female (ba.) in the same yard in Barren Co. (*KW* 88:13/49/60/77, 2012)

50) 9 Nov–11 Dec 2011, ad. female (ba.) in Boyd Co. (*KW* 88:13/49, 2012)

51) 30 Oct 2011–26 Mar 2012, imm. female (ba.) in Simpson Co. (*KW* 88:13/49/77, 2012)

52) 25-26 Aug 2012, ad. male (ph.) in Trigg Co. (*KW* 89:11, 2013)

53) late Aug 2012, ad. male (ph.) nr. Battletown, Meade Co. (*KW* 89:81, 2013)

54) 28 Sep 2012–6 Apr 2013, returning ad. female (*ba.) in the same yard in Barren Co. (*KW* 89:11/49/76, 2013)

55) 13 Oct 2012–6 Apr 2013, returning ad. female (*ba.) in Hart Co. (*KW* 89:11/49/76, 2013)

56) 13 Oct 2012–30 Mar 2013, imm. female (ba.) in Pulaski Co. (*KW* 89:11/49/76, 2013)

57) 26 Oct 2012–19 Apr 2013, imm. female (ba.) in Pike Co. (*KW* 89:11/49/76, 2013)

58) late Oct 2012– 24 Feb 2013, ad. female (ba.) in Wayne Co. (*KW* 89:11/49, 2013)

59) late Oct–mid-Dec 2012, imm. female (ba.) in Menifee Co. (*KW* 89:11/49, 2013)

60) late Sep–last week of Nov 2012, ad. male (ba.) in Lincoln Co. (*KW* 89:11, 2013)

61) fall 2012–late Jan 2013, ad. male (ba.) at Frankfort (*KW* 89:49/50, 2013)

62) fall 2012–9 Apr 2013, imm. male (ba.) in Campbell Co. (*KW* 89:49/76, 2013)

63) 29-31 Jul 2013, ad. male (ph.) at Owensboro, Daviess Co. (*KW* 89:97/104, 2013)

64) 7 Aug 2013–6 Jan 2014, returning female (*ba.) s. of Haywood, Barren Co. (*KW* 90:13/53, 2014)

65) mid-Aug 2013, ad. male (ph.) at Greenville Muhlenberg Co. (*KW* 91:16/36, 2015)

66) late Aug–mid-Sep 2013, ad. male (ph.) in Woodford Co. (*KW* 90:13, 2014)

67) 24 Aug 2013–6 Jan 2014, returning female (*ba.) nw. of Uno, Hart Co. (*KW* 90:13/21/53, 2014)

68) mid-Aug–11 Sep 2013, ad. male (ba.) se. of Hardyville, Hart Co. (*KW* 90:13/20, 2014)

69) early Nov–24 Dec 2013, ad. female (ba.) at Winchester, Clark Co. (*KW* 90:13/53, 2014)

70) early Nov–27 Dec 2013, imm. male (ba.) ne. of Berea, Madison Co. (*KW* 90:13/53/60, 2014)

71) mid-Oct–5 Dec 2013, ad. male (ba.) at Lexington (*KW* 90:13/53, 2014)

72) fall 2013–5 Jan 2014, ad. female (ba.) at Henderson, Henderson Co. (*KW* 90:53, 2014)

73) mid-Oct 2013–6 Jan 2014, ad. female (ba.) nr. Cambellsville, Taylor Co. (*KW* 90:53, 2014)

74) Oct 2014–early Feb 2015, imm. female (ba.) in s. Scott Co. (*KW* 91:11/54, 2015)

75) 21 Nov 2015–13 Apr 2016, imm. female (ba.) at Murray, Calloway Co. (*KW* 92:11/44/65, 2016)

76) 3 Nov 2016–11 Apr 2017, imm. female (ba.) at Salt Lick Bend, Cumberland Co. (*KW* 93:10/50/72, 2017)

77) ca. 13 Nov–19 Dec 2016, imm. male (ba.) at Douglass Hills, Jefferson Co. (*KW* 93:10/50, 2017)

78) Oct 2016–4 Jan 2017, imm. male (ba.) at Taylor Mill, Kenton Co. (*KW* 93:50, 2017)

79) 21 Sep 2017–6 Jan 2018, returning female (*ba.) in Cumberland Co. (*KW* 94:6/56, 2018)

RUFOUS/ALLEN'S HUMMINGBIRD *Selasphorus* spp.

Status: Unidentified female or imm. *Selasphorus* hummingbirds (probably Rufous based on likelihood of occurrence) have been reported on more than 20 additional occasions.

Chronological list of records

1) Nov 1987–5 Feb 1988, imm. female (ph.) at Jeffersontown, Jefferson Co.(*KW* 64:11-12/29, 1988; Palmer-Ball, *KW* 65:24-27, 1989)

2) 17-25 Oct 1989, imm. male in a rural yard nr. Nicholasville, Jessamine Co. (*KW* 66:12, 1990)

3) late Dec 1998–5 Jan 1999, unaged bird at Lexington (Sloan, *KW* 75:32-34, 1999; B. Palmer-Ball, eBird data)

4) late fall 2000–early Jan 2001, unaged bird (presumed to be a *Selasphorus* based on verbal description) at Fort Campbell, Christian Co. (C. O'Neal, pers. comm.)

5) Oct–5 Dec 2002, unaged bird (ph.) in Jessamine Co. (*KW* 79:48, 2003)

6) 12 Oct 2003, unaged bird in Warren Co. (*KW* 80:11, 2004)

7) 23 Oct 2003–16 Jan 2004, unaged female (ph.) at Berea (*KW* 80:11/46, 2004)

8) mid-Dec 2003, probable female (ph.) in Grayson Co. (*KW* 80:46, 2004)

9) Nov–24 Dec 2003, probable female (ph.) in Oldham Co. (*KW* 80:46, 2004)

10) Nov 2003–11 Jan 2004, probable female (ph.) in Jefferson Co. (*KW* 80:46, 2004)

11) Nov 2003–24 Mar 2004, unaged female (ph.) at Lexington (*KW* 80:46/69, 2004)

13) 9 Nov–23 Dec 2004, imm./female (ph.) at Bowling Green (*KW* 81:11/60, 2005)

14) late Oct–23 Dec 2004, imm./female (ph.) in Lyon Co. (*KW* 81:11/60, 2005)

15) late Oct 2012–31 Jan 2013, imm./female (ph.) at Lexington (*KW* 89:49, 2013)

16) 18-20 Apr 2013, female (ph.) s. of Haywood, Barren Co. (*KW* 89:76, 2013)

17) early Dec 2013, unaged bird nr. Utica, Daviess Co. (*KW* 90:53, 2014)

18) Oct 2013–6 Jan 2014, female (ph.) n. of Somerset, Pulaski Co. (*KW* 90:53, 2014)

19) Oct 2013–6 Jan 2014, unaged bird (ph.) s. of Greenville, Muhlenberg Co. (*KW* 90:53, 2014)

20) mid-Oct–18 Nov 2014, probable imm male (ph.) in nw. Spencer Co. (*KW* 91:11, 2015)

21) 20-22 Jan 2016, a probable female (ph.) at Glasgow, Barren Co. (*KW* 92:44, 2016)

Note: There also have been a few additional reports of hummingbirds during winter that have not been identified to genus including birds at Georgetown, Scott Co., Nov–25 Dec 1998 (Sloan, *KW* 75:32-34, 1999) and at Paducah, mid-Oct–15 Dec 2001 (H. Cruse, pers. comm.).

YELLOW RAIL *Coturnicops noveboracensis*

Status: Extremely rare transient. This species is certainly not as rare as the paucity of records indicates, but it is very secretive and difficult to observe, skulking in weed, hay, or grain fields and marshy areas with a predominance of grassy vegetation. There are 16 records (four during spring; 12 during fall), all but two of single birds as listed below.

Chronological list of records

1) 1 Oct 1880, a pair (sp.) in a briar-grown field in Nelson Co. (Mengel:232)

2) 22 Oct 1976, hayfield in ne. Jefferson Co. (Palmer-Ball, *KW* 53:41, 1977)

3) 22-23 Oct 1977, hayfield in ne. Jefferson Co. (Palmer-Ball, *KW* 56:37, 1980)

4) 12 Oct 1986, in a marshy area at the Sauerheber Unit (*KW* 63:8, 1987)

5) 14 Oct 1995, 1 (possibly 2), at the Sauerheber Unit (M. Monroe/B. Monroe, III, pers. comm.)

6) 17-28 Oct 1996, in a weedy area at McElroy Lake (*KW* 73:6, 1997 [dates published erroneously therein as 19-28 Oct (*fide KW* 74:27, 1998)])

7) 28 Oct 1998, in a marshy field in Ohio Co. (*KW* 75:5, 1999)

8) 22 Oct 1999, along a marshy pond margin on the Peabody WMA, Ohio Co. (*KW* 76:5, 2000; D. Roemer, notes)

9) 14/21 Oct 2000, in a moist soils unit at the Sauerheber Unit (*KW* 77:5, 2001)

10) 1-2 Apr 2003, in a hayfield in ne. Jefferson Co. (Palmer-Ball, *KW* 79:91-92, 2003)

11) 23 Mar 2007, 1 or 2 in a grassland in ne. Crittenden Co. (*KW* 83:78, 2007)

12) 19 Oct 2010, in a hayfield in ne. Jefferson Co. (*KW* 87:15, 2011)

13) 29 Mar 2011, (ph.) in a hayfield in ne. Jefferson Co. (*KW* 87:73/86/100, 2011)

14) 23 Oct 2012, in a hayfield in ne. Jefferson Co. (*KW* 89:6, 2013)

15) 4 Nov 2017, Spindletop Farm, Fayette Co. (*KW* 94:6, 2018)

16) 10-11 Apr 2018, (ph.) in ne. Jefferson Co. (*KW* 94:71, 2018)

*KING RAIL *Rallus elegans*

Status: Extremely rare (formerly uncommon) transient, formerly an extremely rare to rare summer resident (perhaps now extirpated). Reported from scattered localities across the state west of the

Cumberland Plateau, but actually has been documented from fewer than ten counties (see below). Encountered in marshes and along the edges of lakes and ponds where cattails and other herbaceous vegetation is abundant. This species has declined over the decades, likely in large part due to habitat loss, and there have only been two confirmed breeding records (Fulton and Henderson cos.) since about 1960 (see below). **State Breeding Status**: Endangered.

Early spring dates: 24 Mar 1928, south-central Kentucky [likely Warren Co.] (*KW* 38:11, 1962); 2 Apr 19—, Hopkins Co. (Mengel:230).

Late fall dates: 11 Nov 1948, Fulton Co. (Mengel:231); 14-22 Oct 19—, Hopkins Co. (Mengel: 231); 22 Oct 2005, Sauerheber Unit (*KW* 82:7, 2006); 22 Oct 2011, Sauerheber Unit (*KW* 88:7, 2012); 21 Oct 2000, Sauerheber Unit (*KW* 77:5, 2001); 20 Oct 2018, Sauerheber Unit (*KW* 95:6, 2019); 18 Oct 2003, Sauerheber Unit (*KW* 80:8, 2004); 17 Oct 1999, Sauerheber Unit (*KW* 76:5, 2000); 14 Oct 2006, Sauerheber Unit (*KW* 83:11, 2007).

Unaccepted records: 26 Oct 2000, Muhlenberg Co. (*KW* 77:5, 2001); 20 May 2002, Muhlenberg Co. (*KW* 78:49, 2002) [no details accompanied these reports].

Summary of breeding records by county

Clinton (Mengel:230)
Daviess (Powell, *KW* 36:26, 1960)
Fulton (Mengel:230; *KW* 60:52-53, 1984)
Henderson (Mengel:230; ad. with 11 chicks at the Sauerheber Unit, 11 Jul 1996 [D. Chaffin, 1996 eBird data])
Jefferson (Mengel:230; *KW* 52:47, 1976)
Warren (Wilson, *KW* 16;18, 1940)

List of additional records by county

Hickman (Mengel:230)
Hopkins (Mengel:230)
Oldham (Mengel:230)

VIRGINIA RAIL *Rallus limicola*

Status: Rare to locally uncommon transient, extremely rare during summer and winter. Recorded from scattered localities across the state, but chiefly west of the Cumberland Plateau. May be fairly widespread during peak migratory periods but very secretive; most often encountered in marshy areas, but also occurs in weedy or grassy fields with dense cover. Peaks of abundance occur from mid-Apr to mid-May and from early Oct to early Nov. This species will occasionally turn up during migration in strange locations such as residential or urban areas (e.g., Stamm, *KW* 48:34, 1972; *KW* 91:7-8, 2015; *KW* 92:58, 2016). Although no definite nesting records exist (Mengel:231), the summer record from Marshall Co. given below may be indicative of at least occasional breeding, and an empty nest was found in Muhlenberg Co. in 2006 (*KW* 82:67-68, 2006). In recent years, small numbers have been found to winter locally in marshes of western Kentucky.

Maximum spring counts: **12** (likely 6 pairs) in se. Muhlenberg Co., 3 May 2006 (*KW* 82:67, 2006); **8** at the Sauerheber Unit, 18 Apr 2004 (*KW* 80:66, 2004); **7** at the Sauerheber Unit, 21 Apr 2007 (*KW* 83:78, 2007); **5-6** at Beckley Creek Park, Jefferson Co., 13 Apr 2018 (*KW* 94:71, 2018); **5** in Oldham Co., 27 Apr 1947 (Mengel:231); at least **5** at the Sauerheber Unit 17 Apr 2010 (*KW* 86:66, 2010).

Maximum fall counts: at least **6** at the Sauerheber Unit, 6 Oct 2007 (*KW* 84:7, 2008); at least **5** at the Sauerheber Unit, 14 Oct 2000 (*KW* 77:5, 2001).

Maximum winter count: **7** total at two sites in se. Muhlenberg Co., 30 Dec 2007 (*KW* 84:44, 2008).

Early spring dates (presumed non-wintering): 27 Mar 2014, (ph.) Fayette Co. (*KW* 90:69, 2014); 6 Apr 1902, Bowling Green (Cooke 1914); 7 Apr 19—, Hopkins Co. (Mengel:231).

Late spring dates (possibly summering birds?): 13 Jun 2003, Pulaski Co. (*KW* 79:81, 2003); 26 May 1989, Ohio Co. (*KW* 65:65, 1989); 22 May 2016, Madison Co. (*KW* 92:58, 2016).

Summer records: 8 Jul 1964, at Lake Peewee (Hancock, *KW* 41:17, 1965); 6 May–25 Jun 1997, a pair of birds in a cattail marsh in Marshall Co. (B. Palmer-Ball, eBird data [initial date erroneously published as 4 May in previous edition of this work]); 1 Aug 2003, Union Co. (*KW* 80:8, 2004); 18 Jun 2014, Sinclair Unit (*KW* 90:88, 2014); 11 Jul–10 Aug 2017, Sinclair Unit (*KW* 93:99, 2017; *KW* 94:6, 2018; eBird data); 23 Jun–13 Jul 2018, Sinclair Unit (*KW* 94:105, 2018).

Early fall dates: 25 Aug 1979, Trimble Co. (*KW* 56:15, 1980); 25 Aug 1988, Trimble Co. (*KW* 65:7, 1989); 25 Aug 2008, Blood River (*KW* 85:13, 2009); 29 Aug 1976, Franklin Co. (*AB* 31:184, 1977); 7 Sep 1980, Louisville (*KW* 57:21, 1981).

Late fall dates (other than known or presumed wintering birds): 12 Nov 1994, Calloway Co. (*KW* 71:4, 1995); 8 Nov 1980, Louisville (*KW* 57:21, 1981).

Out-of-season records (winter): 23 Dec 1950, along the Ohio River in Oldham Co. (Mengel:231; *KW* 27:12/15, 1951); 3 Jan 1999, Shelbyville CBC (*KW* 75:9, 1999); 1-2 Jan 2000, Muhlenberg Co. (*KW* 76:12/30, 2000); 10 Mar 2002, (2) in Marshall Co. where they likely wintered (B. Palmer-Ball, eBird data); 22 Mar 2003, (2) in Marshall Co. where they likely wintered (*KW* 79:67,2003); 30 Dec 2003–3 Jan 2004, (1-2) in Muhlenberg Co. (*KW* 80:19/43, 2004); 2 Jan 2005, (3) in Muhlenberg Co. (*KW* 81:19/58, 2005); 25 Mar 2005, Muhlenberg Co [wintering birds] (*KW* 81:85, 2005); 1 Jan 2006, (3) in Muhlenberg Co. (*KW* 82:19/47, 2006); 15 Jan 2006, Muhlenberg Co. (*KW* 82:47, 2006); 24 Nov 2006–31 Mar 2007, up to 6 total at different locations in Muhlenberg Co. (*KW* 83:11/23/48/78, 2007); 3 Jan 2009, (3) in Muhlenberg Co. (*KW* 85:24/49, 2009); 2/23 Jan 2010, Muhlenberg Co. (*KW* 86:19/43, 2010); 2 Jan 2011, Muhlenberg Co. (*KW* 87:27/61, 2011); winter 2011-2012, Pulaski Co. (*KW* 88:47, 2012); 1 Jan 2012, Muhlenberg Co. (*KW* 88:23/47, 2012); 30 Dec 2012, (3) in Muhlenberg Co. (*KW* 89:22/47, 2013); 14 Dec 2013, (3) heard at the Long Point Unit (*KW* 90:49, 2014); 28 Dec 2013, (3) heard at the Ken Unit Peabody WMA, Ohio Co. (*KW* 90:49, 2014); 29 Dec 2013, (5) heard in Muhlenberg Co. (*KW* 90:23/49, 2014); 1 Jan 2015, 4 total heard in Muhlenberg and Ohio cos. (*KW* 91:19/52, 2015); 3 Jan 2016, Muhlenberg Co. (*KW* 92:20/42, 2016); 26 Feb 2016, heard s. of Clinton, Hickman Co. (*KW* 92:42, 2016); winter 2016-2017, several reports from Muhlenberg and Ohio cos. (*KW* 93:18/48, 2017); 5 Dec 2018, (ph.) Beckley Creek Park, Jefferson Co. (*KW* 95:48, 2019); 30 Dec 2018, Muhlenberg Co. (*KW* 95:23/48 2019); 6 Jan 2019, Sinclair Unit (*KW* 95:48, 2019).

Published error: 24 Aug 1975, Louisville (*KW* 52:47, 1976) pertained to a Sora (*fide* B. Palmer-Ball, notes).

SORA *Porzana carolina*

Status: Uncommon to fairly common transient, extremely rare during summer and winter. Recorded chiefly west of the Cumberland Plateau, but likely not rare in suitable habitat in eastern Kentucky during migration. Widespread in marshes and along pond margins grown up with cattails, sedges, and other dense vegetation, but also occurs in grain, weed and hay fields. Peaks of abundance occur from mid-Apr to early May and from late Aug to late Sep. Like the preceding species, the Sora also may turn up in unusual places during migration. There are a few summer records between the normal spring and fall migratory periods, but breeding has not been documented. Single individuals heard calling from suitable habitat at two locations in Muhlenberg Co. represent the state's first winter records (see below). Usually seen singly, but can be surprisingly numerous in suitable habitat.

Maximum counts: at least **65** at the Sauerheber Unit, 21 Apr 2007 (*KW* 83:78, 2007); **60** at the Sauerheber Unit, 7 Sep 1986 (*KW* 63:8, 1987); **50-60** at the Sauerheber Unit, 20 Apr 1996 (*KW* 72:54, 1996); **40-45+** e. of Morganfield, Union Co., 4 May 2005 (*KW* 81:85, 2005); **40** at the Sauerheber Unit, 6 Oct 2007 (*KW* 84:7, 2008).

Early spring dates: 18 Mar 2007, Sauerheber Unit (C. Crawford, eBird data); 19 Mar 1973, Hopkins Co. (*AB* 27:623, 1973); 21 Mar 1991, a bird picked up dead in Frankfort (R. Cicerello, pers. comm.); 26 Mar 19—, Louisville (Mengel:232); 28 Mar 2014, Fayette Co. (*KW* 90:69, 2014); 29 Mar 2016, Sauerheber Unit (*KW* 92:58, 2016).

Late spring dates: 31 May 2018, Morgan Pond (*KW* 94:71, 2018); 30 May 2008, (ph.) Morgan Pond (*KW* 84:60, 2008); 29 May 2004, Long Point Unit (*KW* 80:66, 2004); 28 May 1981, Louisville (B. Palmer-Ball, eBird data); 26 May 1992, Long Point Unit (M. Stinson, eBird data; date published erroneously as 9 May at *KW* 68;45, 1992); 23 May 2014, Muhlenberg Co. (*KW* 90:69, 2014); 23 May 2016, Jefferson Co. (B. Palmer-Ball, eBird data); 21 May 2005, Boone Co. (*KW* 81:85, 2005); 21 May 2013, Sinclair Unit (*KW* 89:69, 2013).

Early fall dates: 2 Aug 2008, Jefferson Co. (*KW* 85:13, 2009); 3 Aug 2003, Sauerheber Unit (*KW* 80:8, 2004); 9 Aug 2012, Jefferson Co. (*KW* 89:7, 2013); 10 Aug 2003, Sinclair Unit (*KW* 80:8, 2004); 10 Aug 2012, Pulaski Co. (*KW* 89:7, 2013); 13 Aug 2011, Morgan Pond (*KW* 88:7, 2012); 15 Aug 2015, Sand Slough, Henderson Co. (B. Palmer-Ball, eBird data).

Late fall dates: 28 Nov 2014, Anderson Co. (*KW* 91:7, 2015); 9 Nov 2003, Muhlenberg Co. (*KW* 80:8, 2004); 2 Nov 1984, Louisville (*KW* 61:16, 1985).

Out-of-season records (summer): 22 Jun 1974, Larue Co. (*AB* 28:909, 1974); 25 Jun–22 Jul 1963, Barren Co. (Gillenwater, *KW* 40:32-33, 1964); 22 Jul 19—, Louisville area (*KW* 37:29, 1961; Mengel:232); 8 Jul 2010, 2 (hd.) Sinclair Unit (*KW* 86:92, 2010).

Out-of-season records (winter): 2 Jan 2017, single birds (hd.) at two different locations in Muhlenberg Co., with one calling at one of the locales again 17-18 Feb 2017 (*KW* 93:48, 2017).

PURPLE GALLINULE *Porphyrio martinicus*

Status: Extremely rare visitant. There are 25 records of this southern species from widely separated locations across the state. Generally found in marshes and along the marshy borders of lakes and ponds. A vast majority of reports of overshoot birds occur during the first half of May (16 of the 25 records). This species formerly bred at Reelfoot Lake in northwest Tennessee, and has bred in southern Illinois, so the possibility of breeding in western Kentucky should not be overlooked. All records are of single birds.

Early spring dates: 12 Apr 1981, at Goose Pond, Hopkins Co. (*KW* 57:56, 1981); 12 Apr 1996, (ph.) at Jackson, Breathitt Co. (*KW* 72:54, 1996); 23 Apr 1983, at the Ballard WMA (J. MacGregor, notes).

Late fall dates: 25 Sep 2005, a juv. (ph.) nr. Sharkey, Rowan Co. (*KW* 82:7, 2006); 10 Aug 1983, at Back Slough nr. Laketon, Carlisle Co. (J. MacGregor, notes [date published incorrectly as "early Jul" in Monroe, et al. (1988)]).

Out-of-season record (winter): 19 Feb 1983, Shanty Hollow Lake, Warren Co. (*AB* 37:307, 1983).

Tally of records by county

Allen, Ballard, Bell, Boone, Breathitt, Breckinridge, Calloway, Carlisle, Edmonson, Grayson, Henderson (3), Hopkins (3), Jackson/Madison, Jefferson, Lawrence, Letcher, Rowan (2), Trigg, Warren (2).

Chronological list of records

1) 5 May 1964, along the Ohio River nr. Henderson (Rhoads, *KW* 40:55-56, 1964)
2) 8 May 1967, male collected at Caperton's Swamp at Louisville (Monroe and Able, *KW* 44:55, 1968)
3) 7 May 1971, at Goose Pond, Hopkins Co. (Hancock, *KW* 47:44, 1971)
4) 7 May 1972, at Goose Pond, Hopkins Co. (*AB* 26:767, 1972)
5) 9 May 1972, LBL, Trigg Co. (*AB* 26:767, 1972; *KW* 48:43, 1972; W. Gray, pers. comm.)
6) 7-14 May 1973, in Bell Co. (R. Harm, pers. comm.)
7) 15-16 May 1980, on Ky Lake nr. Hamlin, Calloway Co. (*KW* 56:61, 1980)
8) 12 Apr 1981, at Goose Pond, Hopkins Co. (*KW* 57:56, 1981)
9) 9 May 1981, at Owsley Fork Lake, Jackson/Madison Co. (Ritchison, *KW* 57:79-80, 1981)
10) 19 Feb 1983, at Shanty Hollow Lake, Warren Co. (*AB* 37:307, 1983)
11) 23 Apr 1983, at the Ballard WMA (J. MacGregor, notes)
12) 10 Aug 1983, at Back Slough nr. Laketon, Carlisle Co. (J. MacGregor, notes [date published incorrectly as "early Jul" in Monroe, et al. (1988)])
13) 28-29 Apr 1984, (ph.) at Sloan's Crossing Pond, Mammoth Cave National Park (*KW* 60:42, 1984; K. Overman, notes/photographs)
14) 14-24 May 1988, (ph.) at Big Pond Sanctuary, Grayson Co. (K. and H. Clay, *KW* 64:51, 1988)
15) 12 Apr–9 May 1996, (ph.) at Jackson, Breathitt Co. (*KW* 72:54, 1996)
16) 26 Apr 1996, Yatesville Lake WMA, Lawrence Co. (R. Mauro, pers. comm.)
17) 12+ May 1996, nr. Kona, Letcher Co. (J. Kiser, pers. comm.)
18) 15 May–ca. 10 Jun 1996, Yellowbank WMA, Breckinridge Co. (S. McMillen, pers. comm.)
19) 18-25 Sep 2005, a juv. (ph.) nr. Sharkey, Rowan Co. (*KW* 82:7, 2006)

20) 3-4 May 2010, (ph.) at the Sauerheber Unit (*KW* 86:66/76, 2010)
21) 4-8 May 2010, (ph.) at McElroy Lake (*KW* 86:66/76, 2010)
22) 6-8 May 2010, (ph.) along Aurora Ferry Road, Boone Co. (*KW* 86:66/76, 2010)
23) 5-16 Jul 2012, (ph.) nr. Sharkey, Rowan Co. (*KW* 88:94/104, 2012)
24) 10-13 May 2014, s. of Mt. Zion, Allen Co. (*KW* 90:69, 2014)
25) 4-10 May 2017, (ph.) at J.J. Audubon SP, Henderson Co. (*KW* 93:72/84, 2017)

*COMMON GALLINULE *Gallinula galeata*

Status: Rare transient, extremely rare summer resident. Recorded from scattered localities across the state, but chiefly west of the Cumberland Plateau. Usually encountered in marshes or along the marshy borders of lakes and ponds where an abundance of emergent aquatic vegetation is present. Peak of abundance occurs from late Apr to early Sep. Breeding has been confirmed in five counties (see below). Also, summer sightings with unsuccessful or probable nesting have been reported at several additional locations (see below). Usually seen singly or in pairs or family groups. **State Breeding Status**: Threatened.

Maximum counts: **11** at Camp #11, Union Co., 20 Jun 2006 (*KW* 82:81, 2006); **9** at Camp #11, Union Co., 22 Jul 2003 (*KW* 79:81, 2003); at least **8** at the Sauerheber Unit, 25 May 1986 (*KW* 62:42, 1986; B. Palmer-Ball, eBird data); **7-8** at the Sauerheber Unit, 22 May 2006 (*KW* 82:68, 2006); **8** at Morgan Pond, 15 Jun 2011 (*KW* 87:113, 2011); **7** at the Sauerheber Unit, 14 Jul–2 Oct 2004 (*KW* 80:82, 2004; *KW* 81:7, 2005); **7** at the Sinclair Unit, 11 Jun 2016 (*KW* 92:79, 2016).
Early spring dates: 23 Mar 2013, Muhlenberg Co. (*KW* 89:69, 2013); 6 Apr 1952, Louisville (Mengel:233); 11 Apr 1905, Woodford Co. (Cooke 1914).
Late fall dates: 10 Nov 2013, Hart Co. (*KW* 90:8, 2014); 3 Nov 1952, Louisville area (Mengel: 233); 29 Oct 1986, Owsley Fork Lake, Madison/Jackson cos. (*KW* 63:8, 1987); 26 Oct 2014, (ph.) A.J. Jolly Park, Campbell Co. (*KW* 91:7, 2015).

List of confirmed breeding records by county

Henderson (Sauerheber Unit, 2003, 2004, 2010 [*KW* 80:8/82, 2004; *KW* 87:15, 2011])
Muhlenberg (Paradise Power Plant, 1995 [W. James, pers. comm.]; County Rail Trail, 2011 [*KW* 87:113, 2011]; Sinclair Unit, 2016 [*KW* 92:79, 2016])
Ohio (Homestead Unit of Peabody WMA, 1989 [Palmer-Ball and Barron, *KW* 66:76-77, 1990])
Union (Camp #11, 2003, 2005, 2006, 2007, 2009 [*KW* 79:81, 2003; *KW* 81:106, 2005; *KW* 82:81, 2006; *KW* 83:104, 2007; *KW* 85:92, 2009])
Warren (McElroy Lake, 1935 [Wilson, *KW* 16:18, 1940; *KW* 38:11, 1962])

List of additional summer records of probable or unsuccessful breeding by county

Carlisle (Mayfield Creek, 27 Jun 1990 [*KW* 66:86, 1990; C. Peterson, pers. comm.])
Franklin (Pfeiffer Fish Hatchery, summer 1985 [*KW* 61:56, 1985])
Henderson (Sauerheber Unit, summer 1986 (*KW* 62:67, 1986; B. Palmer-Ball, eBird data)
Muhlenberg (Sinclair Unit, 1998 [Palmer-Ball, *KW* 74:86, 1998])
Rowan (Minor Clark Hatchery, summer 1985 [*KW* 61:56, 1985])

*AMERICAN COOT *Fulica americana*

Status: Fairly common to common transient, rare to locally uncommon winter resident, extremely rare to rare during summer (at least three confirmed breeding records). Recorded chiefly west of the Cumberland Plateau, but likely uncommon on reservoirs of eastern Kentucky during migration. Widespread in a great variety of aquatic habitats from small marshes and ponds to the largest lakes and rivers. Peaks of abundance occur from late Mar to late Apr and from late Oct to late Nov. A few birds typically linger into or through summer on ponds, marshes and lakes, but usually do not breed. Breeding has been documented from only three locales (see below). The reliability of additional nesting reports from Crittenden and Union cos. during the first half of the 20th century are unknown (see Wilson, *KW* 18:21, 1942). Most often seen in small to medium-sized flocks of up to a hundred birds, but the species is sometimes present by the hundreds or even thousands, especially during migration. **State Breeding Status**: Endangered.

Maximum counts: **50,000** estimated on Ky Lake, winter 1988-89 (*KW* 65:35, 1989); ca. **10,000** on Lake Barkley, Lyon Co., 30 Mar 2007 (*KW* 83:78, 2007); ca. **8000** at McElroy Lake, 2 Apr 1997 (*KW* 73:54, 1997); **4000-5000** at McElroy Lake, 10-16 Apr 1989 (Palmer-Ball and Boggs, *KW* 67:43, 1991); **4500+** on Cave Run Lake, 27 Oct 2013 (*KW* 90:8, 2014); **4500** on Lake Peewee, late Oct 1984 (*KW* 61:16, 1985); **4000** on Lake Peewee, mid-Nov 1965 (*KW* 42:10, 1966); **3700** on Lake Peewee, 20 Nov 1978 (*KW* 55:15, 1979); **3500** on McElroy Lake, 31 Mar 2018 (*KW* 94:71, 2018; number erroneously published as 4500 therein); **3000** on McElroy Lake, 22 Apr 1939 (Wilson, *KW* 15:31/35, 1939); **3000** on Lake Peewee, 5 Nov 1974 (J. Hancock, notes); **3000** on McElroy Lake, 24 Mar 2015 (*KW* 91:68, 2015); **2500-5000** on Ky Lake, Calloway Co., 7 Nov 1988 (*KW* 65:7, 1989); **2600** on Lake Cumberland, Pulaski Co., 4 Nov 1982 (*KW* 59:15, 1983; date erroneously published as 5 Nov therein); ca. **2500** at Cave Run Lake, 20 Nov 1998 (*KW* 75:5, 1999); **2500** on Barren River Lake, 29 Oct 2014 (*KW* 91:7, 2015); **2500** at the Sauerheber Unit, 7 Apr 2015 (*KW* 91:68, 2015); **2500** on Dale Hollow Lake, Clinton Co., 2 Dec 2017 (R. Bontrager, eBird data).

Summary of breeding records by county

Union (Camp #11, 2002-2003 [Palmer-Ball, *KW* 78:73-75, 2002; *KW* 79:68/81, 2003])
Warren (transient lakes, during the first half of the 20th century [Wilson, *WB* 41:183, 1929; Wilson, *KW* 11:22-23, 1935; Wilson, *KW* 15:36, 1939; Wilson, *KW* 16:18, 1940])
Fayette (1968 [Stamm, *KW* 45:31, 1969])

SANDHILL CRANE *Antigone canadensis*

Status: Rare to locally fairly common transient, typically rare during mid-winter except in the immediate vicinity of a few now traditional roosting areas, accidental during summer. Local in occurrence; seldom seen in eastern and western Kentucky, particularly the former, but fairly numerous along a migratory corridor through the central part of the state that stretches north and south from west of Bowling Green and Leitchfield, Grayson Co., to just west of Somerset, Pulaski Co., and Lexington. Formerly (19th century) perhaps more widespread as a transient, at least in the western part of the state (Mengel:229-230). The frequency of Sandhill Crane sightings in the state has increased dramatically since the late 1970s, apparently as a result of an overall increase in the eastern population. The fall migration often extends so late and the spring migration commences so early that it is unclear how many birds actually winter. Birds now typically remain through the winter at and near Barren River Lake and occasionally elsewhere. Most often seen migrating overhead, when they can be mistaken for geese or swans; however, their long, outstretched legs, kettling behavior, and distinctive, gutteral call eliminate all other species. Flocks are sometimes encountered on the ground, generally resting or foraging in open grain stubble fields and on mudflats. Generally observed in small to medium-sized groups of up to 50 birds, but larger flocks of several hundred or more birds are sometimes seen.

Maximum counts: up to **24,185** at Barren River Lake, 10/11 Feb 2014 (*KW* 90:49, 2014); **22,000** in w. Hardin Co., 18 Feb 2014 (*KW* 90:49, 2014); up to **18,000-20,000** in the vicinity of Barren River Lake 15 Feb 2010 (*KW* 86:43, 2010); **15,300** w. of Cecilia, Hardin Co., 24 Feb 2015 (*KW* 91:52, 2015); **14,570** w. of Cecilia, Hardin Co., 11 Mar 2015 (*KW* 91:69, 2015); **13,600** w. of Cecilia, Hardin Co., 29 Jan 2017 (*KW* 93:49, 2017); **13,000** at Barren River Lake, 19 Dec 2016 (*KW* 93:48, 2017); **12,000** at Barren River Lake, 28 Jan 2016 (*KW* 92:42, 2016); **11,680** at Barren River Lake, 10 Feb 2011 (*KW* 87:61, 2011); **11,000** w. of Cecilia, Hardin Co., 13 Feb 2018 (*KW* 94:56, 2018); ca. **8600** w. of Cecilia, Hardin Co., 3 Feb 2013 (*KW* 89:48, 2013); **7100** w. of Cecilia, Hardin Co., 1 Mar 2010 (*KW* 86:43/66, 2010); **6600** w. of Cecilia, Hardin Co., 8 Feb 2016 (*KW* 92:42, 2016); ca. **6000** in w. Hardin Co., 30 Jan 2007 (*KW* 83:48, 2007); **5130** w. of Cecilia, Hardin Co., 14 Feb 2011 (*KW* 87:61, 2011); ca. **5000** over sw. Jefferson Co., 27 Nov 2009 (*KW* 86:7, 2010); **4000-5000** over Barren River Lake, Barren Co., 15 Nov 1999 (D. Roemer, notes [date published incorrectly as 19 Nov in *KW* 76:5, 2000]); ca. **4500** in w. Hardin Co., 22 Feb 2009 (*KW* 85:49, 2009); **4192** in w. Hardin Co., 3 Mar 2009 (*KW* 85:68, 2009); **3700** over Hart Co., 21 Feb 2000 (*KW* 76:30, 2000); **3500** nr. Lucas, Barren Co., 24 Feb 2008 (*KW* 84:44, 2008); **3000+** over Taylor/Adair cos., 19 Feb 2001 (*NAB* 55:176, 2001); **3000** over Louisville, 27 Nov 1991 (*KW* 68:7, 1992); **2500-3000** over Cumberland Co., 21 Feb 2006 (*KW* 82:47, 2006); **2000-3000** over Louisville, 29 Nov 1992 (*KW*

69:7, 1993); **2150** over Bullitt/Nelson cos., 26 Dec 1999 (*KW* 76:13, 2000); up to **2000** over Elizabethtown, Hardin Co., 14 Dec 2004 (*KW* 81:58, 2005); **1400** at McElroy Lake, 21-22 Feb 1999 (*KW* 75:26, 1999; L. Doyle, pers. comm.); ca. **1400** over Hart Co., 14 Nov 1995 (*KW* 72:5, 1996).

Late spring dates: injured bird lingered into Jun 2004 at McElroy Lake (*KW* 80:66, 2004); 27 May 2017, (ph.) Wayne Co. (*KW* 93:72, 2017; number erroneously published as 3 therein [*fide* R. Bontrager, eBird data]); 3rd week of May 1966, injured bird in Adair Co. (Guthrie, *KW* 42:52, 1966); 22 May 2008, Yatesville Lake WMA, Lawrence Co. (*KW* 84:60, 2008); 22 May 2010, Mercer Co. (*KW* 86:66, 2010); 20 May 2010, (2) in Barren Co. (*KW* 86:66, 2010); 11-15 May 2005, w. Hardin Co. (*KW* 81:85, 2005); 13 May 1989, Hart Co. (*KW* 65:66, 1989); 13 May 2019, (ph.) McElroy Lake (R. Shive, eBird data); 12 May 2008, McElroy Lake (*KW* 84:60, 2008); 11 May 2002, Pulaski Co. (S. Marsh, eBird data); 11 May 2011, McElroy Lake (*KW* 87:86, 2011); 9 May 1948 (Mengel:229); 9 May 2017, Laurel Co. (A. Kayser, eBird data); 8 May 2018, McElroy Lake (*KW* 94:71, 2018); 7 May 2011, Pulaski Co. (*KW* 87:86, 2011); 6 May 2019, Hart Co. (J. Sole, eBird data); 4 May 1980, Louisville (*KW* 56:61, 1980).

Early fall dates: early Aug–22 Aug 2008, Sauerheber Unit (*KW* 85:14, 2009); 16 Aug 2010, Warren Co. (*KW* 87:15, 2011); 29 Aug 1979, Jefferson Co. (*KW* 56:15, 1980); 30 Aug 1998,(2) in Warren Co. (Roemer, *KW* 74:92/94, 1998); 3 Sep 2013, Henderson Co. (*KW* 90:8, 2014); 17 Sep 1960, Falls of the Ohio (Wiley, *KW* 36:68, 1960); 25 Sep 2006, Sauerheber Unit (*KW* 83:11, 2007).

Out-of-season records (summer): 4 Jun 1991, (2) over Hardin Co. (*KW* 67:77, 1991); 5/10 Jul 2008, (ph.) at Morgan Pond (*KW* 84:86, 2008); 28 Jun 2010, McElroy Lake (*KW* 86:92, 2010); 17 Jul 2010, in ne. Jefferson Co. (*KW* 86:92, 2010); 1 Jun–7 Sep 2012, (4) in Union Co. (*KW* 88:93, 2012/*KW* 89:7, 2013); 8 Sep 2012, (4) in Caldwell Co. (possibly/probably same birds?) (*KW* 89:7, 2013); spring/summer 2017, 1-2 lingered in Hart Co. (*KW* 93:72/99, 2017; *KW* 94:6, 2018); 14 Jun 2019, (vt.) Yellowbank WMA, Breckinridge Co. (R. Taylor, video/pers. comm.).

Unaccepted record: 28 Sep 2012, (100) Campbell Co. (eBird data).

e/sWHOOPING CRANE *Grus americana*

Status: Extirpated. Historically this species was apparently encountered regularly during migration in western and central Kentucky to about as far east as Louisville, occurring as late as the mid-1800s (Mengel:229). Audubon reportedly collected several specimens during the early 1800s, but there appears to be no extant specimen for the state (Mengel:229). Over the past decade, an experimental migratory population has been reintroduced in the eastern United States, and this restoration effort has resulted in a few reports of migrants every year. A few individuals are also now wintering in the western part of the state. This population has a long way to go before it is self-sustaining, but so far the cooperaive efforts of government and non-governmental entities seems to be experiencing promising results. **Federal Status**: Endangered.

*BLACK-NECKED STILT *Himantopus mexicanus*

Status: Extremely rare to rare transient and summer resident. Occurs primarily in shallow water pools and along the margins of flooded fields, either with or without emergent vegetation. Prior to 1993, there were only two summer records of vagrant birds in Christian and Franklin cos. (see below). However, during summer 1993, the species was found nesting at Open Pond in western Fulton Co., where at least four pairs successfully raised young (Palmer-Ball and Bennett, *KW* 69: 65-68, 1993). Subsequently, small numbers of birds have been reported most years in the Lower Hickman Bottoms in western Fulton Co. with nesting attempted some years. During the early 2000s, a few birds began showing up in other parts of western Kentucky when suitable habitat was present, and nesting has been documented (Christian and Warren cos.) or suspected (Henderson Co.) at several additional locations. Records of vagrant or migratory birds, primarily during spring, have also increased across central Kentucky over the past 10-15 years, and the species has now been reported from at least 24 counties as far east as Pulaski and Rowan. In recent years, a noticeable fall movement of presumed migratory birds has been detected, mostly during mid- to late Aug across the western third of the state. Most observations are of single birds, pairs, or family groups, although several pairs may occur together in loose breeding colonies when suitable habitat is present.

Maximum counts: **67** in w. Fulton Co., 5 Jul 2004 (*KW* 80:82, 2004); **45-48** in the Lower Hickman Bottoms, 4 May 2018 (*KW* 94:71, 2018; C. Bliznick, eBird data); **37** at Open Pond, Fulton Co., 24 Jun 2002 (*KW* 78:63, 2002); **35-40** on Wolf Island, Hickman Co., 3/8 Aug 2015 (*KW* 92:6/36, 2016); **36** in the Lower Hickman Bottoms, 29 May 2017 (*KW* 93:72, 2017); **29** in the Lower Hickman Bottoms, 10 May 2014 (*KW* 90:70, 2014); **19** at Lake No. 9, 24 Aug 2002 (*KW* 79:8, 2003); **19** at McElroy Lake, 14-27 Jun 2010 (*KW* 86:92, 2010); **19** in the Lower Hickman Bottoms, 8 May 2015 (*KW* 91:69, 2015); **18** at Morgan Pond, 30 Jul 2011 (*KW* 87:113, 2011); **18** in the Lower Hickman Bottoms, 22 May 2013 (B. Lisowsky, eBird data); **16** at Morgan Pond, 16 Jun 2008 (*KW* 84:86, 2008); **15** in McLean Co., 24 May 2011 (*KW* 87:87, 2011); **13** at Lake No. 9, 12 Aug 2009 (*KW* 86:8, 2010); **10** in Lower Hickman Bottoms, 25 Jun 1995 (B. Palmer-Ball, eBird data).

Early spring dates: 20 Mar 2009, Long Point Unit (*KW* 85:68, 2009); 22 Mar 2018, Lower Hickman Bottoms (*KW* 94:71, 2018); 30 Mar 2018, Sauerheber Unit (C. Crawford, eBird data); 31 Mar 2013, Obion WMA (*KW* 89:69, 2013); 1 Apr 2012, Sauerheber Unit (*KW* 88:75, 2012); 1 Apr 2019, (ph.) McElroy Lake (R. Shive, eBird data); 2 Apr 1999, Fulton Co. (J.T. Erwin, pers. comm.); 2 Apr 2017, Sauerheber Unit (*KW* 93:72, 2017); 4 Apr 2008, McElroy Lake (*KW* 84:61, 2008); 4 Apr 2011, McElroy Lake (*KW* 87:87, 2011); 5 Apr 2014, Fulton Co. (*KW* 90:70, 2014); 8 Apr 2013, Ballard WMA & Sauerheber Unit (*KW* 89:69, 2013); 8 Apr 2017, Long Point Unit (H. Chambers/B. Wulker, eBird data); 10 Apr 2015, w. Fulton Co. (*KW* 91:69, 2015); 13 Apr 2014, Sauerheber Unit (*KW* 90:70, 2014); 13 Apr 2019, (ph.) Sauerheber Unit (R. Rold et al., eBird data); 15 Apr 2004, Sauerheber Unit (*KW* 80:67, 2004); 15 Apr 2016, Lower Hickman Bottoms (*KW* 92:59, 2016); 16 Apr 2011, Fulton Co. (*KW* 87:87, 2011); 16 Apr 2015, Scott Co. (*KW* 91:69, 2015); 16 Apr 2012, Union Co. (*KW* 88:75, 2012); 17 Apr 2002, Henderson Co. (C. Crawford, eBird data); 18 Apr 1998, western Fulton Co. (H. Chambers, pers. comm.); 18 Apr 2007, Fulton Co. (*KW* 83:79, 2007).

Late fall dates: 10-24 Oct 2004, Blood River (*KW* 81:8, 2005); 19 Oct 2004, Ohio Co. (*KW* 81:8, 2005); 23 Sep 2011, Muhlenberg Co. (*KW* 88:8, 2012); 19 Sep 2016, Blood River (*KW* 93:7, 2017); 2 Sep 2001, Fulton Co. (*NAB* 56:58, 2002); 29 Aug 1998, Fulton Co. (B. Palmer-Ball, eBird data).

Unaccepted record: 6-7 May 1921, Woodford Co. (see Mengel:521).

Summary of confirmed breeding records by county

Christian (*KW* 84:61/86, 2008; *KW* 87:87/113, 2011; *KW* 88:8, 2012; *KW* 91:85, 2015 [unsuccessful]; S. Arnold/J. Hall et al., 2019 eBird data)

Fulton (Palmer-Ball and Bennett, *KW* 69:65-68, 1993; *KW* 74:72-73, 1998); *NAB* 53:392, 1999 & C. Peterson, 1999 pers. comm.; *KW* 80:82, 2004; *KW* 84:86, 2008; *KW* 85:92, 2009; *KW* 87:16/44, 2011; *KW* 87:113, 2011; *KW* 88:8, 2012; *KW* 89:69/94, 2013; B. Palmer-Ball, 2019 eBird data)

Warren (*KW* 86:67/92, 2010; *KW* 89:69/94, 2013; *KW* 91:69, 2015 [unsuccessful])

Summary of extralimital records by county (non-breeding reports away from western Fulton Co.)

Ballard (30 Apr/3 May 2007 [*KW* 83:79, 2007]; 24 Apr 2008 [*KW* 84:61, 2008]; 8/18 Apr 2013 [*KW* 89:69, 2013]; 8 Aug 2015 [*KW* 92:6, 2016])

Boone (2 May 2004 [*KW* 80:67, 2004])

Calloway (10-24 Oct 2004 [*KW* 81:8, 2005]; 19 Sep 2016 [*KW* 93:7, 2017])

Carlisle (21 Aug 2002 [*KW* 79:8, 2003]; 14-16 Jun 2016 [*KW* 92:79, 2016])

Christian (14 Jul 1991, Morgan Pond [R. English, pers. comm.]; 5 Jun 2003 [*KW* 79:81, 2003]; 25 Apr–11 Jul 2008 [*KW* 84:61/86, 2008]; *KW* 89:69/94, 2013; *KW* 92:59/79, 2016; S. Bell, 2017 eBird data; *KW* 94:105, 2018)

Fayette (3-4 Jun 2001 [*KW* 77:59, 2001; *NAB* 55:439, 2001]; 5 May 2015 [*KW* 91:69, 2015])

Franklin (21 Jul–9 Aug 1976 (Westerman, *KW* 53:17, 1977])

Fulton (annual since mid-1990s)

Hart (27 Apr 2016 [*KW* 92:59, 2016]; 29 May 2017 [L. Craiger/S. Moss, eBird data])

Henderson (17-20 Apr 2002 [*KW* 78:49, 2002; C. Crawford, pers. comm]; 15-20 Apr 2004 [*KW* 80:66-67, 2004]; 13 May 2005 [*KW* 81:86, 2005]; *KW* 83:79, 2007; *KW* 84:61/86, 2008; *KW* 85:92, 2009; *KW* 86:67, 2010; *KW* 88:75, 2012; *KW* 89:69/94, 2013; *KW* 90:70, 2014; *KW* 91:69, 2015; *KW* 92:59/79, 2016; *KW* 93:72, 2017; C. Crawford, et al., 2017 eBird data; *KW* 94:6, 2018; C. Crawford, et al., 2018 eBird data)

Hickman (5 May 1994 [B. Palmer-Ball, eBird data]; *KW* 92:6/36, 2016)

Jefferson (27-28 May 2015 [*KW* 91:69, 2015]; 19-26 Aug 2017 [*KW* 94:6, 2018])

Livingston (5 & 18 Aug 2002 [*KW* 79:8, 2003])

Logan (15 May 2010 [*KW* 86:67, 2010]; 19 Jun/9-12 Jul/13 Jul 2010 [*KW* 86:92, 2010]; *KW* 87:113, 2011; *KW* 89:69/94, 2013; *KW* 91:69, 2015)
McLean (*KW* 87:87, 2011; Palmer-Ball and Huber, *KW* 88:87-91, 2012]);
Muhlenberg (23 Sep 2011 [*KW* 88:8, 2012])
Ohio (19 Oct 2004 [*KW* 81:8, 2004])
Pulaski (11 May 2017 [R. Denton, eBird data])
Rowan (18-21 May 2017 (C. Bliznick et al., eBird data)
Scott (16 Apr 2015 [*KW* 91:69, 2015])
Simpson (4-19 May 2015 [*KW* 91:69, 2015])
Todd (8 Jun 2008 [*KW* 84:86, 2008])
Union (20/30 Jun 2003 [*KW* 79:81, 2003]; 23 May 2007 [*KW* 83:79, 2007]; 18 May 2008 [*KW* 84:61, 2008]; *KW* 88:75, 2012)
Warren (26-27 Apr/31 May–4 Jun 2002 [*KW* 78:49/63, 2002]; 2 Jun 2004 [*KW* 80:82, 2004]; 4 Apr–30 May 2008 [*KW* 84:61, 2008]; *KW* 87:87/114, 2011; S. Bell/T. Quarles, et al., 2018 eBird data; R. Shive, 2019 eBird data)

AMERICAN AVOCET *Recurvirostra americana*

Status: Transient (extremely rare to rare during spring, rare during fall). Reported from scattered localities across the state with sightings from at least 37 counties; has been found most frequently at the Falls of the Ohio where it is observed almost annually. Peaks of abundance occur during mid- to late Apr and from late Jul to early Oct. Usually found resting along the open shores of the larger lakes and rivers, but also occurs on smaller bodies of water and could be found at any good shorebird spot during fall. Flocks are also occasionally observed resting, waterfowl-like, on open water. Avocets typically remain at a location for only a day, but there are records of birds lingering for longer periods a few times during spring and about a dozen times during fall. Most sightings have been of single birds or small flocks of fewer than a dozen individuals.

Maximum spring counts: 67 (ph.) on the Ohio River at Louisville, 25 Apr 2014 (*KW* 90:70, 2014); **48** (ph.) at Morgan Pond, 19 Apr 2015 (*KW* 91:69, 2015 [date erroneously published as 18 Apr therein; *fide* J. Hall, eBird data]); **40** in w. Caldwell Co., 1 May 2003 (*KW* 79:68, 2003); **30** at Lake Carnico, Nicholas Co., 19 Apr 1994 (W. and V. Kingsolver, notes); **24** (ph.) at McElroy Lake, 23 Apr 2011 (*KW* 87:87/99, 2011); **20-25** at Barren River Lake, spring 1997 (M. Vessels, pers. comm.; *fide* D. Roemer, pers. comm.); **21** (ph.) at Ky Dam Village, 28 Apr 2013 (*KW* 89:70, 2013).
Maximum fall counts: **24** (ph.) in Union Co., 23 Jul 2017 (*KW* 93:99, 2017); **18** at the Falls of the Ohio, 28 Aug 1976 (J. Elmore, notes); **13** (ph.) in s. Logan Co., 28 Aug 2012 (*KW* 89:7, 2013); **12** at the Falls of the Ohio, 25 Oct 1975 (*KW* 52:50, 1976).
Early spring dates: 11 Apr 2019, (ph.) Morgan Pond (J. Hall/S. Arnold, eBird data); 12 Apr 2011, McElroy Lake (*KW* 87:87, 2011); 13 Apr 1997, McElroy Lake (Roemer, et al., *KW* 73:79-83, 1997); 14 Apr 1993, Jefferson Co. (*KW* 69:45, 1993).
Late spring dates: 28 May 2019, (ph.) Louisville (T. Lusk, eBird data); 27 May 2017, Lower Hickman Bottoms (*KW* 93:72, 2017); 21 May 2013, Morgan Pond (*KW* 89:70, 2013); 20 May 2000, Falls of the Ohio (B. Etenohan/A. Goldstein, pers. comm.); 20 May 2010, Ballard WMA (*KW* 86:67, 2010); 18 May 2008, Union Co. (*KW* 84:61, 2008); 17 May 2000, Marshall Co. (*KW* 76:45, 2000); 13 May 2015, (ph.) Sauerheber Unit (*KW* 91:69, 2015); 13 May 2018, Jessamine Co. (*KW* 94:72, 2018); 12 May 2015, McElroy Lake (*KW* 91:69, 2015); 11 May 1999, Marshall Co. (*KW* 75:43, 1999); 11 May 2013, McElroy Lake (*KW* 89:70, 2013); 10 May 2013, (ph.) Ky Dam Village (*KW* 89:70, 2013).
Early fall dates: 10 Jul 1994, Falls of the Ohio (W. Dahl, pers. comm.); 14 Jul 1987, Falls of the Ohio (*KW* 63:59, 1987); 14 Jul 2005 (*KW* 81:106, 2005).
Late fall dates: 14-25 Nov 1998, 2-5 (ph.) in Wayne Co. (R. Denton, eBird data; [erroneously published in previous edition of this work as 14-26 Nov]); 13 Nov 1982, Falls of the Ohio (*KW* 59:16, 1983); 10 Nov 2008, (ph.) Green River Lake, Adair Co. (*KW* 85:14, 2009).
Out-of-season record (early summer): 10 Jun 2010, McElroy Lake (*KW* 86:92, 2010).
Published error?: I can find no basis for the inclusion of Adair Co. in the list of counties where the species has occurred as summarized in Monroe, et al. (1988) and believe its inclusion was the result of a transcription error (*fide* A. Stamm, historical archive files). This error pre-dates the 2008 record included below.

Summary of records by county

Adair (*KW* 85:14, 2009)

Allen/Barren (Barren River Lake) (M. Vessels, 1997 pers. comm.; *KW* 65:66-67, 1989; *KW* 73:6, 1997; *KW* 85:68, 2009)

Ballard (B. Palmer-Ball, 1993 eBird data]; *KW* 86:67, 2010)

Barren (*KW* 86:8, 2010)

Boone (*KW* 82:8, 2006; *KW* 86:8, 2010)

Bullitt (L. McMahon, 2019 eBird data)

Caldwell (*KW* 79:68, 2003)

Calloway (J.T. Erwin, 1971 notes; *KW* 76:5, 2000; *KW* 82:8, 2006; *KW* 85:14, 2009; *KW* 95:6, 2019)

Campbell (*KW* 84:86, 2008; J. Ferner, 2011 eBird data)

Carlisle (*KW* 87:16, 2011; *KW* 95:6, 2019)

Carter (*KW* 59:16, 1983)

Christian (*KW* 73:72, 1997; *KW* 88:8, 2012; *KW* 89:70, 2013; *KW* 91:69, 2015; *KW* 93:7, 2017; J. Hall/S. Arnold, 2019 eBird data)

Daviess (*KW* 59:41, 1983; *KW* 76:5, 2000; *KW* 94:6, 2018)

Fayette (*KW* 59:16, 1983; *KW* 85:14, 2009; *KW* 87:16, 2011)

Franklin (Jones, *KW* 41:63-64, 1965; R. Morris, 1975 pers. comm.; *KW* 95:6, 2019)

Fulton (B. Palmer-Ball, 1993 eBird data; J. Wilson, 1994 eBird data; *KW* 85:14, 2009; *KW* 87:16, 2011; *KW* 88:9, 2012; *KW* 91:85, 2015; *KW* 93:72, 2017)

Hardin (*KW* 90:70/84, 2014; *KW* 94:72, 2018; *KW* 95:6, 2019)

Henderson (Mengel:255; mid- to late Oct 1981, Sloughs WMA [R. Dodson, Oct 1981 pers. comm.]; *KW* 88:9, 2012; *KW* 91:69, 2015; *KW* 92:6, 2016; *KW* 93:7, 2017; *KW* 95:6, 2019)

Hickman (*KW* 81:8, 2005 [location erroneously published as Carlisle Co. therein]; *KW* 85:14, 2009; *KW* 92:6, 2016)

Jefferson (essentially annual at the Falls of the Ohio; also *KW* 69:45, 1993; *KW* 90:8, 2014; *KW* 91:8/69, 2015; W. Blodgett, 2019 eBird data; T. Lusk, 2019 eBird data)

Jessamine (*KW* 94:72, 2018)

Laurel (11 Aug 1995, Laurel River Lake [S. Kickert, pers. comm.])

Livingston (*KW* 76:5, 2000; *KW* 88:8, 2012)

Logan (*KW* 89:7, 2013)

Lyon (D. Berry/C. Peterson, 1977 eBird data; *KW* 83:79, 2007)

Marshall (Morse, *KW* 23:5 1947; 1977 eBird data; *KW* 63:8, 1987; *KW* 69:7, 1993; *KW* 75:43, 1999; *KW* 76:45, 2000; *KW* 77:6, 2001; B. Yandell, 2001 pers. comm.; *KW* 80:8, 2004; *KW* 83:74/79, 2007; *KW* 85:68, 2009; *KW* 89:69-70/75, 2013; *KW* 90:8, 2014; *KW* 92:6, 2016; *KW* 93:7, 2017; *KW* 94:6, 2018)

Meade (R. Healy, late 1990s pers. comm.)

Mercer (W. Kemper, 1996 pers. comm./R. Denton, 1996 eBird data; *KW* 80:8, 2004; *KW* 95:6, 2019)

Muhlenberg (*KW* 75:60, 1999; *KW* 76:5, 2000; *KW* 83:12, 2007)

Nelson (*KW* 86:8, 2010)

Nicholas (Kingsolver and Kingsolver, *KW* 54:53, 1978; W. and V. Kingsolver, 1994 notes; *KW* 72:5, 1996)

Pulaski (Elmore, *KW* 59:19, 1983);

Rowan (*KW* 65:7, 1989; *KW* 66:9, 1990; *KW* 78:7, 2002; *KW* 93:7, 2017)

Taylor (8 May 1997, Green River Lake State Park, Taylor Co. (C. Tichenor, pers. comm.)

Todd (*KW* 93:7, 2017; *KW* 94:105, 2018)

Trigg (*AFN* 21:44-45, 1967)

Union (*KW* 84:61, 2008; *KW* 88:9, 2012; *KW* 89:70, 2013; *KW* 91:8, 2015; *KW* 93:97/99, 2017)

Warren (Roemer, et al., *KW* 73:79-83, 1997; *KW* 86:8, 2010; *KW* 86:92, 2010; *KW* 87:87/99, 2011; *KW* 89:70, 2013; *KW* 91:69, 2015)

Wayne (R. Denton, 1998 eBird data; *KW* 93:7, 2017)

BLACK-BELLIED PLOVER *Pluvialis squatarola*

Status: Transient (rare to uncommon during spring, uncommon during fall). Recorded chiefly west of the Cumberland Plateau, but there are several records from the Minor Clark Hatchery in the eastern Knobs and one record from the Cumberland Mountains (13 Oct 1979, Bell Co. [Allaire, *KW*

56:19, 1980]). Peaks of abundance occur during mid-May and from late Aug to mid-Oct. This species is most frequently encountered along the margins of flooded fields during spring; it has been found at least occasionally at all of the better shorebird areas in the state during fall, but most frequently on the open shores and mudflats of the larger lakes and rivers. Generally seen singly or in small groups of up to a dozen birds.

Maximum spring counts: **137** total including flocks of 33 and 51 in w. McLean Co. and ne. Hopkins Co., respectively, 20 May 2011 (*KW* 87:86-87, 2011; Palmer-Ball and Huber, *KW* 88:87-91, 2012); **51** at McElroy Lake, 17 May 1998 (Roemer, *KW* 74:93/94, 1998); at least **45** at McElroy Lake, 20 May 2008 (*KW* 84:60, 2008); at least **42** w. of Buttonsberry, McLean Co., 23-24 May 2011 (*KW* 87:87, 2011); **39** nr. Lake No. 9, 16 May 2018 (*KW* 94:72, 2018); **38** in w. Henderson Co., 20 May 1998 (B. Palmer-Ball, eBird data); **35** at McElroy Lake, 24 May 1950 (*KW* 38:12, 1962); **28** at Open Pond, Fulton Co., 10 May 2015 (*KW* 91:69, 2015); **22** at Parsons Pond, Logan Co., 16 May 2009 (*KW* 85:68, 2009); **19** at Parsons Pond, Logan Co., 16 May 2008 (*KW* 84:60, 2008).

Maximum fall counts: **22** on Ky Lake, Marshall Co., 20 Oct 1980 (*KW* 57:21, 1981); **17** at the Falls of the Ohio, 29 Sep 1962 and 17 Sep 1966 (Stamm, et al., *KW* 43:8, 1967); **9** at Jonathan Creek, 13 Nov 2008 (*KW* 85:14, 2009).

Early spring dates: 7 Apr 2017, (ph.), Fulton Co. (*KW* 93:72, 2017); 11 Apr 1963, Warren Co. (*KW* 40:19, 1964); 12 Apr 2008, Christian Co. (*KW* 84:60, 2008); 13 Apr 2013, Henderson Co. (*KW* 89:69, 2013); 15 Apr 2010, w. Henderson Co. (*KW* 86:66, 2010); 15 Apr 2016, (ph.) Lower Hickman Bottoms (*KW* 92:59, 2016); 16 Apr 1987, Daviess Co. (*KW* 63:49, 1987); 17 Apr 1982, Lower Hickman Bottoms (*KW* 58:50, 1982; B. Palmer-Ball, eBird data); 18 Apr 1970, Warren Co. (*KW* 46:42, 1970); 18 Apr 2009, Chaney Lake (*KW* 85:68, 2009).

Late spring dates: 24 Jun 2008, Fulton Co. (*KW* 84:86, 2008); 19 Jun 2002, Morgan Pond, Christian Co. (*KW* 78:62, 2002); 16 Jun 2014, (ph.) Falls of the Ohio (*KW* 90:88, 2014); 14 Jun 1998, McElroy Lake (Roemer, *KW* 74:94, 1998); 5 Jun 2010, McElroy Lake (*KW* 86:92, 2010); 4 Jun 1994, McElroy Lake (B. Palmer-Ball, eBird data).

Early fall dates: 22 Jul 19—, Louisville area (*KW* 52:48, 1976); 23 Jul 1998, McElroy Lake (Roemer, *KW* 74:94, 1998).

Late fall dates: 14 Dec 2008, Jonathan Creek (*KW* 85:49, 2009); 29 Nov 1969, Ky Lake (Peterson, *KW* 46:47-48, 1970); 27 Nov 1966, Falls of the Ohio (Stamm, et al., *KW* 43:8, 1967).

Unaccepted records: those during spring earlier than the early spring date of 7 Apr given above and including 14 Mar 1994 (*KW* 70:52, 1994); 1 Apr 1991 (*KW* 67:54, 1991); and 1 Apr 1995 (*KW* 71:41, 1995). It is believed that these early-season records represent observations of the following species, which is an earlier spring migrant.

Published error: the late fall date of 2 Dec published in Monroe, et al. (1988) is erroneous, the result of a transcription error (*fide* A. Stamm, historical archive files).

AMERICAN GOLDEN-PLOVER *Pluvialis dominica*

Status: Uncommon to locally fairly common transient, extremely rare during summer. Recorded chiefly west of the Cumberland Plateau, especially during spring when the species is locally distributed from about Louisville and Bowling Green westward and numerous only in the lowlands along the Mississippi River. Easternmost spring reports are from Breathitt Co. (Allaire, *KW* 50:35-40, 1974) and Rowan Co. (*KW* 90:70, 2014). Peaks of abundance occur from late Mar to late Apr and from mid-Aug to early Oct. During spring most frequently observed in extensive fields with sparse vegetation and some bare soil or along shorelines of flooded fields. More widespread during fall, when it is most frequently found on flats and along the margins of bodies of water, but occasionally in open pastures and fields far from water. Most often seen in small groups of fewer than ten birds, but occasionally encountered in large flocks during spring, especially in the extreme western portion of the state where hundreds of birds have been observed in the open agricultural land of western Fulton Co.

Maximum spring counts: at least **2040** in the Lower Hickman Bottoms (including at least 1400 at Open Pond), 15 Apr 2016 (*KW* 92:59, 2016); **1285** in the Upper Hickman Bottoms, 20 Apr 2014 (*KW* 90:70, 2014); **1200** in the Lower Hickman Bottoms, 10 Apr 2018 (*KW* 94:72, 2018); at least **1100** in the Lower Hickman Bottoms, 18 Apr 2010 (*KW* 86:66, 2010); **1000+** in Lower Hickman Bottoms, 5 Apr 1992 (B. Palmer-Ball, eBird data); **900** in scattered flocks in Fulton Co., 1 Apr 1984

(*KW* 60:42, 1984); **700** in the Lower Hickman Bottoms, 5 Apr 2003 (R. Denton, eBird data); **600+** adjacent to Obion WMA, 28 Mar 2013 (*KW* 89:69, 2013); **500+** (probably 1000) in Fulton Co., 23 Apr 1994 (*KW* 70:52, 1994); **500-700** in scattered flocks in Fulton Co., 7 Apr 1996 (B. Palmer-Ball, eBird data); **500** in scattered flocks in Fulton Co., 7 Apr 1984 (*KW* 60:42, 1984); at least **500** in w. Fulton Co., 6 Apr 2003 (*KW* 79:68, 2003); at least **380** in the Pond Creek Bottoms, Hopkins Co., 9 Apr 2014 (*KW* 90:70, 2014); **350** at McElroy Lake, 30 Mar 2011 & 2 Apr 2011 (*KW* 87:87, 2011); **200** at the Sauerheber Unit, 20 Apr 2018 (C. Bliznick, eBird data); **163** in Calloway Co., 29-20 Mar 1947 (Wyatt, *KW* 24:4, 1948); **120** se. of Owensboro, Daviess Co., 19 Apr 2018 (C. Bliznick, eBird data); **110** at McElroy Lake, 7 Apr 2003 (*KW* 79:68, 2003); **100** in the Ohio River bottoms nr. Cincinnati, 14 Apr 1950 (Mengel:237); ca. **100** at McElroy Lake, 4/5 Apr 2008 (*KW* 84:61, 2008); ca. **80** in n. Union Co., 27 Mar 2007 (*KW* 83:78, 2007); **42-80** at Louisville, 27-28 Mar 1955 (Stamm and Krull, *KW* 31:28, 1955).

Maximum fall counts: at least **52** in the Upper Hickman Bottoms, 11 Sep 2013 (*KW* 90:9, 2014); **45** e. of Morganfield, Union Co., 13 Sep 2012 (*KW* 89:7, 2013); **42** at McElroy Lake, 16 Sep 1989 (Palmer-Ball and Boggs, *KW* 67:43, 1991); **42** at Camp #9, Union Co., 24 Sep 2010 (*KW* 87:16, 2011); at least **40** at the Falls of the Ohio, 18 Sep 1960 (Stamm, et al., *KW* 43:8, 1967).

Early spring dates: 3 Mar 1990, McElroy Lake (*KW* 66:56, 1990); 3 Mar 2007, Chaney Lake (*KW* 83:78, 2007); 4 Mar 2003, McElroy Lake (*KW* 79:68, 2003); 7 Mar 2016, McElroy Lake (*KW* 92:59, 2016); 9 Mar 2010, Jonathan Creek (*KW* 86:66, 2010); 9 Mar 2014, McElroy Lake (*KW* 90:70, 2014); 10 Mar 2019, Logan Co. (F. Lyne, eBird data); 11 Mar 2011, McElroy Lake (*KW* 87:87, 2011); 11 Mar 2016, Christan Co. (*KW* 92:59, 2016); 12 Mar 2000, Calloway Co. (*KW* 76:44, 2000).

Late spring dates: 27 May 1995, Lower Hickman Bottoms (B. Palmer-Ball, eBird data); 24 May 2011, McElroy Lake (*KW* 87:87, 2011); 24 May 2011, McLean Co. (Palmer-Ball and Huber, *KW* 88:87-91, 2012); 24 May 2015, McElroy Lake (*KW* 91:69, 2015); 23 May 1989, McElroy Lake (Palmer-Ball and Boggs, *KW* 67:43, 1991).

Early fall dates: 20 Jun 2006, Union Co. (*KW* 82:81, 2006); 27 Jun 1999, Lower Hickman Bottoms (*KW* 76:9, 2000; H. Chambers, notes [date published incorrectly as 22 Jun in *KW* 75:60, 1999]); 5 Jul 2002, Morgan Pond (*KW* 78:62, 2002); 5 Jul 2004, Open Pond (*KW* 80:82, 2004); 9 Jul 2000, Fulton Co. (*KW* 76:56, 2000); 17 Jul 1984, Falls of the Ohio (*KW* 60:53, 1984).

Late fall dates: 3 Dec 2017, (ph.) at the Sauerheber Unit (*KW* 94:56, 2018); 29 Nov 2010, Jonathan Creek (*KW* 87:16, 2011); 26 Nov 2016, (ph.) Todd Co. (*KW* 93:7, 2017); 22 Nov 1967, Falls of the Ohio (Stamm, et al., *KW* 43:8, 1967); 21 Nov 1992, Wayne Co. (R. Denton, eBird data); 21 Nov 2002, McElroy Lake (*KW* 79:8, 2003); 21 Nov 2007, the Sauerheber Unit (*KW* 84:8, 2008); 20 Nov 1982, Minor Clark Hatchery (*KW* 59:16, 1983); 18 Nov 1991, Falls of the Ohio (*KW* 68:7, 1992).

Out-of-season records (mid-summer): 13 Jun 1989, one in non-breeding plumage at McElroy Lake (Palmer-Ball and Boggs, *KW* 67:43, 1991); 17 Jun 2003, one at Open Pond, Fulton Co. (*KW* 79:81, 2003).

Published error: (2) in Fulton Co., 30 May 1999 (*KW* 75:42, 1999) (correction *fide* M. Bennett, pers. comm.).

*KILLDEER *Charadrius vociferus*

Status: Resident; fairly common to common during summer and migration, typically uncommon during winter. Recorded statewide but generally more widespread west of the Cumberland Plateau. Encountered on mudflats and shorelines of a great variety of bodies of water from farm ponds to the shores of the larger lakes and rivers, but may be found in virtually any open situation including some habitats far from water. Peak of abundance occurs from mid-Mar to mid-Nov. Nests on exposed surfaces of dirt, sand, sparse vegetation, and gravel in a variety of habitats including agricultural fields, sandbars, roadsides, parking lots, and urban rooftops. Generally seen singly or in small flocks of up to 30 birds, but larger groups of up to 200 or more are regularly observed during fall.

Maximum counts: at least **1400** at McElroy Lake, 16-17 Jul 2010 (*KW* 86:92, 2010); at least **1340** at McElroy Lake, 31 Dec 2007 (*KW* 84:44, 2008); **1300-1400** in the Upper Hickman Bottoms, 4 Aug 2010 (*KW* 87:16, 2011); **1150** at Barren River Lake, 29 Nov 2010 (*KW* 87:16, 2011); **1000+** at McElroy Lake, 23 Jul 1998 (Roemer, *KW* 74:93/94, 1998); ca. **1000** in the vicinity of Morgan Pond

10-17 Aug 2011 (KW 88:8, 2012); **845** in w. Fulton Co., 16 Jul 2010 (H. Chambers, eBird data); **815** at Barren River Lake, Allen Co., 12 Jan 2008 (*KW* 84:44, 2008); **800** at Mitchell Lake, Ballard WMA, 19 Aug 2010 (*KW* 87:16, 2011); **720+** at McElroy Lake, 21 Nov 2002 (*KW* 79:8, 2003); **620** at Barren River Lake, Allen Co., 14 Dec 2001 (D. Roemer, notes); **561** at Mitchell Lake, Ballard WMA, 11 Aug 2016 (*KW* 93:7, 2017); at least **550** in the vicinity of Morgan Pond, Christian Co., 22 Jul 2010 (*KW* 86:92, 2010); **529** on Green River Lake, Adair Co., 5 Dec 2014 (R. Denton, eBird data); **500+** at Mitchell Lake, Ballard WMA, 27 Jul 2004 (*KW* 80:82, 2004); ca. **500** at Minor Clark Hatchery, 3 Aug 1997 (*KW* 74:7, 1998); **500** in Upper Hickman Bottoms, 9 Sep 1993 (B. Palmer-Ball, eBird data); **500** at Morgan Pond, Christian Co., 3 Aug 1997 (*KW* 74:7, 1998); **500** at Barren River Lake, 23 Nov 2004 (*KW* 81:7, 2005); **475** at Barren River Lake 20 Nov 2016 (*KW* 93:7, 2017); **453** in s. Todd Co., 22 Dec 2017 (A. Troyer, eBird data); **450+** e. of Morganfield, Union Co., 1 Sep 2004 (*KW* 81:7, 2005); **450** at Morgan Pond, 27 Oct 2016 (J. Hall, eBird data); **400** in s. Todd Co., 22 Dec 2015 (J. Hall/A. Troyer, eBird data); **350** at Lake No. 9, 16 Aug 1987 (G. Criswell, eBird data); **350** at Mitchell Lake, Ballard WMA, 3 Aug 2007 (*KW* 84:8, 2008); **350** in the Upper Hickman Bottoms, 4 Aug 2015 (*KW* 92:7, 2016); **332** in Wayne Co., 9 Nov 2015 (*KW* 92:7, 2016); **300** at the Brown Power Plant, Mercer Co., fall 1988 (*KW* 65:7, 1989); **300+** at Spindletop Farm, Fayette Co., 8 Nov 1992 (*KW* 69:7, 1993); **300** at Horseshoe Road Slough, Henderson Co., 14 Jul 2017 (C. Crawford, eBird data).

SEMIPALMATED PLOVER *Charadrius semipalmatus*

Status: Uncommon to fairly common transient, extremely rare during early summer. Recorded chiefly west of the Cumberland Plateau. Encountered in a variety of shallow aquatic habitats; most frequently found along the muddy margins of flooded fields and the shores and mudflats of the larger lakes and rivers, but the species can be expected to occur at least occasionally about any open body of water. Peaks of abundance occur from late Apr to late May and from mid-Aug to mid-Sep. There are several Jun records between the normal spring and fall migratory periods. Generally seen singly or in small groups of fewer than a dozen birds, but loose flocks of 50 or more birds are regularly observed during spring.

Maximum spring counts: **1100-1300** in n. McLean Co., 24 May 2011 (*KW* 87:87, 2011; Palmer-Ball and Huber, *KW* 88:87-91, 2012); **1000-1200** at McElroy Lake, 9 May 2008 (*KW* 84:61, 2008), **800-1000** at McElroy Lake 18 May 2008 (*KW* 84:61, 2008); ca. **500** at McElroy Lake, 21 May 1998 (Roemer, *KW* 74:93/94, 1998); **500** at McElroy Lake, 15 May 2018 (*KW* 94:72, 2018); at least **330** at Horseshoe Road Slough, w. Henderson Co., 30 Apr 2012 (*KW* 88:75, 2012); **300** in w. Henderson Co., 5 May 2005 (*KW* 81:85-86, 2005); **275+** at Horseshoe Road Slough, Henderson Co., 17 May 2007 (*KW* 83:78, 2007); **250+** at McElroy Lake, 20 May 1997 (Roemer, et al., *KW* 73:79-83, 1997); **200+** at McElroy Lake, 15 May 2015 (*KW* 91:69, 2015); at least **200** at Ledford, Fulton Co., 7 May 2010 (*KW* 86:66, 2010); **175+** in western Henderson Co., 20 May 1998 (B. Palmer-Ball, eBird data); **161** s. of Middleton, Simpson Co., 12 May 2015 (*KW* 91:69, 2015); **130** w. of Sonora, Hardin Co., 16 May 2011 (*KW* 87:87, 2011); **120** at Sand Slough, Henderson Co., 29 Apr 2016 (*KW* 92:59, 2016); **110** in s. Jefferson Co., 15 May 2007 (*KW* 83:78, 2007).

Maximum fall counts: "flocks of up to **25-30** birds, several of which are sometimes present at once" at the Falls of the Ohio (Mengel:235); **35-40** at McElroy Lake, 8 Sep 1989 (Palmer-Ball and Boggs, *KW* 67:43, 1991); **25** at Minor Clark Hatchery, 12 Sep 1992 (*KW* 69:7, 1993); **20** at Lake No. 9, 24 Aug 2001 (*KW* 78:7, 2002); **20** at Mitchell Lake, Ballard WMA, 19 Sep 2007 (H. Chambers/R. Denton, eBird data); **20** at the Wildcat Creek embayment of Ky Lake, Trigg Co., 19 Sep 2014 (*KW* 91:8, 2015); **18** at Ky Bend, Fulton Co., 5 Aug 2005 (*KW* 82:8, 2006); **18** at Minor Clark Hatchery, 4 Sep 2014 (*KW* 91:8, 2015); **16** at the Falls of the Ohio, 5 Aug 1985 (B. Palmer-Ball, eBird data); **16** at Lake No. 9, 21 Aug 2000 (R. Denton, eBird data); **16** at Horseshoe Road Slough, w. Henderson Co., 21 Aug 2016 (*KW* 93:7, 2017).

Early spring dates: 5 Apr 2015 (ph.), McElroy Lake (*KW* 91:69, 2015); 7 Apr 2002, McElroy Lake (D. Roemer, notes); 8 Apr 2008, McElroy Lake (*KW* 84:61, 2008); 9 Apr 2012, Fulton Co. (*KW* 88:75, 2012); 10 Apr 2011, Marshall Co. (*KW* 87:87, 2011); 11 Apr 1946, Warren Co. (*KW* 38:12, 1962); 12 Apr 2003, Muhlenberg Co. (*KW* 79:68, 2003); 12 Apr 2005, Warren Co. (*KW* 81:85, 2005); 12 Apr 2019, McElroy Lake (R. Shive et al., eBird data); 13 Apr 1982, Pulaski Co. (*KW* 58:50, 1982); 13 Apr 2013, w. Henderson Co. (*KW* 89:69, 2013); 13 Apr 2018, McElroy Lake (*KW*

94:72, 2018); 14 Apr 1997, McElroy Lake (Roemer, et al., *KW* 73:79-83, 1997); 14 Apr 2003, Sauerheber Unit (R. Morton, eBird data); 14 Apr 2018, s. Jefferson Co. (P. Spaulding, eBird data).

Late fall dates: 24 Nov 2001, Calloway Co. (H. Chambers, notes); 3 Nov 2007, Wayne Co. (*KW* 84:8, 2008); 2 Nov 2011, Freeman Lake (*KW* 88:8, 2012); 30 Oct 2006, Jefferson Co. (*KW* 83:11, 2007); 30 Oct 2015, Calloway Co. (*KW* 92:7, 2016); 26 Oct 1946, Falls of the Ohio (Mengel: 235); 26 Oct 2003, Lake No. 9 (*KW* 80:8, 2004).

Unaccepted record: 24 Mar 1967, south-central Kentucky (*KW* 45:34, 1969).

PIPING PLOVER *Charadrius melodus*

Status: Transient (extremely rare during spring, extremely rare to rare during fall); formerly slightly more regular in occurrence during the latter. All records currently west of the Cumberland Plateau with reports from 14 counties (the farthest east report being from the Minor Clark Hatchery [*KW* 83:12, 2007]). Peaks of abundance occur around the first of May and from mid-Aug to early Sep, but the population of this species has declined in recent decades and it is no longer reported every year. Chiefly encountered on exposed shorelines and bars on the larger rivers and lakes, but the species could occur at any of the better shorebird areas throughout the state. Most older records came from the Falls of the Ohio, but a majority of more recent reports have originated from scattered locales across the western two-thirds of the state (although the species has been found away from the Falls of the Ohio only a few dozen times). Usually seen singly, but more than one have been observed on several occasions. **Federal Status**: Endangered.

Maximum counts: **4** at the Falls of the Ohio, 16 Aug 1978 (*KW* 55:15, 1979); **3** at the Falls of the Ohio, 5 Sep 1964 (Stamm, et al., *KW* 43:8, 1967); **3** at the Falls of the Ohio, 21 Jul 1977 (*AB* 31: 1148, 1977); **3** at McElroy Lake, 21 Aug 1989 (Palmer-Ball and Boggs, *KW* 67:43, 1991).

Early spring dates: 21 Apr 2001, Union Co. (*NAB* 55:306, 2001); 27 Apr 2007, s. Jefferson Co. (*KW* 83:74/79, 2007); 29 Apr 2004 (*KW* 80:66, 2004); 30 Apr 1995, Falls of the Ohio (Palmer-Ball, *KW* 72:65-67, 1996).

Late spring dates: 9 May 2008, McElroy Lake (*KW* 84:61, 2008); 7 May 2002, Morgan Pond, Christian Co. (*KW* 78:49, 2002); 6 May 1996, Ky Dam (Palmer-Ball, *KW* 72:67, 1996); 6 May 2005, Muhlenberg Co. (*KW* 81:86, 2005).

Early fall dates: 12/13 Jul 1994, Warren Co. (B. Palmer-Ball, eBird data); 13 Jul 1987, Lake No. 9 (G. Criswell, eBird data).

Late fall dates: 11 Oct 1971, Falls of the Ohio (*AB* 26:72, 1972); 4 Oct 1986, Jonathan Creek (*KW* 63:8, 1987); 2 Oct 1948, Falls of the Ohio (Mengel:235).

Unaccepted records: 21 May 1933 and 26 May 1937, Warren Co. (*KW* 38:12, 1962; see Mengel: 235).

Published errors: 23 Nov 1997, Marshall Co. (*KW* 74:7, 1998 [see *KW* 74:35, 1998]); also, the inclusion of Kenton Co. in the list of counties where this species has been reported in previous editions of this work was in error; that report technically pertained to Ohio (see Mengel:235).

Summary of records by county

Calloway (*KW* 58:15, 1982; *KW* 79:8, 2003)
Carlisle (*KW* 65:7, 1989; *KW* 82:8, 2006; *KW* 95:7, 2019)
Christian (*KW* 78:49, 2002)
Franklin (*KW* 55:56, 1979)
Fulton (G. Criswell, 1987 eBird data; *KW* 65:7, 1989; B. Palmer-Ball, 2001 eBird data; *KW* 86:92, 2010; *KW* 90:9/21, 2014)
Henderson (*KW* 41:43, 1965)
Jefferson (formerly annual at the Falls of the Ohio; also *KW* 83:74/79, 2007)
Livingston (J. Brunjes, 2009 eBird data)
Marshall (*KW* 63:8, 1987; *KW* 69:7, 1993; Palmer-Ball, *KW* 72:65-67, 1996; *KW* 74:7, 1998)
Muhlenberg (*KW* 75:60, 1999/*KW* 76:9, 2000; *KW* 81:86, 2005; *KW* 83:12, 2007)
Pulaski (*KW* 93:7, 2017)
Rowan (*KW* 83:12, 2007)
Union (Mengel:236; *NAB* 55:306, 2001; *KW* 80:66, 2004; *KW* 83:79, 2007)
Warren (*KW* 38:12, 1962; *KW* 38:12, 1962; Palmer-Ball and Boggs, *KW* 67:43, 1991; Palmer-Ball, *KW* 72:65-67, 1996; B. Palmer-Ball, 1994 eBird data; *KW* 84:61, 2008)

*UPLAND SANDPIPER *Bartramia longicauda*

Status: Transient (rare to [at least formerly] uncommon during spring, rare during fall); extremely rare during summer (one historical breeding record). All records currently from west of the Cumberland Plateau (reports from at least 35 counties; see below), although the species is now reported much less frequently than during the middle of the 20th century. Most often encountered in open fields and pastures with short or sparse vegetation; occasionally observed on mudflats and shorelines. Peaks of abundance occur from mid- to late Apr and from mid-Jul to mid-Aug. A nesting attempt (likely unsuccessful) at the Greater Cincinnati Airport, Boone Co., 4 Jun 1950 (*AFN* 4:278, 1950; Kemsies, et al., *KW* 26:49, 1950) represents the state's only nesting record. In addition, there are several other early summer (Jun) records from scattered localities in north-central Kentucky, but the species is such an early fall migrant that the significance of these records is unclear. Generally occurs singly or in small, loose groups of up to a half-dozen birds. **State Breeding Status**: Historical

Maximum spring counts: **15** at the Louisville airport, 30 Jul 1938 (Monroe and Mengel, *KW* 15:42, 1939); **10** in s. Warren Co., 2 Aug 1938 (Wilson, *KW* 15:10, 1939); **9** in Calloway Co., 12 Apr 1950 (Mengel:242); **8** in Warren Co., 16 Apr 1952 (Wilson, *KW* 28:46, 1952); **8** nr. McElroy Lake, 23 Apr 1983 (*KW* 59:41, 1983); **7** at McElroy Lake, 7 Apr 1939 (Wilson, *KW* 16:19, 1940); **6** at the n. Kentucky airport, Boone Co., 20 Apr 1982 (K. Overman, eBird data).

Maximum fall counts: **15** in Jefferson Co., 30 Jul 1938 (Monroe and Mengel, *KW* 15:42, 1939); **10** in Warren Co., 2 Aug 1938 (Wilson, *KW* 15:10, 1939); **9** at the Owensboro airport, Daviess Co., 5 Aug 1951 (Powell, *KW* 27:64-65, 1951).

Early spring date: 20 Mar 19—, Todd Co. (Mengel:242).

Late spring dates (other than single breeding record): 23 May 2011, ne. of Vandetta, Hopkins Co. (*KW* 87:88, 2011; Palmer-Ball and Huber, *KW* 88:87-91, 2012 [erroneously published as 24 May in the latter]); 17 May 1948, south-central Kentucky (*KW* 38:12, 1962).

Early fall dates (including records of possible summering birds): 20 Jun 1970, Oldham Co. (Croft, *KW* 48:39, 1972); 26/27 Jun 19—, Louisville area (Mengel:242); 27 Jun 1999, Fulton Co. (*KW* 75:60, 1999).

Late fall dates: "early Nov" 1952, Jefferson Co. (Croft, *KW* 48:39-40, 1972); 22 Oct 1950, south-central Kentucky (*KW* 38:12, 1962); 21 Oct 19—, Hopkins Co. (Bacon, *KW* 9:[16], 1933).

Summary of records by county

Allen (*KW* 59:41, 1983)
Ballard (B. Palmer-Ball, 1991 eBird data; *KW* 85:93:2009; *KW* 87:16, 2011)
Barren (*KW* 79:68, 2003)
Boone (Kemsies, et al., *KW* 25:49, 1950; K. Overman, 1982 eBird data)
Boyle (*KW* 64:46, 1988 [Note: original correspondence does not specifically place this report in Boyle Co.])
Bullitt (Mengel:242)
Calloway (Mengel:242; *KW* 63:50, 1987; *KW* 83:79, 2007)
Carlisle (B. Palmer-Ball, 1996 & 1998 eBird data)
Christian (*KW* 86:93, 2010; *KW* 87:114, 2011; *KW* 88:9, 2012; *KW* 92:60, 2016)
Daviess (*KW* 63:50, 1987)
Fayette (Mengel:242; *KW* 58:50, 1982)
Fulton (essentially annual in the w. portion along the Mississippi River)
Hardin (Mengel:242)
Henderson (*KW* 81:86, 2005; *KW* 91:8, 2015; *KW* 93:99, 2017; *KW* 94:7, 2018; *KW* 95:7, 2019)
Hickman (*KW* 64:46, 1988; *KW* 90:9, 2014)
Hopkins (Mengel:243; *KW* 87:88, 2011)
Jefferson (Mengel:242-243; Stamm, et al., *KW* 36:3-8, 1960; Stamm et al., *KW* 43:3-12, 1967; *KW* 60:43, 1984; *KW* 64:17, 1988; *KW* 79:9, 2003; *KW* 83:12, 2007; *KW* 92:7, 2016)
Larue (Mengel:242)
Livingston (B. Palmer-Ball, notes)
Logan (*KW* 90:9, 2014)
Lyon (*KW* 65:7, 1989)
Madison (*KW* 71:41, 1995; *KW* 87:88, 2011; *KW* 88:9/75, 2012)

Marshall (*KW* 64:17, 1988)
McCracken (*KW* 80:67, 2004)
Mercer (*KW* 65:67, 1989; B. Palmer-Ball, 2001 eBird data)
Muhlenberg (M. Vukovich, 2002 eBird data; *KW* 80:9, 2004; *KW* 93:7, 2017)
Oldham (B. Palmer-Ball, 1976 eBird data; *KW* 54:44, 1978: *KW* 59:41, 1983; *KW* 60:43, 1984; (*KW* 63:50, 1987)
Pulaski (*KW* 90:71, 2014)
Rowan (*KW* 83:12, 2007)
Shelby (*KW* 94:7, 2018)
Todd (Mengel:242; *KW* 91:70, 2015; *KW* 94:72, 2018)
Trigg (Mengel:242)
Union (*KW* 91:8, 2015)
Warren (essentially annual at and nr. the transient lakes n. of Woodburn)
Woodford (Mengel:242)

WHIMBREL *Numenius phaeopus*

Status: Extremely rare transient. This species is always a good find, typically occurring for only brief periods when inclement weather grounds migrants. Peak of abundance occurs from mid- to late May. The small number of fall migrants apparently pass through the region largely unnoticed. There are 24 records (22 during spring; two during fall).

Unaccepted records (most or all likely valid, but no details available): 6 May 2000, 3 over Ky Lake and Dam, Marshall Co., and later 2 over n. Lake Barkley, Lyon Co., and (vt.) at Ky Dam Village (*KW* 76:45, 2000; see *KW* 92:89, 2016); 17 May 2000, 1 (vt.) at Smithland Dam (*KW* 76:45, 2000; see *KW* 92:89, 2016); 17 May 2000, 15 birds at the Brown Power Plant, Mercer Co. (*NAB* 54:288, 2000; see *KW* 92:89, 2016); 17 May 2002, 4 at Morgan Pond (*KW* 78:50, 2002; see *KW* 92:89, 2016); 15 Aug 2006, 2 at the Falls of the Ohio (*KW* 83:12, 2007; see *KW* 92:89, 2016)

Chronological list of spring records (one individual unless otherwise indicated)

1) 12 May 1972, in flooded field below Ky Dam, Marshall Co. (Miller, *KW* 48:32-33, 1972)
2) 22 May 1974, in flight nr. Stanton, Powell Co. (*AB* 28:808, 1974)
3) 3 May 1989, (ph.) at Swan Lake WMA (Palmer-Ball, *KW* 66:28-29, 1990)
4) 7 May 1991, in flooded bottomlands west of Barlow, Ballard Co. (B. Palmer-Ball, eBird data)
5) 22 May 1993, 4 in a flooded field east of Fish Pond, Fulton Co. (*KW* 69:45, 1993; B. Palmer-Ball, eBird data)
6) 19 May 1994, 5 at McElroy Lake (B. Palmer-Ball, eBird data)
7) 23 May 1994, 2 at McElroy Lake (*KW* 70:52, 1994)
8) 19 May 1998, 17 (vt.) at McElroy Lake (Roemer, *KW* 74:92/94, 1998)
9) 28 May 1999, below Smithland Dam (*KW* 75:43, 1999)
10) 15 May 2000, 4 on the Ohio River nr. Smithland (F. Bennett, notes)
11) 19 May 2001, 5 (ph.) in the Lower Hickman Bottoms (B. Palmer-Ball/M. Monroe, eBird data)
12) 8 May 2002, (ph.) at McElroy Lake (*KW* 78:50, 2002)
13) 12 Apr 2010, at Lexington (*KW* 86:67, 2010)
14) 15 May 2010, 3 e. of Open Pond, Fulton Co. (*KW* 86:67, 2010)
15) 11 May 2012, 2 (ph.) on Ky Lake, Calloway Co. (*KW* 88:75, 2012)
16) 19 May 2013, (ph.) at Ky Bend, Fulton Co. (*KW* 89:70/74, 2013)
17) 22 May 2013, (ph.) at McElroy Lake (*KW* 89:70, 2013)
18) 22 Apr 2015, (ph.) in the Lower Hickman Bottoms (*KW* 91:70, 2015)
19) 23 Apr 2015, at McElroy Lake (*KW* 91:70, 2015)
20) 7-8 May 2015, 3 (ph.) in the Lower Hickman Bottoms (*KW* 91:70, 2015)
21) 15 May 2019, (ph.) at McElroy Lake (R. Waldrop et al., eBird data)
22) 6 Jun 2019, (ph.) in w. Henderson Co. (C. Crawford, eBird data)

Chronological list of fall records

1) 13 Jul 2010, (vt.) at McElroy Lake (*KW* 86:93, 2010)
2) 21-25 Jul 2013, (ph.) adjacent to Obion WMA (*KW* 89:95/104, 2013)

HUDSONIAN GODWIT *Limosa haemastica*

Status: Extremely rare transient. This species is another large shorebird that is a long-distance migrant that only rarely drops down to rest, most often during inclement weather. There are 13 records (six during spring and seven during fall).

Chronological list of spring records

1) 9 May 1969, collected (sp.) from a flooded field nr. Weir's Creek, ca. three miles south of Providence, Hopkins Co. (Monroe, *KW* 45:63, 1969)
2) 8 May 1971, at the Long Point Unit (Manning and Manning, *Migrant* 42:58-59,66, 1971)
3) 25 Apr 2007, 2 females (ph.) in w. Henderson Co. (*KW* 83:75/79, 2007)
4) 11-12 May 2008, a female (ph.) at McElroy Lake (*KW* 84:62/67, 2008)
5) 18 May 2008, a pair (ph.) at McElroy Lake (*KW* 84:62/66, 2008)
6) 3-4 Jun 2010, 4 (ph.) at McElroy Lake (*KW* 86:93/104, 2010)

Chronological list of fall records

1) 3 Oct 2000, a juv. at Kentucky Bend, Fulton Co. (Leggett, *KW* 77:36-37, 2001)
2) 31 Oct 2002, a juv. (ph.) at the Falls of the Ohio (*KW* 79:9, 2003)
3) 19 Sep 2003, at Blood River (*KW* 80:9, 2004)
4) 17-21 Sep 2009, an ad. (ph.) at Ballard WMA (*KW* 86:8/36, 2010)
5) 30 Aug 2014, an ad. (ph.) at Camp #11, Union Co. (*KW* 91:1/8, 2015)
6) 11 Sep 2014, an ad. (ph.) at Minor Clark Hatchery (*KW* 91:8/36, 2015)
7) 20 Aug 2018, 20 (ph.) over w. Henderson Co. (*KW* 95:7, 2019)

MARBLED GODWIT *Limosa fedoa*

Status: Extremely rare transient. There are 33 records (23 during spring; 10 during fall). This species is another large shorebird that is a long-distance migrant that only rarely drops down to rest, most often during inclement weather. A review of the summary of records for this species included below reveals that on only one occasion has a bird or flock remained for more than a single day.

Early spring dates: 11 Apr 2008, McElroy Lake (*KW* 84:62, 2008); 11 Apr 2011, McElroy Lake (*KW* 87:88, 2011).
Late spring dates: 10 May 1999, Ky Dam Village (*KW* 75:43, 1999); 4 May 2000, Falls of the Ohio (Dever, *KW* 76:50-51, 2000).
Early fall dates: 28 Jun 2013, Ky Bend, Fulton Co. (*KW* 89:95/104, 2013); 12 Jul 2005, at Ky Dam (*KW* 81:106, 2005).
Late fall dates: 25-26 Sep 2005, (ph.) Jonathan Creek (*KW* 82:8, 2006); 25 Sep 2010, Falls of the Ohio (*KW* 87:16, 2011).
Unaccepted record (certainly valid but no details available): 17 Sep 2002, 2 (vt.) below Smithland Dam (*KW* 79:9, 2003).

Chronological list of spring records (one individual unless otherwise noted)

1) 23 Apr 1977, with a flock of 25 Willets at the Falls of the Ohio (*AB* 31:1008, 1977; J. Elmore, notes)
2) 2 May 1983, in a flooded field in Oldham Co. (*KW* 59:41, 1983)
3) 29 Apr 1989, 4 (ph.) with a flock of 43 Willets at McElroy Lake (Palmer-Ball and Boggs, *KW* 67:60, 1991)
4) 19 Apr 1995, 2 at the Falls of the Ohio (B. Palmer-Ball, eBird data)
5) 30 Apr 1995, with a small flock of Willets at Freeman Lake (R. Healy, pers. comm.)
6) 22 Apr 1998, 5 (ph.) with a flock of 11 Willets at the Minor Clark Hatchery (*KW* 74:54, 1998)
7) 10 May 1999, (vt.) with 4 Willets at Ky Dam Village (*KW* 75:43, 1999; D. Roemer, notes)
8) 4 May 2000, at the Falls of the Ohio (Dever, *KW* 76:50-51, 2000)
9) 15 Apr 2001, 8 at Ballard WMA (*NAB* 55:306, 2001)
10) 22 Apr 2001, 15 at the Falls of the Ohio (*KW* 77:49, 2001)
11) 26 Apr 2003, (ph.) at Minor Clark Hatchery (*KW* 79:69, 2003)
12) 28 Apr 2003, 2 in flight over Lake Barkley, Livingston Co. (*KW* 79:69, 2003)

13) 21 Apr 2006, 20 (ph.) at the Paradise Power Plant (*KW* 82:68-69, 2006)
14) 19 Apr 2007, 37 (ph.) at Ky Dam Village (*KW* 83:75/79, 2007)
15) 11 Apr 2008, 10 (ph.) at McElroy Lake (*KW* 84:62, 2008)
16) 26 Apr 2008, at the Falls of the Ohio (*KW* 84:62, 2008)
17) 11 Apr 2011, 3 at McElroy Lake (*KW* 87:88, 2011)
18) 16 Apr 2011, at the WKU Farm, Warren Co. (*KW* 87:88/100, 2011)
19) 16 Apr 2012, (ph.) at the Falls of the Ohio (*KW* 88:75, 2012)
20) 26 Apr 2012, 21 at Blood River (*KW* 88:75, 2012)
21) 14 Apr 2018, 3 (ph.) at Freeman Lake (*KW* 94:72, 2018)
22) 30 Apr 2018, 3 (ph.) at Ky Dam Village (*KW* 94:72/96, 2018)
23) 28 Apr 2019, 5 (ph.) at McElroy Lake (R. Shive, eBird data)

Chronological list of fall records (one individual unless otherwise noted)

1) 9 Aug 1950, at the Falls of the Ohio (*AFN* 5:19, 1951)
2) 29 Aug 1976, at the Falls of the Ohio (*BO*, Sep 1976; J. Elmore, notes)
3) 20 Aug 1989, at Lake No. 9 (G. Knight, pers. comm.; *fide* J. Wilson, notes)
4) 17 Aug 1999, 2 below Smithland Dam (*KW* 77:35, 2001)
5) 1 Aug 2003, (ph.) at the former Camp #11 mine, Union Co. (*KW* 80:9, 2004)
6) 12 Jul 2005, 2 at Ky Dam (*KW* 81:106, 2005)
7) 25-26 Sep 2005, (ph.) at Jonathan Creek (*KW* 82:8, 2006)
8) 25 Sep 2010, at the Falls of the Ohio (*KW* 87:16, 2011)
9) 7 Sep 2012, (ph.) e. of Morganfield, Union Co. (*KW* 89:8, 2013)
10) 28 Jun 2013, (ph.) at Ky Bend, Fulton Co. (*KW* 89:95/104, 2013)

RUDDY TURNSTONE *Arenaria interpres*

Status: Rare to uncommon transient. Recorded chiefly west of the Cumberland Plateau. Most older records originated from the Falls of the Ohio and the transient lakes in Warren Co.; however, the species has now been reported at a few dozen scattered locales across central and western Kentucky. Most frequently encountered along open shorelines, bars, and flats of the larger lakes and rivers, but it should be expected to turn up, at least occasionally, at any of the better shorebird areas in the state. Peaks of abundance occur during mid-May and from mid-Aug to mid-Sep. The observation of a bird on a flat rooftop at Morehead, Rowan Co. (Barbour, *KW* 28:25, 1952) is unique. Most often seen singly or in small flocks of only a few birds, especially during fall.

Maximum spring counts: at least **74** at McElroy Lake, 20 May 2008 (*KW* 84:62, 2008); ca. **55** at McElroy Lake, 21 May 2008 (*KW* 84:62, 2008); **49** at McElroy Lake, 18 May 2008 (*KW* 84:62, 2008); **25** at Morgan Pond, Christian Co., 17 May 2002 (M. Bennett, notes); **22** at McElroy Lake, 22 May 1998 (*KW* 74:54, 1998; L. Doyle, pers. comm.; [number published incorrectly as 16 in *KW* 74:94, 1998]; **20** at McElroy Lake, 17 May 1997 (Roemer, et al., *KW* 73:79-83, 1997); **20** at McElroy Lake, 22 May 2015 (*KW* 91:70, 2015); **19** in McLean and Hopkins cos., 24 May 2011 (Palmer-Ball and Huber, *KW* 88:87-91, 2012); **15** at McElroy Lake, 19 May 1994 (B. Palmer-Ball, eBird data).

Maximum fall counts: **11** at the Falls of the Ohio, 28 Aug 1949 (Mengel:238); **11** at the Falls of the Ohio, 11 Sep 2014 (*KW* 91:8, 2015); **9** in the Upper Hickman Bottoms, 9 Sep 1993 (B. Palmer-Ball, eBird data); **9** at the Falls of the Ohio, 5 Sep 2008 (*KW* 85:14, 2009).

Early spring dates: 18 Apr 1987, Fulton Co. (*KW* 63:50, 1987); 19 Apr 1953, Warren Co. (*KW* 38:12, 1962); 30 Apr 2004, McElroy Lake (*KW* 80:67, 2004); 4 May 1998, McElroy Lake (*KW* 74:54, 1998); 4 May 2008, McElroy Lake (*KW* 84:62, 2008); 4 May 2012, Lake Barkley, Lyon Co. (*KW* 88:76, 2012); 5 May 2019, McElroy Lake (L. Combs/D. Svetich, eBird data); 7 May 1985, Falls of the Ohio (*KW* 61:45, 1985); 10 May 1976, Falls of the Ohio (*KW* 52:48, 1976); 10 May 2009, Chaney Lake (*KW* 85:69, 2009).

Late spring dates: 21 Jun 1998, Open Pond, Fulton Co. (*KW* 74:73, 1998); (ph.) 9 Jun 2010, McCracken Co. (*KW* 86:93, 2010); 6-7 Jun 1984, Falls of the Ohio (*KW* 60:53, 1984; B. Palmer-Ball, eBird data); 6 Jun 1998, McElroy Lake (Roemer, *KW* 74:94, 1998; J. Elmore, pers. comm.).

Early fall dates: 19 Jul 1980, Jefferson Co. (*KW* 56:79, 1980); 26 Jul 1978, Falls of the Ohio (B. Palmer-Ball, eBird data).

Late fall date: 21 Oct 1964 and 1966, Falls of the Ohio (Stamm, et al., *KW* 43:8, 1967).

RED KNOT *Calidris canutus*

Status: Transient (extremely rare during spring [although not conclusively documented; status based on historical sight records], extremely rare [formerly rare] during fall). This species actually has been reported fewer than 30 times in the state. There are only three spring sight records, all at the transient lakes in Warren Co. (see below). Especially the 1974 report lacks any details (including location of observation), and a photo-documented record for spring is highly desirable. Most historical fall records were from the Falls of the Ohio; however, most recent records have come from the western part of the state where shorebird habitat is more prevalent. The species could turn up at least occasionally at any of the better shorebird areas in the state during fall. A peak in abundance formerly occurred from late Aug to mid-Sep. Generally encountered singly, but occasionally in pairs or small flocks. **Federal Status**: Threatened.

Maximum counts: **4** at the Falls of the Ohio, 10 Sep 1959 (Stamm, et al., *KW* 36:6, 1960); **3** at the Falls of the Ohio, 26 Aug 1962 (Stamm, et al., *KW* 43:9, 1967; **3** at McElroy Lake, 2-10 Sep 1989 (Palmer-Ball and Boggs, *KW* 67:60, 1991); **3** in the Upper Hickman Bottoms, 6 Sep 1993 (B. Palmer-Ball, eBird data); **3** at Swan Lake WMA, 18/20 Sep 1993 (*KW* 70:8, 1994 [location erroneously published as Calloway Co. therein; *fide* H. Chambers, notes]/B. Palmer-Ball, eBird data).

Early/late spring dates: see below.

Early fall dates: 1-3 Aug 1978, Ky Lake, Calloway Co. (*KW* 55:15, 1979; J.T. Erwin, notes); 20 Aug 1967, Falls of the Ohio (*KW* 52:49, 1976).

Late fall dates: 19-24 Nov 2000, Marshall Co. (*KW* 77:6, 2001); 4-6 Nov 2000, Marshall Co. (*KW* 77: 6, 2001); 18-20 Sep 1993, Ballard Co. (B. Palmer-Ball, eBird data; *KW* 70:8, 1994 [location erroneously published as Marshall Co. therein]); 16 Sep 1961, Falls of the Ohio (Stamm, et al., *KW* 43: 9, 1967).

Chronological list of spring records

1) 16 May 1956, 1 or 2 [contradictory information on the number of birds in the following cited sources] at McElroy Lake (Wilson, *KW* 32:60-61, 1956; *KW* 38:13, 1962)
2) 20-26 Apr 1963, 1 at Chaney Lake (Wilson, *KW* 40:19, 1964)
3) 20 Apr 1974, 1 at one of the above transient lakes (*KW* 50:42, 1974)

Summary of fall records by county

Ballard (*KW* 65:7, 1989; *KW* 70:8, 1994 [location erroneously published as Calloway Co. therein; *fide* H. Chambers, notes]/B. Palmer-Ball, 1993 eBird data)

Calloway (J.T. Erwin, 1977 notes; *KW* 55:15, 1979; *KW* 76:6, 2000)

Fulton (B. Monroe Jr./M. Monroe, 1983 eBird data; B. Palmer-Ball, 1993 eBird data)

Hickman (H. Chambers, 1997 notes)

Jefferson (Monroe and Mengel, *Wilson Bulletin* 54:138-139, 1942; Stamm, et al., *KW* 36:6, 1960; Stamm, et al., *KW* 43:9, 1967; *KW* 52:49, 1976; *KW* 61:16, 1985/B. Palmer-Ball, 1984 eBird data; *KW* 63:8-9, 1987)

Marshall (*KW* 70:8, 1994; B. Palmer-Ball, 1997 eBird data; *KW* 77:6, 2001; *KW* 84:8, 2008)

Warren (Palmer-Ball and Boggs, *KW* 67:60, 1991)

RUFF *Calidris pugnax*

Status: Extremely rare transient. A definite peak of abundance occurs from late Mar to mid-Apr. As is apparent from the list of records, the species could turn up at any shorebird spot across the state. There are 12 records (10 during spring, one during summer, and one during fall).

Chronological list of records

1) 4 May 1968, on a farm pond in Boyle Co. (Loetscher, *KW* 44:43-44, 1968)
2) 17 Apr 1987, (ph.) at the Long Point Unit (Palmer-Ball, *KW* 64:23, 1988)
3) 1 Apr 1989, presumed male ne. of Harrodsburg, Mercer Co. (*KW* 65:67, 1989; W. Kemper, pers. comm.)
4) 17-18 Apr 1997, a male (ph.) e. of the Sauerheber Unit (*KW* 74:27, 1998; B. Palmer-Ball, eBird data)

5) 17 Apr 1997, a female nr. Geneva, Henderson Co. (*KW* 74:27, 1998; B. Palmer-Ball, eBird data)
6) 7-8 Sep 2001, a juv. (ph.) on the Mississippi River, Carlisle Co. (B. Palmer-Ball, eBird data; *NAB* 56:58, 2002 [date erroneously published as 8-9 Sep therein])
7) 23-28 Apr 2002, a female (ph.) at Morgan Pond, Christian Co. (*KW* 78:50, 2002)
8) 8 Jul 2006, an ad. male (ph.) at Minor Clark Hatchery (*KW* 82:77/82, 2006)
9) 27-28 Apr 2008, a female (ph.) at McElroy Lake (*KW* 84:63/66, 2008)
10) 17 May 2015, a female or "faedor" male (ph.) at McElroy Lake (*KW* 91:70, 2015)
11) 17-18 Mar 2016, a male (ph.) in the Lower Hickman Bottoms (*KW* 92:60, 2016)
12) 1 Apr 2016, a male (ph.) in the Lower Hickman Bottoms (*KW* 92:60/62, 2016)

Unaccepted record: 12 Apr 1969, at Chaney Lake (J. Croft, pers. comm.); this is probably a reliable record, but has been located only in handwritten notes of an anonymous birder who was in the observing party.

STILT SANDPIPER *Calidris himantopus*

Status: Transient (rare to uncommon during spring, uncommon to fairly common during fall). Recorded chiefly west of the Cumberland Plateau. This shorebird is a relatively good find during the spring, but it is more widespread during fall when the species can be relatively numerous in the western third of the state. Encountered in a variety of shallow aquatic habitats but most frequently found along muddy shorelines of lakes, ponds and flooded fields. Peaks of abundance occur during mid-May and from late Jul to late Sep. Generally seen singly or in small groups of fewer than ten birds, often in the company of yellowlegs and dowitchers.

Maximum spring counts: **55** at McElroy Lake, 20 May 1997 (Roemer, et al., *KW* 73:79-83, 1997); **50+** at McElroy Lake, 14 May 2008 (*KW* 84:63, 2008).

Maximum fall counts: **175** at Lake No. 9, 24 Sep 1983 (*KW* 60:17, 1984); **130** at Lake No. 9, 1 Sep 1984 (*KW* 61:16-17, 1985); **94** in w. Henderson Co., 10 Sep 2015 (*KW* 92:7, 2016); **68** adjacent to Obion WMA 20 Jul 2013 (*KW* 89:96, 2013); **42** on the Casey Creek embayment of Green River Lake, Adair Co., 16 Oct 2008 (*KW* 85:15, 2009); **30-35** at McElroy Lake, 2-8 Sep 1989 (Palmer-Ball and Boggs, *KW* 67:61, 1991); **32** at Lake No. 9, 4 Sep 1989 (G. Criswell, eBird data); **31** at Lake No. 9, 7 Aug 1987 (G. Criswell, eBird data); **30** in s. Jefferson Co., 4 Sep 2006 (*KW* 83:13, 2007); **30** at Swallow Spring Pond, Christian Co., 19 Sep 2016 (*KW* 93:8, 2017).

Early spring dates: 5 Mar 2017, Warren Co. (*KW* 93:72, 2017); 12 Mar 1952, McElroy Lake (*KW* 38:13, 1962); 26 Mar 1988, Fulton Co. (*KW* 64:47, 1988); 28 Mar 2014, w. Fulton Co. (*KW* 90:71, 2014); 28 Mar 2016, (ph.) Sauerheber Unit (*KW* 92:60, 2016).

Late spring dates: 2 Jun 2016, (ph.) at Morgan Pond (*KW* 92:79, 2016); 31 May 1996, Fulton Co. (B. Palmer-Ball, eBird data); 30 May 1998, McElroy Lake (Roemer, *KW* 74:95, 1998); 30 May 1999, Henderson Co. (*KW* 75:43, 1999); 30 May 2008, McElroy Lake (*KW* 84:63, 2008).

Early fall dates: 28 Jun 2010, McElroy Lake (*KW* 86:94, 2010); 8 Jul 1998, McElroy Lake (Roemer, *KW* 74:95, 1998); 8 Jul 2009, w. Henderson Co. (*KW* 85:93, 2009); 10 Jul 1994, McElroy Lake (B. Palmer-Ball, eBird data); 11 Jul 2000, Fulton Co. (*KW* 76:56, 2000); 11 Jul 2010, Logan Co. (*KW* 86:94, 2010).

Late fall dates: 30 Nov 1984, LBL (*KW* 61:17, 1985; C. Peterson, pers. comm.); 8 Nov 1983, Marshall Co. (*KW* 60:17, 1984); 6 Nov 1991, Marshall Co. (*KW* 68:8, 1992); 6 Nov 2000, Marshall Co. (*KW* 77:7, 2001); 3 Nov 2010, Union Co. (*KW* 87:17, 2011); 28 Oct 1972, Louisville area (*KW* 52:50, 1976); 28 Oct 1990, Hopkins Co. (*KW* 67:7, 1991).

CURLEW SANDPIPER *Calidris ferruginea*

Status: Accidental vagrant. This Eurasian shorebird has been documented in Kentucky on two occasions.

Chronological list of records

1) 9-11 Jul 1994, an ad. in worn breeding plumage (ph.) at McElroy Lake (Palmer-Ball and Klapheke, *KW* 70:87-88, 1994)
2) 20 Sep 1995, a juv. (ph.) at the Falls of the Ohio (*KW* 73:28, 1997; M. Monroe/B. Palmer-Ball, eBird data)

RED-NECKED STINT *Calidris ruficollis*

Status: Accidental vagrant. This Eurasian species is very infrequently reported in the eastern United States; it has been reported on one occasion in Kentucky.

1) 20-22 Aug 2017, an ad. in worn breeding plumage (ph.) in w. Henderson Co. (Crawford and Palmer-Ball, *KW* 94:37-38, 2018; *KW* 94:7/40, 2018).

SANDERLING *Calidris alba*

Status: Transient (extremely rare to rare during spring, uncommon to fairly common during fall). Recorded chiefly along the Ohio and Mississippi rivers, but regularly occurs at all of the state's better shorebird areas, especially during fall. In contrast, this species is much less numerous during spring, but increased field effort in recent years has shown it to be regular in small numbers, especially during late May. This shorebird prefers bars and shorelines of sand and gravel to any other habitat, but also occurs occasionally on mudflats and rocky shorelines. Generally found singly or in small flocks of up to a half-dozen birds, but occasionally seen in larger groups, especially during fall.

Maximum spring counts: **21** at McElroy Lake, 27 May 1998 (Roemer, *KW* 74:93-94, 1998); **18** (likely a different group) at McElroy Lake, 22 May 1998 (D. Roemer, notes); **17** on the Ohio River, Livingston Co., 24 May 1999 (B. Palmer-Ball, eBird data); **16** in Union Co., 24 May 2001 (B. Palmer-Ball, eBird data).

Maximum fall counts: **56** on the Mississippi River, Carlisle Co., 19 Sep 2000 (*KW* 77:6, 2001); ca. **45** on the Mississippi River, Carlisle Co., 23 Sep 2000 (*KW* 77:6, 2001); **34** on the Mississippi River at Kentucky Bend, Fulton Co., 28 Sep 1999 (*KW* 76:6, 2000); **30** at the Falls of the Ohio, 14 Sep 1980 (*KW* 57:22, 1981); **20-30** at the Falls of the Ohio, [no date] (Monroe and Mengel, *KW* 15:43, 1939); **28** on the Mississippi River, Carlisle Co., 20 Sep 1987 (*KW* 64:17, 1988); at least **18** at Blood River, 23 Sep 2008 (*KW* 85:14, 2009); **16** at the Falls of the Ohio, 7-8 Sep 2011 (*KW* 88:9, 2012).

Early spring date: 19 Apr 1963, Chaney Lake (*KW* 45:35, 1969).

Late spring dates: 10-11 Jun 2009, Mississippi River, Hickman Co. (*KW* 85:93, 2009); 5 Jun 1998, McElroy Lake (Roemer, *KW* 74:94, 1998); 2 Jun 2001, Union Co. (*NAB* 55:440, 2001); 29 May 2014, Hickman Co. (*KW* 90:71, 2014); 27 May 1994, McElroy Lake (B. Palmer-Ball, eBird data); 27 May 1984, Fulton Co. (*KW* 60:43, 1984); 27 May 1999, Ohio River in Union Co. (B. Palmer-Ball, eBird data).

Early fall dates: 12 Jul 1973, Louisville area (*KW* 52:50, 1976); 14 Jul 1994, McElroy Lake (B. Palmer-Ball, eBird data).

Late fall dates: 17 Nov 1995, Rowan Co. (*KW* 72:5, 1996); 10 Nov 1984, Lake Barkley (*KW* 61:16, 1985); 5 Nov 1974, Calloway Co. (Miller and Peterson, *KW* 51:31, 1975 [date published incorrectly as 9 Nov in *KW* 51:32, 1975]; M. Miller, notes).

DUNLIN *Calidris alpina*

Status: Uncommon to locally fairly common transient, extremely rare during mid-summer and mid-winter. Recorded chiefly west of the Cumberland Plateau. Encountered in a variety of shallow aquatic habitats from farm ponds and flooded fields to the shorelines, bars and mudflats of the larger lakes and rivers. Peaks of abundance occur from late Apr to late May and from early Oct to early Nov. This shorebird is a late fall migrant and small numbers occasionally linger into early winter, as evidenced by a number of Dec and several Jan records. In addition, on a few occasions small numbers have appeared to winter during milder years (see below). There are two mid-summer records that have not been accompanied by extensive details, but which have been accepted provisionally herein (see below). Usually seen in small flocks of up to a dozen birds, but occasionally encountered in larger flocks of several dozen or more individuals.

Maximum spring counts: at least **1020** total in scattered flocks (including at least 512 along Narge Creek, Hopkins Co.) in ne. Hopkins Co. and n. McLean Co., 20 May 2011 (Palmer-Ball and Huber, *KW* 88:88, 2012); at least **800** w. of Buttonsberry, McLean Co., 24 May 2011 (Palmer-Ball and Huber, *KW* 88:91, 2012); **539+** at McElroy Lake, 23 May 1998 (D. and J. Elmore, notes; Roemer,

KW 74:93/95, 1998); **350-400** at McElroy Lake, 18 May 2008 (*KW* 84:63, 2008); **300** in w. Fulton Co. (106 at Obion WMA and 194 at Open Pond), 18 May 2018 (*KW* 94:72, 2018; H. Chambers/M. Easley, eBird data); **234** nr. the Sauerheber Unit, 19 May 2006 (*KW* 82:69, 2006); at least **225** at Horseshoe Road Slough, w. Henderson Co., 27 Apr 2012 (*KW* 88:76, 2012); **200** in w. Henderson Co., 5 May 2005 (*KW* 81:87, 2005); **200** at the Sauerheber Unit, 4 May 2018 (*KW* 94:72, 2018); **150+** at McElroy Lake, 14 May 1997 (Roemer, et al., *KW* 73:79-83, 1997); **150+** at Morgan Pond, 19 May 2002 (*KW* 78:50, 2002); ca. **150** at Morgan Pond, 16 May 2016 (*KW* 92:60, 2016); **133** at McElroy Lake, 16 May 2004 (*KW* 80:67, 2004); **117** at the Sauerheber Unit, 18 Apr 2017 (*KW* 93:72, 2017); **103** in the Lower Hickman Bottoms, 4 May 2018 (C. Bliznick, eBird data); **100+** at Jonathan Creek, 10 Mar 1986 (*KW* 62:43, 1986); ca. **100** at the Sauerheber Unit, 3 May 2016 (*KW* 92:60, 2016); **80** in Marshall Co., 28 Mar 1992 (*KW* 68:46, 1992); **80** at McElroy Lake, 17-21 May 2010 (*KW* 86:68, 2010).

Maximum fall counts: **200+** at Minor Clark Hatchery, 29-31 Oct 2002 (*KW* 79:9, 2003); **157** at Blood River, 7 Nov 2017 (*KW* 94:7, 2018); **151** at McElroy Lake, 24 Oct 2002 (*KW* 79:9, 2003); **150** at the Sauerheber Unit, 7 Nov 2017 (*KW* 94:7, 2018); two flocks totaling **136** at the Falls of the Ohio, 29 Oct 2002 (*KW* 79:9, 2003); **112** at the Falls of the Ohio, 29 Oct 1984 (*KW* 61:16, 1985); **99** at Jonathan Creek, 11 Nov 2002 (*KW* 79:9, 2003); **93** at Blood River, 29 Oct 2015 (*KW* 92:7, 2016); **85** at Jonathan Creek, 10 Nov 2006 (*KW* 83:13, 2007); **79** at Fishing Creek, Lake Cumberland, Pulaski Co., 6 Nov 2003 (*KW* 80:9, 2004); **73** at Blood River, 1 Nov 2005 (*KW* 82:9, 2006); **72** at Jonathan Creek, 10 Nov 2015 (*KW* 92:7, 2016); **65** at Green River Lake, Adair Co., 24/31 Oct 2009 (*KW* 86:9, 2010); **54** at Jonathan Creek, 5 Nov 2000 (R. Denton, eBird data); **52** in Union Co., 31 Oct 2010 (*KW* 87:17, 2011); **50** at the Minor Clark Hatchery, 23 Oct 1984 (*KW* 61:16, 1985); **50** at the Sauerheber Unit, 28 Oct 2009 (*KW* 86:9, 2010).

Early spring dates (other than wintering birds): 13 Feb 2003, Blood River (*KW* 79:47, 2003); 16 Feb 2012, Sauerheber Unit (*KW* 88:47-48, 2012); 22 Feb 2003, McElroy Lake (*KW* 79:47, 2003); 26 Feb 2011, Sauerheber Unit (J. Meredig, eBird data); 2 Mar 2017, Sauerheber Unit (*KW* 93:72, 2017); 3 Mar 2003, McElroy Lake (*KW* 79:69, 2003); 8 Mar 2009, Chaney Lake (*KW* 85:69, 2009); (100+) at Jonathan Creek, 10 Mar 1986 (*KW* 62:43, 1986); 13 Mar 2009, Blood River (*KW* 85:69, 2009); 14 Mar 2016, McElroy Lake (*KW* 92:60, 2016); 15 Mar 2010, Chaney Lake (*KW* 86:68, 2010); 21 Mar 1992, Minor Clark Hatchery (*KW* 68:46, 1992); 21 Mar 2016, Sauerheber Unit (*KW* 92:60, 2016); 22 Mar 1992, Henderson Co. (B. Palmer-Ball, eBird data); 22 Mar 2011, McElroy Lake (*KW* 87:89, 2011); 23 Mar 2009, Sauerheber Unit (*KW* 85:69, 2009); 26 Mar 1999, McElroy Lake (D. Roemer, notes); 27 Mar 2007, Union Co. (*KW* 83:80, 2007); 27 Mar 2018, Ohio Co. (*KW* 94:72, 2018); 28 Mar 1992, Fulton Co. (*KW* 68:46, 1992).

Late spring dates: bird with a limp lingered to at least 25 Jun 1997, Morgan Pond (B. Palmer-Ball, eBird data); 15 Jun 2011, McElroy Lake (*KW* 87:114, 2011); 11 Jun 2009, Fulton Co. (*KW* 85:93, 2009); 10 Jun 2005, Union Co. (*KW* 81:106, 2005); 10 Jun 2009, Hickman Co. (*KW* 85:93, 2009); 9 Jun 2015, Morgan Pond (*KW* 91:86, 2015); 8 Jun 1998, McElroy Lake (Roemer, *KW* 74:95, 1998); 7 Jun 2017, Fulton Co. (*KW* 93:99, 2017); 6 Jun 2015, w. Henderson Co. (*KW* 91:86, 2015); 5 Jun 2003, Morgan Pond (*KW* 79:82, 2003); 5 Jun 2009, w. Henderson Co. (*KW* 85:93, 2009); 4 Jun 2005, nr. the Sauerheber Unit (*KW* 81:106, 2005); 2 Jun 2001, Union Co. (B. Palmer-Ball, eBird data).

Out-of-season records (summer): 13 Jul 1996, Ballard Co. (*KW* 72:74, 1996); 4 Aug 1981, Ky Lake (*KW* 58:15, 1982).

Early fall dates: 1 Sep 1973, Falls of the Ohio (*KW* 52:49, 1976; *AB* 28:60, 1974); 4 Sep 1977, Ky Lake, Calloway Co. (J.T. Erwin, notes); 5 Sep 1975, Ky Lake, Calloway Co. (J.T. Erwin, notes); 10-17 Sep 2015, (ph.) w. Henderson Co. (*KW* 92:7, 2016); 14 Sep 1963, Falls of the Ohio (Stamm, et al., *KW* 43:10, 1967); 20 Sep 1978, Ky Lake (*KW* 55:16, 1979); 21 Sep 1983, Green River Lake, Adair Co. (*KW* 60:17, 1984); 24 Sep 1983, Ky Lake, Calloway Co. (*KW* 59:56, 1983; J.T. Erwin, pers. comm.); 26 Sep 1992, Falls of the Ohio (B. Palmer-Ball, eBird data); 25 Sep 2006, Sauerheber Unit (*KW* 83:13, 2007).

Late fall/winter dates: (regularly lingers into mid-Dec with small numbers occasionally lingering into early to mid-Jan): 18 Jan 2001 (2) at Blood River (*KW* 77:29, 2001); (2) at the Sauerheber Unit, 18 Jan 2010 (*KW* 86:44, 2010); 12 Jan 2008, (3) Barren River Lake (*KW* 84:44, 2008); 9 Jan 2004, Barren River Lake (*KW* 80:43, 2004); 30 Dec 2017, Allen Co. (*KW* 94:24, 2018); 26 Dec 2014, (16) at Barren River Lake (*KW* 91:52, 2015).

Out-of-season records (mid-winter): 26 Jan 1983, Brown Power Plant, Mercer Co. (*KW* 59:29, 1983); 27 Jan 1995 (3) at Minor Clark Hatchery (*KW* 71:26, 1995); 29 Jan 1995 (10) at Jonathan

Creek (B. Palmer-Ball, eBird data [erroneously published as 28 Jan in previous edition of this work]);

Unaccepted records: 10-14 Sep 1972, (8) in Hancock Co. (Alsop, *KW* 49:18-19, 1973); 21 Sep 1983, (6) at Minor Clark Hatchery (*KW* 60:17, 1984); in addition, a few of the early fall dates included above were not well-documented, but are accepted provisionally.

Summary of records that appear to demonstrate wintering by county

Allen/Barren (Barren River Lake [winter 2010-2011 (*KW* 87:61, 2011)])
Henderson (Sauerheber Unit [winter 2007-2008 (*KW* 84:44/63, 2008)]; [winter 2012-2013 (*KW* 89:48/71, 2013; J. Meredig/B. Lisowsky/C. Crawford, 2013 eBird data)])
Marshall (Jonathan Creek [winter 1992-93 (*KW* 69:34, 1993)])

BAIRD'S SANDPIPER *Calidris bairdii*

Status: Transient (extremely rare to rare during spring, uncommon during fall). Recorded chiefly west of the Cumberland Plateau, but fairly widespread during the fall migratory season, when it appears to be annual at least as far east as Minor Clark Hatchery. In contrast, the species is not seen annually during spring, when there are only a few photo-documented reports from Louisville westward (see below). Interestingly, the only report from eastern Kentucky occurred during spring (see below). Peaks of abundance occur from late Apr to early May and from mid-Aug to late Sep. Generally encountered on open shorelines and mudflats on the larger lakes and rivers, but seems to occur regularly at all of the better shorebird spots in the state during fall. Usually seen singly or in small groups of only a few birds.

Maximum spring counts: 9 (ph.) in Union Co., 21 Apr 2004 (*KW* 80:67, 2004); 5 at McElroy Lake, 1 May 1997 (Roemer, et al., *KW* 73:79-83, 1997).
Maximum fall counts: 13 at the Falls of the Ohio, 10 Aug 1963 (Stamm, et al., *KW* 43:10, 1967); 11 at Ballard WMA, 17 Aug 1991 (B. Palmer-Ball, eBird data).
Early spring dates: 26/31 Mar 2014, (ph.) at Parson's Pond, Logan Co. (*KW* 90:7/84, 2014); 31 Mar/4 Apr 2005, (ph.) at Chaney Lake (*KW* 81:87, 2005); 4 Apr 1959, Warren Co. (*KW* 38:13, 1962); 12 Apr 1987, (ph.) in Union Co. (*KW* 63:50, 1987).
Late spring dates: 9 May 2008, McElroy Lake (*KW* 84:63, 2008); 9 May 2016, (ph.) at Louisville (*KW* 92:60/63, 2016); 8 May 2002, McElroy Lake (*KW* 78:50, 2002; D. Roemer, videotape/notes); 7 May 1999, (vt.) in Muhlenberg Co. (D. Roemer, notes); 7 May 2002, Walton's Pond, Warren Co. (*KW* 78:50, 2002; D. Roemer, notes); 7 May 2010, Fulton Co. (*KW* 86:68, 2010); 5 May 1997, McElroy Lake (Roemer, et al., *KW* 73:79-83, 1997).
Early fall dates: 22 Jul 1962 (*KW* 52:49, 1976); 22 Jul 2000, Muhlenberg Co. (*KW* 76:56, 2000); 27 Jul 2012, Falls of the Ohio (*KW* 88:94, 2012).
Late fall dates: 26 Nov 1969, Ky Lake, Calloway Co. (Peterson, *KW* 46:47-48, 1970); 8 Nov 1984, Minor Clark Hatchery (*KW* 61:16, 1985); 4 Nov 1984, Falls of the Ohio (*KW* 61:16, 1985); 4 Nov 1983, Fishing Creek, Lake Cumberland, Pulaski Co. (*KW* 60:17, 1984).
Unaccepted records: those during spring/early summer later than the late spring date of 9 May given above and including: 13 Jun 1937, Warren Co. (Mengel: 249); 11 Jun 1968, McElroy Lake (*KW* 45:34, 1969); 14 May 1980, Louisville (*KW* 56:61, 1980); 15 May 1981, Louisville (*KW* 57:57, 1981); 20 May-1 Jun 1990, Rowan Co. (*KW* 66:57/87, 1990); 17 May 1992, Rowan Co. (*KW* 68:46, 1992); 19 May 1999, Rowan Co. (*KW* 75:43, 1999); 14/29 May 2002, Rowan Co. (*KW* 78:50, 2002). Also 9 Nov 1974, (20) in Calloway Co. (Miller and Peterson, *KW* 51:31, 1975).

List of photo-documented spring records by county

Jefferson (9 May 2016 [*KW* 92:60/63, 2016])
Logan (26/31 Mar 2014 [*KW* 90:7/84, 2014; F. Lyne, eBird data])
Muhlenberg (7 May 1999 [D. Roemer, notes])
Union (12 Apr 1987 [*KW* 63:50, 1987; B. Palmer-Ball, eBird data]; 21 Apr 2004 [*KW* 80:67, 2004])
Warren (8 May 2002 [*KW* 78:50, 2002; D. Roemer, notes]; 31 Mar/4 Apr 2005 [*KW* 81:87, 2005])

List of spring records east of Louisville

Breathitt (28 Apr-4 May 1974 [Allaire, *KW* 50:39, 1974])

LITTLE STINT *Calidris minuta*

Status: Accidental vagrant. This Eurasian species is reported very infrequently in the eastern United States; it has been documented only once in Kentucky.

1) 16-20 Aug 2006, an ad. in worn breeding plumage (ph.) at Louisville (Palmer-Ball, *KW* 83:37-40, 2007; *KW* 83:1/13, 2007)

LEAST SANDPIPER *Calidris minutilla*

Status: Common transient, extremely rare to locally uncommon during winter; extremely rare during summer. Generally the most widespread of the peep species other than during mid- to late May when Semipalmated Sandpipers outnumber all others. Encountered in a great variety of shallow aquatic habitats from the margins of farm ponds to mudflats and shorelines of flooded fields and the larger lakes and rivers. Peaks of abundance occur from late Apr to mid-May and from late Jul to early Oct. There are several Jun records between the normal spring and fall migratory periods. Lingering fall birds occasionally remain at favorable locations until the first severe winter weather. Prior to 1998 there was but one mid-winter record; however, in subsequent years the number of winter reports has gradually increased, and wintering has now been demonstrated at no fewer than three sites and most regularly on bays of Ky Lake (see below). The increase in the number of mid- and late winter records has also clouded the arrival date of spring migrants, which seem to be arriving earlier and earlier. Usually encountered in small groups of up to several dozen birds, but occasionally seen in flocks of a hundred or more.

Maximum spring counts: **2000+** at McElroy Lake, 9 May 2008 (*KW* 84:62, 2008); **800-1000+** at McElroy Lake, 18 May 2008 (*KW* 84:62, 2008); ca. **700** at Ledford, Fulton Co., 7 May 2010 (*KW* 86:67, 2010); at least **560** in the Lower Hickman Bottoms (including at least 350 at the Long Point Unit), Fulton Co., 28 Apr 2012 (*KW* 88:76, 2012); **450** at McElroy Lake, 12 May 2018 (*KW* 94:72, 2018); at least **400** at Morgan Pond, 10 May 2013 (*KW* 89:70, 2013); **280** in s. Jefferson Co., 9 May 2016 (*KW* 92:60, 2016); **250-300+** at Swallow Spring Pond, Christian Co., 7 May 2008 (*KW* 84:62, 2008); **250** at McElroy Lake, 5 May 1989 (Palmer-Ball and Boggs, *KW* 67:61, 1991); **220** at the Paradise Power Plant, 11 May 2006 (*KW* 82:69, 2006).

Maximum fall counts: **1059** at Lake No. 9, 23 Sep 2000 (*KW* 77:6, 2001); **750** at Lake No. 9, 4 Oct 1986 (*KW* 63:9, 1987); **500** at Lake No. 9, 21 Oct 1986 (*KW* 63:9, 1987); **475+** in the Upper Hickman Bottoms and **100+** at Open Pond, both 20 Aug 2013 (*KW* 90:10, 2014); ca. **300** at Lake No. 9, 29 Jul 2008 (*KW* 84:87, 2008 [location erroneously published as Open Pond therein]); at least **300** at Open Pond, Fulton Co., 11 Sep 2013 (*KW* 90:10, 2014); **300** in w. Henderson Co., 14 Jul 2017 (*KW* 93:99, 2017).

Maximum winter count: 109 at Jonathan Creek, 29 Jan 2007 (*KW* 83:48, 2007).

Early spring dates (other than probable wintering birds): 13 Feb 2017, w. Fulton Co. (*KW* 93:49, 2017); 16/17 Feb 2008, (4) at Guthrie Swamp, Todd Co. (*KW* 84:44, 2008) with 14 there 2 Mar 2008 (*KW* 84:62, 2008); 16 Feb 2012, (4) Sauerheber Unit (*KW* 88:47, 2012); 18 Feb 2012, (2) in Hart Co. (*KW* 88:47, 2012); 18 Feb 2013, (3) in Hart Co. (*KW* 89:48/70, 2013); 20 Feb 2009, (2) at Chaney Lake (*KW* 85:49, 2009); 21 Feb 2016, McElroy Lake (*KW* 92:43, 2016); 23 Feb 2013, (14) Sauerheber Unit (*KW* 89:48/70, 2013); 24 Feb 2007, (3) Sauerheber Unit (*KW* 83:48, 2007); 27 Feb 2017, (4) nr. the Long Point Unit (*KW* 93:49, 2017); 2 Mar 2008, Sauerheber Unit (*KW* 84:62, 2008); 3 Mar 2018, (6) in Hart Co. (J. Sole, eBird data); 5 Mar 2009, (5) Green River Lake, Adair Co. (*KW* 85:69, 2009); 7 Mar 2003, McElroy Lake (*KW* 79:69, 2003); 7 Mar 2012, (6) Lower Hickman Bottoms (H. Chambers, eBird data); 8 Mar 2003, McElroy Lake (*KW* 79:69, 2003 [date erroneously published as 7 Mar therein]); 9 Mar 2002, (3) at Petersburg, Boone Co. (*KW* 78:50, 2002 [possibly same birds observed 3-24 Nov 2001 at same location (*KW* 78:7, 2002) and wintered?]); 9 Mar 2002, (3) at Green River Lake, Adair Co. (*KW* 78:50, 2002)); 10 Mar 2002, Calloway Co. (H. Chambers, notes); 10 Mar 2016, McElroy Lake (*KW* 92:60, 2016); 11 Mar 2001, Calloway Co. (*KW* 77:49, 2001); 11 Mar 2006, Greenup Co. (*KW* 82:69, 2006); 12 Mar 2010, s. Jefferson Co. (E. Huber, eBird data); 12 Mar 2011, McElroy Lake (*KW* 87:89, 2011); 12 Mar 2014, Logan Co. (*KW* 90:71, 2014); 15 Mar 2002, Henderson Co. (D. Roemer, notes); 15 Mar 2010, (3) at Chaney Lake (*KW* 86:67, 2010); 17 Mar 1990, McElroy Lake (B. Palmer-Ball, eBird data); 17 Mar 2008, McElroy Lake (*KW* 84:62, 2008); 17 Mar 2017, Sauerheber Unit (K. Michalski, eBird data).

Late fall/early winter dates: individuals occasionally linger into early winter, the latest being 9 Jan 2004, (2) at Barren River Lake (*KW* 80:43, 2004); 8 Jan 2003, Muhlenberg Co. (*KW* 79:47, 2003); 6 Jan 1981 at Louisville (*KW* 57:37, 1981); 6 Jan 2002, Calloway Co. (*KW* 78:33, 2002); 5 Jan 2013, Sauerheber Unit (J. Meredig, eBird data); 4 Jan 2004, Lower Hickman Bottoms (*KW* 80:43, 2004); 2 Jan 2000, (7) in Muhlenberg Co. (D. O'Brien, eBird data) and (9) in s. Logan Co. (D. Roemer, notes); 1 Jan 2014 (8) at Guthrie Swamp, Todd Co. (*KW* 90:49, 2014); 1 Jan 2016, Sauerheber Unit (*KW* 92:43, 2016).

Out-of-season records (during mid-winter away from established wintering areas): 30 Jan 1967, (4) at LBL, Trigg Co. (*AFN* 21:425, 1967); 30 Jan 1998, (4) at Jonathan Creek (*KW* 74:33, 1998 [date erroneously published as 30 Dec therein]); 15 Jan 2000, (34) at Jonathan Creek (D. Roemer, notes); 18 Jan 2000, (8) in Ohio Co. and (7) in Muhlenberg Co. (*NAB* 54:184, 2000; D. Roemer, notes); 24 Jan 2000, (2) at Lake Barkley, Lyon Co. (*KW* 76:30, 2000 [date erroneously published as 21 Jan therein (*fide* D. Roemer, notes)]); 4/8 Jan 2003, Muhlenberg Co. (*KW* 79:47, 2003); 14 Jan 2006, (16) in w. Fulton Co. (*KW* 82:47, 2006); 18 Jan 2010, Sauerheber Unit (*KW* 86:44, 2010); 4 Feb 2010, (2) on Cravens Bay, Lake Barkley, Lyon Co. (*KW* 86:44, 2010); 1 Jan 2014, (8) at Guthrie Swamp, Todd Co. (*KW* 90:49, 2014); 17 Jan 2016, (8) at Barren River Lake (*KW* 92:43, 2016); 3-21 Jan 2016, s. Jefferson Co. (*KW* 92:43, 2016); 22 Jan 2017, n. of Franklin Crossroads, Hardin Co. (*KW* 93:49, 2017); 4-11 Feb 2017, Frogue Pond, (ph.) Todd Co. (*KW* 93:49, 2017); 15-17 Jan 2018, Lexington (L. Combs/D. Svetich, eBird data).

Summary of records indicating wintering by county

Allen/Barren (Barren River Lake [*KW* 87:61, 2011])
Calloway (Blood River; many years since the early 2000s)
Marshall (Jonathan Creek; many years since the early 2000s)

WHITE-RUMPED SANDPIPER *Calidris fuscicollis*

Status: Transient (rare to locally fairly common during spring, typically rare during fall). Recorded chiefly west of the Cumberland Plateau; more widespread in the western half of the state, but the species has occurred in eastern Kentucky during both spring and fall. Peaks of abundance occur during mid- to late May and from late Aug to early Oct. This is one of the few shorebird species that is more widespread and numerous during spring, being relatively scarce during fall. Encountered in a variety of shallow aquatic habitats; most frequently found along the muddy margins of flooded fields during spring and has occurred at least occasionally at most of the better shorebird areas during fall. Generally observed in small flocks of fewer than ten birds, usually associating with other species of peeps.

Maximum spring counts: **200+** at McElroy Lake, 22 May 1998 (Roemer, *KW* 74:93-94, 1998); ca. **200** nr. Lake No. 9, 10-11 May 1999 (*KW* 75:43, 1999; D. Roemer, notes); at least **150** at McElroy Lake, 23 May 2008 (*KW* 84:63, 2008); **150** at McElroy Lake, 21 May 2018 (*KW* 94:72, 2018); **100+** birds, McElroy Lake, 20 May 1997 (Roemer, et al., *KW* 73:79-83, 1997); **80** in Fulton Co., 30 May 1985 (*KW* 61:45, 1985); **75+** in Fulton Co., 31 May 1996 (B. Palmer-Ball, eBird data); **75** at McElroy Lake, 4 Jun 2010 (*KW* 86:94, 2010).

Maximum fall counts: **24** (ph.) at the Wildcat Creek embayment of Ky Lake, Calloway Co., 16 Oct 2015 (*KW* 92:8, 2016); **22** (ph.) in s. Jefferson Co., 9 Oct 2015 (*KW* 92:8, 2016); up to **11** e. of Morganfield, Union Co., 17-25 Sep 2018 (*KW* 95:7, 2019); **7** at the Falls of the Ohio, 13 Sep 1950 (Mengel:249); **7** at Jonathan Creek, 11 Sep 1999 (H. Chambers, notes; *KW* 76:6, 2000 [date erroneously published as Sep 4 therein]; **7** at the Fishing Creek embayment of Lake Cumberland, Pulaski Co., 6 Sep 2011 (*KW* 88:9, 2012).

Early spring dates: 19 Apr 2007, w. Henderson Co. (*KW* 83:80, 2007); 23 Apr 1998, McElroy Lake (Roemer, *KW* 74:94, 1998); 25 Apr 1981, Warren Co. (*KW* 57:57, 1981); 25 Apr 1982, Green River WMA, Adair Co. (*KW* 58:50, 1982; J. Elmore, notes).

Late spring dates: a bird lingered at McElroy Lake through 20 Jul 1998 (Roemer, *KW* 74:94, 1998); 30 Jun/21 Jul 2008, Open Pond, Fulton Co. (*KW* 84:87, 2008); 30 Jun 2008, Morgan Pond (*KW* 84:87, 2008); 25 Jun 2018, Morgan Pond (*KW* 94:106, 2018); 21 Jun 2005, w. Henderson Co. (*KW* 81:106, 2005); 19 Jun 1985, Falls of the Ohio (*KW* 61:57, 1985); 19 Jun 2002, Morgan Pond, Christian Co. (*KW* 78:63, 2002); 16 Jun 2001, Peabody WMA, Ohio Co. (R. Denton, eBird data);

15 Jun 2001, Union Co. (B. Palmer-Ball, eBird data); 15 Jun 2011, McElroy Lake (*KW* 87:114, 2011); 14 Jun 2011, s. Logan Co. (*KW* 87:114, 2011).

Early fall dates: 6 Jul 2013 (summering bird?), e. of Morganfield, Union Co. (*KW* 89:95, 2013; *KW* 90:10, 2014); 20 Jul [1967 or 1968?, presumed to be from the Falls of the Ohio] (A. Stamm, notes); 21 Jul 1988, Falls of the Ohio (*KW* 64:63, 1988); 25 Jul 1970, [presumed to be from the Falls of the Ohio] (A. Stamm, notes); 7 Aug 2017, (ph.) Union Co. (*KW* 94:7, 2018); 8 Aug 1982, Falls of the Ohio (B. Monroe, Jr., notes); 11 Aug 1987, Falls of the Ohio (*KW* 64:17, 1988); 11 Aug 1991, Minor Clark Hatchery (*KW* 68:7, 1992).

Late fall dates: 10 Nov 1982, Falls of the Ohio (*KW* 59:16, 1983); 2 Nov 1977, Honker Lake, LBL, Lyon/Trigg cos. (C. Peterson, eBird data); 30 Oct 2016, (ph.) Morgan Pond (*KW* 93:8, 2017); 27-30 Oct 1984, Falls of the Ohio (*KW* 61:16, 1985); 28 Oct 1990, Muhlenberg Co. (*KW* 67:6, 1991).

Unaccepted records: those during spring earlier than the early spring date of 19 Apr given above and including 27 Mar 1965, (10) in south-central Kentucky (Wilson, *KW* 44:41, 1968); also, 10 Sep 1981, (32) in Calloway Co. (*KW* 58:15, 1982).

BUFF-BREASTED SANDPIPER *Calidris subruficollis*

Status: Transient (extremely rare during spring, rare to uncommon during fall). Reported chiefly from west of the Cumberland Plateau, but it has been found at the Minor Clark Hatchery no fewer than five times during fall. Somewhat locally distributed, having been reported from only 21 counties to date. This species migrates north during spring primarily through the Great Plains, and there are only a couple of photo-documented spring records (see below); peak of abundance during fall occurs from late Aug to mid-Sep. Prior to the early 1970s, this shorebird had been reported almost exclusively from the Falls of the Ohio, but it has now been observed at least occasionally at all of the better shorebird areas in the state during fall; small numbers also can occur in open pastures and other open areas with short grass. Generally seen singly or in small flocks of up to ten birds.

Maximum counts: at least **48** along the Mississippi River at the Campbell Dikes, Carlisle Co, 8 Sep 1998 (B. Palmer-Ball, eBird data); at least **21** e. of Morganfield, Union Co., 7 Sep 2001 (B. Palmer-Ball, eBird data); **20** e. of Morganfield, Union Co., 31 Aug 2012 (*KW* 89:9, 2013); **18** along the Mississippi River nr. Laketon, Carlisle Co., 7 Sep 1996 (*KW* 73:7, 1997); **18** at Blood River, 7 Sep 2002 (*KW* 79:9, 2003); at least **16** at McElroy Lake, 4 Sep 1989 (Palmer-Ball and Boggs, *KW* 67: 62, 1991); **16** along the Mississippi River at Watson Point, Fulton Co., 28 Aug 1988 (*KW* 65:8, 1989); **16** at Lake No. 9, 2 Sep 2000 (*KW* 77:7, 2001).

Spring records: 23/24 May 2011, 1/2 (ph.) in flooded bottoms w. of Buttonsberry, McLean Co. (*KW* 87:100, 2011; Palmer-Ball and Huber, *KW* 88:87-91, 2012; B. Palmer-Ball, eBird data); 25 Apr 2016, (ph.) in s. Jefferson Co. (*KW* 92:60/62, 2016).

Early fall dates: 17 Jul 2010, Obion WMA, Fulton Co. (*KW* 86:94, 2010); 24 Jul 1998, McElroy Lake (Roemer, *KW* 74:95, 1998); 26 Jul 2010, Chaney Lake (*KW* 86:94, 2010); 27 Jul 1987, Lake No. 9 (G. Criswell, eBird data); 30 Jul 2015, Upper Hickman Bottoms (*KW* 91:86, 2015); 3 Aug 2013, Upper Hickman Bottoms (*KW* 90:10, 2014); 4 Aug 2010, Upper Hickman Bottoms (*KW* 87:17, 2011); 4 Aug 2015, Upper Hickman Bottoms (*KW* 92:8, 2016); 5 Aug 2015, s. Jefferson Co. (*KW* 92:8, 2016); 6 Aug 2005 (*KW* 82:9, 2006); 7 Aug 1998, Falls of the Ohio (*KW* 75:6, 1999); 7 Aug 2011, Morgan Pond & s. Jefferson Co. (*KW* 88:10, 2012); 7 Aug 2015, Falls of the Ohio (*KW* 92:8, 2016); 8 Aug 1963, Falls of the Ohio (Stamm, et al., *KW* 43:11, 1967); 9 Aug 1997, Falls of the Ohio (*BO*, Sept 1997).

Late fall dates: 3 Nov 2016, (ph.) Morgan Pond (*KW* 93:8, 2017); 1 Oct 2003, Union Co. (*KW* 80:9, 2004); 30 Sep 1990, (ph.) Lyon Co. (*KW* 67:7, 1991); 30 Sep 2011, s. Jefferson Co. (*KW* 88:10, 2012); 28 Sep 2012, Minor Clark Hatchery (*KW* 89:9, 2013).

Unaccepted record: 27 Apr 1918, Warren Co. (Wilson, *WB* 35:118, 1923; *KW* 38:13, 1962; see Mengel:255).

Summary of records by county (status statements refer to fall season)

Adair (Green River Lake [*KW* 84:10, 2008; *KW* 85:16, 2009])
Ballard (likely annual at Ballard WMA)
Calloway (likely annual at Blood River)
Carlisle (likely annual along Mississippi River)

Christian (likely regular at transient ponds [*KW* 81:9, 2005; *KW* 88:10, 2012; *KW* 93:8, 2017])
Fayette (Spindletop Farm [*KW* 93:8, 2017])
Fulton (likely annual along Mississippi River)
Henderson (likely annual at floodplain sloughs along Ohio River)
Hickman (likely annual along Mississippi River [*KW* 81:9, 2005])
Jefferson (annual at Falls of the Ohio; occasional elsewhere)
Livingston (Smithland Dam [*KW* 81:9, 2005; *KW* 87:17, 2011])
Lyon (*KW* 67:7, 1991; *KW* 86:9, 2010)
Marshall (likely annual at Jonathan Creek)
McLean (Palmer-Ball and Huber, *KW* 88:87-91, 2012)
Muhlenberg (Paradise Power Plant [*KW* 76:6, 2000; *KW* 82:9, 2006])
Pulaski (likely annual around Lake Cumberland)
Rowan (likely annual at Minor Clark Hatchery)
Union (likely annual at Camp Mines)
Trigg (likely annual on Lake Barkley [*KW* 79:9, 2003; *KW* 82:9, 2006; *KW* 90:10, 2014])
Warren (likely regular at transient ponds [Palmer-Ball and Boggs, *KW* 67:62, 1991; Roemer, *KW* 75:95, 1998; *KW* 86:94, 2010])
Wayne (*KW* 89:9, 2013; *KW* 93:8, 2017)

PECTORAL SANDPIPER *Calidris melanotos*

Status: Common transient, occasionally lingering into early winter; extremely rare during mid-winter and summer. Widespread in occurrence, but recorded more commonly west of the Cumberland Plateau. This species is one of our most numerous shorebird transients, and it is encountered in a great variety of habitats from farm ponds and moist seeps in pastures to the shorelines of flooded fields and the larger lakes and rivers. Peaks of abundance occur from late Mar to mid-Apr and from mid-Jul to mid-Sep. There are several Jun records between the normal spring and fall migratory periods. Individuals have been documented lingering into early winter on a few occaions, especially in western Kentucky; however, wintering has not been documented. Frequently encountered in flocks of up to 50 birds, but occasionally seen by the hundreds (most often during spring) in suitable habitat.

Maximum spring counts: ca. **2000-2500** in scattered flocks in the Lower Hickman Bottoms, 7 Apr 1996 (B. Palmer-Ball. eBird data); **2000** at the Sauerheber Unit 16 Apr 2005 (*KW* 81:87, 2005); **2000** nr. Blue Pond, Fulton Co., 22 Apr 2014 (*KW* 90:71, 2014); **1500-2000** in the Upper Hickman Bottoms, 28 Mar 2013 (*KW* 89:71, 2013); at least **1450** in the Lower Hickman Bottoms, 1 Apr 2016 (*KW* 92:61, 2016); **1400** at the Sauerheber Unit 16 Mar 2003 (*KW* 79:69, 2003); ca. **1200** at the Long Point Unit, 5 Apr 1992 (B. Palmer-Ball, eBird data); **1100+** at and nr. the Long Point Unit, 7 Apr 2017 (*KW* 93:72, 2017; B. Wulker, eBird data); at least **1030** in w. Henderson Co., 22 Apr 2010 (*KW* 86:68, 2010); **1000** at the Sauerheber Unit, 19 Apr 2014 (*KW* 90:71, 2014); **800** at the Sauerheber Unit, 20 Apr 2018 (*KW* 94:73, 2018); **700+** in w. Fulton Co., 17 Apr 2004 (*KW* 80:67, 2004); ca. **700** in Fulton Co., 9 Apr 2000 (*KW* 76:45, 2000); **700+** in w. Fulton Co., 17 Apr 2004 (*KW* 80:67, 2004); **700** at the Long Point Unit, 8 Apr 2016 (*KW* 92:61, 2016); ca. **650** at Ledford, Fulton Co., 7 May 2010 (*KW* 86:68, 2010); **500** in the Lower Hickman Bottoms, 5 Apr 2003 (R. Denton, eBird data; *KW* 79:69, 2003 [date erroneously published as 6 Apr therein]); **500+** in w. Henderson Co., 19 Apr 2007 (*KW* 83:80, 2007); ca. **500** at Obion WMA, Fulton Co., 3 May 2007 (*KW* 83:80, 2007); **500+** in the Pond Creek Bottoms, Hopkins Co., 9 Apr 2014 (*KW* 90:71, 2014); ca. **500** at McElroy Lake, 21 Mar 2016 (*KW* 92:61, 2016); **500** at the Long Point Unit, 16 Apr 2018 (N. Houlihan/P. Moynahan, eBird data); **450+** in the Upper Hickman Bottoms, 20 Apr 2014 (*KW* 90:71, 2014); ca. **400** in Livingston Co., 16-17 Apr 1989 (*KW* 65:67, 1989); ca. **400** at the Sauerheber Unit, 28 Apr 1989 (B. Palmer-Ball, eBird data); ca. **400** at McElroy Lake, 22 Mar 2008 (*KW* 84:63, 2008); at least **400** at McElroy Lake, 5 May 2010 (*KW* 86:68, 2010); ca. **400** sw. of Rumsey, McLean Co., 24 Mar 2015 (*KW* 91:71, 2015).

Maximum fall counts: ca. **2000** at McElroy Lake, "late summer" 1961 (Wilson, *KW* 39:16, 1963); **1200+** in the Upper Hickman Bottoms, 31 Jul 2015 (*KW* 91:86, 2015); **650** at Lake No. 9, 21 Aug 2006 (*KW* 83:13, 2007); **550** in the Upper Hickman Bottoms, 25 Jul 2013 (*KW* 89:96, 2013); **500** at Lake No. 9, 16 Aug 1987 (G. Criswell, eBird data); **400-500** at Mitchell Lake, Ballard WMA, 25 Aug

2007 (*KW* 84:9, 2008); **475** e. of Morganfield, Union Co., 18 Aug 2017 (B. Palmer-Ball et al., eBird data); ca. **450** at Morgan Pond, 11/13 Aug 2011 (*KW* 88:10, 2012); **400+** at Lake No. 9, 4 Aug 2007 (*KW* 84:9, 2008); **300-350** at McElroy Lake, 20-22 Aug 1989 (Palmer-Ball and Boggs, *KW* 67:61, 1991; **350+** at Mitchell Lake, Ballard WMA, 13 Aug 2005 (*KW* 82:9, 2006).

Early spring dates: 17 Feb 2017, w. of Miller, Fulton Co. (*KW* 93:49, 2017); 21 Feb 2016, McElroy Lake (*KW* 92:43, 2016); 22 Feb 2003, McElroy Lake (*KW* 79:47, 2003); 24 Feb 2013, Sauerheber Unit (*KW* 89:48, 2013); 26 Feb 2007, Chaney Lake (*KW* 83:48, 2007); 27 Feb 2019, Logan Co. (*KW* 95:48, 2019); 1 Mar 2003, Ohio Co. (*KW* 79:69, 2003); 2 Mar 2003, Jonathan Creek (*KW* 79:69, 2003); 3 Mar 2003, McElroy Lake (*KW* 79:69, 2003); 3 Mar 2013, Sauerheber (*KW* 89:71, 2013); 4 Mar 1999, McElroy Lake (D. Roemer, notes); 4 Mar 2007, Sauerheber (*KW* 83:80, 2007); 4 Mar 2014, Nelson Co. (D. Manley, eBird data); 5 Mar 2006, Blood River (*KW* 82:69, 2006); 5 Mar 2007, Pulaski Co. (*KW* 83:80, 2007); 5 Mar 2016, McElroy Lake (*KW* 92:60, 2016); 6 Mar 2000, Warren Co. (D. Roemer, notes); 6 Mar 2016, Jonathan Creek (*KW* 92:60, 2016); 7 Mar 2007, s. Warren Co. (*KW* 83:80, 2007); 7 Mar 2012, s. Jefferson Co. & w. Fulton Co. (*KW* 88:76, 2012); 7 Mar 2014, McElroy Lake (*KW* 90:71, 2014); 7 Mar 2016, Morgan Pond (*KW* 92:61, 2016); 7 Mar 2017, Hart Co. (J. Sole, eBird data).

Late fall/early winter dates: occasionally lingering into late fall/early winter, the latest dates being "count week" of 30 Dec 1961, Lexington CBC (*AFN* 16:191, 1962); 22 Dec 1970, Lake Barkley at Taylor Bay, Trigg Co. (*KW* 47:9-10, 1971); 21 Dec 1985, Lake Barkley (*KW* 62:10, 1986); 18 Dec 1949, Falls of the Ohio [possibly an Indiana record](Summerfield, *KW* 26:26-27, 1950); 30 Nov 1989, Marshall Co. (*KW* 66:10, 1990); 27 Nov 1999, Wayne Co. (R. Denton, eBird data); 26 Nov 1983, Marshall Co. (*KW* 60:17, 1984); 25 Nov 2001, Jonathan Creek (B. Palmer-Ball, eBird data); 25 Nov 2014, Jonathan Creek (*KW* 91:9, 2015); 24 Nov 1982, Rowan Co. (*KW* 59:16, 1983).

Out-of-season record (mid-winter): 9 Feb 1952, Warren Co. (*KW* 38:13, 1962).

Unaccepted record: 18 Dec 2004, (3) Richmond CBC (*KW* 81:25, 2005).

SEMIPALMATED SANDPIPER *Calidris pusilla*

Status: Fairly common to common transient, extremely rare during summer. Recorded chiefly west of the Cumberland Plateau. Encountered in a great variety of shallow aquatic habitats from the margins of farm ponds to mudflats and shorelines of flooded fields and the larger lakes and rivers. Only about a week's period occurs between spring and fall migratory periods (during late Jun) when the species has not been observed in the state. Peaks of abundance occur from mid- to late May and from early Aug to early Sep. This small shorebird winters primarily south of the United States, and late fall and early winter peeps in Kentucky are unlikely to be Semipalmateds. It is also a late spring migrant, and numerous Mar and early Apr reports in the literature are certainly in error. Generally recorded in small to medium-sized flocks of fewer than 25 birds, but flocks of a hundred or more are sometimes seen at favored stopover points, especially in late spring.

Maximum spring counts: **3000-3200** in n. McLean Co., 24 May 2011 (Palmer-Ball and Huber, *KW* 88:91, 2012); **2500-3000** at McElroy Lake 23 May 2008 (*KW* 84:62, 2008); **1500+** at McElroy Lake, 23 May 1997 (Roemer, et al., *KW* 73:79-83, 1997); **1400** at McElroy Lake, 26 May 2018 (*KW* 94: 73, 2018); ca. **1000** in the Upper Hickman Bottoms, 20 May 1999 (D. Roemer, notes); **731** in s. Jefferson Co., 25 May 2012 (*KW* 88:76, 2012); **700-750** at Morgan Pond, 22 May 2016 (*KW* 92:61, 2016); at least **650** in w. Henderson Co., 23 May 2007 (*KW* 83:79, 2007); **500-600** at McElroy Lake and **450-500** at Morgan Pond, both 22 May 2013 (*KW* 89:70, 2013); ca. **500** at McElroy Lake, 21 May 1998 (Roemer, *KW* 74:94, 1998); ca. **500** in se. Muhlenberg Co., 29 May 2006 (*KW* 82:68, 2006); **500+** at McElroy Lake, 15-19 May 2015 (*KW* 91:71, 2015); **425+** at McElroy Lake, 29 May 1989 (Palmer-Ball and Boggs, *KW* 67:60, 1991); ca. **400** in Fulton Co., 22 May 1982 (*KW* 58:51, 1982).

Maximum fall counts: most of ca. 300 peeps at Lake No. 9, 10 Aug 1985 (*KW* 62:6, 1986; B. Palmer-Ball, eBird data); ca. 200 at the Falls of the Ohio, 5 Aug 1985 (*KW* 62:6, 1986); 127 at Lake No. 9, 11 Aug 2001 (R. Denton, eBird data); "a hundred or more are sometimes seen at the Falls of the Ohio" (Mengel:254).

Early spring dates: 16 Apr 2018, (ph.) Frogue Pond, Todd Co. (*KW* 94:73, 2018); 24 Apr 1988, Sauerheber (*KW* 64:46, 1988); 24 Apr 1999, Sauerheber (C. Crawford, eBird data); 24 Apr 2011, McElroy Lake (*KW* 87:88, 2011).

Late fall dates: 18 Nov 2015, (ph.) Jonathan Creek (*KW* 92:8, 2016); 3 Nov 1974, Calloway Co. (Miller and Peterson, *KW* 51:31, 1975); 2 Nov 1950, Warren Co. (Wilson, *KW* 27:5, 1951); 1 Nov 1978, Falls of the Ohio (*KW* 55:16, 1979); 24/28 Oct 1990, Muhlenberg Co. (B. Palmer-Ball, eBird data).

Unaccepted records: those during fall/early winter later than the late fall date of 18 Nov given above and including 15 Dec 1979, (6) in Warren Co. (*KW* 56:3/7, 1980; *AB* 34:499, 1980); 29 Nov 1969, Calloway Co. (*KW* 46:48, 1970); 23 Nov 1969 (*KW* 46:48, 1970); also, 31 Oct 2004, (6-10) in se. Muhlenberg Co. (*KW* 81:8, 2005). Those during spring earlier than the early spring date of 16 Apr given above and including 24 Mar 1967 (*KW* 45:50, 1969; A. Stamm, notes); 27 Mar 1965, Warren Co. (*KW* 45:34, 1969); 31 Mar 1951, Warren Co. (*KW* 38:13, 1962); 6 Apr 1973, (2) Danville (*AC* [2nd ed.], p. 69); 11 Apr 1997, (40) in Fulton Co. (*KW* 73:54, 1997). Also, I can find no details for the report of 16 Apr 1996 included in the previous edition of this work and feel it must be erroneous.

WESTERN SANDPIPER *Calidris mauri*

Status: Transient (extremely rare to rare during spring, uncommon during fall); extremely rare during early summer and winter. Currently, all records are from west of the Cumberland Plateau, although the species has been reported several times at the Minor Clark Hatchery in the adjacent eastern Knobs during fall. The farthest east that the species has been conclusively reported during spring appears to be Louisville (*KW* 87:88, 2011). Most often encountered on mudflats and open shore-lines of the larger lakes and rivers, but occasionally observed along the shores of smaller bodies of water and probably to be expected at any of the state's better shorebirds spots during fall. This species is not numerous, but it occurs fairly regularly during fall, especially in the western portion of the state. The fall migration is strongly bimodal, with a small peak of adults occurring during Jul followed by a larger peak of juveniles during early Sep; many shorebirds show this pattern, but it is especially pronounced in Western. In contrast, the species occurs much less frequently during spring, but small numbers typically occur in western Kentucky during a brief period from early Apr to early May with a peak of abundance in late Apr. Most often seen in small groups of fewer than ten birds, but large fall flocks of peeps in western Kentucky formerly contained dozens of Westerns on occasion.

Maximum spring counts: **19** at McElroy Lake, 2 May 2008 (*KW* 84:62, 2008); **19** at McElroy Lake, 16 Apr 2011 (*KW* 87:88, 2011); **17** at McElroy Lake, 27 Apr 1997 (Roemer, et al., *KW* 73:79-83, 1997); **11** at Chaney Lake, 30 Apr 1997 (D. Roemer, notes); **8** at the Paradise Power Plant, Muhlenberg Co., 28 Apr 2007 (*KW* 83:79, 2007); **6** at McElroy Lake, 20 Apr 1991 (*KW* 67:55, 1991); **6** at McElroy Lake, 23 Apr 1998 (D. Roemer, notes [date published incorrectly as 23 May in *KW* 74:54, 1998]).

Maximum fall counts: **100** at Lake No. 9, 5 Sep 1983 (*KW* 60:16, 1984); **"half or more of 100 peeps"** in Fulton Co., 14 Sep 1966 (Able, *KW* 43:31, 1967); **40+** in the Upper Hickman Bottoms, 9 Sep 1993 (B. Palmer-Ball, eBird data); ca. **35** at McElroy Lake, 4 Sep 1989 (Palmer-Ball and Boggs, *KW* 67:60-61, 1991); **35** on the Mississippi River, Carlisle Co., 14 Aug 1988 (*KW* 65:8, 1989; B. Palmer-Ball, eBird data); **29** at Blood River, 24 Aug 2007 (*KW* 84:9, 2008); **28** (ads.) at McElroy Lake, 12 Jul 1994 (B. Palmer-Ball, eBird data); at least **20** (ads.) in the Upper Hickman Bottoms, 25 Jul 2013 (*KW* 89:95, 2013); **16** (ads.) at McElroy Lake, 17 Jul 2011 (*KW* 87:114, 2011).

Early spring dates: 29 Mar 2016, Lower Hickman Bottoms (*KW* 92:61, 2016); 31 Mar 1951, Warren Co. (*KW* 38:13, 1962); 5 Apr 1987, Fulton Co. (*KW* 63:50, 1987).

Late spring dates: 21 May 2013, Morgan Pond (B. Lisowsky, eBird data); 16 May 2008, McElroy Lake (*KW* 84:62, 2008); 14 May 1950, McElroy Lake (Wilson, *KW* 27:5, 1951); 9 May 2008, McElroy Lake (*KW* 84:62, 2008).

Early fall dates: 2 Jul 2009, Open Pond, Fulton Co. (*KW* 85:93, 2009); 3 Jul 1994, McElroy Lake (B. Palmer-Ball, eBird data).

Late fall dates (other than possible wintering birds): occasionally lingers into early winter, latest being 24 Dec 2015, (2) at Jonathan Creek (*KW* 92:26/43, 2016); 15 Dec 2006, Jonathan Creek (*KW* 83:48, 2007); 14 Dec 2008, Jonathan Creek (*KW* 85:49, 2009); 30 Nov 1990, Lake Barkley, Trigg Co. (*KW* 67:6, 1991).

Out-of-season record (early summer): 12 Jun 1965, Falls of the Ohio (Stamm, et al., *KW* 43:10, 1967).

Out-of-season records (winter): one lingered on mudflats of Green River Lake, Adair Co. 28 Nov 1982–30 Jan 1983 (*KW* 59:16, 1983; *KW* 59:29, 1983); one lingered at Jonathan Creek to 21 Feb 1993 (*KW* 69:34, 1993; B. Palmer-Ball, eBird data); 1 Feb 2008, Jonathan Creek (*KW* 84:44, 2008 [date erroneously published as 1 Jan therein]; B. Hart, notes); 29 Feb 2008, perhaps the same bird not far away at Blood River (*KW* 84:62, 2008); 15 Mar 2007, Jonathan Creek (*KW* 83:79, 2007); 25 Jan 2014, Blood River (*KW* 90:49, 2014).

Unaccepted records: 7-13 Dec 1990, (6) in Marshall Co. (*KW* 66:39, 1990); 19 Dec 1982, (20) in Marshall Co. (*KW* 69:15, 1993); those during spring later than the late spring date of 21 May given above and including 29 May 1953, south-central Kentucky (*KW* 38:13, 1962); 3 Jun 1968, (6) in south-central Kentucky (Wilson, *KW* 44:42, 1968); 30 May 1990, Rowan Co. (*KW* 66:57, 1990); 10-31 May 1991, Rowan Co. (*KW* 67:55, 1991).

Published error: 90 in Fulton Co., 23 Jul 2000 (*KW* 76:56, 2000 [species present, but count incorrect; *fide* H. Chambers, pers. comm.]).

DOWITCHERS *Limnodromus* spp.

Status: The two species of dowitchers both occur regularly in Kentucky, but because they were formerly considered one species, most older records cannot be differentiated. They are difficult to distinguish in some plumages, but well-marked birds in breeding plumage and juveniles during fall show some subtle differences. Also, variation in the timing of fall migration between the two can be helpful in determining their identity. However, the real key to field identification of these species is a distinct difference in their call notes, which unfortunately has not been utilized by many observers in the field. It can be difficult to get Short-billeds to call, but Long-billeds seem to be more vocal, and thus, easier to confirm by voice.

SHORT-BILLED DOWITCHER *Limnodromus griseus*

Status: Uncommon transient. Recorded chiefly west of the Cumberland Plateau but regularly observed at the Minor Clark Hatchery in the adjacent eastern Knobs. Encountered in a variety of shallow aquatic habitats; most often found along the muddy shorelines of flooded fields, lakes and ponds, but regularly occurs at all of the better shorebird areas in the state. Peaks of abundance occur during mid-May and from late Jul to mid-Sep (adults during late Jul and juvs. from mid-Aug to mid-Sep). Usually found singly or in small groups of fewer than a dozen birds.

Maximum spring counts: at least **140** at McElroy Lake, 14 May 2008 (*KW* 84:63, 2008); **102** in Boone Co., 13 May 1989 (McNeely, *KW* 65:76-77, 1989); "**most of 80-85** dowitchers" at McElroy Lake, 9 May 2008 (*KW* 84:63, 2008); at least **75** at Chapman Pond, Warren Co., 10 May 2008 (*KW* 84:63, 2008); ca. **70** at McElroy Lake, 16 May 2010 (*KW* 86:68, 2010); **70** (ph.) in s. Jefferson Co., 13 May 2017 (*KW* 93:73, 2017); **60** at Flaherty, Meade Co., 10 May 1991 (*KW* 67:55, 1991); **50** at McElroy Lake, 14 May 1997 (Roemer, et al., *KW* 73:79-83, 1997); **50** in w. Henderson Co., 13 May 2005 (*KW* 81:87, 2005); ca. **60** at scattered sites in s. Warren Co., 11 May 2004 (*KW* 80:68, 2004).

Maximum fall counts: ca. **40** at the Falls of the Ohio, 22 Aug 1984 (B. Palmer-Ball, eBird data); **25-30** at McElroy Lake, 2 Sep 1989 (Palmer-Ball and Boggs, *KW* 67:62, 1991); **20** in the Upper Hickman Bottoms, 19 Jul 2013 (*KW* 89:96, 2013); **15** in the Upper Hickman Bottoms, 20 Aug 2013 (*KW* 90:11, 2014).

Early spring dates: 5 Apr 1988, Henderson Co. (*KW* 64:47, 1988); 5 Apr 2019, (ph./vo.) McElroy Lake (B. Palmer-Ball, eBird data); 16 Apr 2011, McElroy Lake (*KW* 87:89, 2011).

Late spring dates: 2 Jun 2002, McElroy Lake (*KW* 78:64, 2002); 1 Jun 2002, Walton Stables Pond, s. Warren Co. (*KW* 78:64, 2002); 27 May 1998, McElroy Lake (Roemer, *KW* 74:95, 1998); 27 May 1999, Henderson Co. (B. Palmer-Ball, eBird data); 25 May 1992, Fulton Co. (*KW* 68:46, 1992).

Early fall dates: 26 Jun 2010, McElroy Lake (*KW* 86:94, 2010); 30 Jun 1998, McElroy Lake (Roemer, *KW* 74:95, 1998); 30 Jun 2008, Open Pond, Fulton Co. (*KW* 84:87, 2008); 3 Jul 1994, McElroy Lake (B. Palmer-Ball, eBird data [erroneously published as 2 Jul in previous edition of this work]); 3 Jul 2010, w. Henderson Co. (*KW* 86:94, 2010); 4 Jul 1989, McElroy Lake (Palmer-Ball and Boggs, *KW* 67:62, 1991).

Late fall dates: 10 Oct 2006, Sauerheber (*KW* 83:13, 2007); 30 Sep 1990, Lake Barkley, Trigg Co. (B. Palmer-Ball, eBird data).

Unaccepted records (most probably represent the following species or Wilson's Snipe): 15 Feb 1994, 15 birds at McElroy Lake (*KW* 70:34, 1994); 15 Mar 19—, south-central Kentucky (*KW* 38:13, 1962; *KW* 45:50, 1969); 31 Mar 1972, Woodburn lakes, Warren Co. (Shadowen, *KW* 48:49, 1972); those during fall later than the late fall date of 10 Oct given above and including 20 Oct 19— Louisville area (*KW* 52:50, 1976); 3 Nov 1974, Ky Lake (*KW* 51:32, 1975); and 18 Oct 1981 at Louisville (*KW* 58:15, 1982).

NOTE on subspecies: It appears that the Atlantic or Eastern race (*L. g. griseus*) at least occasionally occurs in the state during spring migration. Reports include three documented with photographs: at McElroy Lake 1-2 Jun 2002 (*KW* 78:64, 2002); in w. Henderson Co., 20 May 2005 (*KW* 81:87, 2005; *KW* 93:106, 2017); and at McElroy Lake, 5-18 May 2008 (*KW* 84:63-64, 2008).

LONG-BILLED DOWITCHER *Limnodromus scolopaceus*

Status: Uncommon transient. All records currently from west of the Cumberland Plateau, but the species has been observed at least once at the Minor Clark Hatchery in the adjacent eastern Knobs (*KW* 90:11, 2014). Encountered in a variety of shallow aquatic habitats; most often found along muddy shorelines of ponds, lakes and flooded fields, but probably regular at all of the better shorebird areas in the state. Occurrence poorly documented historically; two specimens were collected at the Falls of the Ohio: 19 Oct 1946 (Mengel:253) and 10 Oct 1967 (*KW* 52:50, 1976). A number of other records (including most of the ones included below) have been documented by photographs and/or the distinctive call notes. Definitely more numerous than formerly documented, especially in the western part of the state. Peaks of abundance occur from late Apr to early May and during Oct (the fall peak involving juveniles with adults passing through largely unnoticed during Aug and early Sep). Generally seen singly or in small groups of up to ten birds.

Maximum spring counts: ca. **680** in w. Fulton Co. (including 200+ along Midway Church Rd. and ca. 450 at Ky Bend), 28 Apr 2019 (B. Wulker/T. Quarles, eBird data); **225** total at several spots (including 164 at the Long Point Unit) in w. Fulton Co., 14 Apr 2012 (*KW* 88:76, 2012); at least **145** total in three flocks at and nr. the Long Point Unit, 27 Apr 2009 (*KW* 85:69, 2009); **102** at the Long Point Unit, 19 Apr 2017 (*KW* 93:73, 2017); **74** at McElroy Lake, 25 Apr 2011 (*KW* 87:89, 2011); **66** at Lake No. 9, 4 May 2018 (*KW* 94:73, 2018); **60-65** in Hopkins Co., 3 May 1996 (B. Palmer-Ball, eBird data); **52** at the Sauerheber Unit, 29 Apr 2013 (*KW* 89:71, 2013); **most of 52** dowitchers at the Sauerheber Unit, 28 Apr 2007 (*KW* 83:80, 2007); **50** at the Long Point Unit 28 Apr 2015 (*KW* 91:71, 2015); at least **43** at McElroy Lake, 28 Apr 1991 (B. Palmer-Ball, eBird data); probably **most of 45** dowitchers at the Sauerheber Unit, 1 May 2016 (*KW* 92:61, 2016); ca. **40** at McElroy Lake, 3 May 2008 (*KW* 84:64, 2008); **33** at McElroy Lake, 29 Apr 2002 (*KW* 78:50, 2002); **29** nr. Morgan Pond, 2 May 2016 (*KW* 92:61, 2016); at least **28** at McElroy Lake, 29 Apr 2008 (*KW* 84:64, 2008); **27** at the Sauerheber Unit, 30 Apr 2018 (C. Bliznick, eBird data); **25** at Chaney Lake, 3 May 1996 (B. Palmer-Ball, eBird data); ca. **25** at McElroy Lake, 3 May 2010 (*KW* 86:68, 2010); **25** in the Lower Hickman Bottoms, 31 Mar 2013 (*KW* 89:71, 2013).

Maximum fall counts: **56** at Jonathan Creek, 6 Nov 2015 (*KW* 92:9, 2016); **34** at Blood River, 25 Oct 2015 (*KW* 92:9, 2016); **28** at Morgan Pond, 14 Oct 2016 (*KW* 93:9, 2017); **24+** at McElroy Lake, 13 Oct 2002 (*KW* 79:10, 2003); **17** in w. Fulton Co., 19 Oct 2006 (*KW* 83:14, 2007); **11** at Camp #11, Union Co., 31 Oct/3 Nov 2010 (*KW* 87:17, 2011); **11** e. of Morganfield, Union Co., 15 Oct 2017 (*KW* 94:8, 2018); **10** at Lake No. 9, 20 Oct 1985, (*KW* 62:6, 1986).

Early spring dates: 6 Mar 2005, Lake No. 9 (*KW* 81:87, 2005); 10 Mar 2016, McElroy Lake (*KW* 92:61, 2016; A. Hulsey, pers. comm.); 16 Mar 2017, (ph.) Sauerheber Unit (*KW* 93:73, 2017); 21 Mar 2010, s. Warren Co. (*KW* 86:68, 2010); 22 Mar 2008, McElroy Lake (*KW* 84:64, 2008); 22 Mar 2016, Lower Hickman Bottoms (*KW* 92:61, 2016); 23 Mar 2018, Open Pond, Fulton Co. (*KW* 94:73, 2018); 26 Mar 2018, (ph.) Sauerheber Unit (*KW* 94:73, 2018); 27 Mar 2004, Sauerheber Unit (*KW* 80:68, 2004); 28 Mar 2013, Upper Hickman Bottoms (*KW* 89:71, 2013); 28 Mar 2015, Boone Co. (*KW* 91:71, 2015 [date erroneously published as 26 Mar therein]); 28 Mar 2017, (ph.) s. Christian Co. (J. Hall/S. Arnold, eBird data); 30 Mar 2016, Sauerheber Unit (*KW* 92:61, 2016); 31 Mar 2013, Lower Hickman Bottoms (*KW* 89:71, 2013); 30 Mar 2019, Lower Hickman Bottoms (A. Lydeard, eBird data); 2 Apr 2013, Sauerheber Unit (*KW* 89:71, 2013); 4 Apr 2012, Ballard Co. (*KW*

88:76, 2012); 5 Apr 1986, Henderson Co. (*KW* 62:44, 1986); 5 Apr 1992, Fulton Co. (B. Palmer-Ball, eBird data).

Late spring dates: 24 May 2001, Union Co. (B. Palmer-Ball, eBird data); 23 May 2008, McElroy Lake (*KW* 84:64, 2008); 15 May 1967, Boyle Co. (Loetscher, *KW* 43:58, 1967); 15 May 2015, Simpson Co. (*KW* 91:71, 2015).

Early fall dates: 5 Jul 2007, Muhlenberg Co. (*KW* 83:105, 2007); 9 Jul 2014, (ph.) Todd Co. (*KW* 90:89, 2014); 12 Jul 1994, McElroy Lake (B. Palmer-Ball, eBird data); 14 Jul 2010, Morgan Pond, Christian Co. (*KW* 86:94/104, 2010); 19 Jul 2013, Fulton Co. (*KW* 89:96, 2013); 23 Jul 2017, (ph.) Union Co. (*KW* 93:99, 2017); 24 Jul 2016, Union Co. (*KW* 92:79, 2016); 25 Jul 1987, Lake No. 9 (*KW* 63:60, 1987); 25 Jul 2010, Morgan Pond, Christian Co. (*KW* 86:94, 2010); 29 Jul 2006, Pulaski Co. (*KW* 82:82, 2006); 29 Jul 2008, Fulton Co. (*KW* 84:87, 2008); 1 Aug 2003, Union Co. (*KW* 80:9, 2004); 4 Aug 2010, Lake No. 9 (*KW* 87:17, 2011).

Late fall dates: 15 Dec 2005, Pulaski Co. (*KW* 82:47-48, 2006); 27 Nov 2006, [reported as dowitcher sp.] Jonathan Creek (*KW* 83:13, 2007); 24-25 Nov 2001, Marshall Co. (*NAB* 56:58, 2002; H. Chambers, notes); 25 Nov 2006, w. Fulton Co. (*KW* 83:14, 2007); 22 Nov 2003, Blood River [reported as dowitcher sp.] (*KW* 80:9, 2004); 20 Nov 2015, Jonathan Creek (*KW* 92:9, 2016); 13 Nov 2002, Lake No. 9 (*KW* 79:10, 2003); 11 Nov 2010, Blood River (*KW* 87:17, 2011); 11 Nov 2016, Jonathan Creek (*KW* 93:9, 2017); 10 Nov 2006, s. Christian Co. (*KW* 83:14, 2007); 9 Nov 2000, Marshall Co. (*KW* 77:7, 2001); 5 Nov 2008, Sauerheber Unit (eBird data); 3 Nov 2010, Union Co. (*KW* 87:17, 2011); 3 Nov 2013, Sauerheber Unit (*KW* 90:11, 2014); 31 Oct 2017, Hart Co. (*KW* 94:8, 2018); 30 Oct 2007, Wayne Co. (*KW* 84:10, 2008).

Unaccepted records (including dowitcher sp.): (15) [reported as dowitcher sp.] on the Lexington CBC, 27 Dec 1975 (*KW* 52:11, 1976; *AB* 30:170/388, 1976); 28 Feb 1997, (2) [reported as dowitcher sp. – call notes not heard] at the Long Point Unit (*KW* 73:37, 1997).

*AMERICAN WOODCOCK *Scolopax minor*

Status: Uncommon to locally fairly common transient and summer resident, extremely rare to locally rare winter resident. Recorded statewide in a variety of semi-open habitats but most frequently encountered along woodland borders where some weedy or brushy cover and damp ground are present. Peaks of abundance occur during Feb and Nov. Outside of the late winter/early spring courtship season, this species is particularly reclusive and hard to find; it is especially difficult to find during summer and fall prior to the arrival of southbound migrants. Breeding statewide; most numerous on the Cumberland Plateau and in the Shawnee Hills, least numerous in the Inner Bluegrass and Jackson Purchase (Mengel:240). Some birds appear to winter during mild years, especially in the far western part of the state; however, most typically retreat farther south during winter. Nocturnal; usually encountered at dusk or dawn, but can be flushed from the ground by day in appropriate habitat. The unique courtship display can be seen and heard most frequently at dusk during Feb and Mar, when males call from openings in successional fields and along woodland borders. Does not normally flock like the following species, but family groups are sometimes observed.

Maximum counts: perhaps **as many as 100** birds scattered in the woods surrounding Hundred Acre Pond, Hart Co., Feb 1994 (*KW* 70:34, 1994; R. Seymour, pers. comm); ca. **75** at Central Kentucky WMA, Madison Co., 6 Mar 2009 (*KW* 85:72, 2009).

WILSON'S SNIPE *Gallinago delicata*

Status: Fairly common transient, uncommon winter resident, extremely rare during summer. Recorded statewide but less numerous on the Cumberland Plateau and Mountains. Encountered in wet seeps and fields, as well as along the marshy edges of lakes and ponds; sometimes encountered on open shorelines and flats, but typically found much more often around some herbaceous cover. Peaks of abundance occur from mid-Mar to early Apr and from mid-Oct to early Nov. The species is most reliably found during winter across southern and western Kentucky and disappears during mid-winter only during the coldest years. Generally seen singly or in loose groups of up to 25 birds, but occasionally seen during spring migration in loose flocks of 50-100 or more birds in suitable habitat. The unique courtship display can occasionally be encountered during spring.

Maximum counts: at least **325** at the Long Point Unit, 16 Mar 2005 (*KW* 81:87, 2005); **278** total in w. Fulton Co., 7 Mar 2012 (*KW* 88:76, 2012); at least **250** in scattered flocks in w. Fulton Co., 20 Mar 2009 (*KW* 85:72, 2009); **243** in a single flock nr. the Long Point Unit, 27 Jan 2002 (B. Palmer-Ball, eBird data); **232** total (132 e. of Open Pond, Fulton Co., and 100+ at the Long Point Unit), both 26 Mar 2006 (*KW* 82:69, 2006); **220** at McElroy Lake, 28 Mar 2008 (*KW* 84:64, 2008); **200-250** in scattered flocks in Lower Hickman Bottoms, 7 Apr 1996 (B. Palmer-Ball, eBird data); **200** at the Sauerheber Unit, 20 Mar 2017 (*KW* 93:73, 2017); ca. **160** in Fulton Co., 20 Mar 1999 (*KW* 75:43, 1999); **160** e. of Hickman, Fulton Co., 23 Mar 2013 (*KW* 89:71, 2013); **160** se. of Mt. Zion, Allen Co., 19 Mar 2015 (*KW* 91:71, 2015); **156** at the Long Point Unit, 3 Mar 2009 (*KW* 85:72, 2009); **150** in w. Henderson Co. (130 in a single flock), 21 Mar 2007 (*KW* 83:80, 2007); at least **150** at the Sauerheber Unit, 17 Mar 2012 (*KW* 88:76, 2012); **150** adjacent to Ballard WMA, 22 Dec 2015 (*KW* 92:43, 2016); **149** at the Long Point Unit, 15 Apr 2016 (*KW* 92:61, 2016); **144** in the Lower Hickman Bottoms, 27 Feb 2004 (R. Denton, eBird data); ca. **125** at the Sauerheber Unit, 5 Dec 2010 (*KW* 87:62, 2011); **118** counted at the Long Point Unit, 18 Mar 2000 (*KW* 76:45, 2000; H. Chambers, notes); **118** in Hart Co., 4 Mar 2018 (*KW* 94:73, 2018); **110** at and nr. the Long Point Unit, 28 Mar 2014 (*KW* 90:72, 2014); **108** at Petros, Warren Co., 28 Dec 2007 (eBird data); **105** at McElroy Lake, 7 Apr 1997 (C. Sloan, eBird data); at least **101** at the Sauerheber Unit, 16 Feb 2012 (*KW* 88:48, 2012); **101** in Hart Co., 27 Mar 2015 (*KW* 91:71, 2015); as many as **100** on several occasions at McElroy Lake (Wilson, *KW* 16:19, 1940).

Late spring dates: 30 May 2018, (ph.) McElroy Lake (*KW* 94:73, 2018); 27 May 2016, Fayette Co. (*KW* 92:61, 2016); 26 May 1951, south-central Kentucky (*KW* 38:12, 1962); 22 May 2006, w. Henderson Co. (C. Crawford, eBird data); 21 May 2019, McElroy Lake (m. ob., eBird data); 19 May 2000, Pulaski Co. (R. Denton, eBird data); 18 May 19—, Hopkins Co. (Mengel:241).

Early fall dates: 3 Jul 1994, McElroy Lake (B. Palmer-Ball, eBird data); 5 Jul 1996, Sauerheber Unit (B. Palmer-Ball, eBird data); 8 Jul 2009, w. Henderson Co. (*KW* 85:93, 2009).

Out-of-season record (early summer): 19 Jun 1989, McElroy Lake (Palmer-Ball and Boggs, *KW* 67:62-63, 1991).

Unaccepted record: 3 Jun 1990, (2) in Hardin Co. (*KW* 66:87, 1990).

*SPOTTED SANDPIPER *Actitis macularius*

Status: Fairly common to common transient, extremely rare and local summer resident, extremely rare during winter. Recorded statewide, but more widely distributed west of the Cumberland Plateau. This species occurs in a great variety of shallow aquatic habitats from the margins of streams and farm ponds to the shores, mudflats and bars of the larger lakes and rivers. Peaks of abundance occur during early to mid-May and from late Jul to early Sep. Individuals occasionally linger into early winter and several have been documented during mid-winter; in addition, a bird was confirmed wintering in Franklin Co. 2016-2017 (see below). There seem to be a few reports of birds occurring between the normal spring and fall migratory periods every year, and a subset of these reports have included courtship or territorial behavior, perhaps involving nesting attempts (e.g. Mengel:243; *KW* 78:63, 2002; *KW* 66:87, 1990; Palmer-Ball and Boggs, *KW* 67:44-45, 1991). In addition, confirmed breeding has been documented from six counties (see below). Generally occurs singly or in small, scattered groups of fewer than a dozen birds. **State Breeding Status**: Endangered.

Maximum spring counts: **37** along the Barren River, Allen Co., 15 May 2015 (*KW* 91:69, 2015); **30** on the Ohio River at Louisville, 12 May 1991 (B. Palmer-Ball, eBird data); at least **30** at the Falls of the Ohio, 9 May 1999 (B. Palmer-Ball, eBird data).

Maximum fall counts: up to **50** at the Falls of the Ohio (Mengel:244); ca. **50** on the Mississippi River nr. Laketon, Carlisle Co., 31 Aug 1996 (*KW* 73:6, 1997); **43** in w. Fulton Co., 12 Aug 2000 (H. Chambers/M. Easley, eBird data).

Early spring dates: 13 Mar 1991, Ky Dam (*KW* 67:55, 1991); 26 Mar 1995, Chaney Lake (B. Palmer-Ball, eBird data); 29 Mar 19—, Warren Co. (Mengel:243); 30 Mar 1994, Minor Clark Hatchery (*KW* 70:52, 1994); 31 Mar 2003, Ohio River, Campbell Co. (*KW* 79:68, 2003); 1 Apr 2016, Green River Lake, Adair Co. (*KW* 92:59, 2016); 2 Apr 19—, Hopkins Co. (Mengel:243); 3 Apr 2000, Pulaski Co. (R. Denton, eBird data); 3 Apr 2018, Wood Creek Lake, Laurel Co. (*KW* 94:73, 2018); 4 Apr 1995, Pulaski Co. (R. Denton, eBird data); 5 Apr 18—, Nelson Co. (Mengel: 243); 5 Apr

1959, Warren Co. (*KW* 38:12, 1962); 5 Apr 2014, Taylor Co. (*KW* 90:70, 2014); 5 Apr 2015, Ohio River at Louisville (*KW* 91:69, 2015).

Late fall/early winter dates: occasionally lingers into late fall/early winter, latest records being 31 Dec 2007–1 Jan 2008, Ohio River at Dayton, Campbell Co. (*KW* 84:44, 2008); 28 Dec 1974, Lexington CBC (*AB* 29:374, 1975; *KW* 51:14, 1975); 14 Nov & 24 Dec 1987, Falls of the Ohio (*BO*, Dec 1987 & B. Palmer-Ball, eBird data); 19 Dec 2015, (ph.) Franklin Co. (*KW* 92:23/27/42, 2016; J. Snyder, eBird data); 4 Dec 2017, Franklin Co. (*KW* 94:56, 2018); 1 Dec 2000, Lake Barkley, Lyon Co. (*KW* 77:29, 2001; D. Roemer, notes); 23 Nov 2008, Jonathan Creek (*KW* 85:14, 2009 [date erroneously published as 24 Nov therein]); 23 Nov 1969, Louisville (J. Croft, notes).

Out-of-season records (mid-winter): 19 Jan 1986, Campbellsville Lake, Taylor Co. (*KW* 62:28, 1986); 13 Jan 2004, Lake Barkley, Lyon Co. (*KW* 80:43, 2004); 19 Dec 2009 & 25 Jan 2010, Lake Barkley, Lyon Co. (*KW* 86:18/43, 2010); 17 Dec 2016, (2) in Franklin Co. with 1 still there 30 Dec 2016 & 19 Feb/5 Mar/1 Apr 2017 that demonstrated wintering (*KW* 93:21/49/73, 2017 [erroneously published at *KW* 93:49, 2017 as 18 Dec 2016]; G. Sprandel/T. Quarles, eBird data); 20 Jan 2017, Cumberland River, Russell Co. (*KW* 93:49, 2017).

Summary of confirmed breeding records by county

Campbell (*KW* 85:93, 2009)
Fayette (Helton, *KW* 75:74, 1999)
Franklin (Despard, *KW* 30:62-63, 1954)
Henderson (Palmer-Ball, *KW* 76:21-22, 2000; *KW* 81:106, 2005; *KW* 89:95, 2013)
Jefferson (Mengel: 243; Stamm, *KW* 42:3-4, 1966; *KW* 61:57, 1985; *KW* 75:60, 1999)
Pulaski (*KW* 78:63, 2002; R. Denton, 2002 eBird data).

SOLITARY SANDPIPER *Tringa solitaria*

Status: Fairly common transient, extremely rare during summer, accidental during winter. Recorded statewide, but more numerous west of the Cumberland Plateau. Encountered in a variety of shallow aquatic habitats; most commonly found on small ponds and pools including closed-in situations such as semi-wooded streams and tree-bordered ponds; less often observed on open shores and extensive flats. Peaks in abundance occur from late Apr to early May and from late Jul to early Sep. There are several Jun records between the normal spring and fall migratory periods as well as a single report during early winter. Most often seen singly or in small, loose groups of fewer than a dozen birds.

Maximum spring counts: **113** at Chaney Lake, 19 Apr 2006 (*KW* 82:68, 2006); at least **90** at Mitchell Lake, Ballard WMA 3 May 2007 (*KW* 83:79, 2007); **69** at the Long Point Unit, 23 Apr 2002 (*KW* 78:50, 2002); **66** in s. Jefferson Co., 1 May 2018 (*KW* 94:74, 2018); **64+** at the Long Point Unit, 11 Apr 1999 (J. Wilson, notes); as many as **50** at a time in Warren Co. (Wilson, *KW* 16:19, 1940).

Maximum fall counts: **52** at Lake No. 9, 28 Jul 2007 (H. Chambers/M. Easley, eBird data); **40** at Mitchell Lake, Ballard WMA, 26 Aug 2009 (K. Dikun, eBird data).

Early spring dates: 10 Mar 2000, Pulaski Co. (R. Denton, eBird data); 14 Mar 1954, Louisville (Mengel:244); 14 Mar 2018, e. of Hickman, Fulton Co. (*KW* 94:74, 2018); 15 Mar 1952, south-central Kentucky (*KW* 38:12, 1962); 17 Mar 2012, Open Pond, Fulton Co. (*KW* 88:75, 2012).

Late fall dates: 30 Oct 1966, Louisville area (*KW* 52:48, 1976); 29 Oct 2011, Owsley Fork Lake (*KW* 88:9, 2012); 26 Oct 2017, Pulaski Co. (*KW* 94:8, 2018).

Out-of-season record (winter): 17 Dec 2008, Dewey Lake, Warren Co. (*KW* 85:24/49, 2009).

LESSER YELLOWLEGS *Tringa flavipes*

Status: Fairly common to common transient, extremely rare during summer and winter. Recorded statewide, but less numerous on the Cumberland Plateau and Mountains. Encountered in a great variety of shallow aquatic habitats from the margins of flooded fields and farm ponds to open shores and flats on the larger lakes and rivers. Peaks of abundance occur from mid-Apr to early May and from mid-Aug to mid-Sep. The species is occasionally observed during Jun between the normal spring and fall migratory periods and has been encountered a few times during mid-winter.

Generally much more numerous than the Greater Yellowlegs. Typically seen singly or in flocks of up to 25 birds, but occasionally seen in loose flocks of up to a few hundred birds during spring.

Maximum spring counts: at least **1830** in w. Fulton Co. (including 910 at Ky Bend and 575 adjacent to Lake No. 9), 21 Apr 2019 (C. Bliznick et al., eBird data); **1400+** in w. Fulton Co., 8 Apr 2017 (*KW* 93:73, 2017); **1029** in the Lower Hickman Bottoms (including 810 at the Long Point Unit), 29 Apr 2015 (*KW* 91:70, 2015; R. Denton, eBird data); ca. **1000** at the Sauerheber Unit, 15/18 Apr 2017 (*KW* 93:73, 2017/B. Palmer-Ball, eBird data); **800** at the Sauerheber Unit, 26 Apr 2015 (*KW* 91:70, 2015); at least **800** in the Lower Hickman Bottoms, 15 Apr 2016 (*KW* 92:60, 2016); **720** sw. of Rumsey, McLean Co., 26 Apr 2015 (*KW* 91:70, 2015); **684** total in s. Warren Co. (524 at Chapman Pond), 10 May 2008 (*KW* 84:62, 2008); more than **600** in scattered groups in western Fulton Co., 11 Apr 1999 (*KW* 75:43, 1999; M. Bennett, notes); **600** at the Sauerheber Unit, 20 Apr 2018 (*KW* 94:74, 2018); **500+** in the Upper Hickman Bottoms, 20 Apr 2014 (*KW* 90:70, 2014); ca. **500** at McElroy Lake, 12 May 2010 (*KW* 86:67, 2010); **424** in w. Fulton Co., 17 Apr 2004 (H. Chambers, eBird data); **407** at McElroy Lake, 5 May 2008 (*KW* 84:62, 2008); **370+** at the Long Point Unit, 11 Apr 1999 (J. Wilson, notes); "**up to several hundred**" at favorable spots (Mengel:246); **375+** in w. Henderson Co., 13 Apr 2014 (*KW* 90:70, 2014); **370** at McElroy Lake, 30 Apr 2015 (*KW* 91:70, 2015); **350** at the Sauerheber Unit, 4 May 2014 (*KW* 90:71, 2014); **330+** in w. Henderson Co., 29 Apr 2013 (*KW* 89:70, 2013); **300-350** in the Upper Hickman Bottoms, 31 Mar 2013 (*KW* 89:70, 2013); "**hundreds**" in Fulton Co., 6 Apr 1985 (*KW* 61:44, 1985); **300+** in the Upper Hickman Bottoms, 18/26 Apr 2007 (*KW* 83:79, 2007); ca. **300** in Livingston Co., 16-17 Apr 1989 (*KW* 65:67, 1989); 300 in w. Fulton Co., 30 Apr 1984 (*KW* 60:43, 1984); **300** in Fulton Co., 18 Apr 1987 (*KW* 63:49, 1987); **300** at McElroy Lake, 28 Apr 1991 (B. Palmer-Ball, eBird data); at least **300** in w. Henderson Co., 14 Apr 2012 (*KW* 88:75, 2012); **300** at the Long Point Unit, 22 Apr 2014 (*KW* 90:70, 2014); **300** s. of Middleton, Simpson Co., 28 Apr 2015 (*KW* 91:70, 2015); **300** at the Sauerheber Unit, 7 Apr 2016 (*KW* 92:60, 2016).

Maximum fall counts: **185** at a transient pond nr. Hadensville, Todd Co., 21 Sep 2017 (*KW* 94:8, 2018); at least **150** at McElroy Lake, 12 Sep 1989 (Palmer-Ball and Boggs, *KW* 67:44, 1991); **150+** at the Sauerheber Unit, 25 Sep 2006 (*KW* 83:12, 2007); **140+** at Open Pond, Fulton Co., 13 Jul 2008 (*KW* 84:87, 2008).

Early spring dates: 10 Feb 2015, Ballard WMA (*KW* 91:52, 2015); 15 Feb 2019, McElroy Lake (*KW* 95:48, 2019); 16 Feb 2012, Sauerheber Unit (*KW* 88:47, 2012); 19 Feb 2006, w. Henderson Co. (*KW* 82:47, 2006); 19 Feb 2011, w. Henderson Co. (J. Meredig, eBird data); 20 Feb 1982, Fulton Co. (*KW* 58:29, 1982); 20 Feb 2009, Chaney Lake (*KW* 85:49, 2009); 21 Feb 2003, Campbell Co. (*KW* 79:46, 2003).

Late fall/early winter dates: occasionally lingers into early winter, latest records being 15 Dec 2015/9 Jan 2016, Hart Co. (*KW* 92:42, 2016); 5 Jan 2013, Sauerheber Unit (J. Meredig, unconfirmed in eBird data but accepted herein); 29 Dec 1994, Logan Co. (*KW* 71:9, 1995); 19/26 Dec 2011, w. Henderson Co. (*KW* 88:47, 2012/J. Meredig, eBird data); CBC week, Dec 1994, Boyle Co. (*KW* 71:18, 1995); 15 Dec 2001, 5+1 nr. the Long Point Unit (*NAB* 56:181, 2002; C. Sloan, eBird data); 10 Dec 1989, Lake Peewee (*KW* 66:39, 1990); 2 Dec 1990, Lake Peewee (*KW* 67:30, 1991).

Out-of-season dates (mid-winter): 31 Jan 1999, one bird at McElroy Lake (*KW* 75:26, 1999); 3 Feb 2001, Fulton Co. (*NAB* 55:176, 2001); 16 Jan 2011, w. Henderson Co. (*KW* 87:61, 2011).

WILLET *Tringa semipalmata*

Status: Transient (rare to locally uncommon during spring, rare during fall). Recorded chiefly west of the Cumberland Plateau but the species was reported once in Elliott Co. (*KW* 86:67, 2010). Most often encountered on shorelines, mudflats, and bars of the larger lakes and rivers, but the species has been observed on smaller bodies of water and could be seen at any of the better shorebird areas throughout the state. Peaks of abundance occur from late Apr to early May and from mid-Jul to early Sep. Generally encountered singly or in small groups of up to a half-dozen birds, especially during fall, but larger flocks are regularly reported during the peak of spring movement. Like other large shorebirds, flocks of Willets typically remain in an area for only a day before migrating on.

Maximum spring counts: a total of **185** (123 at Ky Dam Village and 62 on Lake Barkley, Lyon Co.) (ph.), 30 Apr 2016 (*KW* 92:59, 2016); **154** (vt.) at Ky Dam Village, 3 May 1999 (*KW* 76:9, 2000; D.

Roemer, notes; [number published incorrectly as five birds in *KW* 75:43, 1999]); **151** (ph.) at Ky Dam Village, 30 Apr 2018 (*KW* 94:74, 2018); **80** (ph.) at Ky Dam Village, 27 Apr 2017 (*KW* 93:73, 2017); **64** (ph.) at Lexington, 28 Apr 2019 (R. Graham, eBird data); **60+** at Freeman Lake, 1 May 2007 (*KW* 83:79, 2007); **56** in ne. Jefferson Co., 2 May 2011 (*KW* 87:88, 2011); **55** at Ky Dam Village, 29 Apr 2017 (eBird data; *KW* 93:73, 2017); **54** at Ky Dam Village, 10 May 2016 (*KW* 92:60, 2016); **53** on Lake Barkley, Lyon Co., 26 Apr 2007 (*KW* 83:79, 2007); **53** (ph.) at Ky Dam Village, 10 May 2013 (*KW* 89:70, 2013); at least **50** at the Minor Clark Hatchery (ca. 12) and Cave Run Lake Dam (ca. 40), 9 May 2009 (*KW* 85:69, 2009); **47** at McElroy Lake, 3 May 2015 (*KW* 91:70, 2015); at least **45** at Ky Dam, 3 May 1991 (*KW* 67:55, 1991); **43** at McElroy Lake, 29 Apr 1989 (Palmer-Ball and Boggs, *KW* 67:44, 1991); **43** on Lake Barkley, Lyon Co., 28 Apr 2003 (*KW* 79:68, 2003); at least **42** in s. Jefferson Co., 25 Apr 2011 (*KW* 87:88, 2011); **41** e. of Cadiz, Trigg Co., 29 Apr 2005 (*KW* 81:86, 2005); **41** at McElroy Lake, 25 Apr 2008 (*KW* 84:62, 2008); **40+** at Barren River Lake, 29 Apr 1989 (*KW* 65:67, 1989); at least **40** at Minor Clark Hatchery, 27 Apr 2013 (*KW* 89:70, 2013); **39** at the Falls of the Ohio, 2 May 2010 (*KW* 86:67, 2010); **38** at Ky Dam Village, 11 May 2007 (*KW* 83:79, 2007 [date erroneously published as 10 May therein]); **38** nr. Morgan Pond, 2 May 2016 (*KW* 92:59, 2016); **38** at Lexington, 28 Apr 2017 (*KW* 93:73, 2017); **37** at the Falls of the Ohio, 5 May 1976 (*KW* 52:49, 1976); **36** on Lake Barkley, Lyon Co., 30 Apr 2003 (*KW* 79:68, 2003); at least **35** at the Falls of the Ohio, 30 Apr 2010 (*KW* 86:67, 2010); **34** at Ky Dam Village, 1 May 2016 (*KW* 92:59, 2016); **31** at Chaney Lake, 25 Apr 2011 (*KW* 87:88, 2011); **29** at the Falls of the Ohio, 25 Apr 2014 (*KW* 90:70, 2014); **28** at Ky Dam Village, 7 May 2003 (*KW* 79:68, 2003); at least **27** at Lake Linville, Rockcastle Co. (*KW* 90:70, 2014); **25** at the Falls of the Ohio, 23 Apr 1977 (*AB* 31:1008, 1977; J. Elmore, notes); **25** at Grayson Lake, Carter Co., 27 Apr 1981 (W. Greene Jr., pers. comm.).

Maximum fall counts: **23** at the Falls of the Ohio, 5 Aug 1985 (*KW* 62:5, 1986); **22** at the Falls of the Ohio, 13 Jul 2005 (*KW* 81:106, 2005); **15** at Ky Dam, 13 Jul 2005 (*KW* 81:106, 2005); **10** at Lake Barkley SRP, Trigg Co., 6 Jul 2010 (*KW* 86:92, 2010).

Early spring dates: 23 Mar 1957, Warren Co. (Wilson, *KW* 33:60, 1957); 30 Mar 1937, Warren Co. (Wilson, *KW* 13:19, 1937); 2 Apr 1939, Warren Co. (Wilson, *KW* 16:19, 1940); 9 Apr 2015, Morgan Pond (*KW* 91:70, 2015); 12 Apr 1995, Madison Co. (*KW* 71:41, 1995); 17 Apr 1978, Falls of the Ohio (*KW* 54:44, 1978); 17 Apr 2013, Upper Hickman Bottoms (*KW* 89:70, 2013); 18 Apr 2008, McElroy Lake (*KW* 84:62, 2008); 19 Apr 1986, Ky Dam (*KW* 62:43, 1986); 19 Apr 2015, s. Christian Co. (J. Hall, eBird data).

Late spring dates: 4 Jun 2013, McElroy Lake (*KW* 89:95, 2013); 29 May 1982, Falls of the Ohio (*KW* 58:50, 1982); 29 May 1999, Marshall Co. (B. Palmer-Ball, eBird data).

Early fall dates: 22 Jun 1986, Smithland Dam (*KW* 62:67, 1986); 22 Jun 2002, Open Pond, Fulton Co. (*KW* 78:63, 2002); 5 Jul 1985, Falls of the Ohio (*KW* 61:57, 1985); 5 Jul 2010, at two locations in s. Warren Co. (*KW* 86:92, 2010); 6 Jul 2010, three locations [e. of Hickman, Fulton Co.; w. Henderson Co.; and Lake Barkley SRP, Trigg Co.] (*KW* 86:92, 2010 [location of the first erroneously published as the Lower Hickman Bottoms therein]); 6 Jul 2013, Union Co. (*KW* 89:95, 2013); 7 Jul 1999, Muhlenberg Co. (M. Bennett, pers. comm.); 8-18 Jul 1998, one to two birds at McElroy Lake (*KW* 74:73, 1998); 8 Jul 2006, Trigg Co. (*KW* 82:81, 2006).

Late fall dates: 17 Nov 1887, Fulton Co. (Mengel: 245); 19 Oct 1977, Pfeiffer Fish Hatchery, Franklin Co. (A. Westerman, pers. comm.); 17 Sep 2008, Ky Lake, Calloway Co. (*KW* 85:14, 2009); 14 Sep 1947, Falls of the Ohio (*KW* 52:49, 1976); 13 Sep 2012, Union Co. (*KW* 89:8, 2013).

Unaccepted records: 28 Feb 1993, Marshall Co. (*KW* 69:34, 1993); 20 Oct 1993, (40) in Madison Co. (*KW* 70:8, 1994).

GREATER YELLOWLEGS *Tringa melanoleuca*

Status: Uncommon to fairly common transient, extremely rare during summer and winter. Recorded chiefly west of the Cumberland Plateau. Encountered in a great variety of shallow aquatic habitats from flooded fields, mudflats, and farm ponds to open shores and flats on the larger lakes and rivers. There are a few Jun records between the normal spring and fall migratory periods, as well as a couple of reports during mid-winter. Peaks of abundance occur during mid-Apr and from late Sep to late Oct. Most often seen singly or in small groups of only a few birds, but sometimes in flocks of up to 25 or more. Generally much less numerous than the Lesser Yellowlegs.

Maximum spring counts: at least **290** in w. Fulton Co. (including 83 along Midway Church Rd. and 100 at Ky Bend), 21 Apr 2019 (C. Bliznick et al., eBird data); ca. **250** at the Sauerheber Unit, 9 Apr 2007 (*KW* 83:79, 2007); at least **214** in w. Henderson Co., 15 Apr 2018 (*KW* 94:74, 2018); **200+** at Obion WMA, Fulton Co., 18 Apr 2007 (*KW* 83:79, 2007); **200** in scattered groups in w. Fulton Co., 11 May 1993 (*KW* 69:45, 1993); **170+** in w. Fulton Co., 22 Apr 2006 (*KW* 82:68, 2006); **140** at the Long Point Unit, 10 Apr 2018 (B. Yandell, eBird data); **128** at the Long Point Unit, 20 Apr 2004 (*KW* 80:67, 2004); **125+** in w. Henderson Co., 13 Apr 2014 (*KW* 90:70, 2014); **120** at and nr. the Long Point Unit, 28 Mar 2014 (*KW* 90:70, 2014); **115** in the Lower Hickman Bottoms 15 Apr 2016 (*KW* 92:59, 2016); ca. **100** in western Fulton Co., 11 Apr 1998 (*KW* 74:53, 1998); **100+** in w. Henderson Co., 22 Apr 2010 (*KW* 86:67, 2010); at least **100** in w. Henderson Co., 14 Apr 2012 (*KW* 88:75, 2012); **100+** in the Upper Hickman Bottoms, 28 Mar 2013 (*KW* 89:70, 2013); **100+** in the Pond Creek Bottoms, Hopkins Co., 9 Apr 2014 (*KW* 90:70, 2014); **100** at the Sauerheber Unit, 26 Apr 2015 (*KW* 91:70, 2015); **100** at the Long Point Unit, 8 Apr 2017 (J. Sole, eBird data); **99** at the Long Point Unit, 31 Mar 2018 (H. Chambers, et al., eBird data); **97** at Morgan Pond, 26 Mar 2018 (J. Hall/S. Arnold, eBird data); at least **87** in w. Henderson Co., 12 Apr 2009 (*KW* 85:69, 2009); ca. **85** in w. Henderson Co., 21 Apr 2004 (*KW* 80:67, 2004); **80+** at the Long Point Unit, 1 Apr 1991 (*KW* 67:55, 1991); **80** at the Sauerheber Unit, 21 Mar 2016 (*KW* 92:59, 2016).

Maximum fall counts: ca. **60** at Ballard WMA, 8 Oct 2007 (*KW* 84:8, 2008); **33** at Jonathan Creek 1 Nov 2005 (H. Chambers, eBird data); **32** at Blood River, 12 Oct 2003 (*KW* 80:8, 2004); **31** at Minor Clark Hatchery, 28 Oct 2004 (*KW* 80:8, 2004).

Early spring dates: 15 Feb 1939, Warren Co. (*KW* 38:12, 1962); 17 Feb 2018, (ph.) Hart Co. (*KW* 94:56, 2018); 18 Feb 2008, McElroy Lake (*KW* 84:44, 2008); 19 Feb 2011, w. Henderson Co. (J. Meredig, eBird data).

Late fall dates: occasionally lingers into late fall/early winter, latest records being 24 Dec 2011, Sauerheber Unit (*KW* 88:47, 2012); 15 Dec 2001, Lower Hickman Bottoms (C. Sloan, eBird data); 11 Dec 1990, Lake Peewee (*KW* 67:30, 1991); (5) in the Lower Hickman Bottoms, 10 Dec 2009 and (4) nr. Open Pond, Fulton Co., 5 Dec 2009 (*KW* 86:43, 2010); 1 Dec 1984, LBL (*KW* 61:30, 1985); 1 Dec 2001, Larue Co. (B. Palmer-Ball, eBird data); 1 Dec 2009, Sauerheber Unit (*KW* 86:43, 2010).

Out-of-season records (mid-winter): 21 Jan 2007, (ph.) Guthrie Swamp, Todd Co. (*KW* 83:48, 2007); 18 Jan 2010, nr. Open Pond, Fulton Co. (*KW* 86:43, 2010).

Unaccepted records: 2 Jan 1971, Henderson CBC [no details provided] (*AB* 25:322, 1971); 19 Dec 1999, Louisville [certainly appeared to be a yellowlegs, but details do not distinguish species] (*KW* 76:13, 2000).

WILSON'S PHALAROPE Phalaropus tricolor

Status: Transient (rare during spring, rare to uncommon during fall); accidental during summer (one nesting attempt). Recorded chiefly west of the Cumberland Plateau, but there are several records from eastern Kentucky including one for Harlan Co. (McKee, *KW* 55:52, 1979). Generally encountered along the shallow water margins of flooded fields and the larger lakes and rivers, but can be expected to occur at least occasionally at all of the state's better shorebird areas during fall. Peaks of abundance occur from late Apr to early May and from late Aug to mid-Sep. The abundance of this species during spring varies greatly from year to year; most years it is quite rare, but occasionally it may be relatively widespread as in 1997, 2008, and 2010 (see below). A nest with eggs was present at McElroy Lake 30 May 2008 (*KW* 84:64, 2008), but it was subsequently destroyed by farming activity (*KW* 64:87, 2008). Most often seen singly, frequently in the company of Lesser Yellowlegs, but there are several records of small flocks of up to a half-dozen or more birds.

Maximum spring counts: at least **85** at Lake No. 9, 29 Apr 2010 (*KW* 86:68, 2010); at least **50** at the Sauerheber Unit, 28 Apr 2010 (*KW* 86:68, 2010); ca. **30** at McElroy Lake, 9 May 2008 (*KW* 84:64, 2008); **20+** at the Long Point Unit, 4 May 1997 (B. Yandell, pers. comm.); **23** total at scattered sites in s. Warren Co., 10 May 2008 (*KW* 84:64, 2008); **18** at McElroy Lake, 4 May 1997 (Roemer, et al., *KW* 73:79-83, 1997); **11** in s. Jefferson Co., 9 May 2014 (*KW* 90:72, 2014).

Maximum fall counts: **7** at the Falls of the Ohio, 22 Aug 1983 (*KW* 60:17, 1984); **5+** (maybe 8-10) at McElroy Lake, 20-27 Aug 1989 (Palmer-Ball and Boggs, *KW* 67:63, 1991).

Early spring dates: 19 Mar 2016, (ph.) Sauerheber Unit (*KW* 92:61, 2016); 30 Mar 1986, Louisville (*KW* 62:44, 1986); 6 Apr 1985, Long Point Unit (*KW* 61:45, 1985); 7 Apr 2017, Sauerheber Unit (*KW* 93:73, 2017).

Late spring dates: 4 Jun 2012, (ph.) Jefferson Co. (*KW* 88:94/104, 2012); 2 Jun 2008, McElroy Lake (*KW* 84:87, 2008; D. Roemer, notes); 28 May 1978, Jessamine Co. (*KW* 54:44, 1978); 27 May 2006, Union Co. (*KW* 82:69, 2006).

Early fall date: 3 Jul 1994, McElroy Lake (B. Palmer-Ball, eBird data).

Late fall date: 28 Sep 1937, Falls of the Ohio (Monroe and Mengel, *KW* 15:43, 1939).

Out-of-season records (summer): 16 Jun 2008, 3 females at Morgan Pond (*KW* 84:87, 2008); 21 Jun 2010, a male at McElroy Lake (*KW* 86:94, 2010).

RED-NECKED PHALAROPE *Phalaropus lobatus*

Status: Extremely rare transient, accidental during summer. There are at least 53 records (19 during spring, two during summer, and 32 during fall). The two "summer" reports occurred between the normal spring and fall migratory periods. Most often seen singly with collections of other shorebirds, but on a few occasions small flocks have been observed resting on open water of reservoirs. Peaks of abundance occur during mid- to late May and from late Aug to late Sep.

Published error: I can find no evidence for the record of a flock of 12 at the Falls of the Ohio, 10 Oct 1948 (*AFN* 3:18, 1949) and believe it must be erroneous.

Tally of records by county

Calloway (3), Christian (5), Fayette, Franklin (2), Fulton (2), Henderson, Jefferson (12), Livingston/ Lyon, Lyon (2), Lyon/Trigg. Marshall (3), McLean (2), Pulaski (2), Rowan (3), Union (5), Warren (9)

Range of spring dates: 3-28 May

Range of fall dates: 24 Aug–30 Oct

Chronological list of spring records (one individual unless otherwise noted)

1) 20-23 May 1989, (ph.) at McElroy Lake (Palmer-Ball, *KW* 66:29-30, 1990)
2) 19 May 1994, at McElroy Lake (*KW* 70:53, 1994)
3) 6 May 1998, at McElroy Lake (Roemer, *KW* 74:92/95, 1998)
4) 24-25 May 2001, (ph.) e. of Morganfield, Union Co. (B. Palmer-Ball, eBird data)
5) 17-19 May 2002, up to 5 (vt.) at Morgan Pond (*KW* 78:50, 2002)
6) 18-19 May 2002, 1-2 at McElroy Lake (*KW* 78:50, 2002)
7) 23 May 2007, (ph.) in w. Henderson Co. (*KW* 83:75/81, 2007)
8) 3-4 May 2008, (ph.) at Morgan Pond (*KW* 84:64/67, 2008)
9) 14/18 May 2008, probably different birds (ph.) at McElroy Lake (*KW* 84:64, 2008)
10) 17 May 2008, 6 (3 males and 3 females) at Morgan Pond (*KW* 84:64, 2008)
11) 20 May 2011, 2 (ph.) e. of Poplar Grove, McLean Co. (Palmer-Ball and Huber, *KW* 88:87-91, 2012; *KW* 87:90, 2011)
12) 23-24 May 2011, w. of Buttonsberry, McLean Co. (Palmer-Ball and Huber, *KW* 88:87-91, 2012; *KW* 87:90, 2011)
13) 4-7 May 2013, 1-2 (ph.) at Hays Kennedy Park, Jefferson Co. (*KW* 89:72/74, 2013)
14) 18 May 2013, at McElroy Lake (*KW* 89:72, 2013)
15) 18-21 May 2013, 1-3 at Morgan Pond (*KW* 89:72, 2013)
16) 23-25 May 2016, (ph.) at Morgan Pond (*KW* 92:61/72, 2016)
17) 26 May 2017, 2 (ph.) in the Lower Hickman Bottoms (*KW* 93:73, 2017)
18) 28 May 2017, (ph.) at Murl Pond, Wayne Co. (*KW* 93:73/84, 2017)
19) 9 May 2018, (ph.) at Talon Winery, s. Fayette Co. (*KW* 94:74, 2018)

Chronological list of summer records

1) 4 Jul 1989, a female at McElroy Lake (Palmer-Ball and Boggs, *KW* 67:63, 1991)
2) 20 Jun 2007, a male (ph.) in Union Co. (*KW* 83:105, 2007)

Chronological list of fall records (all have been juvs.; one individual unless otherwise noted)

1) 24 Aug 1946, Falls of the Ohio (Monroe and Monroe, *KW* 25:65, 1949)
2) 9 Oct 1947, Falls of the Ohio (Monroe and Monroe, *KW* 25:65, 1949)
3) 27 Sep 1953, Falls of the Ohio (Stamm, et al., *KW* 36:7, 1960)
4) 12-13 Sep 1959, Falls of the Ohio (Croft and Wiley, *KW* 36:17-19, 1960)
5) 25 Aug 1963, Falls of the Ohio (Stamm, et al., *KW* 43:11, 1967)
6) 6 Sep 1964, Falls of the Ohio (Stamm, et al., *KW* 43:11, 1967)
7) 26 Aug 1973, Falls of the Ohio (*BO*, Sep 1973)
8) 12 Sep 1975, Blood River (M. Miller, pers. comm.)
9) 19 Oct 1977, Pfeiffer Fish Hatchery, Franklin Co. (A. Westerman, pers. comm.)
10) 30 Oct 1977, Honker Lake, LBL, Lyon/Trigg cos. (D. Berry, eBird data; [erroneously published as 30 Oct–5 Nov in previous edition of this work])
11) fall 1981, Pfeiffer Fish Hatchery, Franklin Co. (G. Wells, pers. comm.)
12) 10-12 Sep 1989, McElroy Lake (Palmer-Ball and Boggs, *KW* 67:63, 1991)
13) 19-20 Sep 1999, Blood River (H. Chambers, eBird data)
14) 14 Oct 2002, McElroy Lake (*KW* 79:10, 2003)
15) 14 Sep 2003, e. of Morganfield, Union Co. (*KW* 80:10, 2004)
16) 15 Sep 2007, (ph.) nr. Prospect, Jefferson Co. (*KW* 84:10 2008)
17) 31 Aug 2008, (ph.) on the Mississippi River, Fulton Co. (*KW* 85:16, 2009)
18) 20-23 Sep 2008, (ph.) at Minor Clark Hatchery (*KW* 85:16/40, 2009)
19) 21-27 Sep 2009, (ph.) at the Falls of the Ohio (*KW* 86:9, 2010)
20) 12 Sep 2010, (ph.) at Blood River (*KW* 87:18, 2011)
21) 19 Sep 2010, 2 (vt.) on Lake Barkley, Livingston/Lyon cos. (*KW* 87:18, 2011)
22) 24-25 Sep 2010, (ph.) e. of Morganfield, Union Co. (*KW* 87:18/44, 2011)
23) 6 Sep 2011, (ph.) at Fishing Creek (*KW* 88:10/40, 2012)
24) 7 Sep 2011, a different bird (ph.) at Fishing Creek (*KW* 88:10, 2012)
25) 5 Oct 2015, at Hays Kennedy Park, Jefferson Co. (*KW* 92:9, 2016)
26) 1-3 Sep 2017, up to 3 (ph.) at the Falls of the Ohio (*KW* 94:8, 2018; Palmer-Ball, *KW* 93:112/113, 2017)
27) 13 Sep 2017, 9 on Ky Lake above Ky Dam (*KW* 94:8, 2018)
28) 13 Sep 2017, on Ky Lake, Marshall Co. (Palmer-Ball, *KW* 93:113, 2017)
29) 17 Sep 2017, (ph.) at Jonathan Creek (*KW* 94:8, 2018; H. Chambers, et al., eBird data)
30) 8 Sep 2018, (ph.) at Minor Clark Hatchery (*KW* 95:7, 2019)
31) 18 Sep 2018, Cave Run Lake (*KW* 95:7, 2019)
32) 4 Oct 2018, (ph.) e. of Morganfield, Union Co. (*KW* 95:7, 2019)

RED PHALAROPE *Phalaropus fulicarius*

Status: Extremely rare fall transient; accidental spring and winter visitant. There are 16 records (14 during fall, one during spring, and one during early winter). A peak of abundance occurs during Sep. Being a pelagic species, this phalarope (as well as the preceding species) can be observed resting on open water of lakes or rivers. Typically seen singly, which makes the report by J.J. Audubon of a flock of 100 all the more extraordinary.

Unaccepted record: given the time of year, a phalarope reported but not conclusively described from s. Jefferson Co., 13 Nov 1991, was likely this species (see *KW* 69:24, 1993).

Tally of records by county

Ballard, Campbell/Kenton, Carlisle, Carroll, Jefferson (8), Marshall (2), Mercer, Warren

Range of fall dates: 11 Aug–15 Nov

Chronological list of fall records (all but one have been juvs.; one individual unless otherwise noted)

1) late Oct 1808, 100 on the Ohio River at Louisville, some of which were shot and eaten by J.J. Audubon – the birds were so tasty that Audubon returned the following day to shoot more, but the flock had departed (Mengel:256)

2) 15 Nov 1938, collected (sp.) on the Ohio River nr. Carrollton, Carroll Co. (Monroe, *Auk* 57:111, 1940)

3) 2 Oct 1948, at the Falls of the Ohio (Mengel:256; *AFN* 3:18, 1949; *KW* 52:50, 1976 [latter source indicates collection of a specimen, but none seems to exist; the reference may pertain to the 1938 bird?])

4) 28 Sep 1949, (ba.) at the Falls of the Ohio (Lovell, *IAQ* 29:6, 1951)

5) 3 Oct 1951, at the Falls of the Ohio (*KW* 52:50, 1976)

6) 1 Nov 1978, at the Falls of the Ohio (*KW* 55:16, 1979)

7) 17-18 Oct 1998, (vt.) at Jonathan Creek (Chambers, *KW* 76:21, 2000)

8) 7-14 Sep 2000, (ph.) at Brown Power Plant, Mercer Co. (*KW* 77:7, 2001; W. Kemper, notes; B. Palmer-Ball, eBird data)

9) 17 Sep 2000, (vt.) nr. Woodburn, Warren Co. (*KW* 77:7, 2001)

10) 13-17 Sep 2003, (ph.) at Jonathan Creek (*KW* 80:10, 2004)

11) 31 Aug 2005, (ph.) on the Ohio River, Campbell/Kenton cos. (*KW* 82:9, 2006)

12) 1-2 Oct 2009, (ph.) in s. Jefferson Co. (*KW* 86:9/36, 2010)

13) 25 Oct 2013, (ph.) on the Mississippi River, Carlisle Co. (*KW* 90:11, 2014)

14) 11 Aug 2015, a molting ad. (ph.) nr. Swan Lake, Ballard Co. (*KW* 92:9/36, 2016)

Spring record

1) 8 May 2013, 2 (ph.) in s. Jefferson Co. (*KW* 89:72/75, 2013)

Winter record

1) 17 Dec 1971, (ph.) found injured in sw. Jefferson Co. (Summerfield, *KW* 48:18, 1972)

POMARINE JAEGER *Stercorarius pomarinus*

Status: Extremely rare fall, winter and early spring visitant. There are six records (one during fall, four during winter, and one during spring).

Chronological list of records

1) 22 Feb–24 Mar 1987, a first-year bird (ph.) at Ky Dam (*KW* 63:37/50 1987; *AB* 41:288, 1987)

2) 23-24 Jan 1999, a sub-ad. bird (vt.) at Ky Dam (*KW* 75:26, 1999; C. Sloan/H. Chambers, notes; D. Roemer, video/notes)

3) 6-7 Feb 1999, a light morph ad. (vt.) at Barkley Dam (*KW* 75:26/49, 1999; J./P. Bell, notes; F. Bennett, video [location published incorrectly as at Ky Dam in *KW* 75:26, 1999])

4) 22-30 Mar 2000, a light morph ad. (vt.) at Barkley Dam (*KW* 76:45, 2000; *NAB* 54:289, 2000; B. Yandell, notes; D. Roemer, video/notes)

5) 3-7 Nov 2005, a juv. (ph.) at Freeman Lake (*KW* 82:9-10, 2006)

6) 14-22 Feb 2014, a likely sub-ad. (ph.) at Green River Lake, Taylor Co. (*KW* 90:49/51, 2014)

PARASITIC JAEGER *Stercorarius parasiticus*

Status: Extremely rare fall visitant. This typically pelagic jaeger has been suitably documented in Kentucky on two occasions.

Chronological list of records

1) 11–14 Sep 2011, a juv. (ph.) at Barren River Lake, Allen/Barren cos. (Chambers et al., *KW* 88:37-38, 2012; *KW* 88:1/12/40, 2012)

2) 13-18 Sep 2017, at least one juv. (ph.) on Ky Lake above Ky Dam (*KW* 94:8/40, 2018; Palmer-Ball, *KW* 93:113-114, 2017)

LONG-TAILED JAEGER *Stercorarius longicaudus*

Status: Extremely rare fall visitant. This typically pelagic jaeger has been suitably documented in Kentucky four times.

Chronological list of records

1) 29 Aug–11 Sep 2004, a juv. (ph.) on Ky Lake above Ky Dam (Chambers, et al., *KW* 81:33-34, 2005; *KW* 81:1/9, 2005)
2) 10-14 Sep 2011, a juv. (ph.) on Barren River Lake, Allen/Barren cos. (Chambers et al., *KW* 88:37-38, 2012; *KW* 88:1/12/40, 2012)
3) 2 Sep 2012, a juv. (ph.) on Ky Lake above Ky Dam, Livingston (*KW* 89:10, 2013)
4) 13-19 Sep 2017, at least one juv. (ph.) on Ky Lake above Ky Dam, Marshall/Livingston cos. (*KW* 94:8/40; Palmer-Ball, *KW* 93:113, 2017)

JAEGERS *Stercorarius* spp.

Status: Jaegers can be extremely difficult to identify reliably to species without excellent study. Individuals that have been reported without sufficent detail to conclusively identify to species have been reported three additional times.

Chronological list of records

1) 3 Dec 1985, a first-year bird on n. Lake Barkley off Boyd's Landing boat ramp, Lyon Co. (*KW* 62:28, 1986)
2) 22 Nov 1996, a first-year bird (probable Pomarine) at Freeman Lake (R. Healy/R. Parker/J. Oliver, notes and drawing)
3) 13-17 Sep 2017, in addition to single individuals confirmed to be Parasitic and Long-tailed Jaegers on Ky Lake above Ky Dam, Livingston/Marshall cos., at least two additional birds were observed on Ky Lake, Marshall Co., but were not confirmed as to identity (*KW* 94:8, 2017; Palmer-Ball, *KW* 93:113-114, 2017)

LONG-BILLED MURRELET *Brachyramphus perdix*

Status: Accidental vagrant. This native of coastal areas of e. Asia has been reported infrequently across North America. It has been reported on one occcasion in Kentucky.

1) 29-30 Oct 2002, (vt./ph.) on the Ohio River at Louisville (*KW* 79:1/11, 2003)

BLACK-LEGGED KITTIWAKE *Rissa tridactyla*

Status: Extremely rare fall and winter transient. This beautiful gull is occasionally encountered during fall migration and early winter, when it has been most frequently encountered at dams on the Ohio River and at LBL. All but one report have been of the boldly marked first-year birds, and all but two reports have been of single birds. There are 17 records, most during Nov and early Dec.

Unaccepted record: 17-18 Feb 1989, a first-year bird on the Ohio River at Louisville (*KW* 65:36, 1989).

Range of dates: 31 Oct–24 Jan

Chronological list of records

1) 6 Nov 1960, a first-year bird on the Ohio River at Louisville (Mengel:518)
2) 10-15 Dec 1966, a first-year bird collected (sp.) on the Ohio River at Louisville (Monroe and Able, *KW* 44:56, 1968)
3) 31 Oct–2 Dec 1967, a first-year bird (2 on 2 Dec) on the Ohio River upstream from and at Louisville (*KW* 52:51, 1976)
4) 9-27 Dec 1967, 1-2 at Ky Dam (*KW* 44:6-7, 1968; Monroe and Able, *KW* 44:55, 1968)
5) 3 Dec 1983, an ad. (ph.) below Ky Dam (*KW* 60:26, 1984)
6) 1-2 Dec 1984, a first-year bird on Ky Lake above Ky Dam (*KW* 61:30, 1985)
7) 17 Nov 1985, a first-year bird below Ky Dam (*KW* 62:6, 1986)
8) 28 Nov 1991, a first-year bird (ph.) on the Ohio River at Louisville (*KW* 68:8, 1992)

9) 25-28 Nov 1995, a first-year bird (ph.) at Green River Lake, Taylor Co. (J. Elmore, notes; B. Palmer-Ball, eBird data)
10) 16-24 Dec 1995, a first-year bird (ph.) at Markland Dam, Gallatin Co. (*KW* 72:19/44, 1996; B. Palmer-Ball, eBird data)
11) 14 Jan 1996, a first-year bird at Ky Dam (B. Palmer-Ball, eBird data)
12) 22-29 Nov 1997, a first-year bird (ph.) at Markland Dam, Gallatin Co. (*KW* 74:8, 1998; B. Palmer-Ball, eBird data)
13) 4 Dec 1999–24 Jan 2000, a first-year bird (vt.) at Meldahl Dam, Bracken Co. (*KW* 76:31, 2000; J. Stenger, pers. comm.)
14) 25 Nov 2000, a first-year bird on Lake Barkley, Lyon Co. (*KW* 77:7, 2001)
15) 4 Nov 2010, a first-year bird on Ky Lake above Ky Dam, Marshall Co. (*KW* 87:18, 2011)
16) 7 Nov 2012, a first-year bird (ph.) on Lake Cumberland, Pulaski Co. (*KW* 89:10, 2013)
17) 11-13 Nov 2012, a first-year bird (ph.) at the Falls of the Ohio (*KW* 89:9/10, 2013)

SABINE'S GULL *Xema sabini*

Status: Extremely rare fall transient and winter visitant. This primarily pelagic gull is probably to be expected only on the larger lakes and rivers and only during fall or early winter. There are at least 15 records (13 during fall and two during winter), and all have been juvs.

Unaccepted record: 5 Sep 2011, Barren River Lake (Stedman 2019) [certainly a reliable record but no details are available for review].

Range of fall dates: 2 Sep–7 Oct

Chronological list of records

1) 8-11 Sep 1984, a juv. (ph.) at the Falls of the Ohio; the same bird (or possibly a different individual) was observed at the same location 30 Sep 1984 & 5 Oct 1984 (Andres and Palmer-Ball, *KW* 60:62-63, 1984)
2) 7 Oct 1999, a juv. on the Ohio River at Metropolis, IL, McCracken Co. (*KW* 77:35, 2001; F. Bennett, notes/drawing)
3) 30 Sep–1 Oct 2000, a juv. on Ky Lake above Ky Dam, Marshall Co. (*KW* 77:7, 2001)
4) 11 Sep–4 Oct 2002, 1-2 juvs. (ph./vt.) on Lake Barkley, Lyon Co. (11 Sep only) and Ky Lake, Marshall Co. (2 present 14-20 Sep) (*KW* 79:11, 2003)
5) 16 Dec 2006–4 Jan 2007, a juv. (vt./ph.) at Honker Bay, Lake Barkley, Lyon Co. (*KW* 83:22/49, 2007; M. Cunningham, pers. comm./photograph)
6) 28-29 Sep 2007, a juv. on Ky Lake, Marshall Co. (*KW* 84:11 2008)
7) 8 Sep 2009, a juv. (ph.) e. of Morganfield,, Union Co. (*KW* 86:10, 2010)
8) 21 Sep 2012, a juv. at Barren River Lake (*KW* 89:9, 2013)
9) 18-19 Sep 2013, a juv.(ph.) on Ky Lake, Marshall Co. (*KW* 90:11/20, 2014)
10) 20 Sep 2014, a juv. on Ky Lake, Marshall Co. (*KW* 91:10, 2015)
11) 12-13 Dec 2015, a juv. (ph.) on a transient pond s. of Murl, Wayne Co. (*KW* 92:43, 2016)
12) 2 Sep 2017, a juv. (ph.) at the Falls of the Ohio (*KW* 94:9, 2018; Palmer-Ball, *KW* 93:112, 2017)
13) 2 Sep 2017, a juv. (vt.) at Jacobson Park, Lexington (*KW* 94:9, 2018; Palmer-Ball, *KW* 93:112, 2017)
14) 13 Sep 2017, a juv. on Ky Lake, Livingston/Marshall cos. (*KW* 94:9, 2018; Palmer-Ball, *KW* 93:113, 2017)
15) 11 Sep 2018, a juv. (ph.) on Lake Cumberland, Russell Co. (*KW* 95:7, 2019)

BONAPARTE'S GULL *Chroicocephalus philadelphia*

Status: Uncommon to fairly common transient, rare to uncommon winter resident, extremely rare during summer. Recorded statewide, but chiefly west of the Cumberland Plateau. Usually encountered on the larger lakes and rivers, but sometimes found resting or feeding on smaller bodies of water and in open agricultural fields, especially during the peak of migratory movements. Wintering was not a regular occurrence historically, but numbers now winter on some of the state's larger reservoirs. The species has been reported once during mid-summer as well as a few times during late summer well before the normal arrival dates in Oct. Most often seen in small groups of fewer than a couple dozen birds, but larger flocks of up to a hundred or more are regularly reported, especially during the peaks of migration during Nov and Apr. In addition, peak counts of wintering birds on the larger lakes and rivers sometimes number more than a thousand birds.

Maximum counts (LBL vicinity): **9000-10,000** in the Kentucky/Barkley/Smithland dams area, early Apr 1989 (*KW* 65:68, 1989); **7000-10,000** on Ky Lake, 11 Feb 2007 (*KW* 83:48, 2007); ca. **6000** on Ky Lake nr. Kenlake State Park, Marshall Co., 20 Jan 2002 (H. Chambers, notes); **5000** on Ky Lake nr. Hamlin, Calloway Co., 31 Dec 1990 (*KW* 67:31, 1991); **4000-5000** on Lake Barkley, Lyon Co., mid-Jan 2009 (*KW* 85:49, 2009); **3500-4000** on Lake Barkley, Lyon Co., 15 Feb 2005 (*KW* 81:59, 2005); ca. **3000** on Ky Lake, Marshall Co., 14 Dec 2008 (*KW* 85:49, 2009); at least **2500** at Lake Barkley, Lyon Co., 1 Mar 2013 (*KW* 89:72, 2013); **2400** at Ky Lake, Marshall Co., 14 Dec 2013 (*KW* 90:49, 2014); **2000+** on Ky Lake, Marshall Co., 29 Dec 2009 (*KW* 84:45, 2008); ca. **2000** at Lake Barkley, Lyon Co., 18 Feb 2012 (*KW* 88:48, 2012); **1500** on Ky Lake, Marshall Co., 16 Dec 2009 (H. Chambers, eBird data); **1450** at Ky Lake, Marshall Co., 17 Dec 2011 (*KW* 88:48, 2012); **1134** at Ky Lake, Calloway Co., 27 Dec 2013 (*KW* 90:49, 2014); **1000** at Ky Dam, 17 Mar 2018 (*KW* 94:74, 2018).

Maximum counts (away from LBL vicinity): **5000** at Barren River Lake, 30 Dec 2017 (R. Bontrager/ L. Bontrager, eBird data); **more than half of 6000** gulls at Barren River Lake, 25 Dec 2012 (*KW* 89:48, 2013); ca. **1900** at Barren River Lake, 13 Feb 2017 (*KW* 93:49, 2017); **1800** at Meldahl Dam on the Ohio River, Bracken Co., 11 Nov 1997 (*KW* 74:7, 1998; date erroneously published as 9 Nov in previous edition of this work); **1600** at Barren River Lake, 14 Nov 2014 (*KW* 91:56, 2015); at least **1100** at Barren River Lake, 25 Dec 2013 (*KW* 90:49, 2014); ca. **1000** at Barren River Lake, 23 Mar 2009 (*KW* 85:72, 2009); at least **1000** at Barren River Lake, 27 Dec 2009/1 Jan 2010 (*KW* 86:44, 2010); **1000** on Honker Bay, LBL, Lyon/Co., 31 Mar 2010 (H. Chambers, eBird data); at least **1000** at Barren River Lake, 23 Nov 2010 (*KW* 87:18, 2011); ca. **1000** on the Fishing Creek embayment of Lake Cumberland, Pulaski Co., 4 Jan 2011 (eBird data); **1000** at Barren River Lake, 2 Jan 2015 (*KW* 91:52, 2015); **900-1000** at Barren River Lake, 4 Jan 2004 (eBird data); **950** on Green River Lake, Adair/Taylor cos., 4 Nov 2017 (*KW* 94:9, 2018); **900+** at Meldahl Dam, Bracken Co., 18 Nov 2002 (*KW* 79:10, 2003); **800** at Barren River Lake, 6 Nov 2006 (*KW* 83:14, 2007); **700** on Lake Cumberland, Russell Co., 18 Feb 2013 (*KW* 89:48, 2013); **600** on the Fishing Creek embayment of Lake Cumberland, Pulaski Co., 16 Mar 2004 (R. Denton, eBird data); **600** in the Lower Hickman Bottoms, 22 Mar 2004 (R. Denton, eBird data); **519** on Lake Cumberland, Wayne Co., 17 Dec 2003 (*KW* 80:44, 2004); **500** at Markland Dam, Gallatin Co., 22 Nov 1997 (B. Palmer-Ball, eBird data); **500** on Lake Cumberland, Pulaski Co., 17 Dec 2003 (R. Denton, eBird data); **500+** at Barren River Lake, 8 Dec 2004 (*KW* 81:59, 2005).

Late spring dates: 2 Jun 1999, Falls of the Ohio (*KW* 75:61, 1999); 1 Jun 1995, Ky Dam (M. Monroe/B. Monroe, III, notes); 27 May 1985, Ky Lake (*KW* 61:45, 1985; B. Palmer-Ball, eBird data); 24 May 1985, Falls of the Ohio (*KW* 61:45, 1985); 23 May 2015, (ph.) Taylorsville Lake, Spencer Co. (*KW* 91:71, 2015).

Early fall dates: 2-7 Aug 1987, (1-3) at the Falls of the Ohio (*KW* 64:18, 1988; L. Rauth, pers. comm.); 11 Aug 1985, Ky Dam (*KW* 62:6, 1986).

Out-of-season records (summer): 24 Jun 2002, an ad. on Barren River Lake (*KW* 78:64, 2002); 13 Jul 2005, a likely first-summer bird on Lake Barkley above the dam (*KW* 81:107, 2005).

Unaccepted records: 28 May 1996, (3) Jonathan Creek (*KW* 72:55, 1996).

BLACK-HEADED GULL *Chroicocephalus ridibundus*

Status: Accidental vagrant. This resident of Eurasia regularly occurs in North America and nests locally in far eastern Canada. It has been documented in Kentucky only once.

1) 15-23 Nov 1995, an ad. (ph.) at the Falls of the Ohio (Palmer-Ball, *KW* 72:1/35, 1996).

LITTLE GULL *Hydrocoloeus minutus*

Status: Extremely rare winter, spring, and summer visitant. This diminutive gull is almost always found in the company of Bonaparte's Gulls. There are eight records (three during spring, four during winter, and one during summer).

Chronological list of records

1) 9-17 Jun 1998, a first-year bird (ph.) at McElroy Lake (Roemer, *KW* 74:92/95, 1998)
2) 4 Apr 2000, a first-year bird on the Ohio River nr. Cincinnati (*KW* 76:45, 2000)
3) 14 Feb–17 Mar 2004, a first-year bird (vt.) on Ky Lake, Marshall Co. (*KW* 80:43-44/68, 2004)
4) 31 Mar–13 Apr 2007, an ad. on Lake Barkley, Lyon Co. (*KW* 83:81, 2007)
5) 23-24 Jan 2010, an ad. (ph.) on Honker Bay, Lake Barkley/LBL, Lyon Co. (*KW* 86:44, 2010)
6) 5 Dec 2012, a first-year bird at Blood River (*KW* 89:48, 2013)
7) 10-25 Feb 2018, a second-year bird (ph.) at Barren River Lake (*KW* 94:56/64, 2018; R. Bontrager, eBird data)
8) 20-28 Apr 2019, a first-year bird (ph.) at Barkley Dam (C. Bliznick et al., eBird data)

LAUGHING GULL *Leucophaeus atricilla*

Status: Rare spring and fall transient/visitant, extremely rare summer visitant and winter visitant/resident. Mengel (p. 521) did not include this species on the accepted state list. It was first recorded conclusively on the Ohio River at Louisville, 16 May 1967 (Monroe and Able, *KW* 44:55-56, 1968). In more recent years this gull has become a regular visitant along the Ohio River (especially at Louisville) and at Ky Lake/Lake Barkley, where it occurs annually in small numbers. In addition, the number of reports from other locales is growing, and the species has now been reported from 27 counties (see below). Most records have occurred from mid-Apr to early Jun and from mid-Jul to mid-Nov, but there are a few mid-summer records. In addition, a few individuals have lingered into early winter, have been seen during mid-winter, and have even wintered on a couple of occastions. It should be noted that the cut-offs in the seasonal summaries below are completely arbitrary. Most spring records are of adults, while most late summer and fall reports are of first-year birds. Usually seen singly, although two to a few are occasionally reported, and most of the state's highest counts have occurred after the passage of the remnants of tropical cyclones.

Maximum counts: **12** total at Barkley/Kentucky/Smithland dams, 27 Sep 2005 (*KW* 82:10, 2006); **10** at Freeman Lake, 31 Aug 2005 (*KW* 82:10, 2006); **7** at Ky Dam Village, 24 Sep 2004 (*KW* 81:9-10, 2005); **6** at the Falls of the Ohio, 2 Sep 2017 (Palmer-Ball, *KW* 93:112, 2017); **4** at Ky Dam and **3** at Smithland Dam, both 5 Sep 2005 (*KW* 82:10, 2006); **5** above Ky Dam, 26 May 1986 (*KW* 62:44, 1986); **5** at Ky Dam Village, 23 May 1998 (*KW* 74:54, 1998); at least **5** on Ky Lake, Marshall Co., 4 Oct 2002 (*KW* 79:10, 2003); **5** at Smithland Dam, 16 Sep 2005 (*KW* 82:10, 2006); **5** at Ky Dam Village, 11 May 2006 (*KW* 82;70, 2006); **5** at Ky Dam Village, 13/19 Sep 2006 (*KW* 83:14, 2007).

Early spring dates (other than known or presumed wintering birds): 11 Mar 2019, (ph.) McElroy Lake (R. Shive, eBird data); 12 Mar 2016, (ph.) Ohio River, Kenton Co. (*KW* 92:61, 2016); 13 Mar 2009, (ph.) Falls of the Ohio (*KW* 85:72, 2009); 21 Mar 2008, (ph.) Lake Cumberland, Pulaski Co. (*KW* 84:64, 2008); 11 Apr 1997, McElroy Lake (Roemer, et al., *KW* 73:82, 1997); 12 Apr 2008, Ky Dam (*KW* 84:64, 2008); 17 Apr 2017, (ph.) Ky Dam Village (*KW* 93:73, 2017).

Late spring dates (arbitrary cut off with summer records given below): 7 Jun 1984, (2) Falls of the Ohio (*KW* 60:53, 1984); 6 Jun 1992, Ky Dam (J. Wilson, eBird data); 6 Jun 2004, Ky Dam Village (*KW* 80:82, 2004); 4 Jun 1986, (2) Ky Dam (*KW* 62:67, 1986); 1 Jun 2000, Newburgh Dam, Henderson Co. (B. Palmer-Ball, eBird data); 1 Jun 2007, (2) Ky Dam (*KW* 83:105, 2007); 30 May 2008, (ph.) Morgan Pond (*KW* 84:64, 2008); 28 May 2009, (ph.) Lake Carnico, Nicholas Co. (*KW* 85: 70/72, 2009)

Early fall dates (arbitrary cut off with summer reports given below): 24 Jul 2003, Ky Dam (*KW* 79:82, 2003); 27 Jul 1989, Lake Barkley above the dam (*KW* 65:87, 1989).

Out-of-season records (summer): 20 Jun 1981, Ballard WMA (*KW* 57:73, 1981); 10-14 Jun 1987, Falls of the Ohio (*KW* 63:60, 1987); 1 Jul 1987, Lake Barkley above the dam (*KW* 63:60, 1987; B. Palmer-Ball, eBird data); 7 Jul 1989, Falls of the Ohio (*KW* 65:87, 1989); 28 Jun 1990, Ohio River at Louisville (*KW* 66:87, 1990); 13 Jul 1998, Ky Dam (*KW* 74:73, 1998); 7 Jul 1999, Ky Dam (*KW* 75:61, 1999); 10-16 Jun 2000, Brown Power Plant, Mercer Co. (*KW* 76:57, 2000); 6 Jul 2002, Lake Barkley, Lyon Co. (*KW* 78:64, 2002); 10 Jul 2005, Ky Lake, Calloway Co. (*KW* 81:107, 2005); 12-15 Jul 2005, up to 3 in the vicinity of Ky Dam (*KW* 81:107, 2005); 26 Jun/13 Jul 2009, Ky Dam (*KW* 85:93, 2009); 13 Jun 2010, McElroy Lake (*KW* 86:94, 2010); 19-21 Jul 2013, Ky Dam Village (*KW* 89:96, 2013); 15 Jun 2015, (ph.) Ky Dam (*KW* 91:86/96, 2015).

Late fall/early winter and out-of-season (winter) dates (occasionally lingers into early winter with a few into mid-winter): 30 Dec 1982–6 Jan 1983, an ad. (ph.) at Ky Dam (*AB* 37:307, 1983; *KW* 59: 29, 1983); 30 Dec 1984, (2 ads.) at Barkley Dam (*KW* 61:30, 1985); 1-26 Feb 1987, an ad. at Ky Dam [likely the same bird at Barkley Dam 22 Feb 1987] (*KW* 63:37, 1987); 13-20 Feb 1988 a first-year bird at Barkley Dam (*KW* 64:29, 1988); winter of 1997-1998, an ad. that remained throughout the season on Ky Lake and Lake Barkley (*KW* 74:13/33/54, 1998); winter 2000-2001, 1-2 ads. observed several times in the vicinity of Ky Dam (*KW* 77:29, 2001; *NAB* 55:176, 2001); 21-29 Dec 2000, Ohio River at Louisville (*KW* 77:11, 2001; B. Palmer-Ball, eBird data); 17 Feb 2001, Markland Dam, Gallatin Co. [possibly same bird that was in Louisville during late Dec 2000] (*KW* 77:29, 2001); 22/29 Dec 2002 & 15 Jan 2003, a first-year bird at Ky Dam (*KW* 79:47, 2003); 14 Dec 2003, Ky Dam (*KW* 80:43, 2004); 26-30 Jan 2006, Barren River Lake (*KW* 82:48, 2006); 15 Dec 2004/10 Jan 2005, Ky Dam (*KW* 81:59, 2005); 29 Dec 2008, nr. Maceo, Daviess Co. (*KW* 85:49, 2009); 21 Dec 2008–12 Jan 2009, (1-2) in the vicinity of Ky Dam (*KW* 85:49, 2009); 5 Dec 2010, Ky Dam (*KW* 87:62, 2011).

Hybrid record: Laughing Gull x Ring-billed Gull, an ad. (ph.) at Ky Dam, 26 Feb 2011 (*KW* 87:62/72, 2011).

Unaccepted record: 31 Jul 2002, Smithland Dam (eBird data [no details are available for review]).

Summary of records by county

Allen/Barren (*KW* 82:10/48, 2006; *KW* 92:9, 2016)
Ballard (*KW* 57:73, 1981; *KW* 85:16, 2009)
Boone (*KW* 79:69. 2003)
Bracken (*KW* 84:10, 2008)
Calloway (Ky Lake; essentially annual)
Campbell/Kenton (mouth of Licking River [*KW* 83:14, 2007])
Carlisle (*KW* 85:16, 2009)
Christian (*KW* 84:64, 2008; *KW* 93:9, 2017)
Daviess (*KW* 85:49, 2009)
Gallatin (*KW* 77:29, 2001)
Hardin (*KW* 82:10, 2006)
Henderson (B. Palmer-Ball, 2000 eBird data)
Jefferson (mostly Falls of the Ohio; annual)
Kenton (*KW* 92:61, 2016)
Livingston (Smithland Dam; essentially annual)
Lyon (Barkley Dam/Lake Barkley; essentially annual)
Marshall (Ky Lake; essentially annual)
Mercer (*KW* 76:57, 2000)
Nicholas (*KW* 85:70/72, 2009)
Ohio (*KW* 82:10, 2006; *KW* 83:81, 2007)
Pulaski (*KW* 82:10, 2006; *KW* 84:64, 2008)
Rowan (*KW* 91:10, 2015)
Russell (*KW* 82:10, 2006)
Trigg (*KW* 82:10, 2006)
Warren (*KW* 70:53, 1994; Roemer, et al., *KW* 73:82, 1997; Roemer, *KW* 74:95, 1998; *KW* 78:50, 2002; *KW* 86:94, 2010; *KW* 87:90, 2011; *KW* 91:72, 2015; *KW* 94:74, 2018)

FRANKLIN'S GULL *Leucophaeus pipixcan*

Status: Rare to locally uncommon transient, extremely rare during summer and winter with only a few records between normal periods of migration. Most of the older records of this species came from the Ohio River at Louisville, but the species occurs regularly on the lower Ohio River, Ky Lake, and Lake Barkley where it is annual, especially during fall migration. This gull is also regular at Barren River Lake during fall, and has now occurred at scattered localities (again, especially during fall migration) in about 20 counties across central and western Kentucky There are also single records for the Cumberland Mountains and Cumberland Plateau, and a few from the adjacent eastern Knobs (see below). Generally observed singly or in small groups of fewer than a half-dozen birds, usually in the company of other gulls.

Maximum spring count: **5** at Ky Dam Village, 12 May 2006 (*KW* 82:70, 2006).

Maximum fall counts: **220** total at scattered locales around the west Ky dam (including 164 below Smithland Dam), 26 Oct 2008 (*KW* 85:16, 2009); **206** at Barren River Lake, 6 Nov 2015 (*KW* 92:9, 2016); **154** at Jonathan Creek, 21 Sep 2014 (*KW* 91:10, 2015); **140** at Barren River Lake, 27 Oct 2010 (*KW* 87:18, 2011); **100** on the Ohio River at Louisville, 2 Nov 1960 (*AFN* 15:45, 1961); at least **100** at Barren River Lake, 28 Oct 2014 (*KW* 91:10, 2015); **64** at the Wildcat Creek embayment of Ky Lake, Calloway Co., 30 Oct 2015 (*KW* 92:9, 2016); **55** at Ky Dam Village, 3 Nov 2015 (*KW* 92:9, 2016); **45** on Ky Lake, Marshall Co., 4 Nov 2001 (*KW* 78:8, 2002); **43** on Ky Lake, Marshall Co., 15 Oct 2001 (*KW* 78:8, 2002); **32** on Barren River Lake, 22 Oct 2007 (*KW* 84:10 2008); **30** at the Sledd Creek embayment of Ky Lake, Marshall Co., 1 Nov 2015 (*KW* 92:9, 2016); **24** on the Ohio River at Louisville, 14 Nov 2000 (*KW* 77:7, 2001); **18** on the Ohio River at Louisville, 12 Nov 2015 (*KW* 92:10, 2016); **15** at Meldahl Dam, Bracken Co., 14 Nov 1998 (*KW* 75:6, 1999); **14** at Blood River, 3 Nov 2003 (*KW* 80:10, 2004 [erroneously published as 15 therein]); at least **13** on Ky Lake above Ky Dam, 7 Oct 1995 (B. Palmer-Ball/M. Monroe, eBird data); **12-20** on the Ohio River at Louisville, 11 Nov 1943 (Lovell and Carpenter, *KW* 21:31, 1945); **12** on Cedar Creek Lake, Lincoln Co., 9 Nov 2013 (*KW* 90:11-12/21, 2014).

Early spring dates: 4 Mar 1989, Lake Barkley (*KW* 65:68, 1989); 5 Mar 2001, Lower Hickman Bottoms (M. Todd, eBird data); 18 Mar 1967, Louisville area (*KW* 52:51, 1976); 18 Mar 2000, Fulton Co. (H. Chambers, notes).

Late spring dates: 10 Jun 2010, McElroy Lake (*KW* 86:94, 2010); 3-7 Jun 2012, (ph.) Jefferson Co. (*KW* 88:94/104, 2012); 4-5 Jun 1985, Falls of the Ohio (*KW* 61:57, 1985); 5 Jun 1998, (2) at McElroy Lake (Roemer, *KW* 74:95, 1998; J. Elmore, notes).

Early fall dates: 30 Jul 2013, Falls of the Ohio (*KW* 89:96, 2013); 9 Aug 1986, Ky Lake, Calloway Co. (*KW* 63:9, 1987); 12 Aug 2009, Barkley Dam (*KW* 86:10, 2010); 29 Aug 1987, sub-adult bird above Barkley Dam (M. Stinson, eBird data); 30 Aug 1998, singles at Smithland Dam and Ky Dam (D. Roemer, notes); 30 Aug 2005, Ky Dam (*KW* 82:10, 2006); 1 Sep 1997, Ohio River, Livingston Co. (B. Palmer-Ball, eBird data); 1 Sep 1998, Minor Clark Hatchery (*KW* 75:6, 1999); 1 Sep 2013, Ky Dam (*KW* 90:11, 2014).; 1 Sep 2017, Ky Dam Village (*KW* 94:9, 2018).

Late fall date: late fall migrants occasionally linger into early winter, the latest being 1 Jan 1958 (*KW* 52:51, 1976).

Out-of-season records (summer): 18 Jul–2 Aug 1987, Falls of the Ohio (*KW* 63:60, 1987; *KW* 64:18, 1988); 5 Jul 1996, Ohio River at Carrollton, Carroll Co. (R. Denton, eBird data); 16 Jun 1998, Ky Dam (B. Palmer-Ball, eBird data); 11-20 Jul 1998, 1-2 at McElroy Lake (Roemer, *KW* 74:95, 1998); 17 Jun 2003, (ph.) Muhlenberg Co. (*KW* 79:82, 2003).

Out-of-season records (winter): 8 Feb 1998, Ky Dam (*KW* 74:33, 1998); 31 Jan 2019, Marshall Co. (*KW* 95:48, 2019).

Published error: 18 Apr 1983, (2) at Ky Dam (*KW* 59:42, 1983; date erroneously published as 18 May therein [(*fide* J. Elmore, notes]).

Summary of records east of the LBL vicinity by county

Adair ([ph.] *KW* 90:11, 2014; [ph.] *KW* 92:10, 2016/R. Denton, 2015 eBird data; *KW* 95:7, 2019)
Allen/Barren (Barren River Lake; essentially annual including some of the state's highest counts)
Bell (13 Oct 1979 [Allaire, *KW* 56:19, 1980])
Bracken (*KW* 75:6, 1999; *KW* 79:10, 2003; *KW* 84:10 2008; *KW* 91:10, 2015)
Campbell (*KW* 92:10, 2016)
Carroll (R. Denton, 1996 eBird data)
Christian ([ph.] *KW* 93:9, 2017)
Fayette ([ph.] *KW* 93:73, 2017)
Gallatin (*KW* 74:7, 1998; *KW* 79:10, 2003; *KW* 87:18, 2011)
Hardin (*KW* 65:6, 1989; *KW* 83:14, 2007)
Harlan (23 Sep 2003 [*KW* 80:10, 2004])
Henderson (*KW* 79:69, 2003)
Jefferson (essentially annual, especially at the Falls of the Ohio)
Lincoln ([ph.] *KW* 90:11-12/21, 2014)
Muhlenberg ([ph.] *KW* 79:82, 2003)
Ohio (*KW* 81:107, 2005)
Pulaski (*KW* 67:7, 1991; *KW* 83:48, 2007)

Rowan (*KW* 66:57, 1990; *KW* 75:6, 1999; [ph.] *KW* 88:77, 2012)
Taylor (*KW* 77:7, 2001; *KW* 90:11, 2014)
Union ([ph.] *KW* 88:11, 2012; [ph.] *KW* 89:10, 2013)
Warren (Mengel:259; Palmer-Ball and Boggs, *KW* 67:63, 1991; Roemer, et al., *KW* 73:79-83, 1997; Roemer, *KW* 74:95, 1998; J. Elmore, 1998 notes; *KW* 86:94, 2010; *KW* 87:90, 2011; *KW* 91:71, 2015; *KW* 94:74, 2018; R. Denton/R. Shive/R. Waldrop, 2019 eBird data)

MEW GULL *Larus canus*

Status: Extremely rare fall visitant. This species is very similar in appearance to Ring-billed Gull in all plumages, and it could be overlooked to some extent; the first two records likely involved the same individual that was observed two years in a row on Barren River Lake. The species has now been documented in Kentucky three times.

Chronological list of records

1) 18 Oct 2009, an ad. (ph.) at Barren River Lake SRP and Barren River Lake, Barren/Allen cos. (*KW* 86:1/10, 2010)
2) 18-24 Oct 2010, an ad. [likely same bird] (ph.) at Barren River Lake (*KW* 87:18,44, 2011)
3) 24 Nov 2018, an ad. (ph.) on Ky Lake above the dam (*KW* 95:7, 2019; C. Bliznick/J. Wheat, eBird data)

RING-BILLED GULL *Larus delawarensis*

Status: Fairly common to common transient and winter resident, rare during summer. Recorded statewide. Most frequently encountered on the larger lakes and rivers, but the species occurs widely and is also reported regularly on smaller bodies of water, especially during peaks of migratory movements; sometimes observed in agricultural fields, at shopping malls, and in other open areas far from water. Peak of abundance occurs from mid-Oct to early Apr. Regularly lingers well into early summer, and at least on occasion remains throughout the summer in small numbers on Ky Lake, Lake Barkley and the lower Ohio River. Away from the larger bodies of water, usually encountered singly or in small flocks of only a few birds, but the species may be seen by the dozens or hundreds in suitable areas. In addition, winter numbers often exceed 10,000 birds on Ky Lake/Lake Barkley.

Maximum counts (Ky Dam vicinity): "**tens of thousands**" on Ky Lake/Lake Barkley, late Jan–mid-Feb 1997 (reported as 50,000+ in *KW* 73:37, 1997; B. Palmer-Ball, eBird data); estimate of at least **45,000** on Ky Lake, 5 Feb 2000 (B. Palmer-Ball, eBird data); **40,000** in the vicinity of Ky Dam, 27 Feb 1991 (J. Wilson, eBird data); ca. **40,000** on Ky Lake, 11 Feb 2007 (*KW* 83:49, 2007); ca. **30,000** on Ky Lake, Marshall Co., 15 Jan 2010 (*KW* 86:44, 2010); ca. **20,000** on Ky Lake above Ky Dam, 15-16 Jan 2015 (*KW* 91:52-53, 2015); **10,000-20,000** on Ky Lake, mid-Feb 1988 (*KW* 64:29, 1988); **14,000** in the vicinity of Ky Dam, 25 Jan 2004 (*KW* 80:44, 2004); nearly **13,000** on Ky Lake/Lake Barkley, 11 Feb 1989 (*KW* 65:35, 1989); ca. **12,000** on Ky Lake/Lake Barkley, 1 Feb 1987 (*KW* 63:37, 1987); **6000** on Lake Barkley, Trigg Co., 29 Jan 2011 (W. Lisowsky, eBird data); ca. **5000** at Jonathan Creek, 30 Jan 2011 (*KW* 87:62, 2011).

Maximum counts (other locations): **7000** at Barren River Lake, 3 Mar 2015 (*KW* 91:72, 2015); **7000** at Barren River Lake, 30 Dec 2017 (R. Bontrager/L. Bontrager, eBird data); **5000** on the Ohio River at Meldahl Dam, Bracken Co., 3 Feb 2003 (J. Stenger, eBird data); **4200** at Barren River Lake, 22 Jan 2010 (D. Roemer, eBird data); ca. **4000** at Green River Lake, 13 Jan 1985 (*KW* 61:31, 1985); ca. **3500** on the Ohio River at Meldahl Dam, Bracken Co., 13 Feb 2011 (*KW* 87:62, 2011); ca. **3500** at Barren River Lake, 1 Dec 2014 (*KW* 91:52, 2015); "**thousands**" at Cave Run Lake 14 Feb 2010 (*KW* 86:44, 2010); **3000** on the Ohio River at Meldahl Dam, Bracken Co., 8 Jan 2001 (*KW* 77:29, 2001); **3000** at Barren River Lake, 28 Feb 2014 (*KW* 90:49, 2014); **2500-3000** at Meldahl Dam, Bracken Co., 19 Feb 2007 (*KW* 83:49, 2007); **2750** at Cave Run Lake/Minor Clark Hatchery, 7 Feb 2015 (*KW* 91:53, 2015); **2650+** at Cave Run Lake/Minor Clark Hatchery, 8 Dec 2013 (*KW* 90:49, 2014); ca. **2500** in the vicinity of Markland Dam, Gallatin Co., 13 Feb 2011 (*KW* 87:62, 2011); **2470** at Green River Lake, Taylor Co., 31 Dec 2013 (*KW* 90:49, 2014); **2000-2500** on the

Ohio River, Bracken Co., 29 Jan 2013 (*KW* 89:48, 2013); **2000** on Lake Cumberland, Pulaski Co., 29 Jan 2001 (R. Denton, eBird data); **2000+** at and nr. Cave Run Lake, 24 Feb 2008 (*KW* 84:45, 2008); ca. **2000** at Cave Run Lake, 4 Feb 2013 (*KW* 89:48, 2013); ca. **2000** on the Ohio River above Markland Dam, Gallatin Co., 12 Feb 2013 (*KW* 89:48, 2013); **1500-2000** at Cave Run Lake, 23 Jan 2009 (*KW* 85:49, 2009); **1500** on Green River Lake, Taylor Co., 26 Nov 1989 (*KW* 66:11, 1990); **1500** on Lake Cumberland, Pulaski Co., 9 Dec 2013 (*KW* 90:49, 2014); ca. **1500** on the Ohio River at Louisville, late Jan–early Feb 2015 (*KW* 91:52, 2015); **1100** nw. of Hadensville, Todd Co., 9 Mar 2015 (*KW* 91:72, 2015); ca. **1000** on Lake Cumberland above Wolf Creek Dam, 18 Feb 2007 (*KW* 83:49, 2007); **1000** on Lake Cumberland above Wolf Creek Dam, 9 Feb 2014 (*KW* 90:49, 2014); ca. **1000** in the vicinity of the Falls of the Ohio, 6 Dec 2008 (*KW* 85:49, 2009); **600-700** nr. Woodburn, Warren Co., 25 Feb 2007 (*KW* 83:49, 2007).

Hybrid record: see Laughing Gull.

CALIFORNIA GULL *Larus californicus*

Status: Extremely rare fall, winter, and spring visitant. This native of western North America has been proven to occur occasionally in Kentucky over the past three decades. Most records have occurred in the LBL area, but indivdiuals have been documented twice on the Ohio River at Louisville and once at Barren River Lake. Perhaps because the adult plumage is the most recognizable, most reports have involved birds of this age. There are 13 records (two during fall, four during winter, and seven during spring).

Chronological list of records

1) 31 Mar 1984, an ad. (ph.) at Ky Dam (Palmer-Ball, *KW* 61:34-36, 1985)
2) 16 May 1984, possibly the same bird at Ky Dam (*KW* 60:43, 1984; *AB* 38:918, 1984)
3) 11 Feb 1996, an ad. (ph.) on an industrial pond along the Tennessee River at Calvert City, Marshall Co. (Palmer-Ball, et al., *KW* 77:22-23, 2001)
4) 15/17 Mar 2001, an ad. (ph.) on Lake Barkley, Lyon Co. (*NAB* 55:306, 2001; *KW* 77:50, 2001)
5) 25 Apr 2001, an ad. at the Falls of the Ohio (*KW* 77:50, 2001)
6) 7 May 2003, a second-year bird at Ky Dam Village (*KW* 79:70, 2003)
7) 17-29 Mar 2004, an ad. (ph.) at Ky Dam (*KW* 80:68, 2004)
8) 17-27 Nov 2007, a first-year bird (ph.) at Ky Dam (*KW* 84:10-11, 2008)
9) 19 Oct–2 Nov 2009, an ad. (ph.) at Barren River Lake (*KW* 86:10/36, 2010)
10) 19 Jan–26 Feb 2010, an ad. (ph.) at Ky Dam [with presumably the same bird on Lake Barkley, Lyon Co., 26 Jan 2010] (*KW* 86:44/52, 2010)
11) 1-7 Mar 2013, an ad. (ph.) on Lake Barkley, Lyon Co. (*KW* 89:72/74, 2013)
12) 28 Feb–1 Mar 2015, an ad. (ph.) on the Ohio River at Louisville (*KW* 91:53/72/79, 2015)
13) 8 Feb–1 Mar 2019, 1-2 ads. (ph.) w. of Calvert City, Marshall Co. (*KW* 95:41/48, 2019; C. Bliznick et al., eBird data).

HERRING GULL *Larus argentatus*

Status: Uncommon transient, uncommon to locally fairly common winter resident, extremely rare during summer. Distribution similar to that of the Ring-billed Gull, except observed much less frequently away from the larger lakes and rivers. An individual or two (typically sub-adult birds) occasionally linger through the summer on the larger lakes and rivers (e.g., *KW* 60:53, 1984; *KW* 62:67, 1986; *KW* 63:60, 1987; *KW* 64:64, 1988; *KW* 88:94, 2012/*KW* 89:9, 2013). Peak of abundance occurs from mid-Nov to mid-Mar. Most often seen singly or in small groups of only a few birds, but occasionally there have been hundreds or thousands of birds reported at the Falls of the Ohio (formerly) and in the vicinity of Kentucky/Barkley/Smithland dams. Generally outnumbers the Ring-billed Gull only during extremely cold, mid-winter weather and only in the Kentucky/Barkley/Smithland dams area and (formerly) at the Falls of the Ohio.

Maximum counts: ca. **5000** on Ky Lake above Ky Dam, 10-17 Feb 1985 (*KW* 61:30, 1985); **3750-5000** on Ky Lake, Feb 1982 (*KW* 58:29, 1982); **3000-5000** at Ky Dam, 26-27 Dec 1989 (*KW* 66:39, 1990); "hundreds, **sometimes thousands**" on the Ohio River at Louisville (Mengel: 257); **300-600**

on the Ohio River at Louisville, winter 1981-1982 (*KW* 58:29, 1982); **580** on the Ohio River at Louisville, 25 Feb 2015 (*KW* 91:53, 2015); **415+** at Meldahl Dam, Bracken Co., 19 Feb 2007 (*KW* 83:49, 2007); ca. **350** at Jonathan Creek, 30 Jan 2011 (*KW* 87:62, 2011).

ICELAND GULL *Larus glaucoides*

Status: Extremely rare transient; rare winter visitant/resident. This species was possibly overlooked historically; it was first conclusively recorded in the state 9-15 Dec 1967, when a first-year bird identified as a "Thayer's Gull" was observed and subsequently collected at Ky Dam (Monroe and Able, *KW* 44:55, 1968). It was not reported again in the state until Feb 1978, when at least one individual was found at the Falls of the Ohio (*KW* 54:29, 1978; *AB* 32:359, 1978), and during the fall/winter 1981-1982, when another first-year bird was observed at the Falls of the Ohio and on the Ohio River at Markland Dam, Gallatin Co. (*KW* 58:16/29, 1982). Since then the species has been found nearly every winter at Kentucky/Barkley/Smithland dams and occasionally on the Ohio River upstream as far as Meldahl Dam, Bracken Co. It probably should not be expected away from the Ohio and Mississippi rivers and larger reservoirs (Palmer-Ball, *KW* 63:3-5, 1987). Individuals in all age-plumages have been seen, but first-year birds and adults predominate. Typically seen singly in association with other large gulls, but a half-dozen or more have been seen in the large mid-winter concentrations of gulls at the Kentucky/Barkley/Smithland dams area during colder years.

Notes on subspecies: For many years Iceland Gull and Thayer's Gull were considered different species; however, in 2017 taxonomists made the decision to "lump" the two taxa into one species. As a result, all reports but those from the past couple of years have been referred to specifically as one or the other. As early as the time of the 1981 report from the Ohio River, however, individuals possessing intermediate plumages have been recognized. In the following summaries, notations indicate which form was reported at the time; these notations simply serve to cross-reference with literature reports to minimize confusion for those using the data in the future. Having spent a few decades recognizing the true rarity of clear-cut "Iceland Gulls" here in Kentucky, I am also some-what hesitant to allow the small number of confirmed reports of that subspecies (*L. g. kumlieni*) to be lost, so included below is a separate listing of seemingly confirmed "Iceland Gulls."

Maximum counts (*L. g. thayeri*): **10-12** of various ages in the vicinity of Kentucky and Barkley dams, 7 Feb 1982 (*KW* 58:29, 1982); at least **9** at Kentucky/Barkley dams, Feb 1985 (*KW* 61:30, 1985).

Early fall dates (*L. g. thayeri* unless otherwise noted): 1-5 Nov 1997, a first-year bird [*L. g. kumlieni*] at Meldahl Dam, Bracken Co. (*KW* 74:8, 1998; J. Dunn, notes); 8 Nov 1984, Falls of the Ohio (*KW* 61:17, 1985); 9 Nov 2009, Ky Dam (*KW* 86:10, 2010); 12 Nov 1988, Ky Dam (*KW* 65:9, 1989).

Late spring dates (*L. g. thayeri* unless otherwise noted): 18 Apr 2013, [possible *L. g. thayer/kumlieni* intergrade] Ky Dam Village (*KW* 89:72, 2013); 11 Apr 1986, Falls of the Ohio (*KW* 62:44, 1986); 6 Apr 1984, Barkley Dam (*KW* 60:43, 1984); 31 Mar 2007, Ky Dam (*KW* 83:31, 2007); 29 Mar 2004, Ky Dam (*KW* 80:68, 2004); 28 Mar 1997, Ky Lake (*KW* 73:54 1997); 28 Mar 2007, [*L. g. kumlieni*] (vt.) on Lake Barkley, Lyon Co. (*KW* 83:81, 2007).

Unaccepted records: details of seven additional reports are not adequate to confirm identity: 9 Feb 1952, an "immature" (*L. g. kumlieni*) [published incorrectly as an ad. by Mengel (pp. 517-518), and as 9 Oct by Monroe (*KW* 45:55, 1969)] along the Ohio River at Louisville (Monroe and Monroe, *KW* 29:13, 1953); 26 Nov 1981, a second-year bird (*L. g. kumlieni*) at the Falls of the Ohio (*KW* 58:16, 1982; *AB* 36:184, 1982); 30 Mar 1982, a second-year bird (*L. g. kumlieni*) at the Falls of the Ohio (*KW* 58:51, 1982; *AB* 36:859, 1982); 1 Apr 1989, Ohio River at Louisville (*KW* 65:68, 1989); 6 Jan 1996, a first-year bird (*L. g. thayeri*) on the Ohio River above Louisville [this report was included in the second edition of this work, but I cannot locate details of the sighting in my notes, so I am including it here];1/5 Feb 1997, an ad. (*L. g. kumlieni*) at Barkley Dam (*KW* 73:38, 1997); 6 Feb 1998, a first-year bird (*L. g. kumlieni*) on Lake Barkley, Lyon Co. (*KW* 74:33, 1998).

Chronological list of accepted records of "Iceland Gull" (*L. glaucoides kumlieni*)

1) 27 Dec 1983–11 Feb 1984, a first-year bird at the Falls of the Ohio (*KW* 60:25, 1984; B. Peter-john, notes)
2) 13 Feb 1988, two first-year birds (ph.) on Lake Barkley above Barkley Dam (*KW* 64:29, 1988; Palmer-Ball, *KW* 65:48-49, 1989)

3) 4 Feb 1996, a first-year bird below Ky Dam, and 5 Mar 1996, probably the same bird below Barkley Dam (B. Palmer-Ball/M. Monroe, eBird data)

4) 26 Jan–15 Feb 1997, a first-year bird (ph.) below Ky Dam (*KW* 73:38, 1997; B. Palmer-Ball, eBird data; F. Fekel, photographs)

5) 1-5 Nov 1997, a first-year bird at Meldahl Dam on the Ohio River, Bracken Co. (*KW* 74:8, 1998; J. Dunn, notes)

6) 25 Jan–26 Feb 2004, a first-year bird (ph.) at Ky Dam (*KW* 80:44, 2004; B. Palmer-Ball, eBird data) (Note: The author considered this bird to be an intergrade *L. g. thayeri* x *L. g. glaucoides*)

7) 28 Mar 2007, a first- or second-year bird (vt.) on Lake Barkley, Lyon Co. (*KW* 83:81, 2007)

8) 26/31 Jan 2009, a first-year bird (ph.) at Ky Dam (*KW* 85:50, 2009)

9) 12/24 Jan 2014, a first-year bird (ph.) at Ky Dam (*KW* 90:52, 2014; B. Palmer-Ball, eBird data)

10) 7/16 Feb 2014, a different first-year bird (ph.) at Ky Dam and Ky Dam Village (*KW* 90:50/52, 2014; B. Palmer-Ball, eBird data)

11) 28 Jan–15 Mar 2015, a first-year bird (ph.) on the Ohio River at Louisville (*KW* 91:53/72, 2015; J. Baker/T. Quarles, eBird data)

12) 10 Jan–12 Feb 2015, a first-year bird (ph.) at Ky Dam (H. Chambers/R. Denton, eBird data; *KW* 91:53/60, 2015)

Chronological list of photograph records of possible or probable intergrades

1) 20 Dec 1997, a first-year bird (ph.) below Ky Dam, 20 Dec 1997 (*KW* 74:13, 1998; B. Palmer-Ball, eBird data; K. Brock/P. Lehman, pers. comm.)

2) 26 Jan/21 Mar 2009, a first-year bird (ph.) at Ky Dam (*KW* 85:50/71/72, 2009; B. Palmer-Ball, eBird data)

3) 6-20 Feb 2011, a second-year bird (ph.) on the Ohio River at Meldahl Dam, Bracken Co. (6 & 20 Feb) and Campbell Co. (13-17 Feb) (*KW* 87:62/72, 2011; L. Keene/W. Hull/R. Foppe/L. Houser, eBird data)

4) 12 Jan–8 Feb 2014, probably 2 different first-year birds at Ky and Barkley Dams (*KW* 90:52, 2014; B. Palmer-Ball/B. Wulker, eBird data)

5) 16 Jan 2015, an ad. (ph.) at Ky Dam (*KW* 91:53, 2015; J. Baker/B. Palmer-Ball/B. Wulker, eBird data)

Summary records away from Smithland Dam, Lake Barkley, & Ky Lake by county

Bracken (6/20 Feb 2011, second-year bird at Meldahl Dam [*KW* 87:62, 2011; correction of age of bird on 20 Feb published therein *fide* J. Stenger, pers. comm.] [Note: I considered this individual a likely intergrade –see above]; 30 Jan 2016, ad. at Meldahl Dam [*KW* 92:43, 2016])

Campbell (13-16 Feb 2011, a second-year bird [ph.] along the New Richmond, OH, waterfront [*KW* 87:62, 2011] [Note: I considered this individual a likely intergrade])

Gallatin (8 Jan 1982, first-year bird at Markland Dam [*KW* 58:29, 1982]; 16-22 Dec 1995, first-year bird [ph.] at Markland Dam [*KW* 72:19/44, 1996; J. Dunn, notes/pers. comm.]; 5 Mar 2014, ad. [ph.] at Craigs Creek [*KW* 90:72/84, 2014])

Jefferson (23 Feb–14 Mar 1978, at least one (probably two) first-year bird(s) at the Falls of the Ohio [*KW* 54:29, 1978; *AB* 32:359, 1978; B. Palmer-Ball, eBird data] [Note: at least one individual was likely a *L. g. kumlieni*, but at that time limited state of knowledge precluded ID to subspecies with certainty]; 21-23 Nov 1981 & 20 Feb 1982, a first-year bird on the Ohio River [*KW* 58:16, 1982; B. Palmer-Ball, 1982 eBird data]; 8-11 Nov 1984, a first-year bird (ph.) at the Falls of the Ohio [*KW* 61:17, 1985]; 21 Jan 1985, a first-year bird at the Falls of the Ohio [*KW* 61:30, 1985]; 10-11 Apr 1986, an ad. (ph.) at the Falls of the Ohio [*KW* 62:44, 1986]; 7-8 Mar 2014, an ad. at the Falls of the Ohio [*KW* 90:72, 2014])

LESSER BLACK-BACKED GULL *Larus fuscus*

Status: Very rare to locally uncommon fall, winter, and spring visitant. First recorded in the state 9 Dec 1967, when an adult was observed on Ky Lake near Ky Dam (Able, *KW* 44:31-32, 1968). Since the winter of 1981-82, when a second-year bird was photographed below Ky Dam (*KW* 58:29, 1982; *AB* 36:860-861, 1982), the species has been documented annually in the vicinity of Ky Lake/Lake Barkley/Smithland Dam. Moreover, during the past decade a number of records (now from nearly 20 counties) have accumulated elsewhere across the central portion of the state east to Meldahl Dam on the Ohio River and Minor Clark Hatchery/Cave Run Lake. This increase in occurrence likely has been related to an increase in the species across eastern North America during the same period. Peak of abundance occurs from mid-Oct to mid-Mar. Generally not to be expected away from the larger lakes and rivers. Typically seen singly in flocks of other gulls, but small numbers are regular on Ky Lake and Lake Barkley.

Maximum counts: at least **17** at Calvert City landfill, Marshall Co., 4 Dec 2018 (*KW* 95:48, 2019); probably **9** at various locations on Lake Barkley, Lyon Co. and Ky Lake, Marshall Co., 9 Feb 2013 (*KW* 89:48, 2013); **8** at various locations on Ky Lake and Lake Barkley, 24 Oct 2016 (*KW* 93:9, 2017); **7** at various locations on Ky Lake and Lake Barkley, 27 Jan 2000 (*KW* 76:30, 2000; D. Roemer, notes); **6** on the LBL CBC, 15 Dec 2001 (H. Chambers, notes); **6** in the vicinity of Ky Dam/Barkley Dam, 8 Oct 2013 (*KW* 90:12, 2014); at least **6** in the vicinity of Ky Dam/Barkley Dam, 8 Feb 2014 (*KW* 90:12, 2014); **5** in the vicinity of Ky Dam, 23 Sep 2008 (*KW* 85:17, 2009); **4** at Kentucky/Barkley dams, 15-16 Dec 1990 (*KW* 67:10/31, 1991); **4** on the Ohio River at Louisville, 31 Jan 2015 [*KW* 91:53, 2015]).

Late spring dates: 12 May 2016, [ph.] Ky Dam Village (*KW* 92:64, 2016); 6-7 May 1991, Calvert City, Marshall Co. (B. Palmer-Ball, eBird data); 5-7 May 1996, (2) Barkley Dams (B. Palmer-Ball, eBird data); 5 May 2014, Ky Dam (*KW* 90:72, 2014); 3 May 2015, (ph.) Ohio River at Louisville (*KW* 91:72, 2015); 3 May 2013, Ky Dam Village (*KW* 89:72, 2013); 1 May 2009, Ky Dam (*KW* 85:72, 2009); 28 Apr 2017, Ky Dam Village (*KW* 93:73, 2017); 26 Apr 2007, Lake Barkley, Lyon Co. (*KW* 83:81, 2007); 23 Apr 2004, Ky Dam (*KW* 80:68, 2004); 23 Apr 2018, Ky Dam Village (*KW* 94:75, 2018); 16 Apr 2000, Ky Lake above the dam (*KW* 76:45, 2000; D. Roemer, notes [location published incorrectly as Barkley Dam in *NAB* 54:289, 2000]).

Early fall dates: 12 Aug 2009, Barkley Dam [possibly summered?] (*KW* 86:10, 2010); 16 Aug 2013, Ky Dam (*KW* 90:12, 2014); 20 Aug 2015, 2 at Ky Dam (*KW* 92:10, 2016); 2 Sep 2001, below Smithland Dam (H. Chambers, notes); 2 Sep 2007, (ph.) Ky Dam Village (*KW* 84:11, 2008) 3 Sep 2008, Ky Lake, Marshall Co. (*KW* 85:17, 2009); 5 Sep 2016, Jonathan Creek (*KW* 93:9, 2017); 8 Sep 2002, below Smithland Dam (*KW* 79:11, 2003); 8 Sep 2010, Barkley Dam (*KW* 87:18, 2011); 11-30 Sep 1990, Lake Barkley nr. Barkley Dam (*KW* 67:7, 1991); 11 Sep 2014, (ph.) Minor Clark Hatchery (*KW* 91:10/11, 2015); 13 Sep 2017, Ky Dam (*KW* 94:9. 2018); 15 Sep 2003, Ky Dam (*KW* 80:10, 2004); 19 Sep 2014, Barkley Dam (*KW* 91:10, 2015); 20 Sep 2011, Ky Dam (*KW* 88:11, 2012); 21 Sep 2005, above Ky Dam (*KW* 82:10, 2006); 21 Sep 2016, Ky Dam (*KW* 93:9, 2017); 22 Sep 2001, Ky Lake, Calloway Co. (H. Chambers, notes); 23 Sep 2012, Lake Barkley, Lyon Co. (*KW* 89:9, 2013); 25-27 Sep 1998, Lake Barkley (*KW* 75:6, 1999).

Summary of records away from Smithland Dam, Lake Barkley, and Ky Lake by county

Adair (3-5 Nov 2013, [ph.] Green River Lake [*KW* 90:12, 2014])

Allen/Barren (8 Oct 2008, [ph.] Barren River Lake [*KW* 85:17, 2009]; 16-31 Oct 2009, [ph.] Barren River Lake [*KW* 86:10, 2010]; 2-3 Mar 2015, Barren River Lake [*KW* 91:72, 2015]; 25 Feb 2018, *KW* 94:57, 2018)

Ballard (19 Dec 2000, an ad. on the Ohio River at Ballard WMA (*KW* 77:12, 2001)

Bracken (4 Nov 2012, Meldahl Dam [*KW* 89:9, 2013]; 25-27 Jan 2013, an ad. on the Ohio River at Meldahl Dam, Bracken Co. [*KW* 89:48, 2013]; 16 Feb 2014, [ph.] Meldahl Dam [*KW* 90:52, 2014])

Campbell/Kenton (18 Feb 2014, Ohio River at Cincinnati [W. Hull, eBird data]; 24 Feb 2015, mouth of Licking River [*KW* 91:53, 2015])

Christian (12 Mar 2019, Swallow Spring Pond [J. Hall, eBird data])

Fayette (5 Mar 2012, [ph.] Jacobson Park [*KW* 88:77, 2012]; 14 Dec 2016–13 Feb 2017, [ph.] Reservoirs #2/#3 [*KW* 93:49, 2017])

Fulton (21 Feb 2005, [ph.] Lower Hickman Bottoms [*KW* 81:59, 2005]; 19 Feb 2008, Lower Hickman Bottoms [M. Todd, eBird data]; 1 Dec 2015, Lower Hickman Bottoms [*KW* 92:43, 2016])

Gallatin (18 Feb 2007, [2] Markland Dam [*KW* 83:49, 2007]; 14/24 Nov 2007, [ph.] Ohio River at Craig's Creek [*KW* 84:11 2008; B. Palmer-Ball, eBird data]; 14 Jan 2011, Ohio River above Craig's Creek [*KW* 87:62, 2011]; 17 Feb 2014, Markland Dam [*KW* 90:52, 2014 (date erroneously published as 16 Feb therein; *fide* J. Stenger, eBird data)]; 5-7 Mar 2014, up to 3 birds [ph.] at Craigs Creek [*KW* 90:72/84, 2014])

Hardin (31 Mar 2013 & [ph.] 3 Dec 2015 Freeman Lake [*KW* 89:72, 2013 & *KW* 92:43, 2016])

Hopkins (2 Mar 2019, Pond River Bottoms [J. Hall/T. Devine, eBird data])

Jefferson (19 Feb 2007, [ph.] Ohio River [*KW* 83:49, 2007]; 22-27 [2 on 26th] Nov 2007, [ph.] Falls of the Ohio [*KW* 84:11 2008]; 30 Jan 2009, Falls of the Ohio [*KW* 85:50, 2009]; 27 Mar 2011, [ph.] Ohio River [*KW* 87:90, 2011]; 14 Feb 2014, Falls of the Ohio [*KW* 90:52, 2014]; 28 Apr 2014, [ph.] Falls of the Ohio [*KW* 90:72, 2014]; 2 Dec 2014–11 Mar 2015, probably at least 5 (ph.) on the Ohio River at Louisville [*KW* 91:53/72, 2015]; 3 May 2015, (ph.) Falls of the Ohio [*KW* 91:72, 2015])
Lincoln (9 Nov 2018, [ph.] Cedar Creek Lake (*KW* 95:7, 2019)
McCracken (31 Dec 2005, Ohio River (*KW* 82:48, 2006)
Pulaski (12 Sep 2018, Fishing Creek embayment Lake Cumberland [*KW* 95:7, 2019])
Rowan (11-14 Sep 2014, [ph.] Minor Clark Hatchery [*KW* 91:10/11, 2015])
Taylor (15-16 Feb 2014, (ph.) Green River Lake [*KW* 90:52, 2014]; 27 Dec 2017, Green River Lake [*KW* 94:56, 2018])
Warren (27-31 Mar 2011, [ph.] McElroy Lake (*KW* 87:90, 2011))

GLAUCOUS GULL *Larus hyperboreus*

Status: Extremely rare to rare transient and winter resident. Currently this gull has been reported almost exclusively along the Ohio River (especially at Louisville) and in the vicinity of Kentucky/ Barkley/Smithland dams where an individual or two can probably be found most every winter. Not likely to be seen away from the larger lakes and rivers. Most are first-year immatures, but older birds – especially adults – have been observed on several occasions at the Falls of the Ohio and at the western Kentucky dams.

Maximum counts: **6** or more in the Ky Dam/Barkley Dam vicinity in late Jan–early Feb 1982 (*KW* 58:29, 1982); **5** at Ky Dam/Barkley Dam, 10 Feb 1985 (*KW* 61:30, 1985); **4** at the Calvert City landfill, 2 Feb 2019 (*KW* 95:48, 2019); **3** at Ky Dam, 22-31 Jan 2009 (*KW* 85:50, 2009); at least **3** in the vicinity of Ky Dam, 28 Jan 2011 (*KW* 87:63, 2011).

Early fall dates: 19 Nov 1967, Louisville area (*KW* 52:50, 1976); 23 Nov 2018, Lake Peewee (*KW* 95:7, 2019); 24 Nov 1995, Ky Dam (B. Palmer-Ball, eBird data); 24 Nov 2018, (ph.) Ky Dam (*KW* 95:7/40, 2019); 30 Nov 2010, Ky Dam (*KW* 87:18, 2011).

Late spring dates: 22 Apr 2009, Ky Dam (*KW* 85:72, 2009); 13 Apr 1997, Lake Barkley, Lyon Co. (*KW* 73:54, 1997); 6 Apr 2008, Ky Dam (*KW* 84:65, 2008); 1 Apr 2016, (ph.) Ky Dam (*KW* 92:64/72, 2016).

List of records away from Ohio River and LBL vicinity by county

Hopkins (23 Nov 2018, a first-year bird (ph.) at Lake Peewee [*KW* 95:7, 2019])
Taylor (15 Feb 2014, first-year bird at Green River Lake [*KW* 90:52, 2014])

GREAT BLACK-BACKED GULL *Larus marinus*

Status: Extremely rare visitant (has been recorded at all seasons, but most have occurred during winter). This large gull has been reported almost exclusively along the Ohio River and in the vicinity of Kentucky/Barkley/Smithland dams where it has been proven to occur at least occasionally. Not likely to be seen away from the larger lakes and rivers. Most reports have involved first-years, but older birds (especially adults) have been observed on several occasions. Most reports have involved a single individual, but two have been reported on four occasions and three individuals were documented once (see below). There are currently at least 46 records (two during summer, eight during spring, four during fall, and 32 during winter).

Unaccepted records: 4 Oct 2001, a first-year bird on Ky Lake, Marshall Co. (*KW* 78:8, 2002; see *KW* 92:89, 2016); 6-10 Jan 2005, a first-year bird at Ky Dam (*KW* 81:59, 2005; see *KW* 92:89, 2016); 23 Nov 2007, a second-year bird below Markland Dam, Gallatin Co. (*KW* 84:11 2008; see *KW* 85:103, 2009).

Summary of records by county (total exceeds 44 because a few birds were thought or known to have been seen at more than one locale):

Boone (Ohio River) (1)
Bracken (Meldahl Dam) (2)
Campbell/Kenton (Ohio River) (2)

Gallatin (Markland Dam) (2)
Jefferson (Ohio River) (10)
Livingston (Smithland Dam) (3)
Livingston/Lyon (Barkley Dam/Lake Barkley) (7)
Livingston/Marshall (Ky Dam/Ky Lake/Calvert City) (23)
Pulaski (Lake Cumberland) (1)

Chronological list of records

1) 18-20 Jul 1976, ad. at the Falls of the Ohio (Stamm, *KW* 53:18, 1977)
2) 29 Jan 1984, first-year bird at the Falls of the Ohio (*KW* 60:25-26, 1984)
3) 14-20 Mar 1984, perhaps the same first-year bird at the Falls of the Ohio (*KW* 60:43, 1984)
4) 10-17 Feb 1985, ad. (ph.) on Ky Lake above Ky Dam (*KW* 61:30, 1985)
5) 22 Jan–12 Feb 1989, ad. (ph.) on Ky Lake above Ky Dam (*KW* 65:36/68, 1989; B. Palmer-Ball, eBird data)
6) 26-27 Dec 1989, ad. and two first-year birds in the vicinity of Ky Dam (*KW* 66:39, 1990)
7) 1 Apr–15 Jul 1990, first-year bird (ph.) in the vicinity of Kentucky and Barkley dams (*KW* 66: 58/87, 1990)
8) 5-8 May 1994, first-year bird at Calvert City [5 May] and Ky Dam [7-8 May] (B. Palmer-Ball, eBird data)
9) 2 May, 1995, ad. at the Falls of the Ohio (B. Palmer-Ball, eBird data)
10) 12 Jan 1996, first-year bird on the Ohio River above Louisville (M. Monroe, notes)
11) 26 Jan 1997, first-year bird below Ky Dam (B. Palmer-Ball, eBird data)
12) 14 Jan–6 Feb 2000, 1-2 first-year birds [one videotaped on 2 Feb; 2 present 2/5/6 Feb] at Smithland Dam (F. Bennett/D. Roemer, notes; B. Palmer-Ball, eBird data; *KW* 76:30, 2000)
13) 21-24 Jan 2000, first- or second-year bird (vt.) on Lake Barkley, Lyon Co. [considered to be a different individual than early Feb birds at Smithland Dam] (*KW* 76:30, 2000; D. Roemer, notes)
14) 13 Feb 2000, second-year bird at Smithland Dam [possibly the 21-24 Jan 2000 Lake Barkley bird] (F. Bennett, notes)
15) 3/22 Mar 2000, probably one of the same first-year birds at Barkley Dam (*KW* 76:45, 2000; D. Roemer, notes)
16) 9/19/29 Sep 2000, first-year (vt.) above Ky dam (R. Denton, eBird data; *KW* 77:7, 2001)
17) 10/17 Mar 2001, first-year bird (vt.) at Barkley Dam (*KW* 77:50, 2001)
18) 11 Jan 2002, first-year bird (vt.) on Ky Lake, Marshall Co. (*KW* 78:34, 2002)
19) 8-17 Feb 2004, first-year bird (ph.) at Ky Dam (*KW* 80:45, 2004)
20) 6-9 Sep 2006, first-year bird (ph.) at the Falls of the Ohio (*KW* 83:14, 2007)
21) 6-7 Feb 2007, second-year bird (ph.) at Ky Dam (*KW* 83:49, 2007)
22) 18 Feb 2007, 2 first-year birds at Markland Dam, Gallatin Co. (*KW* 83:49, 2007)
23) 16-17 Nov 2007, first-year bird in the vicinity of Ky Dam (*KW* 84:11 2008)
24) 18 Mar/6 Apr 2008, possibly the same imm. (first- or second-year) at Ky Dam (*KW* 84:65, 2008)
25) 29 Jan–11 May 2009, first-year bird (ph.) at Ky Dam (*KW* 85:50/72, 2009)
26) 21-26 Nov 2009, first-year bird (ph.) at the Falls of the Ohio (*KW* 86:10-11, 2010)
27) 14 Jan 2010, first-year bird at Smithland Dam, Livingston Co. (*KW* 86:44, 2010)
28) 1 Feb–25 Mar 2010, third-year bird at Ky Dam (*KW* 86:44/69, 2010)
29) 26 Feb–25 Mar 2010, first-year bird (possibly same individual as 14 Jan 2010?) in the vicinity of Kentucky & Barkley dams (*KW* 86:44/69, 2010)
30) 19 Dec 2010–11 Feb 2011, first-year bird (ph.) in the vicinity of Kentucky/Barkley dams (*KW* 87:62/72, 2011)
31) 13 Feb 2011, ad. (ph.) on the Ohio River at Markland Dam, Gallatin Co. (*KW* 87:62, 2011)
32) 8 Mar 2013, first-year bird (ph.) at Ky Dam (*KW* 89:72/73, 2013)
33) 24/30 Dec 2013, first-year bird (ph.) at Barkley Dam (*KW* 90:50/52, 2014) with perhaps the same bird (ph.) at Barkley Dam 7-8 Feb 2014 (*KW* 90:52, 2014) and (ph.) at Ky Dam 16/19 Feb 2014 (*KW* 90:52, 2014)
34) 27 Jan 2014, first-year bird on the Ohio River at Louisville (*KW* 90:52, 2014)
35) 2 Feb 2014, ad. (ph.) on the Ohio River at the mouth of the Licking River, Campbell/Kenton cos. (*KW* 90:52/60, 2014)
36) 14-16 Feb 2014, 1-2 first-year birds (ph.) at Meldahl Dam (*KW* 90:51/52, 2014)

37) 14 Dec 2014 & 10 Jan 2015 & 4/26 Feb 2015, first-year bird (ph.) at Ky Dam (*KW* 91:18/54, 2015, H. Chambers/R. Denton, eBird data)
38) 27 Jan–8 Mar 2015, 1-2 first-year birds (ph.) on the Ohio River at Louisville (*KW* 91:54/72, 2015)
39) 18 Feb 2015, second-year bird (ph.) at Meldahl Dam (*KW* 91:54, 2015) with possibly the same second-year bird on the Ohio River, Campbell Co., 23 Feb 2015 (*KW* 91:54, 2015)
40) 22 Feb 2015, first-year bird on the Ohio River, Boone Co. (*KW* 91:54, 2015)
41) 6-7 Aug 2015, ad. (ph.) at the Falls of the Ohio (*KW* 92:9/10, 2016)
42) 13 Feb 2016, first-year bird (ph.) at Ky Dam (*KW* 92:43, 2016)
43) 10-11 Jan 2018, first-year bird (ph.) on Lake Cumberland, Pulaski Co. (*KW* 94:57, 2018)
44) 17 Feb 2018, first-year bird at Ky Dam (*KW* 94:57, 2018)
45) 20-26 Jan 2019, ad. (ph.) at Calvert City landfill (*KW* 95:48-49, 2019)
46) 31 Jan–2 Feb 2019, first-year bird at Ky Dam (*KW* 95:49, 2019)

SOOTY TERN *Onychoprion fuscatus*

Status: Extremely rare summer and fall visitant. This species seems to be the pelagic waterbird most frequently blown far inland by land-falling tropical cyclones. There are now eight Kentucky records.

Range of dates: 12 Jul–4 Oct

Chronological list of records

1) 4 Oct 2002, 2 and possibly 3 ads. (vt.) on Ky Lake above Ky Dam during the passage of the remnants of hurricane Lili, which had originated in the Caribbean, made landfall on the United States coastline at Louisiana, and moved ne. across western Kentucky (*KW* 79:11, 2003)
2) 4 Oct 2002, an ad. on the Ohio River at Joppa, Illinois, thus in McCracken Co. (*KW* 79:11, 2003)
3) 9 Sep 2004, an ad. found dead on US 119 on Pine Mt., Letcher Co. after the passage of the remnants of Hurricane Frances (Libby, *KW* 81:34-36, 2005)
4) 12-15 Jul 2005, up to 6 (some videotaped) on Ky Lake above the dam during the passage of the remnants of Hurricane Dennis (*KW* 81:107, 2005; Monroe et al., *KW* 82:32-37/40, 2006)
5) 12 Jul 2005, an ad. on Lake Barkley, Lyon Co., during the passage of the remnants of Hurricane Dennis (*KW* 81:107, 2005; Monroe et al., *KW* 82:32-37, 2006)
6) 12 Jul 2005, an ad. on the Ohio River nr. New Richmond, OH, during the passage of the remnants of Hurricane Dennis (*KW* 81:107, 2005; Monroe et al., *KW* 82:32-37, 2006)
7) 13 Jul 2005, 2-3 ads. on the Ohio River below Smithland Dam, Livingston Co., during the passage of the remnants of Hurricane Dennis (*KW* 81:107, 2005; Monroe et al., *KW* 82:32-37, 2006)
8) 13 Sep 2017, 3 ads. (ph.) on Ky Lake above Ky Dam, Livingston/Marshall cos., during the passage of the remnants of Hurricane Irma (J. Baker et al., photographs; Palmer-Ball, *KW* 93:113/114, 2017; *KW* 94:9, 2018)

*LEAST TERN *Sternula antillarum*

Status: Locally uncommon summer resident, otherwise an extremely rare to rare transient or visitant. Recorded chiefly along the Mississippi River and lower Ohio River regularly upstream as far as Daviess, Hancock, and Henderson cos. (rarely to Louisville), but also occurs somewhat regularly on Lake Barkley, Ky Lake, and the lower Tennessee River. There are also scattered records of transient or vagrant birds, mostly from late May to early Aug, as far east as Rowan Co. (see below). Peak of abundance occurs from mid-May to late Aug. Breeding currently limited to along the Mississippi River, the lower Ohio River as far upstream as Livingston Co., and the lower Tennessee River, Marshall Co. Some representative tallies of the nesting population over the past two decades include the following summaries: ca. 250-300 nesting pairs in nine colonies in 1994 (Palmer-Ball, *KW* 71:5-8, 1995); ca. 525 nesting pairs at eight colonies in 2005 (Ciuzio, et al., *KW* 81:99-103); 3-120 nests documented at ten colonies in 2007 (*KW* 83:105, 2007); and more than 1000 nests documented at three sites on the Mississippi and lower Ohio rivers, summer 2014 (*KW* 90:89, 2014) and summer 2017 (*KW* 93:100, 2017). Nesting also has been confirmed at a few additional locations over the years (see below). During years of high water, the species has been found attempting to nest in agricultural fields near the Mississippi and lower Ohio rivers. Generally seen singly or in small flocks of only a few birds away from nesting areas, but nesting colonies occasionally number more than a hundred pairs. **State Breeding Status**: Endangered. **Federal Status**: Endangered.

Maximum counts: **750-1000** active nests on the Mississippi River nr. Watson Point, summer 2013 (*KW* 90:89, 2014); ca. **1000** on the Mississippi River nr. Watson Point, Fulton Co., 14 Aug 2014 (*KW* 91:10, 2015); **400-500** pairs at two different nesting colonies on the Mississippi River, Carlisle and Fulton cos., early Jul 2012 (*KW* 88:94, 2012); **300-400** pairs at a nesting colony on the Mississippi River, Fulton Co., summer 2010 (*KW* 86:94, 2010); ca. **500** on the Mississippi River at Ky Bend, Fulton Co. 11 Aug 2002 (*KW* 79:11, 2003); **400/450** at a nesting colony on the Mississippi River, Fulton Co., 28 Jun/2 Jul 2013 (*KW* 89:96, 2013, J. Brunjes, eBird data); at least **194 pairs** at a nesting colony in Fulton Co., summer 1996 (R. Renken, pers. comm.); **250** at Mitchell Lake, Ballard WMA, 2 Aug 2006 (J. Brunjes, eBird data); **200-300** on the Mississippi River nr. Island No. 1, Carlisle Co., 26 Aug 2004 (*KW* 81:10, 2005); ca. **150** on the Ohio River, Ballard Co., 1 Aug 2006 (*KW* 83:15, 2007); at least **140** below Smithland Dam, 11 Aug 2001 (*NAB* 56:59, 2002).

Early spring dates: 21 Apr 1981, Ky Lake (*KW* 57:57, 1981); 26 Apr 2008, Falls of the Ohio (*KW* 84:65 2008); 28 Apr 19—, Hopkins Co. (Bacon, *KW* 9:[14], 1933).

Late fall dates: 10 Oct 1954, Louisville (Mengel:263); 20 Sep 1998, Mississippi River, Carlisle Co. (B. Palmer-Ball, eBird data); 17 Sep 2005, Mitchell Lake (*KW* 82:11, 2006; H. Chambers, notes); 17 Sep 2006, Mitchell Lake (*KW* 83:15, 2007); 15 Sep 2008, Smithland Dam (*KW* 85:17, 2009); 12 Sep 2004, Mitchell Lake (*KW* 81:10, 2005); 11 Sep 2007, McCracken Co. (*KW* 84:11 2008); 9 Sep 1971, Ohio River, Oldham Co. (*AB* 26:72, 1972); 9 Sep 2009, Mitchell Lake (*KW* 86:10, 2010).

Unaccepted records: 16-17 Oct 1970, location uncertain (*fide* A. Stamm, historical archive files); 14 Apr 1982, 12 birds on Ky Lake (*KW* 58:51, 1982); 5 in Rowan Co., 7 Sep 1983 (*KW* 60:18, 1984).

Published errors: 7 in Marshall Co., 18 Oct 1997 (*KW* 74:8, 1998; correction *fide KW* 74:35, 1998); 3 in Muhlenberg Co. (*KW* 75:61, 1999; correction *fide* D. O'Brien, notes).

Summary of confirmed breeding records by county

Ballard (periodically on dredge spoil islands and natural sandbars on the lower Ohio River; also, at least occasionally in fields adjacent to the river (e.g., Ciuzio, et al., *KW* 81:99-103, 2005; *KW* 84: 88, 2008. *KW* 86:94, 2010])

Carlisle (formerly almost annual, but probably still occasionally, on Mississippi River sandbars [e.g., Ciuzio, *KW* 81:99-103, 2005])

Fulton (annual on Mississippi River sandbars; also, at least occasionally in fields adjacent to the river (e.g., *KW* 84:88, 2008])

Hancock (at least occasionally on an island in the Ohio River below Lewisport astride the Spencer Co., IN, line [e.g., *KW* 83:105, 2007; *KW* 84:88, 2008; *KW* 88:11, 2012])

Hickman (almost annual on Mississippi River sandbars; also, summer 1984, fields nr. Three Ponds [S. Evans, unpubl. rpt.])

Jefferson (early Jul 1967, Falls of the Ohio [Stamm, *KW* 44:49-51, 1968])

Livingston (at least formerly on an annual basis on dredge spoil islands and sandbars in the Ohio River upstream to below Smithland Dam [e.g., Ciuzio, et al., *KW* 81:99-103, 2005])

Marshall (periodically since at least 2003 at an industrial pond at Calvert City [*KW* 80:10, 2004; *KW* 80:83, 2004; Ciuzio, et al., *KW* 81:99-103, 2005; *KW* 83:105, 2007; *KW* 84:88, 2008; *KW* 85:93, 2009; *KW* 86:94, 2010; *KW* 89:96, 2013])

McCracken (mostly formerly, but still occasionally, on dredge spoil islands and sandbars on the Ohio River [J. Brunjes, pers. comm.])

Union (occasional [at least formerly] on Ohio River sand/gravel bars upstream from Dekoven [e.g., Mengel:252; Palmer-Ball, *KW* 71:5-8, 1994; Ciuzio, et al., *KW* 81:99-103]; several times during the 2000s at the Camp #9 Coal Preparation Plant [Ciuzio, et al., *KW* 81:99-103, 2005; *KW* 82:82, 2006; *KW* 90:89, 2014, *KW* 91:10, 2015])

Summary of records away from the Mississippi and lower Ohio rivers (upstream to Louisville), and the LBL vicinity by county (all have occurred mid-May to late Aug)

Christian (1/29-30 Jun 2008 [*KW* 84:88, 2008]; 23 May 2016 [*KW* 92:64, 2016]; 23 May/27 Jun 2016 [*KW* 92:64, 2016/*KW* 92:80, 2016])

Fayette (7 Jul 2014 [*KW* 90:89, 2014])

McLean (24 May 2011 [Palmer-Ball and Huber, *KW* 88:87-91, 2012])
Mercer (4 Aug 2000 & 22 May 2001 [R. Denton, eBird data])
Muhlenberg (22 Jun 2000 [*KW* 76:57, 2000]; 26 Aug 2006 [*KW* 83:15, 2007]; 25 Jul 2007 [*KW* 83: 105, 2007])
Pulaski (3 Aug 2006 [*KW* 83:14, 2007])
Rowan (Busroe, *KW* 61:24-25, 1985; 30 Aug 2017 [*KW* 94:1/9, 2018])
Todd (4/14 Jun 2008 [*KW* 84:88, 2008])
Warren (27 May 1994 [B. Palmer-Ball, 1994 eBird data]; 12 Jun 1998 [*KW* 74:73, 1998]; 14 May 2008 [*KW* 84:65 2008]; 15 Jun 2010 [*KW* 86:94, 2010])

GULL-BILLED TERN *Gelochelidon nilotica*

Status: Accidental vagrant. This typically coastal tern occurs infrequently in the interior of the eastern United States. It has been documented on one occasion in Kentucky.

1) a possible first-year bird (ph.) at the Falls of the Ohio, 27-28 Aug 1994, (Palmer-Ball, *KW* 70:65/86-87, 1994).

Unaccepted record: 16 Apr 1971, reported behind a ferry on the Ohio River, 60 miles e. of Cincinnati [= nr. Maysville, Mason Co.], in the company of a group of gulls, [no details available] (*AB* 25:752, 1971).

CASPIAN TERN *Hydroprogne caspia*

Status: Uncommon to fairly common transient, extremely rare to rare during early summer. Recorded chiefly about the larger lakes and rivers, but occasionally seen on smaller bodies of water. Peaks of abundance occur from early Apr to mid-May and from mid-Aug to mid-Sep. A number of early to mid-Jun sightings, primarily along the Ohio River and on Ky Lake/Lake Barkley, seem to indicate that the species at least occasionally remains throughout the summer. Usually encountered singly or in small groups of fewer than a dozen birds, but occasionally seen in flocks of up to 30 or more birds.

Maximum spring counts: ca. **125** below Ky Dam, Marshall Co., 29 Apr 1998 (*KW* 74:55, 1998); **90** at Ky Dam Village, 23 Apr 2018 (*KW* 94:75, 2018); at least **50** at Calvert City, Marshall Co., 8 May 2009 (*KW* 85:72, 2009); **40+** at Ky Dam Village, 18-23 Apr 2017 (*KW* 93:73, 2017); **40** at Ky Dam, 11 May 2009 (*KW* 85:72, 2009); **34** at the Falls of the Ohio, 17 Apr 1986 (*KW* 62:44, 1986).

Maximum fall counts: **1050** total on Lake Barkley, 3 Sep 2007 (*KW* 84:11 2008); **325** on a single island on Lake Barkley, Trigg Co., late Aug/early Sep 2007 (*KW* 84:11 2008); **300** on Lake Barkley, Lyon Co., 11 Sep 2006 (*KW* 83:15, 2007); **250-300** on Lake Barkley, Lyon Co., 23 Aug 2009 (*KW* 86:10, 2010); **250+** on Lake Barkley, Lyon Co., 30 Aug 2005 (*KW* 82:10, 2006); **200+** on Lake Barkley, Lyon Co., 11 Sep 2002 (*KW* 79:11, 2003); **172** on Lake Barkley above Barkley Dam, 1 Sep 2000 (*KW* 77:7, 2001); **150+** on Lake Barkley nr. Kuttawa, Lyon Co., 27 Aug 2004 (*KW* 81:10, 2005); **130** on Lake Barkley nr. Kuttawa, Lyon Co., 22 Aug 2002 (D. Roemer, notes); **83** on Ky Lake nr. Hamlin, Calloway Co. and **51** at the Wildcat Creek embayment of Ky Lake, Calloway Co., both 18 Aug 2015 (*KW* 92:10, 2016); **51** at Ky Dam Village, 2 Aug 2015 (*KW* 92:10, 2016); **43** at the Falls of the Ohio, 2 Sep 2017 (*KW* 94:9, 2018); **38** at Duck Island, Lake Barkley, Trigg Co., 7 Sep 1996 (B. Palmer-Ball, eBird data); **35** at the Falls of the Ohio, 4 Sep 1972 (J. Pasikowski, notes); **30** at the Paradise Power Plant, 21 Aug 2006 (*KW* 83:15, 2007).

Early spring dates: 25 Mar 2006, Lake Barkley, Lyon Co. (*KW* 82:70, 2006); 27 Mar 2004, Ky Dam (*KW* 80:69, 2004); 27 Mar 2006, Jonathan Creek (*KW* 82:70, 2006); 28 Mar 2004, Jonathan Creek (*KW* 80:69, 2004); 28 Mar 2007, Lake Barkley (*KW* 83:81, 2007); 28 Mar 2008, Lake Barkley (*KW* 84:65 2008); 28 Mar 2018, Frankfort (*KW* 94:75, 2018); 29 Mar 2003, Lake Barkley, Lyon Co. (*KW* 79:70, 2003); 29 Mar 2017, Lyon Co. (*KW* 93:73, 2017); 30 Mar 2002, Lake Barkley, Lyon Co. (*KW* 78:50, 2002); 31 Mar 1934, McElroy Lake (Wilson, *KW* 16:20, 1940); 31 Mar 2015, Ky Lake, Calloway Co. (*KW* 91:72, 2015); 1 Apr 1984, Louisville (*KW* 60:43, 1984); 1 Apr 1990, Ky Lake (*KW* 66:58, 1990); 1 Apr 2011, Lyon Co. (*KW* 87:91, 2011); 1 Apr 2014, Lake Barkley, Trigg Co. (*KW* 90:72, 2014); 1 Apr 2018, Louisville (*KW* 94:75, 2018).

Late fall dates: 19 Nov 1976, Falls of the Ohio (D. Parker, notes; A. Stamm, historical archive files); 17 Novemer 2004, Lake Barkley, Lyon Co. (*KW* 81:10, 2005); 16 Nov 2000, (2) on Ky Lake, Calloway Co. (*KW* 77:7, 2001); 8 Nov 1948, Fulton Co. (Mengel:263).
Unaccepted record: 20 Dec 1981, 2 on Ohio River at Louisville (*KW* 58:7/10/29, 1982).

*BLACK TERN *Chlidonias niger*

Status: Uncommon to (occasionally) fairly common (formerly common) transient, extremely rare during summer (one historical nesting location). Recorded chiefly west of the Cumberland Plateau, but there are a few records from eastern Kentucky (see below). Peaks of abundance occur from mid- to late May and from mid-Aug to early Sep. Most frequently encountered on the larger lakes and rivers, but sometimes observed over smaller bodies of water. Audubon reported nesting of this species at Louisville in the early 1800s, and there was suspected nesting at McElroy Lake in 1927 (Mengel:264). Currently the species is regarded as extirpated as a breeding bird, but it is reported occasionally during early summer between the normal spring and fall migratory periods. Generally observed singly or in small to medium-sized flocks of up to a dozen or so birds, but flocks of several dozen or more birds are occasionally encountered.

Maximum spring counts: **90-100** at McElroy Lake, 26 May 1989 (Palmer-Ball and Boggs, *KW* 67:64, 1991); **80-100** at McElroy Lake, 15 May 2008 (*KW* 84:65 2008); **85** at McElroy Lake, 17 May 2013 (*KW* 89:73, 2013).
Maximum fall counts: **150+** (likely 200-250) on the Mississippi River, Carlisle Co., 17 Aug 1991 (B. Palmer-Ball, eBird data); **150-200** occasionally observed at the Falls of the Ohio during late Aug (Mengel:264); **125+** at McElroy Lake, 6 Aug 1989, 26 May 1989 (Palmer-Ball and Boggs, *KW* 67:64, 1991); **100** at the Falls of the Ohio, 5 Sep 1964 (Stamm, et al., *KW* 43:12, 1967); at least **75** on the Mississippi River, Carlisle Co., 2 Sep 2010 (*KW* 87:19, 2011); **66** on the Ohio River below Markland Dam, Gallatin Co., 31 Aug 2005 (*KW* 82:11, 2006); **60-70** on the Mississippi River, Carlisle Co., 29 Aug 2005 (*KW* 82:11, 2006); **58** at the Falls of the Ohio, 26 Jul 1979 (*KW* 55:56, 1979); **50** on Ky Lake, Calloway co., 17 Aug 2002 (*KW* 79:11, 2003); at least **50** at Barren River Lake, 6 Sep 2008 (*KW* 85:17, 2009).
Early spring dates: 26 Apr 1950, Warren Co. (Wilson, *KW* 27:5, 1951); 30 Apr 2017, (ph.) at the Sauerheber Unit (*KW* 93:73, 2017).
Late fall dates: 12 Oct 19—, Louisville area (Mengel:264); 27 Sep 1979, Ky Lake, Calloway Co. (*KW* 56:16, 1980); 27 Sep 1986, Fishing Creek embayment Lake Cumberland, Pulaski Co. (*KW* 63:10, 1987); 27 Sep 2005, Smithland Dam (*KW* 82:11, 2006).
Unaccepted records: those during spring earlier than the early spring date of 26 Apr given above and including 15 Mar 1989, Warren Co. (Palmer-Ball and Boggs, *KW* 67:64, 1991); and 6 Apr 1955, south-central Kentucky (*KW* 38:14, 1962).
Published error: 7 Apr 1984, Oldham Co. (*KW* 60:44, 1984; should have been 7 May).

List of farthest east records by county

Bell (21 Sep 1985, Pinnacle Overlook, Cumberland Gap NHP [*KW* 61:62, 1985])
Elliott (20 Aug 1992, Grayson Lake [L. Kornman, pers. comm.])
Fleming (B. Wulker/W. Hull, 2017 eBird data)
Perry (Whitt, *KW* 49:45, 1973)
Rowan (essentially annual at Cave Run Lake/Minor Clark Hatchery [first reported 22 Aug 1992; *KW* 69:8, 1993])

COMMON TERN *Sterna hirundo*

Status: Rare to locally uncommon transient, extremely rare during early summer. Recorded chiefly west of the Cumberland Plateau, but the species has been found in eastern Kentucky on a few occasions (see below). Generally encountered on the larger lakes and rivers, but may occasionally turn up on smaller water bodies. Peaks of abundance occur from early to mid-May and from late-Aug to mid-Sep. Generally much less numerous and widespread in occurrence than Forster's Tern. There are a few Jun records between the normal spring and fall migratory periods. Generally encountered in small groups of fewer than a dozen birds, but occasionally seen in larger flocks. This and the following species can be difficult to differentiate, and great care should be exercised when distinguishing between the two (see Mengel:260-261).

Maximum spring counts: at least **280** in the immediate vicinity of Ky Dam Village, 11 May 2006 (KW 82:70, 2006); ca. **75** below Ky Dam, 6-7 May 1997 (B. Palmer-Ball, eBird data); **60-70** at the Falls of the Ohio, 6 May 1991 (J. McCandless and A. Mullen, pers. comm.); **60+** on the Ohio River at Newburgh Dam, Henderson, 5 May 2003 (KW 79:70, 2003).

Maximum fall counts: **137** total on Lake Cumberland, Pulaski/Russell cos., 17 Sep 2018 (KW 95:7, 2019); **98** at the Falls of the Ohio, 13 Sep 1965 (Stamm, et al., KW 43:11, 1967); **70** at the Falls of the Ohio, 11 Sep 1964 (Able, IAQ 43:51, 1965; Stamm, et al., KW 43:11, 1967); **75+** total on the n. ends of Ky Lake and Lake Barkley, 30 Aug 2005 (KW 82:11, 2006); **60** on the Green River at Rochester, Ohio Co., 30 Aug 2005 (KW 82:11, 2006); at least **60** on Ky Lake/Lake Barkley, 25 Sep 2009 (KW 86:11, 2010); **56** at Barren River Lake, 26 Sep 2018 (KW 95:7, 2019); ca. **40** on the Fishing Creek embayment of Lake Cumberland, Pulaski Co., 22 Sep 2002 (KW 79:11, 2003).

Early spring dates: 1 Apr 1939, south-central Kentucky (KW 38:14, 1962); 6 Apr 2012, Lake Barkley, Trigg Co. (KW 88:77, 2012); 9 Apr 1966, Falls of the Ohio (Stamm, et al., KW 43:11, 1967); 14 Apr 1982, Ky Lake, Calloway Co. (KW 58:51, 1982); 24 Apr 2005, Jonathan Creek (KW 81:88, 2005); 24 Apr 2019, Lake Barkley, Lyon Co. (B. Yandell, eBird data); 25 Apr 2002, Ohio River, Campbell Co. (KW 78:50, 2002); 29 Apr 2006, Ky Dam (E. Huber, et al., eBird data).

Late fall dates: 19 Nov 1984, Falls of the Ohio (KW 61:17, 1985); 11 Nov 2003, Jonathan Creek (KW 80:10, 2004); 8 Nov 2013, (ph.) Freeman Lake (KW 90:12/40, 2014); 7 Nov 1999, Mercer Co. (KW 76:6, 2000); 4 Nov 1964, Ohio River at Louisville (Able, IAQ 43:51, 1965; Stamm, et al., KW 43:11, 1967); 1 Nov 1992, Ohio River at Louisville (B. Palmer-Ball, eBird data); 1 Nov 1999, Mercer Co. (KW 76:6, 2000).

Unaccepted records: 26 Dec 1977, Glasgow CBC (KW 54:9, 1978); also, no details exist for the four early Apr reports listed above, and it could be that they should be included here; also 13 & 20 Apr 1991 (KW 67:56, 1991).

List of farthest east records by county

Harlan (Martins Fork Lake [KW 95:7, 2019])
Rowan (Cave Run Lake/Minor Clark Hatchery [Busroe, KW 61:25, 1985; KW 65:68, 1989; KW 68:8, 1992; KW 69:8, 1993/R. Denton, eBird data; KW 70:53, 1994; KW 71:4, 1995; KW 83:15, 2007; KW 88:77, 2012; KW 90:12, 2014; D. Svetich/L. Combs, 2019 eBird data])

FORSTER'S TERN *Sterna forsteri*

Status: Uncommon to fairly common transient, extremely rare during summer and winter. Recorded chiefly west of the Cumberland Plateau, with the easternmost records currently from Cave Run Lake/Minor Clark Hatchery. Most frequently encountered on the larger lakes and rivers, but occasionally observed on smaller bodies of water. Peaks of abundance occur from late Apr to early May and from mid-Aug to late Sep.Generally much more widespread than Common Tern (see Mengel: 262). There are several reports (mostly sub-adults) during Jun between the normal spring and fall migratory periods, typically on the larger lakes and rivers. Prior to the late 1980s, this species was virtually unknown in the state during winter; however small numbers began lingering on Lake Barkley/Ky Lake into late Nov in the late 1980s (e.g., KW 63:10, 1987) and more recently well into Dec (e.g., 19-20 Dec 1992 (KW 69:59, 1993 [date published incorrectly as 24-25 Dec in KW 69:35, 1993]), and small numbers now winter during milder years, primarily on a few embayments on the west side of Ky Lake, Calloway/Marshall cos.

Maximum spring counts: **400+** in the vicinity of Ky Dam, 11 May 2006 (KW 82:70, 2006); at least **170** in the vicinity of Ky Dam, 5 May 2011 (KW 87:91, 2011); **120+** on Lake Barkley above Barkley Dam, 4-5 May 1998 (B. Palmer-Ball, eBird data); **70** on Lake Barkley, Lyon Co., 1 May 2012 (KW 88:77, 2012); ca. **50** at Minor Clark Hatchery, 4 May 1991 (KW 67:56, 1991); ca. **50** on the Tennessee River at Calvert City, Marshall Co., 30 Apr 2016 (KW 92:64, 2016); **40** at the Falls of the Ohio, 5 May 1976 (B. Palmer-Ball, eBird data)

Maximum fall counts: **260+** at Jonathan Creek, 26 Oct 2002 (KW 79:11, 2003); **most of 250-300** *Sterna* terns on Ky Lake nr. Ky Dam, 25 Sep 2009 (KW 86:11, 2010); at least **200** at Jonathan

Creek, 14 Oct 2008 (*KW* 85:17, 2009); at least **200** at Jonathan Creek, 14 Sep 2009 (*KW* 86:11, 2010); at least **200** in the vicinity of Ky Dam and on Ky Lake, Marshall Co., 21/23 Sep 2011, respectively (*KW* 88:12, 2012); ca. **200** on Lake Barkley, Lyon Co., 15 Oct 2007 (*KW* 84:11 2008); ca. **200** in the vicinity of Ky Dam, 26 Oct 2008 (*KW* 85:17, 2009); **180** at Jonathan Creek, 14 Oct 2011 (*KW* 88:12, 2012); **172** at Jonathan Creek, 16 Nov 2007 (*KW* 84:11/72, 2008); **166** at Jonathan Creek, 28 Oct 2006 (*KW* 83:15, 2007); **158** at Jonathan Creek, 27 Sep/10 Oct 2015 (*KW* 92:10, 2016); ca. **140** on Ky Lake, Marshall Co., 25 Sep 2010 (*KW* 87:19, 2011); **130** on the Sledd Creek embayment of Ky Lake, Marshall Co., 25 Sep 2015 (*KW* 92:10, 2016); **125** at Jonathan Creek, 19 Oct 1998 (B. Palmer-Ball, eBird data); **125** at Jonathan Creek, 24 Sep 2004 (*KW* 81:10, 2005); **110** at Ky Dam, 27 Sep 2005 (*KW* 82:11, 2006); **135+** total on Lake Barkley, Lyon Co. (50) and above Ky Dam (85), 12 Oct 2005 (*KW* 82:11, 2006).

Early spring dates (other than recent wintering records, although some may be from wintering populations?): 2 Marc h 2013, Lake Barkley, Lyon Co. (*KW* 89:73, 2013); 6 Mar 2018, Calvert City, Marshall Co. (W. Buechler/W. Gregge, eBird data); 7 Mar 2001, Christian Co. (*KW* 77:50, 2001); 29 Mar 2018, Lexington (D. Svetich, eBird data); 30 Mar 1989, Warren Co. (Palmer-Ball and Boggs, *KW* 67:64, 1991); 30 Mar 2018, Pulaski Co. (T. McNeil, et al., eBird data).

Late spring dates: 3/18 Jun 2004, (2/1) at Calvert City, Marshall Co. (*KW* 80:83, 2004); 14 Jun 2013, Falls of the Ohio (*KW* 89:96-97, 2013); 10 Jun 1987, Falls of the Ohio (*KW* 63:60, 1987); 9 Jun 1994, Smithland Dam (B. Palmer-Ball, eBird data); 4 Jun 2008, Open Pond, Fulton Co. (*KW* 84:88, 2008); 4 Jun 2017, (13) Lexington (*KW* 93:100, 2017).

Early fall dates: 25 Jun 2002, Ky Lake, Calloway Co. (*KW* 78:64, 2002); 25 Jun 2013, (3) nr. Lake No. 9 (*KW* 89:96-97, 2013); 26 Jun 2007, Ohio River, Livingston Co. (*KW* 83:105, 2007); 26 Jun 2009, (2) in the Upper Hickman Bottoms and at Ky Dam (*KW* 85:94, 2009); 27 Jun, 2007, (2) Mississippi River, Fulton Co. (*KW* 83:105, 2007); 28 Jun 2002, nr. Woodburn, Warren Co. (*KW* 78:62, 2002); 28 Jun 2006, Ky Dam (*KW* 82:82, 2006); 28 Jun 2011, McElroy Lake (*KW* 87:115, 2011); 29 Jun 1993, Fishing Creek embayment of Lake Cumberland, Pulaski Co. (*KW* 69:56, 1993).

Late fall dates (away from known wintering sites or nearby): 18 Nov 2009, Barren River Lake (*KW* 86:11, 2010); 10 Nov 2001, Green River Lake, Taylor Co. (*KW* 78:8, 2002); 6 Nov 2002, Lake Cumberland, Pulaski Co. (*KW* 79:11, 2003); 3 Nov 2017, Lake Cumberland, Pulaski Co. (R. Denton, eBird data).

Out-of-season records (winter records other than recent reports of presumed wintering birds): 27 Jan 1983, Falls of the Ohio (*KW* 59:29, 1983); 18 Feb 1998, Barren River Lake, Barren Co. (*KW* 74:34, 1998); 12-13 Dec 2001, (2) on the Ohio River at Louisville (B. Palmer-Ball, eBird data).

Published error(s): a record of four at Grider's Lake, Warren Co., 1 Dec 1956 (Wilson, *KW* 33:15, 1957) was later published as 28 Dec 1956 (*KW* 38:14, 1962) and as 28 Dec 1958 (Stamm and Wiley, *KW* 36:45, 1960), but the correct date is unknown.

SANDWICH TERN *Thallaseus sandvicensis*

Status: Accidental vagrant. This coastal tern is quite rare in the inland eastern United States; it has been documented in Kentucky on one occasion.

1) 5 Sep 2008, (ph.) below Smithland Dam, Livingston Co. (*KW* 85:102, 2009; *NAB* 65:94, 2011).

ᔆBLACK SKIMMER *Rhynchops niger*

Status: Accidental vagrant. This coastal species has occurred infrequently up the Mississippi River valley; it has been documented once in Kentucky.

1) 22 Jul 2004, ad. on the Mississippi River, Fulton Co. (*KW* 80:83, 2004).

RED-THROATED LOON *Gavia stellata*

Status: Extremely rare to rare fall transient, extremely rare winter and spring visitant/transient. There are about 50 records of this loon, mostly during the peak of the species' fall migratory movement during Nov and Dec; however, records during mid-winter and spring have gradually accumulated during the past two decades. Generally to be expected only on the larger lakes and rivers; typically seen singly and sometimes in the company of Common Loons.

Maximum counts: **5** on Ky Lake, Marshall Co., 1 Mar 2019 (B. Wulker/C. Bliznick, et al. eBird data); **3** on Cave Run Lake, 7 Nov 1992 (*KW* 69:4, 1993); **3** on Ky Lake, Marshall Co., 17 Feb 2018 (*KW* 94:57, 2018); **3** on Lake Cumberland, Russell Co., 6/11 Feb 2019 (L. Bontrager/R. Bontrager, eBird data); **3** on McElroy Lake, 8 Apr 2019 (J. Sole, eBird data).

Early fall dates: 31 Oct 2001, Ky Lake, Marshall Co. (*KW* 78:4, 2002); 31 Oct 2004, Paradise Power Plant, Muhlenberg Co. (*KW* 81:5, 2005); 2 Nov 2005, (ph.) Ohio River at Louisville (*KW* 82:5, 2006); 3 Nov 2001, Green River Lake, Adair Co. (R. Denton, eBird data); 4 Nov 2017, Barren River Lake (B. Brand, eBird data); 7 Nov 1992, Cave Run Lake (*KW* 69:4, 1993); 7 Nov 2003, Barren River Lake (*KW* 80:5, 2004).

Late spring dates: 21 May 1939, found dead in Crittenden Co. (Mengel:153); 2 May 2015, Lake Barkley, Lyon Co. (*KW* 91:67, 2015); 14 May 2019, Lexington (D. Svetich, eBird data); 30 Apr 1967, Ohio River at Louisville (Able, *KW* 43:58-59, 1967); 21 Apr 1933, found dead in Fayette Co. (Mengel:153); 16 Apr 2018, Lake Cumberland, Russell Co. (*KW* 94:75, 2018); 8 Apr 2019, McElroy Lake (J. Sole, eBird data); 31 Mar 2013, Cave Run Lake (*KW* 89:66, 2013); 30 Mar 2007, Ky Lake, Marshall Co. (*KW* 83:73, 2007); 28 Mar 2014, Barren River Lake (*KW* 90:67, 2014); 22-25 Mar 2003, Ky Lake, Marshall Co. (*KW* 79:65, 2003); 13-24 Mar 2004, 1-2 on Ky Lake, Marshall Co. (*KW* 80:64, 2004); 23 Mar 2019, Ky Lake, Marshall Co. (J. Hall/S. Arnold, eBird data); 21 Mar 2009, Ky Lake, Marshall Co. (*KW* 85:65, 2009).

Unaccepted records: 2 Jan 1998, Glasgow CBC (*KW* 74:12, 1998; no details were provided with this report); 17 Mar 2018, Marshall Co. (*KW* 94:75, 2018; review of photos by some authorities deem bird to be a Common Loon).

Summary of records by county

Adair (*KW* 73:3, 1997/B. Palmer-Ball, 1996 eBird data; *KW* 74:4, 1998; *NAB* 55:175, 2001; R. Denton/B. Palmer-Ball, 2001 eBird data; *KW* 85:11, 2008; *KW* 88:5, 2012; *KW* 89:4, 2013; *KW* 90:6, 2014; *KW* 94:10, 2018)

Allen/Barren (*KW* 74:4, 1998; *KW* 77:27, 2001; *KW* 78:4, 2002; *KW* 80:5, 2004; *KW* 83:46, 2007; [A. Hulsey, 2007 notes; *KW* 84:43, 2008]; *KW* 90:67, 2014; *KW* 94:24, 2018; *KW* 95:7/24, 2019)

Bath/Rowan (Mengel:153; *KW* 69:4, 1993; *KW* 89:66, 2013; *KW* 91:50, 2015)

Bracken (*KW* 74:4, 1998/B. Palmer-Ball, 1997 eBird data)

Campbell (Mengel:153)

Crittenden (Mengel:153)

Elliott (Greene, *KW* 54:14, 1978)

Fayette (Mengel:153; Frazier, *KW* 51:36, 1975; *KW* 73:35, 1997; *KW* 90:67/84, 2014; C. Osborne, 2019 photos/R. O'Carra et al., 2019 eBird data)

Gallatin (*KW* 91:50/60, 2015)

Hardin (*KW* 89:46, 2013; *KW* 91:50, 2015; *KW* 95:7-8, 2019)

Hopkins (B. Palmer-Ball, 2002 eBird data; A. Morgan, 2002 notes; *KW* 79:4, 2003)

Jefferson (Able, *KW* 43:58-59, 1967; *KW* 54:27, 1978; Bell and Bell, *KW* 67:22, 1991; *KW* 68:12, 1992; J. Parks, 1997 notes and pers. comm.; *KW* 82:5, 2006; *KW* 91:50/67, 2015)

Livingston (*KW* 74:31, 1998)

Lyon (*KW* 69:12-13/32, 1993; *KW* 75:3, 1999/D. Roemer, 1998 notes; *KW* 91:67, 2015; *KW* 94:57, 2018)

Marshall (*KW* 67:11-12/27, 1991; *KW* 68:12, 1992; B. Palmer-Ball, et al., 1995 eBird data; B. Palmer-Ball, 1998 eBird data; *KW* 75:23, 1999; *KW* 78:4, 2002/H. Chambers, 2001 notes; *KW* 79:65, 2003; *KW* 80:17/41/64, 2004; *KW* 83:46/73, 2007; *KW* 84:5, 2008; *KW* 84:43, 2008; *KW* 85:65, 2009; *KW* 92:5/41, 2016; *KW* 94:10/57, 2018; *KW* 95:49, 2019/J. Baker/C. Bliznick et al., 2019 eBird data)

Muhlenberg (*KW* 81:5, 2005)

Ohio (*KW* 85:47, 2009)

Rowan (see Bath)

Russell (*KW* 85:11, 2008; *KW* 91:5, 2015; *KW* 92:5, 2016; *KW* 94:10/57/75, 2018; *KW* 95:49, 2019/L. Bontrager/R. Denton, et al., 2019 eBird data)

Taylor (*KW* 70:15/31, 1994; *KW* 77:3, 2001; B. Palmer-Ball, 2001 eBird data; *KW* 91:50/67, 2015)

PACIFIC LOON *Gavia pacifica*

Status: Extremely rare transient and winter visitant. Separation between this species and the very similar ARCTIC LOON (*G. arctica*) can be extremely difficult in the field; however, the latter has been documented only in western Alaska and along the Pacific coast, and is not considered likely in the eastern United States (see *KW* 68:12, 1992). Moreover, descriptions provided for all of the records listed above have noted the lack of an obvious light flank patch, which is typically a distinctive feature of *G. arctica*. It is unclear whether or not there has been an increase in the occurrence of this loon over the past two decades, or if birders are simply now detecting the species. There are now at least 21 records (13 during fall/early winter, one during mid-winter, and seven during spring).

Early fall dates: 13 Oct 2009, Barren River Lake (*KW* 86:5, 2010); 30 Oct 2015, Green River Lake, Taylor Co. (*KW* 92:5, 2016);
Late spring dates: 13 May 1991, Ky Dam (Stinson, *KW* 68:62-63, 1992; *KW* 67:52, 1991); 13 May 2002, Ky Lake, Marshall Co. (*KW* 78:48, 2002); 6 May 1999, below Ky Dam (B. Palmer-Ball, eBird data)
Unaccepted records: 8-29 Nov 1971, Ohio River at Meldahl Dam [no details available] (*AB* 25:65, 1971; W. Randle, notes); 5 May 1991, Lake Barkley above Barkley Dam, Lyon Co. (D. Parker/B. Palmer-Ball, notes [details of this report cannot be located in author's notes])

Chronological list of records

1) 15-19 Dec 1990, (ph.) on Ky Lake, Marshall Co. (Palmer-Ball and Parker, *KW* 67:47-48, 1991)
2) 3-13 May, 1991, above Ky Dam (Stinson, *KW* 68:62-63, 1992; *KW* 67:52, 1991; *KW* 69:23, 1993)
3) for ca. two weeks 11+ Feb 1995, (ph.) at Freeman Lake (*KW* 71:24, 1995; R. Healy, pers. comm.)
4) 6 May 1999, (ph.) below Ky Dam (B. Palmer-Ball, eBird data)
5) 19-21 Nov 1999, Ky Lake above the dam (*KW* 76:3, 2000; D. Roemer/F. Bennett, notes)
6) 15-19 Nov 2000, (vt.) on Ky Lake above the dam (B. Palmer-Ball, eBird data; *KW* 77:3, 2001 [date erroneously published as 1/19 Nov therein])
7) 30 Mar–13 May 2002, (vt.) on Ky Lake, Marshall Co. (*KW* 78:48, 2002)
8) 24 Nov 2002, above Ky Dam (*KW* 79:4, 2003)
9) 17 Dec 2002, (vt.) Lake Peewee (*KW* 79:44, 2003)
10) 26 Feb/10 Mar 2004, Ky Lake, Marshall Co. (*KW* 80:41/64, 2004)
11) 18 Dec 2004, Lake Barkley, Lyon Co. (*KW* 81:22/57, 2005)
12) 4 Dec 2006, Lake Barkley, Lyon Co. (*KW* 83:46, 2007)
13) 13-17 Oct 2009, (ph.) on Barren River Lake, Allen/Barren cos. (*KW* 86:5, 2010)
14) 16-19 Dec 2009, (vt.) Ky Lake, Marshall Co. (*KW* 86:18/42, 2010)
15) 23-24 Apr 2010, (ph.) at Cave Run Lake, Bath Co. (*KW* 86:64/76, 2010)
16) 2 Apr 2011, Ky Lake, Lyon Co. (*KW* 87:83, 2011)
17) 30 Oct–1 Nov 2015, (ph.) Green River Lake, Taylor Co. (*KW* 92:5, 2016)
18) 13 Dec 2017, (ph.) Dale Hollow Lake, Clinton Co. (*KW* 94:57, 2018)
19) 27-28 Apr 2018, (ph.) Barren River Lake (*KW* 94:75, 2018)
20) 17 Nov 2018, (ph.) Lake Cumberland, Russell Co. (*KW* 95:8, 2019)
21) 20-25 Nov 2018, (ph.) Lake Peewee (*KW* 95:1/8, 2019)

COMMON LOON *Gavia immer*

Status: Fairly common transient, rare to locally uncommon winter resident, extremely rare during summer. Recorded chiefly west of the Cumberland Plateau, although probably uncommon on reservoirs of eastern Kentucky during migration. Generally encountered on the larger lakes and rivers, but sometimes found on smaller bodies of water. Loons are typically found resting on open water, but individuals or loose groups are sometimes observed flying overhead during the day during migratory periods. Individuals occasionally linger into or through summer. Presumed fall migrants occasionally show up during Aug and Sep, but the peak of abundance occurs from early Nov to early Dec. Historically, the species was not known to winter, but in recent years a few birds have wintered on some of the state's larger reservoirs (Dale Hollow Lake, Green River Lake, Ky Lake, Lake Cumberland). Often seen singly or in small groups of up to a dozen birds, but larger groups of up to several dozen birds are occasionally reported.

Maximum fall counts: **1342** on Barren River Lake, 7 Nov 2003 (*KW* 80:5, 2004); ca. **1000** on Barren River Lake, 11-14 Nov 1997 (*KW* 74:4, 1998; L. Doyle, notes); **800+** on Barren River Lake, 16 Nov 2002 (*KW* 79:4, 2003); **637** on Lake Cumberland, Russell Co., 27 Nov 2012 (*KW* 89:5, 2013); **500+** on Cedar Creek Lake, Lincoln Co., 1 Dec 2015 (*KW* 92:41, 2016); ca. **500** on the Ohio River at Louisville and **151** on Lexington Reservoir #4, 17 Nov 1978 (*KW* 55:14, 1979); at least **500** on Barren River Lake, 23 Nov 2010 (*KW* 87:13, 2011); **460** on Green River Lake, Adair/Taylor cos., 27 Nov 2012 (*KW* 89:5, 2013); **330** on Barren River Lake 11 Nov 2011 (*KW* 88:5, 2012); ca. **325** on the Ohio River at Meldahl Dam, 8 Nov 1997 (*KW* 74:4, 1998); **300** over Meldahl Dam, Bracken Co., 8 Nov 1997 (J. Stenger, eBird data); **300** on Lake Cumberland, Russell Co., 21 Nov 2015 (*KW* 92:5, 2016); **240** on the Ohio River above Meldahl Dam, Bracken Co., 18 Nov 2009 (*KW* 86:5, 2010); **190** on Barren River Lake, 7 Nov 2017 (*KW* 94:10, 2018); **150-200** on Barren River Lake, 22 Nov 1975 (Roemer, *KW* 52:16, 1976); **185** on Lake Cumberland, Wayne Co., 15 Nov 2018 (R. Denton, eBird data); **183** on Barren River Lake, 21 Nov 2005 (*KW* 82:5, 2006); **170** on Ky Lake, Marshall Co., 27 Nov 2010 (*KW* 87:13, 2011); **160** on Barren River Lake, 31 Oct 2006 (*KW* 83:9, 2007); **151** on Lexington Reservoir #4, 17 Nov 1978 (*KW* 55:14, 1979); **150+** on Barren River Lake, 26 Nov 2002 (*KW* 79:4, 2003); at least **150** on Green River Lake, 19 Nov 2010 (*KW* 87:13, 2011); at least **150** on Ky Lake, Marshall Co., 9 Nov 2009 (*KW* 86:5, 2010); **154** total on Lake Cumberland, Pulaski/Wayne Cos., 30 Nov 2015 (*KW* 92:5, 2016); **151** on Barren River Lake, 7 Nov 2018 (T. Durbin, eBird data); ca. **120** on the Ohio River, Meade Co., 16 Nov 1941 (Carpenter, *KW* 18:6-7, 1942); **101** on Cave Run Lake and 72 on Dewey Lake, Floyd Co., 7 Nov 1992 (*KW* 69:4, 1993).

Maximum spring counts: **275+** total on Ky Lake/Lake Barkley, 30 Mar 2007 (*KW* 83:73, 2007; location provided as Ky Lake, Marshall Co. in eBird); at least **110** on Ky Lake, Marshall Co., 21 Mar 2009 (*KW* 85:65, 2009); at least **100** on Ky Lake, Marshall Co., 1 Apr 2011 (*KW* 87:83, 2011); at least **87** on Lake Cumberland, Pulaski Co., 3 Apr 2015 (*KW* 91:67, 2015); **83** on Cave Run Lake, 31 Mar 2013 (*KW* 89:66, 2013); **75** on Cave Run Lake, 5 Apr 2012 (*KW* 88:72, 2012); **68** on Lake Cumberland, Pulaski Co. (R. Denton, eBird data); **64** on Barren River Lake, 21 Apr 2013 (*KW* 89:66, 2013); **63** on Cave Run Lake, 23 Apr 2010 (*KW* 86:64, 2010); at least **60** on Barren River Lake, 6 Apr 2009 (*KW* 85:65, 2009); **50-60** on Ky Lake 21 Feb 2007 (*KW* 83:46, 2007); **55-60** on Ky Lake, Marshall Co., 21 Apr 2014 (*KW* 90:67, 2014); **53** on Cave Run Lake, 6 Apr 1990 (*KW* 66:53, 1990); **52** on Cave Run Lake, 15 Apr 2007 (*KW* 83:73, 2007); **51** on Ky Lake, Marshall Co., 29 Mar 2018 (*KW* 94:75, 2018).

YELLOW-BILLED LOON *Gavia adamsii*

Status: Accidental vagrant. This loon typically occurs in northwestern North America but is found infrequently in the eastern United States. It has been documented in Kentucky on one occasion.

1) 13-30 Mar 2004, an imm. (ph.) on Ky Lake nr. Birmingham Point, Marshall Co. (Palmer-Ball and Covert, *KW* 80:59-60, 2004; *KW* 80:37/64-65, 2004).

BAND-RUMPED STORM-PETREL *Hydrobates castro*

Status: Accidental vagrant. This pelagic species should only occur in the state during the passage of the remnants of a tropical cyclone. It has been documented in Kentucky three times. The first was probably deposited with the remnants of "Tropical Depression Two," which dissipated over s. North Carolina, and the latter three occurred with the passage of the remnants of Hurricane Katrina.

Chronological list of records

1) late Jul 1994, picked up dead (sp.) in a yard in e. Anderson Co. (D. Sabree, pers. comm.; Palmer-Ball, *KW* 72:64-65, 1996)
2) 31 Aug 2005, (vt.) at the Falls of the Ohio (*KW* 82:5, 2006; Monroe et al., *KW* 82:32-37)
3) 31 Aug 2005, two (one found dead [sp.] the following day) at the Pfeiffer Fish Hatchery, Franklin Co. (*KW* 82:5, 2006; Monroe et al., *KW* 82:32-37)

BLACK-CAPPED PETREL *Pterodroma hasitata*

Status: Accidental vagrant. This pelagic species should only occur in the state as the remnants of a tropical cyclone pass, and this was the case with the three historic records. The cyclone responsible for this event was called "The Georgia Hurricane of 1898;" it made landfall as a Category 4 storm on the coast of Georgia and came inland through central Kentucky. All three petrels occurred along the Ohio River, 4-5 Oct 1898 (at least one of these individuals was preserved as a voucher specimen [Mengel:156]).

List of records

1) one captured on the river nr. the e. end of Cincinnati [= Campbell Co.] (Lindahl, *Auk* 16:75, 1899)
2) one captured after it struck a light pole on the Ohio–Kentucky roadway bridge at Cincinnati [= Kenton Co.] (Lindahl, *Auk* 16:75, 1899)
3) one captured by a ferry captain nr. Augusta, Bracken Co., and kept alive for several days by force-feeding minnows (Lindahl, *Auk* 16:75, 1899)

GREAT SHEARWATER *Ardenna gravis*

Status: Accidental vagrant. This pelagic species should only occur in the state as the remnants of a tropical cyclone pass, and this was the case with the one record.

1) 15 Jul 2019, (ph.) on Ky Lake above Ky Dam, Marshall Co., present during the passage of the remnants of Hurricane Barry (A. Lydeard/D. Redwine, eBird data)

AUDUBON'S SHEARWATER *Puffinus lherminieri*

Status: Accidental vagrant. This pelagic species should only occur in the state as the remnants of a tropical cyclone pass, and this was the case with the one record.

1) 12 Jul 2005, (vt.) Ky Lake above Ky Dam, Livingston/Marshall cos., present during the passage of the remnants of Hurricane Dennis (Monroe et al., *KW* 82:1/32-37/40, 2006; *KW* 81:105, 2005)

WOOD STORK *Mycteria americana*

Status: Extremely rare summer and fall visitant, accidental during spring and winter. Recorded primarily from scattered localities in the western half of the state with most reports from the Jackson Purchase. Most records for the state came from the late 19th century and first half of the 20th century (Mengel:171), with only 13 documented reports since 1970 (see below). There are only six records, all of single birds, from Louisville eastward (see below). This species can turn up virtually anywhere, but it has been encountered most often in wetlands along the larger river floodplains. Most often seen singly or in small groups of only a few birds, but older records exist that involved flocks of more than 50 individuals (Mengel:171). **Federal Status**: Threatened.

Maximum counts: **250** in Fulton Co., 15 Jul 1887 (Mengel:171); **52** in Webster Co., 21 Jul 1925 (Bacon, *KW* 30:28, 1954); ca. **50** in Ballard Co., Aug–Sep 1875 (Mengel:171); **37** in Hopkins Co., 28 Jul 1925 (Bacon, *KW* 30:28, 1954).
Early summer date: 2 Jul 1941, Fulton Co. (Mengel: 171).
Late fall dates: 27-28 Oct 1975, Paris, Bourbon Co. (*AB* 30:78, 1976); 26 Sep 2000, Ky Lake, Marshall Co. (*KW* 77:4, 2001; P. Ceas, pers. comm.); 23 Sep 19— [assumed to be 1978 in Nelson Co.; see *KW* 55:14/18, 1979]; 20 Sep 2000, McCracken Co. (*KW* 77:4, 2001).
Out-of-season record (winter): 15 Feb 1978, w. side of Lexington, Fayette Co. (*KW* 54:27, 1978).
Out-of-season record (spring): 30 Apr 1983, Minor Clark Hatchery (*KW* 59:40, 1983).
Unaccepted record: 11 Nov 1986–2 Jan 1987, (1-2) on Hopson Bay of Lake Barkley nr. Canton, Trigg Co. (*KW* 63:35, 1987) [details of this record were quite obscure].

List of recent (post-1970) records by county

Ballard (23-24 Jul 2012, 4 (ph.) at Boatwright WMA, Ballard Co. [*KW* 88:92, 2012])
Bourbon (27-28 Oct 1975, Paris [*AB* 30:78, 1976])

Fayette (15 Feb 1978, Masterson Station Park [*KW* 54:27, 1978])

Fulton (9-13 Aug 2006, (ph.) Lake No. 9 [*KW* 83:10, 2007]; 13-15 Sep 2008, up to 11 (ph.) at Lake No. 9 [*KW* 85:12/40, 2008])

Jefferson (30 Jul–23 Aug 2012, (ph.) at Anchorage [*KW* 88:85/92, 2012/*KW* 89:5, 2013])

Livingston (16-18 Jul 2017, (ph.) n. of Bayou [*KW* 93:100, 2017])

Marshall (26 Sep 2000, Ky Lake [*KW* 77:4, 2001; P. Ceas, pers. comm.]; 10-11 Sep 2007, 2 (ph.) at Jonathan Creek [*KW* 84:6-7, 2007])

McCracken (20 Sep 2000, (5) over the Ohio River at Joppa, Illinois [*KW* 77:4, 2001; location erroneously published as Ballard WMA therein [*fide* F. Bennett, pers. comm.])

Nelson (for about two weeks, 9+ Sep 1978, nr. Cox's Creek [*KW* 55:14/18, 1979])

Rowan (30 Apr 1983, Minor Clark Hatchery [*KW* 59:40, 1983])

Trigg (5 Aug 2017, Lake Barkley [*KW* 94:10, 2018])

Summary of records from Louisville and eastward by county

Jefferson (12-18 Aug 1934, Falls of the Ohio [Monroe and Mengel, *KW* 15:39, 1939]; 30 Jul–23 Aug 2012, (ph.) at Anchorage [*KW* 88:85/92, 2012, *KW* 89:5, 2013])

Bourbon (27-28 Oct 1975, Paris [*AB* 30:78, 1976])

Fayette (15 Feb 1978, Masterson Station Park [*KW* 54:27, 1978])

Nelson (for about two weeks, 9+ Sep 1978, nr. Cox's Creek [*KW* 55:14/18, 1979])

Rowan (30 Apr 1983, Minor Clark Hatchery [*KW* 59:40, 1983])

MAGNIFICENT FRIGATEBIRD *Fregata magnificens*

Status: Accidental vagrant. This pelagic and coastal species is typically not encountered inland except during or after the passage of the remnants of a tropical cyclone. It has been documented in Kentucky once during such conditions.

1) 20 Sep 2017, a presumed ad. male (ph.) at the Minor Clark Hatchery (S. Barrett, notes; E. Raglin, photos; *KW* 94:10, 2018; Palmer-Ball, *KW* 93:114-115, 2017). This individual was seen after the passage of the remnants of Hurricane Irma.

NORTHERN GANNET *Morus bassanus*

Status: Accidental vagrant. Thre are two Kentucky records of this coastal and pelagic inhabitant of northeastern North America.

Chronological list of records

1) 7 Dec 1967, an imm. on the Ohio River at Cincinnati (= Kenton/Campbell Co.), later captured in a Cincinnati yard, which proved to be a bird banded on Bonaventure Island, Canada, as a nestling 9 Sep 1967 (*AB* 22:444, 1968)

2) 29 Nov 1987, an imm. observed flying south along Interstate 65, just north of the Tennessee state line, Simpson Co. (Braun, *KW* 64:34-36, 1988)

NEOTROPIC CORMORANT *Phalacrocorax brasilianus*

Status: Extremely rare summer and fall visitant. This cormorant has been turning up with increasing frequency to the north of its traditional range. It has now been documented in Kentucky on six occasions.

Chronological list of records

1) 27 Sep 1998, (vt.) on Lake Barkley, Trigg Co. (*KW* 82:51, 2006)

2) 28 Feb 2007, (ph.) at the Paradise Power Plant, Muhlenberg Co. (Palmer-Ball, *KW* 83:86-87, 2007; *KW* 83:61/88, 2007)

3) 19 Jun–30 Jul 2011, 1-4 (ph.) at Lake No. 9 (*KW* 87:112/124, 2011)

4) 2 Mar 2013, (ph.) on Lake Barkley, Lyon Co. (*KW* 90:92, 2014; E. Huber, photos)

5) 25 Jun 2013, an ad. (ph.) at Lake No. 9 (*KW* 89:93/104, 2013)

6) 24 May 2019, on Lake Barkley, Trigg Co. (H. Chambers, 2019 eBird data)

*DOUBLE-CRESTED CORMORANT *Phalacrocorax auritus*

Status: Uncommon to locally common transient, rare to locally uncommon winter resident, rare to uncommon summer resident/visitant. Recorded chiefly west of the Cumberland Plateau, although seems to be at least uncommon on reservoirs of eastern Kentucky during migratory periods. Generally encountered on the larger lakes, rivers and backwater sloughs, but occasionally seen on smaller bodies of water. Peaks of abundance occur during Apr and from mid-Oct to mid-Nov. Flocks of migrants are not uncommonly seen flying over in wavy lines and can be mistaken for geese. Formerly (prior to the early 1950s) nested with Great Blue Herons and Great Egrets in at least three colonies in western Kentucky (Mengel:157-158). After a period of virtual absence during the middle of the 20th century, the species began increasing during the late 1970s, and by the late 1980s a few birds began summering. Nesting was finally documented again during summer 2000, and has since been confirmed in no fewer than six counties (see below). Large fall flocks often linger into early winter, although extremely cold weather typically results in the species becoming relatively scarce during mid-winter. Most often seen singly or in small groups of fewer than ten birds, but migrant flocks may number up to several hundred or more birds. **State Breeding Status**: Special Concern.

Maximum counts: ca. **15,000** on Lake Barkley, Lyon/Trigg cos., 30 Mar 2007 (*KW* 83:76, 2007); ca. **6000** on Lake Barkley, Trigg Co., 28 Oct 2003 (*KW* 80:6, 2004; date *fide* E. Ray, pers. comm.); ca. **5000** on Lake Barkley, Trigg Co., 25 Oct 2000 (*KW* 77:4, 2001); **4000-6000** on Lake Barkley, Trigg Co., 19 Oct 2004 (*KW* 81:5, 2005); "**several thousand**" over the Ohio River at Uniontown Dam, Union Co., 9 Sep 2008 (*KW* 85:12, 2008); at least **4000** on Taylor Bay, Lake Barkley, Trigg Co., 2 Nov 2009 (*KW* 86:5, 2010); "**a few thousand**" on Lake Barkley, Lyon/Trigg cos., 23 Nov 2008 (*KW* 85:12, 2009); ca. **2500** on Lake Barkley at Kuttawa, Lyon Co., 22 Mar 2008 (*KW* 84:59, 2008); **2500** on Lake Barkley, Trigg Co., 4 Nov 2014 (*KW* 91:5, 2015); at least **2400** on Lake Barkley above the dam, 13 Apr 2000 (B. Palmer-Ball, eBird data); ca. **2400** at Markland Dam, Gallatin Co., 6 Nov 1997 (*KW* 74:4, 1998); **2000** on Lake Barkley, Trigg Co., 30 Mar 2005 (*KW* 81:84, 2005); **2000** on Lake Barkley, Trigg Co., 18 Sep 2007 (*KW* 84:6, 2008; R. Denton, eBird data); **2000** on Lake Barkley at Kuttawa, Lyon Co., 15 Oct 2015 (*KW* 92:5, 2016); **2000** on Lake Barkley, Trigg Co., 29 May & 8 Aug 2017 (A. Trently, eBird data & C. Bliznick/T. Graham, eBird data); **1500-2000** over the Falls of the Ohio, 25 Oct 2007 (*KW* 84:6, 2008); groups of **750** and **1500** at two sites on the Ohio River, Union Co., 24 Oct 2012 (*KW* 89:5, 2013); **1000-1500** over the Long Point Unit, 5 Apr 1992 (B. Palmer-Ball, eBird data); **1200** on Lake Barkley, Trigg Co., 30 Mar 2018 (*KW* 94:75, 2018); ca. **1000** on Lake Barkley nr. Silo Overlook, Trigg Co., 20 Nov 1998 (D. Roemer, notes); ca. **1000** on the Ohio River at Louisville, 11 Oct 1999 (*KW* 76:4, 2000); **1000** on the Ohio River at Louisville, 15 Nov 2005 (*KW* 82:5, 2006); **1000+** on the Ohio River, n. Union Co., 14 Oct 2007 (*KW* 84:6, 2008); **900-1000** over Bowling Green, 6 Apr 2008 (*KW* 84:59, 2008); ca. **900** on the Ohio River at Louisville, 11 Oct 2014 (*KW* 91:5, 2015); **700+** on Mitchell Lake, Ballard WMA, 27 Mar 2009 (*KW* 85:66, 2009); ca. **600** on Lake Barkley at Silo Overlook, Trigg Co., 8 Oct 1993 (*KW* 70:6, 1994); ca. **600** on Lake Barkley at Silo Overlook, Trigg Co., 24 Sep 1994 (*KW* 71:3, 1995); **400+** over Louisville, 20 Oct 1991 (*KW* 68:3, 1992).

List of confirmed breeding records by county (historical)

Ballard (Mengel:157-158)
Fulton (Mengel:157-158)
Henderson (Mengel:157-158)

List of confirmed breeding records by county (recent)

Calloway (Ky Lake at Hamlin; established 2000 [*KW* 78:60, 2002; *KW* 79:80, 2003; *KW* 80:80, 2004; *KW* 81:84/105, 2005; *KW* 82:66, 2006; *KW* 83:76, 2007; Palmer-Ball and Powell, *KW* 91:90-93]; 320 nests [*KW* 92:57, 2016])
Jefferson (Shippingport Island; established 2009 [*KW* 85:66/91, 2009; B. Palmer-Ball, 2018/2019 eBird data])
Jessamine/Mercer (Kentucky River near Shaker Village; established 2018 and 27 active nests in 2019 [B. Lefew/W. Little, pers. comm.])
Lincoln (Cedar Creek Lake; 2019 [T. Nauman, eBird data])

Lyon (Lake Barkley at Kuttawa; established in 2008 [*KW* 84:59/85, 2008; *KW* 85:91, 2009; *KW* 86:64, 2010; *KW* 89:67, 2013; *KW* 90:68, 2014; Palmer-Ball and Powell, *KW* 91:90-93]; at least 500 nests [*KW* 92:57, 2016])

Lyon (Lake Barkley, island above dam; established at least as early as 2015 [Palmer-Ball and Powell, *KW* 91:90-93])

Menifee (Cave Run Lake, Jun 2019 [J. Brunjes, pers. comm.])

Trigg (Lake Barkley, nr. the mouth of the Little River; established in 2008 [*KW* 84:59/85, 2008]; up to 750 nests [*KW* 86:64, 2010; *KW* 87:112, 2011; *KW* 89:93, 2013; *KW* 90:68, 2014; Palmer-Ball and Powell, *KW* 91:90-93]; 1500-2000 active nests [*KW* 92:57, 2016]

Trigg (Lake Barkley off Taylor Bay; [Palmer-Ball and Powell, *KW* 91:90-93]; at least 445 nests [*KW* 92:57, 2016])

*ANHINGA *Anhinga anhinga*

Status: Extremely rare spring and summer visitant (formerly a rare summer resident). Found historically along the Mississippi River, nesting in one colony near Bondurant, Fulton Co. (now on the Long Point Unit), but not reported nesting there since 1950 (Mengel:158-159); in addition, several old records exist for Hopkins Co. (Mengel:159). This species is once again nesting along the Mississippi River in extreme western Tennessee, and its occurrence along the rivers and sloughs of southwestern Kentucky may become more regular. There are now 13 relatively recent records of summer visitants.

Early spring dates: 26 Mar 2009, Ballard Co. (*KW* 85:66, 2009); 7 May 2007, Fulton Co. (*KW* 83:76, 2007); 10 May 2013, Ballard/Carlisle Cos. (*KW* 89:67, 2013); 11 May 2013, Sinclair Unit. (*KW* 89: 67, 2013); 20 May 1949, Fulton Co. (Mengel:158).
Late fall date: 11 Nov 19—, Hopkins Co. (Mengel:159).
Unaccepted records: 23 Oct 1961, Daviess Co. (Powell, *KW* 38:29, 1962); 4 Jun 1964, Ohio River at Louisville (Carpenter, *KW* 40:70-71, 1964; see Monroe, *KW* 52:41, 1976); 8-9 Dec 1985, Ballard Co. (*KW* 62:31, 1986); 7 May 2018, Trigg Co. (eBird data; this record was accepted by the KBRC but details seem unconvincing).
Published error: early spring date of 17 Apr [1938] (*KW* 45:48, 1969) pertains to Tennessee (*fide* Mengel:158).

Chronological list of recent records

1) 1-23 Sep 1995, Breckinridge Co. (*KW* 72:59, 1996; *KW* 73:28, 1997)
2) 15 Jun 1996, a male at Lake No. 9 (J. Wilson, notes)
3) 17-19 Aug 2000, an imm./female (ph.) nr. Audubon State Park, Henderson Co. (Palmer-Ball, *KW* 77:37, 2001)
4) 8 Jun 2004, a female ne. of Hickman, Fulton Co. (*KW* 80:80, 2004)
5) 7 May 2007, 3 males (ph.) over Obion WMA, Fulton Co. (*KW* 83:76, 2007)
6) 26 Mar 2009, nw. of Wickliffe, Ballard Co. (*KW* 85:66, 2009)
7) 13 Jul 2009, a male at the Long Point Unit (*KW* 85:91, 2009)
8) 23 Sep 2011, 2 over Swan Lake vicinity, Ballard Co. (*KW* 88:5, 2012)
9) 10 May 2013, a male (ph.) in a heronry along Mayfield Creek, Ballard/Carlisle Co. (*KW* 89:67, 2013)
10) 11-13 May 2013, a male (ph.) at the Sinclair Unit (*KW* 89:67/75, 2013)
11) 12 Jul 2015, over Ky Lake, Calloway Co. (*KW* 91:84, 2015)
12) 2 Jun 2016, (ph.) nr. Ky Dam, Marshall Co. (*KW* 92:78/92, 2016)
13) 31 May 2017, ad. male along Mississippi River, w. Fulton Co. (*KW* 93:74, 2017)

AMERICAN WHITE PELICAN *Pelecanus erythrorhynchos*

Status: Rare to locally fairly common transient, extremely rare to locally uncommon winter resident/ visitant, extremely rare to locally rare during summer. Recorded chiefly from the Louisville area southwestward. Historically this species was an exceptionally rare vagrant with most reports from the western portion of the state (Mengel:157); however, commencing during the mid-1990s, noticeable spring and fall migratory movements began occurring in far western Kentucky. Migrant flocks initially disappeared during mid-winter, apparently retreating farther south, but as the years have progressed flocks have lingered through the season more and more, especially on Ky Lake and Lake Barkley. In more recent years, a few flocks of non-breeding birds, as well as some known or possibly injured birds, also have begun to summer in far western Kentucky, primarily along the Mississippi River and in the LBL vicinity. There are relatively few records, most of single birds, from east of Louisville, but the species continues to increase and is now being seen several times annually in the central part of the state. Generally encountered on the larger lakes, rivers, and natural floodplain sloughs, but occasionally seen on smaller bodies of water or migrating overhead. Peaks of abundance occur from mid-Mar to mid-Apr and from mid-Oct to early Dec. Most often seen singly or in small flocks of up to a half-dozen birds away from far western Kentucky, where flocks of a hundred or more are not uncommon.

Maximum counts (LBL region and westward; illustrating increase in numbers over past several decades): at least **3229** on the Little River embayment of Lake Barkley, Trigg Co., 15 Oct 2011 (Palmer-Ball, *KW* 89:37-38, 2013); **2000** at Ballard WMA, 10 Mar 2004 (*KW* 80:65, 2004); ca. **2000** on Lake Barkley, Trigg Co., 20 Oct 2010 (*KW* 87:13, 2011); ca. **1800** on the Little River embayment of Lake Barkley, Trigg Co., 20 Sep 2014 (*KW* 91:6, 2015); at least **1600** on Lake Barkley, Trigg, 26 Oct 2008 (*KW* 85:11, 2009); **1500** on the Boyds Branch embayment, Ky Lake, Calloway Co., 29 Mar 2005 (*KW* 81:84, 2005); **1400** on Honker Bay, Lake Barkley, Lyon Co., 20 Oct 2009 (*KW* 86:5, 2010); at least **1200** on Lake Barkley, Lyon/Trigg cos., 20 Oct 2007 (*KW* 84:5, 2008); **1200** at Blood River, 21 Sep 2016 (*KW* 93:5, 2017); **1100** on the Eddy Creek embayment Lake Barkley, Lyon Co., 12 Oct 2018 (*KW* 95:8, 2019); **1000** in the vicinity of Honker Bay, Lake Barkley, Lyon Co., 19/21 Jan 2013 (*KW* 89:46, 2013); **867** along the Ohio River, Livingston Co., 29 Mar 2013 (*KW* 89:67, 2013); **700-1000** at Blood River, 2 Mar 2008 (*KW* 84:58, 2008); **800+** at Blood River, mid-Oct–early Nov 2015 (*KW* 92:5, 2016); **750** at Jonathan Creek, 25 Mar 2015 (*KW* 91:67, 2015); **630+** on Lake Barkley, Trigg Co., 6 Oct 2006 (*KW* 83:9, 2007); **625+** on Lake Barkley between the dam and Eddyville, 30 Mar 2002 (*KW* 78:48, 2002); **600** in the Lower Hickman Bottoms, 2-3 Oct 2004 (*KW* 81:5, 2005; H. Chambers/R. Denton, eBird data); **600+** on Lake Barkley, Trigg Co., 3 Mar 2006 (*KW* 82:66, 2006); at least **600** at Blood River, 9 Mar 2007 (*KW* 83:76, 2007); **550+** at Barkley Dam, 28 Mar 2008 (*KW* 84:59, 2008); **545** at Jonathan Creek, 7 Feb 2012 (*KW* 88:45, 2012); **500+** on Lake Barkley, Lyon Co., 17 Oct 2004 (*KW* 81:5, 2005); **250** on Lake Barkley between the dam and Eddyville, Lyon Co. 23 Feb 2001 (*KW* 77:27, 2001); **245** at Kentucky Bend, Fulton Co., 31 Oct 2000 (*KW* 77:4, 2001); **200-220** on the Ohio River at Birdsville Island, Livingston Co., 25 Mar 1999 (V. Anderson, pers. comm); ca. **200** on Lake Barkley from the dam to Eddyville, 10 Mar 2001 (*KW* 77:48, 2001; D. Roemer, pers. comm.); up to **157** on Lake Barkley above the dam, Lyon Co., in Mar 1998 (*KW* 74:52, 1998); **100-150** in flooded fields north of Hickman, Fulton Co., 16 Mar 1995 (D. Yancy/W. Davis, pers. comm.); **135+** on Lake Barkley above the dam, 10-29 Mar 1998 (*KW* 74:52, 1998); **135** in w. Fulton Co., 11 Aug 1998 (*KW* 75:3, 1999); **113** on Lake Barkley above the dam, 23 Mar 2000 (D. Roemer, notes); **100+** at Duck Island, Lake Barkley, Trigg Co., 25 Mar 1999 (V. Anderson, pers. comm.); up to ca.**100** along the lower Tennessee River, Livingston Co., 30 Mar–17 Apr 1994 (*KW* 70:49, 1994); **84** on Mississippi River, Carlisle Co., 25 Aug 1996 (B. Palmer-Ball, eBird data); up to **83** along the Ohio River, McCracken Co., Apr 1995 (*KW* 71:39, 1995); **83** at Lake No. 9, 30 Jun 1999 (*KW* 75:60, 1999); **50-100** nr. Swan Lake, Ballard Co., 16 Mar 1995 (D. Yancy/W. Davis, pers. comm); **60-65** at Swan Lake, Ballard Co. 6 Mar 1996 (B. Palmer-Ball, eBird data); **20** on Ky Lake, Marshall Co., 15-17 May 1950 (Morse, *KW* 26:48-49, 1950).

Maximum counts (east of the LBL region): ca. **380** in w. Henderson Co., 5 Apr 2013 (*KW* 89:67, 2013); **300** over Hopkins Co., 9 Mar 2011 (*KW* 87:84, 2011); **139** at the Sinclair Unit, 23 Jun 2018 (*KW* 94:107, 2018); **80** on McElroy Lake, 26 Mar 2011 (*KW* 87:84, 2011); ca. **60** on Nolin Lake, Hart Co., 11 Mar 2016 (*KW* 92:57, 2016); ca. **60** over e. Jefferson Co., 26 Sep 2018 (*KW* 95:8, 2019); up to **51** on the Ohio River, w. Henderson Co., Oct 2012 (*KW* 89:5, 2013; W. Flake, eBird data); **51** over the Falls of the Ohio, 21 Sep 2014 (*KW* 91:6/36, 2015); **40** on Lake Peewee, 11 Feb 2016 (*KW* 92:42, 2016); **35** over Allen Co., 10 Mar 2011 (*KW* 87:84, 2011); **31** on Herrington Lake, Garrard/Mercer cos., 28-29 Mar 2012 (*KW* 88:72, 2012); **30** at Guthrie Swamp, Todd Co., 6 Oct 2012 (*KW* 89:5, 2013); **29** at Freeman Lake, Hardin Co., 2 Apr 2018 (J. Snyder, eBird data); **27** over Barren River Lake, 8 Mar 2016 (*KW* 92:57, 2016); **24** on Morgan Pond, 22 Oct 2016 (*KW* 93:5, 2917); **23** on the Ohio River, Campbell/Kenton cos. (*KW* 91:67, 2015); **20** over Warren Co., 14 Mar 2011 (*KW* 87:84, 2011); **17** on Sportsman's Lake, Larue Co., 21 Mar 2012 (*KW* 88:72,

2012); **17** on Barren River Lake, 28 Oct 2017 (R. Stoll/R. Bontrager, eBird data); **15** on the Ohio River at Louisville, 21-22 Mar 2011 (*KW* 87:84, 2011).

Summary of records from Louisville/Hardin Co./Barren River Lake eastward by county

Adair (Green River Lake, 13 Oct 2015 [*KW* 92:5, 2016])

Allen (se. of Mt. Zion, 10 Mar 2011 [*KW* 87:84, 2011])

Allen/Barren (multiple reports now from Barren River Lake; first reports 26 Nov 2002 [*KW* 79:4, 2003]; 19 Apr 2006 [*KW* 82:66, 2006]; 25-27 Oct 2007 [*KW* 84:6, 2008]; 29 Oct–25 Nov 2010 [*KW* 87:13-14, 2011])

Anderson (Taylorsville Lake, 5-13 Aug 1986 [*KW* 63:6, 1987)

Boyle (nr. Lake Herrington, 15 Nov 1929 [Mengel:157])

Bracken (Ohio River, 15-17 Mar 2003 [*KW* 79:65, 2003]; 13 Mar 2011 [*KW* 87:84, 2011]; 19 Apr 2017 [eBird data])

Bullitt (adjacent to Bernheim Forest, (ph.) 1 Mar 2016 [*KW* 92:57/72, 2016])

Campbell (Ohio River, 15-17 Mar 2003 [*KW* 79:65, 2003])

Campbell/Kenton (Ohio River, 24 Jan 2003 [*KW* 79:44, 2003]; 26 Mar 2015 [*KW* 91:67, 2015])

Carroll (K. Nab, 2019 eBird data)

Fayette (Lexington, 25 Mar 2007 [*KW* 83:76, 2007]; 22 Jun 2014 [*KW* 90:88, 2014]; 14 Apr 2018 [J. Ware, eBird data]; 13 Mar 2019 [2019 eBird data; Ben Warren, photos])

Floyd (Dewey Lake, 19 Dec 2016 [*KW* 93:48, 2017])

Gallatin (Ohio River, 19 Feb 2011 [*KW* 87:59, 2011]; 24 Mar 2014 [*KW* 91:16, 2015]; 2 Dec 2014 [*KW* 91:51, 2015]; 1 Apr 2018 [S. Campbell, eBird data])

Garrard/Mercer (Herrington Lake, 28-29 Mar 2012 [*KW* 88:72/84, 2012])

Grant (Cornith Lake, late Oct 1986 [*KW* 63:6, 1987])

Hardin (Freeman Lake, 28 Oct 1996 [*KW* 73:4, 1997; erroneously published therein as 11 birds there 28 Nov 1996; *fide* M. Bennett, notes]; 2 Apr 2018 [J. Snyder, eBird data]; 3 Mar 2019 [J. Snyder, eBird data])

Hart (Nolin Lake, 11 Mar 2016 [*KW* 92:57, 2016])

Jefferson (numerous reports over the years; now annual)

Kenton (Ohio River at Covington, 3 Oct 1996 [*KW* 73:4, 1997])

Larue (Sportsman's Lake, 21 Mar 2012 [*KW* 88:72, 2012])

Madison (Bluegrass Army Depot, 15-16 Mar 2015 [*KW* 91:67, 2015])

Marion (nr. Loretto, 8-12 Sep 2007 [*KW* 84:6, 2008])

Mercer (Shaker Village, 4 May 2015 [*KW* 91:67, 2015])

Nelson (n. of Bloomfield, 13 Sep 2010–mid-Jan 2011 [*KW* 87:13,59-60, 2011])

Pulaski (Lake Cumberland at Burnside, 24 Oct 1987 [*KW* 64:15, 1988]; 11 Nov 2008, Fishing Creek embayment of Lake Cumberland (*KW* 85:11, 2009)

Rowan (Minor Clark Hatchery, 6 Nov 2004 [*KW* 81:5, 2005])

Russell (Lake Cumberland, 25 Oct 1988 [*KW* 65:3, 1989]; 13 Dec 2017 [L. Bontrager, eBird data])

Shelby (nr. Shelbyville, 10 May 2008 [*KW* 84:59, 2008])

Spencer (Taylorsville Lake, 13 Nov 2004 [*KW* 81:5, 2005])

BROWN PELICAN *Pelecanus occidentalis*

Status: Extremely rare visitant. This common coastal resident occurs as an occasional vagrant into the interior eastern United States. Not known as an historical vagrant to the state; all reports have come during the last twenty or so years. There are at least 17 records, some possibly or probably involving the same individual at multiple locations (see below). Of the 17 records, five have occurred during spring, eight during summer, three during fall, and two during winter.

Unaccepted record: Ohio River at Dayton, Campbell Co., ca. 1 May 2008 (*KW* 84:59, 2008).

Tally of records by county

Allen/Barren (2), Bath/Rowan, Campbell, Fayette, Hopkins, Jefferson, Lincoln, Livingston/Lyon (2), Marshall (3), Nicholas, Oldham, Russell, Spencer

Chronological list of records

1) 20-24 Nov 1998, imm. (ph.) at Ky Dam (*KW* 75:3, 1999; D. Roemer, notes)
2) 30 May 1999, imm. at Ky Dam (Dever and Dever, *KW* 75:73-74, 1999)
3) 3 Jun 2006, flying up the Ohio River at the Falls of the Ohio (*KW* 82:80, 2006)
4) 25 Apr 2008, ad. (ph.) below Barkley Dam (*KW* 84:59/66, 2008)
5) 10-22 Dec 2008, sub-ad. (ph.) at Ky Dam (*KW* 85:26/47/60, 2009)
6) 23-25 Apr 2009, imm. (ph.) on Lake Cumberland, Russell Co. (*KW* 85:66/70, 2009)
7) 6/8 May 2009, perhaps the same imm. (ph.) on Cave Run Lake (*KW* 85:66, 2009)
8) 16 May–12 Jun 2009, perhaps the same imm. (ph.) on Lake Carnico, Nicholas Co. (*KW* 85: 66/70/91, 2009)
9) 13 Jul 2009, perhaps the same imm. (ph.) on the Ohio River at Dayton, Campbell Co. (*KW* 85: 91, 2009)
10) 14 Jul 2009, perhaps the same imm. (ph.) on the Ohio River upstream from Charlestown, Indiana, Oldham Co. (*KW* 85:91, 2009)
11) 30 Apr–1 May 2012, sub-ad. (ph.) on Barren River Lake, Allen Co. (eBird data)
12) 8-12 Jul 2017, imm. (ph.) Barren River Lake (*KW* 93:101/116, 2017)
13) 18-20 Jun 2018, imm. (ph.) at Cedar Creek Lake, Lincoln Co. (*KW* 94:107, 2018)
14) 6 Jul 2018, possibly the same imm. (ph.) on Taylorsville Lake, Spencer Co. (*KW* 94:107, 2018)
15) 19 Jul 2018, imm. (ph.) at Lexington (*KW* 94:107, 2018)
16) 11-12 Aug 2018, imm. (ph.) at Lake Peewee (*KW* 95:8, 2019)
17) 5-8 Jan 2019, imm. (ph.) on Lake Barkley, Lyon Co. (*KW* 95:49, 2019)

AMERICAN BITTERN Botaurus lentiginosus

Status: Rare to uncommon transient, extremely rare and local during summer (formerly nested), extremely rare during winter. Recorded chiefly west of the Cumberland Plateau. Most frequently encountered in cattail marshes, but also found during migration in thick vegetation along the shores of lakes and ponds, and occasionally in tall weeds or grass in open fields. Peaks of abundance occur from late Mar to early May and from late Sep to late Oct. Historical breeding was documented in Hopkins Co. (Bacon, *KW* 9:14-16, 1933), where the species has not been reported nesting since 1943. There were a few additional historical records of presumed summering or breeding birds from scattered locations across central and western Kentucky, but none in several decades (Mengel:170; *KW* 38:6-7, 1962). In recent years, a few birds have been found during the winter, but wintering has not been documented. Generally observed singly or in pairs. **State Breeding Status**: Historical.

Maximum counts: **5** at the Sauerheber Unit, 8 Apr 2006 (*KW* 82:66, 2006); **4** on a pond at Peabody WMA, Ohio Co., 25 Sep 2002 (*KW* 79:4, 2003); **4** at the Sauerheber Unit, 12 Apr 2015 (*KW* 91:67, 2015; eBird data); **4** at Green River WMA, Adair Co., 15/17 Apr 2017 (*KW* 93:74, 2017/R. Bontrager, eBird data).

Early spring dates: 14 Mar 1931, Hopkins Co. (Mengel:170); 17 Mar 1948, Louisville area (*KW* 52:42, 1976); 18 Mar 2000, Lawrence Co. (G. Robe, notes); 22 Mar 1939, Warren Co. (Mengel: 170; *KW* 38:7, 1962); 26 Mar 2017, Sauerheber Unit (*KW* 93:74, 2018).

Late spring dates (other than presumed breeding birds): 24 Jun 1958, Louisville (*KW* 52:42, 1976); 11 Jun 2013, Metcalfe Co. (*KW* 91:56, 2015); 30 May 1989, Muhlenberg Co. (*KW* 65:62-63, 1989); 29 May 2002, Sauerheber Unit (C. Crawford, eBird data); 27 May 19—, Warren Co. (Wilson, *KW* 16:16, 1940).

Early fall dates (other than presumed breeding birds): 29 Jun 2017, Taylorsville Lake WMA, Anderson Co. (*KW* 93:101, 2017); 17 Jul 2006, Jefferson Co. (*KW* 82:80, 2006); 2 Aug 2014, ne. Jefferson Co. (*KW* 91:6, 2015); 11 Aug 2009, Long Point Unit (*KW* 86:5, 2010); 25 Aug 2009, s. Jefferson Co. (*KW* 86:5-6, 2010); 1 Sep 1977, Louisville (D. Parker, pers. comm.); 2 Sep 1951, Louisville (Mengel:170); 6 Sep 1977, Jefferson Co. (E. Bagian, pers. comm.).

Late fall dates: occasionally lingering into late fall, latest records being 9 Dec 2006, Sinclair Unit (*KW* 83:47, 2007); 28 Nov 2014, (ph.) Sinclair Unit (*KW* 91:6, 2015); 22 Nov 1917, Bardstown, Nelson Co. (Mengel:170); 17-18 Nov 2012, Muhlenberg Co. Rail Trail (*KW* 89:5, 2013).

Out-of-season records (winter): 16 Dec 1916, Hopkins Co. (Mengel:170); 5 Jan 2002, Sinclair Unit (*KW* 78:21, 2002); 14 Feb 2004, Sinclair Unit (*KW* 80:42, 2004); 1 Jan 2006, Sinclair Unit (*KW* 82:

19/46, 2006); 2 Jan 2011, Muhlenberg Co. (*KW* 87:27/60, 2011); 6 Mar 2012, Ken Unit, Ohio Co. (R. Gundy, eBird data); 10 Jan 2017, (ph.) Fayette Co. (*KW* 93:48, 2017); 8-12 Feb 2017, (ph.) Jefferson Co. (*KW* 93:48, 2017); 15 Dec 2018, (ph.) Long Point Unit (*KW* 95:49, 2019)).

Unaccepted records: 5 in Lyon/Trigg cos., 15 Apr 1966 (eBird data); 4 Sep 1999, Daviess Co. (eBird data); 6 Jul 2016, Kenton Co. (eBird data).

*LEAST BITTERN *Ixobrychus exilis*

Status: Rare transient and summer resident (formerly uncommon). Recorded at scattered localities throughout the state, but chiefly west of the Cumberland Plateau. A report from Lawrence Co., 9 Sep 2003 (*KW* 80:6, 2004) currently represents the only one from the far easterrn part of the state. Peak of abundance occurs from early May to early Sep. This species is almost always encountered in marshes or along edges of lakes and ponds where cattail and other lush aquatic vegetation is present. Nesting has been confirmed in nine counties with probably breeding in an additional 14 (see below). Generally found singly or in pairs, but sometimes nests in loose colonies. **State Breeding Status**: Threatened.

Maximum counts: **11** at Adkins Swamp, Sinclair Unit, 30 Jun 2015 (*KW* 91:84, 2015); **11** at Muck Lake, Sinclair Unit, 23 Jul 2016 (*KW* 92:78, 2016); **8** at Adkins Swamp, Sinclair Unit, 18 Jun 2014 (*KW* 99:88, 2014); **7** in a marsh in Ohio Co., 3 Aug 1989 (*KW* 66:4, 1990); **6** at the Sauerheber Unit, 5 Jul 1996 (B. Palmer-Ball, eBird data); **6** at Muck Lake, Sinclair Unit, 22 Jul 2017 (R. Bontrager, eBird data; *KW* 93:101, 2017); **6** at the Sinclair Unit, 20 Jul 2002 (*KW* 78:61, 2002); **5-6** at the Sauerheber Unit, 10 May 2005 (*KW* 81:84, 2005).

Early spring dates: 6 Apr 19—, Hopkins Co. (Bacon, *KW* 9:[14], 1933); 12 Apr 2011, Sauerheber Unit (*KW* 87:84, 2011); 15 Apr 1995, Minor Clark Hatchery (*KW* 71:40, 1995); 16 Apr 2014, Sinclair Unit (*KW* 90:68, 2014).

Late fall dates: 18 Oct 2003, Sauerheber Unit (*KW* 80:6, 2004); 14 Oct 2006, Sauerheber Unit (*KW* 83:10, 2007); 10 Oct 1992, Sauerheber Unit (*KW* 69:4, 1993); 10 Oct 2009, Sauerheber Unit (*KW* 86:6, 2010); 6 Oct 1978, Jefferson Co. (*KW* 55:14, 1979); 6 Oct 1994, Carlisle Co. (*KW* 71:3, 1995).

Summary of breeding records by county

Carroll (Mengel:169)
Daviess (*KW* 44:61-62, 1968; Stamm, *KW* 45:31, 1969)
Fulton (1991 eBird data; Palmer-Ball, *KW* 74:84-86, 1998)
Henderson (Palmer-Ball, *KW* 74:84-86, 1998)
Hopkins (Hancock, *KW* 30:19, 1954; *AB* 27:875, 1973; Palmer-Ball and Moosman, *KW* 78:40-42, 2002)
Jefferson (Mengel:169)
Muhlenberg (Palmer-Ball, *KW* 74:84-86, 1998; Palmer-Ball and Moosman, *KW* 78:40-42, 2002; *KW* 90:21, 2014; *KW* 92:78, 2016; *KW* 93:101, 2017; *KW* 94:108, 2018)
Nelson (Stamm and Croft, *KW* 44:24, 1968)
Union (*KW* 80:6, 2004; *KW* 81:105, 2005)

Summary of additional summer records of probable breeders by county

Ballard (Mengel:169; Palmer-Ball and Barron, *KW* 58:78, 1982)
Calloway (Mengel:169)
Carlisle (*KW* 66:84, 1990; *KW* 69:55, 1993)
Clinton (Mengel:169)
Crittenden (Mengel:169)
Edmonson (*KW* 38:6, 1962)
Henderson (multiple reports)
Hopkins (*KW* 84:85, 2008; *KW* 86:91, 2010)
Fayette (Mengel:169)
Marshall (Mengel:169)
Muhlenberg (multiple reports)

Ohio (*KW* 65:83, 1989; *KW* 85:91, 2009)
Rowan (*KW* 61:55, 1985)
Union (Palmer-Ball and Moosman, *KW* 78:40-42, 2002)

*GREAT BLUE HERON *Ardea herodias*

Status: Resident; uncommon to fairly common during migration and summer, uncommon to locally fairly common during winter. Recorded chiefly west of the Cumberland Plateau, but can be found statewide especially during the non-breeding season. Encountered in a great variety of aquatic habitats including stream banks, ponds, sloughs, and the shores of the larger lakes and rivers. Breeding formerly was limited to scattered localities from Henderson Co. southwestward (Mengel: 159-160), and the species essentially disappeared from the state during and after the DDT era (1950s-1970s). Subsequent to the banning of DDT and other organochlorine pesticides, the species returned to the far western part of the state and then expanded into central Kentucky during the early 1990s (Palmer-Ball and Thomas, *KW* 75:62-71, 1999). As of 1999, there were 48 nesting colonies consisting of ca. 2235 nesting pairs (Palmer-Ball and Thomas, *KW* 75:62-71, 1999), and by 2004, more than 5200 pairs were nesting at no fewer than 85 distinct colony sites (Palmer-Ball and Ciuzio, *KW* 80:87-96, 2004). During subsequent years, the nesting population has continued to gradually expand across the state. Locally distributed during spring and early summer when most birds remain relatively close to active nesting colonies. Somewhat irregular during winter; scarce in most areas, but locally uncommon to fairly common in central and western Kentucky; least numerous during periods of extremely cold winter weather. Generally seen singly or in small groups of up to 20 birds, but concentrations around favored late summer feeding areas may number more than a hundred birds.

Maximum counts: colony of **697** active nests in Marshall Co., 13 Apr 1993 (B. Pullin, notes); colony of **432** active nests at the Highland Creek Unit, Sloughs WMA, Union Co., 3 Jun 1986 (*KW* 62:65, 1986); **300** at Lake No. 9, 30 Aug 2000 (*KW* 77:4, 2001); **200** at Lake No. 9, 30 Aug 1997 (B. Palmer-Ball, eBird data); **150** nesting pairs at the Long Point Unit, 20 May 1949 (Mengel:160); **155** at McElroy Lake, 14 Jul 2010 (*KW* 86:91, 2010); ca. **150** at the Falls of the Ohio, 12 Jul 2011 (*KW* 87:112, 2011).

Note on white morph birds: There are four records of individuals (presumed not to simply represent leucistic individuals) of the white morph, or GREAT WHITE HERON, of the Caribbean region and south Florida. Such individuals would have to be post-breeding wanderers.

Chronological list of records of white morph birds

1) 21-25 Jul 2000, (ph.) nr. Science Hill, Pulaski Co. (R. Denton, eBird data)
2) 29 Aug–22 Sep 2012, (ph.) at the Falls of the Ohio (*KW* 89:6/21, 2013)
3) 23 Oct 2013, (ph.) at Freeman Lake (*KW* 90:6/40, 2014)
4) 13 Nov 2014, (ph.) LBL, Trigg Co. (*KW* 91:6, 2015; date published erroneously there in [*fide KW* 92:16, 2016])

*GREAT EGRET *Ardea alba*

Status: Uncommon to locally fairly common transient and summer visitant, rare and locally distributed summer resident, extremely rare during winter. Recorded chiefly west of the Cumberland Plateau, although the species has been reported from eastern Kentucky several times. Peak of abundance occurs from early Apr to mid-Oct. Encountered in a great variety of aquatic habitats, but especially on floodplain lakes and sloughs as well as reservoir shorelines. Nesting formerly (early 1950s) occurred at five colonies in the large river floodplains of western Kentucky (Mengel:164-165). The species was absent as a breeder for most of the latter half of the 20th century, but small numbers returned during the late 1980s. In subsequent years, small numbers of nesting birds have come and gone in nesting colonies of other waders, still mostly in the far western part of the state. However, nesting has become established in recent years at a few sites as far northeast as Louisville (see below). Historically there were only a handful of mid-winter records, but during recent years the species has become more regularly seen lingering into early winter. In addition, a few individuals have been documented wintering in recent years. Generally seen singly or in small groups of up to a dozen birds, larger flocks being quite uncommon away from far western Kentucky. **State Breeding Status**: Threatened.

Maximum spring counts: **268** in the Lower Hickman Bottoms 31 May 2017 (*KW* 93:74, 2017; date erroneously published therein as 30 May [*fide* R. Preston, eBird data]); **243** in the Lower Hickman Bottoms, 31 May 2011 (*KW* 87:84, 2011); **158** in the Lower Hickman Bottoms, 14 May 2018 (*KW* 94:76, 2018); **105** at Ky Bend, Fulton Co., 19 May 2013 (*KW* 89:67, 2013); **100** at Obion WMA, Fulton Co., 23 May 2007 (*KW* 83:76, 2007); **70** at the Sauerheber Unit, 15 May 2009 (C. Crawford, eBird data); **70** at the Sauerheber Unit, 20 May 2016 (*KW* 92:57-58, 2016).

Maximum summer/fall counts: **4000-5000** at Lake No. 9, 5 Aug 2008 (*KW* 85:12, 2009); ca. **3000** at Lake No. 9, 14 Sep 1998 (D. Roemer, notes); **2000** at Lake No. 9, 7 Sep 1998 (R. Denton, eBird data); **1600** at Lake No. 9, 30 Aug 2000 (*KW* 77:4, 2001); **1500+** at Island No. 8 Slough, 7 Sep 1998 (B. Palmer-Ball, eBird data); **1500** at Lake No. 9, 27 Aug 2004 (*KW* 81:5, 2005); **1250-1500** at Lake No. 9, 30 Aug–1 Sep 1997 (B. Palmer-Ball, eBird data); **1300** at Island No. 8 Slough, Fulton Co., 26 Jul 2009 (*KW* 85:91, 2009); ca. **1300** at Island No. 8 Slough, Fulton Co., 19 Aug 2010 (*KW* 87:14, 2011); ca. **1000** at Obion WMA and **1200-1300** at Island No. 8 Slough, 18/19 Aug 2010 (*KW* 87:14 2011); ca. **800** at Lake No. 9, late Aug 1994 (J. Wilson, notes); **620** at Horseshoe Road, w. Henderson Co., 19 Aug 2018 (*KW* 95:8, 2019); **500+** at Mitchell Lake, Ballard WMA, early Aug 2004 (*KW* 81:5, 2005); ca. **500** at Lake No. 9 in the late summer of 1984 (*KW* 61:13, 1985); **350-400** in w. Henderson Co., mid-Sep 2003 (*KW* 80:6, 2004); **430** in w. Henderson Co., 31 Aug 2016 (*KW* 93:5, 2017); **238** nr. Morgan Pond, Christian Co., 25 Jul 2018 (*KW* 94:108, 2018); **176** at White City WMA, Hopkins Co., 23 Sep 2010 (*KW* 87:14, 2011); **93** at the Falls of the Ohio, 5 Aug 2012 (*KW* 89:6, 2013); **64** at Taylorsville Lake, Anderson Co., 30 Sep 2016 (*KW* 93:5, 2017).

Early spring dates: 8 Mar 2016, Lake Barkley, Lyon Co. (*KW* 92:57, 2016); 10 Mar 1992, Rowan Co. (*KW* 68:43, 1992); 12 Mar 2016, Campbell/Kenton Co. (D. Johnston, eBird data); 13 Mar 2003, Henderson Co. (*KW* 79:65, 2003; location erroneously published therein as Highland Creek Unit, Union Co. [*fide* C. Crawford, eBird data]); 13 Mar 2010, Lake Cumberland, Pulaski Co. (R. Denton, eBird data); 14 Mar 2008, McCracken Co. (J. Hanfman, eBird data); 15 Mar 2007, Sauerheber Unit (*KW* 83:76, 2007); 15 Mar 2016, Lake Barkley, Trigg Co. (M. Easley, eBird data); 16 Mar 2019, Jefferson Co./Marshall Co. (R. Thunell, eBird data/T. Smith, eBird data); 17 Mar 1999, Fulton Co. (*KW* 75:41, 19`99); 17 Mar 2012, Ky Dam Village (*KW* 88:73, 2012); 17 Mar 2017, Mammoth Cave (S./J. Kistler, eBird data); 17 Mar 2018, Ky Dam and Carroll Co. (*KW* 94:76, 2018); 19 Mar 1959, Louisville (*AFN* 13:373, 1959); 20 Mar 1982, Danville (*KW* 58:48, 1982).

Late fall dates: occasionally lingers into late fall/early winter with scattered records through mid-Dec–early Jan CBC period.

Out-of-season records (winter): 10 Feb 1957, Meade Co. (*KW* 52:42, 1976); 2 Jan 1965, Henderson Co. (*AFN* 19:383, 1965); 1 Jan 1969, Franklin Co. (Brown, *KW* 45:42, 1969); 18 Dec 1987–8 Jan 1988, Minor Clark Hatchery (*KW* 64:14/27, 1988); 13 Jan 1994 and for about a week prior, nr. Kenlake State Park, Marshall Co. (*KW* 70:32, 1994); winter 1997-1998, one wintered along Old Pumphouse Road, Pulaski Co. (R. Denton, eBird data); 8-13 Feb 1998, Lake Barkley (*KW* 74:32, 1998); 4 Feb 2000, (2) in w. Fulton Co. (J.T. Erwin, notes); 4 Jan 2003, (2) in Muhlenberg Co. (*KW* 79:20/44, 2003); 22 Jan 2012, Ky Lake, Calloway Co. (*KW* 88:45-46, 2012); 10 Feb 2012, Madison Co. (*KW* 88:46, 2012); 16 Jan 2016, Woodford Co. (*KW* 92:42, 2016); singles lingered at Guthrie Swamp, Todd Co., and at Lexington, both to 4 Jan 2017 (*KW* 93:48, 2017); 8 & 18 Feb 2017, (ph.) Wayne Co. (*KW* 93:48, 2017); 7 Dec 2017–7 Jan 2018, e. Jefferson Co. (*KW* 94:57, 2018); singles lingered at Shelbyville to 3 Jan 2019 (L. McMahon, eBird data); wsw. of Princeton, Caldwell Co. to 9 Jan 2019 (T. Graham, eBird data); Lake Peewee to 10 Jan 2019 (m. ob., eBird data), at Louisville to 5 Feb 2019 (m. ob., eBird data), and on Lake Barkley, Lyon Co., to 12 Jan 2019 (D. Collins, eBird data); 2 lingered at Barren River Lake to 27 Jan 2019 (L. Craiger/B. Brand, eBird data).

Summary of confirmed breeding records by county (only partial data from recent years for traditional sites)

Ballard (Mengel:164; B. Palmer-Ball, 1993 eBird data; Palmer-Ball and Wethington, *KW* 70:77-83, 1994; Palmer-Ball and Thomas, *KW* 75:62-71, 1999; *KW* 83:103, 2007)
Carlisle (Mengel:164; Palmer-Ball and Ciuzio, *KW* 80:87-96, 2004)

Fulton (Mengel:164; B. Palmer-Ball, 2000 eBird data; *KW* 78:60, 2002; Palmer-Ball and Ciuzio, *KW* 80:87-96, 2004; *KW* 83:103, 2007)

Graves (B. Palmer-Ball, 2000 eBird data)

Henderson (Mengel:164; B. Palmer-Ball, 2000 eBird data)

Hickman (Mengel:164; Palmer-Ball and Wethington, *KW* 70:77-83, 1994; *KW* 78:60, B. Palmer-Ball, 2002 eBird data; Palmer-Ball and Ciuzio, *KW* 80:87-96, 2004; *KW* 83:103, 2007)

Jefferson (*KW* 80:6, 2004; *KW* 81:105, 2005; *KW* 83:103, 2007; *KW* 90:68/88, 2014; B. Palmer-Ball, 2019 eBird data)

Lyon (Palmer-Ball, *KW* 78:72-73, 2002; Palmer-Ball and Ciuzio, *KW* 80:87-96, 2004; *KW* 88:73, 2012; *KW* 90:68, 2014; *KW* 91:68, 2015; Palmer-Ball and Powell, *KW* 91:90-93)

Marshall (Palmer-Ball and Ciuzio, *KW* 80:87-96, 2004)

Muhlenberg (*KW* 83:76, 2007)

Trigg (*KW* 66:5, 1990; Palmer-Ball and Powell, *KW* 91:90-93)

Union (Palmer-Ball and Thomas, *KW* 75:62-71, 1999; B. Palmer-Ball, 2002 eBird data; *KW* 83:103, 2007)

*SNOWY EGRET *Egretta thula*

Status: Extremely rare to locally uncommon transient and summer visitant, extremely rare and local summer resident (currently one nesting locality). Recorded chiefly from the Louisville area south-westward; most frequently encountered along the Mississippi and lower Ohio rivers and associated floodplain wetlands, but found occasionally at scattered localities away from the larger rivers with a few from eastern Kentucky (see below). Peak of abundance occurs from early May to mid-Sep. Generally observed wading in shallow waters of sloughs, ponds and marshes; often found in the company of Little Blue Herons. Breeding recently has been confirmed in a mixed wading bird nesting colony on Lake Barkley, Lyon Co. (see below). Most often encountered singly or in small flocks of up to a half-dozen birds, less frequently in larger groups of up to 15-20 birds in the western part of the state. **State Breeding Status**: Endangered.

Maximum counts: **700** at Lake No. 9, 30 Aug 2000 (*KW* 77:4, 2001); **500+** at Lake No. 9, 1/7 Sep 1997 (B. Palmer-Ball, eBird data); **300** at Lake No. 9, 26 Aug 1994 (eBird data); **260+** at Lake No. 9, 24 Aug 2002 (*KW* 79:5, 2003); **100** at Lake No. 9, 27 Aug 2004 (*KW* 81:5, 2005); **60+** at Mitchell Lake, Ballard WMA, 23 Aug 2007 (*KW* 84:6, 2008); **51** at Mitchell Lake, Ballard WMA, 16 Aug 2016 (*KW* 93:6, 2017); **44** on the Mississippi River at Island No. 1, Carlisle Co., 10 Aug 2002 (*KW* 79:5, 2003); **19** at the Sauerheber Unit, 7 Aug 2004 (*KW* 81:5, 2005).

Early spring dates: 25 Mar 2005, nr. the Long Point Unit (*KW* 81:84, 2005); 3 Apr 2001, Fulton Co. (*KW* 77:48, 2001); 5 Apr 2009, Ballard WMA and the Lower Hickman Bottoms (*KW* 85:66, 2009); 6 Apr 2019, Hardin Co. (J. Snyder, eBird data); 7 Apr 1983, Falls of the Ohio (*KW* 59:39, 1983); 8 Apr 1989, Fulton Co. (*KW* 65:63, 1989); 9 Apr 1995, Falls of the Ohio (B. Palmer-Ball, eBird data); 9 Apr 2017, Cadiz, Trigg Co. (*KW* 93:74, 2017).

Late fall dates: 20 Oct 1990, Marshall Co. (*KW* 67:4, 1991); 17 Oct 2004, Lake Barkley, Lyon Co. (*KW* 81:6, 2005); 17 Oct 2018, s. Jefferson Co. (*KW* 95:8, 2019); 16 Oct 2001, Pulaski Co. (R. Denton, eBird data); 16 Oct 2015, Blood River (*KW* 92:5, 2016); 15 Oct 1997, Fulton Co. (*KW* 74:5, 1998);13 Oct 2013, Freeman Lake, Hardin Co. (B. Jenkins, eBird data); 8 Oct 1995, Lake No. 9 (B. Palmer-Ball, eBird data).

Summary of confirmed breeding records by county

Lyon (Lake Barkley nr. Kuttawa, where at least five nests were present in 2002 (Palmer-Ball, *KW* 78:72-73) and adults were still present in 2004 (Palmer-Ball and Ciuzio, *KW* 80:87-96, 2004). NOTE: The species no longer nests at this colony, but may be nesting at the mixed waterbird colony on Lake Barkley, Trigg Co.

List of easternmost records by county

Greenup (*KW* 83:104, 2007)

Rowan (*KW* 68:44, 1992; *KW* 71:68, 1995; R. Denton, 1998 eBird data; M Greene, 2009 eBird data; *KW* 87:112, 2011)

*LITTLE BLUE HERON *Egretta caerulea*

Status: Rare to locally uncommon transient and summer visitant, extremely rare and local summer resident (currently one nesting locality). Recorded chiefly west of the Cumberland Plateau, but there are a few records from the eastern part of the state. Peak of abundance occurs from early May to late Sep. Encountered in a variety of aquatic habitats, but generally found in the vicinity of shallow sloughs, ponds, and backwater areas. The species has been documented nesting in small numbers with Black-crowned Night-Herons at a few different locations (see below). Adults and pied "calico" first-year birds are seen during spring and early summer, while white-plumaged immature birds predominate during late summer and fall. Large numbers are seen only along the Mississippi and lower Ohio rivers where dozens, and occasionally more than a hundred birds, have been reported. Away from the western counties, generally seen in small groups of up to a half-dozen birds, but formerly in groups of up to 100 at the Falls of the Ohio. **State Breeding Status**: Endangered.

Maximum counts: ca. **500** at Lake No. 9, 7 Sep 1998 (R. Denton/B. Palmer-Ball, eBird data); **400-500** at Lake No. 9, 27 Aug 2004 (*KW* 81:6, 2005); ca. **200** at Lake No. 9, 9 Sep 1994 (*KW* 71:3, 1995); at least **150-200** at roost on Lake Barkley, Lyon Co., 25 Jul 2009 (*KW* 85:91, 2009); ca. **150** at Ballard WMA, 30 Aug 1981 (Palmer-Ball and Barron, *KW* 58:79-80, 1982); formerly (1930s) in "flocks of **ca. 100**" at the Falls of the Ohio (Monroe and Mengel, *KW* 15:38-39, 1939); **80** on nesting/roosting island in Lake Barkley, Trigg Co., 8 Aug 2017 (*KW* 94:10, 2018).

Early spring dates: 18 Mar 1996, Ballard WMA (*KW* 72:52, 1996); 28 Mar 1997, Barkley Dam (B. Palmer-Ball, eBird data); 1 Apr 2011, Lake Barkley, Lyon Co. (*KW* 87:84, 2011); 3 Apr 2007, Ballard WMA (eBird data); 4 Apr 1981, Calloway Co. (*KW* 57:55, 1981); 4 Apr 1992, Fulton Co. (*KW* 68:44, 1992); 4 Apr 1999, Lake Cumberland WMA, Pulaski Co. (R. Denton, eBird data); 5 Apr 2009, Ballard WMA (*KW* 85:67, 2009).

Late fall dates: 23 Oct 2000, Lake No. 9 (*KW* 77:4, 2001); 23 Oct 1988, Rowan Co. (*KW* 65:4, 1989); 21 Oct 1985, Lake No. 9 (*KW* 62:4, 1986).

Unaccepted records: 29 Dec 1995, Hancock Co. (*KW* 72:10, 1996); 1 Aug 2013, Carter Co. [no details available] (eBird data).

Published error: (35) in Marshall Co., 19 Oct 1997 (*KW* 74:5, 1998) (correction *fide KW* 74:35, 1998).

Summary of confirmed breeding records by county

Jefferson (Shippingport Island [*KW* 61:55, 1985; Palmer-Ball and Evans, *KW* 62:75-76, 1986])

Lyon (Lake Barkley [Palmer-Ball and Thomas, *KW* 75:62-71, 1999; *KW* 74:52, 1998; R. Denton, notes; Palmer-Ball and Ciuzio, *KW* 80:87-96, 2004])

Trigg (Lake Barkley [*KW* 57:72, 1981; Thomas, *KW* 58:35, 1982; Evans 1984; Palmer-Ball and Powell, *KW* 91:90-93])

List of easternmost records by county

Laurel (*KW* 92:78, 2016)

Pike (L. Estep, 2002 pers. comm.)

Rowan (multiple reports from Minor Clark Hatchery/Cave Run Lake[*KW* 59:51, 1983; *KW* 71:68, 1995; L. McNeely, 2002 eBird data; *KW* 82:6, 2006; *KW* 89:6, 2013; more recent eBird data])

TRICOLORED HERON *Egretta tricolor*

Status: Extremely rare spring, summer, and fall visitant. It is unclear if the recent increase in the number of reports is tied to a change in regional occurrence or better birding coverage. There are currently 16 records (four during spring, four during summer, and eight during fall).

Unaccepted record: 6 Sep 2000, Lyon Co. [no details available] (*KW* 77:4, 2001).

Chronological list of records

1) 4 Apr 1989, Minor Clark Hatchery (*KW* 65:63, 1989)
2) 19 Jun 1990, Falls of the Ohio (*KW* 66:84, 1990)
3) 23 Jun 1991, (2) at the Falls of the Ohio (*BO*, Aug 1991)

4) 17 Jun 1995, an ad. at Chaney Lake (M. Bierly/G. Foster, notes; *KW* 73:28, 1997)
5) 16-18 May 1996, an ad. (ph.) in s. Jefferson Co. (Bell, et al., *KW* 72:88, 1996)
6) 1 Sep 1997, an imm. at Lake No. 9 (B. Palmer-Ball, eBird data)
7) 16 May 1998, below Smithland Dam (F. Bennett, pers. comm.)
8) 10 Aug–7 Sep 1998, 1-2 imms. (vt. of 1) at Lake No. 9 (*KW* 75:4, 1999; B. Palmer-Ball, eBird data)
9) 30 Sep 2000, n. of Richmond, Madison Co. (*KW* 77:4, 2001)
10) 31 Aug–17 Sep 2001, an imm. at Horse Cave, Hart Co. (*KW* 78:4, 2002; M. Sturgeon/S. Kistler, notes)
11) 4-21 Aug 2005, 1-2 (ph.) at Lake No. 9 (*KW* 82:6, 2006)
12) 30-31 Aug 2008, an ad. at the Eddy Creek embayment of Lake Barkley, Lyon Co. (*KW* 85:12, 2008)
13) 22 Jul 2011, an ad. (ph.) at Fishing Creek (*KW* 87:112/124, 2011)
14) 4 Aug 2012, an imm. (ph.) at Honker Lake, LBL, Trigg/Lyon cos. (*KW* 89:6/20, 2013)
15) 11-13 Aug 2012, an imm. (ph.) at Ballard WMA (*KW* 89:6/40, 2013)
16) 13 Apr 2019, (ph.) at Sand Slough, Henderson Co. (M. Monroe et al., eBird data)

REDDISH EGRET *Egretta rufescens*

Status: Accidental vagrant. This typically coastal wader is reported very infrequently in the inland eastern United States. It has been documented in Kentucky on two occasions.

Chronological list of records

1) 1 Sep 1978, a bird in non-breeding plumage at the Falls of the Ohio (Palmer-Ball, *KW* 58:35-38, 1982)
2) 12 Sep 2004, a juv. (ph.) on the Mississippi River nr. Island No. 1, Carlisle Co. (*KW* 81:6, 2005)

*CATTLE EGRET *Bubulcus ibis*

Status: Extremely rare to rare transient; extremely rare and local summer resident (occurring in numbers only near the few active nesting colonies), extremely rare during winter. As a transient, generally recorded quite irregularly and chiefly west of the Cumberland Plateau, but there are a few records from eastern Kentucky (see below). Peak of abundance occurs from late Apr to mid-Sep. Usually encountered in grassy pastures and meadows, frequently with cattle, but sometimes found along marshy edges of lakes and ponds. First recorded in the state in 1960 (Wilson, *KW* 36:72, 1960). Breeding now has been reported from four counties (see below). Most often seen singly or in small groups of fewer than 30 birds, but flocks of more than a hundred birds are reported near nesting colonies in western Kentucky. **State Breeding Status**: Special Concern.

Maximum counts: **9700** at roost on Lake Barkley nr. Kuttawa, Lyon Co., 6 Sep 2000 (*KW* 77:4, 2001); **4000+** at roost on Lake Barkley nr. Kuttawa, Lyon Co., 25 Sep 1998 (*KW* 75:4, 1999/*KW* 76:9, 2000; B. Palmer-Ball, eBird data); **2000** at roost on Lake Barkley nr. Kuttawa, Lyon Co., 30 Jul 2002 (eBird data); **2000** at roost on Lake Barkley nr. Kuttawa, Lyon Co., 10 Sep 2005 (R. Denton, eBird data; *KW* 82:6, 2006); **1400+** nesting pairs at island in Lake Barkley nr. Kuttawa, Lyon Co., 3 Jun 2004 (Palmer-Ball and Ciuzio, *KW* 80:92, 2004); ca. **1000** over Lake No. 9 on their way to roost, 30 Aug 1997 (B. Palmer-Ball, eBird data); probably **1000+** at Lake No. 9, late Aug–early Sep 1998 (B. Palmer-Ball, eBird data); **1000+** at Lake No. 9, 27 Aug 2004 (*KW* 81:6, 2005); **1000+** at roosting/nesting island on Lake Barkley, Trigg Co., 31 Aug 2013 (*KW* 90:7, 2014).

Early spring dates: 22 Mar 2000, Barkley Dam (*KW* 76:44, 2000); 24 Mar 2002, Fulton Co. (*KW* 78:48, 2002); 30 Mar 1991, McElroy Lake (*KW* 67:52, 1991); 31 Mar 2007, Lake Barkley above the dam (*KW* 83:77, 2007); 1 Apr 2011, Lake Barkley, Lyon Co. (*KW* 87:85, 2011); 2 Apr 2017, Logan Co. (*KW* 93:74, 2017); 6 Apr 1986, Fulton Co. (*KW* 62:41, 1986).

Late fall dates: 19 Dec 1984, (2) Calloway Co. (*KW* 61:28, 1985; C. Peterson, notes); 8 Dec 1984, Madison Co. (*KW* 61:28, 1985); 29 Nov 1984, Ky Dam (*KW* 61:14, 1985); 24 Nov 1982, Minor Clark Hatchery (*KW* 59:13, 1983); 19 Nov 1991, Calloway Co. (*KW* 68:4, 1992); 19 Nov 2003, Barren River Lake (*KW* 80:6, 2004); 16 Nov 1985, Livingston Co. (*KW* 62:4, 1986); 15 Nov 2005, (8) at Russell Springs, Russell Co. (*KW* 82:6, 2006).

Out-of-season records (winter): 22 Feb 1976, nr. Hickman, Fulton Co. (*AB* 30:724, 1976); 2 Jan 1993, Boone Co. (*KW* 69:22, 1993).

Summary of confirmed breeding records by county

Fulton (Mississippi River nr. Lake No. 9 [*KW* 60:51, 1984; Evans 1984])
Jefferson (Shippingport Island [*KW* 61:14, 1985; Evans 1984; *KW* 61:55, 1985; *KW* 62:65,75-76, 1986; *KW* 64:62, 1988; *KW* 94:108/124, 2018])
Lyon (islands in Lake Barkley [B. Palmer-Ball, 1993 eBird data; Palmer-Ball and Thomas, *KW* 75:62-71, 1999; *KW* 78:61, 2002; Palmer-Ball and Ciuzio, *KW* 80:87-96, 2004; *KW* 90:68, 2014; *KW* 91:6, 2015; Palmer-Ball and Powell, *KW* 91:90-93; *KW* 93:6, 2017)
Trigg (s. Lake Barkley [*KW* 57:72, 1981; Thomas, *KW* 58:35, 1982; Palmer-Ball and Wethington, *KW* 70:81, 1994; *KW* 86:65, 2010; *KW* 89:93, 2013; Palmer-Ball and Powell, *KW* 91:90-93])

List of easternmost records by county

Elliott (*KW* 83:10, 2007)
Letcher (*KW* 58:13, 1982)
Pike (*KW* 90:88, 2014)
Rowan (several times at Minor Clark Hatchery)

*GREEN HERON *Butorides virescens*

Status: Uncommon to fairly common transient and summer resident (may be declining), extremely rare during winter. Recorded statewide from a great variety of aquatic habitats from small creeks and farm ponds to marshes, swamps, and the shores of the larger lakes and rivers. Peak of abundance occurs from late Apr to late Sep. Breeding singly or in small, loose colonies throughout the state, usually but not always near water. The species has been found several times during late fall and winter, but presumed wintering has been documented only once (see below). Generally seen singly or in pairs, but loose groups of up to a dozen or more birds are sometimes reported around favored feeding areas.

Maximum counts: **65** at Minor Clark Hatchery, 30 Jul 1983 (*KW* 59:51, 1983); **64** at Minor Clark Hatchery, 24 Aug 1985 (*KW* 62:4, 1986); **56** at Minor Clark Hatchery, 23 Aug 2014 (*KW* 91:6, 2015); **55** at Minor Clark Hatchery, 7 Aug 1989 (*KW* 66:5, 1990); **55** at Minor Clark Hatchery, 29 Jul 1990 (*KW* 66:85, 1990); **51** at Chaney Lake, 11 Aug 1973 (Shadowen, *KW* 49:75, 1973).
Early spring dates: 13 Mar 1982, Ky Lake (*KW* 58:48, 1982); 23 Mar 2017, Camp Ernst Lake, Boone Co. (R. Crice, eBird data); 25 Mar 1945, south-central Kentucky (*KW* 38:6, 1962).
Late fall dates: occasionally lingering to mid- to late Nov with a few early winter records, the latest being 1 Jan 1987, Nelson Co.(*KW* 63:20, 1987); 31 Dec 2011, (ph.) Pulaski Co. (*KW* 88:25/46/60, 2012); and the last week of Dec 1971, nr. Danville (*KW* 48:11, 1972 [location apparently published erroneously as Louisville in *AB* 26:616, 1972]).
Out-of-season dates (mid-winter): 7 Feb 1981, Louisville (*KW* 57:35, 1981); 18 Jan 2016, (ph.) Old Pumphouse Road, Pulaski Co. (*KW* 92:42, 2016); 12/15 Jan & 11/26 Mar 2017, [documenting wintering] Old Pumphouse Road, Pulaski Co. (*KW* 93:48, 2017 & R. Bontrager/R. Denton, eBird data); 12 Jan 2018, Lake Reba, Madison Co. (*KW* 94:57, 2018).
Unaccepted record: 3 Jan 1998, Danville CBC [no details] (*KW* 74:12, 1998).
Published error: the early spring date of 6 Mar [1974] published by Monroe, et al. (1988) is erroneous, the result of a transcription error (*fide* A. Stamm, historical archive files).

*BLACK-CROWNED NIGHT-HERON *Nycticorax nycticorax*

Status: Rare to locally uncommon transient and summer visitant, rare and very locally distributed summer resident, extremely rare winter resident. Found chiefly west of the Cumberland Plateau. Generally encountered regularly only in the vicinity of the few nesting colonies, but occasionally encountered singly or in small numbers elsewhere, especially during late summer and fall during post-breeding dispersal. Peak of abundance occurs from mid-Apr to mid-Sep. Encountered in a variety of aquatic habitats, but most often along secluded lakes, sloughs and slow moving-streams.

Breeding has been documented from about six widely separated counties through the years, but never at more than a few locations at any time (see below). A few individuals regularly linger into early winter (detected during the CBC period), and the species has been reported occasionally during mid-winter. In addition, small numbers have been documented to regularly winter in the Louisville area and at Ky Dam and occasionally elsewhere (see below). Typically encountered singly or in pairs, but loose groups at favored feeding areas may number a few dozen or more. **State Breeding Status**: Threatened.

Maximum counts: colony of ca. **300** active nesting pairs in Jefferson Co., 17 Jun 1988 (*KW* 64:62, 1988); **280** at the Falls of the Ohio, 12 Jul 1985 (*KW* 61:56, 1985); **200** nesting pairs on Lake Barkley island, Lyon Co., 25 Jun 1993 (B. Palmer-Ball, eBird data); **200** at the Falls of the Ohio, 10 Jun 1987 (*KW* 63:59, 1987); **196** at the Falls of the Ohio, 16 Aug 1984 (*KW* 61:14, 1985).

Summary of confirmed breeding records by county

Clark (small upland woodlot in w. part of county 1985-1986 [*KW* 62:66, 1986]; w. of Winchester during 1993 [Palmer-Ball and Wethington, *KW* 70:83, 1994]; and at the Winchester Cemetery 2016 to present [*KW* 92:58/78, 2016; 2017 eBird data; R. Denton, 2018 eBird data])

Greenup (backwater area along the Ohio River from at least 1991 to the mid-1990s [Palmer-Ball and Wethington, *KW* 70:83, 1994; P. Morrison, pers. comm.])

Jefferson (Six-Mile Island from about 1930 to 1948 [Mengel:166]; at and nr. the Falls of the Ohio including Shippingport Island from 1949 to 1992 [Smith, *KW* 26:6-8, 1950; Stamm, et al., *KW* 36:3-8, 1960; F. Stamm, *KW* 36:33, 1960; Wiley, *KW* 40:3-5, 1964; *KW* 64:62, 1988; *KW* 69:55, 1993]; on and nr. the Louisville Zoo and residential areas along Preston Highway 1993–2012 [*KW* 69:55, 1993; G. Michael, pers. comm.; R. Hensel, pers. comm.]; and on Shippingport Island, 2014 to present [*KW* 90:88, 2014; *KW* 91:84, 2015; B. Palmer-Ball, 2018/2019 eBird data])

Lyon (islands in Lake Barkley from nr. Kuttawa to south of the dam since at least 1996 [Palmer-Ball, *KW* 78:72-73, 2002; Palmer-Ball and Ciuzio, *KW* 80:87-96, 2004])

Nicholas (along the North Fork of the Licking River for some period prior to 1950 (Mengel:166-167)

Trigg (islands in Lake Barkley from 1979 to the mid-1980s [*KW* 57:72, 1981; Thomas, *KW* 58:35, 1982; Evans 1984; *KW* 66:5, 1990]; and again as early as 2010 to present [*KW* 86:65, 2010])

Summary of wintering and mid-winter records by county

Fayette (*KW* 79:44, 2003; *KW* 80:42, 2004; *KW* 82:46, 2006)
Greenup (*KW* 88:46, 2012; *KW* 89:47, 2013; *KW* 90:48, 2014)
Jefferson (apparently annual, especially at the Louisville Zoo [e.g. Mengel:167; *KW* 72:14, 1996])
Marshall (annual in recent years below Ky Dam)
Muhlenberg (*KW* 83:47, 2007)

*YELLOW-CROWNED NIGHT-HERON *Nyctanassa violacea*

Status: Extremely rare to rare transient and summer visitant, extremely rare and very locally distributed summer resident. Recorded chiefly west of the Cumberland Plateau, but the species has been documented from as far east as Greenup Co. (*KBBA*:34-35; R. Record, 1985 pers. comm.). Peak of abundance occurs from late Apr to early Sep. Encountered in a variety of aquatic habitats, but especially along secluded, slow-moving streams and in semi-open and forested swamps and sloughs. Nests singly or in small, loose groups of up to a half-dozen pairs, typically in mature bottomland forests and along riparian corridors, but also at least occasionally in wooded, residential areas. Confirmed nesting has been reported from scattered localities in 11 counties across central and western Kentucky (see below). Generally seen singly or in loose groups of up to a half-dozen birds, the latter usually in the vicinity of nesting areas during the late summer post-breeding dispersal period. **State Breeding Status**: Threatened.

Maximum counts: up to **17** at Chaney Lake, late Jul 1998 (Roemer, *KW* 74:92/94, 1998); **14** at the Falls of the Ohio, 9 Jul 1978 (*KW* 54:61, 1978); at least **12** along Cypress Creek, Marshall Co., 5 May 2011 (*KW* 87:85, 2011); **12** at the Grassy Pond-Powells Lake Unit Sloughs WMA, Henderson Co., 21 Aug 2015 (*KW* 92:6, 2016).

Early spring dates: 13 Mar 2019, Louisville (S. Miller, pers. comm./P. Spaulding, eBird data); 23 Mar 1952, Louisville area (*KW* 52:42, 1976); 23 Mar 1967, Hickman Co. (E. Larson, eBird data); 26 Mar 2017, Louisville (*KW* 93:74, 2017); 28 Mar 2017, Sauerheber Unit (C. Crawford, eBird data).

Late fall dates: 21 Oct 1982, Falls of the Ohio (*KW* 59:14, 1983); 20 Oct 2002, Sauerheber Unit (*KW* 79:5, 2003).

Summary of confirmed breeding records by county

Ballard (*KBBA*:34; B. Palmer-Ball, 1993 eBird data)
Boyle (*KW* 54:42, 1978)
Bullitt (*KW* 61:56, 1985; *KW* 64:62, 1988; *KW* 94:76, 2018)
Fayette (Mayfield, *KW* 32:62, 1956; Webster, *KW* 36:30, 1960; *KW* 56:78, 1980; *KW* 59:51, 1983; *KW* 60:52, 1984; *KW* 61:56, 1985; *KW* 62:66, 1986; *KW* 66:85, 1990; *KW* 80:65/81, 2004; *KW* 81:105, 2005; *KW* 82:80, 2006; *KW* 83:77/104, 2007; *KW* 84:59/85, 2008; *KW* 87:85, 2011)
Henderson (*KW* 78:61, 2002)
Hickman (*KW* 64:62, 1988)
Hopkins (*KW* 82:80, 2006; B. Palmer-Ball, 2007 eBird data)
Jefferson (Steilberg, *KW* 25:16, 1949; Halverson, *KW* 31:64-66, 1955; Fitzhugh, *KW* 35:59-65, 1959; Fitzhugh, *KW* 37:20, 1961; Croft and Stamm, *KW* 43:45, 1967; Stamm, *KW* 53:23, 1977; *KW* 61:56, 1985; Palmer-Ball and Evans, *KW* 62:75-76, 1986; *KW* 62:66, 1986; *KW* 64:62, 1988; *KW* 66:54, 1990; *KW* 92:78, 2016; *KW* 93:101, 2017; *KW* 94:76/108/124, 2018)
Marshall (B. Palmer-Ball, 2000 eBird data; *KW* 93:101, 2017; *KW* 94:76, 2018)
Union (*KW* 62:66, 1986; *KW* 87:85, 2011; *KW* 89:68/93-94, 2013; *KW* 90:69/88, 2014; *KW* 93:74, 2017)
Warren (*KW* 38:6, 1962)

WHITE IBIS *Eudocimus albus*

Status: Extremely rare spring, summer, and fall visitant. There are more than 30 records, most during late summer. Depending on habitat conditions in the deep south, modest irruptive flights occur northward into the region (e.g. seven reports during Jul-Aug of 2010). The vast majority of individuals have been juv. birds, but sub-ads. and ads. have been reported on three occasions. Most reports involved single birds, but up to nine individuals have occurred at once. Most reports have come from the western portion of the state, but the species has occurred from as far east as Leslie, Menifee, and Rowan cos. (see below).

Published error: 16 Sep 1993, Warren Co. (*KW* 74:26, 1998) (correction *fide* D. Roemer, pers. comm.).

Spring date: 20 Apr

Range of summer/fall dates: 27 Jun-16 Sep

Late fall date: 11-21 Nov

Tally of records by county

Ballard (3), Calloway, Christian (2), Fulton (9), Jefferson (3), Larue, Leslie, Logan (2), Marshall, McCracken, Menifee, Oldham, Pulaski, Rowan, Taylor, Warren (3), Wayne (2)

Chronological list of records

1) 3-10 Aug 1961, a juv. at Chaney Lake (*KW* 38:7, 1962)
2) 3-9 Aug 1962, a juv. nr. Wendover, Leslie Co. (Muncy, *KW* 38:66, 1962)
3) 9 Aug 1978, 3 juvs. (ph.) on a farm pond at Centerfield, Oldham Co. (Irmscher, *KW* 55:34-35, 1979)
4) 29 Jul 1979, a juv. on Beargrass Creek, Louisville (*KW* 55:55, 1979)
5) 30 Aug 1980, a juv. on Ky Lake, Calloway Co. (*KW* 57:19, 1981)
6) 15 Aug 1982, a juv. at Powersburg, Wayne Co. (*KW* 59:14, 1983; R. Guffey, eBird data)
7) 29 Aug–3 Sep 1983, an ad. on the Ballard WMA (*KW* 60:15, 1984)
8) 13-19 Jul 1990, 2 juvs. (ph.) along Beaver Creek, Menifee Co. (*KW* 66:85, 1990)
9) 12-14 Sep 1990, a juv. (ph.) at the Larue Co. Sportsman's Lake nr. Hodgenville (*KW* 67:4, 1991)

10) 9 Sep 1993, a second-year bird on a flooded backwater area in the Upper Hickman Bottoms (B. Palmer-Ball, et al., eBird data)
11) 20 Apr 1995, an ad. (ph.) nr. Rossington, McCracken Co. (C. Logsdon, eBird data; G. Boaz, photo)
12) 5 Aug 1995, a juv. at Lake No. 9 (G. Criswell, pers. comm.)
13) 30 Aug 1997, 3 juvs. at Lake No. 9 (*KW* 74:5, 1998; J. Wilson, et al., notes)
14) 12 Jul–7 Aug 1998, a juv. (vt.) at McElroy (12 Jul only) and Chaney (22 Jul–7 Aug) lakes (Roemer, *KW* 74:92/94, 1998)
15) 4 Aug 2005, a juv. (ph.) at Lake No. 9 (*KW* 82:6, 2006)
16) 9-13 Aug 2005, a juv. (ph.) at Ballard WMA (*KW* 82:6, 2006)
17) 9-14 Aug 2006, 1-2 juvs. (ph.) at Lake No. 9 (*KW* 83:10, 2007)
18) 28 Jul/10 Aug 2007, a juv. (ph.) at Lake No. 9 (*KW* 83:104, 2007; *KW* 84:6, 2008)
19) 14 Sep 2008, a juv. over the Mississippi River at Wickliffe, Ballard Co. (*KW* 85:12, 2008)
20) 21-22 Aug 2009, a juv. (ph.) at the Melco flood retention basin, Jefferson Co. (*KW* 86:6, 2010)
21) 26-27 Aug, 2009, a juv. (ph.) n. of Campbellsville, Taylor Co. (*KW* 86:6/36, 2010)
22) 11-21 Nov 2009, a juv. (ph.) at Minor Clark Fish Hatchery (*KW* 86:5-6, 2010)
23) 6 Jul 2010, 3 juvs. (ph.) at Lake No. 9 (*KW* 86:91, 2010)
24) 8-21 Jul 2010, a juv. (ph.) at the Falls of the Ohio (*KW* 86:91, 2010)
25) 11-16 Jul 2010, 1-3 juvs. (ph.) in w.-cen. Logan Co. (*KW* 86:91, 2010)
26) 13-18 Jul 2010, 6 juvs. (ph.) at McElroy Lake (*KW* 86:91/104, 2010)
27) 20-22 Jul 2010, a juv. (ph.) at Morgan Pond, Christian Co. (*KW* 86:91, 2010)
28) 5 Aug 2010, a juv. (ph.) at Lake No. 9 (*KW* 87:14, 2011)
29) 18-19 Aug 2010, up to 9 juvs. at Obion WMA, Fulton Co. (*KW* 87:14, 2011)
30) 13 Aug 2011, 3 juvs. nr. Mosley Pond, Logan Co. (*KW* 88:6, 2012)
31) 19 Aug 2011, an ad. in flight s. of Sloans Valley, Pulaski Co. (*KW* 88:6, 2012)
32) 27 Jun 2017, a juv. (ph.) in Wayne Co. (*KW* 93:101/116, 2017)
33) 16 Sep 2017, a juv. at Jonathan Creek (*KW* 94:10, 2018)
34) 13 Jul–early Aug 2019, 2 juvs. (ph.) at Morgan Pond (S. Arnold/J. Hall, et al., eBird data)

GLOSSY IBIS *Plegadis falcinellus*

Status: Extremely rare spring, summer, and fall visitant. There are 14 records (nine during spring; one during summer; and four during fall) that have been conclusively documented by photographs and/or written description. All but three reports have been of single individuals.

Range of spring dates: 21 Apr–19 May

Summer record: 27 Jun

Range of fall dates: 31 Aug–12 Oct

Chronological list of records

1) 17 May 1998, at McElroy Lake (*KW* 74:52, 1998; *KW* 75:48, 1999; M. Bennett/J. Elmore, notes [this individual was videotaped, but only the written description is conclusive to species identity])
2) 12 Oct 2003, 3 (one confirmed by vt.) nr. Woodburn, Warren Co. (*KW* 80:6-7, 2004)
3) 21-25 Apr 2007, (ph.) at the Sauerheber Unit (*KW* 83:74/77, 2007)
4) 3 May 2007, (ph.) at the Long Point Unit (*KW* 83:74/77, 2007)
5) 6 May 2007, apparently a different individual than the 21-25 Apr bird (ph.) at the Sauerheber Unit (*KW* 83:77, 2007)
6) 14 May 2008, 2 (ph.) at McElroy Lake (*KW* 84:59/66, 2008)
7) 10-11 May 2010, (ph.) along Clear Creek, Hopkins Co. (*KW* 86:65/76, 2010 [erroneously published therein as 20 May 2010; *fide KW* 90:93, 2014])
8) 5-9 Oct 2010, (ph.) at Minor Clark Fish Hatchery (*KW* 87:14/44, 2011)
9) 16 Sep 2011, (ph.) at Owsley Fork Lake, Madison Co. (*KW* 88:6, 2012; *KW* 92:87, 2016)
10) 31 Aug 2012, (ph.) e. of Morganfield, Union Co. (*KW* 89:6/40, 2013)
11) 28 Apr 2013, (ph.) at Minor Clark Fish Hatchery (*KW* 89:68/74, 2013)
12) 18-24 May 2013, 1-2 (ph.) at LBL, Trigg Co. (*KW* 89:68/88, 2013)
13) 27 Jun 2015, (ph.) nr. Prospect, Jefferson Co. (*KW* 91:81/84/85, 2015)
14) 19 May 2018, (ph.) at McElroy Lake (*KW* 94:76, 2018; R. Denton, et al., eBird data)

WHITE-FACED IBIS *Plegadis chihi*

Status: Extremely rare spring and fall visitant. There are 13 records (nine during spring and four during fall) that have been conclusively documented by photographs and/or written description. All but one report have been of single birds.

Range of spring dates: 18 Apr–29 May

Range of fall dates: 11 Sep–21 Oct

Chronological list of records

1) 7 Sep 1996, on a pond at Peabody WMA, Ohio Co. (G. and M. Boggs, notes – this record was not accepted by the KBRC [*KW* 75:49, 1999], but details provided with the report include observation of the red iris, a definitive character, and it is accepted herein)
2) 20-21 May 2000, (ph.) at Lake Shelby, Shelby Co. (*NAB* 54:287/289, 2000)
3) 11 Sep 2004, (ph.) in the Lower Hickman Bottoms (*KW* 81:6, 2005)
4) 25-26 Apr 2009, (ph.) at the Long Point Unit (*KW* 85:67/70/80, 2009)
5) 10-15 Oct 2009, an ad. (ph.) at and nr. the Sauerheber Unit (*KW* 86:6/36, 2010)
6) 17 May 2011, 2 nr. the Sauerheber Unit (*KW* 87:85, 2011)
7) 26-27 May 2011, at McElroy Lake (*KW* 87:85, 2011)
8) 24 May 2013, (ph.) at LBL, Trigg Co. (*KW* 89:68/75, 2013)
9) 21 Oct 2015, a molting ad. (ph.) in s. Jefferson Co. (*KW* 92:6/36, 2016)
10) 9 May 2016, (ph.) at Swallow Spring Pond, Christian Co. (*KW* 92:53/58, 2016)
11) 29 May 2017, (ph.) in the Lower Hickman Bottoms (*KW* 93:74/75, 2017)
12) 18 Apr 2018, (ph.) at McElroy Lake (*KW* 94:76, 2018; R. Shive, eBird data)
13) 12 May 2018, (ph.) at Louisville (*KW* 94:76, 2018; P. Bell, eBird data)

GLOSSY/WHITE FACED IBIS *Plegadis* spp.

Status: The two species of *Plegadis* ibis are very similar, especially in juv. and basic plumages, and both species are known to wander north into our region. The presence of hybrids also has been documented. Details of 31 additional records have not been sufficient to positively identify either species.

Chronological list of records

1) 21 Apr 1945, at McElroy Lake (Wilson, *KW* 21:48, 1945)
2) 12 May 1956, at McElroy Lake (Wilson, *KW* 32:59-61, 1956)
3) 20 Mar 1965, a flock of 27 at McElroy Lake (Wilson, *KW* 41:29-30, 1965)
4) 1 May 1963, at Lake Nevin, Bernheim Forest (*KW* 52:42, 1976)
5) 30 Apr 1967, 7 at Ky Dam (Gray, *KW* 43:59, 1967)
6) 7 May 1989, at Lentz's Pond nr. Louisville (*KW* 65:63, 1989)
7) 23 Oct–1 Nov 1991, an imm. (ph.) at the Minor Clark Fish Hatchery (*KW* 68:4, 1992; B. Palmer-Ball, eBird data)
8) 25 Aug 1994, 6 at the Falls of the Ohio (B. Etenohan/A. Goldstein, notes/eBird data)
9) 30 Aug 1999, 3 (ph.) at the Minor Clark Fish Hatchery (*KW* 76:4, 2000; L. Kornman, photos)
10) 17-19 Sep 1999, an imm. (vt.) nr. Franklin, Simpson Co. (*KW* 76:4, 2000; *KW* 77:36, 2001; D. Roemer, notes [review of the video-documentation provided with this record strongly suggests it to be a Glossy Ibis])
11) 21 Nov–4 Dec 2001, an imm. (vt.) at and nr. the Sauerheber Unit (*NAB* 56:57, 2002)
12) 24 Mar 2007, in flight along Cypress Creek, Muhlenberg Co. (*KW* 83:77, 2007)
13) 18/21 Apr 2007, 2/1 at the Sauerheber Unit (*KW* 83:77, 2007/R. Denton, eBird data)
14) 17 Apr 2010, in flight over the Sauerheber Unit (*KW* 86:65, 2010)
15) 8 Sep 2012, at Jonathan Creek (*KW* 89:6, 2013)
16) 7-15 Oct 2012, 1-2 (ph.) (two present 12 Oct) nr. Powderly, Muhlenberg Co. (*KW* 89:6, 2013)
17) 21-22 Oct 2012, nr. Schochoh, Logan Co. (*KW* 89:6, 2013)
18) 23 Oct 2012, at Taylorsville Lake, Spencer Co. (*KW* 89:6, 2013)
19) 10 Oct 2013, 2 (ph.) at Blood River (*KW* 90:7, 2014)

20) 16 Sep 2014, 3 (ph.) e. of Morganfield, Union Co. (*KW* 91:6/36, 2015)
21) 24-26 Oct 2014, (ph.) e. of Morganfield, Union Co. (*KW* 91:6/36, 2015)
22) 18 Apr 2015, 2 (ph.) e. of Hickman, Fulton Co. (*KW* 91:68, 2015)
23) 29 May 2015, (ph.) at the Minor Clark Fish Hatchery (*KW* 91:68, 2015)
24) 13-14 Sep 2015, (ph.) in w. Henderson Co. (*KW* 92:6, 2016)
25) 1 Nov 2015, at the Sauerheber Unit (*KW* 92:6, 2016)
26) 4 Nov 2015, (ph.) in n. Union Co. (*KW* 92:6, 2016)
27) 19-20 May 2016, (ph.) at the Sauerheber Unit (*KW* 92:58, 2016)
28) 26 May 2016, 2 in ne. Union Co. (*KW* 92:58, 2016)
29) 19 Sep 2016, at Swallow Spring Pond, Christian Co. (*KW* 93:6, 2017)
30) 10 Oct 2017, (ph.) e. of Morganfield, Union Co. (*KW* 94:10, 2018)
30) 29 Apr 2018, (ph.) over Hays Kennedy Park, Jefferson Co. (*KW* 94:76, 2018)
31) 17 May 2018, (ph.) at McElroy Lake (*KW* 94:76, 2018)

ROSEATE SPOONBILL *Platalea ajaja*

Status: Extremely rare summer and fall visitant. This unique wading bird typically inhabits coastal wetlands but regularly wanders north after the nesting season. There are eight records, all of juv. or sub-ad. birds.

Range of dates: 28 Jul–17 Sep

Chronological list of records

1) 29 Jul/18 Aug 1989, a juv. (ph.) at Honker Lake, LBL, Trigg Co. (Flam, *KW* 65:96, 1989; *KW* 65:81, 1989)
2) 13-17 Sep 1994, a juv. (ph.) at Lake No. 9 (Parker, et al., *KW* 71:79, 1995);
3) 5 Aug 2005, a juv. over Lake No. 9 (*KW* 82:6, 2006)
4) 11-19 Aug 2007, a juv. (ph.) at Grayson Lake (*KW* 84:1/6, 2008)
5) 4 Sep 2007, a sub-ad. (ph.) at Honker Lake, LBL, Trigg Co. (*KW* 84:6, 2008)
6) 28 Jul 2008, a juv. (ph.) at Lake No. 9 (*KW* 84:85, 2008)
7) 4-13 Sep 2013, a sub-ad. (ph.) at Guist Creek Lake, Shelby Co. (*KW* 90:1/7, 2014)
8) 3-12 Aug 2014, a sub-ad. (ph.) at Long Creek Refuge, LBL, Trigg Co. (*KW* 91:7/36, 2015)

*BLACK VULTURE *Coragyps atratus*

Status: Uncommon to locally fairly common resident (more locally distributed during winter than at other times of the year). Occurs statewide, but recorded chiefly west of the Cumberland Plateau. Somewhat locally distributed at all seasons; regular migratory movements through the state during spring and fall have not been documented, but widely dispersed breeding birds appear to congregate during winter. Encountered in a variety of semi-open habitats with a mixture of forests and farmland. Breeding along cliff lines and in abandoned structures, primarily throughout the western three-quarters of the state; most numerous in semi-open rural areas. Generally encountered singly or in small groups of fewer than a dozen birds, but winter roosts may contain more than a hundred birds. This species has increased dramatically over the past four decades, accounting at least in part for the higher roost counts in recent years.

Maximum counts: **600** total (300 both below Wolf Creek Dam and at Lake Cumberland SRP), Russell Co., 11 Dec 2010 (R. Denton, eBird data); **400+** at Frankfort, 18 Jan 2006 (*KW* 82:46, 2006); at least **400** at Clermont, Bullitt Co., 28 Dec 2008 (*KW* 85:34/48, 2009); **399** on the Frankfort CBC, 16 Dec 2006 (*KW* 83:27/47, 2007); **350+** (ca. one-third of a mixed-species roost of 1100 vultures) at Frankfort, 18 Jan 2007 (*KW* 83:47, 2007); **300-400** at Barren River Lake, 6 Sep 2008 (*KW* 85:13, 2009); **320** at the Falls of the Ohio, 11 Oct 2013 (*KW* 90:7, 2014); **300+** at Germantown, Bracken Co., winter 2012-2013 (*KW* 89:47, 2013); **281** at Barren River Lake, 28 Dec 1999 (*KW* 76:14, 2000); **275** in Grayson Co, 29 Jan 2003 (*KW* 79:44, 2003); at least **250** in Barren Co., 10 Nov 2009 (*KW* 86:6, 2010); ca. **250** below Wolf Creek Dam, 22 Nov 2012 (*KW* 89:6, 2013); **240** in Russell Co., 17 Dec 2012 (R. Denton, eBird data); **225** in s. Jefferson Co., 11 Jan 2012 (*KW* 88:46, 2012); **225** in Trimble Co., 15 Jul 2012 (*KW* 88:93, 2012); **219** at Frankfort, 18 Dec 1999

(*KW* 76:14, 2000); **219** at the Falls of the Ohio, 20 Aug 2018 (*KW* 95:8, 2019); **200** over the Ohio River, Bracken Co., 17 Mar 2003 (*KW* 79:65, 2003); **200** at Taylorsville Lake, Spencer Co., 21 Nov 2003 (R. Allen, eBird data); **192** in Carroll Co., 18 Dec 1999 (*NAB* 54:184, 2000 [location and date published incorrectly as from Boone Co. on 2 Jan 2000 in *KW* 76:14, 2000]); at least **190** below Wolf Creek Dam, 24 Oct 2009 (*KW* 86:6, 2010); **155** in Nelson Co., 26 Dec 1993 (*KW* 70:23, 1994); **135** at the Falls of the Ohio, 24 Aug 2009 (*KW* 86:6, 2010); **133** in Franklin Co., 19 Dec 1982 (*KW* 59:10/28, 1983); **126** on the Falls of Rough CBC, 20 Dec 1997 (*KW* 74:19, 1998); **124** on the Glasgow CBC, 30 Dec 2000 (*KW* 77:14, 2001); **123** on the Louisville CBC, 17 Dec 2006 (*KW* 83:26, 2007); ca. **120** at Wolf Creek Dam, 12 Mar 2011 (*KW* 87:85, 2011); **116** on the Wayne Co. CBC, 19 Dec 2006 (*KW* 83:27, 2007); **113** in Carroll Co., 17 Dec 1994 (*KW* 71:18, 1995).

*TURKEY VULTURE *Cathartes aura*

Status: Resident; fairly common to common during summer and migratory periods, rare to uncommon during winter. Recorded statewide. Encountered in a great variety of habitats, but most numerous in and around semi-open farmland and rural settlement. Breeding along cliff lines and in hollow trees and abandoned buildings throughout the state, but perhaps somewhat more locally distributed on the Cumberland Plateau and Mountains. Peak of abundance occurs from late Mar to late Oct with a somewhat noticeable peak in the presence of migrant flocks during the end of that period. Can be quite locally distributed during winter, when those birds that have not headed farther south often gather into large roosting groups. Generally encountered singly or in small flocks of up to a dozen birds, but occasionally congregates in groups of more than a hundred individuals during migration or near winter roost sites.

Maximum counts: **1200** along the Kentucky River, Jessamine/Mercer cos., 7 Jan 2019 (S. Penner, eBird data); **850** at Barren River Lake, Barren Co., 9 Dec 2001 (S. Stedman/D. Roemer, pers. comm.); ca. **700+** (ca. two-thirds of a mixed-species roost of 1100 vultures) at Frankfort, 18 Jan 2007 (*KW* 83:47, 2007); at least **750** at Barren River Lake, 18 Nov 2009 (*KW* 86:6, 2010); **600+** at Barren River Lake 2 Dec 2002 (*KW* 79:44, 2003); **500-600** at Glasgow, Barren Co., 19 Nov 2003 (*KW* 80:7, 2004); probably **most of 500-600** at Red River Gorge, 24 Feb 1973 (Uterhart, *KW* 49:74, 1973); **500+** in the vicinity of Radcliff, Hardin Co., late Jan 2006 (*KW* 82:46, 2006); **400-500** in Grayson Co., Dec 1995-Jan 1996 (*KW* 72:41, 1996); **400-500** in the vicinity of Cave Run Lake, 18 Mar 2008 (*KW* 84:59, 2008); **425+** at Green River Lake, Taylor Co., 5 Nov 2001 (B. Palmer-Ball, eBird data); **405** on the Glasgow CBC, 28 Dec 1999 (*KW* 76:14, 2000); ca. **400** in Grayson Co., 4 Jan 2003 (*KW* 79:44, 2003); **372** on the Frankfort CBC, 16 Dec 2006 (*KW* 83:27, 2007); ca. **350** nr. Princeton, Caldwell Co., 7 Nov 1988 (*KW* 65:6, 1989); **350** in Grayson Co., 26 Dec 1999 (*KW* 76:14, 2000); **300-400** at Barren River Lake, 6 Sep 2008 (*KW* 85:13, 2009); **325** in Bell Co., 5 Nov 2017 (D. Ledford, eBird data); **300** in Grant Co., 30 Jan 2017 (P. Pratt, eBird data); **285** in Rowan Co., 8 Nov 1984 (*KW* 61:15, 1985); **260** at Frankfort, 18 Dec 1999 (*KW* 76:14, 2000); **244** in Casey Co., 1 Jan 1980 (*KW* 56:31, 1980); **200-300** in Powell Co., 7 Nov 1981 (*KW* 58:14, 1982).

*OSPREY *Pandion haliaetus*

Status: Uncommon to fairly common transient, extremely rare to locally uncommon summer resident, extremely rare during winter. Occurs widely across the state during migration, visiting a great variety of aquatic habitats from the largest lakes and rivers to smaller lakes and ponds; also observed regularly passing overhead during migration, including at prime raptor migration lookouts in the Cumberland Mountains. Nesting was reported from the Falls of the Ohio by Audubon around 1810 (Mengel:219); and from the Blood River embayment of Ky Lake in 1949 (DeLime, *KW* 25:55, 1949) with unsuccessful nesting attempts in Trigg Co. in 1968 (*KW* 45:31, 1969) and Lyon Co. in 1969 (*KW* 46:47, 1970). The Osprey became more regular as a summering bird in the state during the 1980s, assisted to an unknown degree by a restoration program conducted by the Ky. Dept. of Fish and Wildlife Resources 1982-89 (*KW* 58:40, 1982; *KBBA*:50; Ray et al., *KW* 85:3-8, 2009). By 2001, there were at least three dozen active nests in western Kentucky, most on Lake Barkley, but several on Ky Lake and one on the lower Ohio River, Livingston Co. (E. Ray, notes; L. Burford, pers. comm.); during the early 2000s, a few pairs also began nesting in the Green River drainage of Muhlenberg Co. (*NAB* 54:388, 2000; M. Henshaw, pers. comm.) and Hopkins Co. (*KW* 78:62, 2002). By 2011, at least 87 active nesting pairs were present (*KW* 87:113, 2011), with a total of 155 occupied nesting territories by 2017 (Taylor, et al., *KW* 93:87-93, 2018). There may be a few reliable winter records from the larger lakes and rivers (see below), but the species does not typically winter in the state. **State Breeding Status**: Special Concern.

Historical maximum count: "as many as **6 or 7** sometimes present at once" at the Falls of the Ohio (Mengel:219).

Recent maximum count: probably more than **40** in the LBL vicinity, 29 Mar 2017 (*KW* 93:74, 2017).

Early spring dates (note trend for earlier arrivals in recent years): 18 Feb 2012, Ky Dam (*KW* 88:46, 2012); 20 Feb 2018, Taylorsville Lake, Spencer Co. (*KW* 94:57, 2018; location erroneously published as Nelson Co. therein); 23 Feb 2016, (ph.) Ky Dam (*KW* 92:42, 2016); 26 Feb 2018, Ky Dam (*KW* 94:57, 2018); 28 Feb 2007, Lake Barkley, Trigg Co. (*KW* 83:47, 2007); 28 Feb 2009, Honker Lake, LBL, Lyon Co. (*KW* 85:48, 2009); 28 Feb 2017, Ky Dam (*KW* 93:48, 2017); 2 Mar 2011, Lake Barkley, Trigg Co. (*KW* 87:85, 2011); 3 Mar 2016, Ohio River, Greenup Co. (*KW* 92:58, 2016); 5 Mar 2016, Wolf Creek Dam (*KW* 92:58, 2016); 7 Mar 2006, Lake Barkley, Trigg Co., (*KW* 82:67, 2006); 7 Mar 2015, Ky Dam (*KW* 91:68, 2015); 9 Mar 2001, Grayson Co. (*KW* 77:49, 2001); 9 Mar 2008, Lake Barkley, Trigg Co. (*KW* 84:59, 2008); 10 Mar 2002, Trigg Co. (H. Chambers, notes); 10 Mar 2005, Lake Barkley, Lyon Co. (*KW* 81:84, 2005); 10 Mar 2007, Muhlenberg Co. (*KW* 83:77, 2007); 10 Mar 2008, below Smithland Dam, Livingston Co. (*KW* 84:59, 2008); 11 Mar 2012, Muhlenberg Co. (*KW* 88:73, 2012); 14 Mar 2000, LBL (M. Easley, pers. comm.); 14 Mar 2003, Barkley Dam (*KW* 79:67, 2003); 14 Mar 2007, Pulaski Co. (*KW* 83:77, 2007); 18 Mar 2000, Lawrence Co. (L. Towler, pers. comm.); 18 Mar 2007, Minor Clark Hatchery (*KW* 83:77, 2007).

Late fall dates: occasionally lingers into Nov with a few reports into early winter, the latest well-documented reports being 1 Jan 2018, (ph.) at Lexington (*KW* 94:57, 2018); 27 Dec 2010, Ohio River below Meldahl Dam, Bracken Co. (*KW* 87:39/60, 2011); 18 Dec 2010 at Lexington (*KW* 87:40/60, 2011); and 17 Dec 1994, Ohio River, Gallatin Co. (*KW* 71:18, 1995).

Out-of-season records (winter): 14 Jan and 11 Feb 1978, Ohio River in Meade Co. (*AB* 32:358, 1978; *KW* 54:28, 1978); 15 Jan 19—, 27 Jan 19—, and 12 Feb 19—, Louisville (Mengel:219); 3 Jan 2004, Ky Lake, Calloway Co. (*KW* 80:17/42, 2004).

Unaccepted records: most published late fall and winter records (including some older records not included herein) have not been documented sufficiently enough to consider them conclusive; some of the following records may be valid, but some are likely based on confusion with other raptors: 30 Dec 1962, Mammoth Cave National Park (*KW* 39:6, 1963); 22 Dec 1967, LBL CBC (*AFN* 22:245, 1968; *KW* 44:6, 1968); mid-Dec 1972, Louisville CBC (*AB* 27:623, 1973; *KW* 49:9, 1973); 27 Jan 1979, three birds in Crittenden Co. (*KW* 55:30, 1979); 20 Dec 1980, LBL CBC (*KW* 57:8, 1981); 23 Dec 1980, Morehead CBC, Rowan Co. (*KW* 57:11, 1981); 2 Jan 1986, Barren River Lake (*KW* 62:27, 1986); 2 Jan 1988, Boone Co. (*KW* 64:13, 1988); 1 Jan 1996, Crittenden Co. (*KW* 72:10, 1996).

Published error: early Feb 1988, Cumberland Falls State Park (*KW* 64:28, 1988) (correction *fide* S. Kickert. pers. comm.).

Summary of recent county nesting records (away from LBL area) (references to initial nesting records shown)

Fayette (Lexington, 2013 [*KW* 89:68/94, 2013; *KW* 91:85, 2015])
Greenup (Ohio River, 2012 [*KW* 88:73, 2012])
Hopkins (Green River tributaries, 2002 [*KW* 78:62, 2002])
Jefferson (Ohio River at Falls of the Ohio, 2007 [(*KW* 83:77, 2007; *KW* 84:59, 2008; *KW* 85:67/91, 2009])
Laurel (Laurel River Lake, 2011 [Taylor et al, *KW* 92:92, 2017])
Lincoln (Cedar Creek Lake, 2010 [*KW* 86:91, 2010])
McCracken (Ohio River, 2004 [*KW* 80:81, 2004])
Muhlenberg (Green River corridor including Peabody WMA & environs, 2003 [*KW* 79:81, 2003])
Menifee (Cave Run Lake, 2008 [*KW* 85:67, 2009])
Ohio (Green River corridor including Peabody WMA & environs, 2003 [*KW* 79:81, 2003])
Pendleton (Ohio River, 2009 [*KW* 85:91, 2009])
Spencer (Taylorsville Lake, 2017 [Taylor et al, *KW* 92:92, 2017])
Taylor (Green River Lake, 2017 [Taylor et al, *KW* 92:92, 2017])

WHITE-TAILED KITE *Elanus leucurus*

Status: Accidental vagrant. This raptor is typically resident in parts of southern and western North America, occurring infrequently outside of its normal range. It has been documented in Kentucky only once.

1) 5 May 1991, an. ad. (ph.) nr. Hailwell, Hickman Co. (Palmer-Ball and Parker, *KW* 75:35, 1999; *AC* 2nd ed., p. PHOTOS - 3). Photographs of this individual are poor in quality, but suitably document its occurrence along with the written details.

SWALLOW-TAILED KITE *Elanoides forficatus*

Status: Extremely rare spring and summer visitant. Formerly (19th century) apparently a regular transient and summer resident, primarily in western Kentucky, with breeding reported at the Falls of the Ohio by Audubon in the early 1800s (Mengel:204). By early in the 20th century, the species had disappeared from most of the Ohio and Mississippi valleys, perhaps in large part due to clearing of bottomland forests and persecution. During the latter half of the 20th century, the number of reports outside of the much reduced breeding range increased. Consistent with the regional trend for more extralimital sightings, there are 12 recent records of wandering birds in Kentucky.

Unaccepted record: 14 Aug 2013, LBL, Trigg Co. (*KW* 90:7, 2014; see *KW* 92:89, 2016).

Range of dates: 5 May and 8 Jul–7 Sep

Chronological list of recent records

1) 16 Aug–7 Sep 1997, (ph.) spent several weeks in the vicinity of Lawrenceburg, Indiana, and Petersburg, Boone Co. (Renfrow, *KW* 74:24-25, 1998)
2) 31 Jul 2001, Central Kentucky WMA, Madison Co. (*NAB* 55:439, 2001)
3) 12-31 Aug 2003, (ph.) at the Sinclair Unit (*KW* 80:7, 2004)
4) 5 Sep 2008, (ph.) along the Mississippi River, Carlisle Co. (*KW* 85:13, 2009)
5) 15 Aug 2011, along Puncheon Creek, Allen Co. (*KW* 88:6, 2012)
6) 22-23 Apr 2012, (ph.) nr. Rockfield, Warren Co. (*KW*.88:73/84, 2012)
7) 5 May 2012, (ph.) on Ky Lake, Calloway Co. (*KW* 88:73, 2012)
8) 13-19 Aug 2012, (2, ph.) nr. Petersburg, Boone Co. (*KW* 89:6/21, 2013)
9) 12 Aug 2013, se. of Mt. Zion, Allen Co. (*KW* 90:7, 2014)
10) 16 Aug 2015, over Pinchgut Creek, Allen Co. (*KW* 92:6, 2016)
11) 8 Jul 2016, Ft. Campbell, Christian Co. (*KW* 92:79, 2016)
12) 1 Aug 2016, (ph.) nw. of Harrodsburg, Mercer Co. (*KW* 93:6/36, 2017)

GOLDEN EAGLE *Aquila chrysaetos*

Status: Extremely rare to locally rare transient and winter resident, extremely rare during summer. Occurs regularly during winter at a few scattered locations in central and western Kentucky (e.g., Ballard WMA, LBL, Bernheim Forest), occasionally elsewhere. In recent years, better coverage including remote camera surveys and transmitter studies have resulted in a wealth of information regarding this species' occurrence in the region, including establishment of the fact that small numbers winter statewide (see *KW* 85:48, 2009; Palmer-Ball and Smith, *KW* 86:55-62, 2010; *KW* 88:46, 2012; *KW* 90:48-49, 2014; *KW* 91:52, 2015; *KW* 92:42, 2016; Taylor and Slankard, *KW* 94:43-49, 2018). The species is now observed annually at scattered localities throughout the state. Possibly nested formerly (Mengel:215), but now considered a transient and winter resident only.

Maximum counts: 6 at Bernheim Forest 15 Jan 2003 (*KW* 79:46, 2003); 5 at Bernheim Forest, 30 Nov 2003 (*KW* 80:7, 2004); 5 at Bernheim Forest, 3 Jan 2019 (*KW* 95:49, 2019); 3 at LBL, 24-25 Feb 1973 (C. Peterson, pers. comm.; *fide* A. Stamm, historical archive files); 3 at Bernheim Forest, 26 Dec 2000 (*KW* 77:19, 2001); 3 at Bernheim Forest, 22 Dec 2001 (*KW* 78:22, 2002).
Late spring dates: 3 May 2009, Louisville (*KW* 85:68, 2009); 2 May 1995, LBL (*KW* 71:41, 1995); 25 Apr 2009, McCracken Co. (*KW* 85:68, 2009); 23 Apr 2014, Wayne Co. (*KW* 90:69, 2014); 21 Apr 1991, Cave Run Lake (*KW* 67:54, 1991); 19 Apr 2014, Allen Co. (*KW* 90:69, 2014); 15 Apr 2015,

LBL, Lyon Co. (*KW* 91:68, 2015); 8 Apr 2007, Ohio Co. (*KW* 83:78, 2007); 7 Apr 1996, Long Point Unit (B. Palmer-Ball, eBird data); 7 Apr 2013, Lake Cumberland, Russell Co., (eBird data); 5 Apr 2014, Sauerheber Unit (*KW* 90:69, 2014).

Early fall dates: 26 Sep 2014 (transmittered bird), Pike Co. (*KW* 91:7, 2015); 5 Oct 1946, Whitley Co. (Wilson and Browning, *KW* 22:56, 1946; Mengel: 214).

Out-of-season records (summer): 21 Aug 1965, Hancock Co. (Alsop, *KW* 47:61, 1971); early Jun 1992, a wing-tagged bird (probably from a reintroduction program) on the Fort Knox Military Reservation, Hardin Co. (M. Brandenburg, pers. comm./photographs); 17 Jun 1998, Whitley Co. (*FN* 52:454, 1998).

Unaccepted records: 29 Aug 1953 (*AFN* 8:22, 1954); 15 May 1995, Calloway Co. (*KW* 71:41, 1995); also, the validity of high counts of 7 on the LBL CBC, 28 Dec 1971 (*KW* 48:7, 1972) and 5 on the LBL CBC, 23 Dec 1968 (*KW* 45:13, 1969) is unknown, but they are considered unconfirmed herein.

Published errors: a summer record of 4 Jul [1935] (*KW* 45:49, 1969) pertains to Tennessee (*fide* Mengel:215); high counts of multiple birds during the late 1970s and early 1980s at Ballard WMA (e.g., *KW* 54:50-51, 1978; *KW* 55:45, 1979; *KW* 56:32, 1980) were based on confusion with immature Bald Eagles (*fide* L. Burford, pers. comm.).

*NORTHERN HARRIER *Circus hudsonius*

Status: Uncommon transient, uncommon to locally fairly common winter resident, extremely rare and locally distributed summer resident. Recorded statewide; generally absent from heavily forested portions of eastern Kentucky, but occurs regularly at prime raptor migration lookouts in the Cumberland Mountains. Usually encountered singly, working low over open fields and grasslands, but may be observed soaring or steadily flapping high overhead during migration. Spring migrants linger into early Apr and fall migrants begin arriving by late Aug; peak of abundance occurs from late Oct to mid-Mar. Breeding was reported by Audubon in the early 1800s (Mengel:218), and there have been a number of recent reports of nesting, mostly on reclaimed surface mines in west-central Kentucky (see below). A few migrants may linger into late May or early Jun, and reappear during late Jul and early Aug, but summer sightings have increased in frequency in recent years; some may indicate nesting in other parts of the state, especially in open farmland and on reclaimed surface mines. Generally encountered singly or in pairs, but loose congregations of up to a dozen or more birds can be encountered in prime habitat, and the species sometimes roosts communally at night. **State Breeding Status**: Threatened.

Maximum counts: **83** on the Paradise CBC, Muhlenberg/Ohio cos., 30 Dec 1995 (*KW* 72:12, 1996); **83** on the Paradise CBC, 3 Jan 1998 (*KW* 74:18, 1998); at least **46** coming to a roost e of Morganfield, Union Co., 24 Feb 2013 (*KW* 89:47, 2013) with **45** at the same roost, 16 Mar 2013 (*KW* 89:68, 2013).

Summary of confirmed breeding records by county

Hart (Clay and Clay, *KW* 66:99, 1990)
Hopkins (*KW* 82:80/92, 2006)
Muhlenberg (Palmer-Ball and Barron, *KW* 66:74-76, 1990; B. Palmer-Ball, 1998 eBird data; *NAB* 54: 388, 2000; M. Monroe, 2001 notes; *KW* 78:62, 2002; *KW* 79:67/81, 2003)
Ohio (Palmer-Ball and Barron, *KW* 66:74-76, 1990; *KW* 71:41/68, 1995; *KW* 78:62, 2002; *KW* 79: 67/81, 2003)

Summary of additional records of probable breeding by county

McLean (*KW* 65:85, 1989; *KW* 66:86, 1990; *KBBA*:56-57)
Todd (*KW* 65:85, 1990; *KBBA*:56-57)

*SHARP-SHINNED HAWK *Accipiter striatus*

Status: Resident; uncommon to fairly common during migration, uncommon during winter, rare during summer. Recorded statewide. Encountered in a variety of habitats from semi-open farmland and suburban areas to woodland openings and borders; most conspicuous during migration when the species occurs regularly in small numbers at prime raptor migration lookouts in the Cumberland Mountains. Peaks of abundance occur from mid-Mar to late Apr and from mid-Sep to late Oct. Breeding not well documented; the species probably nests at scattered localities throughout more heavily forested areas of the state (Mengel: 206-207), but confirmed breeding records are few (*KBBA*:58). Never numerous, but a dozen or more may be seen in a day's time at favorable locations during migration. **State Breeding Status**: Special Concern.

Maximum counts: **37** in Bell Co., 20 Sep 1981 (*KW* 58:14, 1982); **23** at Bad Branch State Nature Preserve, Letcher Co., 13 Oct 1998 (B. Palmer-Ball, eBird data); **19** over Pine Mt. nr. Oven Fork, Letcher Co., 2 Oct 2011 (*KW* 88:7, 2012).

*COOPER'S HAWK *Accipiter cooperii*

Status: Resident; uncommon to fairly common during migration and winter, rare to uncommon during summer (has increased as a breeder over the past few decades). Recorded statewide. Encountered in a variety of habitats from open farmland and woodland borders to suburban parks and yards; most conspicuous during migration when the species occurs regularly at prime raptor migration lookouts in the Cumberland Mountains. Peak of abundance occurs from early Oct to early Apr. Breeding not well documented; the species probably nests locally across the state, especially in wooded areas and semi-open habitats, but confirmed breeding records are not numerous (see Mengel:207-208; *KBBA*:60). Generally encountered singly, in pairs, or in small family groups.

Maximum counts: **20** on the Louisville CBC, 14 Dec 2014 (*KW* 91:22, 2015); **20** on the Louisville CBC, 18 Dec 2016 (*KW* 93:20, 2017); **17** on the Louisville CBC, 15 Dec 2013 (*KW* 90:29, 2014); **14** on the Lexington CBC, 17 Dec 2011 (*KW* 88:26, 2012).

NORTHERN GOSHAWK *Accipiter gentilis*

Status: Extremely rare fall and winter visitant (although essentially accidental). Most of the few records have originated in semi-open country of north-central Kentucky, but there are a few records from scattered localities throughout the rest of the state. Irregular in occurrence; absent most years, and generally reported only during irruption years when adult birds are more numerous. Most of the published records of this raptor have been accompanied by very few if any details, making it virtually impossible to sort out the reliable data set. Only one report has been documented with photos, and no extant specimen appears to exist. Especially in juvenile plumage the Northern Goshawk can be confused with Cooper's Hawk and Red-shouldered Hawk, and some reports certainly represent misidentifications. Mengel (pp. 205-206) included only a few reports that could be considered well documented. I personally feel that most of the few historical records are valid, but I must question authenticity of most records from the 1970s to the present. Unfortunately, sorting out the poorly documented from the presumably reliable reports is virtually impossible given the overall lack of information.

Unaccepted records: some published reports on various CBCs through the years that have not been supported by any details are not included in the listing below. Also, 31 Dec 1944, a sight record included by Mengel (p. 205), but not by the listed observers in a later publication (*fide* Monroe and Monroe, *KW* 37:28, 1961) suggest the sighting may not have been considered confirmed.

Published error?: based on a review of a number of sources, I believe (but am not certain) that the late spring date of 25 Mar published in Monroe, et al. (1988) is erroneous, the result of a transcription error (*fide* A. Stamm, historical archive files).

Chronological list of published records (validity unassessed, although *italicized* reports occurred during documented irruption years [Newton 2002])

1) early 1800s, several collected (sp.) [specimens no longer extant, but one painting from a specimen published] by J.J. Audubon nr. Henderson, Henderson Co. (Mengel: 205)
2) 1 Dec 1917, an ad. collected (sp.) [specimen no longer extant] near Bardstown, Nelson Co. (Mengel: 205)
3) 2 Feb 1918, sight record of an ad. at Bowling Green (Mengel:205)

4) 19 Dec 1943, sight record of an ad. at Louisville (Stamm, *KW* 22:23-24, 1944)

5) 20 Feb 1946, sight record of an ad. at Louisville (Mengel, *KW* 24:50, 1948)

6) 3-23 Mar 1946, one or two observed n. of Eastwood, Jefferson Co. (Monroe and Monroe, *KW* 37:28, 1961)

7) *17 Dec 1972, sight record of an ad. on the outskirks of Louisville (KW 49:13, 1973; A. Stamm, notes)*

8) 6/28 Dec 1977, sight records of an ad. in e. Shelby Co. (*KW* 54:16, 1978)

9) 2 Jan 1978, sight record of an ad. nr. Ballardsville, Oldham Co. (*KW* 54:16, 1978)

10) 7 Oct 1980, sight record of an ad. at Cumberland Gap National Historical Park, Bell Co. (*KW* 57:20, 1981)

11) *11 Oct 1982, sight record [no details at all] at Fort Knox (KW 59:15, 1983)*

12) *6 Nov 1983, sight record of an ad. in ne. Jefferson Co. (B. Palmer-Ball, eBird data; date erroneously published as 5 Nov in previous editions of this work)*

13) *31 Dec 1983, sight record on the Burlington CBC (KW 60:12, 1984; no details but report included herein because it occurred during a flight year)*

14) 31 Oct 1985, sight record of a presumed ad. at Louisville (*KW* 62:5, 1986)

15) 28 Oct 1988, a juv. (ba./ph.) in Boone Co. (*KW* 65:34, 1989; McNeely, *KW* 81:113-114, 2005)

16) 7 Nov 1999, sight record of a juv. in Bracken Co. (*KW* 76:5, 2000)

17) 20 Oct 2006, sight record of a juv. in Allen Co. (*KW* 83:10, 2007)

*BALD EAGLE *Haliaeetus leucocephalus*

Status: Resident; uncommon to locally fairly common during winter, rare to locally uncommon transient, rare to locally uncommon during summer. Recorded locally throughout the state; encountered chiefly on the larger lakes and rivers, but sometimes found on smaller bodies of water and occasionally observed passing overhead during migration, including at prime raptor migration lookouts in the Cumberland Mountains. Most numerous in the western portion of the state (LBL, Reelfoot Lake area, and corridors of the lower Ohio and Mississippi rivers). but at least a few eagles seem to visit or winter on all of the state's larger reservoirs every year. Formerly, (prior to about 1950), the species nested at several localities in southwestern Kentucky (Mengel:216). After a hiatus spanning more than two decades, there was an unsuccessful nesting attempt at LBL in 1974 (no eggs laid). Then, between 1987 and the early 1990s, successful nesting occurred in Ballard (three sites), Fulton, Henderson and Lyon cos. (L. Burford, unpubl. rpt.). As of 1993, at least 12 nests were active in five counties (the four noted above plus Trigg) (*KW* 69:56, 1993; L. Burford, pers. comm.). The nesting population continued to increase during the remainder of the 1990s, and as of 2001, there were 23 nesting pairs in the following counties: Ballard (5 pairs), Henderson (1), Hickman (2), Hopkins (2), Fulton (3), Lawrence (1; *KW* 76:44, 2000), Lyon (5) and Trigg (4) (L. Burford, unpubl. rpt.). Additional expansion of the nesting population has continued with the following benchmarks: nearly 50 pairs as of 2006 (Palmer-Ball, et al., *KW* 82:59-63, 2006); 84 nesting territories as of 2010 (Heyden, *KW* 86:85-89, 2010); 98 nesting territories as of 2011 (*KW* 87:113, 2011); 131 nesting territories as of 2014 (*KW* 90:88, 2014); and 151 nesting territories as of 2016 (*KW* 92:79, 2016). Typically observed singly or in pairs, but a dozen or more birds may be found together at favored wintering sites, **State Breeding Status**: Special Concern.

Maximum counts: **60+** at a roost at Duncan Lake, LBL, Lyon Co., mid- to late Dec 2017 (M. Cunningham, pers. comm.); **51** at the Long Point Unit, 25 Dec 2017 (*KW* 94:57, 2018); **47** at a roost at Ballard WMA, 2 Jan 2012 (E. Huber, eBird data); **38** at a roost at Ballard WMA, 21 Dec 2009 (*KW* 86:42, 2010).

*MISSISSIPPI KITE *Ictinia mississippiensis*

Status: Uncommon to fairly common summer resident in its limited range in southwestern Kentucky; otherwise, an extremely rare but dramatically increasing spring and summer visitant with breeding range also expanding northeast. Usually encountered in the vicinity of tracts of bottomland forest and along wooded bluffs, but in recent years has shown up regularly in suburban parks and yards with large trees. Peak of abundance occurs from early May to late Aug. Breeding not well documented; the species probably nests at scattered localities throughout the Mississippi and lower Ohio River floodplains of the Jackson Purchase. Confirmed evidence of nesting is limited to only seven counties (see below), but the species' nesting range is expanding, and it appears that many summering birds are likely nesting, especially if they are returning in successive years. Occasional birds were formerly reported outside the normal range at scattered localities across central Kentucky, usually during late spring and summer, but as of the late 2010s, vagrant birds are being reported from several locations annually. A comprehensive list of such birds is included below. Most often seen singly or in small flocks of fewer than ten birds, but larger groups of up to 15-20 or more birds are sometimes observed foraging over favored habitat in western Kentucky. **State Breeding Status**: Special Concern.

Maximum counts: **30** in a loose foraging flock over the Long Point Unit, 17 Jun 1973 (Bierly, *KW* 49:72, 1973); **30** foraging over the Long Point Unit, 15 May 2010 (*KW* 86:65, 2010); **30** at Ballard WMA, 26 Aug 2018 (*KW* 95:8, 2019); **26** in the Lower Hickman Bottoms, 30 May 2017 (*KW* 93:74, 2017); at least **25** adjacent to Ballard WMA, 31 May 2009 (*KW* 85:67, 2009); **25** at Ballard WMA, 5 Aug 2008 (eBird data); **23** at Ballard WMA, 25 Aug 2004 (*KW* 81:6, 2005); **21** over Lake No. 9, 10 Aug 2007 (*KW* 84:7, 2008); **19** in Ballard Co., 3 Aug 1990 (*KW* 67:5, 1991).

Early spring dates: 22 Apr 2019, Todd Co. (D. Hamilton, eBird data); 24 Apr 2004, w. Fulton Co. (H. Chambers/R. Denton, eBird data); 24 Apr 2009, Clarks River NWR and Ballard Co. (*KW* 85:67, 2009); 26 Apr 1989, Long Point Unit (eBird data); 26 Apr 2007, Upper Hickman Bottoms (*KW* 83:77, 2007); 26 Apr 2008, Lower Hickman Bottoms (*KW* 84:59, 2008); 26 Apr 2009, Lower Hickman Bottoms (H. Chambers, eBird data); 27 Apr 2005, Fulton and Hickman cos. (*KW* 81:84, 2005); 27 Apr 2016, Louisville (*KW* 92:58, 2016); 28 Apr 1981, Ballard Co. (*KW* 57:56, 1981); 28 Apr 2001, Fulton Co. (*KW* 77:49, 2001); 28 Apr 2011, w. Fulton Co. (*KW* 87:85, 2011); 28 Apr 2012, Long Point Unit (*KW* 88:73, 2012).

Late fall dates: 17 Oct 2009, nr. the Long Point Unit (*KW* 86:6, 2010); 22 Sep 2007, Paradise Power Plant (*KW* 84:7, 2008); 15 Sep 2008, Carlisle Co. (*KW* 85:13, 2009); 14 Sep 2000, Union Co. (*KW* 77:5, 2001); 14 Sep 2008, w. Fulton Co. (R. Denton, eBird data); 14 Sep 2013, Ballard & Fulton cos. (*KW* 90:7, 2014); 12 Sep 2004, Carlisle Co. (*KW* 81:6, 2005); 11 Sep 1990, Mississippi River, Hickman Co. (B. Palmer-Ball, eBird data); 11 Sep 1997, Lower Hickman Bottoms (B. Palmer-Ball, eBird data).

Unaccepted records: 14 Oct 1996 (*KW* 73:5, 1997 [this observation was made in Tennessee; *fide* C. Peterson, pers. comm.]); at least 50 in a loose, foraging flock nw. of Open Pond, Fulton Co., Jun 1997 (B. Palmer-Ball, notes [I cannot find the date or location of this observation, published in the previous edition of this work]); 3 Oct 2000, Fulton Co. (*KW* 77:5, 2001); 18 Apr 2016, Sauerheber Unit (*KW* 92:58, 2016).

Summary of confirmed breeding records by county (Note: presumed nesting range also includes Hickman, Marshall, and McCracken cos. in the Jackson Purchase)

Ballard (*KW* 60:52, 1984; B. Palmer-Ball, 1993 eBird data)
Carlisle (B. Palmer-Ball, 1995 eBird data)
Fayette (R. Graham et al., 2019 eBird data)
Fulton (*KBBA*:52/C. Peterson, 1987 notes; M. Evans, 1990 pers. comm.; Monroe and Palmer-Ball, *KW* 77:23-24, 2001; *KW* 79:81, 2003; *KW* 80:81, 2004)
Graves (*KW* 87:14, 2011)
Hopkins (*KW* 90:69, 2014)
Jefferson (*KW* 89:94, 2013; *KW* 90:88, 2014; *KW* 91:7/85/96, 2015; *KW* 92:58, 2016; *KW* 93:6/101, 2017)

Summary of records away from known breeding areas and western Kentucky summering range by county

Allen (*KW* 87:85, 2011; *KW* 90:69, 2014)
Barren (*KW* 89:68, 2013)
Boyle (*KW* 80:81-82, 2004)
Bullitt (*KW* 59:40, 1983; D. Striegel, 2019 eBird data)
Butler (*KW* 83:77, 2007)
Calloway (possibly breeding; initial reports have included D. Stephens/L. Potts, 2012 eBird data; H. Chambers, 2013 eBird data; M. Easley/M. Torres, 2016 eBird data; *KW* 94:77, 2018)

Christian (S. Arnold, 2019 eBird data)
Crittenden (*KW* 90:69, 2014)
Daviess (R. Rold, 2018 eBird data)
Grayson (*KW* 64:45, 1988)
Fayette (*KW* 82:7/80, 2006; *KW* 93:101, 2017; *KW* 94:77/109, 2018; m. ob., 2019 eBird data)
Hardin (*KW* 80:66, 2004; *KW* 92:6, 2016; K. Lee, 2019 eBird data)
Henderson (now annual and possibly breeding; initial reports included *KW* 78:62, 2002; *KW* 86:6, 2010)
Hopkins (now annual and breeding; initial reports included *KW* 87:85, 2011; *KW* 89:94, 2013)
Jefferson (now annual and breeding; initial reports included B. Palmer-Ball, 1996 eBird data; *KW* 79: 7, 2003; *KW* 85:67, 2009; *KW* 85:92, 2009; *KW* 86:6/65, 2010)
Jessamine (*KW* 93:101, 2017; m. ob., 2019 eBird data)
Kenton (*KW* 87:113, 2011; *KW* 90:88, 2014)
Lyon (status unclear in LBL; intial reports included *KW* 80:65, 2004; D. Doyle, 2009 eBird data)
McCreary (*KW* 87:85, 2011)
Meade (*KW* 61:44, 1985)
Muhlenberg (now annual and likely breeding; intial reports included *KW* 75:60, 1999/D. Roemer, 1999 notes; *KW* 78:62, 2002; *KW* 79:81, 2003; *KW* 80:7/65/81, 2004; *KW* 84:7/85, 2008; *KW* 85: 67, 2009; *KW* 86:92/104, 2010)
Ohio (R. Denton, 1998 eBird data; *KW* 75:60, 1999; *KW* 76:44, 2000; *NAB* 55:439, 2001; *KW* 88:73, 2012; *KW* 93:74, 2017)
Pulaski (*KW* 93:74, 2017)
Russell (*KW* 86:65, 2010)
Scott (*KW* 83:104, 2007)
Simpson (*KW* 85:77, 2009)
Trigg (status unclear in LBL; initial reports included *KW* 86:6, 2010; *KW* 90:69, 2014; *KW* 94:77, 2018)
Union (now annual and likely breeding; intial reports included B. Palmer-Ball, 2000 eBird data; *KW* 80:81, 2004; *KW* 85:92, 2009).
Warren (*KW* 54:61, 1978; *KW* 76:44, 2000; *KW* 84:59, 2008; R. Shive, 2018/2019 eBird data)
Wayne (*KW* 93:74, 2017)

*RED-SHOULDERED HAWK *Buteo lineatus*

Status: Locally rare to fairly common resident. Recorded statewide; most numerous in and near blocks of lowland forest in the western third of the state. Overall somewhat more locally distributed in central and eastern portions of the state, although not particularly rare in association with tracts of mesic forest; typically quite scarce in extensively cleared areas. Breeding locally throughout the state, chiefly in wooded bottomlands and ravines. There may be perceptible peaks of migratory movement during Mar and Oct, but few transients have been documented at the prime raptor migration lookouts in the Cumberland Mountains. It is unclear how many summer resident birds remain on territory throughout the year, but it seems that most birds present during the winter season are adults. Generally encountered singly, in pairs, or in small family groups.

Maximum counts: **18** on the Louisville CBC, 23 Dec 1950 (*KW* 27:12, 1951); **18** on the Paradise CBC, 30 Dec 2007 (*KW* 84:24, 2008); **16** on the LBL CBC, 17 Dec 1994 (*KW* 71:13, 1995); **15** on the Bernheim Forest CBC, 26 Dec 1999 (*KW* 76:15, 2000); **14** on the Calloway Co. CBC, 1 Jan 1991 (*KW* 67:15, 1991).

*BROAD-WINGED HAWK *Buteo platypterus*

Status: Fairly common transient, locally rare to fairly common summer resident. Widespread and recorded statewide in a great variety of forested and semi-open habitats during migration; quite conspicuous on favorable mid-Sep days including at prime raptor migration lookouts in the Cumberland Mountains. Peaks of abundance occur from late Apr to early May and from mid- to late Sep. Breeding statewide; abundance generally proportional to the amount of drier, upland forest present. Overall most numerous on the Cumberland Plateau, more locally distributed in central and western Kentucky; essentially absent in very open agricultural areas as a breeder. Generally seen singly or in small groups of fewer than a dozen birds, but large autumn flocks of migrants may consist of more than a hundred birds. A dark morph individual was reported at Louisville, 13 May 2010 (*KW* 86:66, 2010).

Maximum counts: **2000-3000** over Pike Co., 24 Sep 1979 (Mayfield, *KW* 56:23, 1980); **2145** over Jefferson Co., 18 Sep 2014 (*KW* 91:7, 2015); **920** over Surrey Hills Farm and **600** over Douglass Hills, Jefferson Co., 17 Sep 2014 (*KW* 91:7, 2015); one-day total of **627** counted at Pine Mt., Letcher Co., 15 Sep 2000 (*KW* 77:5, 2001); ca. **500** in three flocks in Perry Co., 17 Oct 1991 (*KW* 68:6, 1992); **687** in Bell Co. 18-20 Sep 1978 (*KW* 55:15, 1979); **545** in Bell Co., 21 Sep 1976 (*AB* 31:177, 1977); two-day count of **726** in Bell Co., 22/24 Sep 1971 (Stamm, *KW* 48:25-26, 1972); **340** in e. Jefferson Co., 21 Sep 2013 (*KW* 90:7, 2014); **200** at Ownesboro, Daviess Co., 26 Sep 2018 (*KW* 95:8, 2019).

Early spring dates: 17 Mar 1979, Glasgow (*KW* 55:47, 1979); 20 Mar 2013, Allen Co. (*KW* 89:68, 2013); 23 Mar 2011, LBL, Lyon/Trigg cos. (*KW* 87:86, 2011).

Late fall dates: 14 Nov 2013, Ft. Campbell, Trigg Co. (D. Moss, eBird data); 9 Nov 1940, south-central Kentucky (*KW* 38:9, 1962); 9 Nov 1997, Jefferson Co. (B. Palmer-Ball, eBird data).

Unaccepted records: all reports between the late fall and early spring dates given above (see Mengel: 213-214; *AB* 25:323, 1971; *AB* 38:612, 1984) and including 7 Mar 19—, eastern Kentucky (Barbour, *KW* 28:24, 1952); 23 Nov 19— (*KW* 45:49, 1969); 28 Nov 1903, (2), Logan Co. (Mengel: 213); 7 Mar 1953, south-central Kentucky (*KW* 38:9, 1962); 26 Dec 1954, Henderson Co. (*KW* 31: 11, 1955); 25 Nov 1982, Kenton Co. (*KW* 59:15, 1983); 8 Mar 1985, Boyle Co. (*KW* 61:44, 1985).

SWAINSON'S HAWK *Buteo swainsoni*

Status: Extremely rare transient. This raptor is somewhat regularly encountered in the eastern United States, and it has been documented suitably in Kentucky on four occasions.

Unaccepted record: 18 Dec 1977, an ad. in w. Henderson Co. (*KW* 54:4, 1978; R. Dodson, pers. comm.).

Chronological list of records

1) 5 May 1989, four mi. n. of Murray, Calloway Co. (*KW* 65:65, 1989)
2) 8 Apr 2006, an ad. (ph.) over the Sauerheber Unit (*KW* 82:57/67, 2006)
3) 5 May 2011, an ad. over the Natural Arch Scenic Area, McCreary Co. (R. Denton, eBird data; *KW* 90:93, 2014)
4) 1 Sep 2018, an imm. n. of Laketon, Carlisle Co. (*KW* 95:8, 2019)

*RED-TAILED HAWK *Buteo jamaicensis*

Status: Fairly common resident. Widespread throughout the state in a great variety of habitats from mature woodlands to open farmland. Breeding locally statewide; most numerous in semi-open farmland and probably scarcest in extensive areas of forest. Frequently observed perched along rural roadsides or soaring overhead; may hover while hunting on windy days like the Rough-legged Hawk. Peak of abundance occurs from early Nov to mid-Mar. Generally encountered singly or in small family groups, but optimal wintering habitat may attract loose concentrations of a dozen or more birds.

Maximum counts: **75** on the Paradise CBC, Muhlenberg/Ohio cos., 30 Dec 1995 (*KW* 72:16, 1996); **40-50** over the Sauerheber Unit, 27 Oct 2007 (*KW* 84:7, 2008); **38** in w. Fulton Co., 14 Jan 2001 (B. Palmer-Ball, eBird data).

Unaccepted record: Krider's Hawk, 12 Aug 1989 in Ohio Co. (*KW* 66:8, 1990).

Note on subspecies: Numerous records exist, mostly from western Kentucky from Nov through mid-Mar, for individuals of three distinctive western subspecies/morphs: the pale morph of *B. j. borealis* ("KRIDER'S HAWK") and the dark, intermediate and light forms of *B. j. calurus* ("WESTERN" RED-TAILED HAWK), and *B. j. harlani* (HARLAN'S HAWK). All three taxa (as well as some intergrades) appear to occur annually in semi-open to open habitats of about the western half of the state, with *B. j. calurus* seemingly the most numerous and *B. j. harlani* the rarest. Records of these three taxa have occurred from early to mid-Oct through early May. *B. j. calurus* has been reported a little more widely than *B. j. kriderii* and *B. j. harlani*, with a single record of a rufous morph *B. j. calurus* from the Cumberland Plateau (16 Jan 2000 in Boyd Co. [B. Palmer-Ball, eBird data]). A summary of western forms in the state has been previously published (Palmer-Ball and Roemer, *KW* 81:71-80, 2005). Readers should note that some researchers have recently proposed that individuals formerly (and herein) considered to be members of the western subspecies, *B. j. calurus*, may actually be individuals of a previously described subspecies, *B. j. abieticola* that breeds in nw. Canada. If true, this would change identity of individuals referred to as *B. j. calurus* above to *B. j. abieticola*.

ROUGH-LEGGED HAWK *Buteo lagopus*

Status: Irregularly rare to uncommon transient and winter resident (although has decreased in occurrence in recent years); accidental in early summer. Recorded chiefly west of the Cumberland Plateau, but there are reports from near Grayson Lake, Carter Co., 7 Dec 1977 (W. Greene, Jr., pers. comm.) and Greenup Co., 7 Jun 2005 (*KW* 81:105, 2005). Generally encountered in open to semi-open country, perched in open trees or hovering over fields. Irregular in its occurrence from year to year; present in small numbers most winters, but occasionally absent or (formerly) relatively numerous. Peak of abundance occurs from mid-Nov to mid-Mar. Generally seen singly or (formerly) occasionally in loose groups of up to a half-dozen or more birds in suitable habitat. As of 2019, this species has essentially become a rare visitant. Light morph birds are typically observed more often than dark morph birds.

Maximum counts: **33** on the Paradise CBC, Muhlenberg/Ohio cos., 1 Jan 1990 (*KW* 66:21, 1990); **30** on the Paradise CBC, 30 Dec 1995 (*KW* 72:12, 1996); **21** going to roost in Clark Co., 14 Jan 1986 (*KW* 62:27, 1986); **20** in Muhlenberg/Ohio cos., 28 Jan 1996 (B. Palmer-Ball, eBird data); up to **15** nr. Lexington, winter 1977-78 (*KW* 54:28, 1978).

Late spring dates (none have been verified with extensive details [author's latest record is 7 Apr 1992, Ohio Co.]): 21 Apr 1956, south-central Kentucky (*KW* 38:9, 1962); 21 Apr 1979, Louisville (*KW* 55:47, 1979); 20 Apr 1991, Ohio Co. (*KW* 67:54, 1991); 19 Apr 2003, Todd Co. (D. Hamilton, eBird data); 19 Apr 2009, (2) Sinclair Unit (*KW* 85:68, 2009); 18 Apr 1981, Harlan Co. (*KW* 57:56, 1981; 18 Apr 1989, Ohio Co. (*KW* 65:65, 1989); 17 Apr 1996, Fulton Co. (*KW* 72:54, 1996); 16 Apr 1981, Hickman Co. (*KW* 57:56, 1981).

Early fall dates (none well documented): 29 Sep 1960, Mammoth Cave National Park (*AFN* 15:45, 1961); 6 Oct 1979, Calloway Co. (*KW* 56:15, 1980); 5 Oct 1974, Barren Co. (*AB* 29:65, 1975); 12 Oct 1978, Louisville (*KW* 55:15, 1979).

Out-of-season record (summer): 7 Jun 2005, surface mine in e. Greenup Co. (*KW* 81: 105, 2005).

Unaccepted records (very few of the above late spring and early fall records have been well-documented, and at least some probably should be listed here): 7 May 1967, Henderson (*KW* 43:53, 1967); 7 May 1967, Mammoth Cave National Park (*KW* 43:54, 1967); 2 May 1975, two birds nr. Lexington (*AB* 29:860, 1975); 21 Aug 1950, Mammoth Cave area (*KW* 38:9, 1962).

Published error: 11 May 1995, Nicholas Co. (*KW* 71:41, 1995) (correction *fide* W. Kingsolver, pers. comm.).

FERRUGINOUS HAWK *Buteo regalis*

Status: Accidental vagrant. This raptor occurs across much of western North America. It appears infrequently in the eastern United States and has been documented satisfactorily in Kentucky on one occasion.

1) late Jan–12 May 2012, a juv. at the Greater Cincinnati Airport, Boone Co. (Crice and Monroe, *KW* 88:56-58, 2012; *KW* 88:41/50-51/74/84, 2012)

Unaccepted records: 28 Dec 1979, Henderson CBC (*AB* 34:500, 1980); and 29 Dec 1985, (2) Henderson CBC (*AB* 40:796, 1986). These records seem much more likely to have represented northwestern forms of Red-tailed Hawks or Rough-legged Hawks.

*BARN OWL *Tyto alba*

Status: Rare to uncommon (formerly fairly common) resident. Recorded statewide but largely absent from heavily forested portions of eastern Kentucky. Local and secretive, and certainly overlooked to some extent. Seemingly most numerous in semi-open to open farmland and in small rural towns, but also occurs in larger cities. Breeding currently reported from scattered localities west of the Cumberland Plateau, usually in tree cavities and buildings, although a natural cliffline nesting site was documented from along the Barren River, Barren Co., in 1994 (Palmer-Ball, *KW* 72:47-48, 1996). The species may be increasing in abundance with the following benchmarks for nesting: at least 30 territorial pairs documented during 2010 (Heyden, *KW* 86:79-85, 2010); 48 confirmed nesting locations documented during 2013 (Heyden 2014); and 76 confirmed nesting locations and 18 additional non-breeding roosting locations documented during 2016 (Slankard 2016). Seldom encountered during the daytime, when individuals roost in structures, tree cavities, and the dense foliage of trees. Seldom heard other than at or near nesting sites. Generally encountered singly, in pairs, or in small family groups. **State Breeding Status**: Special Concern.

*EASTERN SCREECH-OWL *Megascops asio*

Status: Uncommon to fairly common resident. Recorded statewide. Widespread, occurring in a variety of forested and semi-open habitats from mature woodlands and woodland borders to suburban parks and yards. Breeding statewide in tree cavities and occasionally in artificial nest boxes; most numerous in open woodlands and along woodland borders. Occasionally found during the day, when the species roosts in tree cavities and dense foliage including evergreens. Both rufous and gray morph birds occur (poorly known brown morph either absent or underreported), but one local study indicated that rufous morph birds outnumbered gray morphs by more than 3:1 (R. Brown, pers. comm.). The whinnying calls of this species are most frequently heard during summer and fall. Generally encountered singly, in pairs, or in small family groups.

Maximum count: **12** in sw. Russell Co., 14 Dec 2011 (eBird data).

*GREAT HORNED OWL *Bubo virginianus*

Status: Uncommon to fairly common resident. Recorded statewide; seemingly widespread except in the most heavily forested portions of eastern Kentucky. Inhabits a great variety of forested and semi-open habitats; most numerous in semi-open farmland, but also occurs on forested ridges and in suburban parks. Breeding statewide; generally uses old crow and raptor nests as well as tree cavities, occasionally on bridges and other man-made structures. Usually roosts in dense foliage, most frequently in evergreens where they can sometimes be found during the day. The resonant hoots of adult birds are heard most frequently from late fall through early winter; the screeched begging call of young birds is regularly encountered during spring and summer. Generally encountered singly, in pairs, or in small family groups.

Maximum count: **18** in sw. Russell Co., 14 Dec 2011 (eBird data).

SNOWY OWL *Bubo scandiacus*

Status: Extremely rare and irregular fall and winter visitant. All of the more than three dozen records are from west of the Cumberland Plateau and most are from north-central Kentucky. This partially diurnal species generally inhabits open areas, often near large man-made structures (e.g., industrial buildings, electrical line towers), but also can occur in open farmland. Individuals are usually observed during the day, perched on the open ground or on top of some sort of structure. For the most part this owl occurs in Kentucky only during irruption years when numbers of young birds move south into the United States. Three different individuals were reported in the state during the winters of 1949-50 (*AFN* 4:204, 1950; Mengel:279) and 2001-02 (Caminiti et al., *KW* 78:75-76, 2002); no fewer than six were documented during the winter of 2017-2018 (Palmer-Ball, *KW* 94:92-94, 2018).

Early fall dates: 22 Oct 1960, Erlanger (*KW* 37:2, 1961 [date apparently published incorrectly as 21 Oct in *AFN* 15:45, 1961]); 6 Nov 1937, Jefferson Co. (Brecher, *KW* 14:8-9, 1938); 10/13 Nov 1949, Boone Co. (Monroe, *KW* 26:13, 1950); 10 Nov 1987, Boone Co. (*KW* 64:18, 1988); 10 Nov 2012, (ph.) Louisville (*KW* 89:10/21/40, 2013).

Late spring dates: 8 Apr 2018, (ph.) Taylor Co. (*KW* 94:77, 2018); "Apr" 1810, Nelson Co. (Mengel: 278); 1 Apr 2002, Pendleton Co. (Caminiti et al., *KW* 78:75-76, 2002); 13 Mar 1960, Crittenden Co. (Frazer, *KW* 36:45, 1960); 8 Jan–28 Feb 1977, Louisville (Robertson, *KW* 53:40, 1977).

Unaccepted records: 12 Mar 1950, Mammoth Cave National Park (Hayes, *KW* 37:56, 1961); 13 Feb 1954, Warren Co. (Wilson, *KW* 37:18, 1961) [descriptions of both birds suggest they were Barn Owls]; mid-Dec 1989, in n. Jessamine Co. on the Lexington CBC [no details] (*KW* 66:15/39, 1990; G. Boggs, pers. comm.); 30 Nov 2017, Union Co. (*KW* 94:58, 2018; Palmer-Ball, *KW* 94:92-94, 2018); 17 Apr 2018, Bullitt Co. (Palmer-Ball, *KW* 94:92-94, 2018).

Summary of records by county

Barren (*KW* 38:14, 1962)

Boone (at least five records: Monroe, *KW* 26:13, 1950; *KW* 37:2, 1961; *KW* 64:18, 1988; [ph.] *KW* 94:58, 2018/Palmer-Ball, *KW* 94:92-94, 2018)

Boyle (Lovell, *KW* 26:29, 1950)

Crittenden (two records: Frazer, *KW* 36:45, 1960; *KW* 54:3, 1978)

Daviess (Powell, *KW* 27:64, 1951)

Franklin (S. Hardy, 1996 videotape)

Gallatin ([ph.] *KW* 94:58/64, 2018)

Grant ([ph.] Caminiti et al., *KW* 78:75-76, 2002)

Hancock (Powell, *KW* 36:55, 1960)

Henderson (four records: Mengel:278; *KW* 46:12, 1970; *KW* 53:40, 1977; [ph.] Caminiti et al., *KW* 78: 75-76, 2002; [ph.] *KW* 85:51, 2009)

Hopkins (Oct/Nov 1981, along Pennyrile Pkwy., Hopkins Co. (R. Seelhorst, pers. comm.)

Jefferson (more than 10 records: Mengel:278-279; Brecher, *KW* 14:8-9, 1938; *KW* 37:33, 1961; *KW* 40:15, 1964; *KW* 52:52, 1976/J. Unseld, 1965 pers. comm./fide A. Stamm, historical archive files; 1971 Louisville newspaper article/fide A. Stamm, historical archive files; *KW* 48:10/13, 1972; *KW* 49:13, 1973; *AB* 27:337, 1973; Robertson, *KW* 53:40, 1977; *KW* 57:37, 1981; *NAB* 55:177, 2001; [ph.] *KW* 89:10/21/40, 2013; [2 ph.] *KW* 90:12/52/60, 2014; *KW* 92:47, 2016; [ph.] *KW* 94:58, 2018)

Jessamine ([ph.] *KW* 94:58, 2018)

Kenton (*KW* 37:2, 1961)

Meade (*KW* 37:14, 1961)

Nelson (three records: Mengel:278)

Pendleton ([ph.] Caminiti et al., *KW* 78:75-76, 2002)

Scott (*KW* 65:36, 1989)

Shelby (*KW* 56:10/32, 1980)

Simpson (Mengel:278-279)

Taylor ([ph.] *KW* 94:65/77/94, 2018)

Trimble (two records: *KW* 64:29, 1988; *KW* 68:9, 1992)

Warren (two records: possibly of same bird, Wilson, *KW* 37:17-18, 1961; Funk, *KW* 37:56, 1961)

Washington (Moynahan, *KW* 31:17, 1955)

Wayne ([ph.] *KW* 92:43, 2016)

BARRED OWL *Strix varia*

Status: Uncommon to fairly common resident. Recorded statewide but occurrence varies as follows: numerous in floodplain and riparian forest habitats in western Kentucky; somewhat less wide-spread and numerous across the central part of the state, occurring in tracts of woodland and along riparian corridors but scarce in extensively cleared areas; somewhat locally distributed on the Cumberland Plateau and Mountains, occurring mostly in forested ravines. Generally found in moister forest habitats than Great Horned Owls (Mengel:279-280). Breeding statewide as just des-cribed, usually in tree cavities. Often active during the day when it is not uncommon to hear one calling or see one along a woodland border. When not hunting, typically roosts in tree cavities and dense foliage. The lively hooting calls of this species are most frequently heard during spring and summer; the young produce a raspy begging call from late spring to mid-summer. Usually seen singly or in pairs.

Maximum count: **24** in sw. Russell Co., 14 Dec 2011 (eBird data).

*LONG-EARED OWL *Asio otus*

Status: Extremely rare winter visitant or resident, extremely rare summer resident (one nesting record). Occurrence not well documented; quite secretive and probably overlooked to some extent. The species has been reported from 18 counties (see below). Peak of abundance probably occurs from mid-Nov to mid-Mar. This owl was considered a resident of the native prairies of Kentucky (see Mengel:281), but specific breeding records in the state's historical ornithological record are lacking. A relatively recent breeding record was documented in Muhlenberg Co. in 1993 (see below). This nocturnal species usually roosts in evergreen trees during the day. It is seldom heard on the wintering grounds, although oned was reportedly heard in response to tape playback in Pulaski Co. (R. Denton, 2000 eBird data). Most records involve single birds, but winter roosts may contain several or more individuals. **State Breeding Status**: Endangered.

Maximum counts: **16** at a roost in Muhlenberg Co. (Palmer-Ball, *KW* 70:42-43, 1994); **6** at a roost at the Sinclair Unit, 9 Feb 2012 (*KW* 88:48-49, 2012).
Late spring dates (other than breeding record): 13 Apr 1918, Warren Co. (*KW* 38:14, 1962); 28 Mar 1991, Central Ky WMA, Madison Co. (Ritchison and Able, *KW* 71:72-75, 1995); 23 Mar 2007, Boyle Co. (*KW* 83:82, 2007); 23 Mar 2013, [ph.] Muhlenberg Co. (*KW* 89:73, 2013).
Early fall dates: 1 Nov 1941 at Louisville (Young, *KW* 18:6, 1942); 19 Nov 1983, Nelson Co. (*KW* 60:18, 1984).
Unaccepted records: 30 Apr 1979, Louisville (*KW* 55:48, 1979); 7 Nov 2014, Henderson Co. (eBird data). Also, unspecific reports from Letcher Co. (K. Napier, late 1990s pers. comm.) and Warren Co. (D. Roemer, early 1990s pers. comm.).
Published error: (4) on the Louisville CBC, 22 Dec 1974 (*KW* 51:17, 1975; *fide* NAS CBC data).
Published error?: I can find no basis for the inclusion of Boyle Co. in the list of counties where the species had occurred as summarized in Monroe, et al. (1988) and believe it was the result of a transcription error (*fide* A. Stamm, historical archive files; W. Kemper, pers. comm.). This error predates the Boyle Co. record below.

Summary of breeding records by county

Muhlenberg: an active nest was found 10 May 1993, with successful fledging of at least one young (Palmer-Ball, *KW* 70:42-43, 1994).

Summary of records by county

Allen (*KW* 89:49, 2013; *KW* 94:28, 2018)
Boyle ([ph.] *KW* 83:82, 2007)
Crittenden (Frazer, *KW* 36:45, 1960)
Daviess (Mengel:280)
Franklin (Jones, *KW* 40:41-42, 1964; H. Jones, 1965 pers. comm./*fide* A. Stamm, historical archive files; *KW* 43:19, 1967)
Grant (*KW* 63:37, 1987)
Hardin ([ph.] *KW* 88:48/60, 2012)
Jefferson (Young, *KW* 18:6, 1942; [ph.] Brown, *KW* 58:58, 1982/*KW* 58:29, 1982; *KW* 68:24/35, 1992);
Madison (Abel and Ritchison, *KW* 71:72-75, 1995)
Muhlenberg (J. Hancock, 1970 pers. comm./*fide* A. Stamm, historical archive files; *KW* 65:72, 1989; *KW* 66:18/40, 1990; *KW* 67:31, 1991; *KW* 69:18, 1993; [ph.] Palmer-Ball, *KW* 70:42-43, 1994; *KW* 71:11/26, 1995; *KW* 73:38, 1997; *KW* 77:8, 2001; *KW* 80:11, 2004; *KW* 83:82, 2007; *KW* 86:45, 2010; [ph.] *KW* 88:48-49/77, 2012; [ph.] *KW* 89:10/49, 2013); *KW* 89:49/50/73, 2013)
Nelson (Mengel:280; *KW* 60:18, 1984)
Ohio (*KW* 65:72, 1989; *KW* 66:40, 1990; *KW* 68:9, 1992)

Owen (*KW* 67:31, 1991)
Pulaski (R. Denton, 2000 eBird data)
Shelby (H. Brown, 1984 pers. comm.; *fide* A. Stamm, historical archive files)
Union ([ph.] *KW* 89:49, 2013)
Warren (*KW* 38:14, 1962)
Woodford (*KW* 66:40, 1990)

*SHORT-EARED OWL *Asio flammeus*

Status: Rare to locally uncommon transient and winter resident, extremely rare and local summer resident. Recorded from scattered localities throughout much of the state (43 counties), but chiefly west of the Cumberland Plateau. Most frequent in open farmland and on reclaimed surface mines of central and western Kentucky, but the species has been reported irregularly from suitable habitat on the Cumberland Plateau. Nesting was documented on extensive, grassy reclaimed mines of Muhlenberg and Ohio cos. during a brief period in the late 1980s and early 1990s when habitat was optimal. Nesting is possible in similar habitat anywhere in the state, perhaps particularly following irruption years. Wilson (1923) reported the species as resident in Calloway Co., and it possibly bred occasionally in native grasslands of the western portion of the state. A few have been reported during Oct with most likely arriving by late Nov; numbers appear to linger well into Mar, and there are several Apr records of presumed tardy migrants or lingering birds. This partially diurnal owl is most often observed hunting in harrier-like fashion, low over pastures, hayfields, and other expansive grassy or weedy areas, but it is sometimes seen perched in a tree or on a fencepost, or flushed from daytime roosting spots in tall grass or weeds. It is most often observed hunting at dusk or dawn, but also can be seen occasionally during the daytime, especially when it is cloudy. Usually seen singly or hunting in loose groups of up to a dozen or more birds, and can gather in roosting groups of similar size. **State Breeding Status**: Endangered

Maximum counts: **134** on the Paradise CBC, Muhlenberg/Ohio cos., 30 Dec 1995 (*KW* 72:12, 1996); **126** at the Sinclair Unit, 4 Feb 1996 (B. Palmer-Ball, eBird data); **64** on the Paradise CBC, Muhlenberg/Ohio cos., 1 Jan 1990 (*KW* 66:18, 1990); at least **45** e. of Morganfield, Union Co., 24 Feb 2013 (*KW* 89:49, 2013); up to **35** in Ohio Co., 9-10 Dec 1989 (*KW* 66:40, 1990); **31** at the Homestead Mine, Ohio Co., 31 Dec 1988/13 Mar 1989 (*KW* 65:36/69, 1989); **30** in Ohio Co., 30 Jan 1991 (*KW* 67:31, 1991); up to **30** n. of Clintonville, Bourbon Co., early Dec 2010 (*KW* 87:63, 2011); ca. **25** in Nelson Co., 26 Jan 1999 (R. Healy, pers. comm.); **23** at Masterson Station Park, Fayette Co., 17 Feb 1980 (*KW* 56:32, 1980).

Late spring dates (other than known breeding birds): 4 May 1991, Ohio Co. (*KW* 67:56, 1991); 24 Apr 1958, Warren Co. (*KW* 38:15, 1962); 13 Apr 1975, Calloway Co. (Miller, *KW* 51:34, 1975); 12 Apr 2003, Sinclair Unit (*KW* 79:70, 2003); 11 Apr 2000, Fulton Co. (*KW* 76:46, 2000); 11 Apr 2018, Fayette Co. (*KW* 94:77, 2018); 9 Apr 1989, Livingston Co. (*KW* 65:69, 1989); 8 Apr 1982, Breathitt Co. (Allaire et al., *KW* 58:58-59, 1982).

Summer dates: 1989 nesting birds observed in Muhlenberg Co. as late as 14 Jun 1989 (Palmer-Ball and Barron, *KW* 66:77-78, 1990), and in Ohio Co. as late as 7 Aug, and 3 Sep (*KW* 66:12, 1990).

Early fall dates (other than known breeding birds): 30 Aug 1917, Ballard Co. [a summering bird?] (Mengel: 281); 5 Oct 2003, Sauerheber Unit (*KW* 80:11, 2004); 10 Oct 1940, Oldham Co. (Mengel: 281).

Unaccepted records: 31 Dec 2010, Barren Co. (3) [no details] eBird data); 15 Feb 2011, Monroe Co. (2) [no details] eBird data; *KW* 87:66, 2011).

Published error: date of 9 Oct 1986 (*KW* 63:10, 1987) should be 19 Oct 1986 (see *KW* 63:38, 1987).

Summary of breeding records by county:

Muhlenberg (Palmer-Ball and Barron, *KW* 66:77-78, 1990)
Ohio (Stamm and Clay, *KW* 65:75-76, 1989; Palmer-Ball and Barron, *KW* 66:77-78, 1990)

List of records by county (relatively high probability of being incomplete)

Adair (*KW* 90:53, 2014; *KW* 93:10/50, 2017; *KW* 94:27, 201; D. Coomer, 2017 eBird data; *KW* 95:28, 2019; m. ob., 2019 eBird data)

Allen (*KW* 87:91, 2011; *KW* 90:12/24/53, 2014; *KW* 94:24/28, 2018; R. Stoll, 2018 eBird data)
Ballard (Mengel:281; *KW* 91:10-11, 2015)
Barren (*KW* 38:15, 1962; *KW* 87:19/63/91, 2011)
Bell (*KW* 94:77, 2018)
Boone (*KW* 90:53, 2014; *KW* 92:43, 2016; M. Callan et al., 2018 eBird data)
Bourbon (*KW* 65:36, 1989; *KW* 87:63, 2011)
Boyle (*KW* 44:17, 1968; *KW* 48:11, 1972; *KW* 50:11, 1974; *KW* 55:48, 1979; *KW* 58:29, 1982; *KW* 66:40, 1990; *KW* 93:50, 2017; *KW* 94:77, 2018)
Breathitt (Allaire, et al., *KW* 58:58-59, 1982; *KW* 58:29, 1982)
Calloway (Mengel:281; Miller, *KW* 51:34, 1975)
Campbell (*KW* 72:43, 1996; *KW* 75:26, 1999)
Carroll (*KW* 72:19, 1996; *KW* 73:22, 1997; *KW* 76:20, 2000; *KW* 77:29, 2001)
Christian (*KW* 80:45, 2004)
Clark (*KW* 87:63, 2011)
Daviess (Mengel:281; *KW* 30:7, 1954; *KW* 34:11, 1958; *KW* 36:10, 1960; *KW* 65:36, 1989)
Fayette (*KW* 51:15, 1975; *KW* 53:7, 1977; *KW* 54:29/44, 1978; *KW* 56:16/32, 1980; *KW* 58:29, 1982; *KW* 61:30, 1985; *KW* 85:51, 2009; *KW* 87:19/63/91, 2011; *KW* 90:12-13/53, 2014; *KW* 91:54/73, 2015; *KW* 93:50, 2017; *KW* 94:59/77, 2018; *KW* 95:31, 2019)
Floyd (Mengel:281)
Fulton (Mengel:281; *KW* 76:46, 2000; *KW* 77:29, 2001; R. Denton, 2001 eBird data; B. Palmer-Ball, 2000 eBird data; *KW* 88:48, 2012; *KW* 90:13, 2014)
Graves (Mengel:281)
Grayson (*KW* 67:31, 1991; *KW* 87:28/63, 2011; *KW* 88:48/77, 2012; *KW* 89:10/49/73, 2013; *KW* 90: 25/53, 2014; *KW* 93:50/75, 2017; *KW* 94:11/58, 2018; *KW* 95:23, 2019)
Green (*KW* 67:31, 1991)
Hardin (*KW* 55:16, 1979; *KW* 87:63, 2011; *KW* 90:53, 2014; G. Thompson, 2016 eBird data)
Hart (*KW* 64:29, 1988; J. Sole, 2004 eBird data; J. Rose, 2018 eBird data)
Henderson (*KW* 29:10, 1953; *KW* 31:14, 1955; *KW* 55:7/30, 1979; *KW* 80:11, 2004; *KW* 82:11, 2006; *KW* 83:50, 2007; J. Brunjes, 2008 eBird data; *KW* 85:51, 2009; *KW* 88:12, 2012; *KW* 90:13/72, 2014; *KW* 91:54, 2015; *KW* 93:75, 2017; *KW* 94:77, 2018)
Hopkins (*KW* 83:50, 2007; *KW* 86:45, 2010; *KW* 89:73, 2013; *KW* 90:53, 2014; B. Carrico, 2018 eBird data)
Jefferson (numerous historical reports in Mengel:281; *KW* 54:29, 1978; *KW* 66:12/40, 1990; *KW* 72: 43, 1996; B. Yandell, 1999 eBird data; *KW* 80:11, 2004; *KW* 83:50, 2007; *KW* 87:63/91, 2011; *KW* 90:53, 2014)
Jessamine (*KW* 93:50, 2017; D. Svetich, 2018 eBird data)
Kenton (*KW* 66:12, 1990)
Larue (*KW* 65:69, 1989; *KW* 94:27, 2018)
Livingston (*KW* 65:69, 1989)
Logan (*KW* 87:63, 2011; *KW* 88:48, 2012; *KW* 90:13/23/53, 2014; *KW* 94:11, 2018; *KW* 94:11, 2018)
Madison (*KW* 71:26, 1995; *KW* 75:26, 1999; *KW* 86:70, 2010; *KW* 87:63, 2011)
Marion (*KW* 65:36, 1989)
Marshall (C. Bliznick 2018 eBird data)
Meade (*KW* 94:27, 2018; A. Melnykovych, 2017 eBird data)
Mercer (*KW* 59:29, 1983; *KW* 61:30, 1985; *KW* 92:43, 2016; *KW* 94:11, 2018; S. Penner, 2019 eBird data)
Montgomery (*KW* 65:36, 1989)
Muhlenberg (annual since late 1980s, particularly at Peabody WMA)
Nelson (Mengel:281; *KW* 55:7/10/30, 1979; S. Rogers, 1999 eBird data/R. Healy, 1999 pers. comm.; *KW* 84:45, 2008)
Nicholas (Morford, *KW* 50:30, 1974; *KW* 54:9/29, 1978; *KW* 90:53, 2014)
Oldham (Mengel:281; *KW* 87:63, 2011; *KW* 90:53, 2014; B. Palmer-Ball et al., 2018 eBird data)
Ohio (annual since late 1980s, particularly at Peabody WMA)
Owen (D. Skinner, 2004 notes and photos of remains)
Pike (*KW* 88:48, 2012; *KW* 89:10, 2013; *KW* 92:43-44, 2016)
Pulaski (*KW* 76:7/31, 2000; R. Denton, 1995/1997/2000 eBird data; *KW* 80:45, 2004; *KW* 87:63, 2011)
Rowan (Mengel:281)

Russell (D. Coomer/R. Shive, 2018 eBird data; *KW* 95:28, 2019; R. Denton, 2019 eBird data)
Scott (*KW* 89:76, 2013)
Shelby (*KW* 54:29, 1978; *KW* 61:30, 1985; *KW* 62:28, 1986; *KW* 65:36, 1989; *KW* 76:15, 2000; *KW* 87:19/63, 2011; *KW* 89:49, 2013; *KW* 90:53, 2014; *KW* 93:50, 2017)
Taylor (B. Palmer-Ball, 1999 eBird data; *KW* 76:15/31, 2000; *KW* 94:77, 2018)
Todd (S. Arnold/J. Hall, 2017 eBird data)
Trigg (*KW* 90:13, 2014)
Trimble (*KW* 61:30, 1985)
Union (*KW* 84:12, 2008; *KW* 87:19, 2011; *KW* 89:49/73, 2013; *KW* 90:72, 2014; *KW* 92:44, 2016)
Warren (*KW* 38:14-15, 1962; *KW* 73:8, 1997; *KW* 76:46, 2000; *KW* 87:63, 2011)
Wayne (*KW* 80:45, 2004; *KW* 93:50, 2017; R. Bontrager, 2017 eBird data)

NORTHERN SAW-WHET OWL *Aegolius acadicus*

Status: Extremely rare to rare fall, winter and spring visitant. There are only a few historical records of this small, secretive owl in the state, but recent tape-playback and banding efforts have demonstrated that it is certainly overlooked. It has now been recorded from 25 counties; most frequently from north-central Kentucky, but it likely occurs statewide. This small nocturnal owl roosts by day in cedars, pines and honeysuckle tangles where it can be found only with the most persistent of efforts. The species has been documented breeding on the Cumberland Plateau of eastern Tennessee, so the possibility of nesting should not be overlooked, especially following significant irruption years.

Maximum counts: **20** (ba.) in ne. Jefferson Co., 29-30 Oct 2007 (Monroe and Palmer-Ball, *KW* 84:50-52, 2008); **20** (ba.) in ne. Jefferson Co., 27-28 Oct 2012 (*KW* 89:10, 2013); **17** (ba.) in ne. Jefferson Co., 1-2 Nov 2007 (Monroe and Palmer-Ball, *KW* 84:50-52, 2008); **15** (ba.) in ne. Jefferson Co., 16-17 Nov 2011 (*KW* 88:12, 2012); **15** (ba.) in ne. Jefferson Co., 2-3 Nov 2012 (*KW* 89: 10, 2013); **8** (ba.) at Central Ky WMA, Madison Co., 16 Nov 1999 (Monroe, *KW* 76:37-39, 2000); **6** (hd.) in Pulaski Co., 1 Feb 2004 (*KW* 80:45, 2004); **4** (ba.) at Central Ky WMA, Madison Co., 15 Nov 1999 (Monroe, *KW* 76:37-39, 2000).
Late spring dates: 4 May 2018, (hd.) Pulaski Co. (*KW* 94:77, 2018); 2 Apr 2013, (hd.) Barren Co. (*KW* 89:76, 2013); 31 Mar 1982, Jefferson Co. (*KW* 58:51, 1982); 26 Mar 2000, McCreary Co. (*KW* 76:46, 2000); 18 Mar 1989, Lyon Co. (*KW* 65:69, 1989).
Early fall dates: 2 Oct 1991, Grayson Lake, Elliott Co. (*KW* 68:9, 1992); 12 Oct 1988, Perry Co. (*KW* 65:9, 1989); 17 Oct 2009, Shelby Co. (*KW* 86:11, 2010); 18 Oct 2009, Jefferson Co. (*KW* 86:11, 2010); 21 Oct 1939, Rowan Co. (Barbour, *Auk* 57:254, 1940); 21 Oct 2010, Jefferson Co. (*KW* 87:19, 2011).

Summary of records by county

Barren (*KW* 76:46, 2000; *KW* 79:12, 2003; *KW* 89:76, 2013)
Boone (*KW* 88:36, 2012)
Bracken (*KW* 89:76, 2013)
Bullitt (M. Jones, 1987 notes/pers. comm.)
Christian ([hd.] *KW* 89:49, 2013)
Elliott (*KW* 68:9, 1992)
Fayette (A. Whitt, 1979 pers. comm.; [ph.] *KW* 93:10, 2017)
Franklin ([hd.] *KW* 89:10, 2013)
Gallatin (*KW* 76:20, 2000)
Graves (Woolfenden, *KW* 66:73, 1990)
Grayson (Porter, *KW* 63:24, 1987)
Hart (*KW* 72:6, 1996; S. Kistler, 2000 notes; [hd.] *KW* 89:10, 2013; *KW* 90:13, 2014)
Hopkins (Hancock, *KW* 35:39-40, 1959)
Jefferson (*KW* 32:14, 1956; *KW* 58:51, 1982; Palmer-Ball, *KW* 61:66-67, 1985; *KW* 76:13, 2000; *KW* 78:9, 2002/M. Monroe, 2001 pers. comm.; *KW* 80:11, 2004; *KW* 81:11, 2005; *KW* 82:11, 2006; *KW* 83:15, 2007; Monroe and Palmer-Ball, *KW* 84:50-52, 2008; *KW* 84:65, 2008; *KW* 85:17, 2009; *KW* 87:19, 2011; *KW* 88:12, 2012; *KW* 89:10, 2013; *KW* 90:13, 2014; *KW* 91:11, 2015; *KW* 92:11/44, 2016; *KW* 93:10, 2017; *KW* 94:11, 2018)

Lyon (*KW* 61:17, 1985; *KW* 65:69, 1989)

Madison (Monroe, *KW* 76:37-39, 2000; *KW* 76:46, 2000; *KW* 85:51, 2009; *KW* 86:45, 2010; *KW* 86:70, 2010; [ph.] *KW* 89:49/51, 2013)

McCreary (*KW* 76:31/46, 2000; Stedman, *KW* 77:68-75, 2001; B. Yandell, 2001 notes; R. Denton, 2002 notes; *KW* 83:50, 2007)

Muhlenberg (*KW* 65:36, 1989)

Nelson (*KW* 63:10, 1987/M. Jones, notes)

Nicholas (Kingsolver, *KW* 47:45, 1971)

Pendleton (*KW* 90:13, 2014)

Perry (D. Spencer, 1978 pers. comm.; *KW* 65:9, 1989; *KW* 68:15, 1992)

Pulaski (*KW* 78:51, 2002/R. Denton, 2002 notes; *KW* 79:47, 2003; *KW* 80:45, 2004; *KW* 81:11, 2005; *KW* 84:45, 2008; *KW* 85:51, 2009; *KW* 88:48, 2012; *KW* 94:77, 2018)

Rowan (Barbour, *Auk* 57:254, 1940; Mengel:282)

Shelby (*KW* 86:11, 2010)

*BELTED KINGFISHER *Megaceryle alcyon*

Status: Uncommon to fairly common but somewhat locally distributed resident. Recorded statewide, typically at or near all kinds of bodies of water from small streams and farm ponds to the larger lakes and rivers; generally less numerous in eastern Kentucky. Breeding statewide; nesting in burrows in dirt banks, usually along streams and lake shores, but road cuts, quarry walls and other vertical banks may be used. Can be locally distributed during the breeding season when most birds are tied to nest sites. Most scarce during periods of extremely cold winter weather, when some or many individuals appear to retreat southward. Usually encountered singly or in pairs.

Maximum count: **15** at Cedar Creek Lake, Lincoln Co., 14 Aug 2013 (T. Nauman, eBird data); **11** on Lake Cumberland, Wayne Co., 9 Nov 2006 (D. Miller, eBird data).

*RED-HEADED WOODPECKER *Melanerpes erythrocephalus*

Status: Locally rare to fairly common resident, generally more widespread during the breeding season than at other times of the year. Numbers of this woodpecker within a given region often vary seasonally due to migratory movements that occur in response to changing food supplies. Recorded statewide; most numerous in the bottomland swamps and forests of western Kentucky, somewhat local and not as numerous in central Kentucky, quite local on the Cumberland Plateau and Mountains (*KBBA*:118-119). Encountered in a variety of habitats from open woodlands and along woodland borders to woodlots in open farmland and suburban parks; often occurs near water. Frequently feeds by sallying from open perches to snag flying insects during the breeding season; switches to primarily hard mast (acorns, hickory nuts, beech nuts) during winter. Breeding occurrence similar. Most widespread from late Apr to early May and from mid-Sep through Oct, when transients supplement the breeding population. Somewhat irregular in abundance during winter from year to year, typically scarce in most areas but locally abundant where a good supply of hard mast (acorns, hickory nuts, beech nuts) is present; numbers typically greatest in bottomland hardwood forests of western Kentucky where hundreds of birds winter in loose groups when hard mast food supplies are abundant.

Maximum counts: **357** on the Ballard Co. CBC [most on the Ballard WMA], 29 Dec 1984 (*KW* 61:3, 1985); **265** on the Ballard Co. CBC [most on the Ballard WMA], 23 Dec 2002 (*KW* 79:48, 2003); **125** counted in three days in LBL, Dec 1966 (Able, *KW* 43:32-33, 1967)

*RED-BELLIED WOODPECKER *Melanerpes carolinus*

Status: Fairly common to common resident. Recorded statewide, but less numerous on the Cumberland Plateau and Mountains (*KBBA*:120-121). Breeding statewide in a great variety of forested and semi-open habitats; most numerous and widespread in semi-open farmland and open woodlands, less numerous in heavily forested areas.

Maximum count: **33** in nw. Pulaski Co., 1 Jan 2003 (R. Denton, eBird data).

YELLOW-BELLIED SAPSUCKER *Sphyrapicus varius*

Status: Fairly common transient, uncommon winter resident. Recorded statewide in a variety of forested and semi-open habitats. Irregular in occurrence during winter; typically found in forested areas and present most years in small numbers across most of the state, abundance may be related at least in part to severity of weather and the supply of soft mast food supplies. Sapsuckers are never numerous, but they are conspicuous during Apr and Oct when most of the transients pass through the state.

Maximum counts: **15** at J.J. Audubon SP, Henderson Co., 1 Apr 2017 (*KW* 93:75, 2017); **11** at Otter Creek Park, Meade Co., 29 Dec 2018 (B. Woerner, eBird data); **8** at Iroquois Park, Louisville, 7 Oct 2012 (*KW* 89:11, 2013).

Late spring dates: 4 Jun 1966, Louisville area (*KW* 52:53, 1976); 30 May 19—, Rowan Co. (Barbour, *KW* 28:26, 1952); 24 May 1964, Calloway Co. (E. Larson, eBird data); 15 May 19—, Jefferson Co. (*KW* 52:53, 1976; Mengel:299); 15 May 2019, Sauerheber Unit (P. Blair, eBird data).

Early fall dates: 23 Aug 2011, Lexington (*KW* 88:13, 2012); 2 Sep 2014, Warren Co. (*KW* 91:11, 2015); 12 Sep 2010, Sauerheber Unit (*KW* 87:19, 2011); 13 Sep 2017, Louisville (*KW* 94:11, 2018); 15 Sep 1977, Boone Co. (L. McNeely, notes); 16 Sep 2000, Boone Co. (*KW* 77:8, 2001); 17 Sep 2017, Bernheim Forest (S. Dickman, eBird data); 18 Sep 2010, e. Jefferson Co. (*KW* 87:19, 2011).

Unaccepted records: summer 1944, Black Mt. (Breiding, *KW* 23:38, 1947; see Mengel: 299); 28 Aug 1996, Jefferson Co. (*KW* 73:8, 1997 [no details available]).

Published error?: based on a review of a number of sources, I believe (but am not certain) that the early fall date of 12 Sep [1976] published in Monroe, et al. (1988) is erroneous, the result of a transcription error (*fide* A. Stamm, historical archive files); also, Mengel (p. 299) attributes a late spring record of 17 May 1922 in Warren Co. to G. Wilson, but Wilson does not include the record in his own summary (*KW* 38:15, 1962).

*DOWNY WOODPECKER *Picoides pubescens*

Status: Fairly commmon to common resident. Recorded statewide. Breeding statewide in a great variety of forested and semi-open habitats from mature woodlands and suburban yards to successional woodlots and woodland edges. Typically the most frequent woodpecker at feeding stations.

Maximum count: **29** at West Ky WMA, McCracken Co., 30 Dec 2013 (D. Akers, eBird data).

ᵉRED-COCKADED WOODPECKER *Picoides borealis*

Status: Extirpated. Formerly an extremely rare and local resident. During the first half of the 20th century, this species was not considered particularly rare, occurring in a narrow band of mixed pine-oak forest along the western edge of the Cumberland Plateau (extending locally north to Wolfe and Powell cos. in the Red River Gorge area). However, it appears that harvesting of mature pine during the latter part of the century triggered a decline that continued into the late 1990s. Between 1995 and 2000, small numbers of birds from the southern Coastal Plain were released into parts of the Daniel Boone National Forest in Laurel, McCreary, and Whitley cos. in hopes of bolstering the population. However, a catastrophic infestation of southern pine bark beetles in 2000 decimated the species' habitat, and all remaining birds were relocated to South Carolina and Arkansas in Apr 2001 (K. Feltner, pers. comm.). Immediately prior to disappearing, these woodpeckers were recorded from only a few locations in the southern counties of the western Cumberland Plateau on the National Forest. Generally the species had been associated with mature pine or mixed pine-hardwood forest. This habitat type will continue to be managed for, and birds may be reintroduced into the area in the latter half of the 21st century. There were two records of vagrant (?) birds from similar habitat in Edmonson Co. (Mengel:307; Wilson, *KW* 37:8, 1961; *KW* 38:15, 1962). Most recently encountered singly or in small family groups, although flocks of up to 12-15 birds were reported during the early 1950s (Mengel:307). **Federal Status**: Endangered.

*HAIRY WOODPECKER *Picoides villosus*

Status: Uncommon to fairly common resident. Recorded statewide; most numerous in heavily forested areas, least numerous in the Inner Blue Grass (*KBBA*:124-125). Breeding statewide, mostly in blocks of mature forest. Generally much less numerous than the Downy Woodpecker.

Maximum count: **11** at West Ky WMA, McCracken Co., 30 Dec 2013 (D. Akers, eBird data).

*NORTHERN FLICKER *Colaptes auratus*

Status: Fairly common resident. Fairly widely distributed, although abundance in any given region may vary seasonally due to migratory movements. Recorded statewide, but noticeably less common on the Cumberland Plateau and Mountains. Occurs in a great variety of semi-open to open habitats from open woodlands and farmland to suburban parks and yards. Unlike other woodpeckers, frequently forages on the ground. Perceptable peaks of abundance occur during Apr and from mid-Oct to mid-Nov as migrants pass through. Breeding statewide, often nesting in mature woodlands but preferring to feed in more open areas (*KBBA*:128-129). Generally seen singly or in flocks of up to about ten birds, but larger groups of up to 20 or more individuals are occasionally observed outside of the breeding season.

Maximum count: **100+** in a pasture in Bell Co., 8 Apr 1969 (R. Harm, notes); **30** in a single field in ne. Jefferson Co., 6 Apr 2019 (B. Palmer-Ball, eBird data).

*PILEATED WOODPECKER *Dryocopus pileatus*

Status: Uncommon to fairly common resident. Recorded statewide in a variety of forested habitats; not infrequent in suburban parks and yards with large trees. Breeding statewide, usually in mature forest. Abundance is generally proportional to the amount of mature forest habitat. Generally seen singly, in pairs, or in small family groups.

Maximum counts: **28** at Mammoth Cave, 1 Jun 2004 (S. Kistler, eBird data); **28** at Mammoth Cave, 6 Jun 2009 (S. Kistler, eBird data); **27** at Mammoth Cave, 29 May 2007 (S. Kistler, eBird data).

eIVORY-BILLED WOODPECKER *Campephilus principalis*

Status: Extinct. Not recorded in Kentucky since the latter half of the 19th century, but formerly a resident along the Mississippi and lower Ohio rivers (Mengel: 308). The latest report of the species in the state may have been from the early 1870s in Fulton County (Mengel:308). Unfortunately, it appears that no substantive evidence of the species' occurrence in Kentucky (photograph or specimen) remains extant. **Federal Status**: Endangered.

*AMERICAN KESTREL *Falco sparverius*

Status: Uncommon to fairly common resident. Widespread and recorded statewide throughout the year except in heavily forested portions of eastern Kentucky. Seemingly more numerous during the non-breeding season when transients from farther north supplement the breeding population. Encountered in a great variety of open and semi-open habitats; also observed in small numbers at raptor migration lookouts including those in the Cumberland Mountains. Peak of abundance occurs from late Sep to mid-Mar. Breeding statewide; nests in cavities, usually in rural farmland but also in cities and towns. Generally seen singly or in family groups, most frequently on wires and bare trees, often along highways.

Maximum counts: a loose group of ca. **35** at the Louisville landfill, 16 Jul 2009 (*KW* 85:92, 2009); **36** in w. Wayne Co., 5 Jan 2019 (R. Bontrager, eBird data).

MERLIN *Falco columbarius*

Status: Transient; rare during spring andrare to uncommon during fall; rare winter resident (although has increased in recent years); accidental during summer. Recorded statewide; occurs most regularly in central and western Kentucky. Seldom encountered in the heavily forested portions of eastern Kentucky, but occasionally observed during fall, especially at the prime raptor migration lookouts in the Cumberland Mountains. Encountered in a variety of open and semi-open habitats from open farmland and reclaimed surface mines to suburban parks and cemeteries. Peaks of abundance occur during Apr and from mid-Sep to late Oct. Formerly known primarily as a migrant; however over the course of the past twenty years the species has increased in occurrence, especially during winter, and now appears to regularly winter. Most records are of single birds.

Note on subspecies: most individuals are of the taiga race, *F. c. columbarius*, but the prairie race, *F. c. richardsonii*, is occasionally seen (e.g., *KW* 82:47, 2006; *KW* 84:60, 2008).

Maximum counts: **6** at the Riverqueen Unit Peabody WMA, Muhlenberg Co., 5 Feb 2006 (*KW* 82:47, 2006); **5** over Pine Mt. nr. Oven Fork, Letcher Co., 30 Sep 2011 (*KW* 88:7, 2012); **5** at the Riverqueen Unit Peabody WMA, Muhlenberg Co., 13 Jan 2001 (B. Palmer-Ball, eBird data).

Late spring dates: 13 May 2006, Mason Co. (K. Schwarz, eBird data); 13 May 2018, (ph.) Freeman Lake (*KW* 94:78, 2018); 11 May 2000, Peabody WMA, Muhlenberg Co. (*KW* 76:44, 2000; D. Roemer, notes); 10 May 1951, south-central Kentucky (*KW* 38:11, 1962); 10 May 1997, Warren Co. (D. Roemer, notes).

Early fall dates: 8 Aug 2013, (2) at Bowling Green (*KW* 90:13, 2014); 15 Aug 1955, south-central Kentucky (*KW* 38:11, 1962); 15 Aug 2008, Jefferson Co. (*KW* 85:13, 2009); 16 Aug 2009, Jefferson Co. (*KW* 86:7, 2010); 26 Aug 2015, (ph.) at Louisville (*KW* 92:11, 2016).

Out-of-season records (summer): 17 Jul 2010, McElroy Lake (*KW* 86:92, 2010); 24 Jul 2010, Morgan Pond, Christian Co. (*KW* 86:92, 2010).

Unaccepted records: 26 May 1991, Ohio Co. (eBird data); 2 Jun 2017, Scott Co. (eBird data).

Published error: former early spring date of 13 Mar [1876] (*KW* 45:49, 1969) pertains to Ohio (*fide* Mengel:221).

*PEREGRINE FALCON *Falco peregrinus*

Status: Rare to uncommon (formerly rare) transient, rare winter visitant/resident, extremely rare summer resident. Recorded statewide; usually encountered in open country, often near water where shorebirds and/or waterfowl are concentrated, but regularly observed in heavily forested areas, especially at the prime raptor migration lookouts in the Cumberland Mountains. Peaks of abundance occur from mid-Apr to early May and from mid-Sep to late Oct. Formerly (into first half of the 20th century) bred very locally along rocky cliffs in the southern Cumberland Plateau region (Mengel:220). During the 1990s, the Ky. Dept. of Fish and Wildlife Resources oversaw a reintroduction program that involved the release of hacked young at several central Kentucky locations (L. Burford, unpubl. rpt.). In part as a result of this and similar programs in some Midwestern states, the species has become reestablished as a nester in Kentucky. A pair commenced nesting in Louisville during the mid-1990s (G. Michael, pers. comm./L. Burford, unpubl. rpt.), and as of 2004, five pairs were nesting along the Ohio River in Carroll, Greenup, Jefferson and Trimble (two) cos. (*KW* 80:82, 2004; Dzialak, et al., *KW* 81:39-46, 2005). In subsequent years the nesting population slowly expanded then has perhaps leveled off as optimal habitat has become fully occupied. Most pairs have set up territories at power plants and on bridges along the Ohio River corridor, but two nesting sites have now been documented along the Kentucky River corridor in Franklin and Mercer cos. The latter is situated on a natural cliffline along the Dix River (*KW* 91:73, 2015; *KW* 93:75/81/101, 2017; location of nest site variously published erroneously at *KW* 91:86, 2015 & *KW* 93:75/81/201, 2017 [correct location *fide* T. Nauman, pers. comm.]). Monitoring of the nesting population has documented the following benchmarks in recent years: eight pairs as of 2006 (*KW* 82:67/80-81, 2006; Smith et al. *KW* 83:4-6, 2007; *KW* 83:78/104, 2007); nine pairs as of 2008 (*KW* 84:86, 2008); 11 pairs as of 2009 (*KW* 85:92, 2009); 13 pairs as of 2010 with new pairs in Franklin Co. and Pendleton Co. (*KW* 86:66/92, 2010); 10 territories documented during 2013 (Arnold and Heyden 2013); 14 pairs documented during 2016 (Taylor 2016; *KW* 92:80, 2016); and 17 pairs documented during 2018 (Taylor and Slankard, *KW* 95:38, 2019). The most recent territory to be documented was at Ky Dam (J. Johnson, 2018 pers. comm.). Locally breeding birds appear to remain resident throughout the year. Tyically seen singly as transients. **State Breeding Status**: Endangered.

Maximum count (non-breeding birds): at least **3 and possibly 6** at McElroy Lake, 9 May 2008 (*KW* 84:60, 2008).

Summary of confirmed nesting records by county (initial references)

Boone (*KW* 84:86, 2008)
Campbell (*KW* 82:81, 2006; Smith et al. *KW* 83:4-6, 2007)
Carroll (S. Vorisek, 2002 unpubl. rpt.)
Fayette (Taylor 2016)
Franklin (*KW* 86:66, 2010)
Greenup (S. Vorisek, 2002 unpubl. rpt.)
Jefferson (three pairs; [G. Michael, mid-1990s pers. comm. & *KW* 82:81, 2006; Smith et al. *KW* 83:4-6, 2007 & Taylor 2016; *KW* 92:80, 2016])
Marshall (J. Johnson, 2018 pers. comm.)
Mason (*KW* 82:81, 2006; Smith et al. *KW* 83:4-6, 2007)
Mercer (*KW* 93:75/81/101, 2017 [erroneously published as in Garrard Co. therein])
Meade (*KW* 82:81, 2006 Smith et al. *KW* 83:4-6, 2007)
Pendleton (*KW* 86:92, 2010)
Trimble (S. Vorisek, 2002 unpubl. rpt.)

PRAIRIE FALCON *Falco mexicanus*

Status: Extremely rare winter visitant. Recovery of this species during the post-DDT era, along with an increased level of deforestation along the Mississippi Valley may be responsible for its recent appearance in the state. It has now been suitably documented in Kentucky on at least nine occasions.

Early fall date: 12 Nov 1988, Ohio Co. (Monroe and Monroe, *KW* 65:78-79, 1989).
Late spring date: 27 Mar 1989, Ohio Co. (*KW* 65:65, 1989).
Unaccepted records: 17 Mar 2002, Lower Hickman Bottoms (*KW* 78:49, 2002; see *KW* 92:89, 2016); 28 Aug 2002, Fulton Co. (*KW* 79:7, 2003; see *KW* 92:89, 2016); an unpublished report was also included by Stedman (2019) in Barren Co., apparently during 2012 or 2013.

Chronological list of records

1) a single bird (possibly the same individual) was observed almost every winter from 1988-89 to the mid-1990s on an expansive surface-mined area in southern Ohio Co. nr. Cool Springs. It was reported no fewer than a dozen times (*KW* 67:13/30, 1991; *KW* 69:12/18/34, 1993; *KW* 70:34, 1994; *KW* 71:11, 1995) and was photographed on 28 Jan 1989 (Monroe and Monroe, *KW* 65:78-79, 1989)
2) 18 Dec 1989, (possibly 2) at Munfordville, Hart Co. (Kistler, *KW* 66:28, 1990)
3) 2 Jan 1990, in rural farmland nr. Burgin, Boyle Co. (*KW* 66:26/38 1990)
4) 16 Dec 1997, over the Long Point Unit (*KW* 74:33, 1998)
5) 8 Feb 2001, ad. in western Muhlenberg Co. (*NAB* 55:176, 2001)
6) 4 Dec 2001-9 Feb 2002, a juv. (vt.) in w. Fulton Co. (*KW* 78:33, 2002; D. Roemer/B. Yandell, notes)
7) 15 Feb 2002, ad. (ph.) at the Sinclair Unit (M. Monroe/M. Vukovich, notes)
8) 11 Dec 2013–11 Jan 2014, (ph.) in ne. Hopkins Co. (*KW* 90:50/53, 2014)
9) 3 Dec 2014, (ph.) in ne. Hopkins Co. (*KW* 91:54, 2015)

[e/s]CAROLINA PARAKEET *Conuropsis carolinensis*

Status: Extinct. This parakeet apparently was once a common resident in the Ohio Valley and an undetermined portion of the state, disappearing by the 1860s or 1870s (Mengel:269-271). Unfortunately, it appears that no specimen from Kentucky remains extant.

ASH-THROATED FLYCATCHER *Myiarchus cinerascens*

Status: Accidental vagrant. This inhabitant of the southwestern United States and Mexico is regularly recorded in the eastern United States. It has been documented in Kentucky twice.

Chronological list of records

1) 15 Oct 2000, Bowling Green (Elmore, *KW* 79:74-75, 2003
2) 8-10 Dec 2017, (ph.) Dale Hollow Lake State Resort Park, Cumberland Co. (*KW* 94:41/59, 2018; J. Sole, et al., eBird data)

*GREAT CRESTED FLYCATCHER *Myiarchus crinitus*

Status: Fairly common transient and summer resident. Recorded statewide during migration in a variety of forested and semi-open habitats from mature woodlands and woodland borders to suburban parks and yards. Peak of abundance occurs from late Apr to early Sep. Breeding statewide but somewhat locally distributed in heavily forested portions of eastern Kentucky, apparently due to a preference for the presence of some open structure to the forest. Occurs in a variety of forest types, but most common in xeric upland and mesic bottomland habitats, both of which often offer an open mid-story for foraging. Nests in tree cavities and occasionally in artificial nest boxes.

Maximum count: **36** in Henderson Co., 27 May 2015 (J. Meredig, eBird data).
Early spring dates: 31 Mar 1934, south-central Kentucky (*KW* 38:15, 1962); 3 Apr 2012, Boone Co. (*KW* 88:78, 2012); 6 Apr 1991, Hopkins Co. (*KW* 67:57, 1991).
Late fall dates: 16 Oct 2011 (heard), Louisville (*KW* 88:14, 2012); 13 Oct 2018, Larue Co. (*KW* 95:8, 2019); 4 Oct 19—, Hardin Co. (R. Healy, pers. comm.); 4 Oct 2009 (heard), Adair Co. (*KW* 86:12, 2010); 1 Oct 1933, south-central Kentucky (*KW* 38:15, 1962).
Unaccepted records: 19 Mar 1986, Grayson Co. (*KW* 62:45, 1986); 20 Mar 1996, Hopkins Co. (*KW* 72:56, 1996); 15 Oct 2002, *Myiarchus* sp. in Trigg Co. (*KW* 79:13, 2003); 12 Oct 2014, Greenup Co. (eBird data); 10 Oct 2018, Carter Co. (eBird data).

WESTERN KINGBIRD *Tyrannus verticalis*

Status: Extremely rare spring, summer, and fall visitant. This widespread species of western North America is a regular visitor to the eastern United States. It has nested in west Tennessee, southern Illinois, and southwest Indiana, so the possibility of nesting in western Kentucky should not be overlooked. There are at least nine records (two during spring, two during summer, and five during fall).

Unaccepted records: 21 Oct 2002, Hickman, Fulton Co. (*KW* 79:13, 2003; see *KW* 92:89, 2016); 7 Aug 2008, 2 (nesting pair in adjacent Illinois) along the Ohio River, McCracken Co. (*KW* 85:18, 2009; see *KW* 93:107, 2017).

Chronological list of records

1) 16 Sep 1966, nr. Golden Pond, Trigg Co., LBL (*AFN* 21:45, 1967)
2) 6 Oct 1966, nr. Golden Pond, Trigg Co., in LBL (perhaps different individual than above) (*AFN* 21:45, 1967)
3) 23 Jun 1978, Surrey Hills Farm, Jefferson Co. (Palmer-Ball, *KW* 56:38, 1980)
4) 30-31 Aug 1997, nr. Lake No. 9 (*KW* 74:27/35, 1998 [date erroneiously published as 30-31 Sep in *KW* 74:8, 1998])
5) 9-11 Jun 2008, (ph.) at the Melco Flood Retention Basin, Jefferson Co. (*KW* 84:81/88/100, 2008)
6) 13 Aug 2008, (ph.) s. of Smithland, Livingston Co. (*KW* 85:18, 2009)
7) 9 May 2009, (ph.) s. of Rabbit Hash, Boone Co. (*KW* 85:71/73, 2009)
8) 22 Apr 2010, (ph.) nr. Maynard, Allen Co. (*KW* 86:70/76, 2010)
9) 3 Oct 2011, n. of Dot, Logan Co. (*KW* 88:14, 2012)

*EASTERN KINGBIRD *Tyrannus tyrannus*

Status: Locally uncommon to common transient and summer resident. Recorded statewide during migration in a variety of semi-open to open habitats from woodland borders and lakeshores to suburban parks and open farmland. Peak of abundance occurs from mid-Apr to mid-Aug. Breeding statewide in semi-open to open habitats including parks, the margins of lakes, and residential areas; most numerous in open to semi-open farmland, quite scarce in heavily forested areas. Generally observed singly or in pairs, but occasionally seen during migration in loose flocks of 20 or more birds.

Maximum counts: **550** along the Mississippi River, Hickman Co., 3 Sep 2018 (A. Lydeard/D. Redwine, eBird data [not validated therein]); ca. **100** nr. Dranes Lake, Hardin Co., 3 Aug 2018 (*KW* 95:8, 2019); "**dozens**" along the Mississippi River, Fulton Co., 22 May 1993 (B. Palmer-Ball, eBird data); **57** in a loose flock on Lake Cumberland, Pulaski Co., 24 Aug 2012 (*KW* 89:11, 2013); **71** in e. Calloway Co., 9 May 2009 (H. Chambers, pers. comm.); loose flock of **45** in w. Henderson Co., 6 May 2007 (*KW* 83:82, 2007); loose flock of **25** in Trimble Co., 8-9 May 1984 (*KW* 60:44, 1984).

Early spring dates: 23 Mar 1987, Louisville (*KW* 63:51, 1987); 27 Mar 2015, Hart Co. (*KW* 91:74, 2015); 2 Apr 1954, south-central Kentucky (*KW* 38:15, 1962).

Late fall dates: 27 Nov 1977, Louisville (*AB* 32:213, 1978); 13 Nov 1990, Pulaski Co. (*KW* 67:8, 1991); 7 Nov 1965, LBL, Trigg Co. (Gray, *KW* 42:18-19, 1966; W. Gray, pers. comm. [date published incorrectly as 8 Nov in *KW* 42:18-19, 1966; date published incorrectly as 7-8 Nov in *KW* 45: 51, 1969; location published incorrectly as from Louisville in *AFN* 20:54, 1966; location erroneously published as at Ky Dam Village State Park in Monroe, et al. (1988)]); 30 Oct 2016, Barren Co. (*KW* 93:11, 2017); 13 Oct 1988, Louisville (*KW* 65:9, 1989); early Oct 2012, Louisville airport (M. Autin, pers. comm.); 5 Oct 2002, Logan Co. (*KW* 79:13, 2003); 3 Oct 2016, Jefferson Co. (*KW* 93:11, 2017); 30 Sep 2001, LBL, Trigg Co. (*KW* 77:64, 2001; S. Marsh/V. Brown, notes); 30 Sep 2006, Greenup Co. (*KW* 83:16, 2007); 29 Sep 19—, Danville (Mengel: 309); 29 Sep 1962, Louisville area (*KW* 52:53, 1976); 29 Sep 1991, Bell Co. (*KW* 68:9, 1992); 29 Sep 2016, (ph.) Kenton Co. (*KW* 93: 11, 2017).

Unaccepted record: 9 Mar 2016, Hardin Co. (eBird data).

*GRAY KINGBIRD *Tyrannus dominicensis*

Status: Accidental vagrant. This inhabitant of the Gulf Coast and Caribbean only occasionally turns up north of its traditional range. It has been documented in Kentucky on one occasion.

1) 24-26 Apr 2011, (ph.) sw. of Rabbit Hash, Boone Co. (McNeely, *KW* 87:120-121, 2011; *KW* 87:92/101/124)

*SCISSOR-TAILED FLYCATCHER *Tyrannus forficatus*

Status: Extremely rare spring, summer, and fall visitant, extremely rare summer resident (several recent nesting records). Prior to the early 2000s, there were fewer than ten records in the state; however, since the summer of 2002 there has been sporadic nesting at a few widely separated locales across the western third of the state. Away from the few known nesting territories, there have now been a few dozen additional records of vagrants (all of single birds unless otherwise noted below).

Early spring dates: 2 Apr 2007, Lyon Co. (*KW* 83:82, 2007); 12 Apr 2008, Lyon Co. (*KW* 84:68 2008).

Late fall dates: 11 Oct 2002, Lyon Co. (*KW* 79:13, 2003); 1 Oct 2006, Lyon Co. (*KW* 83:16, 2007); 25 Sep 2011, (ph.) Logan Co. (*KW* 88:14, 2012); 22 Sep 2011, (ph.) Upper Hickman Bottoms (*KW* 88:14, 2012); 16 Sep 2005, Lyon Co. (*KW* 82:12, 2006).

Unaccepted records: 27 Aug 1924, Versailles, Woodford Co. (Pindar, *WB* 37:41, 1925; see Mengel:518); and 6 Aug 1967, (2) at Fort Knox, Hardin Co., see Monroe (*KW* 52:3, 1976).

Summary of breeding records by county

Daviess (2014 [*KW* 90:85/89-90, 2014])

Livingston (2002-2008 [*KW* 78:65, 2002; *KW* 79:13/71/83, 2003; *KW* 80:69/84, 2004; *KW* 81:89/108, 2005; *KW* 82:12/71/82-83, 2006; *KW* 83:106, 2007; *KW* 84:68/88, 2008])

Lyon (2002-2006 [*KW* 78:65, 2002; *KW* 79:13/71, 2003; *KW* 80:69, 2004; *KW* 82:12/71/82-83, 2006; *KW* 83:16, 2007])

Webster (2013 [*KW* 89;89/97, 2013; *KW* 90:14/40, 2014])

Tally of records by county

Adair, Allen, Ballard (2), Bourbon (2), Calloway (3), Carter, Casey, Christian (6), Daviess (2), Franklin (2), Fulton (6), Hardin, Henderson, Livingston (2 + multiple nesting), Logan (2), Lyon (multiple nesting), Muhlenberg, Russell, Shelby (2), Trigg (4), Warren (2), Webster

Chronological list of records away from confirmed nesting territories by county

1) spring 1963, 5 miles west of Owensboro, Daviess Co. (Ford, *KW* 42:31, 1966)
2) 2 May 1966, nr. Forks of Elkhorn, Franklin Co. (Jones, *KW* 42:30-31, 1966)
3) 4 Jun 1977, at Ballard WMA (*AB* 31:1150, 1977)
4) 20 Jun 1983, (ph.) nr. Burna, Livingston Co. (Palmer-Ball, *KW* 59:59-60, 1983 [date erroneously published as 19 Jun therein; *fide* B. Palmer-Ball, eBird data])
5) 27-30 Apr 1992, (ph.) at Grayson Lake headquarters, Carter Co. (*KW* 68:47, 1992; *KW* 69:23, 1993)
6) late 1990s, [an individual seen two or three summers in a row] WKU Farm, Warren Co. (W. Tamminga, pers. comm.)
7) 25 May 1999, Long Point Unit (J. Asher, pers. comm.)
8) 4 Jul 1999, (2) nr. Lake No. 9 (*NAB* 53:394, 1999; J. Wilson, notes)
9) 30 Jun 2001, at Fort Campbell, Christian Co. (*NAB* 55:440, 2001)
10) 18 Jun 2002, LBL, Trigg Co. (*KW* 78:65, 2002; A. Whited, pers. comm.)
11) 19 Jun 2002, (ph.) nr. Bagdad, Shelby Co. (*KW* 78:65, 2002)
12) 27 Apr–31 May 2003, 1-2 birds in ne. Bourbon Co. [apparently members of a pair that had been present at the location since 1999 (*KW* 79:71, 2003; S. Watkins, pers. comm.)]
13) 11 May 2003, (ph.) at the Long Point Unit (*KW* 79:71, 2003; J. Wilson, eBird data)
14) 21 May 2003, (ph.) Sinclair Unit (*KW* 79:71, 2003)
15) 21 May 2004, Murray, Calloway Co.(*KW* 80:69, 2004)
16) 3 Aug/3 Sep 2004, Ft. Campbell, Christian Co. (*KW* 81:12, 2005)
17) 20 May 2005, Ft. Campbell, Christian Co. (*KW* 81:89, 2005)
18) 28 May 2005, nr. Newstead, Christian Co. (*KW* 81:89, 2005)
19) 19 Apr 2006, nw. Bourbon Co. (*KW* 82:71, 2006)
20) 25 May 2006, LBL, Trigg Co. (eBird data)
21) 1 Jun 2008, Morgan Pond (*KW* 84:88, 2008)
22) 26 Apr 2009, w. Fulton Co. (*KW* 85:73, 2009)
23) 20 May 2009, e. Shelby Co. (*KW* 85:73, 2009)
24) 26 Jun 2010, sw. of Hebbardsville, Henderson Co. (*KW* 86:95, 2010)
25) 9-16 Aug 2011, 2 (ph.) s. of Smith's Grove, Warren Co. (*KW* 88:14/40, 2012)
26) 22 Sep 2011, (ph.) Upper Hickman Bottoms (*KW* 88:14, 2012)
27) 25 Sep 2011, (ph.) e. of Auburn, Logan Co. (*KW* 88:14, 2012)
28) 21 Sep 2012, nr. Barren River Lake, Allen Co. (*KW* 89:12, 2013)
29) 22 Apr 2014, (ph.) LBL, Trigg Co. (*KW* 90:73, 2014)
30) 4 May 2014, e. Calloway Co. (*KW* 90:73, 2014)
31) 4 Jun 2015, Ft. Campbell, Christian Co. (D. Moss, eBird data)
32) 15-25 May 2016, (ph.) along Luttrell Creek w. of Dunnville, Adair/Casey/Russell cos. (*KW* 92:65, 2016)
33) 24 May 2016, (ph.) s. of Coldwater, Calloway Co. (*KW* 92:63/65, 2016)
34) 27 May 2016, Ballard WMA (*KW* 92:65, 2016)
35) 21 May 2017, (ph.) Lower Hickman Bottoms (*KW* 93:76, 2017)
36) 28 May 2017, Frankfort (*KW* 93:76, 2017)
37) 2-3 Jun 2017, (ph.) nr. Elizabethtown, Hardin Co. (*KW* 93:101, 2017)
38) 21 Jul–8 Aug 2017, (ph.) nr. Cerulean, Christian Co. (*KW* 93:101, 2017; *KW* 94:12, 2018)
39) 23-26 Jun 2018, nr. Auburn, Logan Co. (*KW* 94:109, 2018)

OLIVE-SIDED FLYCATCHER *Contopus cooperi*

Status: Uncommon transient, extremely rare summer visitant. Recorded statewide in a variety of forested and semi-open habitats including mature woodland borders, forested wetlands and, suburban parks. Peaks of abundance occur from mid- to late May and from late Aug to mid-Sep. Generally seems to be a bit easier to find the farther west one goes in the state. This species is almost always found perched at or near the top of dead snags, sallying out for winged prey, sometimes utilizing the same perch for long periods.

Early spring dates: 18 Apr 2018, Adair Co. (*KW* 94:78, 2018); 24 Apr 1961, Louisville (*KW* 40:54, 1964); 24 Apr 1964, Louisville (Horner, *KW* 40:54, 1964).

Late spring dates: 7 Jun 2017, (ph.) Kentucky Bend, Fulton Co. (*KW* 93:101/102, 2017); 5 Jun 2004, Mammoth Cave National Park (*KW* 80:84, 2004); 4 Jun 1994, Hardin Co. (B. Palmer-Ball, eBird data); 3 Jun 1967, Hickman Co. (Univ. of Louisville collection; K. Able, notes; *KW* 45:52, 1969).

Early fall dates: 2 Aug 2017, (ph.) Warren Co. (*KW* 94:11, 2018); 7 Aug 2005, w. Fulton Co. (*KW* 82:12, 2006); 7 Aug 2009, Fulton Co. (*KW* 86:12, 2010); 12 Aug 1990, Christian Co. (*KW* 67:8, 1991); 14 Aug 1952, Laurel Co. (Mengel:317); 14 Aug 2015, Jefferson Co. (*KW* 92:11, 2016); 15 Aug 1952, Black Mt., Harlan Co. (Mengel:317); 15 Aug 1974, Louisville (*KW* 52:54, 1976; D. McConnell, pers. comm.); 15 Aug 2012, Trigg Co. (*KW* 89:11, 2013).

Late fall dates: 12 Oct 2011, Louisville (*KW* 88:13, 2012); 11 Oct 1973, Louisville area (*KW* 52:54, 1976).

Out-of-season records (summer): 7 Jul 1979, Laurel Co. (Larson, *KW* 55:67, 1979); 24 Jul 1998, Warren Co. (*KW* 74:73, 1998).

Unaccepted records: 11 Oct 2011, Bullitt Co. (eBird data); 19 Jun 2012, (heard only) McCracken Co. (*KW* 88:95, 2012).

*EASTERN WOOD-PEWEE *Contopus virens*

Status: Fairly common to common transient and summer resident. Recorded statewide during migration in a great variety of forested and semi-open habitats from mature woodlands and woodland borders to suburban parks and yards. Peak of abundance occurs from early May to late Sep. Breeding statewide except the more mesic portions of the Cumberland Plateau (Mengel:317; *KBBA*:132-133), usually in mature deciduous trees. This species is seldom numerous, but it can be conspicuous during migration when there seems to be a pewee or two associated with every mixed-species group of passerine transients.

Maximum count: 29 in Metcalfe Co., 6 May 2010 (S. Stedman, eBird data).

Early spring dates: 12 Apr 2002, Muhlenberg Co. (M. Monroe, pers. comm.); 13 Apr 2002, Bernheim Forest (D. O'Brien, eBird data); 13 Apr 2013, Menifee Co. (*KW* 89:76, 2013); 17 Apr 19—, Louisville (Mengel:316).

Late fall dates: 12 Nov 2006, (ph.) Russell Co. (*KW* 83:16, 2007); 6 Nov 2002, road-killed bird in Allen Co. (*KW* 79:12, 2003); 31 Oct 1994, Grayson Co. (*KW* 71:4, 1995); 30 Oct 1997, Hardin Co. (R. Healy, pers. comm.); 29 Oct 1983, Louisville (*KW* 60:18, 1984); 29 Oct 2018, (ph.) e. Jefferson Co. (*KW* 95:8, 2019); 29 Oct 2018, (ph.) Bowling Green (*KW* 95:8, 2019).

Unaccepted record: 31 Dec 1982, (2) on the Redbird CBC (*AB* 37:582, 1983).

EMPIDONAX spp.

Status: The five eastern species of *Empidonax* present great identification problems in the field, and many individuals are identifiable only by their distinctive songs and call notes. Thus, some sightings of *Empidonax* flycatchers during spring, and many during fall, are not safely assignable to species. Moreover, *Empidonax* flycatchers from the western United States are occasionally observed in the east, especially during late fall and winter, and the possibility of western strays should not be overlooked. There are four records of single *Empidonax* flycatchers during Dec (all have been tentatively identified as Least Flycatchers).

Chronological list of records of out-of-season unidentified *Empidonax* sp.

1) 2-12 Dec 1975, Louisville (*AB* 30:726, 1976; J. Elmore, notes)
2) 7 Dec 1975, a different individual elsewhere at Louisville (*AB* 30:726, 1976) [Note: dates for both records were published incorrectly as "2-12 Nov" in *KW* 52:54, 1976]
3) 9 Dec 1979, Cave Hill Cemetery, Louisvillle (*KW* 56:32, 1980)
4) 21-30 Dec 2014, (ph./vt.), Green River State Forest, Henderson Co. (*KW* 91:55, 2015)

YELLOW-BELLIED FLYCATCHER *Empidonax flaviventris*

Status: Uncommon transient. Occurrence not well documented, but probably statewide. Not numerous during either spring or fall, but difficult to consider it a rare find during the peaks of migratory movement from mid- to late May and from late Aug to mid-Sep. Encountered in a variety of forested and semi-open habitats, but most often observed feeding inconspicuously inside the canopy of thickets of young trees or in the understory of mature woodlands.

Note: Validity of reports of this species is very difficult to assess given its general lack of abundance, in combination with its similarity to commoner species of *Empidonax*; subsequently, the following summaries are treated a bit more conservatively than for many species, particularly those during spring.

Early spring date: 8 May 2016, Henderson Co. (*KW* 92:65, 2016).
Late spring dates: 7 Jun 2003, Lexington (*KW* 79:83, 2003); 3 Jun 2002 (banded), Rowan Co. (C. Trombino, notes); 31 May 2006, (hd.) Lee Co. (*KW* 82:71, 2006); 31 May 2015, Pulaski Co. (*KW* 91:73, 2015); 30 May 2006, Christian Co. (*KW* 82:71, 2006); 30 May 2017, (vo.) Fayette Co. (*KW* 93:75, 2017); 29 May 1993, Louisville (*KW* 69:46, 1993); 28 May 1949, Louisville area (*KW* 52:54, 1976); 28 May 1968, Louisville area (*KW* 52:54, 1976); 28 May 1979, Louisville (B. Palmer-Ball, eBird data).
Early fall dates: 7 Aug 1964, south-central Kentucky (*KW* 45:35, 1969); 9 Aug 1971 (ba.), Louisville (B. Monroe, Jr., notes; *KW* 52:54, 1976); 11 Aug 2017, Jefferson Co. (P. Bell, pers. comm./eBird data [report not validated in latter]); 13 Aug 2011, Jefferson Co. (*KW* 88:13, 2012); 14 Aug 1993, Jefferson Co. (*KW* 70:9, 1994).
Late fall dates: 12 Oct 2016, (ph.) LBL, Trigg Co. (*KW* 93:11, 2017); 11 Oct 2006, Warren Co. (*KW* 83:16, 2007); 10 Oct 1959, south-central Kentucky (*KW* 38:16, 1962); 10 Oct 2003, Jefferson Co. (*KW* 80:12, 2004); 10 Oct 2011, Iroquois Park, Louisville (*KW* 88:13, 2012); 9 Oct 2011, Cherokee Park, Louisville (*KW* 88:13, 2012); 8 Oct 2003, Louisville (*KW* 80:12, 2004); 6 Oct 1961, south-central Kentucky (*KW* 38:16, 1962); 6 Oct 2018, Lexington (*KW* 95:8, 2019); 5 Oct 1991, Louisville (B. Palmer-Ball, eBird data); 5 Oct 2002, Caperton Swamp Park, Louisville (B. Yandell, eBird data); 5 Oct 2016, Pulaski Co. (*KW* 93:10, 2017; R. Denton, eBird data).
Unaccepted records: those during spring earlier than early spring date of 8 May given above including 27 Mar 1967 (*KW* 45:35, 1969); 24 Apr 1942, Louisville area (*KW* 52:54, 1976); 28 Apr 1981, Pine Mt. (*KW* 57:57, 1981); and 6 May 1979, Boone Co. (eBird data).
Published error: the late spring date of 3 Jun [1889], published by Monroe (*KW* 45:51, 1969) pertains to Indiana (*fide* Mengel :313).

*ACADIAN FLYCATCHER *Empidonax virescens*

Status: Fairly common to common summer resident. Recorded statewide during migration, but generally uncommon as a transient away from nesting areas; usually encountered in relatively mature, mesic forest during migration. Peak of abundance occurs from late Apr to mid-Sep. Breeding statewide; usually found in tracts of mature, mesic woodlands situated in floodplains, along stream corridors, and within narrow ravines. This species often constructs its nest over water.

Early spring date: 12 Apr 1982, Louisville (*KW* 58:52, 1982).
Late fall dates: 15 Oct 1985, Jefferson Co. (*KW* 62:7, 1986); 12 Oct 2004, Warren Co. (*KW* 81:12, 2005); 10 Oct 1959, south-central Kentucky (*KW* 38:16, 1962).

ALDER FLYCATCHER *Empidonax alnorum*

Status: Transient (uncommon during spring, probably rare to uncommon during fall). Occurrence not well documented; probably statewide, but abundance probably increases as one proceeds westward across the state. Encountered in a variety of semi-open, usually successional habitats; most often found in reverting fields and other open to semi-open areas with scattered patches of young trees. The species was poorly documented in early literature, mostly because it was considered conspecific with the Willow Flycatcher (collectively known as Traill's Flycatcher). Specimens exist for Jefferson Co., 20 Sep 1950 (Mengel:314) and Oldham Co., 20 May 1967 (*KW* 52:54, 1976). Since the mid-1970s the species has received greater attention, and it has been reported annually during spring (identifications based on songs) with records from as far east as Kenton, Pulaski, and Rowan cos. Its occurrence during fall is even more poorly documented, in large part due to the absence of song; a growing number of records based on call notes and responses to taped calls (see below) may accurately represent the species' occurrence during fall migration.

Maximum count: **12+** loosely distributed at Cypress Slough, Henderson Co., 23 May 1997 (B. Palmer-Ball, eBird data).

Early spring dates: 2 May 2014, LBL, Lyon Co. (*KW* 90:73, 2014); 3 May 1981, Kenton Co. (*KW* 57:57, 1981); 3 May 2007, Swan Lake, Ballard Co. (*KW* 83:82, 2007).

Late spring dates: 7 Jun 1998, Taylor Co. (B. Palmer-Ball, eBird data); 6 Jun 2014, Catlettsburg, Boyd Co. (C. Thompson, eBird data); 4 Jun 1976, Danville (F. Loetscher, notes).

Out-of-season records (summer): a bird was singing as if on territory on the Road Creek Mine, Pike Co., 13 May 2010 and was still present and calling 10 Jun 2010 (*KW* 86:70/95, 2010); 30 Jul 2009, a bird softly singing "wee-bee-o" at Shaker Village, Mercer Co. (*KW* 85:94, 2009).

Confirmed fall record: 20 Sep 1950, collected (sp.) at Louisville (Mengel:314).

Fall dates: (accepted provisionally herein if based on the species' distinctive 'pip' call note, as well as, if noted, behavioral response to taped songs/calls of the species; not all of these fall birds have been seen well, but visual confirmation of "Alder/Willow-type" *Empidonax* flycatchers have occurred with most reports; due to the developing nature of this data set, all published reports are included by calendar date): 12 Aug 2001, a calling bird at Lake No. 9, Fulton Co., that came in to a tape of the species' songs/calls (*NAB* 56:59, 2002); 13 Aug 2011, Lake No. 9 (*KW* 88:13, 2012); 14 and 29 Aug 1988, single birds along Mississippi River north of Laketon, Carlisle Co. (B. Palmer-Ball, eBird data); 20 Aug 2013, 4 (one ph.) seen/heard (pip notes)) in w. Fulton Co. (*KW* 90:14/20, 2014); 21 Aug 2003, (hd.) Carlisle Co. (*KW* 80:12, 2004); 24 Aug 2002, one in w. Carlisle Co. and 2 nr. Lake No. 9 (one of the latter two responded with aggressive call notes to a tape of the songs/calls of the species) (*KW* 79:13, 2003); 25-26 Aug 2017, 1-2 (ph.) nr. Lake No. 9 (*KW* 94:11, 2018); 26 Aug 2001, 3 at and nr. Lake No. 9 (2 of which replied with aggressive call notes to a tape of the songs/calls of the species)(B. Palmer-Ball, eBird data; *NAB* 56:59, 2002 [date erroneously published as 25 Aug therein]); 31 Aug 1997, Mitchell Lake, Ballard WMA, (B. Palmer-Ball, eBird data); 2 Sep 2010, (hd.) Fulton Co. (*KW* 87:20, 2011); 3 Sep 1998, Warren Co. (D. Roemer, notes); 5 Sep 2004, Warren Co. (*KW* 81:12, 2005); 11 Sep 1997, nr. Lake No. 9 (B. Palmer-Ball, eBird data); 12 Sep 1997, Swan Lake vicinity, Ballard Co. (B. Palmer-Ball, eBird data); 24 Sep 2013, (ph.) heard calling (pip notes) in Union Co. (*KW* 90:14, 2014); 24-25 Sep 2006, (ph.) Pulaski Co. (*KW* 83:16, 2007).

Unaccepted records: 1 May 1955, Henderson Co., details are inconclusive; must be considered an Alder/Willow-type (*KW* 31:49, 1955); 13 Sep 1997, Mammoth Cave (eBird data [description does not eliminate begging juv. Eastern Wood-Pewee]); 9 Sep 2010, (visual ID plus came in to tape but did not call) Adair Co. (*KW* 87:20, 2011); 6 Oct 2010, a "Traill's Flycatcher" banded in Pulaski Co. (*KW* 87:20, 2011); 24 Sep 2014, Muhlenberg Co. (eBird data).

*WILLOW FLYCATCHER *Empidonax traillii*

Status: Rare to uncommon (and very locally distributed) summer resident. Mengel (pp. 314-315) listed only one nesting and one migrant record for the state. Since that time the species has increased dramatically as a summer resident and now has been recorded breeding at scattered localities throughout most of the state. This flycatcher is seldom encountered as a transient away from nesting areas, but an individual is occasionally found in semi-open habitats, most often in old fields and other open to semi-open areas with scattered patches of young trees; shuns mature forest. Peak of abundance occurs from mid-May to late Jul. Breeding not well documented; the species is present during summer, and probably nests, in moist, early successional habitats at scattered localities across the state (*KBBA*:136-137). It occurs in suitable habitat most frequently across northern Kentucky, being quite locally distributed across the southern portion of the state and in heavily forested areas.

Early spring dates: 28 Apr 2019, (vo.), Henderson Co. (D. Lang, eBird data); 1 May 2007, Calloway Co. (*KW* 83:82, 2007); 2 May 1959, Mammoth Cave National Park (*KW* 38:16, 1962); 2 May 1988, Madison Co. (*KW* 64:48, 1988); 2 May 2015, Henderson Co. (*KW* 92:65, 2016); 2 May 2018, (ph./ba.) Madison Co. (C. Titus/T. McFadden, eBird data).

Late fall dates: 16 Sep 2006, Jefferson Co. (*KW* 83:16, 2007); 15 Sep 1962, at a breeding location at Louisville (Croft, *KW* 38:61, 1962); 7 Sep 2014, (hd.) Muhlenberg Co. (T. Graham, eBird data); 3 Sep 1998, Warren Co. (D. Roemer, notes; included provisionally based on visual ID and call notes).

Unaccepted records: 23 Apr 1963, Mammoth Cave National Park (*KW* 45:35, 1969); 28 Sep 2018, Madison Co. (*KW* 95:8, 2019).

Summary of confirmed breeding records by county

Boone (*KBBA*:136-137)
Campbell (*KBBA*:136-137)
Hardin (M. Monroe, 2000 notes)
Harrison (*KBBA*:136-137)
Jefferson (Mengel:315; Croft, *KW* 37:63-70, 1961; Croft, *KW* 38:59-61, 1962; *KBBA*:136-137)
Mason (*KBBA*:136-137)
McLean (*KW* 65:88, 1989)
Muhlenberg (M. Monroe, 2000 notes)
Nelson (Croft, *KW* 40:27-28, 1964)
Ohio (*KBBA*:136-137; B. Palmer-Ball, eBird data)

*LEAST FLYCATCHER *Empidonax minimus*

Status: Fairly common transient, extremely rare and local summer resident (regular at only one location); accidental elsewhere during summer and during winter. Recorded statewide during migration in a great variety of habitats from mature woodlands and woodland borders to overgrown fields and suburban parks and yards. By far the most numerous species of *Empidonax* in most areas during migration. Small numbers of territorial males have been reported sporadically at the summit of Black Mountain, Harlan Co. (Breiding, *KW* 23:38, 1947; *KW* 59:53, 1983; *KW* 60:54, 1984; *KW* 61: 58, 1985; D. Noonan, 1985 pers. comm.), but breeding has been confirmed only in recent years (see below). In fact, over the past 15 years, the species appears to have expanded and has become annual as a breeder there. **State Breeding Status**: Endangered.

Maximum count: 34 (likely on territory) at the summit of Black Mt., Harlan Co., 10 May 2009 (*KW* 85:73, 2009).

Early spring dates: 17 Apr 19—, Louisville area (Mengel:315; *KW* 52:54, 1976); 19 Apr 2018, (ph.) Lexington (*KW* 94:79, 2018); 21 Apr 2014, Long Point Unit (*KW* 90:73, 2014).

Late spring dates (away from probable breeding areas): 1 Jun 1967, Graves Co. (K. Able, notes); 1 Jun 2006, Pulaski Co. (*KW* 82:82, 2006); 31 May 19—, Louisville area (Mengel:315; *KW* 52:54, 1976); 30 May 1965, Louisville area (A. Stamm, notes); 30 May 1977, Louisville (J. Elmore, notes); 30 May 2017, Henderson Co. (C. Crawford, eBird data).

Extralimital summer record (away from probable breeding areas): 7 Jul 1963, Hancock Co. (Alsop, *KW* 47:64, 1971).

Early fall dates (away from probable breeding areas): 16 Jul 2010, (ba.) Mercer Co. (*KW* 86:95, 2010); 19 Jul 2009, (seen and hd.) Jefferson Co. (*KW* 85:94, 2009); 21 Jul 2001, (ba.) Powell Co. (D. Skinner, notes); 28 Jul 2005, (seen and hd.) Marshall Co. (*KW* 81:108, 2005); 9 Aug 2000, Jefferson Co. (*KW* 77:8, 2001); 9 Aug 2003, (seen and hd.) Louisville (*KW* 80:12, 2004); 11 Aug 2014, Jefferson Co. (*KW* 91:12, 2015); 12 Aug 2009, Jefferson Co. (*KW* 86:12, 2010); 12 Aug 2018, Logan Co. (*KW* 95:8, 2019); 14 Aug 2012, Louisville (*KW* 89:11, 2013).

Late fall dates: 14 Oct 2000, Henderson Co. (seen and heard) (B. Palmer-Ball, eBird data); 7 Oct 2018, (ph.) Metcalfe Co. (*KW* 95:8, 2019); 3 Oct 2018, Hart Co. (S./J. Kistler, eBird data); 3 Oct 2016, Henderson Co. (S./J. Kistler, eBird data); 1 Oct 2016, (ph.) Louisville (J. Wheat, eBird data); 30 Sep 2001 (seen and hd.), Lower Hickman Bottoms (B. Palmer-Ball, eBird data).

Out-of-season record (early winter): 19 Dec 2015, (ph.) seen and call notes heard at Lake No. 9, Fulton Co. (*KW* 92:44, 2016).

Unaccepted records (all considered *Empidonax* sp. due to lack of complete details or no details at all): those during spring earlier than the early spring date of 17 Apr given above and including 6 Apr 1917, south-central Kentucky (*KW* 38:17, 1962); those during fall later than the late fall date of 14 Oct given above and including 2 Nov 1941, south-central Kentucky (*KW* 38:17, 1962) and 21 Oct 19—(Mengel:316); also, 14 Oct 1953, south-central Kentucky (*KW* 38:17, 1962); 14-15 Oct 1972, Lake Cumberland (*KW* 48:68, 1972); and 2 Oct 1976, Carter Caves State Park (*KW* 52:86, 1976); also, 29 Jul 2014, Jefferson Co. (*KW* 90:89, 2014) and 25 Jun 2003, Fulton Co. (*KW* 79:83, 2003).

Published error: 10 in Pike Co., 22 Jun 1996 (*KW* 72:75, 1996) pertained to Acadian Flycatchers (*fide* S. Stedman, pers. comm.).

Summary of confirmed breeding records by county

Harlan (Black Mt. [*KW* 78:51, 2002; *KW* 79:83, 2003; *KW* 81:89/108, 2005; Kuntz and Stedman, *KW* 81:94-96, 2005; *KW* 86:70, 2010; *KW* 87:115, 2011]).

Summary of additional records of possible or probable breeding by county

Bell (nr. Chenoa, Jun/Jul 1989 [*KBBA*:138; A. Barron, notes])
Elliott (27 Jun/3 Jul 1979 [*KW* 55:57, 1979])
Letcher (nr. Whitesburg, Letcher Co., 13-14 Jun 1967 [Croft, *KW* 45:70-71, 1969])
Wolfe (23 Jun 1979 [*KW* 55:57, 1979] and 26 Jun 1980 [*KW* 56:80, 1980]

EASTERN PHOEBE *Sayornis phoebe*

Status: Fairly common transient and summer resident, rare to uncommon winter resident. Recorded statewide during migration in a variety of semi-open habitats from mature woodland openings and along woodland borders to farmland and suburban parks; often found near water. Peak of abundance occurs from mid-Mar to late Oct. Breeding statewide; generally nesting along cliffs and rock overhangs, in buildings, and especially under bridges. A few individuals winter most years, especially along protected streams and lake margins.

Maximum counts: **29** in sw. McCreary Co., 24 Apr 2009 (S. Stedman, eBird data); **27** in Cumberland Co., 27 Sep 2008 (S. Stedman, eBird data); **25** on the Eastern Allen County CBC, 29 Dec 2012 (*KW* 89:28/52, 2013).

SAY'S PHOEBE *Sayornis saya*

Status: Extremely rare fall, winter, and spring visitant. This species is widely distributed across the western United States and it is a fairly regular straggler to the eastern part of the country. There are 12 records (five during fall, six during winter, and one during spring).

Unaccepted record: winter 2012-2013, nr. Barren River Lake, Allen Co. [no additional details available] (M./J. Beachy, pers. comm).

Tally of records by county

Allen (2), Ballard, Barren, Calloway, Fulton, Jefferson, Larue, Logan, Lyon, Nelson, Union

Chronological list of records

1) 30 Dec 1966, along the Ohio River at Joppa, Illinois, flew across the Ohio River into Ballard Co. (*AFN* 21:425, 1967; R. Montgomery, pers. comm.)
2) 28 Dec 1999–17 Jan 2000, (ph.) ca. 3 miles south of Olmstead, Logan Co. (Bennett and Roemer, *KW* 76:61-62, 2000; M. Walter, pers. comm.)

3) 24 Dec 2003, (ph.) w. of Buffalo, Larue Co. (*KW* 80:45/46, 2004; date published erroneously as 26 Dec therein and at *KW* 84:76, 2008)
4) 5 Apr 2008, (ph.) in w. Fulton Co. (*KW* 84:67/68, 2008)
5) 26 Sep 2009, LBL Nature Station, Lyon Co. (*KW* 86:12, 2010)
6) 11 Oct 2009, (ph.) e. of Morganfield, Union Co. (*KW* 86:12/36, 2010)
7) 11 Sep 2010, (ph.) in ne. Jefferson Co. (*KW* 87:1/20, 2011)
8) 4 Jan–7 Mar 2013, (ph.) ne. of Almo, Calloway Co. (*KW* 89:52/60/77, 2013)
9) 20 Oct 2014, in e. Allen Co. (*KW* 91:12, 2015)
10) 18 Sep 2016, se. of Mt. Zion, Allen Co. (*KW* 93:11, 2017)
11) 21 Jan–25 Mar 2017, (ph.) s. of Bloomfield, Nelson Co. (*KW* 93:50/56/75, 2017)
12) 18-22 Dec 2018, (ph.) se. of Austin, Barren Co. (*KW* 95:25/49/60, 2019; L. Bontrager, et al., eBird data)

VERMILION FLYCATCHER *Pyrocephalus rubinus*

Status: Accidental vagrant. This resident of the southwestern United States and Middle America occasionally turns up in the eastern United States. It has been documented once in Kentucky.

1) 8 Oct 1955, an imm. male (sp.) one mile n. of Danville (Loetscher, *Auk* 74:268, 1957).

*LOGGERHEAD SHRIKE *Lanius ludovicianus*

Status: Rare to (very locally) uncommon resident (has decreased remarkably over the past thirty years). Recorded chiefly west of the Cumberland Plateau, although there were occasional sightings in open habitats of eastern Kentucky historically. Occurs in a variety of semi-open and open habitats; most numerous in farmland where it is usually observed on roadside wires and fences. Breeding west of the Cumberland Plateau in semi-open to open farmland, being most numerous in the Jackson Purchase. The eastern subspecies (*L. l. migrans*) occurring in Kentucky has been declining in abundance for several decades and has been considered for federal endangered or threatened status. This decline has included birds residing in Kentucky in recent decades. The species was still relatively well distributed as of the early 1990s (*KBBA*:202-203), but numbers appear to have declined substantially during the subsequent two decades, and it is no longer relatively easy to find anywhere in the state. During severe winter weather, this species will occasionally come to feeding stations to prey on small birds. Generally seen singly or in family groups.

NORTHERN SHRIKE *Lanius excubitor*

Status: Extremely rare fall and winter visitant. This inhabitant of Canada and the northern United States occurs somewhat cyclically south of its normal range, typically appearing during irruptive flights in response to low levels of prey. There are now ten Kentucky records.

Unaccepted records (at least one historical record and two more recent sight records): a bird drawn by Audubon and listed for Henderson, 30 Nov 1812 (Mengel:374), is authentic, but the origin of the specimen may be in question; another shrike caught in Jefferson Co., 30 Dec 1945, was probably this species, although it was identified after the bird was released (Young, *KW* 24:21-23, 1948); finally there was a sight report for the Murray CBC, 26 Dec 1951 (*AFN* 6:116, 1952). The Jefferson Co. report and two other historical records were viewed with skepticism by Mengel (p. 374).

Tally of records by county

Jefferson (2), Muhlenberg (4), Ohio (2), Russell, Union

Range of dates: 2 Nov–23 Mar

Chronological list of records

1) 13-28 Nov 2004, a first-year bird (ph.) at the Sinclair Unit (Chambers, Denton and Easley, *KW* 81:67-68, 2005)
2) 8 Nov 2007, a first-year bird at the Sinclair Unit (*KW* 84:13 2008)

3) 3-4 Feb 2008, a probable ad. at E.P. "Tom" Sawyer State Park, Jefferson Co. *KW* 84:45, 2008)

4) 4-5 Mar 2009, a first-year bird (ph.) at the Melco flood retention basin, Jefferson Co. (*KW* 85: 71/73, 2009)

5) 17 Dec 2012–14 Jan 2013, an ad. (ph.) nr. Helm's Junction, Russell Co. (*KW* 89:52/60, 2013)

6) 30 Dec 2012–27 Jan 2013, a first-year bird (ph.) at the Ken Unit (*KW* 89:22/51/52, 2013)

7) 19-23 Jan 2013 [and possibly 8 Mar 2013], an ad. (ph.) at the Sinclair Unit (*KW* 89:52/60/77, 2013)

8) 16 Feb 2013, an ad. (ph.) on the Ken Unit (*KW* 89:50/52, 2013)

9) 23 Mar 2013, an ad. (ph.) s. of Martwick, Muhlenberg Co. (*KW* 89:77, 2013)

10) 2 Nov 2013, an ad. (ph.) e. of Morganfield, Union Co. (*KW* 90:14/20, 2014)

*WHITE-EYED VIREO *Vireo griseus*

Status: Fairly common to common transient and summer resident, extremely rare in winter. Record- ed statewide during migration in a variety of semi-open habitats from successional woodland borders and old fields to (occasionally) suburban parks and yards; not normally found in mature woodlands. Peak of abundance occurs from late Apr to mid-Sep. Breeding statewide; most nu- merous in overgrown fields and other successional habitats with small trees and brushy cover.

Maximum counts: **42** at Rockcastle River WMA, Pulaski Co., 5 Jul 2014 (R. Denton, eBird data); **38** in ne. Adair Co., 6 May 2008 (R. Denton, eBird data); **37** in LBL, Trigg Co., 19 Sep 2018 (A. Lydeard, eBird data).

Early spring dates: 28 Mar 2012, Allen Co. (*KW* 88:78, 2012); 29 Mar 2012, LBL, Trigg Co. (*KW* 88:78, 2012); 30 Mar 2007, LBL, Lyon Co. (*KW* 83:82, 2007); 30 Mar 2012, Fleming Co. (*KW* 88:78, 2012); 1 Apr 1997, Laurel Co. (*KW* 73:56, 1997); 1 Apr 2006, LBL, Trigg Co. (A. West, eBird data); 1 Apr 2006, Henderson Co. (J. Meredig, eBird data); 1 Apr 2012, LBL, Lyon Co. (J. Poll- peter, eBird data); 1 Apr 2014, LBL, Trigg Co. (*KW* 90:73, 2014); 2 Apr 1938, south-central Ken- tucky (*KW* 38:19, 1962); 2 Apr 1977, Jefferson Co. (*AB* 31:1009, 1977); 2 Apr 2005, Calloway Co. (*KW* 81:89, 2005); 2 Apr 2016, Clarks River NWR, Marshall Co. (*KW* 92:65, 2016).

Late fall dates: 24 Nov 2012 (ph.), Bowling Green (*KW* 89:12/40, 2013); 13 Nov 2006, Jefferson Co. (*KW* 83:16, 2007); 11 Nov 1948, Fulton Co. (Mengel:378); 6-7 Nov 2015, (ph.) Jefferson Co. (*KW* 92:12, 2016); 6 Nov 2006, (ba.) at Frankfort (*KW* 83:16, 2007); 4 Nov 2017, Lexington (*KW* 94:12, 2018); 1 Nov 1977, Louisville (*AB* 32:214, 1978); 1 Nov 2000, Fulton Co. (*KW* 77:8, 2001); 31 Oct 1984, Bowling Green (*KW* 61:18, 1985; J. Callahan, notes); 30 Oct 2018, (ph.) Berea, Madison Co. (*KW* 95:8, 2019); 29 Oct 1984, Central Ky WMA, Madison Co. (*KW* 61:18, 1985; G. Ritchison, pers. comm.); 28 Oct 1984, Pulaski Co. (*KW* 61:18, 1985; J. Elmore, eBird data); 28 Oct 2011, Trigg Co. (*KW* 88:14, 2012); 27 Oct 2017, Fayette Co. (D. Svetich, eBird data); 27 Oct 2018, nr. Lake No. 9 (T. Jones, eBird data); 26 Oct 2012, Pulaski Co. (*KW* 89:12, 2013); 24 Oct 1956, Louisville area (*KW* 52:57, 1976); 24 Oct 2004, Jefferson Co. (*KW* 81:12, 2005); 24 Oct 2008, Pulaski Co. (*KW* 85:18, 2009).

Out-of-season records (winter): 26 Dec 1994, Bernheim Forest (*KW* 71:16, 1995); and 31 Dec 1994, Calloway Co. CBC (*KW* 71:15, 1995); 29 Dec 2006, Bowling Green (*KW* 83:50, 2007); 11 Dec 2009, Kendall Recreation Area, Russell Co. (*KW* 86:45, 2010); 18 Dec 2011 (ph.), Jefferson Co. (*KW* 88:34/49/60, 2012); 26 Nov 2014–5 Jan 2015, (ph.) e. Jefferson Co. (*KW* 91:12/55/60, 2015); 11 Jan 2016, (ph.) at Lexington (*KW* 92:44, 2016); 8 Mar 2016, Cave Run Lake, Rowan Co. (*KW* 92:65, 2016); 16 Dec 2017, (ph.) nr. Danville (*KW* 94:29, 2018); 17 Dec 2018, Ragland, McCracken Co. (*KW* 95:22/49, 2019).

*BELL'S VIREO *Vireo bellii*

Status: Rare to locally uncommon summer resident and extremely rare transient/visitant. Formerly known only as an extremely rare visitant, but in 1980 a small breeding population was discovered in McCracken County, with additional nesting documented at scattered localities across west-cen- tral Kentucky commencing during the late 1980s (primarily on reclaimed mines in Muhlenberg and Ohio cos.) and continuing into the 2000s (primarily in Henderson and Union cos.) (see below). All breeding birds have been found in relatively extensive areas of open habitat with scattered patches of shrubs and small trees. Peak of abundance occurs from late Apr to early Sep. Generally not to be expected in the state away from the limited nesting areas, but as the breeding population has increased and spread (particularly during the past 10-15 years), records of transient and wayward individuals in non-breeding areas have become more frequent. Such records have originated mostly across the western half of the state, but currently as far east as Boyle and Madison cos. (see below). **State Breeding Status**: Special Concern.

Maximum counts: **20** at the Sinclair Unit, 9 May 2007 (eBird data); **20** at the Sinclair Unit, 18 Jun 2016 (T. Graham, eBird data); **15** at the Sinclair Unit, 24 Jun 2000 (C. Sloan, eBird data); **15** at the Sinclair Unit, 22 Jun 2002 (eBird data); **14** at the Sinclair Unit, 12 May 2011 (C. Lituma, eBird data).

Early spring date (at or near breeding areas; see others below): 21 Apr 2009, Sinclair Unit (*KW* 85:73, 2009).

Late fall dates (at or near breeding areas; see others below): 19 Oct 2003, Sinclair Unit (*KW* 80:12, 2004); 25 Sep 2014, Sinclair Unit (*KW* 91:12, 2015); 23 Sep 2018, Ken Unit (*KW* 95:8, 2019); 15 Sep 1997, Ken Unit (*KW* 74:9, 1998; D. Roemer, notes); 15 Sep 2006, Muhlenberg Co. (*KW* 83:16, 2007); 14 Sep 2016, (2) Muhlenberg Co. (*KW* 93:11, 2017); 13 Sep 2010, Sinclair Unit (*KW* 87:20, 2011); 12 Sep 2018, Union Co. (*KW* 95:8, 2019); 10 Sep 2017, (2) Sinclair Unit (*KW* 94, 12, 2018); 9 Sep 2014,(2) Henderson Co. (*KW* 91:12, 2015); 8 Sep 2005, Muhlenberg Co. (*KW* 82:12, 2006); 8 Sep 2015, Muhlenberg Co. (*KW* 92:12, 2016).

Note: some of the additional records listed below (especially during the past 10-15 years) may very well pertain to nesting or territorial birds, but evidence was limited to observations in suitable habitat.

Additional spring records (not known to be at or near nesting areas): 26 Apr 1942 and 29 Apr 1961, Warren Co. (*KW* 38:19, 1962); 23 May 1946, 24 Apr 1948, and 1 May 1949, Jefferson Co. (*KW* 37:36, 1961); 20 Apr 1956, Barren Co. (*KW* 38:19, 1962); 12 Apr 1964, Hancok Co. (Alsop, *KW* 47:65-66, 1971); 3 May 1966, Mammoth Cave NP (*KW* 45:36, 1969); 2 May 1973, Danville (F. Loetscher, notes); 10 Apr 1977, Calloway Co. (*AB* 31:1009, 1977; J.T. Erwin, notes); 11 May 1980, Louisville (*KW* 56:63, 1980); 7 May 1999, Nelson Co. (R. Healy, notes); 13 May 2003, West Ky WMA, McCracken Co. (*KW* 79:71, 2003); 8 May 2009, LBL, Lyon Co. (*KW* 85:73, 2009); 13 Mar 2002, Butler Co. (wintering bird?) (S. Thomas, notes); 8 May 2008, w. Fulton Co. (*KW* 84:68, 2008); 24 May–11 Jun 2009, Jefferson Co. (*KW* 85:71/73/94, 2009); 31 May 2009, Owensboro, Daviess Co. (*KW* 85:73, 2009); 22 May–3 Jun 2010, Jefferson Co. (*KW* 86:70/95, 2010); 18-23 May 2011, Jefferson Co. (*KW* 87:92, 2011); 20 May 2011, sw. of Rumsey, McLean Co. (*KW* 87:92, 2011); 16 May 2012 and 18 May 2012 (different locations), Jefferson Co. (*KW* 88:78, 2012); 16 May 2014, Ft. Campbell, Christian Co. (*KW* 90:73, 2014) 19 May–4 Jun 2014, s. Jefferson Co. (*KW* 90:73, 2014; B. Palmer-Ball, eBird data); 23 May 2016, Big Rivers WMA and SF, Union Co. (*KW* 92:65, 2016); 19 Apr 2017, Graves Co. (*KW* 93:76, 2017); 29-30 May 2017, Ky Bend, Fulton Co. (*KW* 93:76, 2017); 4 May 2018, Long Point Unit (*KW* 94:79, 2018); 11 May 2019, Long Point Unit (H. Chambers, eBird data); late May 2019, nr. Rockfield, Warren Co. (m. ob., eBird data); 26 May 2019, Daviess Co. (R. Rold, eBird data).

Additional summer records (not known to be at or near nesting areas): 27 May–early Jun 1988, Meade Co. (*KW* 64:49, 1988); 5 Aug 1990, Henderson Co. (*KW* 67:8, 1991); 17 Jun 1991, Fort Knox, Bullitt/Hardin Co. (L. Pollock, pers. comm.); 30 Jul 1991, w. Spencer Co. (*KBBA*:208); 21 Jul 2004, Mayfield, Graves Co. (*KW* 80:84, 2004); 22 Jun 2007, nw. of Sonora, Hardin Co. (*KW* 83:106, 2007); 17 Jun 2010, Calvert City, Marshall Co. (*KW* 86:95, 2010); 1 Jun 2014, Ft. Campbell, Trigg Co. (*KW* 90:90, 2014); 13 Jun 2014, Ft. Campbell, Christian Co. (*KW* 90:90, 2014); 22 Jul 2015, Perryville Battlefield State Historic Site, Boyle Co. (*KW* 92:47, 2016; G. Stegner, pers. comm.); 25 Jun 2016, e. side of Paducah (*KW* 92:80, 2016); 6 Jun 2018, Graves Co. (*KW* 94:109, 2018); 23 Jun 2018, nr. Petros, Warren Co. (*KW* 94:109, 2018); 28 Jun 2018, n. of Calhoun, McLean Co. (*KW* 94:109, 2018); 30 Jun 2018, Ballard WMA (*KW* 94:109, 2018).

Additional fall records (not known to be at or near nesting areas): 30 Sep 1967, Jefferson Co. (*KW* 52:57, 1976); 23 Aug 1997, Warren Co. (*KW* 74:9, 1998); 6 Sep 1998, Warren Co. (*KW* 75:6, 1999); 15 Sep 2000, Henderson Co. (*KW* 77:8, 2001); 30 Aug 2013, Ft. Campbell, Trigg Co. (*KW* 90:14, 2014); 25 Aug 2015, Berea, Madison Co (*KW* 92:12, 2016); 9 Sep 2018, Logan Co. (*KW* 95:8, 2019).

Unaccepted records: Mengel (p. 518) notes a report from Fulton Co. during the late 1800s that he did not consider acceptable in the absence of a specimen. He also did not consider the three sight records from Louisville during the 1940s included above as confirmed, and he made no mention of the earlier reports from Barren Co. (1956) and Warren Co.(1942, 1961). It is possible that in the absence of good documentation that none of these reports should be considered acceptable. Also, I cannot find details of a breeding season record listed for Hopkins Co. in the 2nd ed. of this work (B. Palmer-Ball 2001 notes).

Summary of confirmed breeding records by county

Christian (*KW* 82:83, 2006)
Crittenden (*KW* 66:90, 1990; *KBBA*:208-209)
Livingston (*KW* 82:83, 2006)
McCracken (Nicholson, *KW* 57:77-79, 1981; Palmer-Ball and Barron, *KW* 58:76-77, 1982)
Muhlenberg (*KBBA*:208-209; Palmer-Ball and Barron, *KW* 66:78, 1990; *KW* 74:56, 1998; and subsequent years)
Ohio (*KBBA*:208-209; Palmer-Ball and Barron, *KW* 66:78, 1990; and subsequent years)
Union (*KW* 64:65, 1988; *KW* 82:83, 2006; and subsequent years)

Summary of additional summer records of probable nesting birds by county

Butler (*KW* 94:79, 2018; C. Bliznick, et al. 2018 eBird data)
Fulton (*KW* 94:79/109, 2018)
Henderson (*KW* 87:92, 2011; *KW* 88:78, 2012; *KW* 90:73/90, 2014; *KW* 91:12/87, 2015 and subsequent years)
Hopkins (*KW* 82:83, 2006)
Livingston (*KW* 78:65, 2002; *KW* 81:89, 2005; *KW* 84:13/68, 2008; *KW* 85:94, 2009; *KW* 91:87, 2015)

Summary of additional non-breeding records by county (approximate summary of vagrant records above)

Ballard (2018)
Barren (1956)
Boyle (1973; 2015)
Bullitt/Hardin (1991)
Butler (2002)
Calloway (1977)
Christian (2014)
Daviess (2009; 2019)
Edmonson (1966)
Fulton (2008; 2017; 2018; 2019)
Graves (2004; 2017; 2018)
Hancock (1964)
Hardin (2007)
Henderson (1990; 2000; 2011 and subsequent years)
Hopkins (2001; 2006)
Jefferson (1946; 1948; 1949; 1967; 1980; 2009; 2010; 2011; 2012; 2014)
Livingston (2005 and subsequent years)
Logan (*KW* 95:8, 2019)
Lyon (2009)
Madison (2015)
Marshall (2010)
McCracken (2003; 2016)
McLean (2011; 2018)
Meade (1988)
Nelson (1999)
Spencer (1991)
Trigg (2013; 2014)
Union (2016)
Warren (1942; 1961; 1997; 1998; 2018; 2019)

*YELLOW-THROATED VIREO *Vireo flavifrons*

Status: Uncommon to fairly common summer resident. Recorded statewide during migration in a variety of forested and semi-open habitats from mature woodlands and woodland borders to suburban parks, but not especially numerous as a transient away from nesting areas. Peak of abundance occurs from late Apr to late Sep. Breeding statewide in a variety of mature forest types; most numerous on the Cumberland Plateau and Mountains and in the Shawnee Hills, least numerous in the Blue Grass (*KBBA*:212-213).

Maximum count: **17** in n. McCreary Co., 24 Apr 2009 (R. Denton, eBird data).

Early spring dates: 30 Mar 2007, LBL, Trigg Co. (*KW* 83:83, 2007); 1 Apr 2012, Mammoth Cave (*KW* 88:78, 2012); 2 Apr 2007, Calloway Co. (*KW* 83:83, 2007); 2 Apr 2012, Berea Forest (*KW* 88:78, 2012); 3 Apr 2005, Bernheim Forest (*KW* 81:89-90, 2005); 3 Apr 2014, Allen Co. (*KW* 90:73, 2014); 4 Apr 2010, Mammoth Cave (*KW* 86:71, 2010); 5 Apr 2006, LBL, Lyon Co. (*KW* 82:71, 2006); 5 Apr 2014, Pulaski Co. (*KW* 90:73, 2014); 6 Apr 2014, LBL, Trigg Co. (*KW* 90:73, 2014); 7 Apr 2002, Whitley Co. (B. Palmer-Ball, eBird data); 7 Apr 2011, Ohio & Allen cos. (*KW* 87:92, 2011); 8 Apr 1954, south-central Kentucky (*KW* 38:19, 1962); 8 Apr 1981, Calloway Co. (*KW* 57:58, 1981).

Late fall dates: 7 Nov 2007, Jonathan Creek (*KW* 84:13 2008); 24 Oct 1936, south-central Kentucky (*KW* 38:19, 1962).

Unaccepted records: 20 Dec 2003, s. Fayette Co. (*KW* 80:17/48, 2004); 15 Mar 2017, Henderson Co. (*KW* 93:76, 2017; see *KW* 93:107, 2017).

*BLUE-HEADED VIREO *Vireo solitarius*

Status: Uncommon to fairly common transient, rare to locally fairly common summer resident on the Cumberland Plateau and Mountains (accidental or extremely rare elsewhere during summer), extremely rare during winter. Recorded statewide during migration in a variety of forested and semi-open habitats from mature woodlands and woodland borders to suburban parks and yards. Peaks of abundance occur from mid-Apr to early May and from early to mid-Oct. Breeding not well documented; fairly widespread during summer above 3200 ft. on Black Mountain, where Mengel (pp. 380-381) listed a few nesting records; also at scattered localities along the other mountain ridges (Log, Pine, Cumberland) in se. Kentucky (Mengel:381; Croft, *KW* 45:72-73, 1969), where nesting has been confirmed at Cumberland Gap National Historical Park, 19-22 May 1970 (Croft, *KW* 47:24, 1971), and at Pine Mountain SRP, Bell Co., 6-7 May 1972 (D. McConnell, notes) and 15 May 1999 (B. Palmer-Ball, eBird data). More recently the species has expanded into other parts of the Cumberland Plateau, especially in the southern Jellico Mountains and north through the Cliff Section to the Red River Gorge area (e.g., *KBBA*:210; *KW* 71:70, 1995; Yacek and Lacki, *KW* 74: 90-91, 1998; Renfrow, *KW* 75:52, 1999). Potentially territorial birds also have been reported from a few additional localities farther west (see below). Wherever the species occurs during summer, it is associated with extensive tracts of relatively mature forest, often (except at higher elevations in the Cumberland Mountains) with a substantial component of hemlock or pine.

Maximum counts: **21** at Black Mt., Harlan Co., 14 May 2006 (B. Yandell, eBird data); **20** at Wolf Knob, Whitley Co., 2 Apr 2003 (R. Denton, eBird data); **20+** at Black Mt., Harlan Co., 28 Sep 2018 (J. Baker, eBird data).

Early spring dates (note extension of dates in recent years): 13 Mar 2006, (6) McCreary Co. (*KW* 82:71, 2006); 14 Mar 2016, Bell Co. (*KW* 92:65, 2016); 15 Mar 2006, (3) Pulaski Co. (*KW* 82:71, 2006); 15 Mar 2016, Harlan Co. (*KW* 92:65, 2016); 15 Mar 2016, (2) McCreary Co. (*KW* 92:65, 2016); 16 Mar 2013, Pulaski Co. (*KW* 89:77, 2013); 17 Mar 2004, McCreary Co. (*KW* 80:69, 2004); 17 Mar 2011, Pulaski Co. (*KW* 87:92, 2011); 17 Mar 2012, (3) Pulaski Co. (*KW* 88:78, 2012); 17 Mar 2016, (8) McCreary Co. (*KW* 92:66, 2016); 17 Mar 2018, Pulaski Co. (*KW* 94:79, 2018); 18 Mar 2003, Pulaski Co. (*KW* 79:71, 2003); 18 Mar 2011, Madison Co. (*KW* 87:92, 2011); 18 Mar 2012, Madison & Rockcastle cos. (*KW* 88:78, 2012); 18 Mar 2017, Pulaski Co. (R. Bontrager, eBird data); 18 Mar 2018, McCreary Co. (*KW* 94:79-80, 2018); 20 Mar 2004, Powell & Wolfe cos. (*KW* 80:69, 2004); 20 Mar 2009, Pulaski Co. (*KW* 85:73, 2009); 21 Mar 2000, Powell Co. (*NAB* 54:289, 2000); 22 Mar 1997, Wolfe Co. (F. Renfrow, pers. comm.); 22 Mar 2003, McCreary & Wolfe cos. (*KW* 79:71, 2003); 22 Mar 2007, Johnson Co. (*KW* 83:83, 2007); 24 Mar 1985, Cumberland Gap National Park, Bell Co. (*KW* 61:47, 1985).

Late fall dates: 1 Dec 2017, (ph.) Pulaski Co. (*KW* 94:59, 2018); 30 Nov 2002, Louisville (*KW* 79:13, 2003); 27 Nov 1999, McCreary Co. (*KW* 76:7, 2000); 24 Nov 2018, Muhlenberg Co. (*KW* 95:8, 2019); 20 Nov 2004, Jefferson Co. (*KW* 81:12, 2005); 20 Nov 2016, Cumberland Co. (*KW* 93:11, 2017); 18 Nov 1985, Lexington (*KW* 62:8, 1986); 16 Nov 2007, Pulaski Co. (*KW* 84:13 2008); 14 Nov 2004, Pulaski Co. (*KW* 81:12, 2005); 14 Nov 2014, Lexington (*KW* 91:12, 2015); 11 Nov 2001, Warren Co. (*KW* 78:9, 2002).

Out-of-season records (winter): 10 Jan 2001 (hd.), McCreary Co. (S. Thomas, notes/pers. comm.); 6 Dec 2004, (window kill) at Richmond, Madison Co. (*KW* 81:60, 2005); 28 Dec 2005, Taylor Co. (*KW* 82:21/48, 2006); 18 Dec 2017, (ph.) Laurel Co. (*KW* 94:33/59, 2018); 30 Dec 2017, (2) in Allen Co. (*KW* 94:24, 2018); 5 Jan 2019, Marshall Co. (*KW* 95:49, 2019).

Summary of county summer records away from known breeding areas by county

Bullitt (8-16 Jun 2002, Bernheim Forest [*KW* 78:65, 2002])
Christian (1990/1995, Pennyrile State Forest [*KW* 66:90, 1990; *KBBA*:210-211])
Clinton (13 Jun 2009 [*KW* 85:94, 2009])
Edmonson (Jun 1995, [3 males] Mammoth Cave [C. Sloan, pers. comm.])
Oldham (24 Jul 1957, Sleepy Hollow [*KW* 52:57, 1976])

PHILADELPHIA VIREO *Vireo philadelphicus*

Status: Uncommon transient. Recorded statewide in a variety of forested and semi-open habitats from mature woodlands and woodland borders to suburban parks and yards. Although never common, this species can be relatively numerous during the peaks of migration. Peaks of abundance occur during early May and from mid- to late Sep.

Maximum counts: ca. **10** at LBL, Lyon Co., 8 May 2009 (*KW* 85:73, 2009); **10** along the Muhlenberg Co. Rail Trail, 11 Sep 2015 (T. Graham, eBird data); **8** at Minor Clark Fish Hatchery, 15 Sep 2012 (*KW* 89:12, 2013); **8** at Harrods Creek Park, ne. Jefferson Co., 9 May 2018 (P. Bell, eBird data); **8** at the Anchorage Trail, Jefferson Co., 29 Sep 2018 (*KW* 95:8, 2019); at least **6** in a loose group at LBL, Lyon Co., 6 May 2010 (*KW* 86:71, 2010).

Early spring dates: 25 Apr 2018, Muhlenberg Co. (*KW* 94:80, 2018); 25 Apr 2019, Barren Co. & Madison Co. (L. Craiger, eBird data & R. Foster/R. Bates, eBird data); 26 Apr 2014, Mammoth Cave (*KW* 90:73, 2014).

Late spring date: 30 May 1982, Louisville (B. Shannon, pers. comm.; *fide* A. Stamm, historical archive files).

Early fall dates: 16 Aug 2015, Pulaski Co. (*KW* 92:12, 2016); 24 Aug 2018, LBL, Trigg Co. (*KW* 95:8, 2019); 26 Aug 2000, Pulaski Co. (R. Denton, eBird data); 26 Aug 2002, Butler Co. (*KW* 79:13, 2003); 27 Aug 2001, Louisville (*NAB* 56:59, 2002); 29 Aug 2010, se. Jefferson Co. (*KW* 87:20, 2011); 29 Aug 2018, Wayne Co. (*KW* 95:8, 2019); 30 Aug 1942, Oldham Co. (Mengel, *KW* 24:51, 1948).

Late fall dates: 26 Oct 1988, Madison Co. (*KW* 65:10, 1989); 18 Oct 1993, Louisville (*KW* 70:10, 1994); 18 Oct 2017, Louisville (*KW* 94:12, 2018); 18 Oct 2018, Hart Co. (*KW* 95:8, 2019); 17 Oct 1990, Boyle and Jefferson cos. (*KW* 67:8, 1991); 17 Oct 2011, Mammoth Cave (*KW* 88:14, 2012).

Unaccepted records (great care should be exercised to differentiate from Warbling Vireo at extreme dates of occurrence): all of those earlier than the early spring date of 25 Apr given above and including 4 Apr 19—, Louisville area (*KW* 37:37, 1961); 12 Apr 1991, Ky Lake (*KW* 67:58, 1991); 18 Apr 2004, Long Point Unit (*KW* 80:70, 2004); 18 Apr 2006, Calloway Co. (*KW* 82:71, 2006); 20 Apr 19—, Louisville (Mengel:384); 20 Apr 1980, Calloway Co. (*KW* 56:63, 1980); 23 Apr 2003, Calloway Co. (*KW* 79:71, 2003).

Published error: former late fall date of 11 Oct [1936] published by Monroe (*KW* 45:53, 1969) pertains to Ohio (*fide* Mengel: 384).

*WARBLING VIREO *Vireo gilvus*

Status: Uncommon to fairly common transient and summer resident. Recorded statewide during migration, but not especially numerous as a transient away from nesting areas, especially on the Cumberland Plateau and Mountains where the species is quite scarce. Encountered in a variety of semi-open habitats with scattered patches of large trees including isolated woodlots, woodland borders, riparian strips and suburban parks. Peak of abundance occurs from late Apr to mid-Sep. Breeding widespread across central and western Kentucky in such habitats, but quite local in the heavily forested portions of eastern Kentucky (*KBBA*:214-215).

Maximum count: **50** at LBL, Lyon Co., 6 May 2006 (J. Brunjes, eBird data).

Early spring dates: 7 Apr 1995, Hopkins Co. (*KW* 71:43, 1995); 7 Apr 2012, Boone Co. (*KW* 88:78, 2012); 7 Apr 2019, Barren Co. (L. Craiger, eBird data); 8 Apr 19—, Warren Co. (Mengel:385); 8 Apr 2000, Calloway Co. (J.T. Erwin, pers. comm.); 8 Apr 2011, LBL, Lyon/Trigg cos. (*KW* 87:92, 2011); 8 Apr 2016, Henderson Co. (*KW* 92:66, 2016); 8 Apr 2017, Fulton and Marshall cos. (*KW* 93:76, 2017).

Late fall dates: 13 Nov 2016, (ph.) Jefferson Co. (*KW* 93:11/106, 2017); 10 Oct 1980, Oldham Co. (*KW* 57:23, 1981); 8 Oct 2016, Henderson Co. (K. Michalski, eBird data).

Unaccepted record: 18 Oct 2000, (2) in Fulton Co. (*KW* 77:8, 2001).

Published error: 18 Mar 2002, Grayson Co. (*KW* 78:51, 2002) date should have been 18 Apr (*fide* J. Porter, pers. comm.).

*RED-EYED VIREO *Vireo olivaceus*

Status: Fairly common to common transient and summer resident. Recorded statewide during migration in a great variety of forested and semi-open habitats from mature woodlands and woodland borders to suburban parks and yards. Peak of abundance occurs from late Apr to early Oct. Breeding statewide; most common in mature deciduous woodland. This species is one of the most numerous and widespread forest-nesting birds in the state (*KBBA*:216-217).

Maximum counts: **115** in McCreary Co., 24 Apr 2009 (S. Stedman, eBird data); **111** at Natural Arch, McCreary Co., 22 May 2010 (R. Denton, eBird data); **108** in Adair Co., 6 May 2008 (S. Stedman, eBird data); **103** at the Little Lick Rec. Area, Pulaski Co. (B. Stedman, eBird data).

Early spring dates: 31 Mar 2007, Madison Co. (*KW* 83:83, 2007); 1 Apr 1950, south-central Kentucky (*KW* 38:19, 1962); 1 Apr 1987, Rowan Co. (*KW* 63:52, 1987); 1 Apr 2012, Mammoth Cave (*KW* 88:78, 2012); 2 Apr 2012, Trigg Co. (*KW* 88:78, 2012).

Late fall dates: 24 Oct 1886, Nelson Co. (Mengel:384); 23 Oct 2016, Trigg Co. (*KW* 93:11, 2017); (ph.) 19 Oct 2010, Russell Co. (R. Denton, eBird data).

*BLUE JAY *Cyanocitta cristata*

Status: Fairly common to common resident. Recorded statewide in a great variety of forested and semi-open habitats. Breeding statewide; usually in wooded habitats including suburban parks and residential areas. While Blue Jays are found in Kentucky throughout the year, the breeding population is supplemented during the rest of the year by greatly varying numbers of migrants (spring and fall) and winter residents. The species is typically most numerous during migration when it is not uncommon to see large flocks of several dozen birds foraging noisily through the treetops. Also, being a diurnal migrant, Blue Jays frequently can be seen migrating overhead in loose groups during the day, especially during the peaks of their movements from late Apr to early May and again from late Sep to mid-Oct. Winter numbers vary greatly from year to year, typically dependent upon the amount of hard mast (e.g., acorns and beech nuts).

Maximum counts: **750** over the Falls of the Ohio, 30 Sep 2011 (D. Striegel, eBird data); **450** at Wolf Creek Dam, 6 Oct 2018 (*KW* 95:8, 2019); **250** at the Sauerheber Unit, 10 Oct 2009 (R. Denton, eBird data); probably in excess of **200-250** in a few migratory flocks in Lyon Co., 5 Oct 1996 (B. Palmer-Ball, eBird data); **200** at the Lexington Cemetery, 28 Sep 2018 (*KW* 95:8, 2019); **175** at Wolf Creek Dam, 28 Sep 2018 (R. Denton, eBird data); **165** in a single, loose flock at Louisville, 7 Oct 1956 (Stamm, *KW* 33:41, 1957)

Maximum CBC counts: **688** on the Calloway Co. CBC, 2 Jan 1988 (*KW* 64:8, 1988); **688** on the Calloway Co. CBC, 1 Jan 1991 (*KW* 67:16, 1991); **618** on the Lexington CBC, 15 Dec 1990 (*KW* 67:16, 1991); **549** on the Bernheim Forest CBC, 26 Dec 1976 (*KW* 53:8, 1977).

*AMERICAN CROW *Corvus brachyrhynchos*

Status: Fairly common to common resident. Recorded statewide in a great variety of semi-open to open habitats, but much less numerous in heavily forested portions of eastern Kentucky. Breeding statewide, most often in woodlots and forest edge adjacent to farmland. Large roosting flocks of thousands of birds sometimes gather at scattered localities across central and western Kentucky during the non-breeding season.

Maximum counts: estimate of **35,000** on the Henderson CBC, 26 Dec 1953 (*AFN* 8:141, 1954); **30,000** at roost in Shelby Co., 29 Nov 1956 (Stamm and Hardwick, *KW* 34:38-39, 1958); **30,000** at roost at Lexington, Feb 1977 (Hudson, *KW* 53:38-39, 1977); **25,000** in Shelby Co., 18 Nov 1956 (*AFN* 11:30, 1957); "**thousands** frequently seen during winter and early spring" at Bardstown, Nelson Co. (Blincoe, *Auk* 25:412); an estimate of **10,000** at a roost at Corbin, Laurel Co. (J. Flynn, eBird data [unaccepted therein]); **8000** in w. Henderson Co., 1 Jan 2011 (B. Taylor, eBird data).

FISH CROW *Corvus ossifragus*

Status: Locally rare to fairly common summer resident (presumably breeding across much of its limited range in the western portion of the state). The species was first recorded in the Kentucky 24 May 1959 (Coffey, *Migrant* 30:36, 1959) and was subsequently found to be a regular summer bird of the floodplains of the Mississippi River and lower Ohio River as far upstream as Paducah. A specimen record exists for 7 Jun 1966 (Monroe and Able, *KW* 44:56, 1968). During the summer of 1988, an expansion up the Ohio River was documented with sight and voice reports from near Henderson, along the Green River near Pleasant Valley, Henderson/McLean Co. line, near Smithland Dam, and near the Shawneetown Bridge, Union Co. (*KW* 64:65, 1988; *KBBA*:164). In early Apr 1989, additional birds were seen and heard near Smithland, Livingston Co., at Ky Dam, and at Barkley Dam (*KBBA*:164). Since the early 1990s, birds have remained present in all of these areas, as well as having been found southward on Ky Lake (since the early 2000s) and LBL/Lake Barkley (2010s), and the species is occasionally to regularly seen along stream floodplains within the Jackson Purchase. There also have been a couple of extra-limital records outside of this range (see below). Peak of abundance occurs from late Mar to early Oct. Confirmed breeding actually has been documented on only a few occasions (see below), but the species probably nests throughout its limited range. Occasional wintering seems to have been documented in recent years by a handful of mid-winter observations at traditional locations (see below). Calls are distinctive, but care should be taken not to mistake the call of juvenile American Crows as that of this species during late spring and early summer. Usually seen singly or in small groups of fewer than a half-dozen birds, but larger groups of up to 25 or more are sometimes observed. **State Breeding Status**: Special Concern.

Maximum counts: at least **110** in a flock on the Westvaco [Doug Travis] WMA, Carlisle Co., 20 Sep 1998 (B. Palmer-Ball, eBird data); flock of **100+** along Mississippi River nr. Laketon, Carlisle Co., 21 Aug 1999 (*KW* 76:7, 2000); at least **100** along the Mississippi River at Laketon, Carlisle Co., 17 Aug 2005 (*KW* 82:12, 2006); flock of **88+** on Ohio River at Paducah, 12 Aug 1998 (B. Palmer-Ball, eBird data).

Early spring dates: 1 Feb 2017, two locations in Fulton Co. (*KW* 93:50, 2017); 5 Feb 2016, Upper Hickman Bottoms (*KW* 92:44, 2016); 6 Feb 2016, Ky Dam (*KW* 92:44, 2016); 8 Feb 2016, (7) at Fulton, Fulton Co. (*KW* 92:44, 2016); 8 Feb 2017, Upper Hickman Bottoms (H. Chambers, eBird data); 8 Feb 2018, Clarks River NWR, Marshall Co. (*KW* 94:59, 2018); 16 Feb 2000, Hickman Co. (*NAB* 54:285, 2000); 17 Feb 2016, Lower Hickman Bottoms (H. Chambers, eBird data); 18 Feb 2016, Blood River (*KW* 92:44, 2016); 19 Feb 1994, Fulton Co. (*KW* 70:35, 1994).

Late fall dates: 2 lingered at Jonathan Creek to 19 Dec 2015 (*KW* 92:44, 2016); 30 Nov 2015, Jonathan Creek (*KW* 92:12, 2016); 18 Nov 1989, Lyon Co. (*KW* 66:12, 1990).

Out-of-season records (winter): 2 seen and heard at the Wildcat Creek embayment of Ky Lake, Calloway Co., 27 Dec 2008 (*KW* 85:51, 2009); 16 Jan 2015, a calling bird (vo./ph.) at Ky Dam Village (*KW* 91:55, 2015); 17 Dec 2015, Upper Hickman Bottoms (*KW* 92:44, 2016); 14 Jan 2016, Clarks River NWR, Marshall Co. (*KW* 92:44, 2016); 17 Dec 2016, Ky Dam (*KW* 93:50, 2017); mid-Jan–Feb 2019, landfill at Calvert City, Marshall Co. (H. Chambers, et al., eBird data).

List of extralimital reports by county

Boone (27 Apr 2011, (2) seen and heard calling sw. of Rabbit Hash [*KW* 87:92, 2011])
Hopkins (9 Apr 2014, Pond Creek Bottoms [*KW* 90:73, 2014])

*COMMON RAVEN *Corvus corax*

Status: Rare to uncommon (and very locally distributed) resident. Historically this species was apparently a rare resident of the Cumberland Plateau and Mountains, but Mengel (pp. 331-332) listed it as probably extirpated. During the summer of 1969, the species was rediscovered in the rugged mountain country of southeastern Kentucky (Croft, *KW* 46:21-22, 1970), and during subsequent decades ravens have slowly increased in that part of the state. The species is regularly reported from along the crests of Black Mountain, Cumberland Mountain, and others astride the Virginia line, as well as along the entire length of Pine Mountain, which formerly served roughly as a northwestern boundary for regular sightings. During the past couple of decades, reports of ravens have slowly but gradually spread farther north and west into the interior of the Cumberland Plateau, and the species has now been reported from at least 20 counties (see below). The first confirmed nest in Kentucky was found on Pine Mountain at Bad Branch SNP, Letcher Co., in 1984, with subsequent records now documented in four additional counties (see below). Ravens are often heard rather than seen in the heavily forested regions they inhabit; they can probably most easily be seen by scanning from lookouts along the crests of Pine, Cumberland and Black Mountains, but they are least likely to be encountered during the breeding season (Mar through May) when pairs are tied to nesting territories. Generally seen singly or in small family groups of fewer than a half-dozen birds. **State Breeding Status**: Threatened.

Maximum count: **7** at the ICG Mine, Knott Co., 6 Jun 2011 (*KW* 87:115, 2011; B. Palmer-Ball, eBird data).

Summary of confirmed breeding records by county

Knott (Cypress Amax WMA in 1998 [Larkin, et al., *KW* 75:50-52, 1999])
Letcher (Bad Branch SNP in 1984 [*KW* 60:54, 1984; Fowler, et al., *AB* 39:852-853, 1985]; same location in 1989 [*KW* 65:70, 1989] and during susequent years)
Morgan (Paintsville Lake WMA in 2004 [*KW* 80:70, 2004]; same location in 2005 [*KW* 81:90, 2005];)
Perry (Buckhorn Lake in 2015 [*KW* 91:74, 2015]; same location in 2017 [B. Wulker, eBird data])
Pike (nr. Elkhorn City in 2019 [D. Owens et al., eBird data])

Summary of additional records away from Pine Mt. and the Cumberland Mts. by county

Bath (C. Allen, 2017 eBird data; *KW* 94:80, 2018; G. Apte, 2019 eBird data)
Bell (*KW* 86:12, 2010)
Boyd (V. Sandage, 2016 eBird data; *KW* 93:76, 2017; R. Denton, 2018 eBird data)
Breathitt (*KW* 88:14, 2012; *KW* 91:74, 2015; *KW* 94:12, 2018)
Carter (R. Prentki, 2014 eBird data; *KW* 93:50, 2017)
Floyd (*KW* 80:12, 2004; *KW* 86:12, 2010; *KW* 87:20/92, 2011; *KW* 91:74, 2015; *KW* 92:44, 2016; S. Freidhof, 2016 eBird data; *KW* 93:50, 2017)
Greenup (*KW* 93:76, 2017; R. Denton/P. Brown, 2018 eBird data)
Johnson (*KW* 83:83, 2007; *KW* 85:18, 2009; *KW* 92:66, 2016)
Knott (*KW* 82:83, 2006; *KW* 86:12, 2010; *KW* 87:115, 2011; *KW* 88:14, 2012; *KW* 90:14, 2014; *KW* 90:74, 2014; C. Bliznick, 2017 eBird data; L. Anderson, 2019 eBird data)
Lawrence (*KW* 93:50, 2017; *KW* 94:109, 2018)
Leslie (R. Bontrager, 2017 eBird data; D. Lang/J. Sole, 2019 eBird data)
Martin (*KW* 86:45, 2010)
Menifee (G. Sheridan, 2014 eBird data)
Morgan (*KW* 92:12/44, 2016; *KW* 93:50, 2017)
Perry (*KW* 90:73, 2014; D. Svetich, 2017 eBird data)
Pike (*KW* 86:12/71, 2010; *KW* 87:20/92, 2011; *KW* 88:14, 2012; *KW* 89:12/97, 2013; *KW* 91:12/74, 2015; *KW* 92:44/80, 2016; *KW* 93:50, 2017; *KW* 94:12, 2018)
Powell (*KW* 65:70, 1989)
Rowan (*KW* 94:109, 2018)

*HORNED LARK *Eremophila alpestris*

Status: Resident; locally rare to fairly common during migration and summer, irregularly uncommon to fairly common during winter. Recorded essentially statewide in a variety of open habitats with little or no vegetation, but absent from heavily forested portions of eastern Kentucky. Peak of abundance occurs from mid-Nov to mid-Mar. Breeding has been reported locally across the state, most widespread in extensively cultivated areas of central and western Kentucky, but present on reclaimed surface mines and other suitable habitat on the Cumberland Plateau. Much more numerous and widespread during winter when flocks of dozens of birds are not infrequently seen in grain stubble fields in farmland of central and western Kentucky.

Maximum counts: ca. **2000** nw. of Knifely, Adair Co., 29 Jan 2009 (*KW* 85:51, 2009); ca. **2000** nr. Monticello, Wayne Co., 30 Jan 2009 (*KW* 85:51, 2009); **1000** at Ky Bend, Fulton Co., 13 Feb 1971 (Coskren, *KW* 47:31, 1971); **1000** in farmland around McElroy Lake, 3 Feb 1991 (*KW* 67:31, 1991); ca. **1000** in n. Union Co., 2 Jan 2010 (*KW* 86:45, 2010); at least **1000** in Barren Co., 14 Feb 2010 (*KW* 86:45, 2010); flocks of **400-500** not infrequent during winter (Mengel: 319).

Maximum CBC counts: **1942** on the Elkton CBC, 31 Dec 2014 (*KW* 91:24, 2015; R. Stoll, eBird data); **1800** on the Louisville CBC, 23 Dec 1973 (*KW* 50:13/15, 1974); **1455** on the Olmstead CBC (*KW* 81:19/60, 2005).

*BANK SWALLOW *Riparia riparia*

Status: Transient (uncommon to fairly common during spring, rare to uncommon during fall); uncommon and very locally distributed summer resident. Recorded chiefly west of the Cumberland Plateau during migration. Widespread for a brief period during May but seldom seen during fall; generally encountered in small numbers with other swallows, often over water. Breeding at scattered localities in central and western Kentucky, almost exclusively along the banks of the Mississippi and Ohio rivers, but small colonies also have been located in sand and gravel pit banks in several northern and western counties (see below). Nesting colonies may contain from about a dozen burrows up to a hundred or more, and post breeding concentrations (typically in the general vicinity of nesting colonies) may number hundreds of birds. **State Breeding Status**: Special Concern.

Maximum spring counts: **1000+** at McElroy Lake, 11 May 2008 (*KW* 84:68 2008); **1000+** swallows "mostly Bank" in early May 1989 at McElroy Lake (Palmer-Ball and Boggs, *KW* 67:65, 1991); probably ½ of **1000-1500** swallows at Morgan Pond, 18 May 2016 (*KW* 92:66, 2016).

Maximum late summer/fall counts: 80% of ca. **5000** swallows, Hickman Co., 15 Sep 1978 (*KW* 55:16, 1979); most of **3000-5000** swallows on the Mississippi River nr. Island No. 1, Carlisle Co., 19/26 Aug 2001 (B. Palmer-Ball, eBird data); **2000-3000** nr. the Long Point Unit, 26 Jul 2012 (*KW* 88:95, 2012); **2000** on a sandbar on the Mississippi River nr. Lake No. 9, 25 Aug 1988 (*KW* 65:9, 1989); **2000+** in the Lower Hickman Bottoms, 25 Jul 2013 (*KW* 89:97, 2013); nesting colony of **more than 1000** burrows in Henderson Co., 7 Jul 1940 (Mengel:323); at least **1000** nr. Lake No. 9, 18 Aug 2010 (*KW* 87:20, 2011); **1000** on the Mississippi River at Island No. 1, 18 Aug 2018 (*KW* 95:9, 2019); 800-**1000** on Ohio River opposite Shawneetown, Ill., summer 1953 (*AFN* 7:312, 1953).

Early spring dates: 22 Mar 1989, Pulaski Co. (*KW* 65:70, 1989); 24 Mar 2011, Pulaski Co. (*KW* 87:92, 2011); 25 Mar 2011, Bernheim Forest (*KW* 87:92, 2011); 2 Apr 2008, McElroy Lake (*KW* 84:68 2008); 4 Apr 19—, Rowan Co. (Barbour, *KW* 28:26, 1952); 5 Apr 1992, Lower Hickman Bottoms (B. Palmer-Ball, eBird data).

Late fall dates: 24 Oct 2007, (ph.) Pulaski Co. (*KW* 84:13 2008); 10 Oct 1992, Sauerheber Unit (*KW* 69:9, 1993); 2 Oct 1965, Louisville area (*KW* 52:54, 1976).

Unaccepted records: 2 Apr 1991, 3 Apr 1992, and 30 Mar 2002, [no details] Sauerheber Unit (eBird data).

Published errors: a report of nesting in Kenton Co. in 1983 (*KW* 59:53, 1983;) pertained to Northern Rough-winged Swallows (correction *fide* E. Groneman, pers. comm.); the same was true for reports of nesting along the Kentucky River, Mercer and Owen cos. in 1993 (*KW* 69:57, 1993; *fide* K. Prather, pers. comm.).

Summary of breeding records by county

Ballard (Palmer-Ball and Barron, *KW* 58:75, 1982)

Boone (*KW* 57:74, 1981; *KW* 58:84, 1982; *KW* 59:53, 1983; *KW* 60:54, 1984; *KW* 62:68, 1986; *KW* 63:60-61, 1987; *KW* 64:65, 1988; *KW* 65:89, 1989; *KBBA*:154-155; *KW* 79:84, 2003; *KW* 80:84, 2004; *KW* 83:106, 2007)

Campbell (*KW* 83:106, 2007; *KW* 85:94-95, 2009; *KW* 86:95, 2010)

Carlisle (*KBBA*:154-155)

Carroll (*KW* 61:58, 1985; *KW* 62:68, 1986; *KW* 64:65, 1988; *KBBA*:154-155; *KW* 85:95, 2009)

Daviess (*KBBA*:154-155)

Fayette (*KBBA*:154-155)

Fulton (*KW* 60:54, 1984; B. Palmer-Ball, 1995 eBird data; *KW* 74:74, 1998)

Gallatin (*KW* 92:66, 2016)

Henderson (Mengel:323; *KBBA*:154-155)

Hickman (*KW* 55:57, 1979; *KW* 56:80, 1980; *KW* 57:74, 1981; *KW* 62:68, 1986; *KW* 63:61, 1987; *KBBA*:154-155)

Jefferson (Mengel:323; 2001 eBird data)

Lewis (Gelis, *KW* 72:20-25, 1996; *KW* 72:75, 1996; *KW* 79:84, 2003; *KW* 80:84, 2004; *KW* 81:108, 2005; *KW* 83:106, 2007; *KW* 84:68 2008)

Livingston (*KW* 60:54, 1984; *KW* 61:58, 1985; *KW* 62:68, 1986; *KW* 63:61, 1987; *KBBA*:154-155; *KW* 78:66, 2002)

Lyon (*KW* 63:61, 1987)

McCracken (Palmer-Ball and Barron, *KW* 58:75, 1982)

Meade (*KW* 64:65, 1988; *KBBA*:154-155)

Mercer (R. Denton, 2017 eBird data)

Muhlenberg (B. Palmer-Ball, 1998 eBird data; R. Denton, 2002 eBird data)

Oldham (*KBBA*:154-155)

Trimble (B. Monroe, Jr., 1980s pers. comm.; *KW* 61:58, 1985)

Union (Mengel:323; *KBBA*:154-155)

*TREE SWALLOW *Tachycineta bicolor*

Status: Uncommon to fairly common transient, locally rare to fairly common summer resident, extremely rare during winter. Recorded statewide during migration, but seemingly less numerous on the Cumberland Plateau and Mountains; most frequently observed foraging over water. Peaks of abundance occur from late Mar to mid-Apr and from late Sep to mid-Oct. Mengel (p. 322) listed only one uncertain reference to summering and no breeding records. Breeding was first noted in the Cumberland River Valley, Lyon Co., during summer 1965 (Robinson, *KW* 41:61-62, 1965), and at Long Run Park, Jefferson Co., Jun 1975 (Stamm, *KW* 52:13-14, 1976). A general southward expansion continued through the early 1990s (*KBBA*:150-151) and continued into the 2000s, perhaps culminating with confirmed nesting documented in Harlan Co. in se. Kentucky in 2005 (*KW* 81:108, 2005). Now recorded during summer and nesting at scattered localities essentially statewide (although generally still more widespread north than south and west). Initially the species was mostly found nesting along the edges of lakes and ponds with dead trees; more recently Tree Swallows have begun using nest boxes in open areas. Nests singly or in small, loose colonies of up to a half-dozen pairs. The species becomes quite locally distributed after the nesting season (mid-Jul into Oct), being widespread only along the floodplains of the lower Oho and Mississippi rivers where numbers stage before heading south; a noticeable influx of migrants then occurs during Oct, resulting in a short-term increase in distribution and abundance. Generally encountered in flocks of a few to 50 or more birds, but occasionally seen in much larger flocks of hundreds of birds, typically over or near water.

Maximum spring counts: at least **5000** (and possibly 7500–10,000) e. of Morganfield, Union Co., 16 Apr 2012 (KW 88:79, 2012); **3000-5000** e. of Morganfield, Union Co., 12 Apr 2013 (*KW* 89:77, 2013); "**thousands**" at Lake Peewee, last week of Mar 2006 (*KW* 82:72, 2006); **2000** at Barren River Lake, 13 Mar 2017 (*KW* 93:76, 2017; ca. **1000** at Peabody WMA, 13 Apr 2001 (*KW* 77:51, 2001); **1000** at Lake Cumberland, Pulaski Co., 16 Apr 2007 (R. Denton, eBird data); **1000** at Lake Barkley, Trigg Co., 22 Mar 2013 (R. Denton, eBird data); **750-1000** in Hopkins Co., 12 Mar 2006

(*KW* 82:72, 2006); **700** at the Sauerheber Unit 2 Apr 2013 (K. Michalski, eBird data); **500** at the Sauerheber Unit, 26 Apr 2015 (*KW* 91:74, 2015); **500** at the Sinclair Unit, 7 Mar 2017 (T. Graham, eBird data); **450** at Lake Reba, Madison Co., 26-27 Mar 2011 (*KW* 87:92, 2011); **400** at Lexington, 19 Apr 2018 (*KW* 94:80, 2018); **390** at Jonathan Creek, 9 Apr 2016 (H. Chambers/M. Easley, eBird data); **350** at Minor Clark Fish Hatchery, 6 Apr 1990 (*KW* 66:59, 1990).

Maximum fall counts: **3000-5000** in Carlisle Co., 8 Oct 1991 (B. Palmer-Ball, eBird data); up to **3000** at Barren River Lake, 28 Oct 2017 (*KW* 94:12, 2018); **2000+** in Fulton Co., 14 Oct 1996 (*KW* 73:8, 1997); **1500–2000** in Fulton Co., 20 Sep 1986 (*KW* 63:10, 1987); ca. **1500** in the Jackson Purchase, 23 Aug 1980 (Palmer-Ball and Barron, *KW* 58:77, 1982); **1000 + 400** at Green River Lake, Adair Co., 8 Oct 2008 (*KW* 85:18, 2009); **1000** in w. Henderson Co., 14 Oct 2007 (*KW* 84:13, 2008); ca. **1000** at Green River Lake, Adair Co., 14 Oct 2009 (*KW* 86:13, 2010); ca. **800** in Fulton Co., mid-Sep 1966 (Able, *KW* 43:31, 1967); **800** at Green River Lake, Taylor Co., 28 Oct 2017 (R. Denton, eBird data); **700** at Cave Lake, Wayne Co., 22 Sep 2003 (*KW* 80:12, 2004; R. Denton, eBird data); **350** in Gallatin Co., 21 Aug 1999 (*KW* 76:7, 2000).

Early spring dates: 28 Jan 2011, Fulton Co. (*KW* 87:64, 2011); 8 Feb 2017, Todd Co. (*KW* 93:51, 2017); 12 Feb 1965, Louisville (*KW* 52:54, 1976); 13 Feb 2018, Sinclair Unit (H. Chambers et al., eBird data); 13 Feb 2018, Hart Co. (*KW* 94:59, 2018); 15 Feb 2005, Ky Dam (*KW* 81:60, 2005); 16 Feb 1986, Ballard Co. (*KW* 62:28, 1986); 17 Feb 2017, Schochoh, Logan Co. (*KW* 93:51, 2017); 17 Feb 2018, Ky Dam (R. Bontrager, eBird data); 18 Feb 1990, Warren Co. (*KW* 66:40, 1990).

Late fall/early winter dates: occasionally lingers past mid-Nov into early winter, the latest dates being 20 Nov 2018, Lake Peewee (*KW* 95:8, 2019); 22 Nov 1984, Jefferson Co. (*KW* 61:18, 1985); 26 Nov 2008, Sauerheber Unit (*KW* 85:18, 2009); 28 Nov 2018, Ky Lake, Marshall Co. (*KW* 95:8, 2019); 5 Dec 2016, Lake Peewee (*KW* 93:51, 2017); 7 Dec 2000, Ky Lake, Marshall Co. (M. Easley, notes); 19 Dec 1998, two birds on Danville CBC (*KW* 75:9, 1999); 19-20 Dec 2014, Ballard WMA (*KW* 91:55, 2015); 29 Dec 1984, Ballard Co. (*KW* 61:3, 1985); and 31 Dec 1989, Green River Lake, Taylor Co. (*KW* 66:40, 1990; date published erroneously as 30 Dec therein [*fide* J. Elmore, notes]).

Possible hybrid record: See Barn Swallow.

*NORTHERN ROUGH-WINGED SWALLOW *Stelgidopteryx serripennis*

Status: Uncommon to fairly common transient and summer resident. Recorded statewide during migration in a variety of semi-open to open habitats. Peak of abundance occurs from early Apr to early Oct. Breeds statewide, most frequently in crevices in vertical road cuts but also along natural clifflines and dirt banks, and occasionally in holes in bridges and buildings. Nests singly or in small, loose colonies of up to a half-dozen pairs. Most often encountered in small numbers, but as with the Tree Swallow, large flocks of hundreds of birds can be seen during fall, especially along the Mississippi and lower Ohio rivers where numbers stage before heading south.

Maximum spring counts: **140** at Blood River, 11 Apr 2012 (H. Chambers, eBird data); **100** at the Waitsboro Rec. Area, Lake Cumberland, Pulaski Co., 6 Apr 2007 (R. Denton, eBird data); **80** at Minor Clark Hatchery, 4 May 2011 (B. Wulker, eBird data).

Maximum fall counts: **1000+** in Fulton Co., 14 Oct 1996 (*KW* 73:8, 1997); **1000** in the Lower Hickman Bottoms, 2 Oct 2004 (R. Denton/H. Chambers, eBird data); **1000+** in w. Fulton Co., 18 Oct 2006 (*KW* 83:17, 2007); ca. **1000** in Fulton Co., 4 Oct 1981 (*KW* 58:17, 1982); ca. **1000** in the Jackson Purchase, 23 Aug 1980 (Palmer-Ball and Barron, *KW* 58:77, 1982); at least **700** at Ky Bend, Fulton Co, 27 Sep 2013 (*KW* 90:14, 2014); **670** in Fulton Co., 7 Oct 2001 (*KW* 78:9, 2002); **550** in w. Fulton Co., 25 Aug 2011 (*KW* 88:14, 2012); ca. **500** in Fulton Co., mid-Sep 1966 (Able, *KW* 43:31, 1967).

Early spring dates: 13 Mar 2013, Allen Co. (*KW* 89:77, 2013); 14 Mar 2003, Ky Dam Village (*KW* 79:71, 2003); 15 Mar 2001, Warren Co. (J. Elmore, notes); 15 Mar 2011, Ky Dam (*KW* 87:92, 2011); 16 Mar 2001, Lake Barkley, Lyon Co. (R. Denton, eBird data); 16 Mar 2001, Warren Co. (D. Roemer, notes); 16 Mar 2005, Fulton Co. (*KW* 81:90, 2005); 16 Mar 2012, Russell Co. (*KW* 88:79, 2012); 16 Mar 2018, Wolf Creek Dam (*KW* 94:80, 2018); 16 Mar 2019, (ph.) Ky Dam Village (T. Smith, eBird data); 17 Mar 2011, Hart Co. (*KW* 87:92, 2011); 17 Mar 2016, Wood Creek Lake, Laurel Co. (*KW* 92:66, 2016); 17 Mar 2018, Burnside, Pulaski Co. (*KW* 94:80, 2018).

Late fall dates: 28 Nov 2005, (vt.) Fulton Co. (*KW* 82:12, 2006); 10 Nov 2006, Lake Barkley, Lyon Co. (*KW* 83:17, 2007); 10 Nov 2008, Lake Cumberland, Pulaski Co. (*KW* 85:18, 2009); 9 Nov 2007, Fulton Co. (*KW* 84:13 2008); 4 Nov 2017, Cedar Creek Lake, Lincoln Co. (*KW* 94:12, 2018); 1 Nov 2006, Freeman Lake (*KW* 83:16, 2007); 31 Oct 2009, Barren River Lake, Barren Co. (*KW* 86:13, 2010); 29 Oct 2006, Henderson Co. (*KW* 83:17, 2007); 28 Oct 2009, Sauerheber Unit (*KW* 86:13, 2010); 27 Oct 2007, Barren River Lake (*KW* 84:13, 2008); 27 Oct 2010, Sauerheber Unit (*KW* 87:20, 2011); 26 Oct 2003, w. Fulton Co. (*KW* 80:12, 2004); 25 Oct 2006, Barren River Lake (*KW* 83:17, 2007); 25 Oct 2008, Lower Hickman Bottoms (*KW* 85:18, 2009); 25 Oct 2013, Logan Co. (*KW* 90:14, 2014); 24 Oct 2007, Pulaski Co. (*KW* 84:13 2008); 24 Oct 2009, Green River Lake, Adair Co. (*KW* 86:13, 2010); 24 Oct 2012, Union Co. (*KW* 89:12, 2013); 24 Oct 2013, Sauerheber Unit and w. Fulton Co. (*KW* 90:14, 2014).

Unaccepted records: 12 Nov 1983 (15), Rowan Co. (*KW* 60:18, 1984); 10 Dec 2007, Lake Barkley above the dam, Lyon Co., a swallow thought to be this species but unconfirmed (*KW* 84:45, 2008).

*PURPLE MARTIN *Progne subis*

Status: Locally uncommon to fairly common transient and summer resident, accidental during winter. Recorded statewide during migration, usually flying singly or in loose groups over residential areas, farmland, or water. Peak of abundance occurs from late Mar to early Aug. Breeding throughout the state except the heavily forested portions of eastern Kentucky. The species seems to utilize man-made structures exclusively for nesting, so it is primarily found near settlement during the breeding season. Large congregations numbering in the thousands frequently occur at somewhat traditional locales during late summer before the major movement south.

Maximum counts (all at roosts): possibly as many **30,000** at Bowling Green, late Aug 2018 (*KW* 95:8, 2019); **25,000+** at Owensboro, Daviess Co., 20 Aug 1996 (Gorney, *KW* 73:30, 1997); **25,000+** at Lexington, early Aug 2009 (*KW* 86:12, 2010); ca. **25,000** nr. Lake No. 9, 25 Aug 2017 (*KW* 94:12, 2018); **20,000-30,000** at Louisville, mid-Aug 2013 (*KW* 90:14, 2014); **17,000-18,000** on the University of Louisville campus, Aug 1997 (P. Eason, pers. comm.); ca. **15,000** at Lexington, 9 Aug 2014 (*KW* 91:12, 2015); **10,000-15,000** on the University of Louisville campus, 23 Aug 1998 (B. Palmer-Ball, eBird data); **10,000-15,000** in s. Hopkins Co., 4 Aug 2014 (*KW* 91:12, 2015); ca. **10,000** at the Falls of the Ohio, 31 Jul 1978 (*KW* 54:62, 1978); ca. **10,000** at Shippingport Island, Jefferson Co., early Aug 1982 (*KW* 59:17, 1983); ca. **10,000** at Lexington, mid-Aug 2007 (*KW* 84:13 2008); at least **10,000** at Lexington, early Aug 2011 (*KW* 88:14, 2012); ca. **10,000** at Williamsburg, Whitley Co., 30 Jul 2014 (*KW* 90:90, 2014); ca. **10,000** in se. Hopkins Co., 19/23 Jul 2015 (*KW* 91:87, 2015); ca. **10,000** at Wilmore, Jessamine Co. (*KW* 94:109, 2018).

Early spring dates: 16 Feb 1966, Murray, Calloway Co. (E. Larson, eBird data); 17 Feb 1950, Trigg Co. (Mengel:327); 19 Feb 2011, LBL, Lyon Co. (*KW* 87:63, 2011); 22 Feb 2011, Bowling Green (*KW* 87:64, 2011); 23 Feb 2013, Allen Co. (*KW* 89:52, 2013); 24 Feb 2005, se. Monroe Co. (*KW* 81:60, 2005); 25 Feb 2007, Monroe Co. (*KW* 83:50, 2007); 25 Feb 2012, Allen Co. (*KW* 88:79, 2012); 25 Feb 2013, Bowling Green (*KW* 89:52, 2013); 26-27 Feb 2001, Murray (*KW* 77:29, 2001; H. Chambers, notes); 27 Feb 2006, Lewisport, Hancock Co. (*KW* 82:49, 2006); 27 Feb 2011, Allen Co. (*KW* 87:97, 2011); 28 Feb 2013, LBL, Lyon Co. (*KW* 89:52, 2013); 28 Feb 2018, LBL, Lyon Co. (*KW* 94:80, 2018); 29 Feb 2016, LBL, Lyon Co. (*KW* 92:45, 2016); 1 Mar 1992, Grayson Co. (*KW* 68:47, 1992); 1 Mar 2012, LBL, Lyon Co. (*KW* 88:79, 2012); 2 Mar 2004, Bowling Green (*KW* 80:70, 2004); 2 Mar 2008, Bowling Green (*KW* 84:68 2008); 3 Mar 2004, Logan and Marshall cos. (*KW* 80:70, 2004); 3 Mar 2008, Murray, Calloway Co. (*KW* 84:68 2008); 3 Mar 2009, Fulton Co. (*KW* 85:74, 2009); 6 Mar 1964, Louisville area (*KW* 52:55, 1976).

Late fall dates: 16 Oct 2013, Warren Co. (A. Hulsey, eBird data); 11 Oct 2014, Schochoh, Logan Co. (*KW* 91:12, 2015); 3 Oct 1994, Bowling Green (D. Roemer, notes); 28 Sep 18—, Blue Grass region (Mengel: 328); 28 Sep 2014, remarkable count of 195 (ph.) still at Lexington (*KW* 91:12, 2015); 25 Sep 19—, Bowling Green (Mengel:328); 25 Sep 2009, Crittenden Co. (*KW* 86:13, 2010); 24 Sep 2006, Pulaski Co. (*KW* 83:16, 2007).

Out-of-season record (winter): 26 Jan 1967, Louisville (*KW* 52:55, 1976).

*BARN SWALLOW *Hirundo rustica*

Status: Fairly common to common transient and summer resident, extremely rare during winter. Recorded statewide except for the heavily forested portions of eastern Kentucky; widespread as a transient, occurring in a variety of open habitats and over water. Peak of abundance occurs from mid-Apr to mid-Aug. Breeding statewide, but abundance is generally proportional to the amount of settlement; occurs in a great variety of semi-open and open habitats, nesting singly or in small loose colonies in buildings or under bridges. There are a few reports of lingering or wayward birds during winter. Usually seen in small flocks feeding over open areas, but migratory concentrations may number over a hundred birds.

Maximum spring counts ca. **1000** at McElroy Lake, early Apr 1989 (Palmer-Ball and Boggs, *KW* 67:64, 1991); **500** at Morgan Pond, 4 May 2016 (J. Hall, eBird data).

Maximum fall counts: **1000** at Clifty Pond, Pulaski Co., 25 Aug 2001 (R. Denton, eBird data); **500** along Oakhill Road, Pulaski Co., 23 Jul 1980 (eBird data); **500** in n. Warren Co., 20 Aug 2006 (A. Hulsey, eBird data); **500** at the Sinclair Unit, 21 Jul 2017 (R. Bontrager, eBird data); **500** on the Mississippi River at Island No. 1, 18 Aug 2018 (A. Lydeard, eBird data).

Early spring dates: 4 Mar 1934, south-central Kentucky (*KW* 38:17, 1962); 9 Mar 2008, Calloway Co. (*KW* 84:68, 2008); 10 Mar 2001, Barkley Dam (H. Chambers, notes); 10 Mar 2017, Wayne Co. (*KW* 93:76, 2017); 13 Mar 2011, Allen Co. (*KW* 87:93, 2011); 13 Mar 2013, Blood River (*KW* 89:77, 2013); 14 Mar 1983, Calloway Co. (*KW* 59:42, 1983); 14 Mar 2008, Wayne Co. (*KW* 84:68, 2008); 14 Mar 2017, Todd Co. (*KW* 93:76, 2017); 15 Mar 2008, Cedar Creek Lake, Lincoln Co. (R. Denton, eBird data); 16 Mar 2018, McElroy Lake (*KW* 94:80, 2018); 16 Mar 2019, Fulton Co. (C. Bliznick, eBird data); 17 Mar 2001, Pulaski and Wayne cos. (R. Denton, eBird data); 18 Mar 1991, McElroy Lake (*KW* 67:57, 1991); 18 Mar 2000, Pulaski Co. (R. Denton, eBird data); 18 Mar 2006, Hart Co. (*KW* 82:72, 2006); 18 Mar 2016, McElroy Lake (*KW* 92:66, 2016); 18 Mar 2017, Sauerheber Unit (C. Crawford, eBird data); 18 Mar 2019, McElroy Lake (M. Monroe, eBird data).

Late fall dates: 24 Nov 2007, Russell Co. (*KW* 84:13 2008); 11 Nov 1990, Lake Peewee (*KW* 67:8, 1991); 11 Nov 2001, Barren River Lake, Allen/Barren cos. (*KW* 78:9, 2002); 9 Nov 2002, Barren River Lake (*KW* 79:13, 2003); 2 Nov 2004, Minor Clark Fish Hatchery (*KW* 81:13, 2005); 30 Oct 2016, Barren Co. (*KW* 93:12, 2017); 30 Oct 2018, Pfeiffer Fish Hatchery, Franklin Co. (*KW* 95:9, 2019); 29 Oct 2006, Sauerheber Unit (*KW* 83:17, 2007); 27 Oct 2012, Sauerheber Unit (J. Meredig, eBird data); 26 Oct 2007, Barren River Lake (*KW* 84:13 2008); 26 Oct 2009, Barren River Lake (*KW* 86:13, 2010); 26 Oct 2017, Sauerheber Unit (*KW* 94:12, 2018); 25 Oct 2000, Wayne Co. (R. Denton, eBird data); 25 Oct 2005, Wayne Co. (*KW* 82:12, 2006); 25 Oct 2006, Barren River Lake (*KW* 83:17, 2007); 25 Oct 2013, Meade Co. (A. Stark, eBird data).

Out-of-season records (winter): 27 Dec 1977–2 Jan 1978, one bird at the East Hickman Sewage Treatment Plant, Jessamine Co., (*KW* 54:29, 1978; *AB* 32:650, 1978 [location published incorrectly as from "Hickman, Ky." in *AB* 32:359, 1978]); 15 Dec 1999, one bird (vt.) on Ky Lake at Ky Dam Village (*KW* 76:31, 2000); 4-9 Jan 2003, (2 [ph.]) at the Paradise Power Plant (*KW* 79:20/48, 2003); 18 Dec 2011 (ph.), Warren Co. (*KW* 88:23/49, 2012); 17 Feb 2019, Morgan Pond (C. Bliznick/T. Noel, eBird data).

Published error: 22 Oct 2011, Union Co. (*KW* 89:12, 2013; date erroneously published as 21 Oct therein [*fide* A. Newman, et al., eBird data])

Hybrid records: 4 May–17 Jul 2000, a Barn Swallow x Cliff Swallow was observed at a Barn Swallow nesting colony under a bridge over Clear Creek, Hopkins Co. (*NAB* 54:390, 2000; B. Palmer-Ball, eBird data); 29 Jun–3 Jul 2009, a possible Tree Swallow x Barn Swallow in Jefferson Co. (Palmer-Ball, KW 85:81/103-104).

*CLIFF SWALLOW *Petrochelidon pyrrhonota*

Status: Transient (uncommon during spring, rare to uncommon during fall); uncommon to locally common summer resident. Recorded chiefly west of the Cumberland Plateau during migration. Widespread for a brief period during May but seldom seen during fall; generally encountered in small numbers with other swallows. Breeding was formerly (1800s) reported at scattered localities across north-central Kentucky, but the species disappeared by the late 19th century and was absent for many years until the mid-1940s; at that time a colony became established on Ky Dam (Mengel:327; Peterson, *KW* 46:7-9, 1970). In subsequent decades the species has gradually spread throughout the western three-quarters of the state (now documented from more than 70 counties; see below), mostly on dams and under bridges spanning the larger lakes and rivers, but also at least occasionally under bridges of smaller streams and highway overpasses. Nesting colonies typically contain from just a few to up to a hundred or more nests.

Maximum spring counts: **800** at Uniontown Dam, Union Co., 26 Apr 2016 (S. Sorenson, eBird data); probably ½ of **1000-1500** swallows at Morgan Pond, 18 May 2016 (*KW* 92:66, 2016).

Maximum late summer/fall counts: ca. **4000** at Morgan Pond 17 Aug 2011 (*KW* 88:14, 2012); **3000** at Open Pond, Fulton Co., 17 Jul 2004 (J. Wilson, eBird data); ca. **2500** at Guthrie Swamp, Todd Co., 21 Aug 2009 (*KW* 86:13, 2010); likely **1000+** with even more Bank Swallows on the Mississippi River nr. Island No. 1, Carlisle Co., 12 Aug 2001 (B. Palmer-Ball, eBird data); **500-600** nr. Woodburn, Warren Co., 24 Jul 2006 (*KW* 82:83, 2006); **500** in Fulton Co., 11 Jul 1999 (*KW* 75:61, 1999); **500** at Cave Run Lake, 28 Jul 2009 (R. Denton, eBird data); **500** on the Mississippi River at Island No. 1, 18 Aug 2018 (*KW* 95:9, 2019).

Early spring dates: 14 Mar 2006, Barkley Dam (*KW* 82:72, 2006); 15 Mar 2011, Ky Dam (*KW* 87:93, 2011); 17 Mar 2004, Barkley Dam (*KW* 80:70, 2004); 17 Mar 2019, (ph.) Jefferson Co. (S. Thirkannad et al., eBird data); 21 Mar 2004, Ky Dam (*KW* 80:70, 2004); 21 Mar 2007, Barkley Dam (*KW* 83:83, 2007); 23 Mar 1987, Trigg Co. (*KW* 63:51, 1987); 23 Mar 2001, Barkley Dam (B. Palmer-Ball, eBird data); 23 Mar 2003, Ky Lake, Marshall Co. (eBird data); 24 Mar 1917, Mammoth Cave National Park (*KW* 38:17, 1962).

Late fall dates: 29 Oct 2017, Lake Linville, Rockcastle Co. (*KW* 94:12, 2018); 26 Oct 1983, Rowan Co. (*KW* 60:18, 1984); 18 Oct 2006, w. Fulton Co. (*KW* 83:17, 2007); 17 Oct 2009, Lower Hickman Bottoms (*KW* 86:13, 2010); 15 Oct 1997, Fulton Co. (D. Roemer, notes); 14 Oct 2017, w. Hopkins Co. (C. Bliznick, eBird data); 10 Oct 2017, e. of Morganfield, Union Co. (B. Palmer-Ball, eBird data); 7 Oct 2005, Jonathan Creek (*KW* 82:12, 2006); 7 Oct 2012, Allen Co. (*KW* 89:12, 2013); 4 Oct 2009, McElroy Lake (eBird data); 3 Oct 2016, Morgan Pond (*KW* 93:12, 2017); 2 Oct 1965, Louisville area (*KW* 52:55, 1976).

Hybrid record: see Barn Swallow.

Published error: I believe the report of two nesting colonies in Carroll Co. (*KW* 63:61, 1987) actually pertained to Bank Swallow colonies that were present in the county at that time.

Summary of breeding records by county (reference/citation of initial report[s])

Adair (*KW* 58:84, 1982; *KBBA*:156)
Allen (Mason, *KW* 53:40-41, 1977; *KBBA*:156)
Anderson (K. Prather, pers. comm.)
Ballard (*KW* 78:66, 2002)
Barren (Mason, *KW* 53:40-41, 1977; *KBBA*:156)
Bath (*KBBA*:156)
Ballard (*KW* 78:66, 2002)
Boone (*KW* 61:58, 1985; *KBBA*:156)
Bracken (*KBBA*:156)
Breckinridge (*KBBA*:156)
Butler (M. Monroe, 2000 pers. comm.)
Caldwell (*KBBA*:156)
Calloway (*KW* 58:84, 1982; *KBBA*:156)
Campbell (*KW* 84:68, 2008)
Carter (*KW* 55:57, 1979; *KBBA*:156)
Casey (*KW* 63:10-11, 1987; *KBBA*:156)
Cumberland (R. Denton, 2014 eBird data)
Daviess (*KW* 81:108, 2005; *KW* 82:83, 2006)
Elliott (W. Greene, Jr., 1985 pers. comm.)
Fleming (*KW* 64:65, 1988; *KBBA*:156)
Franklin (J. Sole, 2017 eBird data)
Fulton (*KW* 87:116, 2011)
Gallatin (*KW* 63:61, 1987; *KBBA*:156)
Graves (B. Palmer-Ball, 2019 eBird data)
Grayson (*KW* 62:45, 1986; *KBBA*:156)
Green (*KBBA*:156)

Greenup (*KW* 64:19, 1988; *KBBA*:156)
Hart (*KBBA*:156)
Harrison (*KW* 80:70, 2004)
Hart (*KW* 70:10, 1994)
Henderson (*KBBA*:156)
Henry (C. Hummel, 2017 eBird data)
Hopkins (*KBBA*:156)
Jefferson (*KW* 85:74, 2009)
Kenton (*KW* 84:68, 2008)
Knox (*KW* 81:108, 2005)
Larue (B. Palmer-Ball, 2009 eBird data)
Laurel (*KW* 71:69, 1995)
Lawrence (S. Freidhof, 2000 pers. comm.)
Lewis (*KW* 64:19, 1988; *KBBA*:156)
Livingston (Peterson, *KW* 46:7-9, 1970; Peterson, *KW* 49:63-65, 1973; *KBBA*:156)
Logan (S. Tyson, pers. comm./eBird data)
Lyon (*KBBA*:156)
Madison (W. Little, pers. comm.; C. Leftwich, 2019 eBird data)
Magoffin (A. Newman, 2012 eBird data)
Marion (*KW* 68:57, 1992)
Marshall (*KBBA*:156)
McCracken (*KBBA*:156)
McCreary (*KBBA*:156)
Meade (*BO*, Jul 2000)
Menifee (B. Wulker, 2013 eBird data)
Metcalfe (*KW* 73:73, 1997)
Monroe (R. Denton, 2015 eBird data)
Morgan (*KBBA*:156)
Muhlenberg (B. Palmer-Ball, 1993 eBird data)
Nelson (B. Palmer-Ball, 2008 eBird data)
Ohio (*KW* 65:89, 1989; *KBBA*:156)
Owen (*KW* 78:66, 2002)
Pulaski (*KBBA*:156)
Robertson (B. Wulker, 2016 eBird data)
Rowan (*KBBA*:156)
Russell (*KBBA*:156)
Simpson (*KW* 85:94, 2009)
Spencer (M. Autin, pers. comm.; eBird data)
Taylor (*KBBA*:156)
Trigg (*KBBA*:156)
Trimble (B. Wulker, 2016/2018eBird data)
Union (*KBBA*:156)
Warren (*KW* 81:108, 2005)
Washington (*KW* 83:106, 2007)
Whitley (J. Sipiora, 2012 eBird data)
Wolfe (*KW* 55:57, 1979; *KW* 56:80, 1980; *KBBA*:156)

CAVE SWALLOW *Petrochelidon fulva*

Status: Accidental vagrant. This swallow nests primarily in the United States in the southern portion of Texas, but the number of reports of vagrant birds has been on the increase over the past few decades. Currently it has been documented in Kentucky on only one occasion.

1) 4-5 May 2019, (ph.) McElroy Lake (B. Palmer-Ball/L. McMahon, et al., eBird data).

Cliff/Cave Swallow: a pale-rumped swallow, either a tardy Cliff Swallow, or perhaps more likely a vagrant Cave Swallow, was seen at Green River Lake, Adair Co., 7 Dec 2013 (*KW* 90:53-54, 2014; R. Denton, notes).

*CAROLINA CHICKADEE *Poecile carolinensis*

Status: Fairly common to common resident. Recorded statewide in a great variety of forested and semi-open habitats from mature woodlands and woodland borders to semi-open farmland and suburban parks and yards. Breeding statewide in natural tree cavities (typically excavated by the birds) and artificial nesting boxes. This species mixes freely with other small passerines into roving bands that forage together during the non-breeding season.

Maximum counts: **101** (mostly in Nelson Co.) on a portion of the Bernheim Forest CBC, 23 Dec 2006 (B. Palmer-Ball, notes); 70 (mostly in Nelson Co.) on a portion of the Bernheim Forest CBC, 28 Dec 1996 (B. Palmer-Ball, notes); **60** (mostly in Nelson Co.) on the Bernheim Forest CBC, 21 Dec 2014 (B. Davis, eBird data).

BLACK-CAPPED CHICKADEE *Poecile atricapillus*

Status: Extremely rare fall, winter, and spring visitant, apparently occurring on a very irregular basis and only during irruptive years. More than ten records have been documented with photographs and/or in hand measurements; all of these birds have appeared consequent with significant eruptions of birds from se. Canada. Several additional sight records have been documented sufficiently during such flight years to be considered valid. Moreover, the accumulation of these recent records, primarily from ne. Kentucky, suggests that at least some of the historical records (1950s and 1960s) from that part of the state are probably valid; however, many literature reports do not match the developing pattern of occurrence and have not been documented in any way. The similarity of this species with our common Carolina Chickadee, along with the possibility of hybrids between the two, necessitates in-hand measurements, photographs, or very close scrutiny of calls and plumage to confirm identification.

Late spring date: 23 Apr 2000, Boyd Co. (Sweeney, et al., *KW* 76:62-69, 2000).
Early fall date: 9 Nov 1999, Boyd Co. (Sweeney, et al., *KW* 76:62-69, 2000).
Unaccepted records: 15 Dec 1979, (3) at Cumberland Gap NHP (*KW* 56:13, 1980); numerous other vague or poorly documented reports are not addressed herein (see Mengel:522).

Chronological list of records

1) winter 1968-69, (ph.) at Danville (W. Kemper, photographs; Sweeney, et al., *KW* 76:62-69, 2000)
2) 1 Jan 1969, Cumberland Gap NHP, Bell Co. (Croft, *KW* 45:10, 1969; Sweeney, et al., *KW* 76:62-69, 2000)
3) 9 Nov–mid-Dec 1999, (2 ph./ba.) outside of Ashland, Boyd Co. (Sweeney, et al., *KW* 76:62-69, 2000)
4) Nov 1999–23 Apr 2000, (2 ba.) in the sw. corner of Boyd Co. (Sweeney, et al., *KW* 76:62-69, 2000)
5) 22 Nov 1999–7 Mar 2000, (1 ph./ba.) outside Berea, Madison Co. (Sweeney, et al., *KW* 76:62-69, 2000)
6) mid-Jan–12 Apr 2000, (up to 6 [3 ba.]) at Blaine, Lawrence Co. (Sweeney, et al., *KW* 76:62-69, 2000)
7) 11 Mar 2000, nr. Princess, Boyd Co. (Sweeney, et al., *KW* 76:62-69, 2000)
8) 20 Mar 2000, Natural Bridge SRP, Powell Co. (Sweeney, et al., *KW* 76:62-69, 2000)
9) 23 Mar 2000, Carter Caves SRP, Carter Co. (Sweeney, et al., *KW* 76:62-69, 2000)
10) 20 Nov 2001–10 Apr 2002, (5 [3 ph./ba.]) at Blaine, Lawrence Co. (S./M. Freidhof, pers. comm.; B. Palmer-Ball, 2002 eBird data; *KW* 92:87, 2016).
11) 5 Dec 2007, Yatesville Lake WMA, Lawrence Co (*KW* 84:46, 2008)
12) 1 Jan 2008, Siloam, Greenup Co. (*KW* 84:46, 2008; R. Seelhorst, pers. comm.)
13) 28 Dec 2007, (3 [1 ba.]) Ashland, Boyd Co. (*KW* 84:46, 2008; R. Canterbury, notes)
14) 2 Feb–1 Mar 2008, (ph.) Blaine, Lawrence Co. (*KW* 84:46/69, 2008)
15) 26 Dec 2013, (ba.) Ashland, Boyd Co. (*KW* 90:54, 2014; R. Canterbury, notes)
16) late Nov–mid-Dec 1014, (3 ba.), Ashland, Boyd Co. (*KW* 91:55, 2015)
17) 21 Jan–2 Mar 2017, (ph.) Yatesville Lake WMA, Lawrence Co. (*KW* 93:51/76, 2017; B. Palmer-Ball, eBird data)

*TUFTED TITMOUSE *Baeolophus bicolor*

Status: Fairly common to common resident. Recorded statewide in a great variety of forested and semi-open habitats from mature woodlands and woodland borders to suburban parks and yards. Breeding statewide; most commonly utilizes natural tree cavities, but artificial nesting boxes are sometimes used. Usually less numerous than the Carolina Chickadee, but frequently associates with it and other small passerines during the non-breeding season.

Maximum counts: **81** at Otter Creek Park, Meade Co., 29 Dec 2018 (B. Woerner, eBird data); **71** in ne. Calloway Co., 3 Jan 2012 (E. Huber, eBird data); **70** in ne. McCreary Co., 24 Apr 2009 (R. Denton, eBird data).

*RED-BREASTED NUTHATCH *Sitta canadensis*

Status: Uncommon to fairly common but irregular transient and winter resident, extremely rare during summer (currently only one known nesting locality). Recorded statewide during migration when the species is occasionally fairly widespread; most often observed in conifers but sometimes encountered in deciduous forest, particularly during heavy irruptive flights. Irregular and somewhat local in occurrence during winter; numerous some years, nearly absent in others; almost always found in the vicinity of conifers. Peak of abundance occurs from late Oct to mid-Mar. An isolated breeding population occurs in the Red River Gorge, Wolfe Co., with only one additional nesting attempt documented (see below). Usually encountered singly or in small groups of fewer than a half-dozen birds, but occasionally loose flocks of a dozen or more birds are seen during irruption years. **State Breeding Status**: Endangered.

Maximum counts: **110** on the Bernheim Forest CBC, 1 Jan 1987 (*KW* 63:18, 1987); **92** on the Paradise CBC, 30 Dec 2018 (*KW* 95:23, 2019); **86** on the Bernheim Forest CBC, 26 Dec 1983 (*KW* 60:8, 1984); **82** (69 at Otter Creek Park) on the Otter Creek Park CBC, 29 Dec 2018 (*KW* 95:28, 2019); **72** (50 in one pine thicket) on the Paradise CBC, 31 Dec 1993 (*KW* 70:24, 1994).
Late spring dates (away from Wolfe Co. breeding area): 25 May 1978, Louisville (*KW* 54:45, 1978); 18 May 1946/1966, Louisville area (*KW* 52:55, 1976); 18 May 1978, Danville (*KW* 54:45, 1978).
Early fall dates (away from Wolfe Co. breeding area): 25 Aug 1961, Letcher Co. (E. Clark, pers. comm.; *fide* A. Stamm, historical archive files); 26 Aug 2009, Jefferson Co. (*KW* 86:13, 2010); 28 Aug 1993, McCreary Co. (*KW* 70:10, 1994); 28 Aug 2010, Jefferson Co. (*KW* 87:20, 2011); 29 Aug 1999, Nelson Co. (D. Coates, pers. comm.).
Vagrant summer records: (away from the Wolfe Co. breeding area): 16 Jul 1886, collected (sp.) at Bardstown, Nelson Co. (Beckham, *Auk* 3:489, 1886; Mengel:341); 3 Jul 1982, nr. the summit of Black Mt., Harlan Co. (L. Rauth, pers. comm.); 2 Aug 2008, se. Jefferson Co. (*KW* 85:18, 2009).

Summary of breeding records by county

Campbell (Mar-Apr 2000, Evergreen Cemetery (unsuccessful attempt) [Renfrow, *KW* 77:64-67, 2001]);
Wolfe (1996 to present, Red River Gorge [Renfrow, *KW* 72:62-64, 1996; B. Palmer-Ball, 1997 eBird data; *KW* 74:74, 1998; Renfrow, *KW* 75:53-55, 1999; *KW* 76:57, 2000; Renfrow, *KW* 77:64-67, 2001; *KW* 78:52, 2002; *KW* 79:72, 2003; *KW* 81:108, 2005]).

*WHITE-BREASTED NUTHATCH *Sitta carolinensis*

Status: Fairly common resident. Recorded statewide in a variety of forested and semi-open habitats; abundance generally proportional to the amount of mature woodland present. Breeding statewide in natural tree cavities, but occasionally in artificial nest boxes. Usually seen singly or in small groups of fewer than a half-dozen birds, often associating with other small passerines. Frequently seen at feeding stations.

Maximum counts: **34** in w. Wayne Co., 28 Sep 2011 (eBird data); **32** at Otter Creek Park, Meade Co., 29 Dec 2018 (B. Woerner, eBird data).

BROWN-HEADED NUTHATCH *Sitta pusilla*

Status: Extremely rare visitant and resident. This species has very slowly expanded northward from the southeastern Coastal Plain. It prefers open stands of pines, and may associate with flocks of small passerines in the vicinity of such habitat. There are now at least six records including two of nesting.

Maximum counts: **7** at the Marshall Co. nesting location, 6 Nov 2015 (*KW* 92:12, 2016); **7** at the Laurel Co. nesting location, 9 Jun 2018 (*KW* 94:109, 2018; R. Bontrager, eBird data).

Chronological list of records

1) 26 Sep–12 Oct 1999, (ph.) at the Kendall Recreation Area below Wolf Creek Dam (*KW* 76:7, 2000; *NAB* 54:115, 2000)
2) 9-19 May 2008, (ph.) at Ky Dam Village (*KW* 84:67/69, 2008)
3) 18 Jan 2013 to present, a pair and subsequent family groups (ph.) at Ky Dam Village (*KW* 89: 52/60/61/77/88/97, 2013; Renfrow, *KW* 89:82-86, 2013; *KW* 90:15/54/74/90, 2014; *KW* 91:74/80, 2015; *KW* 92:66/72, 2016; *KW* 94:80, 2018; *KW* 95:9, 2019)
4) 16 Sep 2017, KenLake SRP, Marshall Co. (m. ob., eBird data)
5) 15 May 2018 to present, 5-7 including confirmed evidence of nesting at London, Laurel Co. (KW 94:97/109, 2018; *KW* 95:9/49, 2019)
6) 14 Mar 2019+, at least 3 at a different location at London, Laurel Co. (F. Renfrow, pers. comm.)

*BROWN CREEPER *Certhia americana*

Status: Uncommon to fairly common transient and winter resident, extremely rare and local summer resident. Recorded statewide in a variety of forested and semi-open habitats; most frequently encountered in relatively mature woodlands. Peak of abundance occurs from early Nov to mid-Mar. Breeding has been documented from two distinct portions of the state: swamps of far western Kentucky and mature forest in the eastern part of the state; a few additional records may pertain to breeding individuals. Generally encountered singly or in small loose groups of only a few birds, often associating with other small passerines including chickadees, titmice and kinglets. **State Breeding Status**: Threatened.

Maximum count: **50** [19 at Cherokee Park] on the Louisville CBC, 14 Dec 2014 (*KW* 91:24, 2015; R. Lane, eBird data).
Late spring dates (away from known breeding areas): 21 May 19—, Bowling Green (Mengel: 342); 18 May 1966, Louisville (*KW* 52:55, 1976); 7-8 May 2012, singing bird (possibly on territory) in Wolfe Co. [at 2014 nesting location] (*KW* 88:79, 2012); 8 May 1982, Louisville (J. Lewis, eBird data); 7 May 1995, Sauerheber Unit (C. Crawford, eBird data).
Early fall dates (away from known breeding areas): 20 Aug 1972, Cumberland Falls State Park, Whitley Co. (*AB* 27:69, 1973); 23 Aug 1980, Louisville (*KW* 57:22, 1981); 27 Aug 2017, Independence, Kenton Co. (*KW* 94:12, 2018); 1 Sep 1995, [possible post-breeding bird] Carlisle Co. (B. Palmer-Ball, eBird data); 5 Sep 1991, Louisville (B. Palmer-Ball, eBird data).

Summary of breeding records by county

Ballard (Jun 1988, Axe Lake Swamp [Palmer-Ball and Haag, *KW* 65:77-78, 1989])
Harlan (May-Jun 2007, Little Black Mt. [Canterbury, *KW* 91:34, 2015])
Henderson (May 1991, Jenny Hole-Highland Creek Unit Sloughs WMA [*KBBA*: 174])
Marshall (May 1991, Cypress Creek Swamp [*KBBA*:174])
Union (May 1991, Jenny Hole-Highland Creek Unit Sloughs WMA [*KBBA*: 174])
Wolfe (May 2014, Red River Gorge [Renfrow, *KW* 90:99-102, 2014])

Summary of breeding season records by county

Bullitt (20-21 Jul 1999, Ft. Knox [*NAB* 53:394, 1999])
Harlan (summer 1944, several birds on Black Mt. [Breiding, *KW* 23:38, 1947]; viewed with skepticism by Mengel [p. 342] but accepted herein)
Henderson (3 Aug 1981, J.J. Audubon SP [*KW* 58:17, 1982])

Hickman (4 Jun 1977, Murphy's Pond [B. Monroe, Jr., notes]; 14 Jun 2019, Obion WMA [C. Bliznick, eBird data])

Marshall (2 Aug 2014, Cypress Creek (*KW* 91:13, 2015)

Wolfe (9 Jun 1999 & 29 May 2018, Red River Gorge at 2014 nesting location [*KW* 75:61, 1999 & *KW* 94:81, 2018])

ROCK WREN *Salpinctes obsoletus*

Status: Accidental vagrant. This resident of the southwest United States and Middle America occasionally turns up in the eastern United States. It has been documented in Kentucky three times.

Chronological list of records

1) 16 Oct 1965, (reportedly ph.) about four miles w. of Danville (Loetscher, *KW* 44:18, 1968); unfortunately, photographs of this bird could not be located during preparation of this work, and it is unclear if they have been preserved
2) 11 May 2009, (ph.) at Surrey Hills Farm, ne. Jefferson Co. (Palmer-Ball, *KW* 85:78-79, 2009; *KW* 85:61/74/80, 2009)
3) 23 Oct 2018, (ph.) at the Sauerheber Unit (*KW* 95:9/40, 2019)

*HOUSE WREN *Troglodytes aedon*

Status: Uncommon to fairly common transient, locally rare to fairly common summer resident, extremely rare during winter (although has increased in recent years). Recorded statewide during migration in a great variety of semi-open to open habitats with brushy cover. Peak of abundance occurs from late Apr to mid-Oct. The species is absent or breeds very locally throughout a large part of the state, and is widespread only in the Blue Grass (*KBBA*:180-181). Most often found near human habitations, but also occurs in other semi-open habitats including riparian zones cluttered with flood debris. This species has been expanding its breeding range to the south, formerly (1920) nesting only along the northern counties (Mengel:343-345; Stamm, *KW* 27:47-56, 1951). There are occasional reports during mid-winter, but only one occurrence of apparent wintering has been documented (see below). Winter reports have been on the increase, particularly over the past few years (e.g., *KW* 92:45, 2016; *KW* 93:51, 2017), and a few probably do now winter.

Early spring dates (records before about 1 Apr may represent wintering individuals): 12 Mar 1997, Madison Co. (*KW* 73:55, 1997); mid-Mar 1939 (shown as 25 Mar in previous sources; see Mengel:343), Crittenden Co. (Frazer, *KW* 15:30, 1939); 23 Mar 2011, Sauerheber Unit (*KW* 87:93, 2011); 23 Mar 2019, Russell Co. (R. Bontrager/R. Denton, eBird data); 28 Mar 2012, Calloway & McCracken cos. (*KW* 88:79, 2012); 29 Mar 2017, Pulaski Co. (R. Denton, eBird data); 30 Mar 2016, Murray, Calloway Co. (*KW* 92:66, 2016); 31 Mar 19—, Louisville (Mengel:343); 31 Mar 2012, Russell Co. (*KW* 88:79, 2012); 1 Apr 2009, Owsley Fork Lake, Madison Co. (R. Bates/R. Foster, eBird data); 1 Apr 2012, Henderson Co. (*KW* 88:79, 2012); 1 Apr 2018, Jefferson Co. (*KW* 94:81, 2018); 1 Apr 2018, Wayne Co. (R. Bontrager, eBird data); 1 Apr 2019, Hardin Co. (S. Clinning, eBird data); 2 Apr 1939, south-central Kentucky (*KW* 38:18, 1962); 2 Apr 2011, Louisville (*KW* 87:93, 2011); 2 Apr 2018, Freeman Lake (*KW* 94:81, 2018).

Late fall dates: the species occasionally lingers into early winter, with several dozen records into mid- and late Dec, the latest of which are 8 Jan 2014, LBL, Trigg Co. (*KW* 90:54, 2014); 5 Jan 2002, Ohio Co. (*KW* 78:21, 2002); 5 Jan 2016, Lincoln Co. (*KW* 92:45, 2016); 5 Jan 2018, Wayne Co. (R. Denton, eBird data); 3 Jan 2004, Muhlenberg Co. (*KW* 80:46, 2004); 3 Jan 2015, Christian Co. (*KW* 91:55, 2015); 2 Jan 2006, Pendleton Co. (*KW* 82:31, 2006); 2 Jan 2017, (5) in e. Muhlenberg Co. (*KW* 93:51, 2017).

Out-of-season records (mid-winter): 20 Feb 1972, Russell Co. (D. Coskren, pers. comm.; *fide* A. Stamm, historical archive files); 5 Feb 1980, Louisville (*KW* 56:33, 1980); 8 Feb 1987, Louisville (*KW* 63:38, 1987); 10 Feb 2002, Fulton Co. (B. Palmer-Ball, eBird data); 10 Feb 2002, Hickman Fulton Co. (R. Denton, eBird data); 19 Feb 2005, Pulaski Co. (*KW* 81:60, 2005); 4 Mar 2006, Russell Co. (*KW* 82:72, 2006); 16 Feb 2009, LBL, Trigg Co. (*KW* 85:51, 2009); 16 Jan 2010, Barkley Dam, Lyon Co. (*KW* 86:45, 2010); 23 Feb 2014, s. of Smiths Grove, Warren Co. (*KW* 90:54, 2014); 1 Mar 2014, Mercer Co. (*KW* 90:74, 2014); 21 Jan/2 Mar 2017, Yatesville Lake WMA, Lawrence Co. (*KW* 93:51, 2017/B. Palmer-Ball, eBird data); 13/17 Feb 2017, Hickman, Fulton Co. (*KW* 93:51, 2017); 10 Mar 2017, Adair Co. (R. Denton, eBird data); 9 Jan 2018, Crestwood, Oldham Co. (R. Denton, eBird data); 10 Jan 2018, Ken Unit (C. Bliznick, eBird data).

Wintering record: the extensive period of observations of a bird nr. Clifty Pond, Pulaski Co., [22 Dec 2005, 20 Feb 2006, 16 Mar 2006] (*KW* 82:49/72, 2006) seems to establish wintering. Some of the reports above also likely indicate wintering.

WINTER WREN *Troglodytes hiemalis*

Status: Uncommon transient and winter resident, extremely rare during summer. Recorded state-wide. Widespread but rather secretive; most frequently encountered in wooded areas with an abundance of fallen trees and brush, especially along streams and in floodplain areas. Peak of abundance occurs from mid-Oct to early Apr. The few summer records probably represent non-breeding vagrants from nearby Virginia where the species regularly nests; however, occasional nesting at higher elevations in the Cumberland Mountains is possible. This species has remained my favorite bird since I first saw one bobbing and skulking in and out of sight among the exposed roots of large trees along Goose Creek on my family's farm in Jefferson County in 1972.

Maximum count: **20** at and adjacent to the Long Point Unit, 16 Dec 2017 (*KW* 94:59, 2018); **11** at the Long Point Unit, 15 Dec 2018 (C. Bliznick, eBird data).

Late spring dates: 13 May 1997, Whitley Co. (Stedman, *KW* 80:35, 2004); 12 May 2016, (hd.) Lex-ington (*KW* 92:66, 2016); 8 May 1982, Louisville (*KW* 58:52, 1982).

Early fall dates: 8 Sep 1993, Louisville (*KW* 70:10, 1994); 10 Sep 2012, Daviess Co. (*KW* 89:12, 2013); 12 Sep 2012, Hart Co. (*KW* 89:12, 2013); 15 Sep 2006, Louisville (*KW* 83:17, 2007); 17 Sep 2007, e. Jefferson Co. (*KW* 84:14 2008); 17 Sep 2010, Lexington (*KW* 87:21, 2011); 18 Sep 1999, Jefferson Co. (*KW* 76:7, 2000); 21 Sep 1979, Jefferson Co. (*KW* 56:16, 1980).

Out-of-season records (summer): 6 Aug 1939, an imm. (sp.) on Black Mt., Harlan Co. (Barbour, *KW* 17:46, 1941); 26 Aug 1961, nr. Whitesburg, Letcher Co. (E. Clark, pers. comm.); 9 Jul 1996, Black Mt., Harlan Co. (Oliver, *KW* 73:67, 1997).

*SEDGE WREN *Cistothorus platensis*

Status: Rare to uncommon transient, rare summer resident, extremely rare during winter. Recorded chiefly west of the Cumberland Plateau. Fairly widespread but secretive during migration, occurring primarily in hayfields, weedy fields, and other open habitats with thick, grassy cover. Peaks of abundance of migrants occur from late Apr to early May and from late Sep to mid-Oct. Breeding has been reported from hayfields, fallow fields, and sedge meadows at scattered localities across central and western Kentucky (see below). Interestingly, nesting activity has been documented (and may typically peak?) during late summer and fall; these late nestings typically involve birds that have not been present earlier in the summer and are thought to have come south subsequent to earlier nesting efforts farther north. There are several records of single birds or small groups in fields with thick herbaceous vegetation during winter, but wintering likely has been documented only by repeated observations of birds in Oldham Co. during the winter of 1946-47 (see below). Generally seen singly or in small, loose groups of up to a half-dozen birds, but breeding colonies have numbered up to about a dozen pairs. **State Breeding Status**: Special Concern.

Maximum count: at least **55** at a Nelson Co. nesting colony , 25 Aug 1963 (Croft, *KW* 48:40, 1972).

Early spring dates (records before third week of Apr may represent wintering individuals): 2 Apr 1955, south-central Kentucky (*KW* 38:18, 1962); 10 Apr 2001, Fulton Co. (B. Palmer-Ball, eBird data); 12 Apr 2014, Jefferson Co. (*KW* 90:74, 2014); 13 Apr 2017, Jefferson Co. (*KW* 93:77, 2017); 16 Apr 2012, e. Union Co. (*KW* 88:79, 2012); 18 Apr 2004, Sauerheber Unit (eBird data); 22 Apr 2006, Sauerheber Unit (*KW* 82:72, 2006); 27 Apr 1918, Warren Co. (Mengel: 352).

Late fall dates: 26 Nov 2004, Sinclair Unit (*KW* 81:13, 2005); 20 Nov 2003, (4) Sinclair Unit (*KW* 80:13, 2004); 6 Nov 2001, (2) in Ohio Co. (*KW* 78:10, 2002; D. Roemer, notes); 29 Oct 1950, Louisville area (*KW* 52:55, 1976); 29 Oct 2009, Jefferson Co. (*KW* 86:13, 2010); 28 Oct 1998, Ohio Co. (D. Roemer, notes); 28 Oct 2000, Sinclair Unit (R. Denton/D. O"Brien, eBird data); 27 Oct 1977, Louisville (*AB* 32:213, 1978).

Out-of-season records (winter; some of the older records below were not accompanied by any substantive details): 14 Dec 1946–25 Jan 1947, (several) in Oldham Co. (Mengel:353; *KW* 52:55, 1976); 21-22 Dec 1946, (3) on the Providence CBC (*KW* 23:11, 1947); 29 Dec 1949, Providence CBC (*KW* 26:11, 1950); 25 Dec 1950, Marion CBC (*KW* 27:13, 1951); 25 Dec 1951, (2) on Marion CBC (*KW* 28:11, 1952); 28 Dec 1952, Otter Creek Park CBC (*KW* 29:11, 1953); 1 Jan 1955, (3) on the Ashland CBC (*KW* 31:15, 1955); 2 Jan 1960, Greenup Co. (*KW* 36:16, 1960); 21 Dec 1961, Mammoth Cave NP (*KW* 38:18, 1962; Wilson, *KW* 38:35, 1962); 31 Dec 1998, Ohio Co. (*KW* 75: 11, 1999); 12 Jan 2001, Ohio Co. (*NAB* 55:177, 2001); 4 Jan 2003, Sinclair Unit (*KW* 79: 20/48, 2003); 3 Jan 2004, Sinclair Unit (*KW* 80:19, 2004); 13 Mar–17 Apr 2004, Sinclair Unit (*KW* 80:70, 2004); 27 Dec 2005, McCracken Co. (*KW* 82:18/49, 2006); 24 Mar 2006, Ballard Co. (*KW* 82:72, 2006); 26 Mar 2006, se. Muhlenberg Co. (*KW* 82:72, 2006); 16 Dec 2006, (1-2) at the Long Point Unit (*KW* 83:50, 2007); 18 Dec 2006, McCracken Co. (*KW* 83:21/50, 2007); 22 Dec 2008, Mc-Cracken Co. (KW 85:22/51, 2009); 3 Jan 2009, Muhlenberg Co. (*KW* 85:24/51, 2009); 16 Dec 2010, Ken Unit (*KW* 86:45, 2010); 19 Jan 2012, ne. Warren Co. (*KW* 88:49, 2012); 17 Dec 2013, McCracken Co. (*KW* 90:19/54, 2014); 30 Dec 2015, McCracken Co. (*KW* 92:45, 2016); 22 Dec 2017, (ph.) Todd Co. (*KW* 94:24/59, 2018); 23 Dec 2017, (ph.) Bullitt Co. (*KW* 94:29/59, 2018)

Summary of confirmed breeding records by county:

Edmonson (Mengel:352)
Greenup (*KW* 84:14 2008)
Henderson (*KW* 64:65, 1988; *KW* 65:10, 1989; B. Palmer-Ball, 1996/2000 eBird data; *KW* 80:12-13, 2004; *KW* 87:21, 2011)
Jefferson (Mengel:352; *KW* 79:14, 2003; *KW* 81:13, 2005)
Larue (*KW* 60:18, 1984)
Meade (Rowe, *KW* 40:29-31, 1964)
Oldham (Mengel:352)
Nelson (Croft, *KW* 48:40, 1972)
Warren (Wilson, *KW* 27:39, 1951)

Summary of additional summer records of probable breeding by county (many additional summer records exist, but those below seemed more indicative of probable breeding)

Adair (*KW* 86:95, 2010; *KW* 87:21, 2011)
Ballard (*KW* 83:106, 2007; *KW* 84:14, 2008)
Bath (Mengel:352-353)
Calloway (*KW* 60:18, 1984)
Carlisle (*KW* 84:14 2008)
Fulton (*KW* 62:7, 1986; *KW* 82:83, 2006; *KW* 83:17/106, 2007; *KW* 87:21, 2011; *KW* 90:15, 2014)
Green (*KW* 60:18, 1984)
Hardin (*KW* 77:8, 2001; *KW* 83:17, 2007)
Henderson (*KW* 81:13/109, 2005; *KW* 83:17, 2007; *KW* 84:14, 2008; *KW* 92:13, 2016)
Hopkins (*KW* 64:19, 1988)
Jefferson (*KW* 83:106, 2007; *KW* 87:21, 2011)
Knox (Mengel:352-353)
Laurel (Mengel:352-353)
Livingston (*KW* 61:59, 1985)
Morgan (*KBBA*:182-183)
Muhlenberg (*KW* 80:12, 2004; *KW* 93:12, 2017; C. Bliznick, 2017 eBird data)
Ohio (*KW* 81:13, 2005; *KW* 83:106, 2007)
Powell (*KW* 60:18, 1984)
Pulaski (*KW* 86:95, 2010; *KW* 89:12, 2013)
Rowan (Mengel:352-353; *KW* 89:12, 2013)
Trigg (*KW* 91:13, 2015)
Union (Palmer-Ball and Moosman, *KW* 78:40-42, 2002; *KW* 79:14/84, 2003; *KW* 90:15, 2014; *KW* 92:13, 2016)
Wayne (*KW* 56:80, 1980)
Woodford (*KBBA*:182-183)

MARSH WREN *Cistothorus palustris*

Status: Rare to uncommon transient, extremely rare winter resident, extremely rare during summer. Recorded chiefly west of the Cumberland Plateau. Fairly widespread but secretive; most frequently encountered in cattails and other thick vegetation in marshes and along the edges of lakes and ponds, but also can be found in dense, weedy areas. Peaks of abundance occur from late Apr to early May and from late Sep to mid-Oct. There are no confirmed breeding records for the state, but the species has been reported a few times in suitable breeding habitat during summer (see below). A few individuals linger into early winter, and a mounting number of winter records (including a few of birds at the same location for extended periods) apparently demonstrate that the species winters on a somewhat regular basis. Generally seen singly or in pairs, but can be relatively numerous in suitable habitat, occasionally occurring in loose groups of up to a half-dozen or more birds.

Maximum counts: 30+ at the Sauerheber Unit, 6 Oct 2007 (*KW* 84:14 2008); **12-15** at the Sauerheber Unit, 20 Oct 2002 (*KW* 79:14, 2003); **12** at the Falls of the Ohio, 30 Sep 1987 (M. Stinson, eBird data).

Early spring dates (records before early Apr may or probably represent wintering individuals): 13 Mar 2004, Clark Co. (*KW* 80:70, 2004); 17 Mar 2012, Sauerheber Unit (*KW* 88:79, 2012); 17-19 Mar 2011, Allen Co. (*KW* 87:93, 2011); 20 Mar 1999, Henderson Co. (*KW* 75:45, 1999); 20 Mar 2017, Sauerheber Unit (*KW* 93:77, 2017); 26 Mar 2012, (3) in e. Union Co. (*KW* 88:79, 2012); 27 Mar–11 Apr 2004, Sinclair Unit (*KW* 80:70, 2004); 31 Mar 1956, south-central Kentucky (*KW* 38:18, 1962); 31 Mar 2005, Union Co. (*KW* 82:72, 2006); 31 Mar 2015, Sauerheber Unit (*KW* 91:74, 2015); 1 Apr 2019, Sauerheber Unit (C. Crawford, eBird data); 5 Apr 18—, Nelson Co. (Mengel: 351); 5 Apr 2013, Muhlenberg Co. (*KW* 89:77, 2013); 8 Apr 2006, Sauerheber Unit (*KW* 82:72, 2006); 10 Apr 2018, Campbell Co. (*KW* 94:81, 2018); 15 Apr 2000, Russell Co. (S. Marsh, notes); 15 Apr 2004, Henderson Co. (*KW* 80:70, 2004).

Late spring dates: 26 May 2006, Warren Co. (*KW* 82:72, 2006); 19 May 2016, (ph.) Sauerheber Unit (C. Crawford, eBird data); 18 May 2008, Jefferson Co. (*KW* 84:69, 2008; date published erroneously therein as 19 May [*fide* E. Huber, notes]); 18 May 2016, Jefferson Co. (*KW* 92:67, 2016); 17 May 1995, Henderson Co. (B. Palmer-Ball, eBird data); 16 May 2006, w. Henderson Co. (C. Crawford, eBird data); 15 May 1937, nr. Buechel, Jefferson Co. (Mengel: 351).

Early fall dates: 17 Aug 2003, Union Co. (*KW* 80:13, 2004); 23 Aug 2010, (hd.) Jefferson Co. (*KW* 87:21, 2011); 24 Aug 2003, w. Henderson Co. (C. Crawford, eBird data); 29 Aug 1996, Sauerheber Unit (B. Palmer-Ball, eBird data); 30 Aug 2003, Sinclair Unit (*KW* 80:13, 2004); 31 Aug 2015, Muhlenberg Co. (*KW* 92:13, 2016); 1 Sep 2002, Union Co. (*KW* 79:14, 2003); 7 Sep 1986, Henderson Co. (*KW* 63:11, 1987); 9 Sep 2011, Madison Co. (*KW* 88:15, 2012); 10 Sep 1998, Henderson Co. (*KW* 75:7, 1999); 10 Sep 2009, Daviess Co. (*KW* 86:13, 2010).

Late fall dates: 23 Nov-8 Dec 1981, Falls of the Ohio (*KW* 58:17/30, 1982); 28 Nov 2000, (4) e. of Morganfield, Union Co. (B. Palmer-Ball, eBird data); 26 Nov 1984, Rowan Co. (*KW* 61:18, 1985); 26 Nov 2017, Fayette Co. (*KW* 94:13, 2018); 20 Nov 2003, (2) Sinclair Unit (*KW* 80:13, 2004); 20 Nov 2012, Union Co. (*KW* 89:13, 2013); 19 Nov 2005, Sinclair Unit (*KW* 82:13, 2006); 14 Nov 19— Louisville area (Monroe and Monroe, *KW* 37:35, 1961).

Out-of-season records (summer): 30 Jul 1995, Sauerheber Unit (B. Palmer-Ball, eBird data); 3/17 Jul 2000, Clear Creek, Hopkins Co. (B. Palmer-Ball, eBird data); 6 Jul 2003, (hd.) Union Co. (*KW* 79:84, 2003).

Out-of-season dates (winter): 26 Feb 1888, Fulton Co. (Mengel:351); 25 Dec 1941, Marion CBC (*KW* 18:9, 1942); 20 Dec 1952, Henderson CBC (*KW* 29:8, 1953); 23 Dec 1961, Jefferson Co. (Wiley, *KW* 38:40, 1962); 26 Dec 1976, Otter Creek CBC (*KW* 53:5, 1977); 29 Dec 1984, Ballard Co. CBC (*KW* 61:3, 1985); 15 Dec 1994-2 Jan 1995, Muhlenberg Co. (*KW* 71:11, 1995; B. Palmer-Ball, eBird data); 30 Dec 1996-1 Jan 1997, Muhlenberg Co. (*KW* 73:14, 1997; B. Palmer-Ball, eBird data); 2-18 Jan 2000, (two on latter date) Sinclair Unit (*KW* 76:12, 2000; B. Palmer-Ball, eBird data); 2 Jan 2000, Homestead Unit of Peabody WMA, Ohio Co. (*KW* 76:12, 2000); 2 Feb 2001, Sinclair Unit (*NAB* 55:177, 2001; B. Yandell, notes); 16 Feb 2002, Henderson Co. (B. Palmer-Ball, eBird data); 10/17 Mar 2002, Union Co. (B. Palmer-Ball, eBird data); 23 Dec 2002, La Center, Ballard Co. (*KW* 79:18/48, 2003); 4 Jan 2003, Breckinridge Co. (*KW* 79:24/48, 2003); 10 Dec 2005, Ken Unit (*KW* 82:49, 2006); 31 Dec 2005, Pulaski Co. (*KW* 82:17/27/49, 2006); 1 Jan/ 26 Mar 2006, Muhlenberg Co. (*KW* 82:19/49/72, 2006); 11 Mar 2006, Lewis Co. (*KW* 82:72, 2006); 12 Mar 2006, Hopkins Co. (*KW* 82:72, 2006); 23 Mar 2006, Jefferson Co. (*KW* 82:72, 2006); 18

Dec 2006, Ballard WMA (*KW* 83:21, 2007); 30 Dec 2006, (2) Muhlenberg Co. (*KW* 83: 23, 2007); 10 Mar 2007, Muhlenberg Co. (*KW* 83:83, 2007); 21 Dec 2007, Union Co. (*KW* 84:46, 2008); 30 Dec 2007, (2) in se. Muhlenberg Co. and s. Ohio Co. (*KW* 84:46, 2008); 22 Dec 2008, Ballard WMA (*KW* 85:22/51, 2009); 2 Jan 2009, Ken Unit (*KW* 85:51, 2009); 3 Jan 2009, Muhlenberg Co. (*KW* 85:24/51, 2009); 2 & 23 Jan/12 Feb 2010, Muhlenberg Co. (*KW* 86:45, 2010); 2 Jan 2011, (3) in Muhlenberg Co. (*KW* 87:27/64, 2011); 22 Dec 2012 & 23 Jan 2013, Sinclair Unit (*KW* 89:52, 2013); 29 Dec 2013, Muhlenberg Co. (*KW* 90:23/51/54, 2014); 4 Jan 2014, Bullitt Co. (*KW* 90:34/54, 2014); 1 Jan 2015, Muhlenberg Co. (*KW* 91:19/55, 2015); 3 Jan 2016, (2) in Muhlenberg Co. (*KW* 92:20/45, 2016); 9 Mar 2016, Sauerheber Unit (*KW* 92:66, 2016); 2 Jan 2017, Muhlenberg Co. (*KW* 93:18/51, 2017); 23 Dec 2017, Wayne Co. (*KW* 94:59, 2018); 18 Dec 2018, Allen Co. (*KW* 95:25/49, 2019); 30 Dec 2018 & 6 Jan/12 Feb 2019, (1-2) various locales in se. Muhlenberg Co. (*KW* 95:23/49, 2019); 6 Jan 2019 (2), Sauerheber Unit (*KW* 95:49, 2019); 2 Feb 2019, Calvert City, Marshall Co. (*KW* 95:49, 2019).

*CAROLINA WREN *Thryothorus ludovicianus*

Status: Fairly common to common resident. Recorded statewide in a great variety of forested and semi-open habitats with brushy cover. Breeding statewide; often nests in association with human habitations, building nests on porches and in garages and outbuildings of both suburban and rural yards. This species is highly susceptible to severe winter weather, and it may become rare after extremely cold winters when many perish, sometimes being nearly extirpated such as after the winter of 1977-1978 (Monroe, *KW* 54:22, 1978).

Maximum counts: **65** in Cumberland Co., 27 Sep 2008 (S. Stedman, eBird data); **59** at West Ky WMA, McCracken Co., **30** Dec 2013 (D. Akers, eBird data); **56** in sw. Russell Co., 14 Dec 2011 (eBird data)

*[e]BEWICK'S WREN *Thryomanes bewickii*

Status: Extirpated. Formerly an extremely rare to rare and locally distributed summer resident and extremely rare non-breeding season visitant (prior to extirpation, had become very scarce as a transient and absent during winter). Formerly recorded very locally across central and western Kentucky; generally absent from heavily forested portions of the Cumberland Plateau and Mountains. Formerly encountered in a variety of semi-open habitats with brushy cover; occured mostly in rural farmland and settlement, but also in disturbed woodlands (Palmer-Ball, *KW* 69:64-65, 1993). This wren was formerly much more numerous, and as recently as about 1960 it was still regarded as common and widespread (Mengel:348). A steady decline occurred during subsequent decades, and as of the early 2000s the species was being reported only a few times each year. Formerly bred throughout the state, but nesting birds became limited to a few widely separated regions in central and western Kentucky (*KBBA*:178-179). It is unclear whether the southward spread of the House Wren as a breeding species, or some other factor, was involved in this decline (Mengel: 345-348; Monroe, *KW* 54:22, 1978; Hodge and Ritchison, *KW* 83:91-102, 2007). **State Breeding Status**: Historical.

Chronological list of last documented reports of the species in the state (2004 to present)

1) late Apr & 26-27 May 2004, n. of Stamping Ground, Scott Co. (*KW* 80:70, 2004)
2) Jun–1 Jul 2005, territorial bird at same location n. of Stamping Ground, Scott Co. (*KW* 81:108-109, 2005)
3) 28 May–6 Jun 2007, nw. of Beechwood, Owen Co. (*KW* 83:83/106, 2007)
4) 9-23 Jun 1997, se. of Buena Vista, Harrison Co. (*KW* 83:106, 2007)
5) 1 Jul 2008, 2 (a pair?) at Fort Campbell, Trigg Co. (*KW* 84:88, 2008)
6) 4 May 2011, a male singing at Burlington, Boone Co. (*KW* 87:93, 2011)
7) 15 Nov 2011, (2) nw. of Burkesville, Cumberland Co. (*KW* 88:14, 2012)

*BLUE-GRAY GNATCATCHER *Polioptila caerulea*

Status: Fairly common to common transient; fairly common summer resident. Recorded statewide during migration in a great variety of forested and semi-open habitats from mature woodlands and woodland borders to suburban parks and yards. Widespread during spring, especially during early to mid-Apr when pairs or small groups are seemingly everywhere; much less numerous during fall when the species becomes rather inconspicuous by late Sep. Peak of abundance occurs from early Apr to mid-Sep. Breeding statewide in a variety of forested and semi-open habitats, most often in mature woodlands. Generally encountered singly, in pairs, or in small loose flocks of up to a half-dozen birds.

Maximum counts: **86** in McCreary Co., 24 Apr 2009 (S. Stedman, eBird data); **80** in e. Pulaski Co., 8 May 2004 (S. Marsh, eBird data); **71** in w. Henderson Co., 22 Apr 2018 (*KW* 94:81, 2018; J. Meredig, eBird data); **60** in Adair Co., 6 May 2008 (S. Stedman, eBird data); **60** nw. of Powderly, Muhlenberg Co., 17 Apr 2014 (T. Graham, eBird data); **54** in nw. Pulaski Co., 8 May 2004 (R. Denton, eBird data); **40-50** in Calloway Co., 8 Apr 1980 (*KW* 56:63, 1980).
Early spring dates: 16 Mar 2019, Daviess Co./Fulton Co. (R. Rold, eBird data/C. Bliznick, eBird data); 20 Mar 1966, south-central Kentucky (*KW* 45:36, 1969); 20 Mar 1982, Glasgow (*KW* 58:53, 1982); 20 Mar 1990, Jefferson Co. (*KW* 66:59, 1990).
Late fall dates: 29 Nov 2013, (ph.) LBL, Lyon Co. (*KW* 90:15/21, 2014); 11 Nov 1977, Falls of the Ohio (*AB* 32:214, 1978; D. Parker, notes); 10 Nov 2009, Jefferson Co. (*KW* 86:13, 2010); 5 Nov 1965, LBL (A. Stamm, notes); 2 Nov 1974, Louisville (*KW* 52:56, 1976).
Out-of-season records (winter): 22 Dec 2012, sw. Logan Co. (*KW* 89:22/52, 2013); 19/21 Dec 2015, (ph.) Long Point Unit (*KW* 92:45, 2016).
Unaccepted record: 17 Dec 2005, n. Madison Co. (*KW* 82:17/27/49, 2006; see *KW* 88:101, 2012).

GOLDEN-CROWNED KINGLET *Regulus satrapa*

Status: Fairly common to common transient, irregularly uncommon to fairly common winter resident. Recorded statewide in a variety of forested and semi-open habitats from mature woodlands and woodland borders to suburban parks and yards. Irregular in occurrence during winter; numerous some years, somewhat scarce in others; most frequently observed in evergreens and mature woodlands. Peaks of abundance occur from mid- Oct to early Nov and from late Mar to mid-Apr. Generally encountered in loose flocks of up to a dozen birds, often associating with other small passerines.

Maximum counts: count of **98** in McCreary Co., 27 Nov 1999 (*KW* 76:7, 2000); **70** in ne. Calloway Co., 3 Jan 2017 (M. Autin, eBird data); **51** at Cumberland Gap National Historical Park, 26 Nov 1994 (*KW* 71:5, 1995).
Late spring dates: 13 May 2017, Marshall Co. (*KW* 93:77, 2017); 8 May 1976, Louisville area (*KW* 52:56, 1976); 4 May 2019, Lexington (C. Bliznick et al., eBird data); 1 May 2016, Marshall Co. (*KW* 92:66, 2016).
Early fall dates: 30 Aug 2011, Campbell Co. (*KW* 88:15, 2012); 18 Sep 1990, Grayson Co. (*KW* 67: 8, 1991); 23 Sep 1956, Louisville area (*KW* 52:56, 1976).
Unaccepted record: 31 Aug 1966 (*KW* 52:56, 1976); 14 Sep 2002, (2) Fulton Co. (*KW* 79:14, 2003).

RUBY-CROWNED KINGLET *Regulus calendula*

Status: Fairly common to common transient, irregularly rare to uncommon winter resident. Recorded statewide in a variety of forested and semi-open habitats from mature woodlands and woodland borders to suburban parks and yards during migration. Irregular in occurrence during winter; nearly absent some years, generally more numerous during milder years. Always more abundant in the southern and western portions of the state, and seems to have increased in occurrence during winter in recent years. Typically found most frequently in evergreens during winter in most areas, although can be numerous in bottomland forests of western Kentucky. Peaks of abundance occur from early to mid-Apr and from late Sep to mid-Oct. Usually encountered singly or in small loose groups of up to a half-dozen birds, often associating with other small passerines.

Maximum counts: **73** in Rowan Co., 29 Oct 1984 (*KW* 61:18, 1985); **25** in one tree at Louisville, 15 Oct 1972 (L. Brecher, notes); **25** at Morgan Conservation Park, Oldham Co., 19 Apr 2018 (B. Davis, eBird data).

Late spring dates: 24 May 2000, Bowling Green (*NAB* 54:290, 2000); 21 May 2011, Lexington (*KW* 87:93, 2011); 21 May 2013, Lexington (*KW* 89:77, 2013); 19 May 1982, Louisville (*KW* 58:53, 1982); 19 May 2017, Bernheim Forest (C. Root, eBird data); 18 May 1988, Boone Co. (*KW* 64:48, 1988); 17 May 1997, Sauerheber Unit (C. Crawford, eBird data); 17 May 2008, Iroquois Park, Louisville (G. Heath, et al., eBird data); 17 May 2017, Oldham Co. (R. Fischer, eBird data); 16 May 1978, Louisville (*KW* 54:45, 1978).

Early fall dates: 20 Aug 2012, Henderson Co. (*KW* 89:13, 2013); 23 Aug 2015, Jefferson Co. (*KW* 92:13, 2016); 26 Aug 1978, Jefferson Co. (*KW* 55:17, 1979); 30 Apr 2011, Madison Co. (*KW* 88:15, 2012); 5 Sep 1976, Lexington (*AB* 31:185, 1977).

Published error: 31 May 1980, Boone Co. (*KW* 56:63, 1980) should have read 13 May (*fide* L. McNeely, notes).

*EASTERN BLUEBIRD *Sialia sialis*

Status: Locally uncommon to fairly common resident. Recorded statewide, but much less numerous in heavily forested portions of eastern Kentucky. Most often seen on utility lines and fences in rural farmland and settlement, but the species occurs in a variety of semi-open to open habitats including woodland edges, swamps, parks, and reclaimed surface mines. Breeding occurrence similar; most numerous in semi-open farmland. Generally encountered in pairs and family groups during summer; frequently seen during winter in flocks of up to a dozen birds, and occasionally in loose groups of up to 25 or more. Birds from farther north likely supplement the local population during the non-breeding season. This species cannot survive prolonged periods of severe winter weather and may become rare following extremely cold, snowy winters (Monroe, *KW* 54:21-22, 1978).

Maximum counts: **133** in w. Laurel Co., 31 Dec 2010 (R. Denton, eBird data); **118** in w. Wayne Co., 28 Sep 2011 (eBird data); **106** in w. Wayne Co., 5 Jan 2019 (R. Bontrager, eBird data); **96** in w. Laurel Co., 28 Dec 2011 (R. Denton, eBird data); **91** in sw. Russell Co., 14 Dec 2011 (eBird data); at least **82** in a single flock on Fort Knox, Meade Co., 27 Dec 2001 (*KW* 78:24, 2002); **75** in a single flock in Grayson Co., 19 Oct 1990 (*KW* 67:8, 1991); up to **50** in a flock in Meade Co., winter 1984-1985 (Palmer-Ball, et al., *KW* 62:21, 1986).

MOUNTAIN BLUEBIRD *Sialia currucoides*

Status: Accidental vagrant. This resident of the western United States is an occasional fall and winter visitant to the eastern United States. It has been documented in Kentucky one time.

1) 22 Dec 1984–13 Jan 1985, a male (ph.) east of Garrett, in rural Meade Co. (Palmer-Ball, et al., *KW* 62:21-22, 1986). Note: two were erroneously reported 26 Dec 1984 (*KW* 61:31, 1985).

*VEERY *Catharus fuscescens*

Status: Transient (uncommon to fairly common during spring, uncommon during fall); locally rare to common summer resident at higher elevations in the Cumberland Mountains. Recorded statewide during migration in a variety of forested and semi-open habitats; most often found in mature woodlands. Peaks of abundance occur during early May and mid-Sep. The Veery is usually the least numerous species of migrant thrush, especially during fall. Breeding commonly in mature forest above 3000 ft. on Black Mountain, with local summer sightings on nearby Cumberland Mountain, Bell/Harlan cos. (Mengel:366-367; Croft, *KW* 45:72, 1969; Davis and Smith, *KW* 54:73, 1978; Davis, et al., *KW* 56:48, 1980; *KBBA*:188; *KW* 79:84, 2003) and Log Mountain, Bell Co. (*KW* 82:83, 2006). Usually seen singly or in small numbers, often with other transient thrushes.

Maximum counts: **49** on Black Mt., Harlan Co., 18 Jun 1981 (eBird data); **38** on Black Mt., Harlan/Letcher cos., 18 Jun 1981 (B. Palmer-Ball, eBird data); **35** on Black Mt., Harlan Co., 14 May 2006 (eBird data); **28** on Black Mt., Harlan/Letcher cos., 12 Jun 1980 (B. Palmer-Ball, eBird data); **21** on Black Mt., Harlan Co., 20 Jun 2008 (R. Denton, eBird data).

Early spring dates: 12 Apr 1948, Louisville (Mengel:365); 12 Apr 1962, south-central Kentucky (*KW* 45:36, 1969); 18 Apr 1961, south-central Kentucky (*KW* 38:18, 1962); 20 Apr 2008, Berea College Forest, Madison Co. (*KW* 84:69, 2008).

Late spring dates (away from Cumberland Mts.): 4 Jun 1961, south-central Kentucky (*KW* 38:18, 1962); 31 May 1978, Danville (*KW* 54:45, 1978); 31 May 1979, Louisville (B. Palmer-Ball, eBird data); 30 May 1971, Louisville area (*KW* 52:56, 1976); 30 May 1995, Louisville (*KW* 71:42, 1995).

Early fall dates (away from Cumberland Mts.): 25 Aug 1988, Danville (*KW* 65:10, 1989); 27 Aug 1998, Jefferson Co. (B. Palmer-Ball, eBird data); 28 Aug 2011, Allen Co. (*KW* 88:15, 2012); 30 Aug 2014, Allen Co. (*KW* 91:13, 2015); 30 Aug 2015, Pulaski Co. (*KW* 92:13, 2016); 31 Aug 1998, Jefferson Co. (B. Yandell, eBird data); 31 Aug 2015, Allen Co. (*KW* 92:13, 2016); 1 Sep 2010, Pulaski Co. (*KW* 87:21, 2011); 2 Sep 2018, Daviess Co. (*KW* 95:9, 2019).

Late fall dates: 10 Oct 1951, Laurel Co. (Mengel:367); 6 Oct 2018, (hd.) Wayne Co. (*KW* 95:9, 2019).

Unaccepted record: 1 Jan 2004, Falls of Rough CBC (*KW* 80:17/48, 2004).

Published error: 11 Apr 1999, (2) at LBL (*KW* 75:45, 1999) pertained to Hermit Thrushes (*fide* M. Bennett, pers. comm.).

Summary of confirmed breeding records by county

Harlan (Mengel:366-367; *KBBA*:188-189; *KW* 78:52, 2002; R. Denton, 2002 eBird data).

GRAY-CHEEKED THRUSH *Catharus minimus*

Status: Transient (fairly common during spring, uncommon to fairly common during fall); accidental during winter. Recorded statewide in a great variety of forested and semi-open habitats from mature woodlands and woodland borders to suburban parks and yards. Generally much less numerous than the following species in both spring and fall. Peaks of abundance occur during early May and from mid-Sep to early Oct. Usually seen singly or in small numbers with other transient thrushes. No Kentucky specimen appears to be referable to the very locally distributed BICK-NELL'S THRUSH (*C. bicknellii*) (see Mengel:365).

Maximum counts: **150** detected by nocturnal flight calls, 1 Oct 2015, Monroe Co. (*KW* 92:13, 2016); **10-15** in LBL, 12 May 2004 (*KW* 80:70, 2004); **9** at Sloughs WMA, Henderson Co., 10 May 2017 (J. Meredig, eBird data); **8** at LBL, Lyon Co., 4 May 2006 (B. Palmer-Ball, eBird data).

Early spring dates (no records before the early 20s of Apr have been documented well): 11 Apr 1962, south-central Kentucky (*KW* 45:36, 1969); 11 Apr 1965, Louisville area (*KW* 52:56, 1976).

Late spring dates: 6 Jun 1961, south-central Kentucky (*KW* 38:18, 1962); 3 Jun 2004, LBL, Lyon Co., (*KW* 80:84, 2004); 1 Jun 2003, Lexington (*KW* 79:84, 2003).

Early fall dates: 27/31 Aug 2015, Allen Co. (*KW* 92:13, 2016); 30 Aug 2014, Allen Co. (*KW* 91:13, 2015); 31 Aug 2016, Allen Co. (*KW* 93:12, 2017); 2 Sep 2003, Warren Co. (*KW* 80:13, 2004); 2 Sep 2018, (hd.) Wayne Co. (*KW* 95:9, 2019); 3 Sep 2017, (hd.), Wayne Co. (*KW* 94:13, 2018).

Late fall dates: 14 Nov 2015, (window strike), Jefferson Co. 26 Oct 2012, Jefferson Co. (*KW* 89:13, 2013); 23 Oct 19—, Warren Co. (Mengel:365); 20 Oct 1966, Louisville area (*KW* 52:56, 1976); 20 Oct 2007, Cumberland Co. (*KW* 84:14 2008); 20 Oct 2016, Pulaski Co. (*KW* 93:12, 2017).

Out-of-season record (winter): 18 Dec 2016, injured bird (ph.) at Anchorage, Jefferson Co., (*KW* 93:51, 2017).

Unaccepted record: 4 Apr 1981, Calloway Co. (*KW* 57:58, 1981).

SWAINSON'S THRUSH *Catharus ustulatus*

Status: Fairly common to common transient, accidental during summer. Widespread and recorded statewide in a variety of forested and semi-open habitats from mature woodlands and woodland borders to suburban parks and yards. On good migrant days during spring and fall, this species may be quite numerous in forested habitats. Peaks of abundance occur during early May and from early Sep to early Oct. Most often seen singly or in loose groups of fewer than a half-dozen birds, but occasionally encountered in relatively large, loose groups of a dozen or more birds. Commonly heard in flight at night during migration, when this species' questioning "whee" call can be very conspicuous as waves of migrants pass overhead.

Maximum counts: **300** detected by nocturnal flight calls, 1 Oct 2015, Monroe Co. (*KW* 92:13, 2016); **70** detected by nocturnal flight calls, 9 Sep 2018, Wayne (R. Bontrager, eBird data); **55** at Iroquois Park, Louisville, 9 May 2015 (M. Autin et al., eBird data).

Early spring dates: 11 Apr 1965, Louisville area (*KW* 52:56, 1976); 13 Apr 2018, (ph.) Henderson Co. (*KW* 94:81, 2018).

Late spring dates: 8 Jun 1978, Louisville (*KW* 54:62, 1978); 7 Jun 1964, Louisville area (*KW* 52:56, 1976); 4 Jun 2006, Frankfort (*KW* 82:83, 2006); 4 Jun 2016, (ph.) Laurel Co. (*KW* 92:80, 2016); 3 Jun 2004, LBL, Lyon Co. (*KW* 80:84, 2004).

Early fall dates: 22 Aug 2007, Jefferson Co. (*KW* 84:14 2008); 24 Aug 2003, Frankfort (*KW* 80:13, 2004); 25 Aug 1988, Danville (*KW* 65:10, 1989); 26 Aug 1980, Louisville (B. Palmer-Ball, eBird data).

Late fall dates: 17 Nov 2011 (ph.), Bernheim Forest (*KW* 88:15, 2012); 7 Nov 2017, (ph.) Louisville (*KW* 94:13, 2018); 27 Oct 1966, Barren Co. (*KW* 45:36, 1969); 26 Oct 1975, Danville (F. Loetscher, notes); 25 Oct 1975, Louisville (*AB* 30:80, 1976).

Out-of-season record (summer): a spring migrant lingered to 1 Jul 1963 in Warren Co. (Wilson, *KW* 40:19-20, 1964).

Unaccepted records: all between the late fall and early spring dates given above including several on CBCs (e.g., 17 Dec 1995, Louisville [*KW* 72:14/45, 1996]). Being a common migrant through the area, it is not improbable that an occasional bird might linger into winter; however, none of several winter records have been documented convincingly. Also, 4 Apr 1998, Calloway Co. (*KW* 74:56, 1998) and 15 Jun 2012, Russell Co. (eBird data [no details available]).

HERMIT THRUSH *Catharus guttatus*

Status: Fairly common transient, uncommon winter resident. Recorded statewide during migration in a variety of forested and semi-open habitats; most often found in mature woodlands. Generally rare when the other migrant thrushes are moving through in large numbers (i.e., in May and Sep), peaking in abundance during early to mid-Apr and Oct. During winter this species often frequents the cover of cedars, honeysuckle tangles, etc., but also may occur in mature deciduous forest; abundance from year to year and region to region generally proportional to the amount of soft mast food that is present. Generally encountered singly, but occasionally seen in small, loose groups of up to a half-dozen birds.

Maximum counts: **56** at Yatesville Lake WMA, Lawrence Co., 26 Dec 2013 (*KW* 90:54, 2014); **33** at West Ky WMA, McCracken Co., 30 Dec 2013 (*KW* 90:54, 2014); **29** at Yatesville Lake WMA, Lawrence Co., 13 Jan 2011 (*KW* 87:64, 2011); **23** in Pulaski Co. (19 at the Little Lick Rec. Area), 6 Apr 2002 (*KW* 78:52, 2002; R. Denton, eBird data); **18** at the Big South Fork NRRA, McCreary Co., 9 Nov 1997 (S. Steman, notes/pers.comm.); **15** at Louisville, 21 Apr 1983 (*KW* 59:43, 1983).

Late spring dates: 20 May 2006, Boone Co. (*KW* 82:72, 2006); 19 May 1980, Louisville (*KW* 56:62, 1980); 18 May 1963, Louisville area (*KW* 52:56, 1976).

Early fall dates: 25 Sep 1965, Louisville area (*KW* 52:56, 1976); 27 Sep 2014, Blackacre SNP, Jefferson Co. (M. Autin et al., eBird data).

Unaccepted record: 1 Sep 1940, south-central Kentucky (*KW* 38:18, 1962).

*WOOD THRUSH *Hylocichla mustelina*

Status: Fairly common transient, fairly common to common summer resident. Recorded statewide during migration in a variety of forested and semi-open habitats, but typically well outnumbered by other migrant thrushes, especially during fall. Peak of abundance occurs from late Apr to mid-Jul. Breeding statewide in a great variety of forested habitats; occurs in highest densities in extensive tracts of mature woodland (*KBBA*:190-191).

Maximum counts: **64** at Mammoth Cave NP, Edmonson/Hart cos., 31 May 2007 (S./J. Kistler, eBird data); **45** in ne. Pulaski Co., 12 May 2007 (S. Marsh, eBird data); **43** at Mammoth Cave NP, Edmonson/Hart cos., 4 Jun 2010 (S./J. Kister, eBird data).

Early spring dates: 30 Mar 1975, Louisville area (*AB* 29:699, 1975); 1 Apr 2017, Hardin Co. (*KW* 93:77, 2017); 2 Apr 1973, Louisville (*AB* 27:780, 1973); 3 Apr 1957, south-central Kentucky (*KW* 38:18, 1962).

Late fall dates: 4 Nov 2011, Louisville (*KW* 88:15, 2012); 31 Oct 1952, Louisville area (*KW* 52:56, 1976); 28 Oct 2018, Berea (*KW* 95:9, 2019).

Unaccepted records: 30 Dec 1962, Lexington CBC (*AFN* 17:184/329, 1963); 22 Mar 19—, Warren Co. (Mengel:361); 25 Mar 1886, Fulton Co. (Mengel:361).

*AMERICAN ROBIN *Turdus migratorius*

Status: Resident (common during migration and summer, locally uncommon to fairly common during winter). Recorded statewide during migration, occurring ubiquitously. Breeding statewide in a great variety of habitats from mature woodlands and woodland borders to suburban parks and yards. Irregular in occurrence during winter, most years being locally common but occasionally rare or absent in many areas; most numerous in the vicinity of good supplies of soft mast (ornamental trees, cedars, honeysuckle, etc.) during winter. Birds from farther north supplement the local breeding population during the non-breeding season. Loose flocks of a hundred or more are not uncommon during migration; thousands of birds will sometimes gather at night in discrete roosts or mixed with blackbirds and starlings during winter.

Maximum counts: **2,000,000** [?] in Martin Co., Jan 1966 (*KW* 43:24, 1967); up to **90,000** at a roost in Kenton Co., winter 1999-2000 (*KW* 76:32, 2000); **10,000** at a roost in Somerset, Pulaski Co., mid-Nov 1979 (*KW* 56:17, 1980); **9740** in Gallatin Co., 16 Dec 2017 (*KW* 94:32, 2018; T. Towles, 2017 eBird data).

VARIED THRUSH *Ixoreus naevius*

Status: Extremely rare winter and spring visitant. This resident of the northwestern United States and western Canada regularly appears in the eastern United States during winter, when it may occur with flocks of American Robins. There are five Kentucky records.

Unaccepted record: winter 1991-92, at Lexington (W. Enright, pers. comm; *fide* M. Flynn); this report, which apparently involved in-hand identification of a bird that struck a window, was unfortunately accompanied by no written details.

Chronological list of records

1) 15-17 May 1985, a probable male observed in suburban Danville (*KW* 70:13, 1994; W. Kemper, pers. comm.)
2) 19-24 Dec 1993, a male along Mayo Lane, Oldham Co. (Krull, *KW* 70:26, 1994; M. Monroe, pers. comm.)
3) 16-22 Mar 2001, a male (ph.) at Wranglers Camp, LBL, Trigg Co. (Lisowsky, *KW* 78:26-27, 2002; C. Sloan, photographs)
4) 4 Feb–25 Mar 2006, a female (ph.) at Louisville (*KW* 82:49/73, 2006)
5) ca. 6 Feb–14 Mar 2011, a male (ph.) nw. of Sharpe, w. Marshall Co. (*KW* 87:64/72/93, 2011)

*GRAY CATBIRD *Dumetella carolinensis*

Status: Fairly common transient, uncommon to fairly common summer resident, extremely rare during winter. Recorded statewide during migration in a variety of semi-open habitats; usually found where at least some patches of dense, brushy cover are present. Peaks of abundance occur from late Apr to early May and from mid-Sep to early Oct. Breeding statewide but occurrence highest in northern and eastern parts of the state; least numerous in extensively cleared areas (*KBBA*:194-195); most numerous along brushy woodland borders and in overgrown fields, but sometimes present in suburban yards. Individuals occasionally linger into Dec, and wintering has been documented on several occasions (see below). Most numerous during early fall when loose groups of up to a half-dozen or more birds may be seen in suitable habitat.

Maximum count: 35 on Pine Mt., Letcher Co., 2 Oct 2011 (A. Newman/E. Huber, eBird data).

Early spring dates (other than known wintering birds): 16 Mar 2015, Kenton Co. (*KW* 91:75, 2015); 17 Mar 1983, Jefferson Co. (*KW* 59:43, 1983); 18 Mar 2019, Russell Co. (R. Bontrager, eBird data); 19 Mar 2018, Douglass Hills, Jefferson Co. (*KW* 94:81-82, 2018); 23 Mar 2003, Boyle Co. (*KW* 79:72, 2003); 25 Mar 19—, Louisville area (Mengel:355); 25 Mar 1993, Louisville (*KW* 69:47, 1993); 25 Mar 2018, Oldham Co. (B. Davis, eBird data); 27 Mar 2009, Calloway Co. (*KW* 85:74, 2009); 28 Mar 2011, Allen Co. (*KW* 87:93, 2011).

Late fall dates: occasionally lingering into early winter with numerous CBC period reports over the years. As is the case for several other summer residents, winter reports have become more numerous in recent years.

Records of presumed or confirmed records of wintering by county

Jefferson (early Dec 1977–13 Jan 1978, Louisville [*KW* 54:29, 1978]); winter 2016-2017, Anchorage Trail [*KW* 93:51, 2017; T. Quarles, et al., eBird data]; 25 Jan 2015, Anchorage Trail [*KW* 94:59, 2018]; winter 2018-2019, Anchorage Trail [m. ob., eBird data])
Jessamine (6 Feb–late Mar 2010, visiting a suet feeder nr. Wilmore [*KW* 86:45-46/52/71, 2010])
Martin (winter 1959-1960, at Lovely [Reed, *KW* 36:32, 1960])
Warren (mid-winter to 19 Feb 1994, se. of Bowling Green [C. Etkin/E. Moore, 1993-1994 pers. comm.]); 18 Dec 2011–23 Feb 2012, WKU Farm [*KW* 88:49, 2012])

List of additional mid-winter records by county

Elliott (20 Feb 2006, nr. Big Gimlet [*KW* 82:49, 2006])
Franklin (16 Feb 2014, Frankfort [C. Reams, eBird data])
Jefferson (14 Jan 1986, Louisville [*KW* 62:29, 1986]; 16 Feb 2014, Louisville [R. Helfers, eBird data])
Lincoln (30 Jan 2016 [*KW* 92:45, 2016])
Madison (5 Jan 2019, Berea [P. North, eBird data])
Pike (3 Feb 1960, nr. Elkhorn City [Reed, *KW* 36:32, 1960]; 17 Jan 2015, Pikeville [*KW* 91:55, 2015])

*BROWN THRASHER *Toxostoma rufum*

Status: Fairly common to common transient and summer resident, rare to uncommon winter resident. Recorded statewide during migration in a great variety of semi-open habitats with brushy cover. Peak of abundance occurs from early Mar to early Nov. Breeding statewide; most numerous along brushy woodland borders, hedgerows, and fencelines, but also nests in suburban parks and yards. Small numbers winter every year, especially in the western part of the state where a few are generally to be expected in patches of dense, brushy cover with a good supply of soft mast; sometimes visits feeding stations, especially during periods of snowy weather. Typically encountered singly, in pairs, or in family groups, but small groups of up to a half-dozen or more birds are sometimes observed during migration.

Maximum count: 25 in Madison Co., 7 Apr 2013 (J. Polascik, eBird data).

*NORTHERN MOCKINGBIRD *Mimus polyglottos*

Status: Locally uncommon to common resident. Recorded statewide in a great variety of semi-open to open habitats with scattered trees and some dense cover. Breeding statewide, but absent from heavily forested portions of eastern Kentucky (*KBBA*:196-197); most conspicuous about suburban and rural yards in the central and western portions of the state. The presence of an abundance of ornamental trees and shrubs with soft mast fruit in settled areas is largely responsible for the association of this species with homes. Typically observed singly, in pairs, or in family groups.

Maximum counts: 58 in sw. Russell Co., 14 Dec 2011 (eBird data); 56 in s. Pulaski Co., 1 Jan 2015 (eBird data); 45 in sw. Pulaski Co., 11 May 2002 (A. Morton, eBird data).

*EUROPEAN STARLING *Sturnus vulgaris*

Status: Introduced. Locally uncommon to common resident. Recorded statewide but much less numerous in heavily forested portions of eastern Kentucky. Breeding statewide in a wide variety of habitats from urban areas to open farmland and woodland borders. Noisy flocks of dozens to hundreds of immatures characterize the late summer, while large roosts of tens of thousands to over a million birds are scattered throughout central and western Kentucky during winter.

Maximum counts: **2,500,000** at a roost at Ky Dam, 16 Dec 1974 (*KW* 51:10, 1975) and 19 Dec 1976 (*KW* 53:3, 1977); **2,000,000** at a roost nr. Bowling Green, 16 Dec 1972 (*KW* 49:72, 1973).

*CEDAR WAXWING *Bombycilla cedrorum*

Status: Fairly common transient, uncommon to fairly common winter resident, irregularly rare to uncommon summer resident. Recorded statewide during migration and winter in a great variety of forested and semi-open habitats from mature woodlands and woodland borders to suburban parks and yards. Peaks of abundance occur during May (formerly Apr) and from mid-Oct to early Nov. Breeding was formerly regular only on the Cumberland Plateau and Mountains (Mengel:373), but over the past several decades the species has become a still relatively uncommon, but more widespread, nesting bird across central and western Kentucky (*KBBA*: 200-201). Usually nests in semi-open woodlands, parks, and yards. Waxwings are somewhat irregular in occurrence at all seasons, their numbers depending on the abundance of soft mass both here and in adjacent regions. In recent years, the species' presence during winter has been much reduced, especially late in the season, with larger numbers presumably wintering farther south. Frequently encountered in flocks of up to several dozen birds, but occasionally seen by the hundreds during migration and winter.

Maximum counts: ca. **4000** at Murray, 25 Feb 1980 (*KW* 56:33, 1980); **3500** at Mammoth Cave, 18 Dec 2000 (*KW* 77:11/18, 2001); **1200** in one flock at Bernheim Forest 26 Dec 1993 (*KW* 70:20, 1994); ca. **1000** at Shippingport Island, Jefferson Co., 19 May 1986 (*KW* 62:45, 1986); ca. **1000** at Glasgow, Barren Co., 26 Feb 2010 (*KW* 86:46, 2010); **699** on the Otter Creek CBC, 18 Dec 1993 (*KW* 70:20, 1994); **661** on the Bernheim Forest CBC, 23 Dec 1979 (*KW* 56:8, 1980).

*HOUSE SPARROW *Passer domesticus*

Status: Introduced. Locally uncommon to common resident. Recorded statewide throughout the year, but typically found only in association with settlement. Breeding statewide, but much less numerous in heavily forested portions of eastern Kentucky. Quite numerous in cities and towns as well as in rural farmland, but generally absent in unsettled areas.

Maximum count: **500** at Spindletop Farm, Fayette Co., 4 Feb 2011 (J. Swanson, eBird data).

ˢEURASIAN TREE SPARROW *Passer montanus*

Status: Introduced. Accidental vagrant. This Old World species was introduced into the St. Louis, Missouri, area around 1870. It has been reported in Kentucky once.

1) Dec 1977–Jan 1978, one (reportedly ph.) that frequented a feeding station at Lone Oak, a suburb of Paducah, McCracken Co. (*KW* 54:30, 1978). Unfortunately, photographs of the bird could not be located during preparation of this work, and it appears that they were not preserved.

AMERICAN PIPIT *Anthus rubescens*

Status: Uncommon to fairly common transient, rare to locally uncommon during winter (formerly less numerous). Recorded chiefly west of the Cumberland Plateau, but occurs at least occasionally on reclaimed surface mines and in other suitable habitats with sparse vegetation in eastern Kentucky. Peaks of abundance occur from late Mar to mid-Apr and from mid-Oct to mid-Nov. Encountered in a variety of open habitats with short or no ground cover including the margins of flooded fields, freshly tilled fields, grain stubble fields, and pastures. The species was not known to winter historically (Mengel:372); however, a few birds, and sometimes flocks, linger well into winter, and an increase in the frequency of mid-winter observations in recent years (mostly from farmland of south-central and western Kentucky) demonstrates that the species now winters regularly. Most frequently encountered in small to medium-sized flocks of up to 50 birds, but sometimes seen in larger flocks of up to a hundred or more.

Maximum counts: **580** in various flocks in Logan Co., 27 Dec 2005 (*KW* 82:49, 2006); **350** nr. Barren River Lake, Allen Co., 9 Jan 2017 (*KW* 93:51, 2017); **305** in se. Todd Co., 31 Dec 2014 (*KW* 91:55, 2015); **300+** at McElroy Lake, 18 Mar 1991 (*KW* 67:57, 1991); **300+** in Oldham Co., 28 Oct 1993 (*KW* 70:10, 1994); at least **300** at McElroy Lake, 6 May 2008 (*KW* 84:69, 2008); "**a few hundred**" in s. Todd Co., 27 Nov 2006 (*KW* 83:17, 2007); **330** on the Bowling Green CBC, 19 Dec 2016 (*KW* 93:26, 2017); **275** at Bowling Green, 19 Dec 1999 (*KW* 76:32, 2000); **526** total on the Eastern Allen County CBC, 24 Dec 2016 (*KW* 93:26, 2017).

Late spring dates: 27 May 2008, (ph.) McElroy Lake (*KW* 84:69, 2008); 24 May 1994, McElroy Lake (M. Bierly, notes); 21 May 1955, south-central Kentucky (*KW* 38:19, 1962); 19 May 2017, (ph.) w. Henderson Co. (KW 93:77, 2017).

Early fall dates: 22 Aug 1957, Louisville area (*KW* 52:56, 1976); 10 Sep 1960, Louisville area (*KW* 52:56, 1976); 10 Sep 2017, (ph.) Minor Clark Hatchery (*KW* 94:13, 2018).

EVENING GROSBEAK *Coccothraustes vespertinus*

Status: Extremely rare transient and winter resident (formerly irregularly rare to occasionally fairly common). Recorded statewide. Most often observed at feeding stations, but also encountered in deciduous and mixed coniferous-deciduous woodlands, where they feed on fruits and seeds of a variety of trees. Irregular in occurrence; formerly absent or present in very small numbers most years; occasionally more numerous, and in exceptional irruptive years the species was relatively numerous and widespread. Since the late 1990s, the species has been essentially absent with only an occasional report of a transitory bird and two minor irruptions during the winters of 2012-2013 and 2018-2019. Formerly reported in small flocks of fewer than 25 birds, but sometimes seen in flocks of over a hundred birds, especially at feeding stations.

Maximum counts: **150** at Bernheim Forest, winter 1965-66 (Stamm and Wilson, *KW* 42:45, 1966); **125** in Calloway Co., 16 Jan 1986 (*KW* 62:29, 1986); "**hundreds**" in Jefferson Co., winter 1983-84 (*KW* 60:27, 1984); **90-100** in Madison Co., winter 1983-84 (*KW* 60:27, 1984).

Late spring dates: 29 May 1984, [assumed to be at Louisville – see *KW* 60:46, 1984] (A. Stamm, notes); 24 May 1974, Jefferson Co. (*AB* 28:809, 1974); 23 May 1998, Laurel Co. (*KW* 74:59, 1998); 22 May 1984, Jefferson Co. (*KW* 60:46, 1984).

Early fall dates: 22 Sep 2002, Morgan Co. (*KW* 79:17, 2003); 27 Sep 1981, Pine Mt. (*KW* 58:18, 1982); 6 Oct 1978, Jefferson Co. (*KW* 55:17, 1979).

Unaccepted record: 8 Oct 2003, Warren Co. (*KW* 80:16, 2004) [record may be correct but is based only on vocalizations; record at that date/year would be unique in eBird].

Published error: the early fall date of 12 Sep [1979] published in Monroe, et al. (1988) is erroneous, the result of a transcription error (*fide* A. Stamm, historical archive files).

List of recent records (since 2000) by county

Boyd (*KW* 89:16, 2013)
Edmonson (*KW* 89:23/55, 2013)
Franklin (*KW* 95:50, 2019)
Harrison (E. Farmer, 2019 eBird data)
Hart (*KW* 95:50, 2019)
Jefferson (*KW* 89:81, 2013; T. Barnell, 2013 eBird data; *KW* 95:50, 2019)
Lewis (*KW* 89:16, 2013)
Magoffin (*KW* 95:50, 2019)
Morgan (*KW* 89:51/55/81, 2013; D. Hennig, 2018 pers. comm.)
Pulaski (C. Neeley, 2001 eBird data; *KW* 95:50/60, 2019)

*HOUSE FINCH *Haemorhous mexicanus*

Status: Introduced. Locally rare to common resident. This species invaded Kentucky from the northeastern United States, where it was introduced during the 1940s. Small numbers were first recorded in the state at Sandy Hook, Elliott Co., 16 Feb 1977 (*KW* 54:36, 1978) and at Richmond, Madison Co., 18 Jan 1978 (Householder, *KW* 54:35-36, 1978). Although it is now present essentially throughout the state, this finch remains quite scarce in rural farmland and essentially absent in heavily forested areas, apparently preferring suburban areas of cities and towns. Breeding was first observed at Louisville during Apr 1981 (Barron, *KW* 57:64, 1981) and subsequently has been reported from scattered localities throughout most of the state, usually in settled areas (*KBBA*:316-317). Regular at feeding stations, where the species now typically far outnumbers the Purple Finch during winter, especially in urban and suburban areas. This finch flocks during the non-breeding season, when small to medium-sized groups of up to several dozen birds are not uncommon.

Maximum counts: **300+** at a feeding station in Pulaski Co., 17 Jan 1994 (*KW* 70:37, 1994); flock of at least **250** in s. Jefferson Co., 20 Oct 2007 (*KW* 84:16, 2008); **200+** at a feeding station at Eubank, Pulaski Co., 17 Feb 1983 (*KW* 59:30, 1983); **200** at Somerset, Pulaski Co., 16 Nov 1981, (*KW* 58:18, 1982); **200** at Eubank, Pulaski Co., 2/13 Jan 1984 (*KW* 60:27, 1984; J. Elmore, eBird data).

PURPLE FINCH *Haemorhous purpureus*

Status: Uncommon (formerly fairly common to common) transient and winter resident. Recorded statewide in a great variety of habitats from mature woodlands and brushy overgrown fields to suburban parks and rural yards. Irregular in occurrence; present in small numbers most years, but noticeably more common during irruptive years, and occasionally almost absent in others. Often frequents rural feeding stations during winter. Prior to the mid-1980s, this species was much more numerous and widespread during winter, but it has declined substantially (especially in settled areas), perhaps in part due to the dramatic increase in the presence of House Finches. Generally encountered in small flocks of a few to a dozen or so birds, but formerly was sometimes seen in flocks of up to several dozen, especially coming to feeding stations.

Maximum counts: up to **300** in Calloway Co., winter of 1983-84 (*KW* 60:27, 1984); **200** at Eubank, Pulaski Co., 2 Feb 1981 (*KW* 57:38, 1981); **204** on the Mammoth Cave CBC, 21 Dec 2010 (*KW* 87:36/66, 2011); **80+** at a feeding station in Hart Co., 25 Mar 2006 (*KW* 82:75, 2006); **75** at a feeding station in se. Jefferson Co., 7 Mar 2004 (E. Huber, eBird data); **45-50** in Boyd Co., 27 Apr 2013 (*KW* 89:81, 2013).

Late spring dates: 3 Jul 2004, (ph.) se. Jefferson Co. (*KW* 80:86, 2004); 17 Jun 2008, se. Jefferson Co. (*KW* 84:89, 2008); 29 May 2004, Trigg Co. (*KW* 80:73, 2004); 25 May 1982, Grayson Co. (*KW* 58:54, 1982); 22 May 1992, Pulaski Co. (L. McClendon, pers. comm.); 21 May 19—, Louisville area (*KW* 52:62, 1976); 19 May 2008, Franklin Co. (*KW* 84:72, 2008); 17 May 2019, (ph.) Lincoln Co. (J. Elmore, eBird data); 16 May 1996, Boone Co. (*KW* 72:59, 1996); 16 May 2006, e. Jefferson Co. (*KW* 82:75, 2006); 16 May 2019, (ph.) Logan Co. (S. Tyson, eBird data); 15 May 1938, south-central Kentucky (*KW* 38:23, 1962).

Early fall dates: 12 Sep 1979, Jefferson Co. (*KW* 56:17, 1980); 20 Sep 1980, Kenton Co. (*KW* 57:24, 1981); 20 Sep 1985, Pulaski Co. (*KW* 62:8, 1986).

COMMON REDPOLL *Acanthis flammea*

Status: Extremely rare and irregular fall, winter, and spring visitant. This species has been reported fewer than 50 times in Kentucky; most records have originated from the central portion of the state, with none yet from the Cumberland Plateau and Mountains, Typically seen at feeding stations, but occasionally encountered in alder or sweetgum trees in cemeteries as well as in open, weedy fields. Has occurred alone, but more typically in the company of goldfinches or siskins. Irregular in occurrence; absent most years but occasionally present in very small numbers during irruptive years. Usually observed singly, but several older records of small flocks of a half-dozen or more birds exist.

Maximum count: "**25 or 30**" in Nicholas Co., 17-18 Dec 1955 (Mengel: 472).

Late spring dates: 2 Apr 1964, Louisville area (*KW* 52:62, 1976); 29 Mar 1978, Louisville (*KW* 54: 46, 1978); 27 Mar 1966, Jefferson Co. (Stamm and Wilson, *KW* 42:45, 1966).

Early fall dates: 11 Nov 2012, Pendleton Co. (*KW* 89:1/16, 2013); 13 Nov 2007, Owen Co. (*KW* 84: 16, 2008); 25 Nov 1995, Science Hill, Pulaski Co. (J. Elmore, pers. comm); 27 Nov 2015, Lincoln Co. (*KW* 92:16, 2016).

Unaccepted record: 17 Nov 2018, Russell Co. (eBird data).

Published error: the early fall date of 4 Nov [1973] published by Monroe, et al. (1988) is likely erroneous and considered herein to be the result of a transcription error (*fide* A. Stamm, historical archive files).

Summary of records by county (single birds unless otherwise noted)

Boone (two records: 8-9 Jan 1994, (ph.) Middle Creek Road [*KW* 70:37, 1994]; 25 Jan 2009, (2) at Florence [*KW* 85:54, 2009])

Boyle (4 Feb 1978, Danville [Stamm, *KW* 54:30, 1978])

Bullitt (26 Dec 1976, nr. Deatsville, Bullitt Co. [*KW* 53:10, 1977; D. Elmore/L. Rauth, pers. comm.])

Calloway (18 Dec 1983, (3) at Murray (*KW* 60:27, 1984])

Daviess (two records: 1 Jan 1970, [A. Powell, pers. comm./A. Stamm, historical archive files]; 15-16 Mar 1978, Owensboro [*KW* 54:47, 1978])

Edmonson [presumed] (22 Dec 1963, (2), Mammoth Cave NP [Wilson, *KW* 45:38, 1969])

Fayette (three records: 9 Jan–3 Mar 1970, (up to 4), Lexington Cemetery [Morris, *KW* 46:23; R. Morris, pers. comm./A. Stamm notes]; 16 Feb 1972, Lexington [*AB* 26:613, 1972]; mid-Jan–26 Mar 2015, (1-2) Lexington [*KW* 91:56/60/77, 2015])

Franklin (Feb 1899 [Mengel: 472])

Fulton (10-11 Dec 1886, (10+) [Mengel: 472])

Grayson (19-21 Jan 1994, (3) e. of Falls of Rough (*KW* 70:37, 1994])

Jefferson (16 records: last week of Dec 1963, Louisville [C.W. Haberer, pers. comm./A. Stamm, notes]; 2 Apr 1964, Louisville area [*KW* 52:62, 1976]; 29 Jan–9 Mar 1966, (1-3) Louisville [Stamm and Wilson, *KW* 42:45]; 13 Feb 1966, (2) Glenview [Stamm and Wilson, *KW* 42:45]; 27 Mar 1966, (2), Louisville [Stamm and Wilson, *KW* 42:45, 1966]; 6-16 Feb 1977, two Louisville locations [*AB* 31:338, 1972]; 28 Jan 1978, Louisville [*KW* 54:30, 1978]; 29 Jan 1978, Valley Station [*KW* 54:30, 1978]; 29 Jan 1978, Louisville [*KW* 54:30, 1978]; 1-29 Mar 1978, (2), Audubon Park [*KW* 54:46, 1978]; "Mar" 1978, Highlands [*KW* 54:46, 1978]; late Mar 1978, Fern Creek [E. Huber, pers. comm./eBird data]; 22 Mar 1981, (2), Louisville area [*KW* 57:59, 1981]; 7/10 Feb 1982, Cave Hill Cemetery [*KW* 58:31, 1982]; winter 1981-1982, Louisville [*KW* 58:31, 1982]; 12 Dec 2012 (T. Barnell, eBird data)

Kenton (three records: 12 Feb 2012, (ph.) Independence [*KW* 88:53/60, 2012]; 13 Feb 2013, ne. of independence [*KW* 89:54, 2013]; 12 Feb–6 Mar 2016, up to 2 (ph.) at Highland Cemetery, Kenton Co. [*KW* 92:47/52/69, 2016])

Lincoln (27 Nov 2015, (ph.) sw. of Hubble [*KW* 92:16, 2016])

Logan (6-13 Mar 2016, (ph.) Schochoh [*KW* 92:63/69, 2016])

Nicholas (17-18 Dec 1955, (25-30), 7 mi. n. of Carlisle [Green, *KW* 32:18, 1956])

Pendleton (11 Nov 2012, (ph.) 8 mi. n. of Berry [*KW* 89:1/16, 2013])

Pulaski (two records: 16-30 Jan 1994, Science Hill [*KW* 70:37, 1994; eBird data]; 23-25 Nov 1995 [for about a week, *fide* JE], (ph.) Science Hill [J. Elmore, notes/B. Palmer-Ball, photo])

Oldham (26 Dec 1955, (sp.) Harmony Village [Monroe *KW* 32:31, 1956])

Owen (13 Nov 2007 [*KW* 84:16, 2008])

Warren (29 Jan 1964, mouth of Drakes Creek [Wilson, *KW* 45:38, 1969])

Woodford (Feb 1899 [Mengel: 472])

RED CROSSBILL *Loxia curvirostra*

Status: Extremely rare and irregular fall, winter and spring visitant, accidental during summer. This species has been reported fewer than 40 times; most older records originated on the Cumberland Plateau, but the species has now been reported in at least 24 counties across the state (see below). Irregular in occurrence; absent most years but occasionally present in small numbers during irruptive years. Most often encountered in pines, hemlocks, and sweetgums; occasionally comes to feeding stations. Most often seen in small flocks of up to a dozen or so birds.

Note on "call types:" In recent years, much attention has become focused on Red Crossbill "Call Types," which may be indicative of genetically distinctive taxa that may be elevated to full species level in the future. As of the winter 2018-2019, three different Call Types had been identified in birds encountered in Kentucky over the course of the past 6-8 years as determined by interpretion of sound recordings by Cornell University staff. The so-called Type 2 and Type 3 birds seem to be the most regularly occurring, with Type 10 identified on at least one occasion at Lexington (*KW* 89: 54, 2013; R., Denton, eBird data).

Maximum counts: ca. **50** at Louisville, 2 Nov 1973 (Palmer-Ball, *KW* 50:29, 1974); **50** at Louisville, 17 Feb 1982 (*KW* 58:31, 1982); four flocks totaling ca. **60** in Menifee Co., 22 Nov 1969 (Smith, *KW* 46:75, 1970); **26** at Cave Hill Cemetery, Louisville, 21 Feb 2013 (*KW* 89:54, 2013).

Late spring dates: 18 Apr 2018, (ph.) at Ky Dam Village (*KW* 94:82, 2018); 24 Mar [early 1970s], Menifee Co. (L. Smith/J. Pasikowski, pers. comm.; *fide* A. Stamm, historical archive files); 23 Mar 1974, Bernheim Forest (L. Smith, notes).

Early fall date: 12 Oct 1977, Elliott Co. (Greene, *KW* 54:14, 1978).

Out-of-season records (late spring/summer): 7 May 1940, (2) at Louisville (Mengel:475); 21 May 1970, (7) in Bell Co. (*KW* 47:25, 1971); 18 Jun 1974, (2) at Danville (F. Loetscher, notes); mid-May–7 Jun 1991, a small flock coming to feeders in a yard at Elizabethtown, Hardin Co. (*KW* 67: 81, 1991; S. McCloy, pers. comm.); 8 Jun 1991, (8-10) in Red River Gorge, Powell Co. (W. Haag, pers. comm.); 14 Jul 2004, a juv. picked up dead in Kenton Co. (*KW* 80:86, 2004); 10-13 May 2008, (up to 10) at Nolin Lake, Hart Co. (*KW* 84:67/72, 2008); 19 May 2013, Trigg Co. (*KW* 89:81, 2013); 25 May 2013, Marshall Co. (*KW* 89:81, 2013); 16 Jun 2013, Larue Co. (*KW* 89:98, 2013).

Published error: 28 Nov 1990, 8-10 in Jackson Co., (*KW* 67:9, 1991; see *KW* 67:32-33, 1991).

Summary of records by county

Ballard (*KW* 89:54, 2013)
Bell (*KW* 47:25, 1971)
Boyle (F. Loetscher, 1974 notes; *fide* A. Stamm, historical archive files);
Bullitt (L. Smith, 1974 notes; *KW* 73:20/58, 1997)
Calloway (*KW* 86:47/52, 2010)
Christian (Buzzard, *KW* 40:52, 1964; *KW* 50:12, 1974)
Elliott (Greene, *KW* 54:14, 1978)
Fayette (Mengel: 475; *KW* 62:8, 1986; *KW* 89:15/40/54/81, 2013)
Greenup (*KW* 76:9, 2000)
Hardin (*KW* 67:81, 1991/S. McCloy, pers. comm.)
Hart (*KW* 84:67/72, 2008)
Jefferson (Mengel:475; *KW* 47:25, 1971; Palmer-Ball, *KW* 50:29, 1974; *KW* 58:31, 1982; *KW* 89:15-16/51/54/81, 2013)
Kenton (*KW* 80:86, 2004)
Larue (*KW* 89:98, 2013)
Logan (*KW* 77:13/30, 2001)
Lyon (*KW* 89:54, 2013)
Madison (*KW* 76:9, 2000)
Marshall (*KW* 89:81, 2013; *KW* 94:82, 2018)
Menifee (Smith, *KW* 46:75, 1970; L. Smith/J. Pasikowski, early 1970s notes)
Monroe (Mengel: 475)
Nelson (Mengel: 474)
Ohio (*KW* 94:23/59/64, 2018)
Powell (W. Haag, 1991 pers. comm.; *KW* 89:15, 2013)
Pulaski (*KW* 69:36, 1993; *KW* 89:54/81, 2013)
Trigg (*KW* 89:81, 2013; *KW* 94:59, 2018)
Warren (Mengel: 475)

WHITE-WINGED CROSSBILL *Loxia leucoptera*

Status: Extremely rare and irregular fall, winter, and spring visitant. This species has been reported fewer than 40 times in the state. Most records have come from hemlock and sweetgum trees in cemeteries at Louisville and Lexington, but the species also has been reported at a handful of additional sites with natural and planted conifers, as well as feeding stations in suburban and rural yards. There are now reports from 17 widely separated counties (see below). Irregular in occurrence; absent most years but occasionally present in small numbers during irruptive years. Generally seen singly or in small flocks of fewer than a dozen birds.

Maximum counts: ca. **40** at the Lexington Cemetery, 27 Jan 2013 (*KW* 89:54, 2013); **35-40** at the Lexington Cemetery, 7 Feb 2009 (*KW* 85:54, 2009); **25-34** at Bernheim Forest, 24 Mar 1982 (*KW* 58:54, 1982); **25-30** in Hancock Co, 25 Nov 1965 (Alsop, *KW* 47:68, 1971); up to **26** at the Lexington Cemetery, 16 Feb 1972 (R. Morris, notes; *fide* A. Stamm, historical archive files); up to **26** at Cave Hill Cemetery, Louisville, 26 Mar 1972 (J. Pasikowski/L. Smith, notes; *fide* A. Stamm, historical archive files); **25** at Lexington, 6 Dec 1977 (*KW* 54:30, 1978); up to **23** at Louisville during winter of 1954-55 (Slack and Stamm, *KW* 31:17-18, 1955; [number was reported as up to 26 in *AFN* 9:262, 1955]).

Late spring dates: 5-9 May 1982, a male (ph.) at Louisville (*KW* 58:54, 1982); 15-16 Apr 2000, a male (vt.) in Calloway Co. (*KW* 76:47, 2000); 26 Mar 1972, Cave Hill Cemetery, Louisville (*KW* 52:62, 1976).

Early fall dates: 3 Nov 2001, Richmond, Madison Co. (*NAB* 56:60, 2002); 22 Nov 2012, Lexington (*KW* 89:16, 2013); 25 Nov 1965, Hancock Co. (Alsop, *KW* 47:68, 1971).

Unaccepted records (these reports are almost certainly valid, but I can find no details about them other than the dates and locations being noted in Anne Stamm's historical archive files): 4 Mar 1974, 2 at Lexington (A. Stamm, historical archive files); 24 Jan 1979, [#?] at Lexington (A. Stamm, historical archive files).

Summary of records by county (singles unless otherwise noted)

Barren (12-15 Feb 2013, a male (ph.) at Glasgow [*KW* 89:54, 2013])
Breathitt (10 Jan 1978, a male at Jackson [Smith and Allaire, *KW* 54:35, 1978])
Bullitt (24 Mar 1982, (25-34) at Bernheim Forest [Stamm, *KW* 58:54, 1982])
Bullitt (28 Dec 1991, a male at Bernheim Forest [*KW* 68:19, 1992])
Calloway (15-16 Apr 2000, a male in Calloway Co. [Busroe, *KW* 76:47, 2000])
Campbell (four records: 4 Feb 2009, (ca. 12) at Ft. Thomas [*KW* 85:54, 2009]; 5 Feb–15 Mar 2009, (up to 20) at St. Anne's Convent [*KW* 85:41/54/71/76, 2009]; 23 Feb 2009, (at least 25) at Evergreen Cemetery [*KW* 85:54, 2009]; 7-12 Feb & 14 Mar 2013, 1-5 (ph.) at St. Anne's Convent (*KW* 89:54/81/88, 2013)
Fayette (seven records: 24 Jan–10 Feb 1970, (up to 15) at the Lexington Cemetery (Morris, *KW* 46:39, 1970]; 16 Feb 1972, (up to 26) at Lexington (*AB* 26:613, 1972; R. Morris, notes]; 6 Dec 1977–22 Feb 1978, (up to 25) at the Lexington Cemetery [Stamm, *KW* 54:30, 1978]; 24 Jan 1981, (12) at Lexington [Stamm, *KW* 57:38, 1981]; 5-15 Feb 2009, (up to 35-40) [*KW* 85:54, 2009]; 22 Nov 2012–26 Mar 2013, up to 40 (ph.) at the Lexington Cemetery [*KW* 89:16/40/51/54/81, 2013; 29-30 Mar 2013, (3-8) at Spindletop Farm [*KW* 89:81, 2013])
Hancock (25 Nov 1965, (25-30) ca. 1 mi E of Hawesville [Alsop, *KW* 47:68, 1971 & 2009 pers. comm.])
Hardin (30 Jan 2013, (ph.) at Elizabethtown [*KW* 89:54, 2013])
Jefferson (13 records: 27 Nov 1937–6 Feb 1938, (up to 5) at Cave Hill Cemetery [Slack, *KW* 14:17-18, 1938; Mengel:476]; 23 Dec 1954–17 Feb 1955, (up to 23) at Cave Hill Cemetery [Slack and Stamm, *KW* 31:29, 1955; Mengel: 476]; 22 Dec 1963, (6) at Cave Hill Cemetery [Monroe, *KW* 40:15, 1964]; 11 Dec 1965–1 Mar 1966, (up to 15) at Cave Hill Cemetery [Stamm and Wilson, *KW* 42:45, 1966; Able, *KW* 44:56, 1968]; 4 Jan–21 Mar 1970, (up to 15-20) at Cave Hill Cemetery [Stamm, *KW* 46:39, 1970]; 20 Feb 1972, ("a few") at Louisville [*AB* 26:613, 1972; A. Stamm, historical archive files]; 26 Mar 1972, (up to 26) at Cave Hill Cemetery [J. Pasikowski/L. Smith, notes; *fide* A. Stamm, historical archive files]; 2 Jan/11-12 Mar 1978, (up to 8) at Cave Hill Cemetery [Stamm, *KW* 54:30, 1978]; [Stamm, *KW* 54:47, 1978]; 28 Jan 1978, a male at Surrey Hills Farm [Stamm, *KW* 54:30, 1978]; 15 Feb 1982, (10) nr. Cherokee Park [Stamm, *KW* 58:31, 1982]; 5-9 May 1982, a male at Louisville [Stamm, *KW* 58:54, 1982]; 24 Nov–1 Dec 2012, (ph.) at Cave Hill Cemetery [*KW* 89:16/54, 2013]; 4 Apr 2013; 3 (ph.) at Surrey Hills Farm [*KW* 89:81, 2013])

Kenton (8/14 Feb 2009, at Ft. Wright [*KW* 85:54, 2009])
Madison (3 Nov 2001, a first-year male at Richmond [*NAB* 56:60, 2002])
Meade (10 Dec 1981, nr. Muldraugh [Stamm, *KW* 58:31, 1982])
Nelson (28 Dec 1975, (4) at end of Tewell Creek Lane [*KW* 52:9, 1976])
Trimble (winter 1980-1981 [no specific date], (6) at Bedford [Stamm, *KW* 57, 38:1981])
Warren (19 Jan 2002, a female at Shaker Mill [Busroe, *KW* 78:35, 2002])
Wolfe (8 Feb 2009, (14) at Sky Bridge Overlook [*KW* 85:54, 2009])
Woodford (10 Mar 2013, a male (ph.) at Buckley Hills Sanctuary [*KW* 89:81, 2013])

*PINE SISKIN *Spinus pinus*

Status: Irregularly rare to fairly common transient and winter resident, accidental during summer (at least three breeding records). Recorded statewide; most often encountered in pines, hemlocks, and sweetgums in both settled and natural situations, but also observed in a variety of weedy and brushy habitats; also often seen at feeding stations in both rural and suburban yards. Irregular in occurrence; nearly absent some years, but more often present in small to moderate numbers and occasionally quite numerous during irruptive years. Peak of abundance typically occurs from early Nov to mid-Apr, but some years most go farther south, and pronounced peaks of abundance occur at the beginning and end of that period. An individual is occasionally seen during summer (including a few reports in recent years), and breeding has been documented a few times following irruptive years (see below). Most often encountered in small to medium-sized flocks of up to a few dozen birds, but occasionally observed in larger flocks of a hundred or more individuals.

Maximum counts: **250-300** nr. Falls of Rough, Grayson Co., Nov 1989 (*KW* 66:14, 1990); **200-300** at South Williamson, Pike Co., late Jan 2009 (*KW* 85:54, 2009); **200** nr. Falls of Rough, Grayson Co., winter 1980-81 (*KW* 57:38, 1981); ca. **200** at Mt. Zion, Pulaski, 30 Jan 2009 (*KW* 85:54, 2009); "**hundreds**" nr. Big Gimlet, Elliott Co., 1 Feb 2009 (*KW* 85:54, 2009).

Late spring dates: 9 Jul 2009, (ba.) Mercer Co. (*KW* 85:95, 2009); 6 Jul 2015, Rowan Co. (*KW* 91:87/96, 2015); early Jul 2009, Magoffin Co. (*KW* 85:95, 2009); 17 Jun 1992, Louisville (D. Summerfield, notes); 10 Jun 1978, Louisville (*KW* 54:64, 1978); 9 Jun 1979, Louisville (*KW* 55:58, 1979); 7 Jun 2018, Natural Bridge SRP, Powell Co. (*KW* 94:110, 2018); 6 Jun 2009, Pulaski Co. (*KW* 85:95, 2009); 6 Jun 2018, Lincoln Co. (*KW* 94:110, 2018); 5 Jun 2011, Lexington (*KW* 87:116, 2011); 3 Jun 2013, Lee Co. (*KW* 89:98, 2013).

Early fall dates: 17 Sep 2012, Lincoln Co. (*KW* 89:16, 2013); 1 Oct 1990, Grayson Co. (*KW* 67:9, 1991); 1 Oct 2009, Pike Co. (*KW* 86:15, 2010); 5 Oct 1965, Bullitt Co. (Stamm and Wilson, *KW* 42: 44, 1966); 5 Oct 2002, Pike Co. (*KW* 79:17, 2003); 5 Oct 2015, Jefferson Co. (*KW* 92:16, 2016); 8 Oct 2014, Louisville (*KW* 91:16, 2015); 8 Oct 2015, Bullitt Co. (*KW* 92:16, 2016); 9 Oct 1975, Madisonville (*AB* 30:81, 1976).

Out-of-season record (summer): 13 Jul (for circa a week)/11-16 Aug/20-23 Sep 2016, ne. of Defoe, Henry Co. (*KW* 92:81, 2016; *KW* 93:14, 2017); 21 Jul 2019, (ph.) at Schochoh, Logan Co. (S. Tyson, eBird data).

Summary of confirmed breeding records by county

Jefferson (Mar 1978, a nest with one egg at Louisville (unsuccessful) [Palmer-Ball, *KW* 56:38, 1980])
Jefferson (late May 1990, a fledgling was observed being fed at Louisville [*KW* 66:62, 1990; *KBBA*: 318])
Fayette (mid-Apr 2009, two pairs observed gathering nesting material on the se. side of Lexington [*KW* 85:77, 2009])

LESSER GOLDFINCH *Spinus psaltria*

Status: Accidental vagrant. This species is a resident of the western United States and Middle America. It occurs very infrequently in the eastern United States and has been documented in Kentucky on one occasion.

1) 5-7 Dec 1980, a male of the black-backed race (*S. p. psaltria*) (ph.) at feeders in a yard at Elizabethtown, Hardin Co. (*KW* 57:38, 1981; *AB* 35:306, 1981).

*AMERICAN GOLDFINCH *Spinus tristis*

Status: Resident (irregularly fairly common to common during migration, winter, and summer). Recorded statewide in a great variety of semi-open habitats from woodland borders and overgrown fields to suburban parks and yards; frequent at feeding stations. Most years noticeable peaks of abundance occur from mid-Apr to early May and from mid-Oct to mid-Nov as migrants supplement the population. Breeding statewide in a great variety of open and semi-open habitats with scattered small trees. Winter abundance varies from year to year depending on food supplies; substantial numbers linger through the season some years, but the species may be more locally distributed during others. Sometimes encountered in flocks of up to a hundred or more birds during fall and winter.

Maximum count: 1500 in Calloway Co., late Nov 1977 (*AB* 32:214, 1978; J.T. Erwin, notes).

LAPLAND LONGSPUR *Calcarius lapponicus*

Status: Rare to locally uncommon transient and winter resident. Reported chiefly west of the Cumberland Plateau. Most older records originated from farmland near Louisville, but there are now records from at least 44 counties scattered primarily across central and western portions of the state. Sizable winter flocks can be encountered most every winter in particular areas, but widespread influxes occasionally occur during periods of snowy or icy winter weather. Generally encountered in grain stubble fields, but can be found in other types of open habitat with short vegetation, especially when snow cover is present. Usually seen in small numbers with flocks of Horned Larks, but longspurs are sometimes reported in pure flocks of 100-250 or more birds.

Maximum counts: at least **4000** in the Lower Hickman Bottoms, 22 Dec 2008 (*KW* 85:52, 2009); **3921** counted along KY 102, Todd Co., 31 Dec 2014 (*KW* 91:24/56, 2015); **3000** in the Lower Hickman Bottoms, 25 Jan 2018 (*KW* 94:60, 2018); **1100+** at McElroy Lake 2 Dec 2002 (*KW* 79:49, 2003); at least **1000** in the Ohio River bottoms of n. Union Co., 2 Jan 2010 (*KW* 86:47, 2010); ca. **1000** in the Lower Hickman Bottoms 30 Dec 2002 (*KW* 79:49, 2003); ca. **1000** nr. Monticello, Wayne Co., 30 Jan 2009 (*KW* 85:53, 2009); ca. **800** in the Lower Hickman Bottoms, 31 Dec 2000 (D. O'Brien, eBird data); ca. **600** e. of Cedar Creek Lake, Lincoln Co., 8 Feb 2014 (*KW* 90:54, 2014); **550+** at McElroy Lake, 25 Nov 2002 (*KW* 79:17, 2003); more than **500** below Barkley Dam, Lyon Co., 18 Dec 2000 (*KW* 77:30, 2001; D. Roemer, notes); at least **500** at each of two locations in Pulaski Co., 29/30 Jan 2009 (*KW* 85:53, 2009); ca. **500** in Calloway Co., 30 Dec 2000 (*KW* 77:17, 2001; H. Chambers, notes); **410** in sw. Daviess, 1 Jan 2012 (*KW* 88:49, 2012); ca. **350** w. of Woodburn, Warren Co., 7 Feb 2014 (*KW* 90:54, 2014); ca. **300** nr. Open Pond, Fulton Co., 16 Dec 1997 (D. Roemer, notes; *KW* 74:34, 1998 [location erroneously published as the Long Point Unit therein]); **320** on the Olmstead, Logan Co. CBC, 28 Dec 2000 (*KW* 77:17, 2001); **300** s. of Petersburg, Boone Co., 15-16 Dec 2013 (*KW* 90:54, 2014); ca. **250** in ne. Jefferson Co., 14-18 Jan/9 Feb 1982 (*KW* 58:31, 1982); **200** sw. of Owensboro, Daviess Co., 8 Jan 2014 (*KW* 90:54, 2014); at least **200** in Pulaski Co., 4 Feb 2009 (*KW* 85:53, 2009); ca. **200** in Fayette Co., 8 Jan 2014 (*KW* 90:54, 2014); **200** nr. Dot, Logan Co., 2 Dec 2015 (*KW* 92:45, 2016).

Late spring dates: 26 Apr 2015, singing bird heard ne. of Jewell City, McLean Co. (*KW* 91:75, 2015 [location erroneously published as Hopkins Co. therein]); 11 Apr 2002, McElroy Lake (*KW* 78:53, 2002); 7 Apr 1984, Fulton Co. (*KW* 60:46, 1984); 3 Apr 1959, south-central Kentucky (*KW* 38:23, 1962).

Early fall dates: 11 Oct 2002, Carter Co. (*KW* 79:17, 2003); 13 Oct 2009, Warren Co. (*KW* 86:15, 2010); 14 Oct 2004, McElroy Lake (*KW* 81:15, 2005); 21 Oct 1998, Warren Co. (*KW* 75:8, 1999); 23 Oct 2015, Jefferson Co. (*KW* 92:13, 2016); 24 Oct 1982, Louisville (*KW* 59:18, 1983).

Out-of-season record (late spring): 24 May 1950, McElroy Lake (*KW* 38:24, 1962) [Mengel:514-515 did not include this report, so its validity has never been assessed].

Summary of records by county

Adair (*KW* 85:53, 2009)
Allen (*KW* 90:54, 2014)
Ballard (annual)
Barren (D. Roemer, 2010 eBird data; *KW* 86:47, 2010)

Boone (probably annual)
Bourbon (*KW* 84:47, 2008)
Boyle (*KW* 58:31, 1982)
Calloway (*KW* 90:54, 2014)
Carter (*KW* 79:17, 2003)
Campbell (*KW* 77:30, 2001)
Christian (*KW* 90:54, 2014; J. Hall, 2016 eBird data)
Daviess (*KW* 79:49, 2003; *KW* 88:49, 2012; *KW* 90:54, 2014; C. Bliznick, 2018 eBird data)
Elliott (*KW* 85:53, 2009)
Fayette (annual)
Fulton (annual)
Gallatin (*KW* 77:30, 2001; *KW* 79:49, 2003)
Hardin (*KW* 84:47, 2008; *KW* 87:64, 2011; *KW* 88:49, 2012; G. Heath, 2012 eBird data; B. Wulker, 2014 eBird data; B. Palmer-Ball, 2016 eBird data; m. ob. 2018 eBird data)
Henderson (likely annual)
Hickman (*KW* 88:49, 2012)
Hopkins (*KW* 90:54, 2014; J. Sole, 2013 eBird data; B. Wulker, 2014 eBird data)
Jefferson (annual)
Larue (*KW* 84:47, 2008; *KW* 89:52, 2013)
Lawrence (*KW* 84:47, 2008)
Lincoln (*KW* 85:53, 2009; *KW* 90:54, 2014)
Livingston (B. Wulker, 2018 eBird data)
Logan (annual)
Lyon (*KW* 77:30, 2001)
Marshall (M. Autin, 2014 eBird data; *KW* 94:13, 2018; C. Bliznick et al., 2017/2019 eBird data)
McCracken (D. Akers, 2013 eBird data; T. Wolff, 2016 eBird data)
McLean (*KW* 91:75, 2015 [location erroneously published as Hopkins Co. therein])
Muhlenberg (likely annual)
Nelson (*KW* 87:64, 2011; D. Manley, 2018 eBird data)
Ohio (2002/2005/2009 eBird data)
Oldham (*KW* 90:54, 2014; m. ob. 2018 eBird data)
Pulaski (R. Denton, 2000/2001/2017 eBird data; *KW* 85:52-53, 2009; D. Svetich/L. Combs, 2017 eBird data)
Rowan (*KW* 85:52, 2009; *KW* 90:15, 2014)
Russell (*KW* 85:52, 2009)
Shelby (*KW* 77:30, 2001; *KW* 84:47, 2008; *KW* 86:47, 2010; *KW* 87:64, 2011)
Simpson (R. Denton, 2015 eBird data)
Todd (annual in recent years)
Trigg (*KW* 77:30, 2001; B. Lisowsky, 2014 eBird data)
Union (*KW* 86:47, 2010; *KW* 89:13, 2013)
Warren (annual)
Wayne (*KW* 85:53, 2009)

SMITH'S LONGSPUR *Calcarius pictus*

Status: Extremely rare visitant. Based on the regularity of occurrence of this species in adjacent states, it cannot be considered accidental, and it is remarkable that a few birds are not found at least occasionally in farmland of the western part of the state. Only one record has been documented in Kentucky.

1) 11-14 Mar 1998, a male (ph.) nr. Open Pond, western Fulton Co. (Roemer, *KW* 74:63, 1998).

SNOW BUNTING *Plectrophenax nivalis*

Status: Extremely rare to rare transient and winter visitant. Most historical records originated at the Falls of the Ohio and more recently in open farmland near Louisville, but the species has now been reported from at least 36 counties across the state, including at least two records from the Cumberland Plateau (see below). Single birds or small flocks occasionally appear during fall, but almost all reports have occurred during periods of snowy or icy conditions during mid- to late winter. The flocks that appear during such events typically vanish as soon as the snow or ice cover disappears. This species is occasionally seen along open shores of the larger lakes and rivers, but more frequently in grain stubble fields or other open habitats with short vegetation. It usually occurs in the company of Horned Larks and Lapland Longspurs, but the larger mid-winter flocks may contain only Snow Buntings. Usually encountered in small numbers of up to a dozen or so birds, but larger flocks have been observed on a few occasions.

Maximum counts: **770+** in one flock in ne. Jefferson Co., 10 Feb 1982 (B. Palmer-Ball, eBird data [number incorrectly published as "400" in *KW* 58:31, 1982]); ca. **200** in ne. Jefferson Co., 12 Dec 1977 (*KW* 54:31, 1978); at least **50** in each of two different flocks in Boone Co., 9 Mar 2008 (*KW* 84:71, 2008); at least **97** in ne. Jefferson Co., 8 Feb 2014 (*KW* 90:54, 2014); **75-80** in ne. Jefferson Co., 1 Feb 2004 (*KW* 80:48, 2004); ca. **70** in Fayette Co, 5-6 Feb 2009 (*KW* 85:53, 2009); **60** in Boone Co., 19 Feb 2007 (*KW* 83:52, 2007); **51** in ne. Jefferson Co., 28 Jan 2009 (*KW* 85:53, 2009); **50+** in Boone Co., 31 Jan 2014 (*KW* 80:48, 2004.

Late spring date: 8 Mar 1978, Jefferson Co. (*KW* 54:47, 1978).

Early fall dates: 23 Oct 1977, Elliott Co. (Greene, *KW* 54:14, 1978); 24 Oct 2014, Union Co. (*KW* 91:13, 2015); 6 Nov 2017, (ph.) w. Henderson Co. (*KW* 94:13, 2018); 8 Nov 1975, Pfeiffer Fish Hatchery, Franklin Co. (A. Gilchrist, pers. comm.; *fide* A. Stamm, historical archive files); 12 Nov 1944, Ky Lake area (Mengel:515); 12 Nov 2006, Falls of the Ohio (*KW* 83:20, 2007).

Unaccepted records: 4-9 Oct 1965, Ft. Knox (*AFN* 20:54, 1966; *KW* 52:64, 1976) [I cannot find any details of this observation and feel it best be listed here]; Mengel (p. 516) includes a few other vague historical references.

Summary of records by county

Adair (R. Denton, 1996 eBird data; *KW* 85:53, 2009)
Boone (*KW* 70:37, 1994; *KW* 75:27, 1999; B. Palmer-Ball, 2000 eBird data; *KW* 80:48, 2004; *KW* 83: 52, 2007; *KW* 84:71, 2008; *KW* 85:53, 2009; *KW* 90:54, 2014)
Bourbon (*KW* 90:54, 2014)
Boyd (*KW* 35:10, 1959)
Bracken (*KW* 83:52, 2007)
Calloway (*KW* 86:47, 2010)
Campbell (Mengel:515; *KW* 75:27, 1999; *KW* 80:48, 2004)
Carroll (*KW* 67:9, 1991)
Christian (*KW* 59:9, 1983)
Daviess (*KW* 77:17, 2001; eBird data)
Elliott (Greene, *KW* 54:14, 1978; *KW* 85:53, 2009)
Fayette (*KW* 58:31, 1982; *KW* 85:53, 2009; *KW* 87:64, 2011; *KW* 90:54, 2014)
Franklin (A. Gilchrist, pers. comm., *fide* A. Stamm, historical archive files; *KW* 85:53, 2009; *KW* 86: 47, 2010)
Jefferson (numerous reports)
Gallatin (*KW* 83:52, 2007; *KW* 90:54, 2014)
Grant (Davis, *KW* 40:33, 1964)
Harrison (*KW* 90:54, 2014)
Henderson (*KW* 90:54, 2014; [ph.] *KW* 94:13, 2018)
Lewis (*KW* 86:47, 2010; *KW* 87:64, 2011)
Lincoln (*KW* 85:53, 2009)
Lyon (*KW* 85:53, 2009)
Marion (Webster, *KW* 37:18, 1961)
Marshall (Mengel:515 [location given as Ky Lake therein]; B. Palmer-Ball, 1995 eBird data; *KW* 77:17, 2001 [location given as LBL CBC therein]; *KW* 85:53, 2009)
Meade (*KW* 77:17, 2001/B. Palmer-Ball, 2000 eBird data)
Muhlenberg (*KW* 66:18/41, 1990)
Ohio (*KW* 79:49, 2003)
Oldham (*KW* 85:53, 2009; *KW* 90:54, 2014)
Pulaski (*KW* 85:53, 2009)
Rowan (*KW* 78:13, 2002/L. Kornman, photo; *KW* 83:52, 2007; *KW* 85:53, 2009; *KW* 89:53, 2013)

Russell (*KW* 85:53, 2009)
Shelby (*KW* 54:31, 1978; *KW* 60:11, 1984; *KW* 63:12, 1987; *KW* 65:12, 1989; *KW* 77:30, 2001; *KW* 87:64, 2011)
Spencer (*KW* 85:53, 2009)
Union (*KW* 91:13, 2015)
Warren (*KW* 75:27, 1999; *KW* 77:30, 2001; *KW* 79:49, 2003)
Wayne (*KW* 85:53, 2009)
Woodford (*KW* 85:53, 2009)

*BACHMAN'S SPARROW *Peucaea aestivalis*

Status: Extremely rare and local (formerly uncommon) summer resident. Formerly recorded state-wide, but more numerous west of the Cumberland Plateau, breeding in a variety of open, scrubby habitats; apparently was most numerous in overgrown fields where there were scattered patches of small trees (often conifers), briars, and bare ground (Mengel:492). Some evidence suggests that the species may not have been widespread at the time of European settlement, but that it expand-ed into the state in response to forest clearing during the late 1800s and early 1900s (Mengel:491-492). Subsequent to a dramatic population decline that appeared to commence during the early to mid-1960s, this species could only be found in a few locations in western Kentucky by the mid- to late 1980s (*KBBA*:282-283). For about a decade it was thought to be extirpated from Kentucky, but recent work on the Fort Campbell Military Reservation, Trigg Co. (as well as adjacent areas in Tennessee), has documented the presence of a limited but seemingly persistent breeding popu-lation) (e.g. *NAB* 55:441, 2001; *KW* 78:67, 2002; *KW* 80:85, 2004; *KW* 84:89, 2008; *KW* 85:95, 2009; *KW* 86:73, 2010; *KW* 92:81, 2016; *KW* 94:110, 2018; D. Moss, eBird data). On Fort Camp-bell, the species is utilizing fields of mostly native grasses and forbs that are frequently burned (D. Moss, pers. comm.). **State Breeding Status**: Endangered.

Early spring dates: 13 Mar 1948, nr. Louisville (Mengel:490); 18 Mar [unknown year], Nelson Co. (Mengel:490); 20 Mar 1889, Eubank, Pulaski Co. (Mengel:490); [recent] 17 Apr 2009, Ft. Camp-bell, Trigg Co. (*KW* 85:75, 2009; D. Moss, eBird data).
Late fall dates: 1 Oct 1950, nr. Louisville (Mengel:492); 26 Sep 1889, Eubank, Pulaski Co. (Mengel:493); 17 Sep 1950, (sp.) Jefferson Co. (Mengel:492); 30 Aug 2013, Ft. Campbell, Trigg Co. (*KW* 90:17, 2014; D. Moss, eBird data).
Unaccepted record: 3 Jun 1984, Henry Co. (*KW* 60:56, 1984).

*GRASSHOPPER SPARROW *Ammodramus savannarum*

Status: Uncommon to locally fairly common summer resident, extremely rare during winter. Known primarily as a summer bird, being quite uncommon and inconspicuous as a transient away from nesting areas, although migrants are occasionally flushed from grassy or weedy fields. Peak of abundance occurs from late Apr to mid-Aug. Breeding throughout the state except the heavily forested portions of eastern Kentucky; utilizes hayfields, reclaimed surface mines, and other open habitats with an abundance of grassy vegetation. There are a few winter records, mostly of single birds, in extensive grassy habitats. This species declined dramatically during the 1970s (Monroe, *KW* 54:21, 1978; *KBBA*:294), but that decline appears to have leveled off during the past two dec-ades (*KBBA*:294; BBS data). Generally encountered singly or in pairs.

Early spring dates: 22 Mar 2012, (hd.), Hart Co. (*KW* 88:82, 2012); 26 Mar 19—, Nelson Co. (Mengel:481); 26 Mar 1921, south-central Kentucky (*KW* 38:23, 1962); 4 Apr 2017, Jefferson Co. (*KW* 93:77, 2017).
Late fall dates: 8 Dec 2014, (possibly lingered to winter?) n. of Dot, Logan Co. (*KW* 91:56, 2015); 22 Nov 1984, Madison Co. (*KW* 61:18, 1985); 7 Nov 18— or 19—, Nelson Co. (Mengel:482); 2 Nov 2009, Jefferson Co. (*KW* 86:15, 2010); 2 Nov 2016, Logan Co. (*KW* 93:13, 2017).
Out-of-season records (winter): 28 Dec 1965, Otter Creek Park CBC, Meade Co. (*KW* 42:14, 1966; *AFN* 20:238, 1966); 23 Dec 1973, Louisville CBC (*KW* 50:15, 1974); 22-23 Dec 1984, (3) ne. of Flaherty, Meade Co. (*KW* 61:31, 1985; B. Palmer-Ball, eBird data); 1 Jan 2006, one on the former Gibraltar Mine, Muhlenberg Co. (*KW* 82:19, 2006); 6-10 Mar 2012, Allen Co. (possibly early mi-

grant) (*KW* 88:81, 2012); 11 Nov 2015–14 Feb 2016, (ph.) Logan Co. (*KW* 92:15/46, 2016); 31 Jan 2019, (ph.) in s. Jefferson Co. (*KW* 95:50, 2019).

Unaccepted records: records of up to ten birds lingering into early winter in Henderson Co., as reported on several CBCs in the 1950s and 1960s (*KW* 31:11, 1955; *AFN* 10:147, 1956; *AFN* 11: 152, 1957; *AFN* 13:172, 1959; *AFN* 14:187, 1960; *AFN* 18:202, 1964; *AFN* 21:228, 1967; and *AFN* 23:271, 1969), are considered herein to likely refer to Le Conte's Sparrows.

*LARK SPARROW *Chondestes grammacus*

Status: Rare spring transient and summer resident (formerly more numerous), extremely rare during late summer and fall; accidental during winter. Most records are from west of the Cumberland Plateau, although one was recently documented in Perry Co. (L. Anderson, 2019 eBird data/photos). Known primarily as a summer bird, but occasionally encountered during migration in fallow fields and pastures or along open roadsides where some bare ground is present. Confirmed breeding has been documented from only a dozen counties (see below). In addition, there are summer sightings from scattered locations, primarily in open farmland, in other parts of central and western Kentucky that could be indicative of breeding (e.g., Mengel:489-490; *AB* 30:964, 1976; *KW* 60:56, 1984; *KW* 62:69, 1986; *KW* 64:66, 1988; *KBBA*:290; *KW* 70:56/71, 1994; and additional recent reports, many in eBird). Usually seen singly or in pairs. **State Breeding Status**: Special Concern.

Maximum count: flock of at least **10** in w. Henderson Co., 19 Apr 2008 (*KW* 84:71, 2008).

Early spring dates: 27 Mar 19—, Warren Co. (Mengel:489); 2 Apr 2011, Hart Co. (*KW* 87:95, 2011).

Late fall dates: 5 Nov 1977, ne. Jefferson Co. (*AB* 32:214, 1978; eBird data); 24 Oct 2016, Woodford Co. (*KW* 93:14, 2017); 20 Oct 2000, Lyon Co. (*KW* 77:10, 2001); 18 Oct 1919, Warren Co. (Mengel:490; *KW* 38:23, 1962).

Out-of-season records (winter): 20-23 Jan 2016, ne. of Defoe, Henry Co. (*KW* 92:46, 2016); 16-18 Feb 2016, (ph.) Georgetown, Scott Co. (*KW* 92:46/52, 2016); 2 Jan 2017, (ph.) n. Fayette Co. (*KW* 93:53, 2017).

Unaccepted records: (2) in Trigg Co., 15 Dec 1946 (Wyatt, *KW* 23:44, 1947); flock of 12 below Ky Dam, 19 Jan 1997 (*KW* 73:39, 1997); 24 Feb 2000, Grayson Co. (*KW* 76:32, 2000).

Summary of confirmed breeding records by county

Butler (D. Harker, 1983 pers. comm.)
Calloway (Mengel:489)
Harrison (Mengel:489)
Henderson (*KW* 84:71, 2008; *KW* 85:95, 2009; *KW* 87:116, 2011; *KW* 88:95, 2012; *KW* 90:90, 2014; *KW* 92:68, 2016)
Hopkins (Mengel:489)
Jefferson (Mengel:489)
Monroe (*KBBA*:290)
Muhlenberg (B. Palmer-Ball, 1998 eBird data)
Nelson (Mengel:489)
Shelby ([carrying nesting material] *KW* 89:97-98, 2013)
Trigg (J. Giocomo/D. Moss, 2001/2002 notes; *KW* 79:85, 2003; *KW* 80:85, 2004; *KW* 88:95, 2012; *KW* 91:87, 2015; *KW* 92:81, 2016)
Warren (Wilson, *KW* 22:9, 1946; *KW* 74:74, 1998; *KW* 84:89, 2008)

LARK BUNTING *Calamospiza melanocorys*

Status: Accidental vagrant. This species breeds across the western United States and rarely shows up in the eastern United States. It has been documented in Kentucky on one occasion.

1) 6-7 Aug 2017, an adult male molting out of breeding plumage (ph.) in w. Henderson Co. (*KW* 94:14/40, 2018)

*CHIPPING SPARROW *Spizella passerina*

Status: Fairly common to common transient and summer resident, rare to locally uncommon during winter (formerly quite rare, but more frequent in recent years). Recorded statewide during migration in a variety of semi-open to open habitats with scattered trees and short vegetation or bare ground. Peaks of abundance occur during the first half of Apr and from mid-Oct to mid-Nov. Breeding statewide in a variety of similar habitats, but most frequent in suburban and rural yards and park-like areas with conifers and shrubs; only occasionally observed in its natural habitat, mixed pine-hardwood forest with an open sub-canopy layer. Historically, only a few individuals would linger into or through winter, but over the past few decades the species has become a locally distributed, but not paricularly rare, winter resident. Habitats used during winter are simiar to those used at other times of the year; occasional at feeding stations. Most older winter records pertained to single birds, often in the company of Dark-eyed Juncos or other sparrows, but in recent years flocks of up to a couple of dozen or more birds have become somewhat regular. Migrant flocks can containe up to a few dozen or more individuals.

Maximum spring count: **80** at the Lexington Cemetery 11 Apr 2016 (C. Bliznick/J. Sole, eBird data).

Maximum fall counts: a flock of **200+** in Jefferson Co., 1 Nov 2006 (*KW* 83:19, 2007); **150** at the Maysville Cemetery, Mason Co., 30 Oct 2011 (K. Schwarz, eBird data); a flock of at least **125** in LBL, Trigg Co., 31 Oct 2002 (*KW* 79:16, 2003); **120** at Evergreen Cemetery, Campbell Co., 24 Oct 2004 (*KW* 81:15, 2005); **102** at the Fishing Creek Recreation Area, Pulaski Co., 25 Oct 2004 (R. Denton, eBird data); **100** at the Lexington Cemetery, 13 Nov 1985 (*KW* 62:8, 1986).

CLAY-COLORED SPARROW *Spizella pallida*

Status: Extremely rare transient. This species has been encountered in a variety of habitats from suburban parks and yards to weedy fields and woodland borders. An eastward expansion of its breeding range has resulted in a slight uptick in the frequency of reports of migrants in Kentucky, but it continues to be an exceptional find during both spring and fall. There are 20 records (eight during spring; 12 during fall).

Unaccepted records [some of the following reports are certainly valid, but insufficient or lacking documentation has resulted in their lack of acceptance after KBRC review]: 24 Aug 2003, Jefferson Co. (*KW* 80:15, 2004; see *KW* 92:89, 2016); 7 May 2004, Nicholas Co. (see *KW* 88:101, 2012); 15 Oct 2005, (2) in Jefferson Co. (*KW* 82:15, 2006; see *KW* 85:103, 2009); 25 Sep 2006, Jefferson Co. (*KW* 83:19, 2007; see *KW* 92:89, 2016); 7 Oct 2006, Jefferson Co. (*KW* 83:19, 2007; see *KW* 85:103, 2009); 15 Oct 2010, Jefferson Co. (*KW* 87:23, 2011; see *KW* 88:101, 2012); 18 Oct 2011, (2) Louisville (*KW* 88:17, 2012; see *KW* 92:89, 2016); 5 Sep 2017, Jefferson Co. (*KW* 93:107, 2017).

Tally of records by county

Barren, Boone, Fayette (3), Jefferson (7), Lincoln, Logan, Marshall, Muhlenberg, Pulaski, Shelby, Warren, Wayne

Chronological list of records

1) 7 May 1978, Lexington (*KW* 54:47, 1978)
2) 17 May 1989, (ph.) Louisville (Palmer-Ball, *KW* 66:47-48, 1990)
3) 11 May 1998, Louisville (*KW* 74:58, 1998; *KW* 75:49, 1999)
4) 24 Oct 1998, Warren Co. (*KW* 75:8, 1999)
5) 30 Apr 2001, (at least one, possibly two) in Jefferson Co. (J./P. Bell, pers. comm. /B. Palmer-Ball, eBird data; *KW* 92:88, 2016)
6) 29 Apr 2002, Boone Co. (*KW* 78:53, 2002)
7) 7 Oct 2002, Peabody WMA, Muhlenberg Co. (*KW* 79:16, 2003); [erroneously published as 17 Oct in *KW* 82:52, 2006]
8) 10 Nov 2003, Mt. Zion, Pulaski Co. (*KW* 80:15, 2004)
9) 4 Nov 2004, nr. Hardin, Marshall Co. (*KW* 82:16, 2006 [date erroneously published as 5 Nov therein; *fide KW* 85:102-103, 2009])
10) 10 May 2006, Barren River Lake SRP, Barren Co. (*KW* 82:74, 2006; *KW* 84:77, 2008)

11) 15-28 Sep 2007, (at least three; one ba./another ph.) in southern Jefferson Co. (*KW* 84:15/36 2008)
12) 3 Oct 2008, Jefferson Co. (*KW* 85:20, 2009; *KW* 88:100, 2012)
13) 8 May 2009, (up to four, one ph.) at the Lexington Cemetery (*KW* 85:71/75, 2009)
14) 8 May 2011, (ph.) at Shippingport Island, Louisville (*KW* 87:95/100, 2011)
15) 3 May 2016, (ph.) at Waddy, Shelby Co. (*KW* 92:73/81, 2016)
16) 17 Oct 2016, ne. of Powersburg, Wayne Co. (*KW* 93:14/106, 2017)
17) 30 Aug 2017, (ph.) at Lyndon, Jefferson Co. (*KW* 94:14, 2018)
18) 30 Sep–6 Nov 2017, (ph.) at Schochoh, Logan Co. (*KW* 94:14, 2018)
19) 22 Oct 2017, (ph.) at Spindletop Farm, Fayette Co. (*KW* 94:14, 2018)
20) 12 Oct 2018, (ph.) nr. Stanford, Lincoln Co. (*KW* 95:9/40, 2019)

*FIELD SPARROW *Spizella pusilla*

Status: Fairly common to common resident, somewhat less widespread but perhaps no less numerous during winter when migrants join local nesting birds in foraging flocks. Recorded statewide in a great variety of semi-open to open habitats with some grassy or weedy cover. Breeding throughout the state in successional habitats with thick, grassy vegetation and weeds, especially those with scattered patches of shrubs and saplings. Migrants seem to appear most commonly during Oct and from mid-Mar to early Apr. Usually seen in small numbers with other sparrows, but sometimes encountered in flocks of 25 or more birds during migration and winter.

Maximum count: at least **300** at the Sinclair Unit, 12 Oct 2013 (KW 90:17, 2014).

Note on subspecies: The gray faced, western subspecies, (*S. p. arenacea*), occurs occasionally, probably most frequently in the western portion of the state. Mengel (pp. 500-501) listed a few specimen records, and there two sight records from Henderson Co.: 3 Mar 1996 (B. Palmer-Ball, eBird data) and 17 Mar 2012 (*KW* 88:81, 2012).

BREWER'S SPARROW *Spizella breweri*

Status: Accidental vagrant. This resident of arid shrublands of the western United States is an extremely rare vagrant in eastern North America. It has been documented in Kentucky on one occasion.

1) 30 Apr 2019, (ph.) at Louisville (P. Spaulding, eBird data)

FOX SPARROW *Passerella iliaca*

Status: Uncommon to fairly common transient, uncommon winter resident. Recorded statewide but much less numerous in heavily forested portions of eastern Kentucky. Encountered in a variety of semi-open habitats with an abundance of weeds and brush, most often along woodland borders with tangles of dense growth. Peaks of abundance occur from late Oct to early Nov and from late Mar to early Apr. Usually encountered singly or in small numbers with other sparrows, cardinals, and towhees; often visits feeding stations during winter, especially during snowy periods.

Maximum counts: "**dozens**," nr. Louisville, Mar 19— (Mengel:504); at least **50** in a single flock ne. of Canmer, Hart Co., early Feb 2011 (*KW* 87:65, 2011); **60** (most in two loose groups) on the Paradise CBC, 2 Jan 2011 (*KW* 87:27, 2011); ca. **45** s. of Mt. Zion, Allen Co., 26 Dec 2010 (*KW* 87:97, 2011); at least **30** at a feeding station in se. Jefferson Co., 27 Jan 2011 (*KW* 87:65, 2011); **26** at Lake Cumberland WMA, Pulaski Co., 30 Dec 2000 (R. Denton, eBird data); **25** in a single flock ne. of Boston, Nelson Co., 26 Dec 2010 (*KW* 87:65, 2011); **25** at Lake Cumberland WMA, Pulaski Co., 1 Jan 2014 (R. Denton, eBird data); **25** on the Ken Unit, 8 Dec 2016 (J. Baker, eBird data); **25** at Taylorsville Lake WMA, Anderson Co., 18 Mar 2017 (*KW* 93:78, 2017).
Late spring dates: 28-30 May 2019, Warren Co. (A. Hulsey, eBird data); 25 Apr 1978, Louisville (*KW* 54:47, 1978); 24 Apr 2005, Henderson Co. (J. Meredig, eBird data); 22 Apr 2010, Jefferson Co. (*KW* 86:73, 2010); 18 Apr 1957, Louisville (*KW* 52:64, 1976).

Early fall dates: 28 Sep 1979, Louisville (*KW* 56:18, 1980); 7 Oct 2010, Jefferson Co. (*KW* 87:23, 2011); 9 Oct 2010, Sauerheber Unit (R. Denton et al., eBird data); 11 Oct 1980, Boone Co. (L. McNeely, notes); 12 Oct 2010, Louisville (*KW* 87:23, 2011); 13 Oct 19—, Warren Co. (Mengel: 504).

Unaccepted records: other than the confirmed late May 2019 report, those during spring later than the late spring date of 25 Apr given above and including 24 May 1975, Cumberland Gap National Historical Park (*KW* 51:53, 1975); 7 May 1944, south-central Kentucky (*KW* 38:24, 1962); 7 May 1961, Henderson (*KW* 37:54, 1961); 5 May 1974, Henderson (*KW* 50:45, 1974); 4 May 1958, Louisville (*KW* 34:42, 1958); and 2 May 1976, Henderson (*KW* 52:30, 1976); those during fall earlier than the early fall date of 28 Sep given above and including 22 Sep 1943, south-central Kentucky (*KW* 38:24, 1962); also 4 Oct 2011, (hd.) at Louisville (*KW* 88:18, 2012; *fide* B. Palmer-Ball, pers. comm.)

AMERICAN TREE SPARROW *Spizelloides arborea*

Status: Uncommon to fairly common but somewhat irregular winter resident. Recorded chiefly west of the Cumberland Plateau, the only reports from the eastern part of the state being a few from the northern portion of the Cumberland Plateau. Abundance greatest in north-central Kentucky, decreasing as one proceeds south. Encountered in a variety of semi-open to open habitats; most frequently found in open fields and along fencerows with an abundance of weeds. Irregular in occurrence from year to year; usually present in small numbers, but occasionally fairly numerous. This species is often more widespread and numerous during cold, snowy weather when numbers sometimes turn up at feeding stations. Peak of abundance occurs from early Nov to mid-Mar. Usually observed with other sparrows in small flocks of up to a dozen birds, but occasionally found in pure flocks of a few dozen or more birds.

Maximum counts: **743** (200 or more in a single flock in Ohio Co.) on the Paradise CBC, Muhlenberg/Ohio cos., 30 Dec 2000 (*KW* 77:18, 2001; R. Rold, et al., pers. comm); **331** on the Burlington CBC, 30 Dec 2000 (*KW* 77:17, 2001); **300** on the Louisville CBC, 31 Dec 2000 (*KW* 77:17, 2001); **281** on the Otter Creek CBC, 27 Dec 2000 (*KW* 77:17, 2001); **109** at the West Ky WMA, McCracken Co., 30 Dec 2013 (*KW* 90:55, 2014); **100** in ne. Hart Co., 7 Feb 2009 (J. Sole, eBird data); **100** at the Sauerheber Unit, 16 Jan 2008 (eBird data); **80** at a feeding station in ne. Jefferson Co., 30 Jan–5 Feb 2014 (*KW* 90:55, 2014); **70+** at the Sinclair Unit, 5 Feb 2007 (*KW* 83:51, 2007); **65** in ne. Jefferson Co., 6 Feb 2010 (*KW* 86:46, 2010); **63** at a feeding station in Jefferson Co., 3 Feb 2009 (*KW* 85:52, 2009).

Late spring dates: 14 Apr 2018, Daviess Co. (*KW* 94:82, 2018); 13 Apr 1957, south-central Kentucky (*KW* 38:23, 1962); 10 Apr 19—, Louisville (Mengel:496); 7 Apr 2011, Louisville (*KW* 87:95, 2011); 5 Apr 2013, Sauerheber Unit (*KW* 89:79, 2013); 3 Apr 2001, Daviess Co. (M. Thompson, pers. comm.); 2 Apr 2014, Lincoln Co. (*KW* 90:76, 2014); 1 Apr 2019, Jefferson Co. (P. Bell, eBird data); 31 Mar 1950, Fayette Co. (Mengel:496); 30 Mar 1996, Louisville (B. Palmer-Ball, eBird data).

Early fall dates: 11 Oct 1989, Louisville (*KW* 66:13, 1990); 12 Oct 18—, Nelson Co. (Mengel: 496); 14 Oct 1988, Rowan Co. (*KW* 65:11, 1989); 15 Oct 1955, nr. Louisville (Mengel:496).

Unaccepted records: those during spring later than the late spring date of 14 Apr given above and including 28 Apr 19—, Louisville area (Mengel:496); 7 May 1961, Henderson (*KW* 37:54, 1961); 6 May 1973, Louisville (*KW* 49:58, 1973); 6 May 1978, Boone Co. (*KW* 54:48, 1978); 3rd week of May 1983, Warren Co. (*KW* 59:45, 1983); 5 May 1990, Louisville (*KW* 66:61, 1990); also, those during fall earlier than the early fall date of 11 Oct given above and including 4 Oct 1965, Louisville area (*KW* 52:63, 1976) and 3 Oct 1976, Carter Co. (*KW* 52:86, 1976; A. Stamm, notes).

*DARK-EYED JUNCO *Junco hyemalis*

Status: Fairly common to common transient and winter resident, rare to uncommon summer resident at higher elevations of the Cumberland Mountains. Recorded statewide during migration and winter in a great variety of semi-open and open habitats with weeds and brush including woodland borders, weedy fields and fencerows, and suburban parks and yards (where it is frequent at feeding stations); only occasionally observed in the understory of mature woodlands. Peak of abundance occurs from late Oct to early Apr. Breeds in numbers only near the summit of Black Mountain, where the species occurs in second-growth woodland and successional growth. This species is one of our most numerous winter residents and is often encountered in flocks of 25 or more birds. **State Breeding Status**: Special Concern.

Maximum counts: **230** at West Ky WMA, McCracken Co., 30 Dec 2018 (D. Akers, eBird data); **180** in w. Laurel Co., 29 Dec 2012 (R. Denton, eBird data); **180** in Calloway Co., 3 Jan 2012 (E. Huber, eBird data).

Late spring dates (outside Cumberland Mts.): 25 May 1963, Louisville area (*KW* 52:63, 1976); 23 May 1983, Pulaski Co. (*KW* 59:45, 1983); 21 May 2008, (ph.) at Lexington (*KW* 84:71, 2008); 20 May 1961, Louisville (*AFN* 15:416, 1961); 16-18 May 2009,(ph.) at Lexington (*KW* 85:76, 2009); 15 May 1993, Jefferson Co. (*KW* 69:48, 1993).

Early fall dates (outside Cumberland Mts.): 11 Sep 1979, Okolona, Jefferson Co. (*KW* 56:18, 1980); 18 Sep 1977, Louisville (*AB* 32:214, 1978); 21 Sep 1981, Louisville (B. Palmer-Ball, eBird data).

Out-of-season records (non-breeding summer): along the crest of Pine Mt., Bell Co. (R. Cassell, 1980s pers. comm.); 12 Jul 1988, sw. of Willard, Carter Co. (*KW* 64:66, 1988; *KBBA*: 300).

Unaccepted record: 3 Aug 1966, Louisville area (*KW* 52:63, 1976).

Hybrid record: see White-throated Sparrow.

Summary of confirmed breeding records by county

Harlan (Lovell, *Auk* 67:107, 1950; Mengel:494; R. Denton, 2014/2016 eBird data)

Bell/Harlan (18 Jun 2003, 6 males on territory and a juvenile observed being fed at high elevations in Cumberland Gap National Historical Park, Bell/Harlan cos. [*KW* 79:85, 2003]; 25 Sep 2003, a male still present in the same area [*KW* 80:15, 2004].

Note on subspecies: Breeding birds, and the vast majority of transients and winter residents, pertain to the eastern group (formerly known as the SLATE-COLORED JUNCO – *J. h. carolinensis* and *J. h. hyemalis*); however, there are a few specimen/photograph records and numerous sight records of individuals of the western groups (OREGON JUNCO – *J. h. oreganus* and PINK-SIDED JUNCO – *J. h. mearnsi*) mostly during winter; the former occurs annually in small numbers, but the latter appears to be quite rare and is represented by only a few reports.

Photograph records of western subspecies

J. hyemalis mearnsi

1) 30 Dec 2000–9 Jan 2001, nr. Science Hill, Pulaski Co., (*NAB* 55:178, 2001; R. Denton, eBird data)

J. hyemalis oreganus

1) 2 Feb 2015, Long Run Park, Jefferson Co. (*KW* 91:56/60, 2015)
2) 26 Oct 2015–11 Mar 2016, Douglass Hills, Jefferson Co. (*KW* 92:15/46/47/68, 2016); returning winter 2016-2017 (*KW* 93:13/53, 2017; B. & M. Yandell, eBird data), winter 2017-2018 (*KW* 94:14/60/83, 2018; B. & M. Yandell, eBird data), and winter 2018-2019 (*KW* 95:9, 2019; B. & M. Yandell, eBird data)
3) 18 Dec 2017, Goshen, Oldham Co. (*KW* 94:60, 2018); B. Davis, eBird data)

WHITE-CROWNED SPARROW *Zonotrichia leucophrys*

Status: Uncommon to fairly common transient and winter resident, accidental during summer. Recorded statewide but generally absent from heavily forested portions of eastern Kentucky. Encountered in a variety of semi-open and open habitats; most numerous in open farmland where the species frequents weedy fencerows and fields, and pastures with scattered patches of weeds and small trees. Also frequently occurs at feeding stations in the vicinity of such habitat. Peak of abundance occurs from mid-Oct to early May. Generally encountered in small to medium-sized flocks of up to a dozen or more birds.

Maximum counts: **310** in Boone Co., 20 Dec 2003 (*KW* 80:48, 2004); **267** in n. Boone Co., 16 Dec 2006 (*KW* 83:51, 2007); **195** on the Hodgenville CBC, 4 Jan 2008 (*KW* 84:47, 2008); **192** on the Somerset CBC, 30 Dec 2006 (*KW* 83:51, 2007); **191** on the Yelvington, Daviess Co., CBC, 17 Dec 1988 (*KW* 65:14, 1989); **155** on the Danville CBC, 20 Dec 2003 (*KW* 80:48, 2004).

Late spring dates: 28 May 1938, south-central Kentucky (*KW* 38:24, 1962); 28 May 1992, Grayson Co. (*KW* 68:48, 1992); 26 May 1976, Louisville (*KW* 52:63, 1976; B. Palmer-Ball, eBird data).

Early fall dates: 13 Sep 2017, Louisville (*KW* 94:14, 2018); 26 Sep 1948, Meade Co. (Mengel: 502); 26 Sep 2010, Henderson Co. (*KW* 87:23, 2011); 26 Sep 2013, McCracken Co. (*KW* 90:17, 2014); 27 Sep 1997, Louisville (B. Yandell, eBird data).

Out-of-season records (summer): 5 Jul 1965, (ba.) in Oldham Co. (Young, *KW* 43:65, 1967); 15 Jun 2012, Madison Co. (*KW* 88:95, 2012); 21 Jul 2013, Jefferson Co. (*KW* 89:98, 2013).

HARRIS'S SPARROW *Zonotrichia querula*

Status: Extremely rare late fall, winter, and spring visitant. Recorded chiefly west of the Cumberland Plateau. There have been nearly 30 reports of this species from 17 widely scattered counties as far east as Morgan Co. (see below). This species is typically found in the company of White-crowned Sparrows, which share the same habitat preferences. Most records have come from feeding stations, but they also have been found in open, weedy areas.

Maximum counts: **4** in Henderson Co., 21 Dec 1952 (Benson, *KW* 29:13-14, 1953; *KW* 29:8/11, 1953 [date and number of birds apparently given incorrectly in the latter as 20 Dec and one, respectively]; **3** on the Henderson CBC, 26 Dec 1953 (*KW* 30:9, 1954).

Late spring dates: 6 May 2006, Daviess Co. (*KW* 82:75, 2006); 6 May 2018, (ph.) ne. Jefferson Co. (*KW* 94:83, 2018); 5 May 2004, Ballard Co. (*KW* 80:72, 2004); 4 May 2015, Logan Co. (*KW* 91:76, 2015); 4 May 1958, Louisville (Sommers, *KW* 34:45, 1958); 31 Mar 2018, Graves Co. (*KW* 94:83, 2018); 30 Apr 2015, Muhlenberg Co. (*KW* 91:76/80, 2015); 30 Apr 2019, Logan Co. (S. Tyson, eBird data); 26 Apr 2001, Fulton Co. (*KW* 77:53, 2001); 22 Mar 1988, Lexington (*KW* 64:49, 1988; D. Svetich, pers. comm.).

Early fall dates: 18-22 Nov 1984, Morgan Co. (M./G. Elam, notes); 18 Nov 2018, Schochoh, Logan Co. (*KW* 95:9, 2019); 4 Dec 1966, Daviess Co. (*KW* 43:15, 1967).

Unaccepted records: I can find absolutely no source for the date of 19 Mar [year unkown; presumed to be 1960s], location also unknown, published in the occurrence bar graph at *KW* 45:55, 1969; late Dec 1983, (7) in Crittenden Co. (*KW* 60:4, 1984). Also, 24 May 2015, Pulaski Co. (*KW* 91:76, 2015; see *KW* 92:89, 2016).

Summary of records by county

Ballard (mid-Feb–5 May 2004 [*KW* 80:48/72, 2004])

Bath (5 Mar 2006 [*KW* 82:75, 2006])

Crittenden (last week of Dec 1960 [*KW* 37:9, 1961]; 4 Jan 1981 [*KW* 57:13, 1981/A. Stamm, historical archive files])

Daviess (4 Dec 1966–2 Jan 1967 [*KW* 43:15, 1967]; 28 Dec 1973 [Isles, *KW* 50:29, 1974]; 17 Dec 2000 [*KW* 77:13, 2001]; late Dec 2005–6 May 2006 [*KW* 82:50/56/75, 2006])

Fayette (24 Dec 1987–22 Mar 1988 [*KW* 64:49, 1988/D. Svetich, eBird data])

Franklin (14-29 Dec 1957 [Jones, *KW* 34:45, 1958]; 19 Dec 1982–end of Feb 1983 [*KW* 59:10/30, 1983; R. Morris, pers. comm.])

Fulton (3 Feb–26 Apr 2001 (ph.) [*KW* 77:30/53, 2001/B. Palmer-Ball, et al., eBird data])

Graves (20 Jan–31 Mar 2018 (ph.) [M. Coleman, eBird data; *KW* 94:60/64/83, 2018])

Henderson (15-17 Dec 1952 (2) and 21 Dec 1952 (4 at a different locales) [Benson, *KW* 29:13-14, 1953/*KW* 29:8, 1953]; 26 Dec 1953 (3) [*KW* 30:9, 1954]; 29 Dec 1960 [*KW* 37:11, 1961])

Hopkins (26 Feb 1965 [J. Hancock, 1965 notes])

Jefferson (9-23 Dec 1956 [Krull, *KW* 33:57, 1957]; 4 May 1958 [Sommers, *KW* 34:45, 1958]; 3-19 Feb 1980 [*KW* 56:34, 1980]; 5-6 May 2018 (ph.) [*KW* 94:83, 2018])

Jessamine (25 Jan 1990 [*KW* 66:41, 1990])

Logan (8 Dec 2014–4 May 2015 (ph.) [*KW* 91:37/56/76, 2015]; 18 Nov 2018–30 Apr 2019 [*KW* 95:50, 2019; S. Tyson et al., eBird data])

Morgan (3rd week Nov 1984 [M./G. Elam, 1984 notes/A. Stamm, historical archive files])

Muhlenberg (26-30 Apr 2015 (ph.) [*KW* 91:76/80, 2015])
Oldham (23 Dec 1956 [*KW* 33:13, 1957/eBird data]; 13 Mar 1965 (ba.) [Young, *KW* 43:65, 1967]; 3-30 Jan 2010 [*KW* 86:46/52, 2010])
Trigg (19 Dec 2011–23 Feb 2012 (ph.) [*KW* 88:52/60, 2012])

WHITE-THROATED SPARROW *Zonotrichia albicollis*

Status: Common transient and winter resident, accidental during summer. Recorded statewide in a variety of forested and semi-open habitats with an abundance of weeds and brush, especially woodland borders; seldom observed well out in open weed fields, preferring more substantial cover. Peak of abundance occurs from mid-Oct to early May. This species is one of our most numerous winter residents and is frequently observed at feeding stations. Typically encountered in flocks of up to a couple of dozen birds, often in the company of Northern Cardinals and Eastern Towhees. It is unclear why there has been an increase in the number of reports during summer in recent years.

Maximum counts (CBC tallies not included): **293** in Rowan Co., 29-30 Oct 1985 (*KW* 61:19, 1985); **270** at West Ky WMA, McCracken Co., 30 Dec 2013 (D. Akers, eBird data); **270** at West Ky WMA, McCracken Co., 30 Dec 2017 (T. Wolff, eBird data).

Late spring dates (some could represent summering birds): 3 Jul 2019, (ph.) Lincoln Co. (J. Elmore, eBird data); 13 Jun 2018, (vo.) in Madison Co. (*KW* 94:110, 2018); 8 Jun 2004, (ph.) Jefferson Co. (*KW* 80:85, 2004); 6 Jun 2005, Louisville (*KW* 81:109, 2005); 5 Jun 2019, Pulaski Co. (R. Bontrager, eBird data); 4 Jun 2018, Lincoln Co. (*KW* 94:110, 2018); 3 Jun 2010, Louisville (*KW* 86:96, 2010); 2 Jun 1887, Pulaski Co. (Mengel:503); 1 Jun 1998, Pulaski Co. (R. Denton, eBird data); 1 Jun 2007, Richmond (*KW* 83:107, 2007); 31 May 2010, Bernheim Forest (S. Ward/ M. Kahn, eBird data).

Early fall dates: 18 Aug 2018, (ph.) in Jefferson Co. (*KW* 95:9, 2019); 28 Aug 2002, Lexington (*KW* 79:16, 2003); 28 Aug 2004, Jefferson Co. (*KW* 81:15, 2005); 31 Aug 1955, Louisville area (*KW* 52:63, 1976); 3 Sep 2005, Boone Co. (*KW* 82:16, 2006); 8 Sep 1964, Louisville area (*KW* 52:63, 1976).

Out-of-season records (summer): 2 Aug 1962, Louisville area (*KW* 52:63, 1976); 6/12 Aug 2005, Jefferson Co. [possible summering bird; see above, *KW* 81:109, 2005] (*KW* 82:16, 2006); late May –17 Jul 2006, (1-2) in Jefferson Co. (*KW* 82:84, 2006); 15 Jun 2008, Henderson Co. (*KW* 84:89, 2008); 26 Jun 2008, St. Matthews, Jefferson Co. (*KW* 84:89, 2008); 15 Jul 2012, Mason Co. (*KW* 88:95, 2012); 14 Jun 2013, Garrard Co. (*KW* 89:98, 2013 [location erroneously published as Mercer Co. therein; *fide* T. Nauman, eBird data]); 16-18 Jun 2013, Louisville (*KW* 89:98, 2013); 2 Jul 2017, J.J. Audubon SP, Henderson Co. (*KW* 93:102, 2017); 24 Jun 2018, (ph.) at Louisville (*KW* 94:110, 2018).

Hybrid record: a White-throated Sparrow x Dark-eyed Junco at Lake Jericho, Henry Co., 26 Nov 1976 (*AB* 31:186, 1977).

SAGEBRUSH SPARROW *Artemisiospiza nevadensis*

Status: Accidental vagrant. The Kentucky record is one of only two ever reported east of the Great Plains. Field marks appear to eliminate Bell's Sparrow (*Artemisiospiza belli*), formerly a separate subspecies of Sage Sparrow now elevated to full species status.

1) 18 Apr 2006, (ph.) in ne. Warren Co. (Hulsey, *KW* 84:77-79/80, 2008)

*VESPER SPARROW *Pooecetes gramineus*

Status: Uncommon transient, extremely rare summer resident (formerly locally uncommon, but possibly or probably no longer breeding), extremely rare during winter. Recorded statewide during migration but generally more numerous west of the Cumberland Plateau; widespread in a variety of open to semi-open habitats including grain stubble fields, pastures, and open roadsides. Peaks of abundance occur from mid-Mar to early Apr and from mid-Oct to early Nov. Formerly reported breeding at scattered localities in north-central Kentucky on rocky, hillside pastures and may have been even more widespread in central Kentucky during the 1800s (see Mengel:487-488). Nesting has not been documented in recent years; in fact, there are only a few recent summer records (see below). The species was not known to be present during winter historically (Mengel:488), but during recent years an uptick in well documented reports indicates that a few birds may now be wintering, particularly in the southwestern portion of the state. Generally encountered in small flocks of up to a half-dozen birds during migration. **State Breeding Status**: Endangered.

Maximum counts: **40+** in Pulaski Co., 28 Mar 1981 (*KW* 57:60, 1981); **30+** total at scattered locales in Warren Co., 23 Mar 2005 (*KW* 81:92, 2005); **23** at the Minor Clark Fish Hatchery, 1 Nov 1991 (*KW* 68:10, 1992); flock of at least **20** in Jefferson Co., 23 Mar 2008 (*KW* 84:71, 2008).

Early spring dates (also see winter records below): 16 Feb 2015, Allen Co. (*KW* 91:56, 2015); 17 Feb 1882, Nelson Co. (Mengel:487); 23 Feb 1891, Pulaski Co. (Mengel:487); 1 Mar 1952, south-central Kentucky (*KW* 38:23, 1962).

Late spring dates (away from limited breeding areas): 1 Jun 19—, Louisville area [summer vagrant?] (*KW* 52:63, 1976); 30 May 2012, w. Henderson Co. (J. Meredig, eBird data); 26 May 2006, w. Fulton Co. (*KW* 82:74, 2006); 21 May 2015, Boyd/Greenup Co. line (*KW* 91:76, 2015); 20 May 2008, (2) (ph.) [on territory?] in w. Henderson Co. (*KW* 84:71, 2008); 16 May 2010, Lyon Co. (*KW* 86:73, 2010); 14 May 2011, e. Mason Co. [on territory?] (*KW* 87:95, 2011); 10 May 2008, Harrison Co. [on territory?] (*KW* 84:71, 2008); 9 May 1952, Laurel Co. (Mengel:487); 8 May 1976, Louisville area (*KW* 52:63, 1976); 8 May 2010, Jefferson Co. (*KW* 86:73, 2010); 6 May 1943, Louisville area (*KW* 37:42, 1961); 6 May 1979, Louisville area (A. Stamm, notes); 6 May 2005, w. Henderson Co. (*KW* 81:92, 2005); 6 May 2007, w. Henderson Co. (*KW* 83:85, 2007); 6 May 2008, McElroy Lake (*KW* 84:71, 2008); 6 May 2014, Mercer Co. (N. Houlihan, eBird data).

Early fall dates (away from limited breeding areas): 17 Aug 2005, Bernheim Forest (*KW* 82:15, 2006); 20 Aug 2017, Sandy Watkins Park, Henderson Co. (*KW* 94:14, 2018); 11 Sep 2004, Bernheim Forest (*KW* 81:15, 2005); 12 Sep 18—, Nelson Co. [summering bird?] (Mengel:488); 22 Sep 1982, Boone Co. (L. McNeely, notes); 23 Sep 2011, Hart Co. (*KW* 88:17, 2012); 24 Sep 2011, w. Fulton Co. (*KW* 88:17, 2012); 29 Sep 1979, Oldham Co. (*KW* 56:17, 1980); 7 Oct 19-, Warren Co. (Mengel:488); 7 Oct 1979, Daviess Co. (*KW* 56:18, 1980); 8 Oct 2011, Madison Co. (*KW* 88:17, 2012); 10 Oct 1942, south-central Kentucky (*KW* 38:23, 1962); 14 Oct 1949, Louisville area (*KW* 52:63, 1976).

Late fall dates (early winter): occasionally lingers into mid- to late Nov with a couple of dozen reports (some well-documented) into early winter: 16 Dec 2016, (8) nw. of Zion, Todd Co. (*KW* 93:28/53, 2017); 26 Dec 2015, Allen Co. (*KW* 92:46, 2016); 30 Dec 2011, (2) in McCracken Co. (*KW* 88:52, 2012); 30 Dec 2014, (ph.) McCracken Co. (*KW* 91:56/60, 2015); 31 Dec 1965, Bowling Green (*KW* 45:38, 1969); 31 Dec 2018, McCracken Co. (*KW* 95:50, 2019); 1 Jan 1997, Muhlenberg Co. (*KW* 73:14, 1997); 1 Jan 2004 (3), Trigg Co. (*KW* 80: 47, 2004); 1 Jan 2008, McCreary Co. (*KW* 84:47, 2008); 3 Jan 1999, (2) Shelbville CBC, Shelby Co. (*KW* 75:9, 1999).

Out-of-season records (mid-winter): 23 Jan 1957, south-central Kentucky (*KW* 38:23, 1962); 6 Jan/12 Feb 1999, at Mt. Zion, Pulaski Co. (R. Denton, eBird data); 10 Feb 2001, (flock of 8) at the Long Point Unit (R. Denton, et al., eBird data) and one n. of Open Pond, Fulton Co. (M. Bennett, notes); 9 Jan/1 Feb 2010, (4/1) (ph.) in Livingston Co. (*KW* 86:46, 2010); 15-16 Jan 2012, (up to 10) in Trigg Co. (*KW* 88:52, 2012); 19-20 Jan 2016, (up to 6) in Logan Co. (*KW* 92:46, 2016); 14-15 Dec 2016 & 16-23 Feb 2017, up to 5 (ph.) e of Guthrie, Todd Co. (*KW* 93:53, 2017); 8 Jan–19 Feb 2017, (up to 6) (ph.) n. of Dot, Logan Co. (*KW* 93:53, 2017); 19 Dec 2017–6 Jan 2018, (up to 4) in s. Logan Co. (*KW* 94:60, 2018).

Unaccepted records: 4 Feb 1981, (25) in Calloway Co. (*KW* 57:38, 1981).

Confirmed breeding records by county

Franklin (Moore, *KW* 45:56-57, 1969)

Historical probable breeding records by county

Boone (Mengel:487-488)
Campbell (Mengel:487-488)
Gallatin (Mengel:487-488)
Grant (Mengel:487-488)
Harrison (Mengel:487-488)

Kenton (Mengel:487-488)
Mercer (Mengel:487)
Pendleton (Mengel:487-488)
Woodford (Mengel: 487)

Post-1980s breeding season records by county

Bourbon (22 Jun 1991 [*KBBA*:288])
Henderson (18/21 Jul 2009 [*KW* 85:95, 2009])
Nicholas (26 Jun 1995 [Kingsolver, *KW* 71:48/71 1995])

LE CONTE'S SPARROW *Ammospiza leconteii*

Status: Extremely rare to rare transient and winter resident. Recorded from nearly two dozen counties scattered across central and western Kentucky as far east as Madison Co. Generally most numerous across the western third of the state. This species typically skulks in weedy and grassy fields; it is most often found in dense, matted grass near water or in low, damp areas. Reported most frequently as a fall transient, but an increased amount of survey work in recent years during the winter season has confirmed that small numbers winter in suitable habitat (at least some years) across the western third of the state. Generally hard to flush, often requiring a diligent effort to observe well. Usually seen singly or in small, loose groups of several birds.

Maximum counts: ca. **20** in Marshall Co., 11-16 Apr 1950 (Mengel:484); at least **12** at the Sinclair Unit, 30 Dec 2000 (*KW* 77:18, 2001); at least **11** at the Cape Hills Unit, Sloughs WMA, Henderson Co., 17 Mar 2012 (*KW* 88:82, 2012); at least **8-10** at the Long Point Unit, 18 Dec 2010 (*KW* 87:65, 2011); at least **8** at the former Gibraltar Mine, Muhlenberg Co., 23 Mar 2013(*KW* 89:80, 2013).

Late spring dates: 6 May 1979, Calloway Co. (*KW* 55:50, 1979); 3 May 1950, Calloway Co. (Mengel:484); 2 May 2001 (ba.), Muhlenberg Co. (B. Palmer-Ball, eBird data).

Early fall dates: 2 Oct 2007, Jefferson Co. (*KW* 84:15 2008); 6 Oct 1963, south-central Kentucky (*KW* 45:38, 1969).

Historical winter records (pre-late 1980s): 28 Dec 1904, Logan Co. (Mengel:484); 31 Dec 19—, location uncertain (*KW* 45:55, 1969); 27 Dec 1980, Henderson Co. (*KW* 57:9, 1981); 16 Feb 1986, Ballard Co. (*KW* 62:29, 1986); also, see Unaccepted records under Grasshopper Sparrow above.

Published error: erroneously included on 2016-2017 CBC table as a count week (cw) bird on the Henry County CBC (*KW* 93:29, 2017).

Summary of records by county

Allen (*KW* 88:18, 2012)
Ballard (*KW* 62:29, 1986; [wintering documented 2005-2006] *KW* 82:18/50, 2006; *KW* 83:21/51, 2007; *KW* 86:17/46, 2010; *KW* 87:25/65, 2011; *KW* 89:18/53, 2013; *KW* 93:53, 2017; *KW* 95:22/ 50, 2019)
Bullitt (*KW* 77:19, 2001)
Butler (*KW* 83:51, 2007; *KW* 84:47, 2008)
Calloway (Mengel:484; *KW* 55:50, 1979; *KW* 79:73, 2003; *KW* 83:51, 2007; *KW* 91:56, 2015);
Christian (*KW* 74:10, 1998)
Fulton (Mengel:484; [wintering documented 1997-1998] (*KW* 74:34, 1998; B. Palmer-Ball, 1997/1998 eBird data), *KW* 75:8, 1999; [wintering documented 2000-2001] (*KW* 77:30, 2001; H. Chambers/B. Palmer-Ball, 2001 eBird data); [wintering documented 2008-2009] (*KW* 85:52/76, 2009); *KW* 87:65, 2011; *KW* 90:17/55, 2014; M. Greene, 2016 eBird data; *KW* 93:53, 2017; *KW* 94:60, 2018)
Henderson (*KW* 57:9, 1981; *KW* 64:49, 1988; nearly annual at Sloughs WMA since late 1980s)
Hopkins (*KW* 88:52, 2012)
Jefferson ([ph.] *KW* 56:17, 1980; *KW* 57:24, 1981; *KW* 58:18, 1982; [ph.] *KW* 82:15/74, 2006; *KW* 83: 19, 2007; *KW* 84:15, 2008; *KW* 88:82, 2012; *KW* 94:83, 2018)
Logan (Mengel:484; (ph.) *KW* 89:15, 2013; *KW* 94:14, 2018)
Lyon (*KW* 82:50, 2006; *KW* 83:19/22/51, 2007)
Madison (13 Nov 1991 [*KW* 68:10, 1992])
Marshall (Mengel:484; *KW* 69:36, 1993/B. Palmer-Ball, eBird data; *KW* 86:46, 2010; *KW* 88:82, 2012)

Meade (*KW* 82:20/50, 2006)
McCracken ([wintering documented 2002-2003] (*KW* 79:18/49/73, 2003);*KW* 80:17/47, 2004; *KW* 81:
93, 2005; *KW* 85:22/52, 2009; *KW* 90:55, 2014; *KW* 92:18/46, 2016); [wintering documented 2016-
2017] *KW* 93:16/53, 2017; *KW* 94:60, 2018)
Muhlenberg (Mengel:484; *KW* 70:18, 1994; *KW* 73:14, 1997; *KW* 76:8, 2000; [wintering documented
1999-2000] *KW* 76:12/32, 2000/B. Palmer-Ball, 2000 eBird data; [wintering documented 2000-
2001] (ba./ph.) *KW* 77:10/18/53, 2001/B. Palmer-Ball, 2001 eBird data; (ba.) 2 May 2001 (M. Monroe, banding data; B. Palmer-Ball, eBird data); [wintering documented 2001-2002] *KW* 78:12/21/
34, 2002/B. Palmer-Ball, 2002 eBird data; *KW* 79:73, 2003; *KW* 80:15/72, 2004; *KW* 81:15, 2005;
KW 82:19/50, 2006; *KW* 83:23/51, 2007; *KW* 86:46, 2010; *KW* 88:23/52, 2012; *KW* 89:22/53/80,
2013; *KW* 90:23/55, 2014; *KW* 91:19/56, 2015; *KW* 92:46, 2016; *KW* 93:18/53, 2017; *KW* 94:14/
83, 2018)
Muhlenberg/Ohio [published only as "Peabody WMA" so county uncertain] (*KW* 75:8, 1999; *KW* 76:
32, 2000; *KW* 78:34, 2002)
Nelson (*KW* 82:15, 2006)
Ohio (*KW* 75:11, 1999; B. Palmer-Ball, 2001 eBird data; *KW* 78:12, 2002; *KW* 94:60/83, 2018); *KW*
95:24/50, 2019)
Trigg (Mengel:484; *KW* 83:19, 2007)
Warren (Mengel:484; *KW* 74:10, 1998)

NELSON'S SPARROW *Ammospiza nelsoni*

Status: Transient (extremely rare during spring, extremely rare to rare during fall); accidental during
winter. There are currently about 50 records (all but three during fall), mostly from a narrow window
of time during the peak of the species' fall migration during Oct. Most of the records have come
during concerted efforts to find this inhabitant of dense, marshy vegetation. The species has now
been reported from 13 counties, all west of the Cumberland Plateau. Generally to be expected in
dense weeds and grasses, especially along the margins of water bodies and in marshy areas.
Most records are of single birds, but two or more in loose association with one another have been
encountered on several occasions.

Maximum counts: at least **6** (some ph.) at the Sauerheber Unit, 22 Oct 2005 (*KW* 82:15, 2006); **5** at
the Sauerheber Unit, 28 Oct 2000 (B. Yandell, eBird data).
Early fall dates: 16 Sep 2007, (ph.) Jefferson Co. (*KW* 84:15 2008); 19 Sep 2006, Daviess Co. (*KW*
83:19, 2007); 23 Sep 2012, Minor Clark Hatchery (*KW* 89:15, 2013); 26 Sep 2006, ne. Jefferson
Co. (*KW* 83:19, 2007); 26 Sep 2011 (ph.), Louisville (*KW* 88:18, 2012); 3-6 Oct 2005, Jefferson
Co. (*KW* 82:15, 2006); 3 Oct 2016, Morgan Pond (*KW* 93:13, 2017); 6 Oct 2007, Sauerheber Unit
(*KW* 84:15, 2008); 6 Oct 2012, Bullitt Co. (*KW* 89:15, 2013).
Late fall dates: 30 Oct 2008, Ohio Co. (*KW* 85:20, 2009); 28 Oct 2000, Sinclair Unit (*KW* 77:10,
2001; D. O'Brien/R. Denton, eBird data]); 28 Oct 2000, Sauerheber Unit (B. Yandell, eBird data).
Out-of-season record (winter): 16 Dec 2012–19 Apr 2013, one (ba./ph.) at Louisville (Palmer-Ball,
KW 89:58-59, 2013; *KW* 89:33/53/60/80, 2013).
Spring records: 20 May 1989, McElroy Lake (Palmer-Ball, *KW* 66:30-31, 1990); 12 May 2012, (ba./
ph.) Cave Hill Cemetery, Louisville (*KW* 88:82/84, 2012).
Unaccepted records: 27 May 2001, Peabody WMA, Muhlenberg Co. (*NAB* 55:307, 2001; [not re-
viewed by KBRC]); two earlier records were regarded by Mengel (p. 519) as hypothetical: 15 Nov
1910, Woodford Co. and 30 Apr 1940, Louisville (Carpenter and Lovell, *KW* 16:48, 1940).

Summary of records by county

Bullitt (6 Oct 2012 [*KW* 89:15, 2013])
Christian (3 Oct 2016 [*KW* 93:13, 2017])
Daviess (19 Sep 2006 (ph.) [*KW* 83:19, 2007])
Fayette (11/14 Oct 2008 [*KW* 85:20, 2009]; 17-19 Oct 2015 (2) (ph.) [*KW* 92:15/36, 2016])
Henderson (12 Oct 1986 (2) [*KW* 63:11-12, 1987]; 11 Oct 1987 (ph.) [*KW* 64:19, 1988; Palmer-Ball,
KW 66:30-31, 1990]; 21 Oct 1989 [*KW* 66:14, 1990]; 10 Oct 1992 [*KW* 69:11, 1993]; 16 Oct 1993
[*KW* 70:11, 1994]; 23 Oct 1994 (2) [*KW* 71:5, 1995]; 12-13 Oct 1996 [*KW* 73:11, 1997]; 12 Oct
1997 [*KW* 74:11, 1998]; 17 Oct 1999 (2) [*KW* 76:8, 2000]; 14 Oct 2000 (4) [*KW* 77:10, 2001]; 21

Oct 2000 [R. Denton/H. Chambers, eBird data]; 28 Oct 2000 (5) [B. Yandell, eBird data]; 20 Oct 2001 [*KW* 78;12, 2002]; 20 Oct 2002 (3) [*KW* 79:16, 2003]; 9 Oct 2004 (2) (ph.) [*KW* 81:15, 2005]; 22 Oct 2005 (6) [*KW* 82:15, 2006]; 14 Oct 2006 (2) [*KW* 83:19, 2007]; 6 Oct 2007 [*KW* 84:15, 2008]; 10 Oct 2009 [*KW* 86:15, 2010]; 21 Oct 2012 (ph.) [*KW* 89:15, 2013]; 15 Oct 2016 (ph.) [*KW* 93:13, 2017])

Jefferson (21 Oct 1977 (ph.) [Parker, *KW* 54:15, 1978]; 3-6/16 Oct 2005 [*KW* 82:15, 2006]; 26 Sep 2006 [*KW* 83:19, 2007]; 16 Sep 2007 & 20-21 Oct 2007 (both ph.) [*KW* 84:15 2008]; 26 Sep 2011 (ph.) [*KW* 88:18, 2012]; 12 May 2012 (ba./ph.) [*KW* 88:82/84, 2012]; 16 Dec 2012–19 Apr 2013 (ba. and later ph.) [Palmer-Ball, *KW* 89:58-59, 2013; *KW* 89:33/53/60/80, 2013]; 7 Oct 2015 (ph.) [*KW* 92:15, 2016]

Livingston (16 Oct 2001 (2) (ph.) [*KW* 78:12, 2002])

Muhlenberg (26 Oct 2000 (3) [*KW* 77:10, 2001]; 28 Oct 2000 (2) [*KW* 77:10, 2001; D. O'Brien/R. Denton, eBird data]; 21 Oct 2001 [*KW* 78:12, 2002; D. O'Brien, eBird data]; 19 Oct 2003 [*KW* 80:15, 2004])

Nelson (11 Oct 2005 (2) [*KW* 82:15, 2006])

Ohio (8 Oct 2000 [*KW* 77:10, 2001; B. Palmer-Ball, eBird data]; 9 Oct 2001 & 18 Oct 2001 (2) (ph.) [*KW* 78:12, 2002]; 7 Oct 2002 [*KW* 79:16, 2003]; 10 Oct 2005 [*KW* 82:15, 2006]; 30 Oct 2008 [*KW* 85:20, 2009])

Oldham (20 Oct 1990, (sp.) [Elmore and Palmer-Ball, *KW* 67:69-70, 1991; USNM 608658]);

Rowan (23 Sep 2012 [*KW* 89:15, 2013])

Warren (20 May 1989 [Palmer-Ball, *KW* 66:30-31, 1990]; 8 Oct 1997 [*KW* 74:11, 1998])

HENSLOW'S SPARROW *Centronyx henslowii*

Status: Locally rare to uncommon summer resident, rare transient, extremely rare during winter. Recorded statewide, but generally more widely distributed west of the Cumberland Plateau. Known primarily as a summer bird, being quite scarce and inconspicuous as a transient away from nesting areas. However, migrants are occasionally heard singing in non-breeding areas during spring (mid-Apr to early May) and a few have been flushed from weedy or grassy fields during fall (mid-Oct to early Nov). Prior to about 1980 the species was known during summer from only the middle third of the state (primarily in north-central Kentucky). More recently, however, scattered summer records and probable nesting have been reported from a number of localities on the northern Cumberland Plateau, and westward across central and western Kentucky to as far west as Caldwell Co. (*KBBA*:296-297), and Calloway and Graves cos. (B. Palmer-Ball, 2000 eBird data). There are, however, very few actual confirmed breeding records. Generally breeds in fallow hayfields, on reclaimed surface mines, and in other grassy habitats with scattered small trees and tall weeds. The species has been found during winter at least a couple of times, but wintering has not been documented. Generally encountered singly, but loose nesting colonies may contain up to a dozen or more pairs. **State Breeding Status**: Special Concern.

Maximum count: an estimated total of at least **120 nesting pairs** nr. Sonora, Hardin Co., summer 2005 (*KW* 81:109, 2005).

Early spring dates: 17 Mar 2006, Jefferson Co. (*KW* 82:74, 2006); 26 Mar 1939, Louisville area (*KW* 52:63, 1976); 27 Mar 2004, Jefferson Co. (*KW* 80:72, 2004); 27 Mar 2017, Jefferson Co. (B. Palmer-Ball, eBird data; *KW* 93:77, 2017 [date erroneously published as 28 Mar therein]); 29 Mar 2002, Calloway Co. (R. Head, pers. comm.); 29 Mar 2017, Sinclair Unit (*KW* 93:77, 2017); 31 Mar 2005, Calloway Co. (*KW* 81:92, 2005); 3 Apr 2012, Mercer Co. (*KW* 88:82, 2012); 5 Apr 2000, Taylor Co. (*NAB* 54:290, 2000).

Late fall dates: 6 Nov 2001, Sinclair Unit (*NAB* 56:59, 2002); 3 Nov 2009, Sinclair Unit (*KW* 86:15, 2010); 2 Nov 1978, Louisville (*KW* 55:17, 1979).

Out-of-season records (winter): 26 Dec 1963–2 Jan 1964, (4) nr. Glasgow, Barren Co. (*KW* 40:13, 1964; *KW* 45:55, 1969) [details of this observation are somewhat convincing; however, the habitat and number reported cause some skepticism]; 13 Jan 2001, (ba./ph.) Sinclair Unit (*NAB* 55:178, 2001); 4 Mar 2012, (possible early migrant?) in Allen Co. (*KW* 88:82, 2012); 19 Dec 2016, West Ky WMA, McCracken Co. (*KW* 93:53/107, 2017).

Unaccepted records: 3 Mar 1945, south-central Kentucky (*KW* 38:23, 1962); 4 Nov 1984, (4) in Rowan Co. (*KW* 61:18, 1985); 12 Mar 1987, (2) in Rowan Co. (*KW* 63:52, 1987).

Summary of confirmed breeding records by county

Hardin (M. Monroe, 2000 notes)
Jefferson (*KW* 91:87, 2015)
Meade (Wiley and Croft, *KW* 40:39-41, 1964)
Muhlenberg (M. Monroe, 2000/2001 notes)
Ohio ([carrying food] Palmer-Ball and Barron, *KW* 66:78-79, 1990)
Oldham (Mengel:485)
Taylor (M. Monroe, 2000 notes)

*SAVANNAH SPARROW *Passerculus sandwichensis*

Status: Fairly common transient, rare to uncommon winter resident, rare and local summer resident. Recorded statewide but generally absent from heavily forested portions of eastern Kentucky. This species occurs in a wide variety of open and semi-open, grassy habitats, typically avoiding tall, thick weeds and grass. Encountered during migration in a variety of open habitats, usually in open fields with scattered patches of bare ground and weeds or grasses where the species can be surprisingly numerous. Occurs locally during winter; abundance somewhat variable from year to year, scarce in most areas, but occurs with increasing regularity and abundance to the south and west. Usually found in extensive weedy and grain stubble fields with some patches of dense ground cover. Peaks of abundance occur from late Apr to early May and from mid-Oct to early Nov. Breeding has been documented in open grasslands and pastures in several counties of central Kentucky (see below). There are also a few scattered reports of birds during early summer (perhaps some territorial) as far west as Livingston Co. (see below). Generally encountered in loose flocks of from a few to more than a dozen birds during migration and winter. **State Breeding Status**: Special Concern.

Maximum counts: "hundreds" on roadsides in Livingston Co., 1 Feb 2010 (*KW* 86:46, 2010); "**hundreds**" on roadsides in Barren Co., 14 Feb 2010 (*KW* 86:46, 2010); ca. **225** below Barkley Dam, Lyon Co., 17 Nov 2010 (*KW* 87:23, 2011); **200+** at McElroy Lake, 14 Oct 1996 (*KW* 73:11, 1997); **100** in Cherokee Park, Louisville, 15 Oct 1972 (L. Brecher, notes); **85** in s. Jefferson Co., 2 Oct 2010 (*KW* 87:23, 2011); **90** on the Paradise CBC, 1 Jan 1999 (*KW* 75:11, 1999).

Late spring dates (away from limited breeding areas): 10 Jun 1990, Livingston Co. (summer vagrant?) (B. Palmer-Ball, eBird data); 8 Jun 2012, Wayne Co. (eBird data); 4 Jun 2019, Henderson Co. (C. Crawford, eBird data); 3 Jun 2018, Hardin Co. (*KW* 94:110, 2018); 1 Jun 1995, Ohio Co. (eBird data); 27 May 2006, w. Henderson Co. (*KW* 82:74, 2006); 26 May 2016, Christian Co. (G. Gerdeman, eBird data); 25 May 2005, w. Henderson Co. (*KW* 81:92, 2005).

Early fall dates (away from limited breeding areas): 17 Aug 2012, Boone Co. (*KW* 89:14, 2013); 18 Aug 2001, Union Co. (B. Palmer-Ball, eBird data); 26 Aug 2017, w. Henderson Co. (J. Snyder, eBird data); 1 Sep 2004, Union Co. (*KW* 81:15, 2005); 1 Sep 2013, Allen Co. (*KW* 90:17, 2014); 6 Sep 2006, Pulaski Co. (*KW* 83:19, 2007); 6/10 Sep 2011, Madison Co. (*KW* 88:17-18, 2012); 7 Sep 1997, Pulaski Co. (R. Denton, eBird data); 8 Sep 2005, Pulaski Co. (*KW* 82:15, 2006); 10 Sep 2000, Jonathan Creek (R. Denton, eBird data); 11 Sep 2004, McCreary Co. (*KW* 81:15, 2005); 12 Sep 1959, Louisville area (*KW* 37:41, 1961).

Summary of confirmed breeding records by county

Adair (*KW* 84:89, 2008; *KW* 85:95, 2009)
Casey (*KW* 91:87, 2015; R. Denton, 2014/2015 eBird data)
Fayette (*AB* 27:878, 1973; *KBBA*:292; numerous subsequent years)
Lewis (*KW* 64:66, 1988; *KBBA*:292-293)
Oldham (Stamm and McConnell, *KW* 47:45, 1971)

Summary of additional summer records of possible/probable breeding by county

Adair (*KW* 90:90, 2014)
Barren (2013 eBird data; *KW* 90:90, 2014)
Boone (*KW* 75:61, 1999; L. McNeely, 1998/2001 notes)
Boyle (*KBBA*:292-293)

Bourbon (*KBBA*:292-293)
Garrard (*KW* 88:95, 2012)
Hardin (*KW* 94:110, 2018)
Hart (*KW* 91:87, 2015; *KW* 92:81, 2016)
Jefferson (*KBBA*:292-293; *KW* 86:96, 2010)
Jessamine (*KW* 82:84, 2006)
Larue (*KW* 81:109, 2005; *KW* 84:89, 2008;*KW* 91:87, 2015)
Logan (*KW* 87:116, 2011)
Mercer (*KW* 86:73, 2010; *KW* 87:95/116, 2011)
Muhlenberg (*KW* 90:90, 2014)
Oldham (*KBBA*:292-293; *KW* 86:96, 2010)
Shelby (*KW* 83:106-107, 2007)
Woodford (*KBBA*:292-293; D. Lang, 2017 eBird data)

*SONG SPARROW *Melospiza melodia*

Status: Fairly common to common transient and winter resident, locally rare to common summer resident. Recorded statewide during migration and winter in a great variety of semi-open to open
habitats with at least some patches of weeds and brush. Peak of abundance occurs from mid-Oct
to early Apr. Breeding statewide except portions of the Jackson Purchase and southern Highland
Rim (*KBBA*:298-299), occurring in a great variety of habitats from brushy woodland borders and
overgrown fields and fencerows to suburban parks and yards. Encountered singly or in small
groups of up to a dozen birds, but occasionally seen in loose flocks of up to a few dozen birds.

Maximum counts: **258** in sw. Todd Co., 22 Dec 2017 (A. Troyer, eBird data); **221** at Buck Creek NP,
Pulaski Co., 21 Nov 2006 (R. Denton, eBird data); **212** at West Ky WMA, McCracken Co., 30 Dec
2013 (D. Akers, eBird data).

LINCOLN'S SPARROW *Melospiza lincolnii*

Status: Uncommon transient, extremely rare during winter. Recorded statewide in a variety of semi-
open, weedy and brushy habitats with some dense cover (often along woodland borders) where
the species can be somewhat shy and hard to observe well. Peaks of abundance occur during
early May and Oct. The species is occasionally reported during winter, but it certainly does not regularly overwinter. Few older records during winter were suitably documented (see Mengel:505 and
below), but the frequency of reports has increased in recent years and a number of well documented ones now exist. Most often encountered singly, but loose flocks of up to a half-dozen or
more birds are occasionally seen during fall.

Maximum counts: **34** at the Sinclair Unit, 12 Oct 2013 (*KW* 90:17, 2014); at least **20** at Surrey Hills
Farm, Jefferson Co., 2 Oct 2004 (*KW* 81:15, 2005); **17** at Louisville, 3 Oct 1964 (Able, *KW* 41:18,
1965); **12** in s. Jefferson Co., 16 Oct 2010 (*KW* 87:23, 2011; E. Huber, eBird data); **11** at Pum-
phrey Farm, Pulaski Co., 20 Oct 2006 (*KW* 83:19, 2007); **10+** in Fulton Co., 2 May 1992 (*KW* 68:
48, 1992).

Early spring dates: 25 Mar 2001 (a wintering individual? – see Mengel:505), Lower Hickman Bottoms (B. Palmer-Ball, eBird data); 26 Mar 2004, Mammoth Cave National Park (*KW* 80:72, 2004);
10 Apr 1993, LBL (*KW* 69:48, 1993); 14 Apr 2014, (ph.) Sauerheber Unit (*KW* 90:76, 2014); 14 Apr
2017, Muhlenberg Co. (*KW* 93:78, 2017); 15 Apr 2018, s. Jefferson Co. (*KW* 94:83, 2018); 17 Apr
2016, Jefferson Co. (*KW* 92:68, 2016); 18 Apr 19—, Louisville area (Mengel:505).

Late spring dates: 7 Jun 1937, Christian Co. (Mengel:505); 1 Jun 1977, Jefferson Co. (B. Palmer-
Ball, eBird data); 30 May 1979, Louisville (eBird data; J. Elmore, notes); 23 May 2017, Lexington
(D. Svetich, eBird data); 23 May 2017, Franklin Co. (*KW* 93:78, 2017).

Early fall dates: 7 Sep 1905, Fayette Co. (Mengel:505); 12 Sep 1959, Louisville area (Mengel: 505);
12 Sep 2012, Pulaski Co. (*KW* 89:15, 2013).

Late fall dates (birds occasionally linger into early winter, although it is unclear if CBC period birds
during mid- to late Dec may winter; latest reports include the following): 1 Jan 2009, Pulaski Co.
(*KW* 85:52, 2009); 31 Dec 19—, Louisville area (*KW* 52:64, 1976); 31 Dec 1996, Barren Co. (eBird

data); 31 Dec 2017, Ohio Co. (*KW* 94:60, 2018); 30 Dec 2013, (2) West Ky WMA, McCracken Co. (*KW* 90:55, 2014); 30 Dec 2016, West Ky WMA, McCracken Co. (*KW* 93:53, 2017); 30 Dec 2017, West Ky WMA, McCracken Co. (*KW* 94:60, 2018).

Out-of-season records (mid-winter): 9 Feb 1985, at a feeding station at Elizabethtown (eBird data; J. Noel/R. Healy, pers. comm.); 29 Jan 2004, Pulaski Co. (*KW* 80:48, 2004); 9 Feb 2004, Barren Co. (*KW* 80:48, 2004); 9 Jan 2010, (ph.) St. Matthews, Jefferson Co. (*KW* 86:46/52, 2010); 18 Jan 2012, LBL, Lyon Co. (*KW* 88:52, 2012); 21 Jan 2012, Nelson Co. (*KW* 88:52, 2012); 10-11 Mar 2012 (wintering bird?), (ph.) Sinclair Unit (*KW* 88:82, 2012); 29 Jan 2013, Fulton Co. (*KW* 89:53, 2013).

Unaccepted records: all during winter for which there appear to be no substantiating details and that lie between the late fall and early spring dates given above; these would include 12 Feb 1959, south-central Kentucky (*KW* 38:24, 1962); 18 Mar 19—, Louisville area (*KW* 52:64, 1976); 31 Aug 1989, Falls of the Ohio [published location is in Indiana] (*KW* 66:14, 1990); 27 Dec 1981, (3) Henderson CBC (*KW* 58:9, 1982); 2 Sep 2016, Edmonson Co. (eBird data).

SWAMP SPARROW *Melospiza georgiana*

Status: Fairly common to common transient and winter resident. Recorded statewide but much less numerous in heavily forested portions of eastern Kentucky. Encountered in a variety of semi-open to open, weedy or marshy habitats with dense herbaceous cover; most numerous in dense vegetation over water or in low, damp ground. Peak of abundance occurs from mid-Oct to mid-Apr. Usually encountered in small groups of from several to more than a dozen birds, but occasionally seen in loose flocks of up to several dozen or more birds, especially during the peak of fall migration in Oct.

Maximum counts: **400** at the Sauerheber Unit, 17 Oct 1999 (R. Denton/H. Chambers, eBird data); **200-300** in Henderson Co., 12 Oct 1986 (*KW* 63:12, 1987; Palmer-Ball, *KW* 66:30, 1990); **275** in Henderson Co., 12 Oct 1997 (*KW* 74:11, 1998); **200** in the Lower Hickman Bottoms, 11 Feb 2001 (*KW* 77:30, 2001); **200** at the Sauerheber Unit, 18 Oct 2003 (R. Denton, eBird data); **200** at the Sauerheber Unit, 20 Oct 2013 (J. Sole, eBird data); **200** at the Sauerheber Unit, 17 Oct 2015 (J. Baker et al., eBird data); **178** at Buck Creek NP, Pulaski Co., 20 Oct 2006 (*KW* 83:19, 2007).

Late spring dates: 5 Jun 1977, Louisville (*AB* 31:1150, 1977); 3 Jun 2001, Nicholas Co. (BBS data; V. Kingsolver, notes); 1 Jun 1976, Louisville (*AB* 30:850, 1976).

Early fall dates: 14 Sep 1922, south-central Kentucky (*KW* 38:24, 1962); 18 Sep 2012, Allen Co. (*KW* 89:15, 2013); 22 Sep 2013, w. Henderson Co. (K. Michalski, eBird data); 22 Sep 2015, Jefferson Co. (*KW* 92:15, 2016); 23 Sep 2012, Falls of the Ohio (*KW* 89:15, 2013); 24 Sep 1995, Mercer Co. (*KW* 72:9, 1996).

GREEN-TAILED TOWHEE *Pipilo chlorurus*

Status: Accidental vagrant. This resident of the western United States and Middle America occasionally shows up in the eastern United States, and it has been documented once in Kentucky.

1) 6-9 May 1992, one (ph.) at a feeding station at Central City, Muhlenberg Co. (Neace, *KW* 68:51, 1992)

SPOTTED TOWHEE *Pipilo maculatus*

Status: Extremely rare winter visitant/resident. This species was formerly considered a subspecies of the Rufous-sided (Eastern) Towhee, but it was taxonomically elevated to full species status a couple of decades ago. There are six Kentucky records.

Chronological list of records

1) 31 Dec 1989–4 Feb 1990, a male (ph.) nr. Garrett in rural Meade Co. (Palmer-Ball and Cassell, *KW* 66:98-99, 1990)
2) 23 Dec 1995, a male at Bernheim Forest along Wilson Creek, Nelson Co. (*KW* 72:14, 1996)

3) 30 Dec 2003–17 Apr 2004, a male (ph.), in western McCracken Co. (*KW* 80:17/47/72, 2004); presumably this same bird returned the following winter and was observed 21 Dec 2004 (*KW* 81: 18/60, 2005) and returned the following year and was seen 27 Oct 2005–27 Jan 2006 (*KW* 82: 15/17/29/49, 2006)
4) 3 Jan–27 Feb 2004, a male in e. Muhlenberg Co. (*KW* 80:19/47, 2004; *KW* 84:77, 2008)
5) late Dec 2005–24 Apr 2006, a male in ne. Hart Co. (*KW* 82:21/49/74, 2006) and 12 Dec 2006– 15 Apr 2007 (*KW* 83:31/51/84, 2007; *KW* 85:102, 2009)
6) 18 Dec 2012–30 Jan 2013, a male (ph.) on and adjacent to the West Ky WMA, McCracken Co. (*KW* 89:18/41/53, 2013)

*EASTERN TOWHEE *Pipilo erythrophthalmus*

Status: Fairly common to common resident. Recorded statewide in a great variety of semi-open habitats with at least some brushy, dense cover. Breeding statewide in a variety of brushy habitats; most numerous along woodland borders and in successional thickets and overgrown fields. The breeding population is probably supplemented by migrants that winter locally, making the species slightly more numerous from late Oct to early Apr. Usually encountered in pairs or loose groups of up to a dozen birds during migration and winter.

Maximum count: 55 at Berea College Forest, Madison Co., 8 Apr 2018 (R. Bates et al., eBird data).

*YELLOW-BREASTED CHAT *Icteria virens*

Status: Fairly common to common summer resident, accidental during winter. Recorded statewide during migration, but generally uncommon as a transient away from nesting areas, especially during fall when the species is seldom observed. Transient individuals occur in a variety of semi-open and open, successional habitats with some brushy cover. Peak of abundance occurs from late Apr to mid-Jul. Breeding statewide in a variety of open, brushy habitats with scattered trees including forest clear cuts, overgrown fields, and woodland borders. The species has been reported once during winter.

Maximum counts: 75 at the Road Creek Mine/Fishtrap WMA, Pike Co., 15 May 2012 (A. Newman, eBird data); 49 in nw. Pulaski Co., 8 May 2004 (R. Denton, eBird data); 44 in w. Henderson Co., 23 May 2018 (*KW* 94:83, 2018).
Early spring dates: 10 Apr 2017, Wayne Co. (R. Bontrager, eBird data); 14 Apr 2017, McCreary Co. (*KW* 93:78, 2017); 15 Apr 2012, Allen Co. (*KW* 88:81, 2012); 16 Apr 1945, south-central Kentucky (*KW* 38:21, 1962); 17 Apr 2017, (ph.) Sauerheber Unit (*KW* 93:78, 2017).
Late fall dates: 21 Oct 1965, Louisville area (*KW* 52:60, 1976); 20 Oct 1990 (tower kill), Oldham Co. (Elmore and Palmer-Ball, *KW* 67:69, 1991); 17 Oct 1990 (tower kill), Adair Co. (Elmore and Palmer-Ball, *KW* 67:69, 1991); 13 Oct 2007, Laurel Co. (*KW* 84:15 2008); 10 Oct 2013, Washington Co. (*KW* 90:16, 2014); 9 Oct 2004, Jefferson Co. (*KW* 81:15, 2005); 7 Oct 2011, Jefferson Co. (*KW* 88:17, 2012); 3 Oct 2017, LBL, Trigg Co. (*KW* 94:14, 2018); 3 Oct 2018, Warren Co. (*KW* 95: 9, 2019); 1 Oct 1950/1960, Louisville area (*KW* 37:39, 1961); 30 Sep 2011, Lexington (*KW* 88:17, 2012); 29 Sep 1945, south-central Kentucky (*KW* 38:21, 1962); 29 Sep 2002, Menifee Co. (*KW* 79: 16, 2003).
Out-of-season record (winter): 17 Jan 2016, McMillan's Landing, Monroe Co. (*KW* 92:46, 2016).

YELLOW-HEADED BLACKBIRD *Xanthocephalus xanthocephalus*

Status: Extremely rare visitant (has occurred in every month except Jul). There are nearly 40 records of this unique blackbird from 21 widely scattered counties as far east as Rowan Co. (see below). Records are spread rather evenly among spring, fall and winter seasons, with one in early Jun; most records are of single birds and only for brief periods, but two males wintered in Union Co. in 2001-2002. This species can be expected to occur just about anywhere, but usually with other blackbirds; most records have been of the conspicuous males, including a few at feeding stations.

Late spring dates: 3 Jun 1987, (ph.) Louisville (*KW* 63:61, 1987); 3 Jun 2004, Shaker Village, Mercer Co. (*KW* 80:86, 2004; KBRC accepted 2019); 30 May 2008, Christian Co. (*KW* 84:71, 2008); 24 May 1998, Warren Co. (*KW* 74:59, 1998); 19 May 1963, Oldham Co. (Horner, *KW* 39:46, 1963); 18 May 1998, McElroy Lake (*KW* 74:59, 1998); 12 May 2008 (*KW* 84:67/71, 2008); 8 May 2016, (ph.), Elliott Co. (*KW* 92:62/68, 2016); 30 Apr 2013, (ph.) Fulton Co. (*KW* 89:75/80, 2013).

Early fall dates: 18 Aug 2017, w. Henderson Co. (*KW* 94:14, 2018); 19 Aug 1981, (ph./ba.) Logan Co. (Twedt, *KW* 58:59-60, 1982); 24 Aug 1973, Lexington (Westerman, *KW* 49:73, 1973); 5 Sep 1983, Fulton Co. (B. Palmer-Ball, eBird data); 13 Sep 2017, (ph.) Wayne Co. (*KW* 94:14, 2018); 25 Sep 2014, e. Shelby Co. (*KW* 91:15, 2015); 27 Sep 2003, Union Co. (*KW* 80:15, 2004); 2 Oct 1976, Barren Co. (Mason, *KW* 52:81, 1976); 13 Oct 1952, Louisville (Stamm, *KW* 28:58, 1952).

Unaccepted record: I cannot find details of a report from Morgan Co. in 1989 (M./G. Elam, notes) included in the previous edition of this work.

Summary of records by county

Barren (2 Oct 1976 [Mason, *KW* 52:81, 1976])

Christian (30 May 2008 [*KW* 84:71, 2008])

Elliott (8 May 2016 (ph.) [*KW* 92:62/68, 2016])

Fayette (24 Aug 1973 [Westerman, *KW* 49:73, 1973]; late Feb 1985 [*KW* 61:32, 1985]; 24-27 Apr 2002 (ph.) [*KW* 80:96, 2004])

Franklin (6 Feb 1977 [*AB* 31:338, 1977])

Fulton (5 Sep 1983 [B. Palmer-Ball, eBird data (erroneously published as 6 Sep in earlier editions of this work)]; 12 May 2008 (ph.) [*KW* 84:67/71, 2008]; 30 Apr 2013 (ph.) [*KW* 89:75/80, 2013])

Hardin (27 Apr 1988 [*KW* 64:50, 1988]; 16 Feb 1991 *KW* 67:32, 1991])

Henderson (3 Nov 2008 [*KW* 85:20, 2009]; 18 Aug 2017 [*KW* 94:14, 2018])

Hopkins (20 Dec 2013 [*KW* 90:55/95, 2014])

Jefferson (19 Apr 1940 [Brecher, *KW* 16:27-28, 1940]; 13 Oct 1952 [Stamm, *KW* 28:58, 1952]; 19 Apr 1973 [Harm, *KW* 49:46, 1973]; 7 Dec 1984 (ph.) [*KW* 61:32, 1985/B. Palmer-Ball, eBird data]; 10 Jan–14 Feb 1985 [*KW* 61:32, 1985; eBird data]; 3 Jun 1987 (ph.) [*KW* 63:61, 1987])

Logan (19 Aug 1981, (ph./ba.) [Twedt, *KW* 58:59-60, 1982])

Meade (31 Dec 1999 [*KW* 76:18, 2000; B. Palmer-Ball, eBird data])

Mercer (10 Jan 1992 [*KW* 68:36, 1992]; 3 Jun 2004 [*KW* 80:86, 2004; KBRC accepted 2019])

Muhlenberg (20 Jan 1994 [S. Neace, eBird data]; 16 Oct 2012 [*KW* 89:15, 2013]; 17 Jan 2018 (ph.) [*KW* 94:60, 2018])

Oldham (19 May 1963 [Horner, *KW* 39:46, 1963])

Rowan (12 Apr 1933 (a flock[?]) [Barbour, *KW* 28:28, 1952])

Shelby (25 Sep 2014 [*KW* 90:95, 2014/*KW* 91:15, 2015])

Union (19/27 Oct 2001 [two present on latter date], 3/23 Nov 2001, 27 Feb 2002 (ph.), 10/17 Mar 2002 [*KW* 78:13, 2002/B. Palmer-Ball, et al., eBird data]; 27 Oct 2002 [*KW* 79:17, 2003]; 27 Sep/5 Oct/29 Oct 2003 [*KW* 80:15, 2004])

Warren (10 Mar 1990 [*KW* 66:62, 1990]; 18 May 1998 [*KW* 74:59, 1998]; 24 May 1998 [*KW* 74:59, 1998])

Wayne (13 Sep 2017 (ph.) [*KW* 94:14, 2018]

Webster (8 Nov 2007 (ph.) [*KW* 84:16, 2008; B. Palmer-Ball, eBird data])

BOBOLINK *Dolichonyx oryzivorus*

Status: Transient (uncommon to locally fairly common during spring, uncommon during fall); extremely rare and local summer resident. Recorded chiefly west of the Cumberland Plateau during migration but can be found in suitable habitat statewide; most frequently encountered in open hayfields in farmland, but occurs in a variety of open, grassy habitats. Peaks of abundance occur during early May and from late Aug to late Sep. Breeding has been documented from only a few localities in north-central Kentucky (see below), typically in extensive hayfields and lightly grazed pastures. A few spring migrants regularly linger into Jun, perhaps accounting for additional records during early summer from widely scattered localities away from the north-central part of the state. Most often encountered during spring migration in small to medium sized flocks of up to a couple of dozen birds, but the species passes through largely unnoticed during fall, many individuals being noted only by call notes as they pass overhead. **State Breeding Status**: Special Concern.

Maximum spring counts: ca. **1500** in the Lower Hickman Bottoms, 6 May 1996 (B. Palmer-Ball, eBird data) with **500-1000** in the Lower Hickman Bottoms, 4 May 1996 (*KW* 72:59, 1996); ca. **825** in the Lower Hickman Bottoms, 3 May 2014 (*KW* 90:77, 2014); ca. **500** in the Lower Hickman Bottoms, 15 May 2010 (*KW* 86:73, 2010); at least **500** in the Lower Hickman Bottoms, 4 May 2018 (*KW* 94:83, 2018).

Maximum summer/fall counts: ca. **150** w. of Henderson, Henderson Co., 6 Sep 1949 (Mengel: 437); **75** at Shaker Village, Mercer Co., 19 Jul 2014 (*KW* 90:90, 2014); at least **60** in Bourbon Co., 2 Sep 2007 (*KW* 84:16, 2008); ca. **60** at Spindletop Farm, Fayette Co., 13 Sep 2014 (*KW* 91:15, 2015); at least **52** over Wolf Creek Dam, Russell, 18 Sep 2016 (*KW* 93:14, 2017); ca. **50** at Spindletop Farm, Fayette Co., 17 Aug 1993 (*KW* 70:12, 1994); **50** at Spindletop Farm, Fayette Co., 12 Sep 2011 (*KW* 88:19, 2012); **40** in the Louisville area, 2 Sep 1956 (Stamm, *KW* 33:41, 1957); at least **40** in Jefferson Co., 3 Sep 2010 (*KW* 87:23, 2011); **35-40** in w. Henderson Co., 10-17 Sep 2015 (*KW* 92:16, 2016); ca. **35** in Boyle Co., 12 Sep 2010 (*KW* 87:23, 2011); ca. **30** at Spindletop Farm, Fayette Co., 2 Aug 2009 (*KW* 86:15, 2010); **25** at Falling Springs Park, Woodford Co., 16 Aug 2018 (*KW* 95:9, 2019); **24** in ne. Jefferson Co., 12 Sep 2004 (*KW* 81:16, 2005); **23** nr. Rochester, Butler Co., 24 Sep 2009 (*KW* 86:15, 2010); **20-25** at South Shore WMA, Greenup Co., 9 Sep 2007 (*KW* 84:16, 2008).

Early spring dates: 14 Apr 2012, Fulton Co. (*KW* 88:82, 2012); 15 Apr 1972, Warren Co. (*KW* 48:28, 1972); 16 Apr 1955, Louisville area (*KW* 52:60, 1976); 17 Apr 2004, Fulton Co. (*KW* 80:72, 2004).

Late spring dates (away from probable or possible breeding sites): 26 Jun 2017, Madison Co. (G. Sheridan, eBird data); 24 Jun 2018, Mason Co. (*KW* 94:110, 2018); 20 Jun 1997, Ohio Co. (B. Palmer-Ball, eBird data); 15 Jun 2017, Scott Co. (B. Stern, eBird data); 14 Jun 2003, Sinclair Unit (*KW* 79:85, 2003); 9 Jun 2018, Morgan Co. (*KW* 94:110, 2018); 8 Jun 1980, [presumed] Henry Co. (*KW* 56:81, 1980); 8 Jun 2012, Allen Co. (*KW* 88:95, 2012); 7 Jun 1987, Shelby Co. (*KW* 63:61, 1987); 6 Jun 1993, Pulaski Co. (*KW* 69:59, 1993); 6 Jun 2010, Pulaski Co. (*KW* 86:96, 2010); 6 Jun 2011, Montgomery Co. (*KW* 87:116, 2011); 5 Jun 1983, n. Taylor Co. (*KW* 59:54, 1983; B. Palmer-Ball, eBird data).

Late fall dates: 31 Oct 2010, Sauerheber Unit (*KW* 87:23, 2011); 30 Oct 2005, Jefferson Co. (*KW* 82:16, 2006); 24-30 Oct 2006, Jefferson Co. (*KW* 83:20, 2007); 27 Oct 1982, Oldham Co. (B. Palmer-Ball, eBird data).

Published error?: it is possible that the early spring date of 15 Apr [19—], published by Monroe, et al. (1988) and included above may represent a recent misinterpretation from the list published in *KW* 48:28, 1972 for 15-16 Apr 1972 in Warren Co.; however, unlike the similar Dickcissel report, no other sources exist to check this information against.

Summary of confirmed breeding records by county

Boyle (*KW* 69:59, 1993; *KW* 74:74, 1998; *KW* 80:86, 2004)

Fayette (*AB* 29:982, 1975; *KW* 54:63, 1978; *KW* 61:47/60, 1985; *KW* 62:70, 1986; *KW* 71:71, 1995; *KW* 74:74, 1998; *KW* 79:85, 2003; *KW* 86:73, 2010)

Jessamine (M. Burns, 1999-2002 notes/photographs; *KW* 78:67, 2002; *KW* 82:84, 2006; *KW* 91:87, 2015; *KW* 92:81, 2016; [*KW* 93:102, 2017; T. Noel/N. Braun, et al., 2017 eBird data; *KW* 94:110, 2018])

Mercer (*KW* 82:84, 2006; [nest] *KW* 83:85/107, 2007; *KW* 90:90, 2014)

Oldham (Croft, *KW* 48:40-41, 1972; *KW* 54:63, 1978; *KW* 56:81, 180; *KW* 58:85, 1982; *KW* 59:54, 1983)

Summary of probable breeding records by county (most likely represent breeding)

Bath/Montgomery (*KW* 84:89, 2008; R. Denton, 2017 eBird data)

Bourbon (*KBBA*:302; *KW* 74:59, 1998; *KW* 83:107, 2007; *KW* 92:81, 2016; R. Denton, 2017 eBird data)

Boyle (*KBBA*: 302; *KW* 65:91, 1989; *KW* 70:71, 1994; *KW* 81:110, 2005; *KW* 84:89, 2008)

Clark (*KW* 73:57-58/75, 1997; *KW* 76:58, 2000; *KW* 83:107, 2007; *KW* 94:110, 2018)

Fayette (*KW* 66:92, 1990; *KW* 89:80/98, 2013; *KW* 90:90, 2014; *KW* 91:87, 2015; *KW* 92:81, 2016; T. Noel, et al. 2017 eBird data; *KW* 94:110, 2018)

Garrard (*KW* 88:95, 2012)

Henry (*KW* 58:85, 1982; *KW* 59:54, 1983; *KW* 82:84, 2006)

Jessamine (*KW* 81:110, 2005; *KW* 89:80/98, 2013: *KW* 90:90, 2014)
Madison (*KW* 92:81, 2016; *KW* 94:110, 2018)
Mercer (*KW* 80:86, 2004; *KW* 82:84, 2006; *KW* 85:76/95, 2009; *KW* 86:96, 2010; *KW* 91:87, 2015)
Nicholas (*KW* 88:95, 2012; R. Denton, 2017 eBird data)
Oldham (*KW* 68:58, 1992)
Owen (Jones, *KW* 51:20, 1975)
Pulaski (*KW* 86:96, 2010)
Shelby (*KBBA*:302; *KW* 64:66, 1988; *KW* 79:85, 2003; *KW* 81:110, 2005; *KW* 82:84, 2006; *KW* 83:107, 2007; *KW* 94:110, 2018)
Washington (*KW* 81:110, 2005)
Woodford (*KW* 83:107, 2007; *KW* 90:90, 2014; *KW* 91:87, 2015; *KW* 93:78, 2017; B. Wulker/D. Lang, et al., 2017 eBird data)

*EASTERN MEADOWLARK *Sturnella magna*

Status: Uncommon to fairly common resident. Recorded statewide in farmland and other open habitats with an abundance of grassland. Breeding statewide in a variety of grasslands including hayfields, pastures, reclaimed surface mines, and roadway rights-of-way; absent in heavily forested areas. Migrants from farther north appear to supplement the breeding population during migration and winter. Numbers may fluctuate during winter in response to the severity of weather (see Monroe, *KW* 54:20, 1978). Outside of the breeding season, the species is generally more locally distributed, but can be found in loose flocks of up to a few dozen birds.

Maximum counts: **143** in Hart Co., 14 May 2011 (J. Kistler, eBird data); **128** in ne. Wayne Co., 5 Jan 2013 (R. Denton, eBird data); **104** in ne. Pulaski Co., 13 May 2000 (L. Kamperman, eBird data).

*WESTERN MEADOWLARK *Sturnella neglecta*

Status: Extremely rare to locally rare visitant or transient, extremely rare winter resident, extremely rare breeder (two records). Doubtlessly overlooked to some extent; this species has been reported only several dozen times in the state. Oddly, prior to the mid-1980s most reports were from the Louisville area where the species has not been reported in several decades. In recent years small numbers have been found to occur somewhat regularly during winter and early spring in the open farmland of western Fulton Co., where a few birds appear to winter and two nesting attempts have been documented (see below). Single individuals have also been reported occasionally elsewhere in the western half of the state, and the species has now been documented from 16 counties as far east as Jefferson, Oldham, and Washington cos. (see below). Based on the accumulating body of information, a perceptible peak of spring migrants may occur during late Mar and early Apr.

Maximum counts: **15-20** (some ph./vo.) wsw. of Cayce, Fulton Co., 13 Feb 2017 (*KW* 93:53, 2017); at least **13** in the Lower Hickman Bottoms, 5 Apr 1992 (B. Palmer-Ball, eBird data); **10** in one flock in w. Fulton Co., 3 Feb 1996 (B. Palmer-Ball, eBird data); ca. **10** in Lower Hickman Bottoms, 10-11 Mar 1998 (*KW* 74:59, 1998); **10** wsw. of Cayce, Fulton Co., 29 Jan 2013 (*KW* 89:54, 2013).

Late spring dates (away from limited breeding areas): 1 Jun 1968, Breckinridge Co. (*KW* 46:44, 1970/B. Monroe, Jr., notes; eBird data); 19 May 1957, nr. Springfield, Washington Co. (Croft, *KW* 37:59-60, 1961); 18 May 1957, Louisville (Croft, *KW* 37:59-60, 1961); 12 May 2003, w. Fulton Co. (*KW* 79:74, 2003); 4 May 1949, (sp.) at Chaney Lake (Mengel:441; Monroe, *KW* 35:43, 1959); 4 May 1958, Henderson Co. (*KW* 34:0, 1958); 4 May 1963, Bowling Green (*KW* 45:37, 1969); 18 Apr 1954, Hopkins Co. (Hancock, *KW* 30:47-48, 1954); 7 Apr 1996, Lower Hickman Bottoms (B. Palmer-Ball, eBird data); 1 Apr 2011, McElroy Lake (*KW* 87:96, 2011); 30 Mar 1958, Louisville (*KW* 37:40, 1961); 27 Mar 1988, Lower Hickman Bottoms (*KW* 64:50, 1988).

Early fall dates: 2 Oct 19—, [year and location unknown] (*KW* 45:54, 1969); 15 Oct 1998, Open Pond, Fulton Co. (eBird data); 15 Oct 2015, (ph.) in Union Co. (*KW* 92:16, 2016; J. Baker, eBird data); 21 Oct 1959, Warren Co. (*KW* 38:22, 1962); 31 Oct 2010, Union Co. (*KW* 87:23/44, 2011); 8 Nov 2007, (ph.) Sinclair Unit (*KW* 84:16, 2008); 12 Nov 1966, nr. Worthington, Jefferson Co. (*KW* 52:60, 1976; A. Stamm, historical archive files).

Unaccepted records: 30 Jun 1969, one on Hodgenville BBS route (*KW* 46:44, 1970; BBS data; [this record was included by Monroe, et al. (1988) but in the absence of details it is not included herein]; 14 Dec 2014, Warren Co. (*KW* 91:19, 2015 [report likely accurate but no details available]). Several CBC and Big Spring List reports through the years have also been published without details.

Chronological list of breeding records

1) Fulton: May 1992, a pair was observed carrying food in a fallow field about a mile ne. of Open Pond; it is unknown if this nesting was successful as a nest could not be located (Palmer-Ball, *KW* 89:101, 2013; B. Palmer-Ball, eBird data)
2) Fulton: Apr and May 2013, a singing male was on territory wsw. of Cayce, with an active nest containing two eggs located; the nest was destroyed by farming activities before the eggs hatched (Palmer-Ball, *KW* 89:101/103/104, 2013; *KW* 89:80, 2013)

Summary of records by county

Allen (*KW* 86:73, 2010)

Ballard (*KW* 88:21/52, 2012; [ph./vo.] *KW* 89:54/80, 2013)

Barren ([vt.] *KW* 86:47, 2010)

Breckinridge (*KW* 46:44, 1970/B. Monroe, Jr., notes/eBird data)

Fulton ([now annual] *KW* 64:49-50, 1988; *KW* 66:41, 1990; *KW* 68:48, 1992; *KW* 74:59, 1998; *KW* 75:27, 1999; *KW* 76:32/47, 2000; *KW* 77:30, 2001: *KW* 79:74, 2003; *KW* 85:53, 2009; *KW* 86:47, 2010; *KW* 87:65, 2011; *KW* 88:52, 2012; [ph.] *KW* 89:54/80, 2013; [ph.] *KW* 90:17/55, 2014; *KW* 91:15, 2015; [ph./vo.] [vo.] *KW* 93:53/78, 2017; *KW* 94:60, 2018; *KW* 95:9/50, 2019)

Henderson (*KW* 34:40, 1958; *KW* 35:52, 1959)

Hopkins (Hancock, *KW* 30:47-48, 1954)

Jefferson (Mengel:441; *KW* 35:7, 1959; *KW* 37:40, 1961; Croft, *KW* 37:59-60, 1961; *KW* 40:15, 1964; *KW* 52:10, 1976; *KW* 52:60, 1976)

Lyon (*KW* 58:54, 1982; *KW* 60:46, 1984)

McCracken ([ph.] *KW* 77:12, 2001; location erroneously published as Ballard Co. therein)

Muhlenberg ([ph.] *KW* 84:16, 2008)

Oldham (Mengel:441 [Note: some Louisville CBC reports listed under Jefferson Co. above could pertain to Oldham Co.])

Todd (*KW* 94:60, 2018)

Union (*KW* 87:23/44, 2011; *KW* 92:16, 2016/J. Baker, eBird data)

Warren (Mengel:441; Wilson, *KW* 33:58, 1957; *KW* 38:22, 1962; *KW* 45:37, 1969; B. Palmer-Ball, 1991 eBird data; J. Baker, 1996 eBird data; D. Roemer, 1999 notes; *KW* 76:47, 2000; *KW* 87:96, 2011; [ph.] *KW* 89:80, 2013; [ph.] *KW* 90:50/55, 2014; *KW* 94:84, 2018)

Washington (Croft, *KW* 37:59-60, 1961)

*ORCHARD ORIOLE *Icterus spurius*

Status: Fairly common transient and summer resident; accidental during winter. Recorded statewide during spring migration in a variety of semi-open to open habitats from mature woodland borders to suburban parks and yards; generally not found in mature woodlands. This species departs very early during fall, most birds disappearing by the end of Aug; as a result it is essentially absent as a fall migrant later in the season. Peak of abundance occurs from late Apr to mid-Aug. Breeding statewide, but much less numerous in heavily forested portions of eastern Kentucky (*KBBA*:312-313); generally occurs in rural farmland and other open to semi-open habitats with scattered trees. Occasionally seen in flocks of up to a half-dozen or more birds during spring migration, otherwise typically found singly or in family groups.

Early spring dates: 28 Mar 1988, Calloway Co. (*KW* 64:50, 1988); 5 Apr 2014, Boone Co. (Z. De-Bruine, eBird data); 6 Apr 1986, LBL (*KW* 62:46, 1986); 8 Apr 1969, Callway Co. (E. Larson, eBird data); 9 Apr 1980, Hamlin, Calloway Co. (*KW* 56:64, 1980); 10 Apr 1965, south-central Kentucky (*KW* 45:37, 1969); 10 Apr 1978, Calloway Co. (*KW* 54:46, 1978; J.T. Erwin, notes).

Late fall dates: 21 Sep 2003, Lyon Co. (*KW* 80:16, 2004); 12 Sep 2011, Lexington (*KW* 88:19, 2012); 11 Sep 1997, Fulton Co. (B. Palmer-Ball, eBird data).

Out-of-season record (winter): 27 Jan–mid-Mar 2010, an ad. male in a yard at Richmond, Madison Co. (*KW* 86:74, 2010).

Unaccepted records: those during fall later than the late fall date of 21 Sep given above and including 3 Oct 1942, south-central Kentucky (*KW* 38:22, 1962).

HOODED ORIOLE *Icterus cucullatus*

Status: Accidental vagrant. Although orioles occasionally appear in the caged bird trade, Kentucky's single report has been considered to be of natural origin.

1) 29 Nov 2008, an ad. male (ph.) at Woodville, McCracken Co. (Rowe, *KW* 85:58-59, 2009; *KW* 85:1/20-21, 2009 [location erroneously published as Ballard Co. therein; *fide* J. Rowe, pers. comm.])

BULLOCK'S ORIOLE *Icterus bullockii*

Status: Accidental vagrant. Although orioles occasionally appear in the caged bird trade, Kentucky's single report has been considered to be of natural origin.

1) mid-Jan–8 Apr 2005, a male (ph.) at feeders in a yard at Lawrenceburg, Anderson Co. (*KW* 81:61-62/93, 2005; Palmer-Ball, *KW* 81:113/116, 2005)

*BALTIMORE ORIOLE *Icterus galbula*

Status: Fairly common transient, locally uncommon to fairly common summer resident, extremely rare during winter. Recorded statewide during migration in a variety of semi-open habitats from mature woodlands and woodland borders to suburban parks and yards; much less numerous during fall when the species is most conspicuous during early Sep. Peak of abundance occurs from late Apr to early Sep. Breeding statewide, but somewhat local in occurrence across southern and eastern Kentucky (*KBBA*:314-315); most frequently encountered in open to semi-open habitats with scattered large deciduous trees including rural farmland, riparian corridors, parks, and the margins of tracts of mature forest. There are at least 16 records of individuals lingering into winter, mostly at feeding stations, but wintering has not been documented. Details of several winter records are not complete, and could possibly pertain to Bullock's Oriole. Occasionally seen in flocks of up to a half-dozen or more birds during migration (especially spring); otherwise typically found singly or in family groups.

Maximum counts: perhaps as many as **150** in Calloway Co, 3 May 1979 (*KW* 55:50, 1979); **24-30** nr. Hamlin, Calloway Co., 4 May 1983 (*KW* 59:44, 1983).

Early spring dates: 7 Apr 1979, Louisville (*KW* 55:50, 1979); 7 Apr 1991, Jefferson Co. (*KW* 67:59, 1991); 10 Apr 1968, Louisville area (*KW* 52:61, 1976); 12 Apr 1919, Warren Co. (Mengel:446); 12 Apr 2019, (ph.) Grant Co. (B. Wulker, eBird data).

Late fall dates: 29 Nov 2018, (ph.) at Schochoh, Logan Co. (*KW* 95:9, 2019); 27 Nov 1999, Danville (N. Eklund, pers. comm); 18-26 Nov 1975, Breathitt Co. (*AB* 30:70, 1976); 25 Nov 2006, (ph.) in Rowan Co. (*KW* 83:20, 2007); 26 Oct 1945, Louisville (Mengel:447); 29 Sep 2012, Edmonson Co. (S. Spencer, eBird data).

Out-of-season dates (winter): 21 Dec 1952–2 Jan 1953, female at Louisville (specimen) (*KW* 29:12, 1953; *KW* 52:61, 1976); 19 Dec 1964–3 Jan 1965, female at Lexington (*KW* 41:13, 1965); 22 Jan 1973, female at Richmond (Schroeder and Schroeder, *KW* 49:73, 1973); 26 Dec 1975, female or imm. at Murray (Peterson, *KW* 52:15, 1976); 16 Dec 1979, ad. male at Somerset (Elmore, *KW* 56:22, 1980); 26-27 Dec 1979, female at Danville (*KW* 56:33, 1980; F. Loetscher, notes); winter 1979-80, Hardin Co. (*KW* 56:33, 1980); 28 Dec 1980–5 Jan 1981, Jefferson Co. (*KW* 57:38, 1981); 29 Dec 1984, ad. male in Ballard Co. (*KW* 61:3, 1985); 21 Dec 1985, female in Daviess Co. (*KW* 62:11, 1986); 9-21 Jan 1991, female (ph.) at Lexington (*KW* 67:32, 1991; *KW* 68:13, 1992); mid-Jan–mid-Feb 2007, female (ph.) at Frankfort (*KW* 83:52, 2007); 19 Dec 2009, an ad. male at Lyndon, Jefferson Co. (*KW* 86:47, 2010); 4-28 Jan 2014, male (ph.) at Lexington (*KW* 90:55, 2014); 1

Jan 2016, (ph.) Murray, Calloway Co. (*KW* 92:47, 2016); 20 Jan–7 Feb 2016, female (ph.) ne. of Goshen, Oldham Co (*KW* 92:47/52, 2016); 28 Jan 2016, female (ph.) at Bardstown, Nelson Co. (*KW* 92:47, 2016).

Unaccepted record: four males at Lexington, 2 Jan 1965 (*KW* 41:13, 1965).

SCOTT'S ORIOLE *Icterus parisorum*

Status: Accidental vagrant. Although orioles occasionally appear in the caged bird trade, Kentucky's single report has been considered to be of natural origin.

1) 29 Jan–23 Apr 2007, a female (ph.) at feeders in a yard north of Frankfort, Franklin Co. (Palmer-Ball, *KW* 83:56-57, 2007; *KW* 83:41/60, 2007)

*RED-WINGED BLACKBIRD *Agelaius phoeniceus*

Status: Resident; fairly common to common during summer and migration, locally rare to fairly common during winter. Recorded statewide in a great variety of open to semi-open habitats; most numerous in farmland and wetlands with an abundance of herbaceous cover. Breeding statewide in overgrown fields, meadows, hayfields, and marshy areas. Irregular during winter; rare or absent in many areas, but sometimes numerous in the general vicinity of large blackbird roosts. Generally more widespread and numerous in the western portion of the state during winter.

Maximum counts (numerous literature and eBird reports of multiple tens of thousands): ca. **1,500,000** in the Louisville area during the winter of 1957-58 (*AFN* 13:298, 1959); ca. **600,000** estimated in a large blackbird roost at Bowling Green, winter 1968-69 (*AFN* 23:488, 1969).

*BROWN-HEADED COWBIRD *Molothrus ater*

Status: Resident; fairly common during summer and migration, locally rare to fairly common during winter. Recorded statewide in a great variety of habitats from dissected tracts of mature woodlands and farmland to suburban parks and yards. Peak of abundance occurs from late Mar to late Aug. Breeding statewide except the heavily forested portions of eastern Kentucky. This species is a brood parasite, laying its eggs in the nests of a wide variety of songbirds (Mengel:452-456; *KBBA*: 310; *KW* 90:90, 2014). Irregular in occurrence from late summer through winter; as soon as the breeding season ends, flocks begin to form and overall distribution becomes scattered. The species becomes rare or absent in most areas during the winter, but can be numerous in the general vicinity of large blackbird roosts. Typically seen singly, in pairs, or in small flocks of up to a dozen birds during the breeding season; flocks of several hundred birds are not uncommon during the non-breeding season.

Maximum count: ca. **200,000** estimated at a roost at Bowling Green, Dec 1972 (*KW* 49:12, 1973); ca. **50,000** estimated at a roost at Somerset, Pulaski Co., 4 Jan 1981 (*KW* 57:13, 1981); **6100** on the Elkton CBC, Todd Co., 31 Dec 2014 (R. Stoll, eBird data; *KW* 91:26, 2015); **5000** estimated to be at a blackbird roost in Union Co., 3 Nov 2001 (R. Denton, eBird data).

RUSTY BLACKBIRD *Euphagus carolinus*

Status: Uncommon to locally fairly common transient and winter resident (although has decreased in recent decades). Recorded chiefly west of the Cumberland Plateau; more numerous in western Kentucky but always somewhat locally distributed. Usually encountered in swampy woods and wet fields with pools of standing water, but also occurs along stream and pond margins, in feedlots and in grain stubble fields; occasional at feeding stations during winter. This species is often found segregated from other blackbirds, but it sometimes mixes in with other species in open farmland. The population of this species has been in severe decline for a few decades, resulting in reduced numbers being seen in our region during winter. Usually seen in small to medium-sized flocks of up to a hundred birds.

Maximum counts (many of the highest counts are based on rough percentages of this species in large blackbird roosts and could represent over-estimates): ca. **450,000** estimated at a blackbird roost at Bowling Green, 21 Dec 1967 (*AFN* 22:245, 1968); ca. **200,000** estimated at a blackbird roost at Bowling Green, Dec 1972 (*KW* 49:12, 1973); possibly up to ca. **150,000** estimated at blackbird roosts at Louisville, [no specific data] (*KW* 52:61, 1976); **5000** estimated at a blackbird roost at Somerset, Pulaski Co., 4 Jan 1981 (*KW* 57:13, 1981); **2000** estimated at a blackbird roost at Somerset, Pulaski Co., 16 Dec 1979 (*KW* 56:9, 1981); ca. **1500** on the Louisville CBC, 22 Dec 1985 (*KW* 62:15, 1986); **1400** on the Danville CBC, 20 Dec 1986 (*KW* 63:19, 1987); **1000** estimated at a blackbird roost at Somerset, Pulaski Co., 1 Jan 1986 (*KW* 62:15, 1986); **1000-1500** total at scattered locales in w. Henderson Co., 20 Mar 2005 (*KW* 81:93, 2005); ca. **1000** in s. Jefferson Co., Jan 1990 (*KW* 66:41, 1990); ca. **1000** on the Olmstead CBC, 22 Dec 2012 (*KW* 89: 22/54, 2013); **800-1000** in w. Henderson Co., 14 Mar 2004 (*KW* 80:72, 2004); **700** in s. Warren Co., 4 Dec 2007 (*KW* 84:47, 2008); **620** in w. Hardin Co., 5 Feb 2012 (*KW* 88:52, 2012); **530** on the Hart County CBC, 17 Dec 2011 (*KW* 88:32/52, 2012); at least **500** at Bowling Green, 21 Dec 2010 (*KW* 87:65, 2011); ca. **500** in Hart Co., 18 Feb 2012 (*KW* 88:52, 2012); **500** at the Highland Creek Unit Sloughs WMA, Union Co., 29 Dec 2015 (*KW* 92:47, 2016).

Late spring dates: 20 May 2006, Greenup Co. (*KW* 82:75, 2006); 14 May 2005, Louisville (B. Yandell, eBird data); 12 May 1985, Louisville (*KW* 61:48, 1985); 10 May 1975, Louisville area (*KW* 52:61, 1976).

Early fall dates: 9 Oct 1983, Jefferson Co. (*KW* 60:19, 1984); 9 Oct 2010, Sauerheber Unit (*KW* 87: 23, 2011); 10 Oct 2006, e. Jefferson Co. (*KW* 83:20, 2007); 17 Oct 2000, Warren Co. (*KW* 77:11, 2001); 17 Oct 2013, Minor Clark Hatchery (*KW* 90:17, 2014); 18 Oct 2018, s. Jefferson Co. (B. Palmer-Ball, eBird data); 19 Oct 1985, Ky Dam (*KW* 62:8, 1986); 20 Oct 1973, Bernheim Forest (*KW* 52:61, 1976; B. Monroe, Jr., notes); 20 Oct 2018, Sauerheber Unit (C. Bliznick et al., eBird data).

Unaccepted records: those during fall earlier than the early fall date of 9 Oct given above and including 27 Aug 1926, south-central Kentucky (*KW* 38:22, 1962) and 10 Sep 1977, Louisville (*AB* 32:214, 1978).

BREWER'S BLACKBIRD *Euphagus cyanocephalus*

Status: Rare to locally uncommon transient, extremely rare to rare winter visitant/resident. Currently recorded only west of the Cumberland Plateau. Most frequently encountered in open farmland, especially in feedlots, pastures, and freshly tilled fields; typically segregates from other blackbirds, but occasionally mixes in loosely with other species. Seems to be regular in small numbers in the western third of the state, irregular to only occasional elsewhere in central Kentucky (reports from 34 counties). Many winter reports are considered erroneous, but small numbers have now been documented to have remained throughout the winter at a few locations in south-central and western Kentucky. Usually seen in small flocks of up to a dozen or so birds.

Maximum spring counts: **600** in ne. Hopkins Co., 27 Nov 2018 (*KW* 95:9, 2019); ca. **500** in e. Hopkins Co., 9 Mar 2018 (*KW* 94:84, 2018); at least **350** (perhaps 500) along Frostburg Road, Hopkins Co., 23 Mar 2013 (*KW* 89:81, 2013); **300+** nr. McElroy Lake, Warren Co., 25 Mar 1997 (Roemer, et al., *KW* 73:83, 1997); at least **150** in the Pond Creek Bottoms, Hopkins Co., 5 Apr 2015 (*KW* 91:76, 2015); **100-150** in scattered flocks in southern Warren Co., 31 Mar 1991 (B. Palmer-Ball, eBird data); **110** in Warren Co., 29 Mar 2002 (*KW* 78:53, 2002); **100-150** coming into a roost e. of Morganfield, Union Co., 16 Apr 2012 (*KW* 88:83, 2012); probably more than **100** e. of Morganfield, Union Co., 31 Mar 2011 (*KW* 87:96, 2011); **75-100** nr. Hailwell, Hickman Co., 3 Apr 1990 (*KW* 66: 62, 1990); **85** in the Lower Hickman Bottoms, 27 Mar 2013 (*KW* 89:81, 2013).

Maximum fall/winter counts: **600** in e. Hopkins Co., 27 Nov 2018 (*KW* 95:9, 2019); **80-100** in e. Grayson Co., 10 Jan 2010 (*KW* 86:47, 2010); **54** at Open Pond, Fulton Co., 11 Feb 2002 (R. Denton, eBird data); **53** nr. Oscar, Ballard Co., 20 Nov 2005 (*KW* 82:16, 2006); at least **50** e. of Cadiz, Trigg Co., 22 Nov 2009 (*KW* 86:15, 2010); at least **50** e. of Madisonville, Hopkins Co. (*KW* 87:24, 2011); **40** n. of Oscar, Ballard Co., 21 Dec 2004 (*KW* 81:18/61, 2005); ca. **40** in Hopkins Co., 9 Dec 2007 (*KW* 84:47, 2008); **21** in Ballard Co., 17 Dec 2007 (*KW* 84:18, 2008 [number erroneously published as "2 & 9" therein (should have read "2 & 19")]); **21** in e. Hopkins Co., 13 Dec 2017 (*KW* 94:61, 2018); **19** in Warren Co., 16 Nov 2004 (*KW* 81:16, 2005).

Late spring dates: 3 May 1967, south-central Kentucky (*KW* 45:37, 1969); 26 Apr 1997, Warren Co. (Roemer, et al., *KW* 73:83, 1997); 21 Apr 2000, Sauerheber Unit (*KW* 76:47, 2000); 21 Apr 2007, w. Henderson Co. (*KW* 83:85, 2007).

Early fall dates: 17 Sep 1956, Louisville (Stamm, *KW* 33:41, 1957); 16 Oct 1950, Louisville (Mengel: 449); 18 Oct 1959, Warren Co. (*KW* 38:22, 1962); 22 Oct 2005, Sauerheber Unit (*KW* 82:16, 2006); 24 Oct 2014, Union Co. (*KW* 91:15, 2015); 25 Oct 1982, Jefferson Co. (*KW* 59:18, 1983).

Unaccepted records (after acquiring a great deal of knowledge about the occurrence of this cryptic species in Kentucky, I am hesitant to include a number of reports appearing in the state's ornithological literature; several reports included by Mengel [p. 449] that he notes as unconfirmed are not included herein; I have also omitted a number of winter reports included on CBC lists that are accompanied by no details; some may be correct, but confusion with both Common Grackles and Rusty Blackbirds is probably responsible for many of these undocumented reports): 4 Sep 1949, Henderson Co. (Mengel:449); 3 May 1967, south-central Kentucky (*KW* 45:37, 1969); 12 May 1938, Woodford Co. (Mengel: 449); 20 Dec 1981, (100) Henderson CBC (*KW* 58:9, 1982); 18 Dec 1982, (40) Lexington CBC (*KW* 59:9, 1983); CBC period 1987-1988, West Liberty CBC (*KW* 64:9, 1988); 17 Dec 1988, (300) Lexington CBC (*KW* 65:19, 1989); 26 Apr 1993, Morehead, Rowan Co. (*KW* 69:48, 1993); 20 Feb 1995, (8) Jefferson Co. (*KW* 71:27, 1995); 23/25 Feb 1996, (10-15) Jefferson Co. (*KW* 72:44, 1996); 1 Jan 1998, Sorgho CBC (*KW* 74:17, 1998); 26 Dec 1988, (30) Yelvington CBC (*KW* 75:17, 1999); 2 Jan 1999, (11) Sorgho CBC (*KW* 75:17, 1999); 28 Dec 1999, Glasgow CBC (*KW* 76:17, 2000); 29 Dec 2001, Danville CBC (*KW* 78;14, 2002); 14 Dec 2002, (3) LBL CBC and (20) Richmond CBC (*KW* 79:25/49, 2003); 26 Oct 2011, (30) in LBL, Lyon Co. (eBird data); as well as some additional late spring dates included on historical Big Spring Lists. I also cannot find details of reports listed in the previous edition of this work from Bourbon Co. (D. Coskren, 1975 notes) and Mercer Co. (W. Kemper/F. Loetscher, pers. comm.).

Published error: 63 birds on Sorgho CBC, 1 Jan 2012 (*KW* 88:30, 2012; correction *fide* J. Howard, compiler).

Summary of records by county

Adair ([ph.] *KW* 90:77, 2014)

Allen (*KW* 88:83, 2012; *KW* 89:15, 2013)

Ballard (B. Palmer-Ball, 1996 eBird data; *KW* 80:48, 2004; essentially annual since the mid-2000s)

Barren (*KW* 86:74, 2010)

Boone (*KW* 64:9/13, 1988; *KW* 79:28/49, 2003; *KW* 87:66, 2011; *KW* 89:35/54, 2013)

Boyle (*KW* 57:38, 1981; *KW* 59:9/30, 1983; *KW* 62:15/46, 1986; *KW* 63:19/38, 1987; *KW* 64:9, 1988; *KW* 67:17, 1991)

Calloway (*KW* 85:53, 2009)

Christian (*KW* 92:68, 2016)

Clark (*KW* 62:29, 1986)

Daviess (R. Denton, 2019 eBird data)

Fayette (*KW* 54:30, 1978; *KW* 62:15, 1986; *KW* 86:15, 2010)

Fulton (*KW* 58:54, 1982; *KW* 59:44, 1983; [wintering documented 2001-2002 (C. Sloan, 2001 eBird data; B. Palmer-Ball, 2002 eBird data); essentially annual since the early 2000s)

Grayson (*KW* 58:54, 1982; *KW* 69:36, 1993; [wintering documented 2009-2010] (*KW* 86:19/47/73, 2010; [wintering documented 2010-2011] *KW* 87:36/65-66, 2011; *KW* 88:30/33/52, 2012; *KW* 89: 54, 2013); [wintering documented 2013-2014] (*KW* 90:25/55, 2014)

Hardin (*KW* 84:47, 2008; *KW* 87:66, 2011; *KW* 90:17, 2014)

Hart (*KW* 89:81, 2013)

Henderson (*AB* 32:360, 1978; *KW* 76:47, 2000; *KW* 82:16, 2006; *KW* 83:85, 2007; *KW* 87:24, 2011; *KW* 89:15, 2013; *KW* 91:56, 2015)

Hickman (E. Larson, 1966 eBird data; *KW* 66:62, 1990; *KW* 67:59, 1991; *KW* 90:17, 2014; *KW* 92: 47, 2016)

Hopkins (*KW* 84:47, 2008; *KW* 86:47, 2010; *KW* 87:24, 2011; *KW* 88:52, 2012; *KW* 89:81, 2013; [[wintering documented 2013-2014] *KW* 90:17/55/77, 2014; *KW* 91:5/76, 2015; *KW* 94:84, 2018)

Jefferson (Mengel:449; *KW* 57:59, 1981; *KW* 59:18, 1983; *KW* 60:19/26, 1984; *KW* 65:72, 1989; *KW* 90:77, 2014; *KW* 91:76, 2015; *KW* 93:78, 2017; *KW* 94:61/84, 2018)

Larue (*KW* 88:33/52, 2012)

Logan (*KW* 75:10, 1999; *KW* 89:30/54, 2013; [ph.] *KW* 91:56, 2015; *KW* 92:68, 2016; essentially annual for past 6-8 years)

Lyon (*KW* 83:85, 2007)

Marshall (*KW* 59:44, 1983; *KW* 92:16, 2016)

McLean (*KW* 90:77, 2014; *KW* 91:76, 2015; *KW* 94:61/84, 2018)

Meade (*KW* 67:32, 1991; [ph.] *KW* 94:27/61, 2018; *KW* 95:28, 2019)

Muhlenberg (*KW* 74:18, 1998)

Ohio (*KW* 89:54/81, 2013; *KW* 90:32/55, 2014)

Oldham (Mengel:449; *KW* 59:30, 1983; *KW* 74:11, 1998; *KW* 82:16, 2006)

Simpson (R. Bontrager, 2018 eBird data)

Trigg (*KW* 86:15/47, 2010; *KW* 89:54, 2013)

Union (*KW* 87:24/96, 2011; *KW* 88:83, 2012; *KW* 89:15, 2013; *KW* 90:17, 2014)

Warren (*KW* 59:44, 1983; *KW* 65:72, 1989; *KW* 66:41/62, 1990; essentially annual since the early 1990s)

Wayne (R. Denton, 2002 eBird data; *KW* 90:55, 2014; *KW* 92:47, 2016; R. Bontrager, 2017 eBird data; *KW* 95:29, 2019)

Webster (*KW* 87:66, 2011)

*COMMON GRACKLE *Quiscalus quiscula*

Status: Resident; fairly common to common during summer and migration, locally rare to fairly common during winter. Recorded statewide in a great variety of habitats from mature woodlands and farmland to suburban parks and yards. Breeding statewide, but essentially absent in heavily forested portions of eastern Kentucky (*KBBA*:308-309). Irregular during winter; rare or absent in most areas, but often quite numerous in the vicinity of large blackbird roosts. Typically seen in flocks of several to several dozen birds during the breeding season; often nests in loose colonies (Jones, *KW* 45:1-8, 1969). During fall and winter, it is not unusual to see flocks of thousands of birds in the western part of the state. Data accumulated during the 1960s and 1970s indicated this to be the most numerous nesting bird in Kentucky at the time (Monroe, *KW* 51:43, 1975; BBS data).

Maximum counts: many of **3,000,000** blackbirds at a roost in Pulaski Co., winter 1979-80 (*KW* 56:33, 1980); ca. **1/2 of 5,000,000** in a roost at Bowling Green, winter 1971-72 (Shadowen, *KW* 48:55, 1972); ca. **2,000,000** estimated at a roost at Bowling Green, Dec 1972 (*KW* 49:12, 1973); ca. **1,350,000** estimated to be in a roost at Bowling Green, winter of 1968-69 (*AFN* 23:488, 1969).

*OVENBIRD *Seiurus aurocapilla*

Status: Fairly common transient, locally uncommon to common summer resident, extremely rare during winter. Recorded statewide during migration in a great variety of forested and semi-open habitats including suburban parks and yards where individuals sometimes perish after striking glass windows and doors. Peaks of abundance occur during early May and from mid- to late Sep. Breeding statewide but abundance varies greatly as follows: widespread on the Cumberland Plateau and Mountains; scattered and very local in larger tracts of more mature forest through central Kentucky west to LBL; essentially absent from the Jackson Purchase (*KBBA*:252-253). Breeds in relatively mature woodlands; most numerous in drier forest types of uplands and upper slopes. There are a few reports during winter, including one of a bird that apparently wintered successfully.

Maximum counts: **76** in McCreary Co., 24 Apr 2009 (S. Stedman, eBird data); **74** on Black Mt., Harlan Co., 12 Jun 1980 (eBird data); **71** on Black Mt., Harlan/Letcher cos., 12 Jun 1980 (B. Palmer-Ball, eBird data); **65** at Mammoth Cave, 31 May 2007 (S./J. Kistler, eBird data); **61** in Pulaski Co., 5 Jun 2010 (B. Stedman, eBird data).

Early spring dates: 29 Mar 2017, Mammoth Cave (*KW* 93:78, 2017); 3 Apr 1888, Pulaski Co. (Mengel:421); 4 Apr 2012, Mammoth Cave (*KW* 88:79, 2012); 5 Apr 2009, Pulaski Co. (*KW* 85:75, 2009); 6 Apr 2002, Pulaski Co. (R. Denton, eBird data); 8 Apr 1922, south-central Kentucky (*KW* 38:21, 1962).

Late fall dates: 23 Nov 2018, (ph.) Jefferson Co. (*KW* 95:10, 2019); 11 Nov 2002, (fresh window-kill) Louisville (*KW* 79:15, 2003); 9 Nov 1975, Louisville (*KW* 52:59, 1976); 7 Nov 1984, Pulaski Co. (J. Elmore, eBird data); 6 Nov 1936, Louisville (Mengel:422); 5 Nov 19—, Louisville area (*KW* 52:39,

1961); 27 Oct 1886, Pulaski Co. (Mengel:422); 27 Oct 1966, south-central Kentucky (*KW* 45:37, 1969); 25 Oct 1967, Boyle Co. (eBird data); 25 Oct 2002, Pualski Co. (C. Neeley, eBird data).

Out-of-season records (winter): Dec 1972–15 Jan 1973, Louisville (*KW* 49:13, 1973; *KW* 52:59, 1976); 20-21 Dec 1975, Oldham Co. (*KW* 52:10/59, 1976); 21 Dec 1989, Louisville (*KW* 66:41, 1990); 15 Dec 1990, Louisville (*KW* 67:32, 1991); 19 Mar 1991 [possibly a wintering bird], Louisville (*KW* 67:59, 1991); mid-Nov 1995–23 Feb 1996 (ph.), Kenton Co. (*KW* 72:45, 1996; *KW* 73:29, 1997).

*WORM-EATING WARBLER *Helmitheros vermivorum*

Status: Locally uncommon to fairly common summer resident. Recorded statewide during migration in a variety of forested and semi-open habitats, but generally uncommon as a transient away from nesting areas; most often encountered in mature woodlands. Peak of abundance occurs from late Apr to mid-Jul. Breeding statewide but abundance varies greatly as follows: widespread on the Cumberland Plateau and Mountains, less numerous and more local to the west, being quite local in the Blue Grass and Jackson Purchase (*KBBA*:248-249). Nests primarily in mature forest, most commonly on moist slopes. Contrary to what is sometimes read, this species is seldom observed on the ground; it is most often observed foraging in shrubs and trees at low to mid-story levels, investigating clumps of dead leaves for invertebrate prey, and sometimes creeping along tree branches like a Black-and-white Warbler.

Maximum counts: **47** in McCreary Co., 24 Apr 2009 (S. Stedman, eBird data); **35** at Mammoth Cave, 6 Jun 2009 (S./J. Kistler, eBird data); **30** at Pennyrile State Forest, Chrisitan Co., 26 Apr 2016 (T. Graham, eBird data).

Early spring dates: 5 Apr 2006, Lyon Co. (*KW* 82:73, 2006); 5 Apr 2017, Hopkins Co. (*KW* 93:78, 2017); 6 Apr 1986, Mammoth Cave National Park (*KW* 62:45, 1986); 7 Apr 2012, Pulaski Co. (*KW* 88:79, 2012); 8 Apr 1945, south-central Kentucky (*KW* 38:20, 1962); 8 Apr 2012, Trigg Co. (*KW* 88:79, 2012); 8 Apr 2013, LBL, Lyon Co. (*KW* 89:78, 2013); 9 Apr 2005, McCreary Co. (*KW* 81:92, 2005); 9 Apr 2011, Pulaski Co. (*KW* 87:95, 2011); 9 Apr 2014, Lexington (*KW* 90:75, 2014); 9 Apr 2015, Pulaski Co. (R. Denton, eBird data); 10 Apr 1999, McCreary Co. (R. Denton, eBird data); 10 Apr 2005, Monroe Co. (T. Campbell, eBird data); 10 Apr 2011 at Mammoth Cave and in Jackson Co. (*KW* 87:95, 2011); 11 Apr 2014, Mammoth Cave (*KW* 90:75, 2014); 12 Apr 2010, Edmonson Co. (*KW* 86:72, 2010); 12 Apr 2018, LBL, Lyon Co. (*KW* 94:84, 2018).

Late fall dates: 1 Nov 1945, Ohio River bank opposite Campbell Co. (Mengel:393); 10 Oct 1886, Nelson Co. (Mengel:393); 6 Oct 1957, Louisville area (*KW* 37:37, 1961).

Unaccepted records: 3 Apr 19—, Warren Co. (see Mengel:392).

*LOUISIANA WATERTHRUSH *Parkesia motacilla*

Status: Uncommon to fairly common summer resident. Recorded statewide during migration in a variety of forested and semi-open habitats, but seldom seen as a transient away from nesting areas, especially during fall when the species departs early and is rarely encountered after the end of Jul. The few migrants that are seen in non-breeding areas typically occur along streams and swampy margins in woodlands. Peak of abundance occurs from late Mar to mid-Jul. Breeding statewide; probably most numerous along the streams of eastern and central Kentucky but also widespread along the slow-moving creeks and margins of swamps across the western third of the state.

Maximum counts: **36** along the Nolin River, Edmonson Co., 3 Jul 2006 (R. Denton, eBird data); **26** along Buck Creek, Pulaski Co., 13 Apr 2006 (R. Denton, eBird data).

Early spring dates: 12 Mar 2011, Hart Co. (*KW* 87:95, 2011); 14 Mar 2007, Pulaski Co. (*KW* 83:84, 2007); 15 Mar 2012, in Allen, Calloway, Hart, & Pulaski cos. (*KW* 88:79, 2012); 15 Mar 2016, Bath Co. (*KW* 92:67, 2016); 16 Mar 2006, Calloway Co. (*KW* 82:74, 2006); 16 Mar 2012, Russell Co. (R. Denton, eBird data); 16 Mar 2012, LBL, Trigg Co. (H. Chambers, eBird data); 16 Mar 2016, Calloway and Pulaski cos. (*KW* 92:67, 2016); 17 Mar 2012, Henderson Co. (E. Huber, eBird data); 17 Mar 2016, McCreary Co. (*KW* 92:67, 2016); 18 Mar 1948, Louisville (*KW* 52:59, 1976); 18 Mar 1996, LBL (R. Healy, pers. comm.); 18 Mar 2010, Calloway Co. (*KW* 86:72, 2010); 18 Mar 2017,

LBL, Trigg Co. (*KW* 93:78, 2017); 18 Mar 2018, Marshall Co. (*KW* 94:84, 2018); 19 Mar 1961, south-central Kentucky (*KW* 38:21, 1962).

Late fall dates: 18 Oct 19—, Warren Co. (Mengel: 424); 14 Oct 1918, south-central Kentucky (*KW* 38:21, 1962); 28 Aug 2012, LBL, Trigg Co. (H. Chambers, eBird data).

NORTHERN WATERTHRUSH *Parkesia noveboracensis*

Status: Uncommon to fairly common transient; accidental during summer. Recorded statewide in a variety of forested and semi-open habitats; most often encountered along streams and standing water margins near cover, but sometimes found in dense vegetation well away from water, especially during fall. Typically more numerous in relatively open areas with young trees rather than mature forest. Peaks of abundance occur during late Apr to early May and from late Aug to mid-Sep. This waterthrush typically far outnumbers the previous species in most areas during migration.

Maximum counts: **19** in Henderson Co., 5 May 2007 (J. Meredig, eBird data); **17** in Henderson Co., 2 May 2008 (J. Meredig, eBird data).

Early spring date: 1 Apr 1933, (sp.) Rowan Co. (Mengel:422).

Late spring dates: 1 Jun 1979, Louisville (*KW* 55:58, 1979); 31 May 1971, Jefferson Co. (eBird data, *KW* 52:59, 1976; B. Monroe, Jr., notes).

Early fall dates: 5 Aug 2018, (ph.) Clay Co. (*KW* 95:10, 2019); 7 Aug 2002, Louisville (*KW* 79:15, 2003); 8 Aug 1971 (ba.), Louisville (*AB* 25:865, 1971; B. Monroe, Jr., notes); 12 Aug 2012, Pulaski Co. (*KW* 89:13, 2013).

Late fall dates: 14 Nov 2016, Louisville (*KW* 93:12, 2017); 4 Nov 2003, Jefferson Co. (*KW* 80:14, 2004); 30-31 Oct 2004, Pulaski Co. (*KW* 81:14, 2005); 25 Oct 1975, Louisville (*KW* 52:59, 1976; B. Palmer-Ball, eBird data).

Out-of-season records (summer); 30 Jun 2006, (ba.) at Clarks River NWR, Marshall (*KW* 82:84, 2006); 22 Jul 2015, (ba.) at Shaker Village (*KW* 91:87, 2015).

Unaccepted records (I have doubts about reports of this species prior to the second week of Apr. Assuming the specimen record given above is correct, it is hard to invalidate other reports from the first part of the month, but I feel confident that most are misidentified Louisiana Waterthrushes. My personal early Northern Waterthrush in the state is 12 Apr 2011 in w. Henderson Co. [*KW* 87:95, 2011]. The following records, like a number of additional reports that are in the eBird data set for early Apr, are accompanied by no or insufficient details to rule out Louisiana Waterthrush): 31 Mar 1953, south-central Kentucky (*KW* 38:21, 1962); 28 Mar 1971, nr. Lake Cumberland (*AB* 25:587, 1971); 1 Apr 1983 Ballard Co. (*KW* 59:44, 1983); 3 Apr 2016, Jefferson Co. (eBird data).

^eBACHMAN'S WARBLER *Vermivora bachmanii*

Status: Extinct. Recorded in Kentucky only during the springs of 1905 and 1906 in n. Logan Co. (Embody, *Auk* 24:41-42, 1907; Mengel:396). These records include the collection of five specimens and the location of a nest. The species probably was locally distributed as a breeding bird, occurring in mature forests with thick understory vegetation, particularly giant cane in floodplains. **Federal Status**: Endangered.

*GOLDEN-WINGED WARBLER *Vermivora chrysoptera*

Status: Uncommon transient (seems to have declined in recent years), extremely rare and very locally distributed summer resident. Recorded statewide during migration in a variety of habitats from mature woodlands and woodland borders to overgrown fields and suburban parks. Peaks of abundance occur during early May and Sep. Breeding not well documented; summering has been reported from several locations in the Cumberland Mountains and adjacent areas on the Cumberland Plateau; a 2003-2005 study in southeastern Kentucky detected nesting birds at several scattered sites, primarily on reclaimed surface mines in Bell, Harlan, and Pike cos. (Patton 2007), but the breeding population has been in steep decline and may now be extremely scarce or extirpated (see below). **State Breeding Status**: Endangered.

Maximum counts: **10** at Louisville, 12 May 1948 (Mengel: 394); **10** in Lyon & Marshall cos., 2 May 2014 (*KW* 90:75, 2014); **10** at Mt. Zion, Allen Co., 20 Sep 2014 (*KW* 91:13, 2015); **8** at Louisville, 5 Sep 1991 (B. Palmer-Ball, eBird data); **7** se. of Mt.Zion, Allen Co., mid-Sep 2015 (*KW* 92:13, 2016); at least **6** at Cherokee Park, Louisville, 13 Sep 2013 (*KW* 90:15, 2014); **6** se. of Mt. Zion, Allen Co., 15 Sep 2013 (*KW* 90:15, 2014); **6** at Mammoth Cave 16 Sep 2016 (*KW* 93:13, 2017).

Early spring dates: 11 Apr 1965, south-central Kentucky (*KW* 45:36, 1969); 17 Apr 1960, Louisville area (*KW* 52:57, 1976); 17 Apr 2000, Calloway Co. (M. Todd, eBird data).

Late spring date (away from known or probable breeding areas): 20 May 1948, Louisville area (*KW* 37:37, 1961).

Early fall dates (away from breeding areas): 15 Aug 2012 (*KW* 89:13, 2013); 18 Aug 1991, Louisville (*KW* 68:10, 1992); 19 Aug 1991, Pulaski Co. (R. Denton, eBird data); 23 Aug 1980, Louisville (*KW* 57:23, 1981); 23 Aug 1992, Louisville (*KW* 69:10, 1993); 23 Aug 2009, Jefferson Co. (*KW* 86:13, 2010).

Late fall dates: 15 Oct 2005, Pulaski Co. (*KW* 82:13, 2006); 14 Oct 2017, Mahr Park, Hopkins Co. (*KW* 94:15, 2018); 12 Oct 2017, Jefferson Co. (P. Bell, eBird data); 10 Oct 1986, Louisville (*KW* 63:11, 1987); 8 Oct 1982, Louisville (*KW* 63:10, 1987); 8 Oct 2017, Hart Co. (S./J. Kistler, eBird data).

Vagrant summer record (away from breeding areas): 10-12 Jun 1946, Hopkins Co. (Hancock, *KW* 23:4, 1947).

Note on hybrids: Blue-winged and Golden-winged warblers hybridize, resulting in two regularly encountered forms as well as various backcrosses. The dominant hybrid form between these species, known as the **BREWSTER'S WARBLER**, is a rare transient in the state. In addition, three older summer records exist: 15 Jun 1952, a singing male (sp.) in Laurel Co. (Mengel: 396); 15 Jul 1988, a singing, territorial male in Lawrence Co. (*KW* 64:66, 1988; *KBBA*: 327); and 31 Jul 1991, a female or immature in Laurel Co. (*KBBA*:328). More recently, studies on breeding Golden-winged Warblers in se. Kentucky have detected a number of territorial and nesting Brewster's Warblers and a few Lawrence's Warblers (Patton, et al., *KW* 80:73-75, 2004; *KW* 80:85, 2004; *KW* 81:109, 2005; *KW* 82:83, 2006; *KW* 84:89, 2008; *KW* 86:95, 2010). The recessive cross, known as the **LAWRENCE'S WARBLER**, has been reported at least a couple of dozen times in the state: 22 May 1968, Otter Creek Park, Meade Co. (*KW* 45:55, 1969; A. Stamm, historical archive files); 24 Apr 1972, Louisville (*KW* 52:58, 1976); 6 May 1978, Louisville (Elmore, *KW* 54:54, 1978); 5 May 1984, nr. Falls of Rough, Grayson Co. (K. Clay, notes); 2 Sep 1988, Louisville (*KW* 65:10, 1989); 11 May 1991, Boone Co. (*KW* 69:23, 1993); 9 Jul 1991, Pike Co. (*KBBA*:327-328); 7 May 1993 (ph.), Jefferson Co. (*KW* 69:47, 1993); 7 Sep 1996, Louisville (B. Yandell, eBird data); 17 Sep 1997, Louisville (B. Yandell, eBird data); 4 Jun 2003, Knox Co. (*KW* 79:84, 2003; L. Palmer, pers. comm.); 6 Jun 2003, Pike Co. (*KW* 79:84, 2003; eBird data); 9-10 May 2008, Louisville (*KW* 84:69, 2008); 13 Sep 2011, Louisville (*KW* 88:15, 2012); 30 Apr 2013, Lexington (*KW* 89:78, 2013); 29 May 2013, Bell Co. (Ky. Dept. of Fish and Wildlife data); 30 Aug 2013, Pulaski Co. (*KW* 90:15-16, 2014); 7 Sep 2013, Allen Co. (*KW* 90:16, 2014); 21 Apr 2015, Minor Clark Fish Hatchery (*KW* 91:75, 2015); 1 Jun 2016, Bell Co. (Ky. Dept. of Fish and Wildlife data); 15 May 2018, Whitley Co. (S. Barker/L. Tayor, eBird data); 6 Jun 2018, Harlan Co. (*KW* 94:111, 2018).

Summary of confirmed and probable breeding records by county

Bell (*KW* 54:63, 1978; Patton, et al., *KW* 80:73-75, 2004; five active nests [*KW* 80:85, 2004]; two active nests [*KW* 81:109, 2005]; two active nests [*KW* 82:83, 2006]; *KW* 85:95, 2009; *KW* 86:95, 2010; *KW* 87:116, 2011)

Bell/Harlan (1967-1969, several locations in the Cumberland Mts., along Pine Mt., and in valleys in between [Croft, *KW* 45:74, 1969; R. Harm, 1969 notes; Croft, *KW* 47:24, 1971; 5 Jun 1973 & 4 Jun 1978, (B. Monroe, Jr., & S. McKee, Cumberland Gap BBS data)])

Breathitt (22 Jun 1975, (2) [A.L. Whitt, Pine Ridge BBS route data])

Harlan (Black Mt. [Mengel:394; Croft, *KW* 45:74, 1969; *KBBA*:220; *KW* 87:116, 2011]; 17 Jun 1981, (fledgling being fed) nr. Cumberland [B. Palmer-Ball, eBird data]; Patton, et al., *KW* 80:73-75, 2004; active nest [*KW* 80:85, 2004]; two active nests [*KW* 81:109, 2005]; *KW* 85:95, 2009; *KW* 86:95, 2010; S. Barker/L. Taylor, 2018 eBird data)

Letcher (*KBBA*:220)
McCreary (May 2002 [Stedman, *KW* 79:90-91, 2003; Patton, et al., *KW* 80:73-75, 2004]; *KW* 87:116, 2011)
Pike (6 Jun 1979 [D. Bystrak, Phelps BBS data]; *KBBA*: 220; Patton, et al., *KW* 80:73-75, 2004; *KW* 85:95, 2009; *KW* 86:95, 2010)
Whitley (Patton, et al., *KW* 80:73-75, 2004; active nest [*KW* 80:85, 2004]; two active nests [*KW* 81: 109, 2005]; nine active nests [*KW* 84:89, 2008]; *KW* 86:95, 2010; *KW* 87:116, 2011)

List of additional summer records by county

Wolfe or Breathitt (22 Jun 1975 [Pine Ridge BBS data])
Bell or Harlan (5 Jun 1973 and 4 Jun 1978 [Cumberland Gap BBS data])

*BLUE-WINGED WARBLER *Vermivora cyanoptera*

Status: Uncommon to fairly common transient, locally rare to fairly common summer resident. Recorded statewide during migration in a variety of habitats from mature woodlands and woodland borders to overgrown fields and suburban parks. Peaks of abundance occur from late Apr to early May and from late Aug to mid-Sep. Breeding statewide, but rather scarce across most of central and western Kentucky (*KBBA*:218-219). Most frequently encountered in semi-open, successional habitats; most numerous in moist, brushy or scrubby openings in or near more mature forest.

Maximum counts: **40** at Fishtrap WMA, Pike Co., 15 May 2012 (A. Newman, eBird data); at least **25** at Yatesville Lake WMA, Lawrence Co., 9 May 2012 (B. Palmer-Ball, eBird data); **18** at Tygarts SF, Carter Co., 27 Apr 2013 (R. Denton, eBird data); **17** at Park Lake Mt. NP, Fleming Co., 4 May 2014 (B. Wulker, eBird data); **15** at Beaver Creek Wetlands, Menifee Co., 27 Apr 2014 (B. Wulker, eBird data); **13** at Louisville, 29 Apr 1983 (*KW* 59:43, 1983).

Early spring dates: 27 Mar 1989, Grayson Co. (*KW* 65:71, 1989); 1 Apr 2012, Allen Co. (*KW* 88:79-80, 2012); 2 Apr 2007, LBL, Trigg Co. (*KW* 83:83, 2007); 2 Apr 2012, LBL, Trigg Co. (*KW* 88:80, 2012); 4 Apr 2012, Pulaski Co. (*KW* 88:80, 2012); 6 Apr 1964, Calloway Co. (E. Larson, eBird data); 7 Apr 2006, LBL, Trigg Co. (*KW* 82:73, 2006); 7 Apr 2010, LBL, Trigg Co. (*KW* 86:71, 2010); 7 Apr 2011, Bernheim Forest (*KW* 87:93, 2011); 8 Apr 1948, Hopkins Co. (Hancock, *KW* 24:48, 1948); 8 Apr 2001, Warren Co. (*KW* 77:51, 2001); 8 Apr 2012, Madison Co. (*KW* 88:80, 2012); 9 Apr 1963, south-central Kentucky (*KW* 45:36, 1969); 9 Apr 2001, Mammoth Cave National Park (*KW* 77:51, 2001).

Late fall dates: 16 Oct 2002, Bowling Green (*KW* 79:14, 2003); 14 Oct 1998, Fulton Co. (*KW* 75:7, 1999); 11 Oct 1989, Falls of the Ohio [IN/KY line] (*KW* 66:13, 1990); 10 Oct 1986, Louisville (*KW* 63:11, 1987).

Unaccepted records: 20 Dec 1980, Frankfort CBC (*KW* 57:15, 1981; *AB* 35:542, 1981).

*BLACK-AND-WHITE WARBLER *Mniotilta varia*

Status: Fairly common transient, locally rare to fairly common summer resident; extremely rare during winter. Recorded statewide during migration in a great variety of habitats from mature woodlands and woodland borders to suburban parks and yards. Peaks of abundance occur from late Apr to early May and from late Aug to mid-Sep. Breeding statewide but abundance varies greatly as follows: widespread on wooded slopes and uplands throughout the Cumberland Plateau and Mountains; much more locally distributed in the central part of the state, where the species is fairly numerous in tracts of mature deciduous woodland in the Knobs section of the Blue Grass; and quite scarce throughout the western third, occurring regularly only at Pennyrile Forest and LBL (*KBBA*:242-243). There are a few recent records during early winter, but the species is not known to winter.

Maximum counts: **71** in McCreary Co., 24 Apr 2009 (S. Stedman, eBird data); **48** elsewhere in McCreary Co., 24 Apr 2009 (R. Denton, eBird data).

Early spring dates: 19 Mar 2012, LBL, Trigg Co. (*KW* 88:80, 2012); 20 Mar 2013, LBL, Trigg Co. (*KW* 89:78, 2013); 21 Mar 2012, Madison Co. (*KW* 88:80, 2012); 22 Mar 2003, Wolfe Co. (*KW* 79:73, 2003); 23 Mar 2002, Fayette Co. (J./P. Bell, pers. comm.; eBird data); 23 Mar 2011, LBL,

Lyon Co. (*KW* 87:94, 2011); 24 Mar 1998, Pilot Knob State Nature Preserve, Powell Co. (M. Hines/ A. Covert, pers. comm.); 25 Mar 2012, Cumberland Gap NHP, Bell Co. (A. Newman, eBird data); 26 Mar 1949, south-central Kentucky (*KW* 38:19, 1962); 26 Mar 2000, McCreary Co. (R. Denton, et al., eBird data); 26 Mar 2012, Pulaski Co. (R. Denton, eBird data).

Late fall dates: 4 Dec 2017, (ph.) at Alexandria, Campbell, Co. (*KW* 94:61, 2018); 26 Nov 2001, (vt.) Warren Co. (*NAB* 56:59, 2002; eBird data); 6 Nov 2017, Pulaski Co. (*KW* 94:15, 2018); 3 Nov 1978, Jefferson Co. (*KW* 55:17, 1979); 22 Oct 1963, Louisville area (*KW* 52:57, 1976); 22 Oct 1967, Boyle Co. (Kemper, *KW* 44:19, 1968); 22 Oct 2010, Lexington (C./G. Tremoulet, eBird data).

Out-of-season records (winter): 20 Dec 2014, Raven Run Sanctuary, Fayette Co. (*KW* 91:31/56, 2015); 9 Jan 2016, (ph.) Raven Run Sanctuary, Fayette Co. (*KW* 92:45/52, 2016); 16 Dec 2018, (ph.) e. Jefferson Co. (*KW* 95:32/50, 2019).

*PROTHONOTARY WARBLER *Protonotaria citrea*

Status: Locally uncommon to fairly common summer resident. Recorded chiefly west of the Cumberland Plateau but a few have been found on reservoirs in eastern Kentucky (see below). Encountered in a variety of forested habitats during migration, but rare to uncommon as a transient away from nesting areas; usually encountered in woodlands near water. Peak of abundance occurs from late Apr to early Aug. This species is a widespread and conspicuous breeding bird of wetland forests and riparian corridors throughout the western third of the state, especially in the Jackson Purchase; somewhat local in central Kentucky east to the edge of the Cumberland Plateau (*KBBA*:246-247).

Maximum counts: **106** along the Barren River and Long Creek, e. Allen Co., 15 May 2015 (*KW* 91:75, 2015); **46** in w. Henderson Co., 23 May 2018 (*KW* 94:84, 2018); **44** in w. Henderson Co., 7 Jun 2017 (J. Meredig, eBird data); **38** in w. Henderson Co., 12 May 2015 (J. Meredig, eBird data); **37** at Lake Cumberland WMA, Pulaski Co., 2 Aug 2003 (*KW* 80:14, 2004); **30** at LBL. 22 Apr 1995 (*KW* 71:44, 1995); loose group of **30** at Blood River, 4 Aug 2006 (*KW* 83:19, 2007).

Early spring dates: 30 Mar 1995, Logan Co. (eBird data); 1 Apr 1961, south-central Kentucky (*KW* 38:19, 1962); 2 Apr 2009, Calloway and Muhlenberg cos., (*KW* 85:75, 2009).

Late fall dates: 12 Nov 2011, Henderson Co. (*KW* 88:16, 2012); 9 Oct 2008, Sauerheber Unit (*KW* 85:20, 2009); 8 Oct 2011, Madison Co. (*KW* 88:16, 2012); 7 Oct 1967, Louisville area (*KW* 52:57, 1976).

Easternmost records by county

Carter (D. Lang, et al., 2011 eBird data)
Johnson (*KW* 69:58, 1993)
Lawrence (S. Freidhof, 2000/2001 notes)
Lewis (*KW* 83:106, 2007)
Perry (G. Bolton, 2010 eBird data).

*SWAINSON'S WARBLER *Limnothlypis swainsonii*

Status: Rare to locally uncommon summer resident; nearly unrecorded as a transient. Occurrence not well documented; recorded chiefly as a summer bird from scattered localities throughout southern and eastern Kentucky as follows: in bottomland forests of the Jackson Purchase, especially where an abundance of cane occurs in the understory; occasionally at scattered localities in bottomland forests of south-central Kentucky where they have been found in cane or other dense understory vegetation (Christian, Edmonson, Hopkins and Warren cos.); and from scattered localities in eastern and southeastern Kentucky in moist, rhododendron-filled ravines from Elliott, Lee, Menifee and Powell cos., south to McCreary Co. on the southern Cumberland Plateau and Bell, Harlan and Letcher cos. in the Cumberland Mountains. Peak of abundance occurs from late Apr to mid-Jul. Although the species is present throughout the summer, there are only a few reports documenting evidence of nesting (see below). Reports of birds other than at presumed nesting areas are extremely rare, but a few sight records and one tower-killed specimen exist.

Maximum counts: **13** total at scattered sites in McCreary Co., 2 Jun 2011 (S. Stedman, eBird data); **9** in sw McCreary Co., 28 May 2018 (*KW* 94:85, 2018); **8** at and nr. the Little Lick Rec. Area, Pulaski Co., 17 Jun 2015 (*KW* 91:87, 2015); **7** in Powell/Wolfe cos., 7 May 2012 (*KW* 88:80, 2012); "up to **6** or more" singing along the Bee Rock Trail, DBNF, Pulaski Co., 3 Jun 2007 (*KW* 83:106, 2007 [location erroneously published as Laurel Co. therein; *fide* T. Houghton, eBird data]); **6** at the Little Lick Rec Area, Pulaski Co., 19 Jun 2004 (R. Denton, eBird data); **6** in the DBNF, Wolfe Co., 14 Jun 2009 (D. Slager, eBird data).

Early spring dates: 10 Apr 2010, Powell Co. (*KW* 86:72, 2010); 15 Apr 1981, Calloway Co. (*KW* 57:58, 1981); 16 Apr 2012, Laurel Co. (*KW* 88:80, 2012); 18 Apr 2015, Wolfe Co. (*KW* 91:75, 2015); 17 Apr 2008, McCreary Co. (*KW* 84:70, 2008 [date erroneously published as 19 Apr therein; *fide* D. Crotser, eBird data]); 17 Apr 2017, Wolfe Co. (*KW* 93:79, 2017); 18 Apr 2018, Blood River (*KW* 94:85, 2018); 19 Apr 2019, McCreary Co. (R. Bontrager, eBird data); 20 Apr 1977, Wolfe Co. (D. Coskren, notes; *fide* A. Stamm, historical archive files); 20 Apr 2017, Wolfe Co. (M. Harvey, eBird data); 21 Apr 2012, Wolfe Co. (*KW* 88:80, 2012); 23 Apr 2006, Wolfe Co. (*KW* 82:74, 2006); 23 Apr 2016, (5) Wolfe Co. (*KW* 92:67, 2016).

Late fall dates: 11 Oct 1990, tower kill in Adair Co. (Elmore and Palmer-Ball, *KW* 67:69-70, 1991); 12 Sep 2009, McCreary Co. (*KW* 86:14, 2010); 4 Sep 2017, Blood River (*KW* 94:15, 2018); 14 Aug 1958, Mammoth Cave (Wilson, *KW* 34:58, 1958); 14 Aug 2003, Pulaski Co. (*KW* 80:14, 2004); 2 Aug 2000, Pulaski Co. (*KW* 77:10, 2001); 2 Aug 2006, (ba.) in Powell Co. (*KW* 83:19, 2007); 27 Jul 2002, Pulaski Co. (R. Denton, eBird data); 26 Jul 2003, (3) Laurel Co. (*KW* 79:85, 2003).

Vagrant records (away from likely breeding areas): 27 Jun 1937, Bernheim Forest, Bullitt Co. (Carpenter, *KW* 13:32, 1937); 11 Oct 1990, tower kill in Adair Co. (Elmore and Palmer-Ball, *KW* 67:69-70, 1991); 6 May 2011, Madison Co. (*KW* 87:95, 2011); 2 Jun 2017, Green Co. (*KW* 93:102, 2017); 4 May 2018, (ph.) Lexington (*KW* 94:85, 2018); 12 May 2018, below Wolf Creek Dam, Russell Co. (*KW* 94:85, 2018).

Unaccepted records: 9 Oct 1981, Louisville (*KW* 58:18, 1982); 12 Sep 2011, (2) Bell Co. (*KW* 88:16, 2012).

Published error: the late fall date of 1 Sep [1938] published by Monroe (*KW* 45:53, 1969) likely pertains to Illinois (*fide* Mengel:391).

Summary of confirmed breeding records by county

Letcher (8 Jun 2001, ad. carrying food at Bad Branch SNP (B. Palmer-Ball, eBird data)

Powell (5 Jun 1993, ad. carrying food in the Red River Gorge (*KW* 69:58, 1993)

Pulaski (2 Aug 2000, ads. carrying food [*KW* 77:10, 2001]; 27 Jul 2002, ads. carrying food [*KW* 78:66, 2002]; 8 Jul 2006, ads. carrying food [R. Denton, eBird data])

Wolfe (27 Jun 1988, a family group observed in the Red River Gorge vicinity [*KBBA*:250; *KW* 64:66, 1988 (date published incorrectly as Jul in the latter; *fide* T. Towles, notes)])

Wolfe (7 Jul 1998, begging juv. in the Red River Gorge [F. Renfrow, notes])

TENNESSEE WARBLER *Leiothlypis peregrina*

Status: Fairly common to common transient, extremely rare during winter. A widespread and numerous transient across most of the state during both spring and fall, although somewhat less numerous across eastern Kentucky. Peaks of abundance occur during early May and from mid-Sep to mid-Oct. Encountered in a great variety of habitats from mature woodlands and woodland borders to weedy fields and suburban parks and yards. The species has been recorded three times during winter. Generally encountered singly or in small groups of up to a dozen birds, but occasionally seen in flocks of up to several dozen birds during fall.

Maximum counts: **100-150** at LBL, Lyon Co. 6 May 2003 (*KW* 79:72, 2003); **100+** at LBL, Lyon Co., 30 Apr 2004 (*KW* 80:71, 2004); **75** at Audubon SP, Henderson Co., 8 May 2011 (J. Meredig, eBird data); **75+** at Mammoth Cave NP, 15 Sep 2002 (*KW* 79:14, 2003).

Early spring dates: 10 Apr 1965, south-central Kentucky (*KW* 45:36, 1969); 10 Apr 2011, two locations in Bath Co (B. Wulker, eBird data); 13 Apr 1991, LBL (*KW* 67:58, 1991); 13 Apr 2006, LBL, Lyon Co. (J. Pollpeter, eBird data).

Late spring dates: 14 Jun 1981, Louisville (B. Palmer-Ball, eBird data); 9 Jun 1980, Lexington (*KW* 56:81, 1980); 6 Jun 2009, Mammoth Cave NP (S. Kistler, eBird data); 4 Jun 1994, Louisville (*KW* 70:55, 1994).

Early fall dates: 5 Aug 2007, Pulaski Co. (*KW* 84:14 2008); 7 Aug 2005, Pulaski Co. (C. Neeley, eBird data); 16 Aug 1998, Louisville (B. Yandell, eBird data); 17 Aug 1975, Louisville area (*KW* 52: 58, 1976); 17 Aug 1977, Louisville (A. Stamm, notes); 18 Aug 1991, Louisville (*KW* 68:10, 1992); 18 Aug 1998, Pulaski Co. (R. Denton, eBird data); 18 Aug 2006, Madison Co. (*KW* 83:18, 2007).

Late fall dates: 8 Dec 2017, Pulaski Co. (R. Denton, eBird data); Dec 2003, Owensboro (*KW* 80:47, 2004); 28 Nov 2008, (ph.) Taylor Co. (*KW* 85:19, 2009); 17 Nov 2018, Ky Dam Village (*KW* 95:10, 2019); 14 Nov 2014, Lexington (*KW* 91:13, 2015); 12 Nov 1989, Grayson Co. (*KW* 66:13, 1990); 11 Nov 2000, Letcher Co. (*KW* 77:9, 2001); 9 Nov 2002, Louisville (*KW* 79:14, 2003); 8 Nov 1965/1975, Louisville area (*KW* 52:58, 1976).

Out-of-season records (winter): 2-5 Jan 1977, Louisville (B. Palmer-Ball, eBird data); 15 Dec 1979 and 27 Jan 1980, Louisville (B. Palmer-Ball, eBird data); 2 Feb 2013, (ph.) at Louisville (*KW* 89: 53/60, 2013).

ORANGE-CROWNED WARBLER *Leiothlypis celata*

Status: Transient (rare during spring, rare to uncommon during fall); extremely rare during winter. Occurrence not well documented; probably occurs statewide but likely increasing in abundance as one proceeds from east to west. This species occurs in a variety of semi-open habitats; most often found in weedy or brushy areas, but sometimes in woodlands, especially during spring. Peaks of abundance occur during late Apr and from mid-Oct to early Nov. In recent years, there has been a remarkable increase in the number of sightings, particularly during winter. Prior to the winter of 2015-2016, there were fewer than 20 reports during that season, but the past few years have yielded at least ten reports each winter. In addition, the species has shown up earlier in spring and lingered later in fall than previously documented. In fact, the presence of extremely early spring birds and lingering fall birds now clouds the normal dates of arrival and departure of spring and fall migrants, respectively.

Maximum count: at least **8** in LBL, Lyon/Trigg cos., 24 Apr 2013 (*KW* 89:78, 2013).

Early spring dates (reports prior to second week of Apr could be wintering individuals): 20 Mar 2011, Madison Co. (*KW* 87:94, 2011); 21 Mar 2012 (2), LBL, Trigg Co. (*KW* 88:80, 2012); 1 Apr 2012, Henderson Co. (*KW* 88:80, 2012); 1 Apr 2016, w. Fulton Co. (*KW* 92:67, 2016); 2 Apr 2002, Louisville (J./P. Bell, notes); 5 Apr 2014, Jefferson Co. (*KW* 90:75, 2014); 7 Apr 1958, south-central Kentucky (*KW* 38:20, 1962); 8 Apr 2018, Jefferson Co. (*KW* 94:85, 2018); 10 Apr 1981, Calloway Co. (*KW* 57:58-59, 1981).

Late spring dates: 19 May 1960, south-central Kentucky (*KW* 38:20, 1962); 19 May 19—, Louisville (Mengel: 397); 17 May 2005, Lyon Co. (*KW* 81:91, 2005).

Early fall dates: 30 Aug 2006, Jefferson Co. (*KW* 83:18, 2007); 5 Sep 2003, Mammoth Cave National Park, Barren Co. (*KW* 80:13, 2004); 8 Sep 1990, Louisville (*KW* 67:8, 1991); 8 Sep 2007, Bernheim Forest (*KW* 84:14 2008); 9 Sep 2011, Pulaski Co. (*KW* 88:16, 2012); 10 Sep 2006, Trigg Co. (*KW* 83:18, 2007); 11 Sep 1958, south-central Kentucky (*KW* 38:20, 1962); 11 Sep 2005, Jefferson Co. (*KW* 82:14, 2006); 13 Sep 2012, Mammoth Cave (*KW* 89:13, 2013); 14 Sep 1995, Louisville (B. Palmer-Ball, eBird data).

Late fall dates (has become impossible to distinguish between late migrants and wintering birds in recent years; birds listed here were not subsequently reported at listed locations): 8 Dec 2015, Jefferson Co. (*KW* 92:45, 2016); 8 Dec 2016, Ohio Co. (*KW* 93:52, 2017); 7 Dec 2017, McCracken Co. (*KW* 94:61, 2018); 5 Dec 1998, two different locations at Louisville (*KW* 75:27, 1999; B. Yandell, eBird data); 28 Nov 2017, Louisville (*KW* 94:15, 2018); 27 Nov 2016, (ph.) Grant Co. (*KW* 93: 13, 2017); 26 Nov 2017, Jefferson Co. (P. Bell, eBird data); 19 Nov 1995, Louisville (B. Yandell, eBird data); 19 Nov 2003, (ph.) Warren Co. (*KW* 80:13, 2004); 17 Nov 2016, Lexington (*KW* 93:13, 2017); 14 Nov 2017, Warren Co. (A. Hulsey, eBird data); 11 Nov 2011, Henderson Co. (*KW* 88:16, 2012).

Out-of-season records (winter): 7 Feb 1971, Lexington (*AB* 25:587, 1971); 4 Jan 1972, Lexington (*AB* 26:612, 1972); 19 Dec 1981, LBL CBC (*KW* 58:3, 1982); 3 Jan–10 Mar 1988, one visiting a sugar water feeder at Jeffersontown, Jefferson Co. (*KW* 64:30, 1988; Palmer-Ball, *KW* 65:24-27, 1989); 1 Jan 1997, Muhlenberg Co. (*KW* 73:14, 1997); 11 Jan 1998, Louisville (M. Autin, pers. comm.); 14 Feb 1998, Louisville (B. Yandell, eBird data); 19 Dec 1999, Louisville (*KW* 76:13/32, 2000; date erroneously published as 21 Dec on latter page no.); 9 Mar 2002, Long Point Unit (B.

Palmer-Ball, eBird data); 16 Dec 2002, Pulaski Co. (*KW* 79:48, 2003); 16 Mar 2005, Hickman Co. (*KW* 81:91, 2005); 2+ Jan 2007, ne. Hart Co. (*KW* 83:51, 2007); 1-4 Jan 2009, Lexington (J. Pulliam, eBird data); 30 Dec 2009, Logan Co. (*KW* 86:18/46, 2010); 31 Jan 2010, Jefferson Co. (*KW* 86:46, 2010); early Jan–late Feb 2012, one coming to feeders in a yard in Boone Co. (*KW* 88:49, 2012); 6 Feb 2012, Warren Co. (*KW* 88:49, 2012); mid-Dec 2012–Feb 2013, likely the same bird returning to yard in Boone Co. (*KW* 89:35/53, 2013); 28 Jan 2014, (ph.) at Murray, Calloway Co. (*KW* 90:54/60, 2014); 11 Dec 2015, Louisville (*KW* 92:45, 2016); 15 Dec 2015/30 Jan & 1 Apr 2016, Goshen, Oldham Co. (*KW* 92:45/67, 2016); 17 Dec 2015, Fish Pond, Fulton Co. (*KW* 92:45, 2016); 19 Dec 2015, (4) in w. Fulton Co. (*KW* 92:45, 2016); 20 Dec 2015, Louisville (*KW* 92:28/45, 2016); 22 Dec 2015, Ballard WMA (*KW* 92:18/28/45, 2016); 22 Dec 2015, 2 (ph.) nr. Elkton, Todd Co. (*KW* 92:28, 2016); 30 Jan 2016, Jefferson Co. (*KW* 92:45, 2016); 3-15 Feb 2016, Frankfort (*KW* 92:45, 2016); 6 Mar 2016, Muhlenberg Co. (*KW* 92:67, 2016); mid-Dec 2016–late Feb 2017, at least 13 reports from Ballard (3), Fayette, Fulton (2), Henderson, Jefferson (2), Marshall, McCracken, Pulaski, and Warren cos. (*KW* 93:52/56/79, 2017); 5 Mar 2017, Goshen, Oldham Co. (B. Davis, eBird data); 8 Mar 2017, (ph.) Louisville (B. Woerner/D. Stewart, eBird data); 16 Dec 2017, Warren Co. (*KW* 94:61, 2018); 21 Dec 2017, (2) on the Barren River Lake CBC (*KW* 94:24, 2018); 30 Dec 2017, Allen Co. (*KW* 94:24, 2018); 30 Dec 2017, (ph.) nr. Austin, Barren Co. (R./L. Bontrager, eBird data); 8 Jan 2018, Ken Unit (*KW* 94:61, 2018); late winter 2018, single birds visited feeders in yards at Louisville and at Murray, Calloway Co. (*KW* 94:61/85, 2018); 8/18 Feb 2018, Louisville (E. Hope, eBird data); 9 Feb 2018, Lexington (C. Tremoulet, eBird data); 6/16 Mar 2018, Warren Co. (*KW* 94:85, 2018); 4 Jan 2019, Pulaski Co. (*KW* 95:28, 2019; R. Denton, eBird data); 16 Jan 2019, (ph.) Hickman, Fulton Co. (C. Bliznick et al., eBird data).

NASHVILLE WARBLER *Leiothlypis ruficapilla*

Status: Fairly common transient, extremely rare during winter. Recorded statewide in a great variety of habitats from mature woodlands and woodland borders to weedy fields and suburban parks and yards. Peaks of abundance occur from late Apr to early May and from late Sep to mid-Oct. There are three winter records. Occasionally seen in small flocks of several individuals, especially during fall.

Maximum counts: **20** at the Lexington Cemetery, 29 Apr 2012 (S. Bonner, eBird data); **15** at Audubon SP, Henderson Co., 30 Apr 2008 (J. Meredig, eBird data).

Early spring dates: 7 Apr 2013, Calloway Co. (*KW* 89:79, 2013); 8 Apr 2012, Trigg Co. (*KW* 88:80, 2012); 9 Apr 2000, Henderson (B. Palmer-Ball, eBird data); 9 Apr 2007, Jefferson Co. (*KW* 83:84, 2007); 10 Apr 2005, Calloway Co. (*KW* 81:91, 2005); 11 Apr 1981, Danville (*KW* 57:59, 1981); 11 Apr 2019, Hopkins Co. (D. Stricklin, eBird data); 12 Apr 2014, Allen Co. (*KW* 90:75, 2014); 13 Apr 1991, LBL (*KW* 67:58, 1991); 13 Apr 2001, Louisville (B. Yandell, eBird data); 13 Apr 2017, Trigg Co. (*KW* 93:79, 2017).

Late spring dates: 1 Jun 1952, Oldham Co. (Stamm, et al., *KW* 29:21-28, 1953); 25 May 2008, Jefferson Co. (Beckham Bird Club, eBird data); 25 May 2014, LBL, Trigg Co. (I. Ferrell, eBird data); 25 May 2016, Audubon SP, Henderson Co. (J. Meredig, eBird data).

Early fall dates: 9 Aug 2015, Jefferson Co. (*KW* 92:14, 2016); 15 Aug 1992, Louisville (*KW* 69:10, 1993); 15 Aug 2008, Jefferson Co. (*KW* 85:19, 2009); 18 Aug 2012, Louisville (*KW* 89:13, 2013); 19 Aug 2006, Bernheim Forest (Beckham Bird Club, eBird data); 20 Aug 1985, Falls of the Ohio (*KW* 62:8, 1986); 20 Aug 2001, Louisville (*NAB* 56:59, 2002); 21 Aug 2010, Louisville (*KW* 87:22, 2011); 23 Aug 2005, Louisville (*KW* 82:14, 2006); 24 Aug 1986, Louisville (*KW* 63:11, 1987).

Late fall dates: last week of Nov 2006, Jefferson Co. (*KW* 83:18, 2007); 12 Nov 2014, Muhlenberg Co. (*KW* 91:13, 2015); 17 Nov 1986, Berea (*KW* 63:11, 1987); 11 Nov 2000, Louisville (B. Yandell, eBird data); 7 Nov 2017, (ph.) Louisville (*KW* 94:15, 2018); 6 Nov 1991, Louisville (*KW* 68:10, 1992).

Out-of-season records (winter): 1-5 Jan 1977, Louisville (Palmer-Ball, *KW* 56:38, 1980; B. Palmer-Ball, eBird data); 27 Dec 2008, Boone Co. (*KW* 85:36/52, 2009); 16 Dec 2017, Louisville (*KW* 94:31, 2018; J. Souder, notes).

Unaccepted record: 14 Aug 1981, Lexington (eBird data).

CONNECTICUT WARBLER *Oporornis agilis*

Status: Transient (rare during spring, extremely rare during fall). Occurrence relatively poorly documented but probably statewide; likely to be less numerous westward, especially during fall when there are no well-documented records from the western third of the state. Relatively secretive and hard to observe, occurring in a variety of forested and semi-open habitats with some thick cover in the shrub layer. Most often encountered in the dense understory of successional thickets and mature woodlands where the species forages on the ground like an Ovenbird. Peaks of abundance occur during mid-May and from mid-Sep to early Oct. During fall the vast majority of individuals migrate to the east of the Appalachian Mountains, but the species is reported annually, mostly from the more heavily birded central part of the state.

Maximum count: **8** in ne. Jefferson Co., 11 May 1995 (B. Palmer-Ball, eBird data).

Early spring dates: 2 May 2012, Louisville (*KW* 88:80, 2012); 7 May 2018, Freeman Lake (*KW* 94: 86, 2018); 7 May 2018, (ph.) Cherokee Park, Louisville (*KW* 94:86, 2018); 9 May 2002, Warren Co. (R. Denton, eBird data).

Late spring dates: 4 Jun 1949, Louisville (*KW* 52:59, 1976); 3 Jun 2006, Fulton Co. (*KW* 82:84, 2006); 2 Jun 2012, Wayne Co. (eBird data).

Early fall dates: 23 Aug 2015, Louisville (*KW* 92:14, 2016); 28 Aug 2012, Louisville (*KW* 89:14, 2013); 2 Sep 2006, Boone Co. (*KW* 83:19, 2007); 5 Sep 2010, Boone Co. (*KW* 87:22, 2011); 5 Sep 2015, Hart Co. (*KW* 92:14, 2016); 6 Sep 1979, Louisville (*KW* 56:17, 1980); 6 Sep 1998, Warren Co. (*KW* 75:7, 1999); 7 Sep 2010, Jefferson Co. (*KW* 87:22, 2011).

Late fall dates: 16 Oct 2005, Mammoth Cave (*KW* 82:14, 2006); 14 Oct 1984, Fort Knox area (*KW* 61:18, 1985).

Unaccepted records: those in spring earlier than the early spring date of 2 May given above and including 19 Apr 1964, south-central Kentucky (*KW* 45:37, 1969); 24 Apr 19—, Rowan Co. (Barbour, *KW* 28:26, 1952); 25 Apr 1965, Louisville area (*KW* 52:59, 1976); 27 Apr 1958, south-central Kentucky (*KW* 38:21, 1962); and 28 Apr 19—, Louisville (Mengel:426). Also, 6 Oct 1983, Russell Co. (W. Zwartjes, eBird data [no details available]).

MOURNING WARBLER *Geothlypis philadelphia*

Status: Rare to uncommon transient; extremely rare during early winter. Recorded statewide in a variety of semi-open habitats with brushy, dense cover; most numerous in successional thickets and along brushy woodland borders where the species forages low to the ground and can be quite difficult to observe. Peaks of abundance occur during mid-May and from late Aug to mid-Sep. There are two Dec records of presumed lingering fall migrants.

Maximum count: **7** in Jefferson Co., 20 May 1983 (*KW* 59:44, 1983); **5** se. of Mt. Zion, Allen Co., 29 Aug 2012 (KW 89:14, 2013).

Early spring dates: 25 Apr 1953, south-central Kentucky (*KW* 38:21, 1962); 30 Apr 2014, Louisville (*KW* 90:75, 2014); 3 May 19—, Louisville area (Mengel:426); 3 May 1990, Calloway Co. (*KW* 66: 60, 1990); 3 May 2014, Louisville (*KW* 90:75, 2014).

Late spring dates: 12 Jun 1980, two widely separated singing males along crest of Black Mt., Harlan/Letcher cos. (considered herein to be lingering spring migrants) (B. Palmer-Ball et al., eBird data); 3 Jun 1959, Warren Co. (Wilson, *KW* 35:54, 1959); 31 May 1979, Jefferson Co. (B. Palmer-Ball, eBird data).

Early fall dates: 6 Aug 2014, (ba./ph.) at Shaker Village (*KW* 91:14, 2015); 22 Aug 1998, Louisville (B. Yandell, eBird data); 22 Aug 1999, Louisville (J. Elmore, notes); 22 Aug 2012, Louisville (*KW* 89:14, 2013); 23 Aug 2015, Louisville (*KW* 92:14, 2016); 24 Aug 1977, Louisville (J. Elmore, notes); 24 Aug 2015, Frankfort (*KW* 91:14, 2015); 25 Aug 1959, Louisville area (*KW* 52:60, 1976).

Late fall dates: 23 Oct 1970, Oldham Co. (*AB* 25:66, 1971); 18 Oct 2009, Berea College Forest, Madison Co. (R. Bates/R. Foster, eBird data); 7 Oct 2012 (ph.), Kenton Co. (R. Crice, eBird data); 4 Oct 1981, (sp.) Pulaski Co. (eBird data).

Out-of-season records (early winter): 9 Dec 2003, Warren Co. (*KW* 80:47, 2004); 17 Dec 2005, Marshall Co. (*KW* 82:18/49, 2006).

Unaccepted record: 16 Apr 1977, LBL (*AB* 31:1009, 1977).

*KENTUCKY WARBLER *Geothlypis formosa*

Status: Uncommon to fairly common summer resident. Recorded statewide during migration in a variety of forested habitats, but generally uncommon as a transient away from nesting areas, especially during fall when the species departs early and is seldom observed. Peak of abundance occurs from early May to mid-Jul. Breeding statewide in mature woodlands with some thick understory cover in the shrub layer; generally more numerous in moister forest types, least widespread in the Bluegrass and Highland Rim (*KBBA*:256-257). Does not require particularly large blocks of forest habitat, so it is a bit more widespread than some other forest breeding warblers.

Maximum counts: **36** at Mammoth Cave, 31 May 2007 (S. Kistler, eBird data); **31** at Mammoth Cave, 5 Jun 2009 (S. Kistler, eBird data).

Early spring dates: 3 Apr 1988, Madison Co. (*KW* 64:49, 1988); 4 Apr 1885, Nelson Co. (Mengel: 424); 10 Apr 2016, Berea College Forest, Madison Co. (*KW* 92:67, 2016).

Late fall dates (none other than the last [5 Oct] have any supporting documentation): 18 Nov 1965, south-central Kentucky (*KW* 45:37, 1969); 18/31 Oct 1986, Barren Co. (*KW* 63:11, 1987 [dates erroneously published as 16 and 31 Oct therein; *fide* A. Stamm, historical archive files]); 12 Oct 1961, south-central Kentucky (*KW* 38:21, 1962); 7 Oct 1975, Louisville area (*KW* 52:59, 1976); 6 Oct 1973, Louisville, (A. Stamm, historical archive files); 5 Oct 2013, Berea College Forest, Madison Co. (*KW* 90:16, 2014).

Published error: the early spring date of 4 Mar published by Monroe (*KW* 45:54, 1969) should have read 4 Apr (*fide* A. Stamm, historical archive files).

*COMMON YELLOWTHROAT *Geothlypis trichas*

Status: Fairly common to common transient and summer resident, extremely rare during winter. Recorded statewide during migration in a variety of brushy or weedy, semi-open to open habitats. Peaks of abundance occur from late Apr to early May and during Oct. Breeding widespread across the state except the heavily forested portions of eastern Kentucky; most numerous in overgrown fields, along fencerows and the margins of wetlands, woodland borders, and other habitats where an abundance of grassy vegetation, weeds, and brush occur. Prior to the early 2000s, there were only a few records of birds lingering into winter, but during recent years the species has been reported annually during early winter (mostly during the CBC period). Despite the increase in reports, wintering has not been documented.

Maximum counts: **100** in w. Henderson Co., 9 May 2013 (J. Meredig, eBird data); **87** in Pulaski Co., 8 May 2004 (R. Denton, eBird data); **83** in Henderson Co., 12 May 2015 (J. Meredig, eBird data).

Early spring dates (reports prior to the first week of Apr may be wintering indivdiuals): 23 Mar 2012 (ph.), Sauerheber Unit (*KW* 88:80, 2012); 26 Mar 2017, Sauerheber Unit (*KW* 93:79, 2017); 30 Mar 2013, Sauerheber Unit (*KW* 89:79, 2013); 3 Apr 19—, Louisville area (Mengel:427); 3 Apr 2012, Henderson Co. (*KW* 88:80, 2012).

Late fall dates (only one record has been documented after early Jan): 6 Jan 2019, (ph.) Sauerheber Unit (*KW* 95:50, 2019); 3 Jan 1988, Morgan Co. (*KW* 64:14, 1988); 2 Jan 2008 (different location from 30 Dec 2007), Ohio Co. (*KW* 84:20/46, 2008); 2 Jan 2010, Muhlenberg Co. (*KW* 86: 19/46, 2010); 2 Jan 2017, Muhlenberg Co. (*KW* 93: 18/52, 2017); 1 Jan 1996, Nelson Co. (B. Palmer-Ball, eBird data); 31 Dec 2011, Pulaski Co. (*KW* 88:29/49, 2012); 30 Dec 2007, Ohio Co. (*KW* 84:20/46, 2008); 27 Dec 2014, Meade Co. (*KW* 91: 28/56, 2015); 26 Dec 2013, Lawrence Co. (*KW* 90:55, 2014); 24 Dec 2016, Warren Co. (*KW* 93: 52, 2017); 23 Dec 2018, Boyd Co. (R. Canterbury, notes); 22 Dec 1990, Ft. Knox, Meade Co. (*KW* 67:19/32, 1991); 22 Dec 2015, Lexington (*KW* 92:45, 2016); 21 Dec 2009, Ballard Co. (*KW* 86:46, 2010); 15 Dec 2018, (ph.) Long Point Unit (*KW* 95:50, 2019); 11 Dec 2010, Russell Co. (*KW* 87:65, 2011); 6 Dec 2017, Wayne Co. (*KW* 94: 61, 2018); 5 Dec 2006, Pulaski Co. (*KW* 83:51, 2007); 27 Nov 2016, Sauerheber Unit (*KW* 93:13, 2017); 26 Nov 2005, Henderson Co. (*KW* 82:15, 2006); 19 Nov 1978, Louisville (B. Palmer-Ball, eBird data); 18 Nov 1975, Jefferson Co. (J. Elmore, notes).

Out-of-season record (mid-winter): 28 Jan 2017, w. Henderson Co. (*KW* 93:52, 2017).

Published error?: based on a review of a number of sources, I believe (but am not certain) that the late fall date of 23 Nov 1975 published by Monroe (*KW* 52:60, 1976) is erroneous, the result of a transcription error (*fide* A. Stamm, historical archive files).

*HOODED WARBLER *Setophaga citrina*

Status: Locally rare to common summer resident. Recorded statewide during migration, but generally uncommon as a transient away from nesting areas, especially during fall when the species is seldom observed; usually encountered foraging low in mature woodland understory during migration. Peak of abundance occurs from late Apr to mid-Aug. Breeding widespread, but abundance varies greatly as follows: common on the Cumberland Plateau and Mountains; much less numerous and very locally distributed to the west, occurring in some abundance only in the more extensively forested areas of the Knobs section of the Blue Grass and along the Dripping Springs Escarpment in the Shawnee Hills (*KBBA*:260-261). This species is typically associated with extensive tracts of forest that have at least scattered patches of dense vegetation in the shrub layer.

Maximum counts: **129** in McCreary Co., 24 Apr 2009 (eBird data); **84** in n. McCreary Co., 24 Apr 2009 (R. Denton, eBird data); **58** at the Little Lick Rec. Area, DBNF, Pulaski Co. (R. Denton, eBird data).

Early spring dates: 5 Apr 19—, Jefferson Co. Forest (*fide* A. Stamm, historical archive files); 6 Apr 2018, Pulaski Co. (*KW* 94:86, 2018); 7 Apr 2012, Pulaski Co. (*KW* 88:80, 2012); 8 Apr 1890, Pulaski Co. (Mengel:429); 8 Apr 2013, Allen Co. (*KW* 89:79, 2013).

Late fall dates: 8 Nov 1995, Louisville (B. Yandell, eBird data); 3 Nov 2003, Boyd Co. (*KW* 80:14, 2004); 27 Oct 2016, Lexington (*KW* 93:13, 2017); 17 Oct 1964, south-central Kentucky (*KW* 45:37, 1969); 17 Oct 2011, Mammoth Cave (*KW* 88:16, 2012).

*AMERICAN REDSTART *Setophaga ruticilla*

Status: Transient (fairly common during spring, fairly common to common during fall); locally rare to fairly common summer resident; extremely rare during winter. Recorded statewide during migration in a great variety of habitats from mature woodlands and woodland borders to overgrown fields and suburban parks and yards. At times one of the most numerous transient warblers, especially in early to mid-Sep when loose flocks of a half-dozen or more birds are not uncommon. Peaks of abundance occur from early to mid-May and from late Aug to late Sep. Breeding in both mature and successional deciduous woodlands as follows: fairly widespread on the Cumberland Plateau and Mountains, occurring mostly along riparian corridors and ravine slopes; very locally distributed through central and western Kentucky, generally occurring sparingly in forested riparian and floodplain zones along rivers and streams (*KBBA*:244-245). There are three winter records of presumed lingering fall transients.

Maximum count: **30** along the Anchorage Trail, Jefferson Co., 17 Sep 2013 (J. Galitzine, eBird data).

Early spring dates: 4 Apr 1919, Warren Co. (Mengel:434; *KW* 38:21, 1962); 8 Apr 2015, Floyd Co. (*KW* 91:75, 2015); 9 Apr 2013, Berea, Madison Co. (*KW* 89:79, 2013); 12 Apr 1890, Pulaski Co. (Mengel:434); 12 Apr 2015, DBNF, Menifee Co. (D. Cormier/I. Pratte, eBird data).

Late fall dates: 28 Oct 1981, Louisville (*KW* 58:18, 1982); 25 Oct 1959, Louisville (Mengel:435; *KW* 52:60, 1976).

Out-of-season records (winter): 1 Jan 1980, below Wolf Creek Dam (Elmore, *KW* 56:22, 1980); 4-8 Jan 2012, s. of Red Hill, Allen Co. (*KW* 88:49, 2012); 5 Dec 2015–9 Jan 2016, (ph.) nr. Mt. Zion, Pulaski Co. (*KW* 92:29/45, 2016).

Hybrid record: see Chestnut-sided Warbler.

CAPE MAY WARBLER *Setophaga tigrina*

Status: Transient (uncommon to fairly common during spring, uncommon during fall); accidental during summer and winter. Recorded statewide but generally more numerous in eastern Kentucky and relatively scarce in the west, especially during fall. This species is found in a variety of forested and semi-open habitats including mature woodlands and woodland borders; it also occurs in suburban parks and yards, where surprising numbers can sometimes be found in large spruce or pine trees, especially during spring. Peaks of abundance occur during early May and from mid-Sep to early Oct. Somewhat variable in abundance from year to year. Usually seen singly or in small numbers with other transient warblers, but occasionally seen in loose flocks of a half-dozen or more birds.

Maximum count: 30 to possibly 50 in a tree at Frankfort, first week of May 2007 (*KW* 83:84, 2007).

Early spring dates: 15 Apr 2017, Lexington (*KW* 93:79, 2017); 17 Apr 2017, Jessamine Co. (S. Penner, eBird data); 17 Apr 2018, two locations in Madison Co. (*KW* 94:86, 2018); 18 Apr 2016, Lexington (*KW* 92:67, 2016); 19 Apr 19—, Warren Co. (Mengel:402); 19 Apr 2013, Allen Co. (*KW* 89:79, 2013); 19 Apr 2017, Mammoth Cave (J. Rose, et al., eBird data); 20 Apr 2000, Lexington (eBird data).

Late spring dates: 24 May 1977, Danville (*AB* 31:1009, 1977); 21 May 2002, Pulaski Co. (R. Denton, eBird data); 21 May 2014, Lexington (J. Sole, eBird data).

Early fall dates: 23 Aug 2008, Louisville (*KW* 85:19, 2009); 24 Aug 2010, Pulaski Co. (*KW* 87:22, 2011); 27 Aug 2011, Lexington (*KW* 88:16, 2012); 28 Aug 2005, Louisville (*KW* 82:14, 2006); 28 Aug 2008, Louisville (*KW* 85:19, 2009); 28 Aug 2014 (D. Stewart, eBird data); 30 Aug 1998, Marshall Co. (B. Palmer-Ball, eBird data); 30 Aug 2012, Jefferson Co. (*KW* 89:14, 2013); 31 Aug 2017 (*KW* 94:16, 2018)..

Late fall dates: 12 Nov 1993, Muhlenberg Co. (B. Palmer-Ball, eBird data); 4 Nov 2010, Pike Co. (*KW* 87:22, 2011); 2 Nov 2000, Warren Co. (*KW* 77:9, 2001); 2 Nov 2004, Boone Co. (*KW* 81:14, 2005); 25 Oct 1983, Pulaski Co. (*KW* 60:19, 1984).

Out-of-season records (summer): 23 Jun 1974, Louisville (*KW* 52:58, 1976); 26 Jul 2016, (ph.) Kenton Co. (*KW* 92:81/92, 2016).

Out-of-season records (winter): 16 Dec 2006, (ph.) in Trigg Co. (*KW* 83:22/51, 2007); 22 Dec 2016–25 Jan 2017, (ph.) at Horse Cave, Hart Co. (*KW* 93:52/107, 2017); 4-5 Dec 2018, (ph.) at Crestwood, Oldham Co. (*KW* 95:50, 2019).

*CERULEAN WARBLER *Setophaga cerulea*

Status: Locally rare to fairly common summer resident. Recorded statewide during migration, but generally rare to uncommon as a transient away from nesting areas; usually encountered in mature woodlands. Breeding statewide in mature deciduous woodlands, but occurrence varies remarkably by region. It is somewhat locally distributed across the entire state but generally more widespread on the Cumberland Plateau and Mountains (*KBBA*:240-241). Across central and western Kentucky, where Mengel (pp. 408-409) considered it fairly common to common and even more numerous than in the eastern part of the state, the species has declined substantially and it is now primarily restricted to a few of the most extensive tracts of mature forest (e.g. Mammoth Cave NP). This species often forages high in the tallest forest trees and is often detected only by its distinctive song. Peak of abundance occurs from late Apr to early Jul. This warbler leaves the breeding grounds very early, most birds being gone from Kentucky by mid-Aug. Only a handful of well-documented sightings exist after the first of Sep.

Maximum counts: **35** on Wolf Knob, Whitley Co., 4 Jun 2005 (S. Stedman, eBird data); **34** on Wolf Knob, Whitley Co., 4 Jun 1996 (R. Denton, eBird data); **27** along the Little Shepherd Trail, Harlan Co. (eBird data).

Early spring dates: 4 Apr 1981, Calloway Co. (*KW* 57:59, 1981); 5 Apr 1892, Pulaski Co. (Mengel: 408); 7 Apr 1964, south-central Kentucky (*KW* 45:36, 1969); 10 Apr 1882, Nelson Co. (Mengel: 408); 10 Apr 2015, Laurel Co. (J. Muller, eBird data).

Late fall dates: 20 Oct 1886, (sp.) Nelson Co. (Mengel:410); 14 Oct 1934, south-central Kentucky (*KW* 38:20, 1962); 6 Oct 1946, Whitley Co. (Mengel:410).

*NORTHERN PARULA *Setophaga americana*

Status: Uncommon to fairly common summer resident (seems to have increased in recent decades). Recorded statewide during migration in a variety of forested habitats, but relatively uncommon as a transient away from nesting areas. Peaks of abundance occur from late Apr to early May and during Sep. Breeding statewide in mature woodlands, usually in bottomland or riparian habitats but also on mesic slopes; most numerous on the Cumberland Plateau and Mountains and in the Jackson Purchase, scattered locally throughout the rest of the state, mostly along river and stream corridors (*KBBA*:222-223).

Maximum counts: **41** in McCreary Co., 24 Apr 2009 (S. Stedman, eBird data); **40** in LBL, Lyon Co., 18 Apr 2017 (B. Palmer-Ball et al., eBird data).

Early spring dates: 20 Mar 2012, LBL, Trigg Co., and Oldham Co. (*KW* 88:80, 2012); 21 Mar 2012, Mammoth Cave (*KW* 88:81, 2012); 26 Mar 2007, Hart & Warren cos. (*KW* 83:84, 2007); 26 Mar 2012, Lyon & Pulaski cos. (*KW* 88:81, 2012); 27 Mar 2012, Allen Co. (*KW* 88:81, 2012); 28 Mar 1990, Louisville (*KW* 66:60, 1990); 28 Mar 1991, Edmonson Co. (*KW* 67:58, 1991); 28 Mar 2011, Louisville (*KW* 87:94, 2011); 28 Mar 2018, Mercer Co. (*KW* 94:86, 2018).

Late fall dates: 26 Oct 1975, Boyle Co. (eBird data); 15 Oct 2010, Hickman Co. (*KW* 87:22, 2011); 15 Oct 2014, LBL, Trigg Co. (*KW* 91:14, 2015); 15 Oct 2016, LBL, Trigg Co. (*KW* 93:13, 2017); 14 Oct 2006, Sauerheber Unit (eBird data); 14 Oct 2015, Lexington (*KW* 92:14, 2016); 13 Oct 2013, Jefferson Co. (eBird data); 12 Oct 2016, Ballard Co. (P. Hunt, eBird data); 11-12 Oct 1990 (3; tower casualties), Adair Co. (Elmore and Palmer-Ball, *KW* 67:67-71, 1991).

MAGNOLIA WARBLER *Setophaga magnolia*

Status: Transient (fairly common during spring, fairly common to common during fall). Recorded statewide in a great variety of habitats from mature woodlands and woodland borders to overgrown fields and suburban parks and yards; favors young, dense woodland and edge. Peaks of abundance occur during May and from late Aug to late Sep. This species is one of the most numerous transient warblers, especially during early fall when it is not uncommon to encounter a half-dozen or more birds in loose groups in suitable habitat.

Maximum count: **26** in Pulaski Co., 24 Sep 2004 (R. Denton, eBird data).

Early spring dates: 18 Apr 1969, Bell Co. (R. Harm, notes); 19 Apr 2014, Audubon SP, Henderson Co. (K. and J. Anderson-Bricker, eBird data); 20 Apr 1980, Calloway Co. (*KW* 56:63, 1980); 21 Apr 19—, Louisville area (*KW* 52:58, 1976); 21 Apr 2001, Grayson Co. (*KW* 77:52, 2001).

Late spring dates: 6 Jun 1992, Owen Co. (*KW* 68:57, 1992); 5 Jun 1979, Louisville (*KW* 55:58, 1979); 5 Jun 2013, Lexington (*KW* 89:97, 2013).

Early fall dates: 18 Aug 2012, Allen & Jefferson cos. (*KW* 89:14, 2013); 20 Aug 1977, Falls of the Ohio (eBird data; A. Stamm, notes); 20 Aug 2000, Warren Co. (*KW* 77:9, 2001); 21 Aug 1954, Louisville area (*KW* 52:58, 1976); 21 Aug 1983, Pulaski Co. (*KW* 60:19, 1984).

Late fall dates: 18 Nov 2006, Hart Co. (*KW* 83:18, 2007); 4 Nov 2010, Russell Co. (*KW* 87:22, 2011); 2 Nov 2018, Adair Co. (*KW* 95:10, 2019); 31 Oct 2009, Louisville (S. Ward/M. Kahn, eBird data); 29 Oct 2006, Jefferson Co. (*KW* 83:18, 2007); 28 Oct 1984, Pulaski Co. (*KW* 61:18, 1985); 28 Oct 2016, Lexington (*KW* 93:13, 2017).

Unaccepted records: 2 Apr 1994, (2) in Grayson Co. (*KW* 70:55, 1994); 7 Apr 1956, south-central Kentucky (*KW* 38:20, 1962)

BAY-BREASTED WARBLER *Setophaga castanea*

Status: Uncommon to fairly common transient (although may be declining). Recorded statewide in a great variety of forested and semi-open habitats including woodland borders and suburban parks and yards, but most often found in mature woodlands where the species usually frequents the midstory and lower canopy. Peaks of abundance occur from early to mid-May and from mid-Sep to early Oct. This species was seemingly more common in the past, when it typically outnumbered all other species in mature deciduous forest during fall migration (Mengel:414).

Maximum count: **20** in the Daniel Boone NF, Rowan Co., 22 Sep 2013 (B. Wulker, eBird data).

Early spring dates: 14 Apr 1934, south-central Kentucky (*KW* 38:21, 1962); 19 Apr 19—, Rowan Co. (Mengel:414); 24 Apr 1993, Scott Co. (D. Lang, eBird data); 24 Apr 2009, Boone Co. (R. Ripma, eBird data); 24 Apr 2015, Cumberland Falls SRP, Whitley Co. (A. Xeira, eBird data); 24 Apr 2016, Lexington (*KW* 92:67, 2016).

Late spring dates: 30 May 1977, Louisville (eBird data; J. Elmore, notes); 29 May 1979, Louisville (*KW* 55:49, 1979); 28 May 1949, Louisville (*KW* 52:59, 1976); 28 May 1979, Jefferson Co. (*KW* 55:49, 1979).

Early fall dates: 7 Aug 1966 (summer vagrant?), Hancock Co. (Alsop, *KW* 47:67, 1971); 19 Aug 2012, Jefferson Co. (*KW* 89:14, 2013); 21 Aug 1977, Louisville (J. Elmore, notes); 21 Aug 2013, Louisville (*KW* 90:16, 2014); 22 Aug 1978, Louisville (B. Palmer-Ball, eBird data); 22 Aug 1999, Louisville (J. Bell, notes).

Late fall dates: 16 Nov 1985, Boone Co. (*KW* 62:8, 1986); 15 Nov 1986, Louisville (*KW* 63:11, 1987)

*BLACKBURNIAN WARBLER *Setophaga fusca*

Status: Uncommon to fairly common transient, rare (but possibly increasing) summer resident at higher elevations on Black Mountain, and perhaps elsewhere at the highest elevations in the Cumberland Mountains (see recent reports below). Recorded statewide during migration in a great variety of forested and semi-open habitats from mature woodlands and woodland borders to suburban parks and yards. Peaks of abundance occur during early May and from late Aug to late Sep. Breeding not well documented; the species is present during summer in mature woodland above 3000 ft. on Black Mountain, but no nests have been located. In fact, breeding has been confirmed only on the basis of the observation of fledglings being fed by parents on one occasion, 29 Jun–5 Jul 1951 (Mengel:410-411). A presumed lingering migrant reported in early Dec represents the state's only winter record. **State Breeding Status**: Threatened.

Maximum count: **30-35** seen/heard on Black Mt., Harlan Co. 14 May 2010 (*KW* 86:72, 2010); **12** at Veterans Park, Lexington, 29 Aug 2011 (*KW* 88:17, 2012); **12** at the Lexington Cemetery, 29 Aug 2014 (M. Tower, eBird data); **12** at Big Bone Lick SP, Boone Co., 6 Sep 2016 (*KW* 93:13, 2017); **12** at Bernheim Forest, 3 May 2017 (B. Palmer-Ball, eBird data).

Early spring dates: 1 Apr 1942, south-central Kentucky (*KW* 38:20, 1962); 3 Apr 1882, Nelson Co. (Mengel:410); 11 Apr 2019, Hopkins Co. (D. Stricklin, eBird data); 16 Apr 2012, Audubon SP, Henderson Co. (*KW* 88:81, 2012); 17 Apr 1957, Louisville area (*KW* 52:59, 1976).

Late spring dates (away from breeding areas): 5 Jun 1977, Louisville (B. Palmer-Ball, eBird data); 3 Jun 2006, se. Jefferson Co. (*KW* 82:83, 2006).

Early fall dates (away from breeding areas): 2 Aug 2015, Louisville (*KW* 92:14, 2016); 6 Aug 2014, Mt. Zion, Pulaski Co. (*KW* 91:14, 2015); 12 Aug 2007, Warren Co. (*KW* 84:15 2008); 13 Aug 2000, Louisville (B. Yandell, eBird data); 13 Aug 2012, Jefferson Co. (*KW* 89:14, 2013); 14 Aug 2011, Louisville (*KW* 88:17, 2012); 14 Aug 2015, Jefferson Co. (*KW* 92:14, 2016); 15 Aug 1992, Louisville (*KW* 69:10, 1993); 15 Aug 2015, w. Franklin Co. (*KW* 92:14, 2016); 16 Aug 1979, Louisville (*KW* 56:17, 1980); 16 Aug 1998, Louisville (B. Yandell, eBird data); 17 Aug 1957, Louisville area (Croft, *KW* 34:46, 1958).

Late fall dates: 3 Nov 1946, Jefferson Co. (*KW* 52:59, 1976); 28 Oct 1984, Pulaski Co. (*KW* 61:18, 1985); 27 Oct 1996, Louisville (B. Yandell, eBird data)..

Out-of-season record (early winter): 5 Dec 1976, Louisville (B. Palmer-Ball, eBird data).

Summary of probable breeding records away from Black Mountain by county

Bell/Harlan (summer 2003, several territorial males at higher elevations in Cumberland Gap National Historical Park [*KW* 79:84, 2003])
Harlan (14 Jun 2007, singing bird on Pine Mountain, Harlan Co., 14 Jun 2007 (*KW* 83:106, 2007).

*YELLOW WARBLER *Setophaga petechia*

Status: Fairly common transient, locally rare to fairly common summer resident. Recorded statewide during migration in a variety of semi-open to open habitats with scattered trees including suburban parks and yards. This species is an early fall migrant, most birds leaving by early Sep. Peaks of abundance occur from late Apr to early May and during mid- to late Aug. Breeding widespread throughout eastern Kentucky, but quite locally distributed across the western two-thirds of the state (*KBBA*:224-225); utilizes a variety of semi-open habitats, most frequently near water in patches of young trees.

Maximum counts: **20** at Rough River SP, Grayson Co., 7 May 2007 (J. Brunjes, eBird data); **15** in w. Henderson Co., 5 May 2007 (J. Meredig, eBird data).

Early spring dates: 28 Mar 19—, Rowan Co. (Mengel:400); 1 Apr 1933, (sp.) Rowan Co. (Mengel:400); 3 Apr 19—, Louisville (Mengel:400); 4 Apr 2013, Trigg Co. (*KW* 89:79, 2013).

Late fall dates: 13 Nov 1983, Pulaski Co. (*KW* 60:19, 1984); 4 Nov 2004, Trigg Co. (*KW* 81:14, 2005); 19 Oct 1935, south-central Kentucky (*KW* 38:20, 1962); 14 Oct 2009, Sauerheber Unit (*KW* 86:14, 2010); 11 Oct 1990 (tower kill), Adair Co. (Elmore and Palmer-Ball, *KW* 67:69-70, 1991).

*CHESTNUT-SIDED WARBLER *Setophaga pensylvanica*

Status: Fairly common transient, uncommon to fairly common summer resident at higher elevations in the Cumberland Mountains, extremely rare and local summer resident in portions of the Cumberland Plateau. Recorded statewide during migration in a great variety of habitats from mature woodlands and woodland borders to suburban parks and yards. Peaks of abundance occur during early May and from early to late Sep. Historically the species was known to breed only at higher elevations on Black Mountain; more recently, breeding also has been confirmed elsewhere in the Cumberland Mountains, along the crest of Pine Mountain, and at a couple of locations on the Cumberland Plateau (see below). Breeds in brushy, successional growth of both natural and artificial woodland openings including utility rights-of-way, regenerating timber harvest areas, and forest damaged by fire or storms.

Maximum counts: **86** on Black Mt., Harlan/Letcher cos., 12 Jun 1980 (B. Palmer-Ball, eBird data); **67** on Black Mt., Harlan/Letcher cos., 18 Jun 1981 (B. Palmer-Ball, eBird data); **61** on Black Mt., 15 May 2005 (*KW* 81;91, 2005); **58** on Black Mt., 9 May 2004 (*KW* 80:71, 2004); **50** at Mammoth Cave, 14 Sep 2002 (eBird data); **43** along the Little Shepherd Trail, Harlan Co., 10 May 2005 (eBird data).

Early spring dates: 13 Apr 1958, south-central Kentucky (*KW* 38:20, 1962); 13 Apr 2011, Bernheim Forest (*KW* 87:94, 2011); 18 Apr 1965, Louisville area (*KW* 52:59, 1976).

Late spring dates (away from breeding areas): 16 Jun 2002, Louisville (M. Stickel, notes); 10 Jun 1999, Rowan Co. (*KW* 75:61, 1999); 6 Jun 2010, Pulaski Co. (*KW* 86:95, 2010); 3 Jun 1992, Ft. Knox, Bullitt Co. (B. Palmer-Ball, eBird data; erroneously reported as in Hardin Co. in 2nd edition of this work); 2 Jun 2012, Wolfe Co. (*KW* 88:95, 2012); 1 Jun 2003, Lexington (*KW* 79:84, 2003); 31 May 1966/1976, Louisville area (*KW* 52:59, 1976); 31 May 2010, Lee Co. (*KW* 86:72, 2010).

Early fall dates (away from breeding areas): 21 Jul 2004, Mammoth Cave (*KW* 80:85, 2004); 13 Aug 2000, Louisville (B. Yandell, eBird data); 16 Aug 1998, Louisville (B. Yandell, eBird data); 16 Aug 2012, Owen Co. (*KW* 89:14, 2013); 16 Aug 2017, Jefferson Co. (*KW* 94:16, 2018); 18 Aug 2007, Pulaski Co. (*KW* 84:14 2008); 18 Aug 2012, Jefferson Co. (*KW* 89:14, 2013); 18 Aug 2013, Jefferson Co. (*KW* 90:16, 2014); 19 Aug 2003, Pulaski Co. (*KW* 80:13, 2004); 21 Aug 2006, Pulaski Co. (*KW* 83:18, 2007); 21 Aug 2009, Louisville (*KW* 86:14, 2010; 21 Aug 2012, Lexington (L. Thomas, eBird data).

Late fall dates: 9 Nov 1975, Louisville (*KW* 52:59, 1976); 31 Oct 2004, Jefferson Co. (*KW* 81:14, 2005); 25 Oct 1975, Jefferson Co. (A. Stamm, historical archive files; J. Elmore/D. Parker, notes); 23 Oct 2011, Taylorsville Lake SP, Spencer Co. (Beckham Bird Club, eBird data).

Hybrid record: 5 May 1995, male Chestnut-sided Warbler x American Redstart observed in LBL, Trigg Co. (B. Palmer-Ball, notes; R. Healy, drawing).

Unaccepted records: 11 Jun 2005, Wolfe Co. [no details available] (J. Habig, eBird data); 8 Jun 2008, Martin Co. [no details available] (T. Czubek, eBird data)

Summary of confirmed breeding records by county

Bell/Harlan (Log and Cumberland mts. including in Cumberland Gap NHP on latter [Croft, *KW* 45:76, 1969; Davis and Smith, *KW* 54:73, 1978; Davis, et al., *KW* 56:50, 1980; *KBBA*:226; *KW* 65:90, 1989; *KW* 79:84, 2003])
Harlan/Letcher (Black Mt. [Mengel:413-414])
Leslie (7 Jul 1989, s. of Helton [*KBBA*:226; *KW* 65:90, 1989])

List of other possible/probable breeding records away from Cumberland Mts. by county

Harlan/Letcher (crest of Pine Mt. [*KW* 70:70, 1994; J. Ferner, eBird data; *KW* 80:71, 2004; *KW* 81:91, 2005])
Lewis (Jun 1991 [*KBBA*:226]; 26 Jul 1998 [*KW* 74:74, 1998]; 30 Jun 1999 [*KW* 75:61, 1999])
McCreary/Whitley (1994-1999, Wolf Knob [*KW* 70:70, 1994; *KW* 71:70, 1995; *KW* 72:76, 1996; 1997–1999 eBird data; 8 May 2004, Jellico Mt. [*KW* 80:71, 2004])]
McCreary (10 Jun 2007, DBNF [*KW* 83:106, 2007]; 30 May–4 Jun 2011 [*KW* 87:116, 2011; R. Denton, eBird data])
Wolfe (21 May–19 Jun 2005 and 10-13 Jun 2006, Sky Bridge [*KW* 81:91/109, 2005; *KW* 82:83, 2006])

BLACKPOLL WARBLER *Setophaga striata*

Status: Transient (fairly common during spring, extremely rare to rare during fall). Recorded state-wide in a great variety of habitats from mature woodland and woodland borders to suburban parks and yards. Peaks of abundance occur from early to mid-May and from mid-Sep to early Oct. Wide-spread during spring, when the species occurs statewide but is particularly numerous across the western half of the state. In contrast, this species migrates primarily east of the Appalachian Mountains in fall, accounting for its scarcity in Kentucky at that time. Small numbers seem to be regular in about the eastern half of the state during fall, especially on the Cumberland Plateau and Mountains, but it is decidedly scarce in central Kentucky and essentially absent in the western third of the state, where there are only a few records (see below).

Maximum spring count: at least **50** at LBL, Lyon Co., 2 May 2007 (B. Palmer-Ball, eBird data).

Maximum fall count: **6** at Fredericks Landing Park, Kenton Co., 5 Oct 2016 (*KW* 93:13, 2017).

Early spring dates: 14 Apr 2011, Allen Co. (*KW* 87:94, 2011); 15 Apr 2017, Mammoth Cave (J. Rose, eBird data); 17 Apr 1982, Grayson Co. (*KW* 58:53, 1982); 17 Apr 1983, Louisville (*KW* 59: 44, 1983); 17 Apr 2011, Mammoth Cave (*KW* 87:94, 2011); 17 Apr 2013, at Lexington and at LBL, Trigg Co. (*KW* 89:79, 2013).

Late spring dates: 4 Jun 2005, Henderson Co. (*KW* 81:109, 2005); 31 May 1973, Lake Cumberland (A. Byrd, notes); 30 May 1973, Bernheim Forest (*KW* 52:59, 1976; B. Monroe, Jr., notes); 30 May 2005, Pike Co. (*KW* 81:91, 2005).

Early fall dates: 1 Sep 2017, (ph.) Lincoln Co. (J. Elmore, eBird data); 2 Sep 2012, (ph.) Doe Run Lake Park, Kenton Co., (R. Crice, eBird data); 3 Sep 2012, Boone Co. (*KW* 89:14, 2013); 3 Sep 2017, Jefferson Co. (*KW* 94:16, 2018); 6 Sep 1988, Boyle Co. (*KW* 65:11, 1989); 9 Sep 2011, Boone Co. (*KW* 88:17, 2012); 10 Sep 1988, Louisville (*KW* 65:11, 1989).

Late fall dates: 7 Nov 2017, Mahr Park, Hopkins Co. (D. Stricklin, eBird data); 18 Oct 2005, Pulaski Co. (*KW* 82:14, 2006); 15 Oct 2005, Franklin Co. (*KW* 82:14, 2006); 13 Oct 2002, Warren Co. (*KW* 79:15, 2003); 13 Oct 2008, se. Jefferson Co. (*KW* 85:19, 2009); 12 Oct 1981, Louisville (*KW* 58:18, 1982); 12 Oct 2011, (ph.) Pulaski Co. (*KW* 88:17, 2012).

List of fall records west of Louisville and Bowling Green by county

Henderson (21 Sep 1990, tower kill (sp.) at Henderson [Palmer-Ball and Rauth, *KW* 66:98, 1990])
Hopkins (31 Oct/7 Nov 2017, Mahr Park [D. Stricklin, eBird data])
Livingston (17 Sep 2006, nr. Barkley Dam [*KW* 83:18, 2007])
Trigg (8 Oct 2006, LBL [*KW* 83:19, 2007])

*BLACK-THROATED BLUE WARBLER *Setophaga caerulescens*

Status: Rare to uncommon transient, locally uncommon to fairly common summer resident in the Cumberland Mountains, especially at higher elevations. Recorded statewide during migration but very infrequent in the western half of the state and nearly absent in the Jackson Purchase. Most often seen in mature forest understory, but generally rare as a transient away from nesting areas. Peaks of abundance occur during early May and from mid-Sep to early Oct. Breeding widespread in mature forest above 3000 ft. on Black Mountain, and scattered locally on the higher portions of Cumberland Mountain, Bell/Harlan cos. and on Pine Mountain, Letcher Co.(see below).

Maximum counts: **42** on Black Mt., Harlan/Letcher cos., 12 Jun 1980 (B. Palmer-Ball, eBird data); **37** on Black Mt., Harlan/Letcher cos., 18 Jun 1981 (B. Palmer-Ball, eBird data); **28** on Black Mt., 12 Jun 1980 (eBird data); **10** on Black Mt., 26 May 2002 (R. Denton, eBird data).

Early spring dates: 1 Apr 1963, south-central Kentucky (*KW* 45:36, 1969); 7 Apr 2013, Lexington (J. Howell, eBird data); 12 Apr 2015, Natural Bridge SRP, Powell Co. (*KW* 91:76, 2015 [date erroneously published as 11 Apr therein; *fide* J. Muller, eBird data]); 12 Apr 2015, Mammoth Cave (*KW* 91:76, 2015); 12 Apr 2017, Bad Branch SNP, Letcher Co. (*KW* 93:79, 2017); 13 Apr 2017, Mammoth Cave (S. & J. Kistler, eBird data); 20 Apr 2007, Trigg Co. (*KW* 83:84, 2007); 20 Apr 2016, Black Mt., Harlan Co. (*KW* 92:68, 2016); 22 Apr 2015, Lexington (G. Tremoulet, eBird data); 23 Apr 1944, south-central Kentucky (*KW* 38:20, 1962); 23 Apr 1966, Louisville area (*KW* 52:58, 1976).

Late spring dates (away from breeding areas): 9 Jun 1990, Pendleton Co. (*KW* 66:91, 1990); 31 May 2005, Pulaski Co. (eBird data); 27 May 2016, Fayette Co. (D. Svetich, eBird data).

Early fall dates (away from breeding areas): 23 Aug 2009, Louisville Co. (*KW* 86:14, 2010); 28 Aug 1981, Louisville (*KW* 58:18, 1982); 31 Aug 2012, Jefferson Co. (*KW* 89:14, 2013).

Late fall dates: 22 Nov 2001, Berea (*NAB* 56:59, 2002); 25 Oct 1943, south-central Kentucky (*KW* 38:20, 1962); 22 Oct 1983 (tower kill), Adair Co. (*KW* 60:19, 1984); 22 Oct 2017, (ph.) at Berea, Madison Co. (*KW* 94:16, 2018).

Summary of confirmed/probable breeding records by county

Bell/Harlan (Cumberland Mt. [Croft, *KW* 45:75, 1969; Davis and Smith, *KW* 54:73, 1978; Davis, et al., *KW* 56:50, 1980; *KBBA*:228-229; *KW* 79:84, 2003])
Harlan (Black Mt. [Mengel:403; *KW* 74:74, 1998])
Letcher (Bad Branch SNP [*KBBA*:228-229; B. Palmer-Ball, 2001 eBird data]).

List of farthest west documented records by county

Calloway (10-14 Oct 1963 [E. Larson, eBird data]; 16 Sep 2007 [*KW* 84:15 2008]; 4 May 2019 [H. Chambers, eBird data])
Livingston (R. Bontrager, 2019 eBird data)
Lyon (7 May 1998 [W. Ealding, eBird data]; 12 May 2005 [*KW* 81:91, 2005]; 10 May 2010 [*KW* 86:72, 2010]; 16 May 2011 (ph.) [*KW* 87:94, 2011]; 3 May 2013 [*KW* 89:79, 2013])
Marshall (23 Apr 1981 [*KW* 57:59, 1981]; 13 Sep 2003 [*KW* 80:14, 2004])
Trigg (20 Apr 2007 [*KW* 83:84, 2007]; 26 Sep 2015 [*KW* 92:14, 2016])

PALM WARBLER *Setophaga palmarum*

Status: Fairly common to common transient, extremely rare to rare winter visitant/resident. Recorded statewide during migration in a variety of semi-open and open habitats including woodland edges, fencerows and weedy fields, but sometimes seen in open woodlands with other warblers. This species also forages on the open ground where it can be mistaken for an American Pipit. Peaks of abundance occur during late Apr and from late Sep to mid-Oct. A few birds occasionally linger well into winter, some of which winter during milder years (see Mengel:420; *KW* 59:30, 1983). Sometimes encountered singly, but more often observed in loose flocks of up to a dozen or so birds. Most winter records are for single birds, but small flocks have been reported on several occasions.

Maximum spring/fall counts: 60+ at Danville, 24 Sep 1992 (*KW* 69:10, 1993); **45** in s. Jefferson Co., 2 Oct 2010 (M. Autin, eBird data); **45** nr. Shepherdsville, Bullitt Co., 11 Oct 2014 (Beckham Bird Club et al., eBird data); **43** at Beckley Creek Park, Jefferson Co., 25 Sep 2014 (P. Bell, eBird data); at least **30** in LBL, Lyon Co., 18 Apr 2017 (B. Palmer-Ball/T. Graham, eBird data).

Maximum winter counts: flock of at least **35** (ph.) in Meade Co., 30 Dec 2016 (*KW* 93:19/52, 2017); **26** on the Russell/Adair cos. CBC, 16 Dec 2017 (*KW* 94:27, 2018); **22** in e. Allen Co., 28 Dec 2013 (*KW* 90:30/55, 2014); **21** in w. Allen Co., 14 Dec 2013 (*KW* 90:30/55, 2014); **20** (including a flock of 8) in Russell Co., 16 Dec 2017 (R. Bontrager, eBird data); **16** (ph.) at Lexington, 31 Dec 2011 (*KW* 88:52, 2012).

Late spring dates: 30 May 1968, Louisville (A. Ricketts, pers. comm; *fide* A. Stamm, historical archive files); 26 May 2018, (ph.) at KenLake SRP, Marshall Co. (*KW* 94:87, 2018); 25 May 1968, Louisville area (*KW* 52:59, 1976); 25 May 2011, (ph.) Mercer Co. (*KW* 87:94, 2011).

Early fall dates: 22 Aug 2012, Lexington (*KW* 89:14, 2013); 29 Aug 1982, Falls of the Ohio (*KW* 59:18, 1983); 2 Sep 2001, Fulton Co. (B. Palmer-Ball, eBird data); 2 Sep 2017, Henderson Co. (*KW* 94:16, 2018); 3 Sep 2017, Jefferson Co. (*KW* 94:16, 2018); 4 Sep 1988, Falls of the Ohio (*KW* 65:11, 1989); 4 Sep 2003, Jefferson Co. (*KW* 80:14, 2004); 4 Sep 2010, Cave Run Lake (*KW* 87:22, 2011).

Unaccepted record: 26 Nov 2012, Yellow Palm Warbler se. of Mt. Zion, Allen Co. (*KW* 89:14, 2013; see *KW* 92:89, 2016).

Note on subspecies: There are seven documented records of the relatively distinctive eastern subspecies, known as the YELLOW PALM WARBLER (*D. p. hypochrysea*).

Summary of records of *D. p. hypochrysea* by county

Barren (20 Oct 2006, (ph.) in Barren Co. [*KW* 83:18, 2007]; 12 Oct 2009 [*KW* 86:14, 2010]; 13 Oct 2009 [*KW* 86:14, 2010])
Jefferson (2 Apr 2017, (ph.) [*KW* 93:80/84, 2017])
Meade (30 Dec 2016–4 Jan 2017, (ph.) [*KW* 9319/52, 2017])
Muhlenberg (28 Oct 2000 [B. Palmer-Ball, eBird data])
Russell (11 Dec 2010 [*KW* 87:65, 2011])

*PINE WARBLER *Setophaga pinus*

Status: Locally uncommon to fairly common summer resident, extremely rare to rare winter resident. Recorded statewide during migration in a variety of forested and semi-open habitats, but generally quite scarce as a transient away from nesting areas. Migrants are found most regularly in pines but occasionally in deciduous woodlands. Breeding widespread on the Cumberland Plateau and lower Cumberland Mountains in association with stands of pine; also breeds locally across central and western parts of the state as follows: west through the Knobs section of the Blue Grass and Shawnee Hills regions, and in pine plantings into the Jackson Purchase (*KBBA*:236-237). A few birds regularly linger into winter (especially through the CBC period). There are also scattered records during Jan and first half of Feb, mostly in association with stands of pines or feeding stations, that demonstrate wintering, which is now likely annual. Spring migrants and returning summer residents seem to begin to appear during the first half of Feb. Typically encountered singly or in small, loose flocks of up to about a dozen birds (the latter especially during fall).

Maximum counts: ca. **50** at Bernheim Forest, 30 Sep 1989 (*KW* 66:13, 1990); **35** at and nr. Nolin Lake, Hart Co., 31 Aug 2017 (*KW* 94:16, 2018); **30** at Bernheim Forest, 9 Oct 1976 (*BO*, Nov 1976).
Maximum winter counts: 12 on the Calloway Co. CBC, 3 Jan 2017 (*KW* 93:52, 2017); 8 in Muhlenberg Co., 21 Jan 1995 (*KW* 71:26, 1995).

YELLOW-RUMPED WARBLER *Setophaga coronata*

Status: Common transient, irregularly uncommon to fairly common winter resident. Recorded statewide during migration in a great variety of habitats from mature woodlands and woodland borders to overgrown fields and suburban parks and yards. Peaks of abundance occur from mid-Apr to early May and from mid-Oct to early Nov. This is the only species of warbler to winter regularly in the state, occurring at that season primarily in deciduous or mixed forest, cedar thickets, and other habitats where trees, shrubs, and vines bearing soft mast are present. Generally seen in loose flocks of up to a dozen birds, but sometimes encountered in larger flocks of several dozen or more both during migration and winter.

Maximum counts: 200+ at Minor Clark Hatchery, 25 Oct 1984 (*KW* 61:18, 1985); ca. **200** at Minor Clark Hatchery, 14 Oct 1988 (*KW* 65:11, 1989); **150** at Jacobson Park, Lexington, 29 Apr 2012 (A. Newman/M. Buschow, eBird data).
Late spring dates: 22 May 2002, Jefferson Co. (B. Palmer-Ball, eBird data); 21 May 2002, Boone Co. (*KW* 78:52, 2002); 21 May 2006, Mammoth Cave (Beckham Bird Club, eBird data); 21 May 2008, Marshall Co. (*KW* 84:70, 2008); 21 May 2017, Lexington (*KW* 93:80, 2017); 20 May 1997, Louisville (B. Yandell, eBird data); 20 May 2006, (5) Boone Co. (*KW* 82:73, 2006 [date erroneously published as 21 May therein; *fide* L. McNeely, eBird data]); 20 May 2013, LBL, Trigg Co. (*KW* 89:79, 2013).
Early fall dates: 8 Sep 2012, Boyd Co. (C. Thompson, eBird data); 11 Sep 1976, Louisville (*AB* 31:185, 1977); 12 Sep 1979, Louisville (*KW* 56:17, 1980).
Unaccepted records: 5 Sep 19—, Warren Co. and 6 Sep 1920, Madison Co. (see Mengel:404); 20 May 2006, (10) Greenup Co. (eBird data); 21 Dec 1996, two birds of western subspecies, AUDUBON'S WARBLER (*KW* 73:19, 1997).

Note on subspecies: There are two documented records of the subspecies of western North America, also known as the AUDUBON'S WARBLER (*S. c. auduboni*).

List of records of *S. c. auduboni* by county

Jefferson (23-24 Sep 2007, Melco flood retention basin, Jefferson Co. [Palmer-Ball, *KW* 84:33-35 2008])

Warren (16-23 Apr 2018, Bowling Green [*KW* 94:122/124, 2018; R. Shive, eBird data])

*YELLOW-THROATED WARBLER *Setophaga dominica*

Status: Uncommon to fairly common summer resident, accidental during winter. Recorded statewide during migration when it is usually encountered in mature woodlands, but generally scarce as a transient away from nesting areas. Peak of abundance occurs from early Apr to mid-Sep. Breeding statewide in three distinct habitat types: in the floodplains of the Mississippi and lower Ohio rivers and their tributaries, where the species is found most frequently in association with bald cypress in bottomland and swamp forests; throughout much of the rest of the state, but especially most of western and central Kentucky, where it occurs in association with sycamores in bottomland and riparian forest; and in the Cumberland Plateau (and locally elsewhere statewide), where it occurs in upland forests in association with pines (*KBBA*:234).

Maximum counts: **46** along Buck Creek, Pulaski Co., 13 Apr 2006 (R. Denton, eBird data); **41** at Fishing Creek Rec. Area, Pulaski Co., 18 Apr 2007 and 15 Jun 2009 (R. Denton, eBird data).

Early spring dates: 14 Mar 2015, Lexington (*KW* 92:47, 2016); 18 Mar 2012, Allen Co. (*KW* 88:81, 2012); 19 Mar 2012, Lyon/Trigg, Pike, & Rowan cos. (*KW* 88:81, 2012); 20 Mar 2012, Bath, Laurel, & Pulaski cos. (*KW* 88:81, 2012); 21 Mar 1948, south-central Kentucky (*KW* 38:20, 1962); 21 Mar 2012, Mammoth Cave & Pulaski Co. (*KW* 88:81, 2012).

Late fall dates: 26 Nov 2009, Logan Co. (*KW* 86:14, 2010); 18 Nov 2012, Calloway Co. (*KW* 89:14, 2013); 10-11 Nov 1986, Berea (*KW* 63:11, 1987); 30 Oct 2005, Warrern Co. (A. Hulsey, eBird data); 24/26 Oct 1977, [location unknown] (*fide* A. Stamm, historical archive files); 21 Oct 2000, Jefferson Co. (*NAB* 55:60, 2001); 21 Oct 2009, w. Henderson Co. (C. Crawford, eBird data); 18 Oct 2015, e. Jefferson Co. (*KW* 92:15, 2016); 17 Oct 1984, Pulaski Co. (*KW* 61:18, 1985).

Out-of-season record (winter): 20-21 Dec 2016, WKU Farm, Warren Co. (*KW* 93:52/107, 2017).

*PRAIRIE WARBLER *Setophaga discolor*

Status: Fairly common summer resident, extremely rare during winter (including one apparent record of wintering). Recorded statewide during migration in a variety of semi-open, successional habitats, but generally uncommon as a transient away from nesting areas. Peak of abundance occurs from mid-Apr to mid-Sep. Breeding statewide, but less numerous in extensively cleared areas in the Inner Blue Grass, Highland Rim, Shawnee Hills, and Jackson Purchase (*KBBA*:238-239). Generally breeds in association with old fields, clear cuts, or other open, brushy habitats with small trees.

Maximum counts: **62** in Adair Co., 6 May 2008 (S. Stedman, eBird data); **58** in Pulaski Co., 8 May 2004 (S. Marsh, eBird data); **50** at Pennyrile State Forest, Christian Co., 22 Apr 2016 (B. Palmer-Ball/T. Graham, eBird data)

Early spring dates: "late Mar" 1976, eastern Kentucky (*AB* 30:720, 1976); 31 Mar 2012, Adair Co. (*KW* 88:81, 2012); 1 Apr 2012, Hancock, McCreary, & Trigg cos. (*KW* 88:81, 2012); 3 Apr 2012, Allen Co. (*KW* 88:81, 2012); 4 Apr 1994, Grayson Co. (*KW* 70:55, 1994); 4 Apr 2006, Warren Co. (*KW* 82:73, 2006); 4 Apr 2007, LBL, Trigg Co. (*KW* 83:84, 2007); 4 Apr 2012, Pulaski Co. (*KW* 88:81, 2012); 5 Apr 2005, LBL, Trigg Co. (*KW* 81:91, 2005); 5 Apr 2017, Jefferson and McCreary cos. (*KW* 93:80, 2017); 6 Apr 1921, Warren Co. (*KW* 38:21, 1962).

Late fall dates: 4 Dec 2017, Louisville (*KW* 94:61, 2018); 1 Dec 2017, Carlisle Co. (*KW* 94:51, 2018); 28 Nov 2008, Jefferson Co. (*KW* 85:19, 2009); 11/16 Nov 2001, Grayson Co. (*KW* 78:11, 2002); 12 Nov 2005, (ph.) Lincoln Co. (*KW* 82:14, 2006); 6 Nov 2015, (ph.) Louisville (*KW* 92:15, 2016); 24 Oct 1965, Bullitt Co. (*KW* 52:59, 1976).

Out-of-season records (winter): 30 Dec 1965, Madisonville (*KW* 42:10, 1966); 9 Dec 1967, LBL, Trigg Co. (Able, *KW* 45:42, 1969); 22 Dec 1990, Meade Co. (*KW* 67:19/32, 1991); 30 Nov 1992-3

Feb 1993, Carlisle, Nicholas Co. (*KW* 69:35, 1993); 18 Dec 1999, Warsaw, Gallatin Co. (*KW* 76:20/32, 2000); 14 Dec 2012, w. Allen Co. (*KW* 89:23/53, 2013); 14 Dec 2015, (ph.) at Paducah (*KW* 92:45/46, 2016).

BLACK-THROATED GRAY WARBLER *Setophaga nigrescens*

Status: Accidental vagrant. This warbler is a widespread breeding bird in the western United States and relatively regular vagrant to the eastern states. It has been suitably documented in Kentucky on two occasions.

Unaccepted record: 3 May 1941, Louisville (Carpenter, *KW* 18:17, 1942; see Mengel:518).

Chronological list of records

1) 28 Nov 1986–14 Jan 1987, a probable imm. female (ph.) at the Lexington Cemetery (*KW* 63:1/ 11/38, 1987; Andres and Palmer-Ball, *KW* 63:41-42, 1987)
2) 4 Nov–6 Dec 2015, an imm. female (ph.) at Louisville (*KW* 92:1/15/46, 2016)

*BLACK-THROATED GREEN WARBLER *Setophaga virens*

Status: Fairly common transient, uncommon to fairly common but somewhat locally distributed summer resident, extremely rare in early winter. Recorded statewide during migration in a great variety of habitats from mature woodlands and woodland borders to suburban parks and yards. Peaks of abundance occur from late Apr to early May and from mid-Sep to mid-Oct. Breeding locally throughout the Cumberland Plateau and Mountains, generally occurring wherever hemlocks are numerous in the forests, but also at least occasionally present and presumably breeding in deciduous forest. Confirmed breeding records are scarce; in fact, the state's first two records of actual nests were only recently reported from Wolfe Co., 13 May 1998 (Yacek and Lacki, *KW* 75:30-31, 1999) and 22 May 2000 (*KW* 76:46/58, 2000). There are two early winter records of presumed lingering fall transients.Typically seen singly or in small numbers with other migrant warblers, but occasionally encountered in loose groups of up to a half-dozen or more birds.

Maximum counts: **70** in McCreary Co., 24 Apr 2009 (S. Stedman, eBird data); **58** at Bee Rock Rec. Area, Pulaski Co., 15 Apr 2016 (R. Denton, eBird data); **56** at Natural Arch Scenic Area, DBNF, McCreary Co., 22 May 2010 (R. Denton, eBird data); **55** at Red River Gorge, Wolfe Co., 23 Apr 2007 (B. Wulker, eBird data); **52** in Pulaski Co., 10 Apr 2004 (*KW* 80:71, 2004).
Early spring dates: 20 Mar 1982, McCreary Co. (*KW* 58:53, 1982); 20 Mar 2004, DBNF, Wolfe Co. (*KW* 80:71, 2004); 20 Mar 2012, Lee Co. (*KW* 88:81, 2012).
Late spring dates (away from breeding areas): 10 Jun 1975, Hopkins Co. (*AB* 29:982, 1975); 9 Jun 1965, Hancock Co. (Alsop, *KW* 47:67, 1971); 5 Jun 1997, Logan Co. (B. Palmer-Ball, eBird data).
Vagrant summer records (away from breeding areas): 14 Jul 1882, Nelson Co. (Mengel:407); 22 Jul, 1966, Hancock Co. (Alsop, *KW* 47:67, 1971); 29 Jun 1991, Woodford Co. (*KBBA*:13); 10 Jul 2011, Hart Co. (*KW* 87:116, 2011); 31 Jul 2014, Anderson Co. (P. Graber, eBird data).
Early fall dates (away from breeding areas): 10 Aug 2003, Bowling Green (*KW* 80:14, 2004); 13 Aug 19—, Louisville (*KW* 52:58, 1976; Mengel:407); 13 Aug 2008, e. Jefferson Co. (*KW* 85:19, 2009).
Late fall dates: 5 Nov 1961, Louisville area (*KW* 52:58, 1976); 5 Nov 1979, Louisville (B. Palmer-Ball, eBird data); 5 Nov 2005, Louisville (*KW* 82:14, 2006).
Out-of-season records (early winter): 19 Dec 1965, LBL, Trigg Co. (Able, *KW* 42:18, 1966); 30 Nov–1 Dec 1975, (sp.) at Alvaton, Warren Co. (Shadowen, *KW* 52:16, 1976).

*CANADA WARBLER *Cardellina canadensis*

Status: Uncommon transient, rare to locally uncommon summer resident at higher elevations in the Cumberland Mountains. Recorded statewide during migration in a variety of forested and semi-open habitats; usually encountered in the understory of wooded areas, but also seen in successional thickets and along woodland borders. Peaks of abundance occur during mid-May and from late Aug to mid-Sep. Breeding has been documented only at the highest elevations in the Cumberland Mountains (see below). **State Breeding Status**: Special Concern.

Maximum counts: **14** on Black Mt., 18 Jun 1981 (eBird data); **12** on Black Mt., Harlan/Letcher cos., 12 Jun 1980 (B. Palmer-Ball, eBird data); **7** at Gunpowder Creek Nature Park, Boone Co., 19 May 2010 (Beckham Bird Club, eBird data); **7** at Surrey Hills Farm, Jefferson Co., 18 May 2012 (*KW* 88: 81, 2012); **7** at LBL, Trigg Co., 14 May 2015 (B. Lisowsky, eBird data).

Early spring dates: 19 Apr 1976, Boyle Co. (F. Loetscher, notes; *fide* A. Stamm, historical archive files); 24 Apr 1963, south-central Kentucky (*KW* 45:37, 1969); 27 Apr 1958, south-central Kentucky (*KW* 38:21, 1962); 28 Apr 19—, Warren Co. (Mengel:433); 30 Apr 1944, Louisville (Mengel:433); 1 May 1994, Owen Co. (D. Lang, eBird data).

Late spring dates (away from breeding areas): 11 Jun 1998, Cumberland Co. (eBird data); 4 Jun 2005, Jefferson Co. (*KW* 81:109, 2005); 31 May 2009, Lee Co. (*KW* 85:75, 2009); 31 May 2016, Jefferson Co. (*KW* 92:68, 2016); 30 May 1948, Louisville area (*KW* 52:60, 1976); 30 May 1977, Louisville (J. Elmore, notes).

Early fall dates (away from breeding areas): 2 Aug 2006, (ba.) in Marshall Co. (*KW* 83:19, 2007); 5 Aug 2002, Louisville (*KW* 79:15, 2003); 12 Aug 2007, Warren Co. (*KW* 84:15 2008); 15 Aug 2014, Lexington (*KW* 91:14, 2015); 17 Aug 2013, Allen Co. (*KW* 90:16, 2014); 18 Aug 1957/1966, Louisville area (*KW* 52:60, 1976); 18 Aug 2011, Pulaski Co. (*KW* 88:17, 2012); 18 Aug 2012, Allen Co. (*KW* 89:14, 2013); 18 Aug 2015, Jefferson Co. (*KW* 92:15, 2016).

Late fall dates: 14 Oct 2016, (ph.) Sauerheber Unit (*KW* 93:13, 2017); 12 Oct 1963, south-central Kentucky (*KW* 45:37, 1969).

Summary of confirmed/probable breeding records by county

<u>Bell/Harlan</u> (locally along the crest of Cumberland Mt. [Croft, *KW* 45:76, 1969; Davis, et al., *KW* 56: 51, 1980; *KBBA*:262; *KW* 79:85, 2003]

<u>Harlan/Letcher</u> (in deciduous forest above 3600 ft. on Black Mt. [Lovell, *KW* 26:63, 1950; Mengel: 433]

WILSON'S WARBLER *Cardellina pusilla*

Status: Uncommon transient, accidental during winter. Recorded statewide in a variety of semi-open habitats with an abundance of brushy, dense growth and weeds; most numerous in successional thickets of young trees and along woodland borders, but occasionally observed in mature woodland understory. Peaks of abundance occur during mid-May and from late Aug to mid-Sep. There are three records of presumed lingering fall transients during early winter. Typically seen singly or in small, loose groups of only a few birds.

Maximum counts: flock of **9** in Warren Co., 17 Sep 1997 (*KW* 74:10, 1998); at least **9** at LBL, Lyon Co., 8 May 2009 (*KW* 85:75, 2009).

Early spring dates (only one of the reports prior to the last few days of Apr have been accompanied by any details): 20 Apr 1965, south-central Kentucky (*KW* 45:37, 1969); 22 Apr 1939, south-central Kentucky (*KW* 38:21, 1962); 22 Apr 2018, (ph.) at Lexington (*KW* 94:88, 2018); 24 Apr 1964 & 1965, Louisville area (*KW* 52:60, 1976); 27 Apr 2019, Lexington (C. Vellios, eBird data); 28 Apr 2012, LBL, Lyon Co. (*KW* 88:81, 2012); 28 Apr 2015, Lexington (*KW* 91:76, 2016); 29 Apr 1958, Louisville area (*KW* 37:39, 1961); 29 Apr 2012, w. Henderson Co. (*KW* 88:81, 2012).

Late spring dates: 5 Jun 2012, Calloway Co. (*KW* 88:95, 2012); 31 May 1986, Rockcastle Co. (*KW* 62:45, 1986).

Early fall dates: 12 Aug 2018, Louisville (*KW* 95:10, 2019); 16 Aug 1985, Pulaski Co. (*KW* 62:8, 1986); 17 Aug 2012, Jefferson Co. (*KW* 89:14, 2013); 22 Aug 2015, Jefferson Co. (*KW* 92:15, 2016); 22 Apr 2017, Jefferson Co. (*KW* 94:17, 2018).

Late fall dates: 30 Nov 1986, nr. Ky Dam, Livingston Co. (*KW* 63:11, 1987 [location erroneously published as Marshall Co. therein; *fide* J. Robinson, notes]); 3 Nov 2015, Muhlenberg Co. (*KW* 92: 15, 2016); 24 Oct 2004, Louisville (*KW* 81:15, 2005); 24 Oct 2018, (ph.) Boyd Co. (*KW* 95:10, 2019); 23 Oct 1979, Louisville (B. Palmer-Ball, eBird data); 21 Oct 1965, Louisville area (*KW* 52: 60, 1976).

Out-of-season records (early winter): 8 Dec 1974–5 Jan 1975, Louisville (*KW* 52:60, 1976); 13 Dec 2003, Berea, Madison Co. (*KW* 80:47, 2004); 14 Dec 2015, (ph.) at Paducah (*KW* 92:46, 2016).

Published error: 19 Apr 2002, Pulaski Co. (*KW* 78:53, 2002) (correction *fide* R. Denton, notes).

Unaccepted record: 18 Apr 19—, Warren Co. (see Mengel:432).

*SUMMER TANAGER *Piranga rubra*

Status: Locally uncommon to fairly common summer resident, accidental during winter. Recorded statewide during migration in a variety of forested and semi-open habitats, but usually not numerous as a transient away from nesting areas; found most frequently along mature woodland edges. Peak of abundance occurs from late Apr to mid-Sep. Breeding throughout the state in a great variety of forest types, but generally prefers relatively mature woodland on drier slopes and uplands. During spring and summer, second-year males may appear in a variety of pied red-and-yellow plumages.

Maximum count: 45 in Adair Co., 6 May 2008 (S. Stedman, eBird data).

Early spring dates: 20 Mar 2009, Marshall Co. (*KW* 85:75, 2009); 26 Mar 2012 (heard), Mammoth Cave (*KW* 88:82, 2012); 9 Apr 2013, Allen Co. (*KW* 89:80, 2013); 10 Apr 1938, south-central Kentucky (*KW* 38:22, 1962); 10 Apr 1994, Grayson Co. (*KW* 70:56, 1994).

Late fall dates: 7 Nov 2012, Boone Co. (*KW* 89:15, 2013); 7 Nov 2017, (ph.) Benton, Marshall Co. (*KW* 94:17, 2018); 7 Nov 2017, Daviess Co. (*KW* 94:17, 2018); 3-4 Nov 1984, Louisville (*KW* 61:18, 1985); 28 Oct 2015, Trigg Co. (*KW* 92:16, 2016); 25 Oct 1994, Grayson Co. (*KW* 71:5, 1995); 25 Oct 2016, (ph.) Jefferson Co. (*KW* 93:14, 2017); 24 Oct 2004, Pulaski Co. (*KW* 81:15, 2005); 23 Oct 1948, Louisville (Mengel:461); 23 Oct 1966, Louisville area (*KW* 52:61, 1976); 23 Oct 1971, Louisville (*KW* 52:61, 1976; B. Monroe, Jr., notes).

Out-of-season records (winter): 19 Dec 2009–4 Jan 2010, a female (ph.) at Frankfort (*KW* 86:47/52, 2010; M. Schillhahn, photos); early Dec 2018–early Jan 2019, a female (ph.) at Frankfort (*KW* 95:50/51, 2019).

*SCARLET TANAGER *Piranga olivacea*

Status: Fairly common transient, locally uncommon to fairly common summer resident. Recorded statewide during migration in a variety of forested and semi-open habitats from mature woodlands and woodland borders to suburban parks and yards; typically far outnumbers the Summer Tanager in most areas during migration. Peaks of abundance occur from late Apr to early May and from mid-Sep to early Oct. Breeding statewide in mature deciduous and mixed deciduous-coniferous forests as follows: most numerous on the Cumberland Plateau and Mountains, less common and widespread to the west, where it occurs in greatest numbers in extensive tracts of forest (*KBBA*: 268-269).

Maximum counts: 50 at Mammoth Cave, 16 Jun 1996 (S./J. Kistler, eBird data); **25** at Dale Hollow Lake SRP, Cumberland Co., 14 Sep 2017 (*KW* 94:17, 2018).

Early spring dates: 31 Mar 2012, Russell Co. (*KW* 88:82, 2012); 5 Apr 1978, Calloway Co. (*KW* 54:46, 1978); 7 Apr 2012, Pulaski Co. (R. Denton, eBird data); 7 Apr 2012, Lexington (D. Chesnut, eBird data).

Late fall dates: 22-23 Nov 1992, Trimble Co. feeding station (*KW* 69:10, 1993); 20 Nov 2013, Yatesville Lake WMA, Lawrence Co. (*KW* 90:17, 2014); 2 Nov 1967, Boyle Co. (Kemper, *KW* 44:19, 1968); 26 Oct 1978, Jefferson Co. (*KW* 55:17, 1979).

Published error: 26 Nov 1996, Hopkins Co. (*KW* 73:10, 1997) (correction *fide* J. Hancock, notes)

WESTERN TANAGER *Piranga ludoviciana*. Accidental spring visitant. This songbird is a widespread summer resident through much of western North America, and it is regularly found as a vagrant in the eastern United States. It has been suitably documented three times in Kentucky.

Unaccepted record: 14 May 1962, a male at Cherokee Park, Louisville (Carpenter, *KW* 38:50-51, 1962).

Chronological list of records

1) 27-29 Mar 2013, a male (ph.) nr. Lawrenceburg, Anderson Co. (*KW* 89:80/88, 2013)
2) 29 Apr 2013, a male (ph.) at the Lexington Cemetery (*KW* 89:80/88, 2013)
3) 5 May 2016, a male at Hestand, Monroe Co. (*KW* 92:68, 2016)

*NORTHERN CARDINAL *Cardinalis cardinalis*

Status: Common resident. Recorded statewide wherever at least a few patches of dense vegetation exist. Breeding statewide in a great variety of habitats including mature woodland understory, brushy edges and fencelines, and suburban parks and yards. Occasionally encountered during winter in loose groups of a few dozen or more birds, especially along brushy woodland borders.

Maximum counts: **180** in sw. Russell Co., 14 Dec 2011 (eBird data); **168** in nw. Pulaski Co., 1 Jan 2011 (R. Denton, eBird data).

*ROSE-BREASTED GROSBEAK *Pheucticus ludovicianus*

Status: Fairly common transient, uncommon summer resident at higher elevations on Black Mountain (accidental or extremely rare elsewhere during summer), extremely rare during winter. Recorded statewide during migration in a great variety of forested and semi-open habitats from mature woodlands and woodland borders to suburban parks and yards; regularly visits feeding stations during the height of spring migration, less commonly during fall. Peaks of abundance occur during early May and from late Sep to mid-Oct. Breeding regularly in numbers only in deciduous forest above 3000 ft. on Black Mountain, but also likely somewhat regular in small numbers along the crest of Cumberland Mountain in Cumberland Gap National Park and occasional in Boone Co. (see below) Generally encountered singly or in loose groups of up to a dozen birds during migration. **State Breeding Status**: Special Concern.

Maximum counts: at least **85** at Lake Cumberland WMA, Pulaski Co., 27 Sep 2012 (*KW* 89:15, 2013); at least **80** along Pointer Creek Road, Pulaski Co., 7 Oct 2012 (*KW* 89:15, 2013); at least **50** at a feeding station nr. Hartford, Ohio Co., early May 2007 (*KW* 83:85, 2007); **50** at a feeding station at Central Kentucky Wildlife Refuge, Boyle Co., early May 2007 (*KW* 83:85, 2007); a flock of **40** in Pulaski Co., 9 Oct 2016 (*KW* 93:14, 2017); **30-40** at a feeding station at Central City, Muhlenberg Co., early May 2007 (*KW* 83:85, 2007); **35** at the Lexington Cemetery, 2 May 2012 (A. Newman, eBird data).

Early spring dates: 10 Mar 1975, at Carlisle, Nicholas Co. (*AB* 29:699, 1975); 12 Mar 2018, (ph.) Murray, Calloway Co. (*KW* 94:88, 2018); 20 Mar 1938, south-central Kentucky (*KW* 38:22, 1962); 24 Mar 1990, Jefferson Co. (*KW* 66:61, 1990); 24 Mar 2003, Grayson Co. (*KW* 79:73, 2003); 24 Mar 2009, Scott Co. (*KW* 85:76, 2009).

Late spring dates (away from known breeding areas – some may represent summer vagrants): 9 Jun 1977, Lexington (B. Howard, notes); 8 Jun 1986, Grayson Co. (*KW* 62:45, 1986); 6 Jun 1982, Edmonson Co. (*KW* 58:85, 1982); 5 Jun 2004, Louisville (B. Yandell, eBird data); 5 Jun 2007, Woodford Co. (*KW* 83:107, 2007); 4 Jun 2012, (ph.) Pendleton Co. (*KW* 88:95, 2012); 1 Jun 1995, Owen Co. (*KW* 71:71, 1995); 1 Jun 2010, Bath Co. (*KW* 86:96, 2010).

Early fall dates (away from known breeding areas): 4-5 Aug 2016, (ph.) at Berea, Madison Co. (*KW* 93:14, 2017); 5 Aug 2017, Jefferson Co. (T. Lusk, eBird data); 14 Aug 1975, Louisville area (*KW* 52:61, 1976).

Late fall dates: 15 Dec 2018, Pulaski Co. (*KW* 95:51, 2019); 12-13 Dec 2015, (ph.) Lexington (*KW* 92:47, 2016); 10 Dec 2018, Fayette Co. (*KW* 95:51, 2019); 7 Dec 2018, (ph.) Hopkins Co. (*KW* 95:51, 2019); 3 Dec 2007, Calloway Co. (*KW* 84:47, 2008); 1 Dec 2004, Nelson Co. (*KW* 81:61, 2005); 26-28 Nov 1990, (vt.) Bowling Green (*KW* 67:9, 1991); 21-23 Nov 2011 (ph.), Lexington (*KW* 88:18, 2012); 15 Nov 2017, Lincoln Co. (*KW* 94:17, 2018); 13 Nov 2007, Pike Co. (*KW* 84:16 2008); 7 Nov 1999, Louisville (J. Pasikowski, notes); 7 Nov 2000, Warren Co. (*KW* 77:10, 2001); 4 Nov 2012, Pulaski Co. (*KW* 89:15, 2013); 1 Nov 2012, Franklin Co. (*KW* 89:15, 2013); 31 Oct 1960, south-central Kentucky (*KW* 38:22, 1962).

Vagrant summer records (outside of normal breeding range and without evidence of nesting): 10 Jul 1976, male in Jefferson Co. (*BO*, Aug 1976 [date published incorrectly as 10 Jun in *AB* 30:964, 1976]); 21 Jun 1997, Rowan Co. (F. Renfrow, notes; *KW* 73:74, 1997 [date erroneously published as 2 Jun therein]); mid-Jun 2007, Kenton Co. (*KW* 83:107, 2007); 21 Jun 2015, Hardin Co. (*KW* 91:87, 2015); 15-16 Jun 2016, Canton, Trigg Co. (*KW* 92:81, 2016); 23 Jun 2016, Riverpointe, Campbell Co. (*KW* 92:81, 2016).

Out-of-season records (winter): 14 Nov 1998 (*KW* 75:8, 1999) and (assuming same bird) 31 Dec 1998–3 Jan 1999, imm. male at feeders at Short Creek, Grayson Co. (*KW* 75:9/47, 1999); 26 Feb– 2 Mar 2016, ne. of Defoe, Henry Co. (*KW* 92:68, 2016).

Unaccepted records: 23 Dec 1936, (7) at Glasgow (*KW* 36:14, 1960); 31 Dec 1959, (14) in Barren Co. (*KW* 36:14, 1960); 30 Dec 1961, (3 males) at Lexington (*AB* 16:191, 1962); 9 Mar 2001, (2) in Green Co. (R. Sullivan, notes);

Summary of confirmed breeding records by county

Boone (summer 1991 [McNeely, et al., *KW* 67:86, 1991]; *KW* 71:71, 1995; *KW* 73:74, 1997; *KW* 75: 61, 1999; *KW* 86:96, 2010; May 2011 (two separate reports) [*KW* 87:96, 2011])
Daviess (summer of 1985, nr. Maceo [M. Brown, notes])
Harlan (numerous years, Black Mt. [Mengel:463-464; *KBBA*:272])

Summary of additional records of probable breeding by county

Bell/Harlan (17 Jun 1989, Cumberland Gap National Historical Park [*KBBA*:272]; mid-Jun 2003, Cumberland Gap National Historical Park [*KW* 79:85, 2003])
Boone (23 May 2009, (pair copulating) [*KW* 85:76, 2009]; 3 Jun 2012 (pair) [*KW* 88:95, 2012]);
Lewis (summer 1991; two singing males; *KBBA*:272)
Rowan (summer 2003; *KW* 79:85, 2003)

BLACK-HEADED GROSBEAK *Pheucticus melanocephalus*

Status: Extremely rare winter and spring visitant. This widespread summer resident of western North America States is occasionally found in the eastern United States. It has been documented in Kentucky on four occasions (twice during winter and twice during spring).

Chronological list of records

1) 21-29 Dec 1975, an imm. male at Louisville (Palmer-Ball, *KW* 52:34, 1976)
2) 15-16 Apr 1978, an ad. male (ph.) at a feeding station at Jeffersontown, Jefferson Co. (Mathes, *KW* 54:55, 1978; [unfortunately, photographs of this individual could not be located during preparation of this work, and it is unclear if they have been preserved])
3) mid-Jan–late Mar 1986, an imm. or female (ph.) at a feeding station in n. Jessamine Co. (*AB* 40: 480, 1986; B. Maxson, notes [date and location published erroneously as "mid-Apr" and at Lexington, respectively, in *KW* 62:45, 1986])
4) 2 May 2009, a male at Frankfort (*KW* 88:101, 2012; J. Fries, pers. comm.)

*BLUE GROSBEAK *Passerina caerulea*

Status: Uncommon to fairly common summer resident. Known primarily as a summer bird, although migrants are regularly encountered, especially during spring. Usually occurs in semi-open habitats with scattered trees and brush; also occasionally comes to feeding stations, especially during the peak of spring migration during late Apr and early May. Mengel (pp. 465-466) listed only a few spring and summer sightings and considered the breeding population to be negligible as of the late 1950s. However, a dramatic range expansion occurred during subsequent decades (Ritchison, *KW* 60:29-31, 1984), and the species now occurs at least somewhat regularly in suitable habitat statewide. The species also now breeds throughout all of the state except the most heavily forested portions of southeastern Kentucky, but it remains most numerous in the western and southern portions of the state (*KBBA*:274-275). Breeds in farmland, on reclaimed surface mines, and in other semi-open habitats with brushy edges and scattered small trees. Typically seen singly, in pairs, or in family groups.

Maximum count: **30** in Clinton Co., 16 Aug 2003 (S. Stedman, eBird data).
Early spring dates: 3 Apr 1953, Caldwell Co. (Counce, *KW* 30:14, 1954); 11 Apr 2014, Logan Co. (*KW* 90:76, 2014); 12 Apr 1981, Calloway Co. (*KW* 57:59, 1981); 13 Apr 1964, south-central Kentucky (*KW* 45:37, 1969); 13 Apr 1979, Hopkins Co. (KW 55:50, 1979); 13 Apr 1983, Hopkins Co. (*KW* 59:44, 1983); 13 Apr 2001, Sauerheber Unit (C. Crawford, eBird data); 13 Apr 2011, Allen Co. (*KW* 87:96, 2011); 13 Apr 2019, Henderson Co./Todd Co. (M. Stickel, pers. comm./D. Hamilton, eBird data).

Late fall dates: 31 Oct 2011 (ph.), Henderson Co. (*KW* 88:18, 2012); 30 Oct 2013, Pulaski Co. (C. Neeley, eBird data); 30 Oct 2016, (ph.) Logan Co. (*KW* 93:14, 2017); 25 Oct 2010, Sauerheber Unit (*KW* 87:23, 2011); 24 Oct 1998, Butler Co. (*KW* 75:8, 1999); 23 Oct 1994, Henderson Co. (*KW* 71:5, 1995); 23 Oct 2010, ne. Jefferson Co. (*KW* 87:23, 2011); 23 Oct 2012, Pulaski Co. (*KW* 89:15, 2013); 21 Oct 2004, Pulaski Co. (*KW* 81:16, 2005); 21 Oct 2007, Jefferson Co. (*KW* 84:16 2008); 21 Oct 2009, Pulaski Co. (C. Neeley, eBird data).

*INDIGO BUNTING *Passerina cyanea*

Status: Common transient and summer resident, extremely rare during winter. Recorded statewide during migration, occurring in a great variety of semi-open to open habitats; sometimes visits feeding stations during the peak of spring migration during late Apr and early May. Breeding statewide in a great variety of habitats from mature woodland openings to brushy woodland borders, overgrown fields, and shrubby fencerows. This species is one of the most widespread nesting birds in the state; except in urban areas, the attentive birder is seemingly never out of hearing range of a territorial male during summer. There are about a dozen winter records, some at feeding stations, including at least two of individuals that were known to winter. Usually encountered singly or in pairs, although flocks of migrants may number up to a few dozen or more birds, especially during spring.

Maximum counts: at least **300** along the Mississippi River levee nr. Lake No. 9, Fulton Co., 6 May 1996 (B. Palmer-Ball, eBird data); tally of **164** in Metcalfe Co., 6 May 2010 (S. Stedman, eBird data); tally of **158** in Cumberland Co., 9 Jul 2006 (S. Stedman, eBird data); tally of **155** in w. Henderson Co., 15 Jul 2015 (J. Meredig, eBird data); "probably at least **100**" at Barren River Lake, Barren Co., 12 Oct 2010 (*KW* 87:23, 2011).

Early spring dates (records earlier than the first week of Apr may represent wintering individuals): 7-15 Mar 1975, Corydon, Henderson Co. (*AB* 29:699, 1975); 17-19 Mar 1981, Bowling Green (*KW* 57:59, 1981); 18 Mar 2002, Pulaski Co. (R. Denton, eBird data); 30 Mar 2017, (2) w. Fulton Co. (*KW* 93:80, 2017); 4 Apr 2014, Pulaski & Trigg cos. (*KW* 90:76, 2014); 5 Apr 2008, Logan Co. (*KW* 84:71, 2008); 5 Apr 2012, Marshall Co. (*KW* 88:82, 2012); 6 Apr 2012, Bourbon Co. (*KW* 88:82, 2012); 9 Apr 2006, w. Fulton Co. (*KW* 82:75, 2006); 9 Apr 2008, Madison Co. (*KW* 84:71, 2008); 9 Apr 2013, Pulaski Co. (R. Denton, eBird data); 9 Apr 2015, Allen Co. (*KW* 91:76, 2015); 10 Apr 2011, Mammoth Cave (*KW* 87:96, 2011); 10 Apr 2013, Marshall Co. & LBL, Lyon Co. (*KW* 89:80, 2013 & J. Pollpeter, eBird data); 10 Apr 2017, Mammoth Cave (*KW* 93:80, 2017); 11 Apr 1964, south-central Kentucky (*KW* 40:53, 1964); 11 Apr 2013, Allen Co. (*KW* 89:80, 2013); 11 Apr. 2015, Calloway Co. (M. Torres, eBird data); 11 Apr 2019, Madison Co. (D. Pritchard, eBird data).

Late fall/early winter dates: occasionally lingering into Dec with more than ten records during early winter: 14 Dec 1946, Jefferson Co. (Mengel:467; *KW* 35:6, 1959); 26 Dec 1988, at least four birds in a flock in sw. Butler Co. (*KW* 65:14/37, 1989); 15 Dec 1990, Fayette Co. (*KW* 67:10, 1991); 12 Dec 1998, nr. Laketon, Carlisle Co. (B. Palmer-Ball, eBird data); 4 Dec 2004, w. Fulton Co. (*KW* 81:61, 2005); 17 Dec 2011 (ph.), w. Henderson Co. (*KW* 88:52, 2012); 24 Dec 2011, Allen Co. (*KW* 88:32/52, 2012); 12 Dec 2012, (ph.) at Owensboro, Daviess Co. (*KW* 89:50/53, 2013); 30 Dec 2012, (ph.) at Melbourne, Campbell Co. (*KW* 89:53, 2013); 1 Jan 2014, (ph.) Pulaski Co. (*KW* 90: 33/50/55, 2014); 31 Dec 2016, Pulaski Co. (*KW* 93:29/53, 2017); unspecified date in Dec 2016, Allen Co. (*KW* 93:53, 2017); 3 Jan 2018, w. Allen Co. (*KW* 94:28, 2018).

Out-of-season records (mid-winter): 21 Jan 1956, Owensboro, Daviess Co. (Sutton, *KW* 32:31, 1956); 13 Dec 1958–18 Jan 1959, (3) Jefferson Co. (*KW* 35:6, 1959; *AFN* 13:172/298, 1959); Feb–Mar 1970, Hancock Co. (Alsop, *KW* 47:68, 1971); 23 Jan 1976, Warren Co. (Shadowen, *KW* 52:16, 1976); 8 Dec 1982–14 Apr 1983, (ph.) at Louisville (*KW* 59:30, 1983); 18 Feb–4 Mar 2002, Owensboro, Daviess Co. (*KW* 78:35, 2002; M. Thompson, notes); 31 Dec 2005–12 Jan 2006, probable male (ph.) in Pulaski Co. (*KW* 82:17/50, 2006); 1 Jan–9 Feb 2010, at Anchorage, Jefferson Co. (*KW* 86:47, 2010); 28 Jan–22 Apr 2010, (ph.) nr. Cadiz, Trigg Co. (*KW* 86:47/73, 2010); 29-31 Jan 2019, (ph.) Monroe Co. (*KW* 95:51, 2019).

PAINTED BUNTING *Passerina ciris*

Status: Extremely rare spring and summer visitant. This inhabitant of the southern United States and Mexico occurs somewhat regularly as a vagrant to the north of its established range. Although the species regularly appears in the caged bird trade, none of Kentucky's reports have been considered to be of unnatural origin. It has been documented on ten occasions in Kentucky.

Range of dates: (28 Mar–23 Jul & "Aug")

Chronological list of records

1) Aug 1892, a male in Fulton Co. (Mengel:518-519; considered hypothetical therein)
2) 27 Apr 1997, female at a feeder at Mt. Zion, Pulaski Co. (R. Denton, eBird data; *KW* 88:101, 2012)
3) 30 Apr–23 Jul 2003, a male (ph.) on territory at Miller, Fulton Co. (Palmer-Ball and Monroe, *KW* 79:89-90, 2003; *KW* 79:77/92, 2003)
4) 26 May 2006, a male (vt.) at Burkesville, Cumberland Co. (*KW* 82:75/76, 2006)
5) 12 May 2007, a male and a female at Bethlehem, Henry Co. (*KW* 83:85, 2007; *KW* 85:102, 2009)
6) 1 May 2008, a female at Berea, Madison Co. (*KW* 84:71, 2008; *KW* 85:102, 2009)
7) 9 May 2009, a male north of Murray, Calloway Co. (*KW* 85:76, 2009; *KW* 88:101, 2010)
8) 26 Apr 2012, a male (ph.) at Crestwood, Oldham Co. (*KW* 88:82/84, 2012)
9) 28 Mar–1 Apr 2017, a male (ph.) at Ravenna, Estill Co. (*KW* 93:80/84/107, 2017)
10) 1 May 2019, (ph.) ne. Jefferson Co. (D. Menefee, eBird data)

*DICKCISSEL *Spiza americana*

Status: Irregularly rare to fairly common (and locally distributed) summer resident, extremely rare during winter. Recorded chiefly west of the Cumberland Plateau during migration, when this species is generally rare to uncommon as a transient away from nesting areas. Typically encountered in hayfields and other grassy or weedy habitats in open areas during migration. Peak of abundance occurs from early May to mid-Aug. Breeding chiefly west of the Cumberland Plateau, although the species has been found nesting in open habitats (mostly reclaimed surface mines) in eastern Kentucky in recent years (e.g., Claus, et al., *KW* 64:41, 1988; *KW* 70:71, 1994; *KW* 81:110, 2005; *KW* 86:96, 2010; *KW* 87:116, 2011; *KW* 90:76/90, 2014; *KW* 92:81, 2016; L. Anderson, 2019 eBird data). Through central and western Kentucky the species is encountered primarily in open farmland, where it uses hayfields, grain fields, and fallow fields, but other grassy or weedy areas are also utilized including reclaimed surface mines and roadway rights-of-way. Irregular in abundance from year to year and tending to occur locally in small, loose colonies. Fairly widespread in the western quarter of the state where it seems to be numerous every year; less numerous and more local to the north and east where the species is scarce some years, but occasionally fairly common. There are about ten winter records, mostly from feeding stations and mostly from the western half of the state.

Maximum spring count: **210** in the Lower Hickman Bottoms, 10 May 2014 (R. Lane, eBird data).
Maximum fall counts: "probably **hundreds**" in a field in Henderson Co., 5-6 Sep 1949 (Mengel: 470); **15-20** in a loose group in Hopkins Co., 4 Sep 2010 (*KW* 87:23, 2011).
Early spring dates: 14 Apr 2012, Fulton Co. (*KW* 88:82, 2012); 16 Apr 1965, south-central Kentucky (*KW* 45:37, 1969); 16 Apr 1972, Warren Co. (*AB* 26:768, 1972); 17 Apr 2015, sw. Graves Co. (M. Coleman, eBird data).
Late fall dates: 26 Nov 2014, (ph.) sw. Logan Co. (*KW* 91:15, 2015); 9-22 Nov 1973, Owensboro, Daviess Co. (Bowne, *KW* 50:18, 1974; A. Stamm, historical archive files); 7 Nov 2015, Logan Co. (*KW* 92:16, 2016); 3 Nov 2018, (ph.) Jefferson Co. (*KW* 95:10/40, 2019); 29 Oct 2011, Sauerheber Unit (*KW* 88:18, 2012); 29 Oct 2018, (ph.) Lincoln Co. (*KW* 95:10, 2019); 26 Oct 2009, Sauerheber Unit (*KW* 86:15, 2010); 24 Oct 1971, Bullitt Co. (*KW* 52:62, 1976; *AB* 26:73, 1972); 24 Oct 2011, Madison Co. (*KW* 88:18, 2012).
Out-of-season records (winter): 27 Dec 1958, Ashland CBC, Boyd Co. (not confirmed; see *KW* 35: 9-10, 1959); 25 Dec 1969–22 Feb 1970, Owensboro, Daviess Co. (*KW* 46:16, 1970; Isles, *KW* 46: 22, 1970; *AB* 24:510, 1970); 1 Jan 1970, Henderson CBC (*KW* 46:12, 1970); 29 Dec 1979, Hen-

derson CBC (*KW* 56:9, 1980); 10-13 Jan 1988, Hardin Co. (*KW* 64:30, 1988); 19 Feb–13 Mar 1982, Murray, Calloway Co. (*KW* 58:30/54, 1982); 29 Dec 1984, (2) on the Ballard Co. CBC (*KW* 61:3, 1985); 21/23 Jan and 3 Mar 2001 (ph.), Lexington (*NAB* 55:178, 2001; L. Royse, pers. comm.); 16-17 Jan 2009, Trigg Co. (*KW* 85:53, 2009); 14 Dec 2009, Russell Co. (*KW* 86:17/31/47, 2010); 13 Dec 2017–3 Jan 2018, (ph.) at Union, Boone Co. (*KW* 94:29, 2018).

Published errors: based on a review of a number of sources, I believe (but am not certain) that the date of 3 Dec [19—] published by Monroe, et al. (1988) is erroneous, the result of a transcription error (*fide* A. Stamm, historical archive files); also, the early spring date of 15 Apr [19—], published by Monroe, et al. (1988) appears to represent a recent misinterpretation from the list published in *KW* 48:28, 1972 for 15-16 Apr 1972 in Warren Co.; this assessment is based on the publication of 16 Apr 1972 as the more likely date in *AB* 26:73, 1972 (*fide* A. Stamm, historical archive files).

HYPOTHETICAL LIST

Species included in the following list have been reported in Kentucky, but records have not been documented with suitable detail to warrant inclusion on the official list or they involve only one single-observer sight record.

BARROW'S GOLDENEYE *Bucephala islandica.* One single-observer sight record: 11 Dec 2009, a female reported on Ky Lake above Ky Dam, Marshall Co. (*KW* 86:41, 2010).

BROAD-BILLED HUMMINGBIRD *Cynanthus latirostirs.* One record: late Oct–early Nov 2010, (ph.) at Madisonville, Hopkins Co. (*KW* 87:19, 2011). This resident of Mexico and Central America wanders widely, accounting for nearly a dozen records in the eastern United States and Canada, mostly during summer. *Note: This report was not accepted by the KBRC (KW 88:101, 2012), but it has been accepted herein as Hypothetical based on assessment of the report by several authorities on hummingbird identification.*

BLACK RAIL *Laterallus jamaicensis.* One single-observer sight record: 24 Apr 2001, Sinclair Unit (*KW* 77:49, 2001).

ESKIMO CURLEW *Numenius borealis.* A few vague historical records (Mengel:517).

LONG-BILLED CURLEW *Numenius americanus.* Several records: at least three historic references in Mengel (p. 517); also, 25 Aug 1976, one reported from the Sloughs WMA, Henderson Co. (B. Burnley, notes).

SPRAGUE'S PIPIT *Anthus spragueii.* One single-observer sight record: 16 Apr 1955, one nr. Louisville (Mengel:518; *KW* 52:56, 1976).

PINE GROSBEAK *Pinicola enucleator.* Two single-observer sight records: several reported during the winter of 1888 at Hickman, Fulton Co. (Mengel: 519); 21 Dec 1975, a male at Cherokee Park, Louisville (Stamm, *KW* 52:35, 1976; *KW* 52:62, 1976).

KIRTLAND'S WARBLER *Setophaga kirtlandii.* One single-observer sight record: 15 May 1968, a male observed at Danville (Loetscher, *KW* 44:51, 1968).

OTHER SPECIES NOT INCLUDED OR REMOVED
FROM PREVIOUS LISTS

BARNACLE GOOSE *Branta leucopsis*. Two sight records: 13 Jan 1983, one feeding with Canada Geese at the Sauerheber Unit (*KW* 59:27, 1983); and mid-Jan 1987, another with Canada Geese at the Sauerheber Unit (B. Palmer-Ball, notes). Apparently wild and migratory individuals in the interior eastern United States are often birds that have escaped captivity, but their status remains uncertain (Ryff, *Birding* 16: 146-154).

MASKED DUCK *Nomonyx dominicus*. A published record of a first-year male at the Long Point Unit of Reelfoot NWR, Fulton, Co., 15 Apr 1974 (Fintel, *Migrant* 45:47-48, 1974) is considered invalid. This bird was observed several times (and photographed) during a five-day period (11-15 Apr 1974) on a small pond just south of the state line in Tennessee; however, on two occasions on 15 Apr it was seen flying out to the north over the Kentucky portion of the refuge (P. Crawford, pers. comm.). Based on reassessment of the documentary photographs, the bird is now believed not to have been a Masked Duck (see *KW* 88:101, 2012).

RING-NECKED PHEASANT *Phasianus colchicus*. This native species of Europe has been introduced into North America and established populations are present in the northern portions of Illinois, Indiana, and Ohio. Local introductions also occur at hunting preserves in Kentucky on an occasional basis. All reports of pheasants in Kentucky are considered to be of local origin and are not included in the fauna of the state.

PURPLE SANDPIPER *Calidris maritima*. A single-observer sight record at the Falls of the Ohio, 18 Dec 1949 (Summerfield, *KW* 26:26-27, 1950) involved a bird tentatively identified at the time and regarded as hypothetical by Mengel (p. 517). In the company of two Dunlin and three Pectoral Sandpipers, this unusual-looking bird was studied at close range for some time. Because mid-Dec would be a likely time for the occurrence of this species in the state, it would seem that this record is authentic. However, details concerning the location of the sighting contained in the published account would clearly place the bird within the Indiana portion of the Falls of the Ohio. According to the author (D. Summerfield, pers. comm.), the birds were seen to fly out over the water on several occasions, thus perhaps putting them within Kentucky, but this cannot be conclusively established. Purple Sandpipers prefer algae-covered rocks along the edges of lakes and rivers, and close scrutiny of stone breakwaters and dams, especially during winter, could turn up an occasional individual in the state.

FORK-TAILED FLYCATCHER *Tyrannus savana*. An historical record from late Oct during the early 1800s in considered invalid. The bird was reported near Henderson by J.J. Audubon (Mengel:309-310). Although Mengel accepted this record, the origin of the specimen painted by Audubon is in question, and it would seem best to consider this record as unconfirmed for that reason (see *Birding* 31:314-315, 1999).

EUROPEAN GOLDFINCH *Carduelis carduelis*. This Eurasian species has been released intentionally and unintentionally a number of times in the United States as early and the mid-1800s. The most recent release of significance occurred during the early 2000s at Chicago, Illinois. These birds apparently have survived and bred, establishing a somewhat self-sustaining population, possibly accounting for a few recent reports in Kentucky during the past few years.

CITED SOURCES

Arnold, M., and K. Heyden. 2013. 2013 Kentucky Peregrine Falcon Report. Ky. Dept. of Fish and Wildlife Resources. Frankfort, KY.

Chesser, R.T., K.J. Burns, C. Cicero, J.L. Dunn, A.W. Kratter, I.J. Lovette, P.C. Rasmussen, J.V. Remsen, Jr., D.F. Stotz, and K. Winker. 2019a. *Check-list of North American Birds* (online). American Ornithological Society. http://checklist.aou.org/taxa. Accessed May 3, 2019.

Chesser, R.T., K.J. Burns, C. Cicero, J.L. Dunn, A.W. Kratter, I.J. Lovette, P.C. Rasmussen, J.V. Remsen, Jr., D.F. Stotz, and K. Winker. 2019b. Sixtieth supplement to the American Ornithological Society's *Check-list of North American Birds*. *Auk: Ornithological Advances* 136 in press.

Cooke, W. 1914. Distribution and migration of North American rails and their allies. Bulletin of the U.S. Dept. of Agriculture, No. 128, Sept. 25, 1914. Washington, D.C., US. 50 pp.

Evans, Sherri. 1984. The Distribution and Status of Heron Rookeries in Kentucky. Ky. Dept. of Fish & Wildlife Resources, unpubl. rpt. Frankfort, KY.

Heyden, K. 2014. 2013 Barn Owl Inventory Report. Unpubl. rpt. Ky. Dept. of Fish and Wildlife Resources. 30 January 2014. Frankfort, KY. 10 pp.

Kentucky State Nature Preserves Commission (KSNPC). 2000. Endangered, Threatened, Special Concern, and Historic Biota of Kentucky. *Journal of the Kentucky Academy of Science* 61:115-132.

Monroe, B.L., Jr., A.L. Stamm, and B.L. Palmer-Ball, Jr. 1988. Annotated Checklist of the Birds of Kentucky, 1st ed. Kentucky Ornithological Society. Louisville, KY.

Newton, I. 2002. Population limitation in holarctic owls. Pp. 3-29 in "Ecology and conservation of owls," I. Newton, R. Kavenagh, J. Olsen, and I. Taylor, eds. CSIRO Publishing, Collingwood, Australia.

Palmer-Ball, B.L., Jr. 2003. Annotated Checklist of the Birds of Kentucky, 2nd ed. Kentucky Ornithological Society. Louisville, KY.

Patton, L. 2007. Comparative ecology of the Golden-winged Warbler and Blue-winged Warbler on reclaimed mines in southeastern Kentucky. M.S. Thesis. University of Kentucky, Dept. of Forestry. Lexington, KY.

Slankard, K. 2016. 2016 Barn Owl Inventory Report. Unpubl. rpt. Ky. Dept. of Fish and Wildlife Resources. Frankfort, KY. 10 pp.

Stedman, S. 2019. Web site: https://birdsandbutterfliesoftheuppercumberlandregion.com. Accessed March 3, 2019.

Taylor, L. 2016. 2016 Kentucky Peregrine Falcon report. Ky. Dept of Fish and Wildlife Resources, Frankfort, KY. 19 pp.

INDEX TO COMMON NAMES

NOTES

NOTES

NOTES

CPSIA information can be obtained
at www.ICGtesting.com
Printed in the USA
LVHW101622140620
658048LV00009B/1168

9 780578 550770